Robert F. Spencer

THE NORTH ALASKAN ESKIMO

A Study in Ecology and Society

Dover Publications, Inc.
New York

LETTER OF TRANSMITTAL

SMITHSONIAN INSTITUTION,
BUREAU OF AMERICAN ETHNOLOGY,
Washington, D. C., December 27, 1957.

SIR: I have the honor to transmit herewith a manuscript entitled "The North Alaskan Eskimo: A Study in Ecology and Society," by Robert F. Spencer, and to recommend that it be published as a bulletin of the Bureau of American Ethnology.

Very respectfully yours,

M. W. STIRLING, *Director.*

DR. LEONARD CARMICHAEL,
Secretary, Smithsonian Institution.

Published in Canada by General Publishing Company, Ltd., 30 Lesmill Road, Don Mills, Toronto, Ontario.

Published in the United Kingdom by Constable and Company, Ltd., 10 Orange Street, London WC2H 7EG.

This Dover edition, first published in 1976, is an unabridged republication of the work originally published by the United States Government Printing Office, Washington, 1959, as *Bulletin 171* of the Bureau of American Ethnology, Smithsonian Institution (House Document No. 249, 85th Congress, 1st session).

International Standard Book Number: 0-486-23369-3
Library of Congress Catalog Card Number: 76-19601

Manufactured in the United States of America
Dover Publications, Inc.
180 Varick Street
New York, N.Y. 10014

CONTENTS

PAGE

Introduction — 1
The problem — 6
The land and the people — 9
The land — 9
North Alaskan Eskimo settlements — 13
Human relation to the biota — 23
Flora — 23
Fauna — 25
Summary — 38
Language — 39
Houses and settlements — 43
Houses of the nuunamiut — 44
Houses of the tareumiut — 49
Family and kinship — 62
Introduction — 62
The nuclear family — 63
The extended family — 65
Kinship terminology — 66
Lineal and nuclear consanguines — 66
Consanguineal kin—collaterals — 67
Affinal kin — 68
Step- and adoptive relationships — 69
Combined kin terms — 69
Factors in the system — 70
Collective responsibility — 71
Marriage — 75
Divorce — 82
Wife lending and wife exchange — 83
qataŋuutigiit — 84
Adoption — 87
Abandonment — 92
Conclusion — 95
Customary law — 97
Economy and society — 124
Introduction — 124
Human ecology of the Alaskan Arctic slope — 126
1. nuunamiut and tareumiut — 126
2. The nuunamiut — 132
3. The tareumiut — 139
Summary: nuunamiut vs. tareumiut — 146
Property, wealth, and status — 147
Ownership — 147
Wealth — 151
Competition and cooperation — 159

	PAGE
Voluntary associations	166
Partnerships	167
Joking partnerships	172
Women's partnerships	177
The hunting group and the umealiq	177
The karigi	182
Trade	193
Open trade	193
Structured trade	198
The Messenger Feast (kimŋic)	210
Conclusion	227
The individual and the life cycle	229
Introduction	229
Pregnancy	229
Birth	231
Infancy	234
Childhood	237
Puberty	241
Sexual behavior	244
Marital behavior	249
Old age	251
Death	252
Conclusion	253
The supernatural	255
Introduction	255
Cosmic view	257
Dwarfs, mermen, monsters, and other supernatural beings	259
Relation to animals	264
Land animals	267
Sea animals	272
Songs	277
Charms and amulets	282
Names	286
Ghosts and souls	291
Dreams and portents	293
Masks	293
Summary	294
The wiivaksat—Strangers in the Sky	296
Shamanism	299
Examples of shamanistic behavior	315
The treatment of disease	327
The cults	331
The cult of the whale	332
Whaling charms and songs	338
Taking the whale	342
Greeting the whale	344
Close of the whaling season	347
nalukataq	350
The cult of the caribou	353
Culture change	358
Sources of money (1888–1948)	360
Seasonal activities	366

Culture change—Continued PAGE
- Food 371
- Meals 375
- Family and budgets 376
- Summary of modern economic life 377
- Christianity 378

Folklore 383
- The folktales 384
- Texts 428
- Children's stories 438

Conclusions 440
- Ecology and society in North Alaska 440
- The place of North Alaska in Eskimo culture 446
- North Alaska and Eskimo culture history 452

Bibliography 455
Appendix 1. Tobacco 462
Appendix 2. Dogs 465
Appendix 3. Pottery 470
Appendix 4. Time reckoning; enumeration 475
Index 479

ILLUSTRATIONS

(All plates follow page 477)

PLATES

1. Informants at Point Barrow.
2. Barrow village today.
3. *a*, A sod house in use at Point Lay. *b*, The iccellik, tent of the nuunamiut. *c*, Storage racks, meat cache, and umiak frame, Point Lay.
4. *a*, The 1953 summer settlement of nuunamiut at Anaktuvuk Pass. *b*, A house ruin at Tikeraaq (Point Hope). *c*, Summer house of the Barrow village people at piγiniq (Birnirk), the duck shooting station.
5. *a*, The spring whaling camp at an ice lead near Barrow village. *b*, An umiak in tow, stern foremost. *c*, Barrow village men shooting walrus from an ice floe.
6. *a*, Barrow village women engaged in skinning a polar bear. *b*, nalukataq. The "blanket toss" celebration held at the close of a successful spring whaling season. *c*, Informant and interpreter Mr. Alfred Hopson, shown with his daughter.
7. *a*, Chorus of men singing at a social dance at Barrow village. *b*, The traditional Eskimo tambourine. *c*, Women join the men in singing, seated near or behind them.
8. *a*, Informants at Anaktuvuk Pass. Nuunamiut man and wife. *b*, Sikvayuŋgaq shown with the box drum used in the Messenger Feast.
9. Ayaraq (string figure). *a*, Sawiaxlukak carrying his kayak. *b*, Aakluq, the two brown bears. *c*, Amawk. the wolf.

TEXT FIGURES

PAGE

1. Maritime Eskimo house: *a*, floor plan; *b*, cross section (facing) 49
2. The old town of utkeaaγvik, about 1895 50

MAPS

1. Local groups of North Alaskan Eskimo 8
2. Travel routes, Point Barrow area (facing) 198
3. Aboriginal trade routes, North Alaska (facing) 200
4. Route taken by Naval Expedition, 1886 (Stoney, 1900) 202

INTRODUCTION

Ethnographic studies among the North Alaskan Eskimo were carried on in the summer and early fall of both 1952 and 1953. The work was made possible in 1952 through a contract between the University of Minnesota and the United States Navy, Office of Naval Research, while in 1953 the research was supported by the Arctic Institute of North America and the Office of Naval Research. Fieldwork was carried on through the facilities of the Arctic Research Laboratory, located at Point Barrow, Alaska, and logistic support was provided by the Laboratory. The sincere thanks of the writer are due both the Office of Naval Research and the Arctic Institute of North America for making the research possible. A special debt is due the Arctic Research Laboratory and its director, Dr. Ira L. Wiggins, for aiding the investigations. It is difficult to conceive of a more ideal research climate than that provided by the Laboratory. It is hoped that the research results which are recorded here will in some measure justify the support which these investigations were accorded.

It is to be regretted that the press of duties elsewhere prevented an observation of the year-round cycle and pattern of life of the North Alaskan Eskimo. It is hoped that at some future time this may be accomplished. Since, however, the primary concern of this research lies with the aboriginal North Alaskan Eskimo culture, much of the data obtained had to be dependent on the memory of older living informants. In the contemporary culture there is much to suggest the undisrupted native past, but many institutions have been subjected to change and it is only from the older peoples, those whose memories reach back to the last decades of the 1800's, that the facts of the integrated and untouched native society can be elicited.

The original aim of this project was the examination of patterns of contemporary social behavior among the Eskimo of northern Alaska. The 1952 season was devoted to the community of Barrow itself, Barrow Village, the town most intimately involved in the naval petroleum project on the Naval Petroleum Reserve IV. An original point of interest was the examination of the changes which have come about as a result of the introduction of a moneyed economy. It was thought that this, the result of employment of many Eskimo by the Arctic Contractors, Ltd., would have far-reaching effects, both in the native economic system and in social organization. Indeed, a point of much concern to the Alaska Native Service and to many serious-minded civic and welfare groups in the territory was that the Barrow Eskimo would be greatly corrupted by the effects of the high wages made available to them by their new employment. It was felt, for example, that men employed at the naval installation, and thus unable to devote the proper amount of time to hunting, would bring some privation to themselves and their families. Among so many of the American Indians located on reservations in all parts of the United States, such social change has worked a serious hardship. An initial attempt of the present study was to evaluate the effects of the changing economy.

But the introduction of money into the native economy did not have quite the effects which were predicted, and disorganization both of society and of personality was not so rampant as some of the welfare services believed. A point often forgotten when the Barrow naval project and its relation to them is considered, is that the Eskimo had long been aware of money, both through the 19th-century contacts with the traders and Euro-American whaling vessels, and later through the fur industry. Field research quickly revealed that much more of the aboriginal patterns of life remained than was expected. Instead of a disorganized society, a smoothly functioning one was encountered, one in which many older precontact institutions were still actively operative. Money and modern industrialized technology, it is true, had made inroads and changes; both modern education and Christian missionizing had effected modifications of some patterns. But the native social structure was one in which cooperative institutions had to be brought to the fore. The Eskimo of North Alaska had solved the problem of living together by establishing a strong cooperative kinship bond. This remains, despite the collapse of some other social forms, and in remaining, continues to provide the keystone of the social structure, a nuclear point around which all other institutional aspects constellate. Family and kinship are thus primary, and it seems safe to predict that this social entity cannot be considered disorganized until the breakdown of the family system itself. When the present investigations were conducted, this had not yet taken place.

As soon as the nature of the social organization and of the integrative function of the family became clear in the field, attention was given primarily to the aboriginal culture. If the changes which have come about as the result of contact with the dominant culture of the United States are to be observed, it follows that as clear a picture of the native organization of the precontact native past must be obtained. A complete ethnographic study of the Eskimo of northern Alaska had not in any case been undertaken. When the area was visited by the Point Barrow Expedition of 1881–82, many ethnographical observations were made. Both Lieutenant Ray and John Murdoch were keen observers and able to elicit a great deal of information on the lives of the people. But the fact that neither man knew the language resulted in primary attention to material culture and to museum collections. Murdoch's report (1892) stresses technology and presents only a small section on society and other nonmaterial aspects. An earlier description of life at Point Barrow had been published by Dr. John Simpson, R. N. (1855), who had spent several seasons in the area 30 years before and who proved to be a somewhat keener observer than either Ray or Murdoch. Important though the analysis of the material culture might be, the present writer felt that his own research might be directed to the analysis of the social structure in view of the absence of any systematic treatment of it elsewhere.

The season of 1952 was thus devoted to the Barrow community and to the reconstruction of aboriginal culture patterns among the people formerly known as the utkeaviŋmiut and the nuwuŋmiut. Considerable data on their economy, society, and religion were collected between mid-June and the end of September of that year. When the results of the 1952 field season were considered, however, it became clear that to treat the Barrow area out of context from its neighboring areas led to certain false impressions. The peoples of the northern villages, utkeaaγvik and nuwuk, had contacts both down the coasts and with a great many groups of inland Eskimo. There were permanent settlements between Point Hope (tikeraaq) and Point Barrow but little by way of permanent settlement along the northern Alaskan coasts to the east of Barrow. Indeed, once the North Alaskan Eskimo are left behind, there is evidence that populations were very scanty until the mouth of the McKenzie was reached. The apparent reason for the development of settlements on the northwest coast of Alaska lay in the presence of the baleen whales. The coastal settlements of the area were thus preoccupied with whaling, and it is possible to define a maritime whaling province, an area marked not only by common habits, customs, and language, but also by ties of kinship.

There remains, however, the problem of the inland Eskimo, the groups variously called nuunamiut, nunataγmiut, nunatarmiut, etc. These were always somewhat of a problem for the early Alaskan investigators, and their cultural position has never been adequately understood. They were inland Eskimo who had evolved a dependence on interior caribou hunting and who were thus wholly differently oriented from their coastal neighbors. Moreover, these groups were in some measure dependent on the maritime peoples with the result that a remarkable balance of society and economy was achieved. When this interaction between the two groups was understood, it became evident that the culture area of whaling (in which whales were the primary focus of ceremonial activity, although a variety of other sea mammals were hunted as well) had to be examined in respect to the interrelationships between its villages and that the inland Eskimo likewise had to be described in order to comprehend the nature of the contacts between the two groups. The season of 1953 was devoted to this problem.

The data collected at Barrow were a starting point for further analysis of the area at large. The 1953 investigations were again carried on primarily at Barrow, although opportunities were found to visit other communities for short periods of time. As a result of the employment offered to the Eskimo by the naval installation, a large group of North Alaskan Eskimo had assembled at the town of Barrow. Individuals and families had come from as far away as Kotzebue to the south, not to mention Cape Prince of Wales and some other southern communities, as well as from Barter Island to the east. Virtually all the communities of North Alaska were represented in the Barrow situation, not only by younger employable people but by the members of an older generation who had accompanied them. Inland as well as maritime communities were represented. This being so, it was possible to obtain at Barrow the services of a representative sample of good respondents from all areas concerned. Indeed, care had to be taken to avoid the all too willing services of individuals whose backgrounds lay outside the area. An examination of the web of kinship, of genealogical backgrounds, and of point of origin of each informant made selection fairly readily possible. Aside from casual contacts made with scores of individuals, about 35 respondents from all communities were questioned intensively.

The informants, ranging in age from the mid-thirties to the very aged, were selected primarily because of their conservatism, which tended to preserve as well as possible the precontact institutions (pl. 1, *a–d*). Of these, 20 were men and women who had been born and raised in the Barrow area (utkeaaγvik and nuwuk) itself; 5 came from Wainwright, considering themselves kuγmiut, attached to the maritime village but with wide inland experience as well; 4 Point Hope people served as informants, although one of them was associated with the town of Point Lay, a modern settlement or colony of Point Hope. The remainder were inland Eskimo, those who had lived and moved along the Colville drainage, along the mountain slopes of the Brooks Range, and as far west as the Noatak and Kobuk Rivers.

These informants, located at Barrow for the reasons indicated, were supplemented by several others in the local communities themselves. A visit to the killiγmiut, located in Anaktuvuk Pass in the

Brooks Range in the summer of 1953, was unfortunately cut short because of the writer's illness, but not before some 10 days of work with this highly unacculturated band. The Alaska Native Service supplies the communities of the Arctic coast with materials for the stores, schools, and hospitals. Once a year, usually in early September, the towns are visited by a supply ship, which makes the quick voyage during the period when the ocean is essentially free of ice. Through the courtesy of the Alaska Native Service, it was possible to travel with this vessel, the *SS North Star*, and to obtain some further perspective on the native communities to the south and west of Point Barrow. Some 6 days were spent at Point Hope, for example, and contacts were readily made with relatives of individuals with whom contacts had been made in the Barrow area. A debt of appreciation to the captain and the crew of the *SS North Star* is acknowledged. Thus, although the data from the area were obtained principally at Barrow village, from informants who were either native there or who had come to Barrow relatively recently, it was possible to secure an integrated perspective. The North Alaskan culture area with its twofold ecology emerges as a unit, and it is possible to understand the forces which shaped it.

The native language remains the primary means of communication in the area even today. In spite of the efforts of the Government schools, the North Alaskan dialect of Eskimo remains in force as the language of the home and virtually all interpersonal intercourse. Interpreters were employed. Any ethnographer who has elicited information through an interpreter is aware of the pitfalls. It is only when the investigator himself begins to achieve sufficient knowledge by way of auditory comprehension that a check can be made on the reliability of the interpreter. The latter must be trained not to impose his own value judgments and not to color the situations which he describes. The writer found himself particularly fortunate in this regard, having the services of a woman of middle age whose father was a European. She possessed a remarkable curiosity about the older culture and felt herself sufficiently detached from it as to interpret exactly. A later check revealed her remarkable reliability. Several other interpreters were used from time to time. Needless to say, in the interest of maintaining good community relations and of not violating confidences so freely given no purpose is served here by naming either the informants or the interpreters. Other interpreters were men, one from the Utokak area, another from Barrow itself, a third from the group formerly settled along the Ikpikpuk River, and a fourth from the Anaktuvuk Pass region. Of these, none proved so satisfactory as their female counterpart, serving better as informants than as interpreters. While it is possible to develop an adequate comprehension of spoken Eskimo in a few months, the morphological intricacies in the language do not lend themselves to freedom of expression for the beginner. An interpreter is a necessity in the field situation.

The present writer, with his research assistant Marietta B. Spencer, is pleased that the work which was undertaken proved so fruitful insofar, at least, as obtaining full data is concerned. Speaking personally, the writer wishes to note that of the various field experiences which he has had, none has proved more satisfying or rewarding than this one in Alaska. The people, with their great personal dignity and integrity, as well as their joyous but subtle humor and individual warmth, make for ideal respondents. Theirs is an almost scientific objectivity; in all cases there was encountered a virtual passion for truth and accuracy. The informants reacted at once to the idea that some of the older traditions should be preserved in writing. To this they brought a desire to cooperate and an eagerness for accurately conceived data. It is to them, the North Alaskan Eskimo, and particularly, to the informants whose time and thoughts were so freely given that this work is dedicated.

THE PROBLEM

Since the shift was made from attention to the contemporary life to that of the past, several significant problems suggest themselves. In the main, these rest in the theoretical implications of Eskimo ethnology. When the limits of the north Alaskan area, as a cultural focus, became clear, the primary problem which emerged was that of the analysis of two differing ways of life operating within the framework of a common culture. As may be noted, there is the same language, the same world view, the same cultural preoccupations—in short, the same overall ethos; but there are differences which rest in environment. The coastal peoples have adapted themselves to their environment in one particular way, the inland groups in another. Basically, one might say that the social understandings characteristic of the groups are different in degree only, being no more than variations on a common theme. But it is evident that such differences exist and that they are in large measure predicated on adjustments to the terrain and to the business of making a living within it. A question which this study asks is: what is the relation between economy and society? This is thus a study in differing patterns of human ecology.

In no sense, however, may it be understood that environment is anything more than a limiting factor in human development. The stress which has been laid on the Eskimo as a group operating in the face of a hostile environment has a point, to be sure, but one may agree with Kroeber (1939, p. 1) that the causes of cultural phenomena are other cultural phenomena. That culture and society are rooted in nature cannot be denied. Among the groups in question, the environment played a significant part in placing severe limitations on activities and in providing the raw materials on which the groups depended to keep alive. Even in an area in which the limitations are so onerous, however, there is a choice. The culture history of the Eskimo has permitted the realization of certain kinds of mechanisms by which their society can perpetuate itself. The keynote became cooperation, but, as will be seen, a kind of particularly structured cooperation, one in which choices were made which have little or no relationship to the environment. As a means of understanding the culture of north Alaska an attempt has been made to analyze the cooperative devices at work in the society, the particular selections which were made in the creation of institutional forms. As society relates to the ecology, it is examined in detail. This is first a study in social structure and social culture. It aims at the analysis of the culture whole and attempts to show how a basic culture oriented itself around the two contrasting ecological patterns of whaling and caribou hunting.

There is a further consideration. This study seeks to balance the two ecological patterns and to provide some point of common focus for them. It seeks to bring the data on the inland Eskimo collected by Lieutenant Stoney (1900), by the archeologists Giddings (1952), Irving (1951), and Solecki (1951), and by the zoologist Rausch (1951), into somewhat broader perspective. Similarly, the early descriptions of the maritime groups by Murdoch (1892), Ray (1885b, c), John Simpson (1855), and some others, such as Stefansson (1914), can be supplemented. For the same area, an attempt is made to fit Rainey's excellent study of Point Hope (1947) into the area at large. Hitherto, the inland and maritime groups were treated as two essentially separate entities. It is Larsen and Rainey (1948) who begin to suggest the essential interdependence between the two, even if the conclusions which they reach are not perhaps wholly warranted. There is thus raised again the old problem of Eskimo temporal sequence, the question which has aroused so much attention for so long. Given the two ecological systems, can any statement be made as to the priority of one over the other? Do the inland Eskimo represent an earlier developmental stage of Eskimo history and the maritime life a later specialization? An examination of the data on the nature of the socioeconomic interdependence between the two, as well as on the kinds of specializations developed by each group, may in part serve to refocus the problem. It may serve to shed some ethnological light on the matter of the temporal sequence of the Eskimo cultures. It is to be hoped that the data supplied here will speak for themselves.

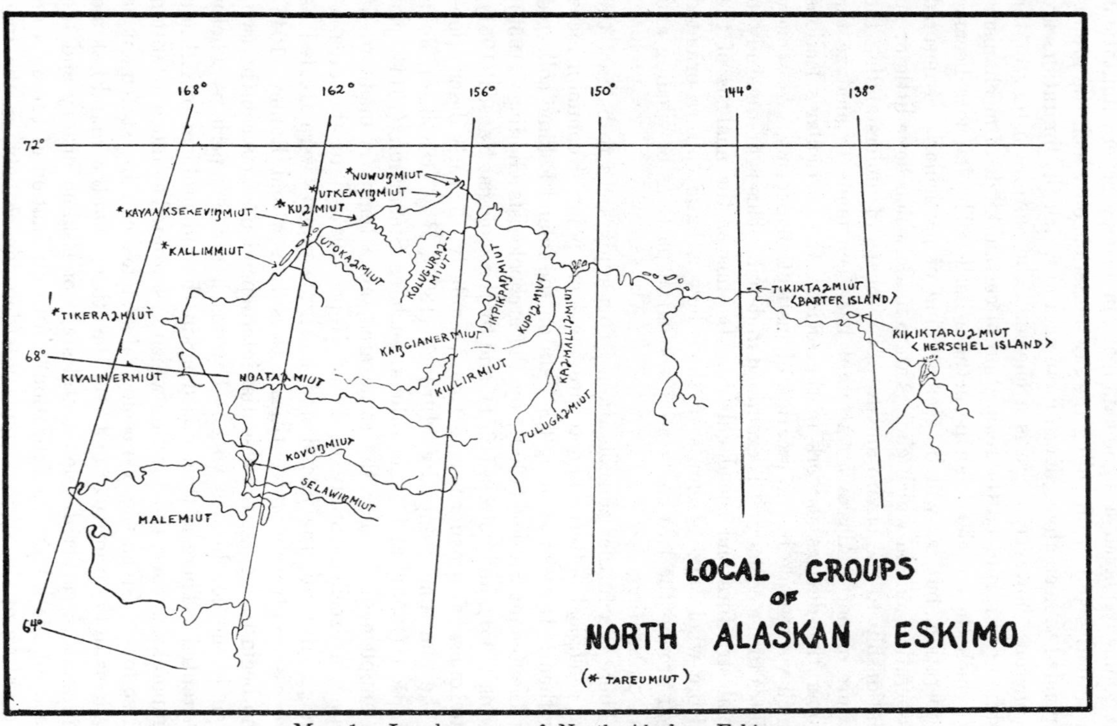

Map 1.—Local groups of North Alaskan Eskimo.

THE LAND AND THE PEOPLE

THE LAND

In northwestern North America, between the Brooks Range and the Arctic Ocean, lie some seventy-odd thousand square miles of tundra. Wholly within the Arctic Circle, this region is bounded on the east by the Colville Delta, on the south by the jagged peaks of the glaciated Brooks Range, on the north by the Arctic Ocean itself. The western sections of the region, likewise bounded by the ocean, incline from northeast to southwest, and form, at the southern end, a point at which mountain and sea come together. This axis, beginning at Point Barrow, ending at Point Hope in the southwest, constitutes the Arctic slope of northwestern Alaska. In this area of tundra, a desert of cold, are to be found two configurations of aboriginal Eskimo culture, a situation which throws the caribou hunters of the inland regions sharply into contrast with the whalers of the coastal slope.

Physiographically, this vast area may be divided into three major zones. These provinces run generally in an east-west direction and consist of the Brooks Range, the Arctic foothills, and the Arctic coastal plain.

The Brooks Range, the northwesternmost extension of the main continental mountain system of North America, forms a topographic barrier, setting off the forested lands which flank the Yukon tributaries to the south from the treeless Arctic plain. It forms a continental divide, its streams going either north, meandering lazily across the tundra, or southward, joining the great river systems of central Alaska. The highest peaks of the Brooks Range are found in the eastern sections, where, perennially snow covered, they rise to heights of 9,000 feet. In its western end, the range splits, being flanked by the smaller De Long Range and by the Baird Mountains. Near the general area of Point Hope, east of Cape Lisburne, the Brooks Range has given way to a series of rolling highlands across which the peaks of the De Long Mountains loom large (cf. Smith and Mertie, 1930; Schrader, 1904; Solecki, 1951).

The Brooks Range province is roughly 600 miles long. The range itself consists of heavily weathered yet resistant Paleozoic rock still marked by the presence of numerous small glaciers. Several large stream-fed lakes are to be found along the northern edge of the range. These, in turn, contribute to the rivers flowing northward to the

Arctic Ocean across the tundra. The Brooks Range is characterized by rugged peaks and numerous hanging valleys. Except for three well-defined passes which serve to connect the drainages on both north and south, the mountains are most difficult of access. These three passes in the middle of the range—the Howard, the Survey, and the Anaktuvuk—serving as routes for the caribou movements, have been vital to human residence in the area. In the passes and along the lakes there is evidence of a long period of Eskimo habitation (Solecki, 1951, pp. 478–492; cf. also Giddings, 1944, 1952; W. Irving, 1951). Icebound in winter, and subject to extremes of wind and cold, the areas of human settlement in the mountains have proved wholly adequate for hunting and fishing. Indeed, it is in the summer that the range province becomes less tolerable with its marshes and its clouds of mosquitoes.

To the north of the mountains lies the province of the foothills, an area intermediate between the range itself and the Arctic plain. The general pattern is one of a gradual descent from south to north, there being no sudden break on the northern slopes of the Brooks Range. The southern foothills range from 2,500 to 3,500 feet in height, and taper off in the northern sections to ridges alined in an east-west direction and no higher than 200 to 600 feet. In the main, the zone of foothills has not been glaciated, although wind and weather and the seasonal freezing and thawing combine to create some deformation. A Mesozoic complex, warped and folded especially on the southern side, the foothills were subjected to less violent warping in the north. Here the slope becomes gentle, the streams sluggish and beginning to take on the diffuse drainage aspect which characterizes the Arctic plain. In the northern foothills, hard layers, more impervious to weathering, top the ridges.

As the Arctic coastal plain is reached, the streams begin to wander at random, and there is the formation of numerous lakes and marshes. The area, extending to a depth of about 70 miles from the coast, is wholly flat except for a few isolated hummocks and knobs. Until recent geologic time this province was submerged (Solecki, 1951, p. 476; Smith and Mertie, 1930, p. 238). It is characterized by alluvial deposits of sands, clays, and gravels, and by perpetually frozen ground, the permafrost so characteristic of the typical Arctic. This phenomenon, also evident in the foothills and in the glacial silts of the mountain passes, reaches a depth of several hundred feet. Only in the short summer does the ground thaw and then only to a depth of a few inches (Wiggins, 1953, pp. 8–9). The flat plain is poorly drained and is thus, in summer, marked by its stagnant pools, its marshes, and its haphazard, meandering water courses. Although, like the foothills, the Arctic plain has not been subjected to glaciation, frost wedges, accumulations of subsurface ice, have formed and remain present through the year. In many places along the coasts the shoreline is ill defined, although here and there beach ridges, some rising 30 to 40 feet in height, have been formed as a result of the action of pack ice driven in against the land. Along the coasts, too, some windblown deposits of sand appear. This loess, the so-called Gubik Sands, has been found rich in Pleistocene fossils and it has been suggested that some evidence of early human remains, paralleling the discoveries of artifacts already made in the pass and foothill regions, may yet be found here (Solecki, 1951, p. 476). The plain is not characterized by any well-defined series of marine deposits (Smith and Mertie, 1930, p. 238).

In the truest sense, the Alaskan Arctic plain is a desert. Rain and snowfall are very slight, averaging no more than 5 to 7 inches per year. It has been suggested that this limited precipitation is the primary factor in hindering the spread of glaciers northward. The principal basis for seasonal differentiation lies not in rainfall, but in the differing intensity of temperature and in the length of daylight. The brief summer season is marked by a thaw and, for a 2-month period, by 24-hour sunshine. The transition from 24 hours of sunlight in late July to the fall equinox is most rapid, and, again, the shift from the equinox to the winter solstice involves the change in a short period from 12 hours of daylight to total darkness. At Point Barrow, for example, at 71° 23′ N., 72 days of winter darkness, beginning November 15, are the rule. Temperature changes cannot be regarded as extreme. In summer, the averages hover somewhat above freezing, although highs of 60° or 65° F. may be reached for short periods. From this, there is a gradual shift to the winter temperatures. These are not so extreme as might be imagined, particularly along the coast where 30° F. below zero may be regarded as essentially average. As Larsen and Rainey (1948, p. 23) point out, the winter temperatures of the region, while by no means so cold in comparison with the 50° to 70° below zero readings of the deeper interior, as in the forested zones of continental type climate, are nonetheless infinitely more severe as a result of intensity of wind. In the Arctic plain and foothills, a somewhat more adequate adjustment on the part of humans in terms of clothing and housing is a necessity. The frigid winters are very long and the summer brief. Physiographic change is slow and little climatic variation has been noted since the 1880's when climatic data were compiled for the first time and the coastal temperatures at Point Barrow were found to average on a yearly basis 8° F. above zero (Murdoch, 1892, p. 30). Streams and lakes are blocked with ice for much of the year and usually by November the ice has begun to form on the ocean, creating a pack which may remain unbroken until the following summer, often as late as August or September, or later.

Travel in the area is thus fairly limited and comes to depend on particular types of specialization. Throughout the long winter season, travel by dog sled is everywhere possible throughout the region. Summer travel is arduous except by the watercourses. The prevailing method remains the skin boat, the Eskimo umiak, both for travel along the rivers and on the open sea. As the limited snow melts, the land forms characteristic of the tundra, the polygonal ground, appear. These polygons, shapes caused on the surface by alternate freezing and thawing, create small depressions in which undrained water rests. Boggy areas are formed in this way; they are crossed on foot only with difficulty. Inland travel along the water courses follows the configuration of the foothills and ridges, being east and west in accord with the axes of the higher ground. The great Colville system, for example, moves eastward along the foothill base until it turns northward to fan out into the plain. The Colville rises from a divide in the west. Here, at Howard Pass, the eastward moving Colville tributaries are set off from the Noatak system which flows south and west into Kotzebue Sound.

The entire region of northwestern Alaska, from the bare northern flanks of the Brooks Range northward to the Arctic Ocean, has been described as barren, treeless, and monotonously dun colored. But this is hardly a fair description. Not only do the land forms gradually change from mountain to plain, but the many streams and lakes, the knolls and hummocks, create considerable diversity in physiographic pattern. It is true that winters are marked by sufficient snowfall as to present a vast white land, but the driving polar winds clear patches of ground, leaving bare black ridges and forming the small deposits of snow into random and sometimes heavy drifts. Along the coasts, the pack-ice crushes in along the beaches and, reaching surprising heights as the result of action of wind and wave, creates a temporary landscape full of amazing shapes as one berg piles up against another. As the winds shift, so also do the configurations of land and sea. Nor is the landscape monotonous in summer. As the tundra thaws, the shallow rooted vegetation begins to sprout in abundance, hastily to enjoy its brief life in the 24-hour sunshine. There are no trees, to be sure, and except for a few clumps of stunted willow that are prominent in the foothills and mountain passes but increasingly less significant in the plain, the plant life reaches no marked growth. On the other hand, the many species of flowering plants, minute though they are, and the many varieties of lichens and mosses cover the tundra in all directions and offer a meadowlike prospect. Seasonal changes, contrasts between light and darkness, between wind, storm, fog, and sunshine, not to mention the richness of plant and animal life, combine to make the tundra regions an area of great fascination. One shading moves into another, day by day, season by season, subtly, but perceptibly.

NORTH ALASKAN ESKIMO SETTLEMENTS

Throughout this great area live the scattered groups of Eskimo. These represent a people settled over centuries but not the first groups in the region. Since Alaska formed the land bridge by which man entered the New World from Asia, there is widespread evidence of human antiquity, of the Paleo-Indian, the precursors of the pre-Columbian Indian tribes of North and South America. In northern Alaska, through the area which has been described, there was a backwash of the main stream of movement. The archeologist has given considerable attention to this and his researches have shed much light on the important problem of the origin of man in the Americas. The interior regions of Alaska are especially rich in remote prehistoric remains, the most ancient levels being characterized by flint tools of types which correlate with sequences established elsewhere in the Americas and which, in many instances, are suggestive of Asia. Evidence of Folsom culture—polyhedral core and lamellar flake industries—has come to light in northwestern Alaska; the so-called "Mesolithic" forms have been detected in the northern foothills; and along the coasts, at Cape Denbigh on Norton Sound, the recent discoveries of burins point to an origin in Asia (Solecki, 1951, pp. 478–493). As the evidence is weighed and new data are collected, man's antiquity in Alaska is shown to be remote.

But in addition to these and many other ancient remains, there is the tremendous richness of the prehistory of the Eskimo themselves. While not so remote in time, the Eskimo cultures of the past pose a good many as yet unsolved problems. The Eskimo cultures might be resolved in terms of varying degrees of specialization and of influences emanating from distant culture centers. Thus, while the remoter prehistory of the region indicates an orientation toward the hunting of land animals, a sequence which carries through into the prehistoric Eskimo cultures of the inland regions, such a culture as that of the Ipiutak at Point Hope has been described as marginal to a central Siberian bronze and iron age culture (Larsen and Rainey, 1948, p. 160; Collins, 1951, p. 432). However this may be, the Eskimo cultures of the past are never simple, and the various suggestions as to their origin are being clarified slowly as new data come to light. Even in the general prehistoric picture, however, the question of the human ecology, of specializations on land or sea and of degrees between, needs resolution. In Alaska, at least, the archeological evidence presupposes the ethnological development. Northern Alaska demonstrates the interaction, both in the prehistoric past and in the ethnological present, of groups each reflecting a major ecological pattern. These are two, the nuunamiut, people of the land, whose life developed around the caribou, and the tareumiut, the people of the sea, whose primary orientation was toward sea mammal hunting, and in the area of the Arctic slope, at least, especially toward whaling. Whatever may be said of the local specializations of the cultures of northwestern Alaska in the past, whether the concern is with the Ipiutak, the Old Bering Sea, the Birnirk, or whatever, these are maritime cultures set off against inland caribou hunting cultures. The generalized Thule culture, typologically definable, basically maritime but orienting itself as well toward caribou hunting, does not, in Alaska, modify this basic ecological picture. There remains, in the historic present, the inland nomad set off against the village dweller at the sea.

While a fuller discussion of the two groups is yet to be given, the general pattern of geographic settlement must be kept in mind in order properly to designate the peoples of the region. The terms nuunamiut (nuunataγmiut) and tareumiut are of course derivative of native designations for the two ecological groupings. These terms are descriptive of a way of life and cannot be regarded as tribal designations. As is well known, aboriginal Eskimo society consisted of aggregates of individuals that formed bands or villages. Since membership and residence in either depended pretty much on the choice of the individual, and since the size of the group could expand or contract depending on local circumstances, it is difficult to do other than to point out certain of the major groupings and to define them at a particular point in time. The situation today is atypical, Barrow village having grown inordinately as the result of the employment opportunities afforded by the naval installation there. Today, moreover, the delicate balance that once existed between the inland peoples and those on the sea has been completely disrupted. Except for a small band that still chooses to reside in the foothills and the passes of the Brooks Range and another which moves about in the Kobuk-Noatak region, the inland cultures are virtually extinct. To obtain a proper perspective on the distribution of peoples in the area, the stage must be set at a century ago, in the period when mutual interdependence of inland and maritime life was still paramount and before the distortions in the native economy took place as a result of the presence of European whalers, the growth of the governmentally sponsored schools, and missionization.

It is considerably easier to discuss the settlements of the coastal groups where a greater degree of permanence was achieved. Coastal villages were well integrated around dance houses and the concept of the whaling crew and its leader. Moreover, the maritime villages came to have fairly well-defined territories in which their respective residents moved. Not that these were in any sense owned; in the main, this came about as the result of exploitation of familiar terrain. It was possible, and still remains so, to determine a man's place of origin by noting who his relatives were and also by his speech, since each village had its own phonetic idiosyncrasy. The inland peoples, while in the main definable as to local territory, tended to lack the incipient formalization of the concept of chieftainship. Because, as bands, they tended to move much more widely and to lack fixed villages, they become somewhat more difficult to name. This is complicated further by the fact that although such local groups had names for themselves, the name might or might not coincide with the name applied to them by the coastal peoples. There was by no means uniformity of names, either as designations for local bands or for topographic and geographic features. And it must also be emphasized that Eskimo culture requires an exactness of names in respect both to ethnic groups and places. There has thus been some confusion of Eskimo group names, much depending on the point of reference from which the name is applied.

All the native peoples of the region, however, are agreed on the basic nomenclature distinguishing caribou from sea mammal hunter. Local groups within each classification can be recognized and it is suggested here, for purposes of convenience, that the names applied by the natives of Barrow village to their neighbors be selected as standard. The major settlements and groupings of the coastal regions are as follows.

At the Point, on the northernmost tip of land of the North American mainland, was the now abandoned village of nuwuk, the people of which were known as the nuwuŋmiut. In 1852–53, nuwuk had 54 inhabited houses, with a population of 309, 166 of which were men (John Simpson, 1855, p. 237). In 1854 a fuel shortage had reduced the number of inhabited houses to 48. Dr. John Simpson, whose observations these are, believed the population to be declining, a fact which he substantiated by the presence of an abandoned dance house at nuwuk and of several ruined dwellings. Forty persons had died of influenza in 1851, and again, in 1853–54, there were 27 deaths, mainly the result of starvation. When the next observations were made, in 1882–83, nuwuk had a population of 150 (Ray, 1885 b, p. 38).

Down from nuwuk, on the sea side, were several campsites. All of these bore names, designations which apply still, but none were sufficiently large or continuously inhabited to merit their being called villages. The site of piγinik, from which the archeological horizon of Birnirk is named, was not inhabited in the recent period, although families have been known to reside there the year round and the location forms the duck hunting reserve of the Barrow Eskimo.

Several village units combined into one at the site of the modern Barrow village (pl. 2, *a*). This is the location of the older town of utkeaaγvik, the people of which were known up and down the coast as the utkeaviŋmiut. Like nuwuk, this village grew and declined in population depending on circumstances. Simpson lists 40 houses and 250 people in 1852–53, with a decline as a result of famine in 1853–54, 40 deaths having occurred (J. Simpson, 1855, p. 237). Ray and Murdoch, in 1882–83, record 23 families present at Cape Smythe (utkeaaγvik) with a total population of 130 (Ray, 1885 b, pp. 33, 39).

Moving southward from Cape Smythe, one passes considerable distance down the coast to the next historic settlement, although again scattered houses and families might be met at any point. All campsites, and indeed, any significant location of any kind, whether creek mouth, high bank, or gully, was named, a reflection of a major cultural preoccupation with geography. Individuals and families, moreover, were designated as coming from a particular place, the name of which was at once familiar. Ray records 8 families and 50 individuals resident at Point Belcher on the sea side south and west of Peard Bay (ibid., p.38). These he terms the Sidarumiut. As nearly as can be judged, this was not a permanent settlement in historic times. Groups moved in and out of the Point Belcher area, this being a favored location for summer caribou hunting. Several groups are described as having lived at and near Peard Bay, from sinaraat (Skull Cliff) to the Wainwright Inlet.

At the modern village of Wainwright, the Kuk River empties into a lagoon; the people are hence designated as the kuγmiut. Ten families are listed as resident there in 1882–83, with a total population of 80 persons (ibid., p. 38). Kuk means simply "river."

Leaving Wainwright, one passes another area of extremely sparse population before the next major settlement is reached. This is Icy Cape, a village which was very important a century ago as a native whaling center but which was abandoned no later than 1890. The building of the whaling station at Cape Smythe by New England whalers evidently caused the desertion of several previously inhabited hamlets and villages. It also increased momentarily the population of Barrow village. Icy Cape was known as kayaakserevik, the residents as the kayaaksereviŋmiut. No census data are available, but the group was unquestionably small, there being only one dance house there in the recollection of living informants.

South of Icy Cape, the long narrow lagoon, known as kasegaluk, was formed by the alluvial reefs deposited by the Utokuk River. At the mouth of the Utokuk itself lay a quasipermanent settlement, likewise abandoned in the late 19th century, also known as utokuk. The people who derive their name from this settlement, the utokaγmiut, are a recognized nuunamiut grouping who came to the sea periodically for trading and for social activities such as the Messenger Feast. They were not drawn into the whaling complex. This group was allegedly the largest of the inland Eskimo north of the mountains.

At the southern end of the kasegaluk lagoon, on the coast itself, is the modern village of Point Lay. This was a hamlet consisting of a house or two until 1929–30, when a group of Eskimo from Point Hope "colonized" there (Rainey, 1947, p. 236). Point Lay bears the name kalli, the people being the kallimmiut. The residents of this village hunt seal, some walrus, and an occasional beluga, but do not engage in whaling, the coastline being indented away from the usual course taken by whales.

It is now a considerable distance to the south until the next village is reached. As before, several hamlets lay between—not the least of which was at Cape Lisburne, a point known as wiivak (place of return). Point Hope was the next major settlement, the southern limit of intensive whaling, a large village, comparable to nuwuk and utkeaaγvik in the north. It had an estimated population of 250 in 1880, a number which it retains today very closely (ibid., p. 236). The village is located on a sand and gravel bar formed by the Kukpuk River and is thus somewhat comparable in location to nuwuk, a village resting on the long narrow spit of Point Barrow itself. Point Hope is known as tikeraaq (index finger) and the people living there as the tikeraγmiut.

Point Barrow marks the northern limit of the area of intensive whaling, Point Hope the southern. The principal groupings of peoples in this area of the Alaskan Arctic Slope are thus those listed. Southward from Point Hope and eastward from Point Barrow other groups are encountered, it is true; these, however, reflect a different ecological adjustment and are allied more closely with the aboriginal inland groupings. Although to the east of Barrow there are numerous campsites, they are for the most part remains left by the utkeaviŋmiut and the nuwuŋmiut as they traveled to the mouth of the Colville for trade with the inland Eskimo. No permanent settlements are indicated. Nor do there seem to have been people permanently resident at neγłiq, on the Colville Delta, or at Oliktok Point, the sites of trading assemblages. The next major settlement to the east is Barter Island (tikixtak, tikixtaγmiut) and beyond this, on the Canadian side, is Herschel Island (kikiktaaruk), both suggesting a Thule type culture with different orientations. The nearest neighbors of the modern Point Hope group are those of the village to the south along the coast. This village bears the name kivaliina (to the east), and the people are designated as the kivalinermiut. This is a recent village, founded at the turn of the present century by a group of inland Eskimo who pushed to the sea (ibid., pp. 236–237). The orientation of this group is virtually wholly toward the inland regions and they may be properly regarded as nuunamiut. Except for some sealing and the hunting of an occasional beluga, the kivalinermiut depend basically on caribou hunting in the western foothills. The various groups farther to the east and south may also be regarded as inland Eskimo even though many bands formerly settled on the coast for various periods of time.

In summary, therefore, the people classed as the tareumiut are specifically those residing in permanent coastal villages, devoting themselves primarily to sea mammal hunting, particularly to whaling, and building a series of complex social and religious patterns around the whale. These groups consist of the nuwuŋmiut, the utkeaviŋmiut, the kuγmiut, the kayaaksereviŋmiut, the recently established group of kallimmiut, and the tikeraγmiut. To these may be added the many minor settlements, some wholly temporary, some of longer duration, inhabited by a family or two for a time and then abandoned. In such cases, the people were designated either with the name of the place where they chose to reside or continued to bear the name of the group from which they originally came.

These temporary hamlets along the coasts tend to render the matter of population estimates somewhat difficult. As has been seen from the estimates provided by the different 19th century explorers of the region, population fluctuated greatly. That it may have been considerably greater in the remote past is indicated by the richness of archeological materials, the 600 dwellings at Ipiutak, for example, the large and presumably communal houses at Birnirk, and the many ruins, both near modern and ancient, scattered along the coasts. According to the census obtained in 1881–83 by the Point Barrow Expedition, and adding these to the known figures for the Point Hope-Point Lay area for the same period, population of slightly less than 1,000 may be supposed for the coastal villages in the late 19th century (Ray, 1885 b, p. 38; Rainey, 1947, p. 236). This would represent a considerable decrease, perhaps by as many as 500, from the period of the 1850's, a loss attributable in large measure to the European diseases to which the Eskimo lacked resistance, such as measles, influenza, and tuberculosis, and to famine. In the recent period, the tendency has been to abandon the scattered dwellings and to converge on the towns. This has been the result of the building of schools, mission churches, and hospitals established either by mission bodies or the United States Department of the Interior. Educational and medical care provided at Barrow, for example, effectively brought about the end of the nuwuk settlement, the people having gradually given up residence there and built new homes at Barrow village. The process of change was a slow one, to be sure, but the number of coastal settlements is now limited to four along the Arctic slope.

Throughout the 20th century, it would appear that the coastal villages have held their own in terms of population. This is true, however, only in a superficial sense. The establishment of coastal villages as administrative centers has affected the resettlement of inland Eskimo with the result that the nuunamiut have virtually ceased to exist. Many have now chosen to live on the coast in the four whaling villages of Barrow, Wainwright, Point Lay, and Point Hope, or they have elected to settle on the coast farther to the south, such as at kivaliina, on the Noatak River, or at Kotzebue at Hotham Inlet. Thus, if the coastal population has remained stable, it has been at the expense of the marked decrease of inland groups. The situation at Barrow village is further anomalous, the population here having swelled out of all proportion in the period of 1946–1953, a result of the employment opportunities offered by the naval installation on the petroleum reserve of northern Alaska. Census returns will vary with the year; in the most recent period, Barrow population has averaged about 1,500, while the other towns have fewer inhabitants. According to the count of the Alaska Native Service, an administrative arm of the United States Indian Bureau, Wainwright, in the most recent period, has had 180 inhabitants, Point Lay 90, and Point Hope 240. All intermediate settlements were abandoned in the period after 1900, the last family resident at nuwuk having moved to Barrow village in 1942. Other coastal settlements had disappeared somewhat earlier.

The inland Eskimo are thus virtually gone. There is a vanishing group still resident north of the Brooks Range. This is an alliance of two formerly fairly large bands, the killiγmiut, a group taking its name from the Killik River, and the tulugaγmiut, residents of Anaktuvuk Pass and named from Lake Tulugak, in the lower reaches of the pass. When visited by the writer in 1953, this group consisted of 58 persons. The group hunts over a wide area, from Chandler Lake to the many watercourses of the Colville. It has thus far resisted schools and medical care, although it has been Christianized, and it seems a matter of a few years at most before the group vanishes completely (pl. 4, *a*).

In the western foothills, however, there are still Eskimo groups, all of them small, located along the Noatak, Kobuk, and Selawik Rivers. No adequate census figures for these groups can be given, however, although 200 is probably excessive, for the reason that this is a floating population. The people have ties to the now fairly large town of Kotzebue and look to this center as a source of cash and various necessities. Families are known to move about hunting and fishing for extended periods of time, 2 years and more, and then to return for a like period to a settlement. Unlike the group resident in the Anaktuvuk area, these inland peoples no longer retain the sense of group autonomy.

As the more recent history of the inland zone is considered, however, it is seen that the ethnic groups were once fairly large. Because of the diffuse nature of the way of life, it is again difficult to obtain either an accurate census or adequate designations for the groups themselves. The principal basis for estimates of population must come from natives themselves who can recall the assemblages at the height of the season of trading. Although these congregations varied in size from year to year, there is no doubt that the majority of the inland Eskimo visited them, being forced by necessity to go at least once yearly to the coast to obtain the necessary commodity of seal oil. The earliest census is that given by McLenegan in 1885 for the people of the Noatak area. This suggests 225 noataγmiut (Healy, 1887, p. 75). But this does not take into account the many Eskimo who may have been absent from the settlements at the time. Larsen's informant, the utokaγmiu, qamaq, describes a convocation of the utokaγmiut at utokuk at the mouth of the river. He recalls two rows of 80 tents each and estimates 10 persons to a tent. Larsen and Rainey, although they believe the estimate excessive, are of the opinion that even if this number were halved, there would still be a possibility of 800 people in the assemblage (Larsen and Rainey, 1948, p. 31). Stefansson (1914 b, p. 10) believes that the utokaγmiut formed the largest grouping of inland Eskimo.

To these figures may be added the groupings further to the east. Names for these groupings tend to vary somewhat depending on the point of reference. The utkeaviŋmiut, for example, referred to the Colville River as kupik; any grouping along the Colville proper was thus called kupiγmiut. This might be broken down further depending on the specific locale or tributary with which the grouping was usually associated. Thus the groups along the ikpikpuk were the ikpikpaŋmiut; those along the Meade River (koluγuraak), the koluγuraγmiut, or more specifically, since the modern Meade River village bears the name of the old campsite, tikereeluq, as the tikereluγmiut. A term commonly used to refer to the Colville River people was kaŋgianermiut, essentially synonymous with the kupiγmiut of Barrow usage. Others might be listed that are subdivisions of these, groups which draw their names from various localities, especially from streams, but the designations are by no means exact. Of importance, for example, are the still surviving killiγmiut, or, farther to the east, the now vanished kaγmalliγmiut, a grouping visited and described by Stefansson.[1]

At the mouth of the Colville, on one of the arms of the delta, was the site of neγłiq, where the utkeaviŋmiut and the nuwuŋmiut met with the inland Eskimo in July and August for purposes of trade. Living informants who went there as traders in the early years of the present century are agreed that an amazing number of people made the trip down the Colville from the inland regions. qiwaq, an utkeaviŋmiu, counted over 400 tents pitched there by the many groups from all areas, including those to the mouth of the McKenzie, Herschel and Barter Islands, and was unable to complete a count. When it is remembered that people came to neγłiq from as far away as noatak, as well as from virtually every stream across the tundra, the assemblage of 1,500 there is not too surprising. When, however, this is added to the parallel assemblage held at Hotham Inlet between inland Eskimo farther to the south and those from the coast from Wainwright to Point Hope, the numbers of inland Eskimo begin to emerge somewhat more clearly. Larsen and Rainey estimate the population of the inland regions in the period of roughly 1895 to 1905 as 3,000. This figure agrees with that arrived at by the present writer. This would, however, include the groups located on the western plateaus of the Brooks Range and those of the Hotham Inlet region, the people of the Noatak (noataγmiut), of the Kobuk (kovuŋmiut), and the Selawik (selawiŋmiut) Rivers. On this basis, the ratio between tareumiut and nuunamiut would be about one to three.

But the groups of inland Eskimo have gradually dropped away. Even in 1924, Rasmussen encountered about 500 Eskimo at the Colville mouth (Rasmussen, 1927, p. 317). This area is wholly deserted today. As is noted above, the populations of the Noatak-Kobuk-Selawik drainages can hardly be said to be permanent, a fact which suggests to the present writer a grouping of about 200 more or less fixed Eskimo. Actually, a count of 1939 reveals 1,400 residents of interior Alaska north and west of the Brooks Range, and a decade ago Larsen and Rainey suggest the inland populations as being about 900 (Larsen and Rainey, 1948, p. 31). Although there is unquestionably great mobility of population, the Alaska Native Service has done all in its power to draw the inland groups to the coast for administra-

[1] Stefansson (1914 a, p. 9) This author differentiates the kupiγmiut from the kaŋgianermiut, placing the latter on the upper reaches of the Colville, the former on the lower.

tive purposes. Coupled with this is the recent employment incentive at Barrow. The inland populations today do concentrate along the westward flowing rivers. The peoples to the north of the Brooks Range, in the Anaktuvuk Pass area, remain as a small group of conservative diehards. The modern Meade River village, not far from Barrow, is wholly recent and has a mixed nuunamiut-tareumiut population settled there to work a coal mine. It is, however, an old nuunamiut station. Various factors—an imposed administrative situation, the introduction of a money economy, and not the least, the health problem—have combined to decimate the inland Eskimo. As may be seen, however, the maritime villages have not grown correspondingly.

The chief problem associated with the determining of groupings of the inland Eskimo arises from the ephemeral nature of their organization. Rainey argues convincingly for the designation of both tareumiut and nuunamiut groupings as tribes, thereby implying a fixed territory, common interests, and essential group stability (Rainey, 1947, p. 240). All of this was certainly true but because the so-called tribes were secondary to the emphasis placed on kinship, and because the ties of kinship cut across tribal lines, this designation is perhaps not the most favorable. Since these peoples lacked any unifying force beyond kinship, and since each individual was free, either with or without his immediate relatives, to settle where he chose, provided he could establish some claim of kinship, the concept of tribe is wholly subordinated. That there were certain unifying institutions which went beyond kinship can be established. In no case, however, were these inclusive of all of the population of a grouping. The whaling crew on the coast, and the communal caribou hunt inland serve as a locus of interests and are non-kin associations. It is thus difficult to discover any activity in which a grouping engaged as a whole. Some sense of rivalry existed between the maritime villages, especially with regard to intervillage contests arising at the time of the major socioeconomic festival, the Messenger Feast. Even here, however, the majority of the village inhabitants merely occupied the role of spectators. Statuses were fixed, but not in relation to a village group; these, too, tended to cut across residence lines. The upshot of this situation permits a designation of the various groupings only in terms of activity that produce localized culture areas. The basic distinction of nuunamiut as against tareumiut is permissible as a basic ecological and cultural division. Other than this, one can only refer to the various subgroupings by name and with the understanding that these are meaningful only in the sense of geographical divisions within each culture and ecological area. Far more important is the interlocking of circles of kinship and the significant fact that nuunamiut is distinguished from tareumiut not only on the basis of way of life but also because of the absence of kinship ties between them. Kinship extends within an ecological area, never across its boundaries. For convenient reference, it is possible to designate the coastal settlements as villages, and the contracting and expanding inland groupings as bands.

HUMAN RELATION TO THE BIOTA

FLORA

In the exploitation of the resources of his domain, the aboriginal Eskimo chose to be selective and to make exclusive capital of the products of hunting. Meat, whether of sea mammals, of the various mammalian species taken on land, of fowl, or of fish, remains the basis of human diet in the area of northern Alaska. One result of the primary orientation toward meat was the neglect of almost all plant foods and the restriction of their use chiefly to cases of dire emergency. Plants were used more to meet certain utilitarian needs than as food. The attention to plant foods was indirect, in that the partially digested stomach contents of the various kinds of herbivorous game was frequently eaten. The various mosses on which the caribou depend, the seaborne plankton that forms the basis of subsistence for the baleen whales, created side dishes in the Eskimo diet. But in terms of actual use, the flora of the region yields a small inventory only.

Of the two human ecological orientations, the nuunamiut, the peoples of the inland regions, made far greater use of the available plant life. For example, the many species and varieties of berries collected on the mountain slopes may be regarded as forming the most important contribution of vegetable foods to the native diet. Mixed with caribou fat, soaked in seal oil, or pounded into meat to make a pemmican, such berries became an important item in the aboriginal trade between the interior and the coast. The most complete list of the various berries used is that made by Lieut. George M. Stoney (1900, p. 99) in his explorations of the region in 1885. He does not, however, identify these beyond noting the native name, nor does he specify the localities in which the berries are picked. Stoney gives 10 different species, the chief of which were the salmonberry (aakpuk) and the various blueberries (pawnraat). He notes that all are preferred with oil or meat and are sometimes eaten before meat. Only in cases of extreme need would the inland peoples subsist solely on berries. Stoney notes that at isiyuq, on the lower Colville, there is an edible clay which is sometimes eaten with oil and berries (ibid., p. 100).

Apart from berries, there was random use of various plants as food. So indifferent are the native peoples to these, as well as to berries, that they could not be persuaded, at Anaktuvuk Pass, for example, to locate some of the edible plants for purposes of identification.[2] The most important root vegetable was a knotweed, faintly resembling a parsnip (*Polygonum bistortum*), known by the native term "masu," which was gathered in the passes and foothills. This was eaten raw or boiled, and the leaves also were sometimes gathered and soaked in oil. The same treatment was given to a kind of rhubarb, to willow shoots, and, in Stoney's observation, to a dozen other plants, including roots and grasses (Stoney, 1900, p. 99).

Beyond the use of the paunch contents of herbivores, and the berries obtained by trade from the nuunamiut, the coastal Eskimo had no plant foods. Edible seaweeds were collected south of Point Hope but as nearly as can be judged, they did not find their way northward. The seaweeds did travel to the inland peoples by trade. One especially, naγkuwik, found its way inland along the Kobuk and Noatak routes. Stoney (1900, p. 99) remarks of this that it had to be boiled in seal oil; to eat it raw caused crossed eyes.

Among the inland bands, there was extensive use of plants for other purposes than as food. Spruce bark, for example, was shredded and used to enforce cordage, and the spruce roots were sometimes eaten. The various willows had many uses, not the least of which was as fuel in the passes and foothills. The heavier willows (konuŋyuq) are still used to make snowshoe frames, and as was formerly the case bows were made from them when birch (ulaaleluq) was scarce. The smaller willows were differentiated as waakpiq, akutuaq, and nuwuŋyuq. The latter was used to make a red dye, its bark being finely scraped and soaked in water. A generic term for the willow is ukpiq.

Along the coasts, there was some employment of mosses for various purposes. The rich sphagnum moss which grows in areas of decayed animal matter, such as at abandoned campsites, was used to line the interior of boots. The tareumiut preferred shredded baleen for this purpose. Mosses were regularly used for infant diapering and for the wick of the ubiquitous lamp.

The exploitation of plant resources was somewhat increased when tobacco was introduced to the Eskimo south of Bering Strait. This took place in the early 19th century, and within a short time tobacco was obtainable by the north Alaskan groups through the processes of trade. So valuable a commodity had at all costs to be saved as

---

[2] An amusing illustration of this was provided at Anaktuvuk Pass. An old informant, queried on plant foods, indicated both his lack of interest and distaste for them. He had lived for a time with a married daughter in Fairbanks, but had returned to the north because, as he said, "I couldn't stand eating them flowers all the time; I wanted meat". He went on to say that he ate no "flowers" now.

long as possible. Traded always in leaf form, the tobacco was made ready for smoking—the principal use to which the Eskimo applied it—by adulterating it with cottonwood bark, willow bark, fungi, and grasses. Even in this instance, however, dog or caribou hair was frequently mixed with tobacco and was in any case always placed at the bottom of the pipe bowl as a filter.

Along the coasts, the only source of wood was that which drifted in on the beaches. This was found in surprisingly large quantities and came to serve as the source of supply for the making of house beams, planking, sleds, weapons, and many other things. Even the inland Eskimo came to depend on this source of supply, obtaining logs and planks by trade from the coast. Unconcerned with plants as food, and dependent on driftwood for meeting various important needs, the maritime Eskimo made no effort to utilize the local vegetation. Even if the inland Eskimo made greater use of plants, it is clear that some needs which might have been met by a fuller use of vegetable products were filled in other ways.

FAUNA

The Eskimo food quest was thus centered wholly in the wildlife of the region. It is this, in its various manifestations, which underlies adjustments in ecology and culture. In the patterned dichotomy of existence are seen the differences of inland nomadism, of bands organized around caribou hunting, as against the settled village life with its whaling emphasis. In both settings, despite the uniformities of language and kinship organization, there were vast differences in the social forms which went beyond kinship and in ceremonial life. The relations of man to the native fauna must accordingly be conceived in terms of the two primary orientations. Of the two, the maritime Eskimo had the far richer life, able as they were to direct attention to inland hunting on the tundra when not engaged in sea mammal pursuit. Thus, they hunted caribou in the summer and fall, fished extensively in the fresh-water streams, and were skilled in the uses of the various traps. In some measure, they thus acquired the skills of inland life while the reverse was not true; the inland Eskimo were not prepared to deal with the hazards of the sea, of whaling in the ice leads, or of sealing at breathing holes in the ice. But for the maritime Eskimo, inland hunting was largely an individual matter; it did not call for the communal enterprise characteristic of the nuunamiut or for the same ceremonial orientations. The various animals known and used, a wide variety, are best listed and some evaluation of their role in the native economy given.

1. *The whale.*—This is the polar, or bowhead, whale (*Balaena mysticetus* Linn.)[3] which begins to swim up through the Bering Strait as soon as the ice permits free movement. Herds of these animals feed through the summer along the edges of the polar cap, returning southward in the fall when the ocean ice begins to thicken. Today as in the past, the baleen whales appear in the off-shore ice leads beginning in late April. They may still be sighted in early June. Whaling camps were set up on the edges of the leads and the crews pursued the whales in umiaks, each with several harpoons with two seal-bladder floats on each. The attempt was made to place as many harpoons as possible in the whale. When the animal tired and rose for air in the limited space of the ice lead, it was lanced, a special lance with a large stone head being used for this purpose. An attempt was made to spear the whale in the heart, lungs, or brain and so to kill it. The carcass was then towed back to the camp at the edge of the lead, tugged by communal effort on the ice, and divided. It is in respect to this whole activity that an extremely elaborate series of ceremonial usages arise and that a basis for extra-kin associations is seen.[4]

The general teım for the common baleen whale is aaγvik. An especially large specimen—and it is worth noting that some exceed 60 feet in length and that a rough computation can be made of 1 ton per foot—is called qayrelik. Smaller specimens, the poggy whales, 20 to 30 feet in length, with 3 or 4 feet of baleen, and reflecting a varietal difference, are iŋutuk. A larger specimen of this type is iŋutuvak.

The northern villages engaged in whaling in the fall also, when the herds began to move south again. But this season cannot be considered important since it affected only nuwuk and utkeaaγvik. Even for these towns, no elaboration of ceremonial activity took place in the fall, this being reserved for the earlier season. At this time, whales were hunted in the open water, obviously a much more difficult undertaking in the fragile umiak. Two or three animals might be captured at this time, although this by no means compares with a successful spring season, when as many as 25 whales, representing hundreds of tons of meat, might be brought in.

---

[3] Murdoch (1885 a, p. 101). The faunal nomenclature has in most instances been drawn from Murdoch's treatment of the natural history of the region and from data obtained at the Arctic Research Laboratory at Point Barrow. These were checked against G. S. Miller, Jr., and R. Kellogg's "List of North American Recent Mammals," 1955. Identifications of inland faunae have been made by Rausch (1951) and Murie (1935).

[4] Ibid., p. 101. Murdoch mentions the introduction of techniques derived from European whalers as well as their equipment. By 1881, the Eskimo at Cape Smythe (Barrow) were using steel lances and whaling bombs. A resistance to these methods arose in 1883, the prevailing attitude being that the stone-headed lance should still be used to dispatch the whale and barring this, an ivory harpoon should strike the whale first. When this was done, steel harpoons could safely be used. By 1900, this custom had fallen away.

The meat was divided in various ways between participating crews. It was carefully stored in ice cellars after being distributed according to well-defined regulation and ceremony. Use was made of virtually every part of the whale carcass. Apart from the especially prized skin—the delicate muktuk, eaten raw and boiled—and the blubber and meat, the bones were used much as wood, in making house beams, sleds, and many other artifacts, and the baleen, the long-fringed strainers in the mouth of the plankton-eating whales, was likewise used for many purposes, including the making of ornaments and amulets, of sledges, and of armor. Oil in great quantities, for use as food and fuel, was stored in seal bladders and skins. The upshot of the whaling, given an average year, made for considerable surplus of food and a basic ease of life. If, however, the herds changed their course for a year or two, the result was often starvation, or at least, limited rations. The population of a coastal community rose with a successful year, and declined markedly if few whales were taken, as the inhabitants struck out alone or in small groups to wrest a living from other sources.

2. The caribou.—What the whale was to the tareumiut, the caribou was to the nuunamiut. Its presence was vital to inland life and, like the whale on the coast, it became the keystone of economic, social, and religious activity, involved with an infinite number of restrictions, attitudes, and modes of treatment. The caribou (*Rangifer arcticus stonei* (Allen)), Eskimo tuttu, spreads widely over the American Arctic and sub-Arctic, appearing in herds of literally thousands. Through the north Alaskan regions the migrations of these animals are quite complex and the relations of the Brooks Range herds to those farther to the south are only imperfectly understood. (Rausch, 1951, pp. 186–87). The caribou move through the passes of the Brooks Range, not once, but often several times yearly, the movements themselves being quite irregular and erratic. The unpredictability of the caribou migrations has long affected the patterning of settlement of the inland Eskimo, inasmuch as these groups are obliged to cover wide areas both in search of the herds and to follow them for long distances once they have been located. The animals tend to move northward through the passes between January and June, a definite sequence beginning with cows and calves, followed by bulls, and lastly, old bulls, having been noted by Rausch (ibid., pp. 187–88). Calves are born on the Arctic slope side between April and June. By October, the entire herds move southward again. These movements are usual but by no means consistent or wholly predictable. Nor do the herds remain stable in numbers, small herds sometimes returning to the place where an extremely large herd had been sighted the previous year. In the Central Brooks Range, a not unusual pattern is seen in the movement northward along the Killik River, while the southward trek takes place along the Anaktuvuk River, through the pass of that name, and so to the south along the John River (ibid., p. 187). Whatever the route of movement, one may expect to encounter herds of caribou along the foothills and adjacent tundra plain in the spring. The rutting season of these animals is generally in October. The animals, having milled about the tundra, feeding on moss, have begun to move southward in order, as the Eskimo say, to escape the mosquitoes.

On the Arctic plain, the herds tend to break into eastern and western sections. Some stragglers remain in or near the passes, while advance guards may reach the coasts at various points. The patterning of movement has evidently changed in recent years. Murdoch mentions the presence of caribou in spring along the Ikpikpuk, Meade, and Kuaru Rivers, but indicates that the herds do not come to the coast or near it (Murdoch, 1885 a, p. 98). In recent years, however, fairly large herds have regularly been seen along the beaches to the south of Barrow village, along the Kuk River and Peard Bay. Since they appear in the areas close to the coast, they become an important source of food supply to the modern coastal Eskimo. Farther to the south, the noataγmiut and the utokaγmiut have been wholly dependent on the westward movements of caribou herds and remain so.

There appears to be no evidence that the caribou herds are disappearing. Indeed, the killiγmiut indicate that the herds today are larger than they were a quarter of a century and more ago. In fact, hunting by the Eskimo, with the disappearance of the inland bands, is not nearly so intensive as it was formerly. There is always the threat to the herds brought on by wolves and other predators, but this, as may be anticipated, seems cyclical. The introduction of reindeer blood lines, as the result of the failure of the reindeer industry in northern Alaska, appears not to have modified the caribou population.

More significant is the disappearance of the inland Eskimo. This has come about, not, as has been suggested by some, because of decimation of the caribou herds, but rather because the peoples of the coast discontinued the patterns of trade on which the nuunamiut so vitally depended. Once this took place, the inland Eskimo were forced to come to the coast and to revise their mode of life.

That the caribou movements are erratic is indicated by the experiences of the Anaktuvuk Eskimo in the summer of 1953. The spring had not been successful in that the caribou had failed to materialize in the Central Brooks Range. The small group of remaining Eskimo were at short rations and were later obliged to move to the east in order to catch the southward movement. This has been the usual situation, with the result that inland Eskimo life has always been precariously balanced between feast and famine.

The inland Eskimo regularly undertook their intensive caribou hunting in the spring. The meat was usually jerked, being hung on racks. As soon as the weather permitted this, the great drives began to take place. This was usually by April, which meant that much of the hunting was directed toward the younger bulls, a preferred quarry because of their greater fat storage. In the past, cows and calves were hunted less for meat and more for the hides. These skins especially were important as a main item of trade with the coast, being in demand for making into undergarments.

Eskimo terms for the caribou vary in differentiating both age and sex and the lexicon is large. The general term "tuttu" applies to any adult caribou, but bulls, pukniq, are distinguished from cows, kulavaq, and the younger animals ranked as to age. There is a general term for calf, nuγaq, and for a young bull, nukataγaq; young bulls with fully grown antlers, nukataγaakruq, are distinguished from yearlings, aŋayukl^{y}aakruq.

The hunting of caribou among the inland Eskimo reached a high degree of specialization in aboriginal times, skills being involved in which the peoples of the coast did not wholly share. Caribou hunting by the tareumiut was more frequently an individual matter, or at least one in which several men might informally share. In the inland sections, however, the hunting was elaborated and communal, providing the basis for the structuring of lines of authority and prestige. The great spring hunt was undertaken by means of one of two well-defined methods involving activity on the part of virtually every member of the community. The first technique was the impound drive, the second, a variation of the first, a lake drive.

Each inland band, having its defined hunting area, chose several sites within this territory, depending on the route of caribou migration, for the erection of a corral. The impound itself, kaŋiγak, was located at a point beyond a ford and concealed, if possible, behind a ridge. The corral itself was made from different materials depending on the season. A spring corral was often made with stones and willow branches, while in the late fall or early spring, walls of ice were erected. A usual technique was to build several roughly parallel walls at the far end of the corral, leaving openings through which the caribou might advance, only to be caught by snares in the further spaces. While the area covered by the corral might vary, the average might run to as much as 50 yards in width and from 75 to 100 yards in length. The herds of caribou were led into the corral by converging lines of posts set up at intervals of 30 to 100 yards apart and leading directly to the ford and the corral entrance. These were logs, cairns of stones, or piles of brush, often covered with discarded clothing or with pieces of skin which flapped in the breeze. These were known as in^{y}uksuk (like a man, i. e. a scarecrow) and were stretched out for as much as 5 miles away from the corral opening. The men of the hunting party often remained in blinds along the way; when the caribou began to move into the row of in^{y}uksut they would run behind the herd to prevent its milling and breaking through the rows of uprights. Once the caribou forded the stream and had begun to enter the corral, men stationed in blinds at the entrance emerged to close the entrance with brush and to begin shooting with arrows into the milling caribou. The animals in the corral, many caught at the snares at the far end, others milling and trampling, could then be dispatched at leisure.

Using this method, the hunters most frequently killed the animals in the corral with arrows. Boys who had not previously participated in the caribou drive were accorded the privilege of shooting the first arrows. The animals caught in the snares at the end of the corral were dispatched with spears. When the colder weather had begun, the corrals were made of mounds of snow and were covered with discarded clothing as in the case of the spring and summer in^{y}uksut, the hunting method being essentially the same. The sod, willow, and stone corrals of the spring hunt were kept permanently in place and could be repeatedly used. It can be readily noted that large numbers of caribou could be taken by this method and large amounts of meat obtained. It would, however, be difficult to estimate the average catch, the size of the herds themselves being so variable from year to year. The process could be repeated over several days or weeks, and it would appear possible that 200 to 300 animals could be taken in a day's hunting, and the corral cleared and made ready for the following day.

A variant of the impound method was the water drive. In this, the tuttusiuvaktuat, the in^{y}uksut led to a small lake or lagoon. The caribou were driven as before and forced into the water. Here, hunters in kayaks awaited them, spearing the animals as they began swimming. If the body of water was small, a stockade was erected on the far side so that any that escaped were ensnared as they regained the land. The tareumiut knew this method and used it along the Arctic plain. The more elaborate stockade, however, was preferred in the passes and foothills.

When the caribou were collected, the women of the group went to the work of skinning them. The meat was cut in strings for drying and pounding with fat and berries, and the leg bones were cracked for marrow. The paunch and intestines were emptied of their contents and this vegetable matter was eaten. Foetuses were also boiled and eaten. The choice parts of the caribou were the marrow bones.

The leg bones were cracked for the marrow and stored with fat in the emptied paunch. This favored combination (akutuq) made a light and easily transportable food. Caribou meat was divided according to well-defined regulation, each family receiving a share. The usual practice was to strip the meat, dry it, and cache it. A family that left the group during the summer season regularly left some of the dried meat at the usual campsite, taking the remainder as provender for any journey. The tareumiut treated the caribou differently, not stripping the meat, but preserving it intact in the ice cellars in a frozen state. Between the two groups, there was also marked difference in ceremonial usage; the inland Eskimo always removed the head of the caribou at once, "lest the animal suffer," while this practice was not followed on the coast.

Several other methods of taking caribou were known and employed. Individual hunters set up traps on the tundra, often in defiles through which the caribou must pass. Depending on the nature of the terrain, looped cords were fixed to catch either the antlers or the legs of the caribou. Murdoch (1885 a, p. 99) mentions the pitfall as a means of taking caribou, but living informants do not recall this. A preferred time for individual hunting was in the rutting season. At this time the caribou become curious and will approach a man.

With the introduction of firearms, the older methods of caribou hunting tended to fall by the way. Only older residents of the area recall the use of corrals or the water drive, while Murdoch notes that the Barrow Eskimo of 1883 were hunting with guns, circling the herds and firing into them from a distance (ibid., p. 99). Rausch (1951, p. 192) remarks that the natives of the Anaktuvuk area have not used the corral for about 75 years. Stefansson (1914 a, p. 385) obtained the details of a corral from Point Hope informants and indicates the use of the corral had fallen by the way at the time of his visits with Anderson in the first decade of the present century.

Thus, in the treatment of the whale and caribou, the two primary foci of the patterning of human ecology of the Alaskan Arctic slope are considered. To do justice to the elaborate exploitation of the faunal resources, however, some listing of the animals associated with each setting is necessary. The tareumiut, able to draw the bulk of their food from the sea, were nevertheless intimately involved in the hunting of many land animals. On the other hand, the nuunamiut, while they hunted a great variety of animals widely and successfully, were obliged to depend primarily on the caribou, the only animal which could be taken in quantity. The following treatment does not attempt to do other than note those animals that were of marked economic importance to either group. It is perhaps sufficient to note that there are numerous small animals and birds which assumed little or no economic role in Eskimo life. The rodents and nonmigratory fowl, for example, played little part in native life. Those to which attention is given are significant as contributing vitally to the food supply of either ecological setting or are important as objects of ritual behavior. In a general way, ritualism and economic importance coincide, although this is not always the case.

3. The wolf, Canis lupus tundrarum (Miller), Eskimo amawk, and amaruq, was trapped by both tareumiut and nuunamiut, although it was more important to the economy of the latter. The traps were of many different kinds, their use being hemmed in with innumerable restrictions of a supernatural kind. Wolfskins were valuable as items of trade, the outer parka and trousers often being made of them. A thick fur was valued as a facepiece on a parka hood. Wolf skulls were prized as whaling charms by the tareumiut. Both groups ate the flesh.

4. Foxes, Vulpes fulva alascensis (Merriam), appear in several varieties—the red fox, kayaktuq; the cross fox, kenraq; the silver fox, kerenektaq; the blue fox, kenraktunuq; ciriganeak, so-called "white fox," possibly *Alopex lagopus innuitus* (Merriam). The attitudes and treatment of foxes parallel that directed toward wolves.

5. The wolverine, *Gulo luscus luscus* (Linn.).—This animal is fairly frequent in the mountains. The fur was much valued as a decoration for clothing and for parka facepieces. As such, wolverine pelts became an important trading item and reached the coasts via the inland trade routes. The taking of the wolverine was also hemmed in with considerable ritual.

5. Grizzly bear (Arctic grizzly), Ursusrich ardsoni (Swainson), Eskimo aakluq. This animal is fairly widely distributed on the northern slopes of the Brooks Range (Rausch, 1951, pp. 165–170). In aboriginal times, these bears were evidently frequently met not only by the nuunamiut, but also by parties of tareumiut, and there are records of such bears having wandered into the various coastal villages. The hunting of such bears was surrounded with a particularly elaborate ritual.

6. Polar bear, Thalarctos maritimus (Phipps).—This animal is very common along the coastal Arctic slope, is principally a water feeder and inhabits the moving ice, rarely coming ashore. Polar bear (Eskimo, naanuk) meat is particularly favored by the maritime Eskimo.

7. Seals. Excepting the bearded seal, these animals were taken on the winter ice pack at breathing holes (aadłuk) either with nets or by spearing. Nets were set out across the lagoons and stream mouths in summer. Three principal species are taken by this method. They are:

(a) *Phoca vitulina richardii* (Gray), the harbor seal, Eskimo kasigeaq; (b) *Phoca hispida beaufortiana* (Anderson), ringed seal, Eskimo necik, nunuq; (c) *Phoca fasciata* (Gill), the ribbon seal, Eskimo kayxolik. Of the three, the ringed seal is by far the most common. It remains through the year along the Arctic coast but is most plentiful on the winter ice. All the ingenuity attributed to the Eskimo reaches its peak in respect to the hunting of seals. Largely an individual matter, the hunter strings his nets under the winter ice, scratching with seal claws to attract the animals. The baleen nets strangle the seal or may break the animal's neck when dragged in. Formerly, as the ice receded and the seals rested on the rotten ice, alternately napping and waking, the hunter, equipped with harpoon, crept up on them, timing his movements with those of his quarry. With whale, seals formed a significant part of the maritime Eskimo diet. The skins were used for clothing and the oil was carefully collected for use as food, fuel, and as an important item of trade.

The bearded seal is somewhat less common than the ringed seal and is of seasonal occurrence. It is found on the ice from the end of the whaling season in late spring and is still taken up to the time the ice recedes in late summer. The maritime Eskimo sought this animal eagerly in view of the valuable skin, six of which were sufficient to cover an umiak frame. The bearded seal, *Erignathus barbatus nauticus* (Pallas.), Eskimo ugruk, was hunted communally, unlike the other seals that were taken as the result of individual effort.

8. The walrus, Odobaenus rosmarus divergens (Illiger), Eskimo ayvuq, Pacific walrus. This animal, appearing in herds, is seasonal, coming with the movement of ice floes northward at midsummer. It has been noted that the majority of animals taken along the Arctic coast are males, principally old bulls. The cows and calves have evidently split off from the bulls and summer on the Siberian side. Hunting was done with umiak, as a group venture, and the walrus harpooned. The ivory was much sought, but the meat, while useful and plentiful, was not valued as food for human consumption. Flipper parts and certain of the internal organs were eaten, the former being allowed to sour before cooking. Walrus meat went largely to the maintenance of dogs. Calfskins were used for the manufacture of whaling lines, the whole skins of grown animals, carefully thinned by scraping, sometimes being employed as umiak covers, three to four skins serving to cover a frame.

9. Beluga (*white whales*), *Delphinapterus leucas* (Pallas), Eskimo, kil^{y}elluaq, sisuak. This small whale has never been too plentiful in the northern sections of the coastal Arctic slope and is considerably more important to the maritime Eskimo farther down the coast, such as at

Icy Cape, Point Lay, and Point Hope. Indeed, the kivalinermiut, for all that they are an original nuunamiut grouping, have taken to hunting the beluga somewhat intensively. Formerly, the beluga skins were valued as whaling and walrus lines and as boot soles. The animals, traveling in schools, were harpooned in shallow water, sometimes being driven into waiting hunters on a beach or spit. At present, they are shot rather than harpooned.

10. The killer whale, Orca orca (Linn.); *Grampus rectipinna* (Cope.), the Pacific killer whale, Eskimo, aaxłu. Never economically significant, never purposely hunted, in fact, the killer whale is worth noting in view of the numerous tales which have arisen around it and the anxieties which it still produces.

11. Mountain or Dall sheep, Ovis dalli dalli (Nelson), Eskimo, inmaeq.—The mountain sheep were snared in the mountains by the nuunamiut. On rare occasions, a party of tareumiut would hunt them for sport in the mountains to the east, and on the coast just south of Barter Island. The sheep were not obtained in sufficient numbers by either group to be economically important, but their horns were eagerly sought, serving as caribou spearheads and dippers, and becoming an important item of trade.

The list of mammals might be extended at length. The smaller mammals, however, become less important to the native economy although their use might depend on emergency. The nuunamiut made some use of the various squirrels (*Citellus parryii barrowensis* (Merriam), the marmots, weasels, and hares, all of which might be snared when caribou was scarce and the skins of which were used for underclothing and for children's garments. Similarly, the tareumiut, when traveling inland, might trap squirrels and rabbits (*Lepus arcticus arcticus* (Ross) if these were found in abundance. Weasels (ermine) were snared for their pelts, which were used as decoration on parkas with matched skins. The various lemmings seem to have had no economic value, no record being obtainable of anyone having eaten the flesh of lemmings. The myth persists that the lemming comes from the clouds, this bit of folklore also having been noted in Scandinavia. A few larger mammals might also be mentioned but likewise are economically not significant. The coastal natives know both the narwhal (*Monodon monoceros* (Linn.)) and various porpoises but are not concerned with them. The former remain as a memory but no living Eskimo were encountered who recall seeing one. A porpoise was taken at Barrow in the summer of 1952 but is otherwise very rare. Both groups know the musk ox (*Ovibos moschatus* (Gmel.)) and skulls turn up from time to time on the tundra, but the species appears to be extinct north of the Brooks Range, or, indeed, in all of Alaska. Mountain lions are known south of the Brooks Range as are moose, but they are generally removed from the Eskimo sphere of interest. In summary, the mammalian domain of the North Alaskan Eskimo was not large. But if the species hunted were few, the quantity taken more than compensated for the variety.

Fowl.—In the area of bird hunting, the Eskimo of the region also tended to be selective. The fowl that formed a part of the native diet were principally the ducks and the geese, the hunting of which became a preoccupation of the maritime Eskimo, although it was not limited to them, and the various species of ptarmigan, to which the nuunamiut directed their primary attention. Ptarmigan abound in the watercourses flowing out from the foothills and are found back into the mountain passes. They are principally the *Lagopus albus* (Aud.), the willow ptarmigan. There are other species as well, however, chief among them being the *Lagopus rupestris* (Leach), the rock ptarmigan. The nuunamiut decoyed them into nets and snares, using stuffed birds during the mating season. These were attacked by live birds, which became enmeshed in the spread nets. Noose traps, nets, the latter of baleen traded from the coast and strung in lines, and many other devices were used in the trapping. The nuunamiut also used baleen nets to take waterfowl on the lakes, sinking the nets and enmeshing the birds as they dove. Small spears were used for geese and ducks during the moulting season.

The many species of waterfowl which flew along the coasts provided an important secondary food source for the tareumiut. The most sought after of these ducks were the various eiders which continue to fly across Elson Lagoon across the Point Barrow spit and which fly in flocks down the Arctic coast. Most tareumiut groups maintained camps where families might go, particularly during the summer months, for duck hunting. At utkeaaγvik and nuwuk, for example, the old site of piγiniq was used as a shooting station (pl. 4, *c*). Similarly, there were duck shooting stations along the lagoons south of Icy Cape which were periodically used by the people of the various southern villages. At Point Barrow, the eider ducks were hunted with the bola as they flew low over the sandspit, but, as in the inland regions, there was also intensive netting and snaring. The utkeaviŋmiut and nuwuŋmiut erected a series of in^y^uksut, similar to the scarecrows used by the nuunamiut in caribou hunting, along the south side of Elson Lagoon, the purpose being to drive the ducks over the sandspit, thus preventing them from swinging to the south. These devices were evidently wholly successful. The principal eider ducks taken in this manner are *Somateria spectabilis* (Linn.), the king eider, Eskimo kin^yaluk; *Somateria V-nigra* (Gray), the Pacific eider, Eskimo amawlik ("like a wolf"); *Arctonetta fischeri* (Brandt), the spectacled eider, Eskimo tuttuluk ("like caribou"). Others, including the brant geese, *Bernicla nigricans* (Lawr.), involve the squaw duck, *Harelda glacialis* (Leach), Steller's duck, *Polysticta stelleri* (Brandt), Eskimo ignikawktuq, and many others.

Important though the various fowl are to the native food supply, it is of interest to note that few integrated usages appear in association with them. Of the two principal types of fowl, those of the land, the various ptarmigan, play a much more significant role in folklore and legend. On the coasts, the ducks were preserved in oil and fat. When needed, they were skinned rather than plucked and the fat eaten carefully. Essentially similar treatment was accorded the ptarmigan among the inland groups, although the facilities for storing the birds were not so readily available.

Fish.—Like fowl, fish formed part of the secondary diet of the peoples of the area. Lacking the reserves of fat, fish were never a staple food, serving to supplement the diet of meat. Not much fishing was actually done in the sea by the maritime people and then only when certain species came up the coasts in schools and could be obtained in quantity. These were principally the tomcod (*Boreogadus saida*), a winter fish, obtained through holes in the ice, and the eulachon (candlefish), obtainable in summer. While other species were available from the sea, they could not be obtained in sufficient quantity to be of economic importance.

Fishing, for both the nuunamiut and the tareumiut, was focused on the fresh water of the inland lakes and streams. Here, fish of many kinds could be had in sufficient quantity to justify an intensive activity. The nuunamiut fished both summer and winter, fishing through the ice in the latter season, while the tareumiut limited their fishing, except for the seaborne tomcod, to the summer months when the streams were open. Only rarely would a family remain at a fishing site into the fall or winter, although it was of course possible to continue fishing into the dark of the year. In general, fishing was a woman's activity, although men would assist in setting out the nets. Families from both ecological settings would remain at fishing camps for part of the year, the men engaging in caribou hunting while the women, with their smaller children, would congregate at the river or lake banks, drawing in the nets, gutting and drying or freezing the catch. Fish were stored by the tareumiut in ice cellars in a frozen state and were dried and cached by the nuunamiut.

Fish known to the area may be listed as follows:[5]

Fish—gen.	ikaaluq	
Fishing activity	ikaluneaktuak	
Small fishes	ikallowayaat	
Arctic lamprey	nimmeaq (var. nimmereaq)	*Lampetra japonica*
Dog salmon	ikalluguruaq	*Oncorhynchus keta*
Humpback salmon	amaktuq	*O. gorbuscha*
Arctic char	ikaluukpiq	*Salvelinus alpinus*
Dolly Varden	ikaluukpiq	*S. malma*
Lake trout	ikaluakpuq	*S. namaycush*
Grayling	sulukpawak	*Thymallus signifer*
She-fish	siiriroaq	*Stenodus* spp.
White fish (gen.)	ikallupeaq	
White fish (round)	anaakłiq	*Prosopium* spp.
White fish (Coregonus)	piγuktuuk	*Coregonus* spp.
White fish (Autumnalis)	kaktuq (var. tipu)	*Leucichthys autumnalis*
White fish (Sardinella)	ikalusaaq	*L. sardinella* complex
Smelt	ixγoaaniq	*Osmerus dentex*
Smelt larvae	irituunʸiq	
Capeling	paŋmageruq	*Mallotus villosus*
Herring	uxruxtuq	*Clupea pallasi*
Pike	siiyuliq	*Esox lucius*
Blackfish	ixluγukiniq	*Dallia pectoralis*
Sucker	milluweaq	*Catostomus* spp.
Freshwater cod	tittaliq	*Lota maculosa*
Polar cod (tomcod)	ikalluwaq	*Boreogadus saida*
Siberian cod	uuγaq	*Eleginus* spp.
Flounder	nataaγnaq	Pleuronectidae (fam.)
Sculpin	qanayuq	Cottidae (fam.)
Stickleback	kakiilʸesuq	*Pungitius pungitius*
"Eel-port" (Lycoides)	kuγurawnaq	Lycoidae (fam.)

Of the above, the white fishes, the grayling, and the various trout formed the principal items in the native diet. Fish taken in the summer were frequently left at the site where the fishing had been done until the onset of winter. With sled, accompanied by sufficient number of dogs, a man would go out in winter to return the summer's catch. If a family planned on it, they traveled to the fishing station by umiak and made it back to the settlement before the winter freeze set in.

Each grouping, whether basically oriented toward the sea or the land, tended to move to the same general fishing areas. This meant that the foothill and plain provinces were dotted with established camps where the fishing took place. It is not to be implied that these were in any sense owned by any one group; in the course of summer travel by families over familiar routes certain places were selected as sites for fishing. In the summers, small communities

[5] The writer is indebted to Dr. Norman Wilmovsky, Stanford University, for the identification of the various piscine forms, as well as for the location of the various fishing stations of the maritime groups.

often grew up around them, dispersing when the winter freeze began. Some, it is true, remained behind for as long as they chose. Among the maritime people, those from the larger villages, it was not unusual, nor is it today, for a family to build a semipermanent house at such a fishing camp, returning there summer after summer. Some, indeed, went so far as to build an ice cellar at the site, storing both the fish taken by the women and the caribou shot by the men.

While it would be of marked interest to offer details of the location of each fishing camp of each group, it was not found possible to list these. It may, however, suffice to note those to which the natives of utkeaaγvik and nuwuk were regularly accustomed to go and which remain important at present for fishing activity. The camps, varying in size and location, are often some days' journey from the Point Barrow villages and could be reached only by water in summer or by dog sled in winter. They are as follows (cf. map 2.):

suŋoγaraq	71°2′25″N, 156°28′30″W.
poleaq	70°54′10″N, 156°18′30″W.
iiviksuq	70°53′40″N, 156°37′W.
nawłat	70°52′40″N, 156°53′10″W.
opiksuq	70°41′30″N, 156°36′20″W.
kaveiarat	70°40′30″N, 157°1′W.
wiireiaq	70°18′30″N, 157°24′40″W.
payuuγvit	70°51′N, 156°24′30″W.
tupaaγaruq	70°40′N, 155°50′W.
avirławvik	Near latter on Chipp River.
aalaktak	70°46′30″N, 155°3′W.
piŋuuguruaarevic	70°53′5″N, 156°43′5″W.
puleyiceax	70°55′5″N, 156°13′20″W.
aatut	70°39′N, 157°14′W.
uyaraalik	?

SUMMARY

As may be seen, the human relation to the biota was a selective one, the exploitation being of those animals of which considerable quantity could be obtained. Each setting came to stress the game most readily available and was intent on amassing surplus supplies of food, not only as insurance against the ever present threat of famine, but also because possession of surplus food and goods counted as wealth and underlay the status system for both nuunamiut and tareumiut. In the course of the utilization of the resources which the land provided, it was inevitable that small groups were most effective, both because the supply potential was limited and because the game, in its general seasonal movements, was sporadic and unpredictable. Given this kind of limitation, the social units alined themselves, structured themselves, and created a high degree of order.

LANGUAGE

Eskimoan or Eskimo-Aleut, as is well known, constitutes a wholly independent linguistic grouping. Efforts to relate Eskimo to any of the other North American language families, to the Hyperborean languages of Northeastern Siberia, or to some of the better formulated stocks of northern and central Eurasia, such as to Tungusic or Finno-Ugric, have proved fruitless. A recent suggestion, made by the Danish linguist Hammerich that Eskimoan and Indo-European may have a common root, likewise seems untenable, although of course the idea is a stimulating one (Hammerich, 1951b). While there is a distinct difference between Eskimo and Aleut, the two being wholly mutually unintelligible, there are sufficient common points in both morphology and cognates to permit the formulation of a relationship. The languages spoken by the Eskimo themselves, ranging from Greenland to southern Alaska, suggest dialects rather than separate tongues. The natives of Barrow recall that when Rasmussen and some Greenland Eskimo visted in 1924, Rasmussen himself delivered an address in Greenlandic which was intelligible to the north Alaskan people. The absence of any sharp dialectic distinctions or of a series of well-defined different languages might point to a relatively recent dissemination of the Eskimo-speaking peoples across the American Arctic.

That there are local dialects must be considered. These tend to be based on phonological and lexical differences rather than on morphological or syntactical ones. Throughout the Eskimo area, and certainly on the north Alaskan slope, there is considerable consciousness of language. A man's speech usually served as a criterion of his birthplace. The utkeaviŋmiut, for example, the people of Barrow, were said to speak more slowly and evenly, while those of Point Hope, the tikeraamiut, are alleged to speak rapidly and with a much more marked intonation pattern. But even in such closely situated villages as nuwuk, utkeaaγvik, and piγiniq, or between local settlements anywhere, there were reputedly some dialectical differences. Not that the dialects digressed so far as to become mutually unintelligible; it was often a matter merely of certain lexical selections. It is not known why this should have come about. The fact that a group dropped a word in favor of another for the same object or concept could conceivably have a supernatural basis but no data were to be had regarding word taboos. In certain communities words took on a fadlike character, particularly in nouns designating animals, birds, and plants. This process is by no means gone. New words are continually evolving. Such may depend on the fondness for puns and word play which the groups share. When it is recalled that the cultures placed a great emphasis on compulsive formulas in the form of songs, it is perhaps not difficult to see that lexicon might in some measure be affected.

This would point to the present continuing importance of the native language. Today, despite the efforts of the local schools to develop a written and spoken knowledge of English, Eskimo is spoken in the home and remains the language of social usage among old and young alike. This has meant that any ethnographer, the writer included, has been obliged to make use of an interpreter in dealing with informants. A comparative few speak English adequately.

The Eskimoan dialects have been so completely analyzed that there is little point in attempting a further description here. The Danes, with their interests in Greenland, have perhaps done the most complete summary of Eskimo linguistics, although the field has by no means been neglected by American scholars. A recent reconstruction of proto-Eskimo by Swadesh (Swadesh, 1951, 1952 a–d), as well as a number of comprehensive descriptive statements, make Eskimo one of the most intensively studied languages of native North America. Interesting though the specific analysis of the north Alaska dialects might be, this area not having been adequately worked linguistically in comparison with other regions, and while the writer is convinced that language offers aids in the elicitation of culture patterns, the present investigation could give no more than cursory attention to linguistic patterns. By working through an interpreter for several hours daily, the present ethnographer was able to attain some degree of comprehension of spoken Eskimo. But a complete linguistic analysis prevents attention to other aspects; little time was given to language except as an ethnographic aid.

In the sections which follow, native terms are given. There are also three folk tales which were transcribed in Eskimo as well as a number of songs. It was found possible to resolve the phonology but little attention could be given either to morphology or syntax. It is, however, possible to define the morphological unit or word. There is a high degree of inflection, both of nouns and verbs, the principal constructions involving root suffixation. Nouns and verbs offer a tremendous number of possible inflections, with numerous noun cases, as well as complex verb constructions involving mode, tense, negation, validity, and the like. The verbal system stresses the validity of an action primarily and is only secondarily concerned with factors of tense. In the following sections, where nouns are given, they appear as constructs, as absolutatives rather than as nominatives. Dual and plural number are given where necessary.

The language permits great facility of expression, is rich in metaphor and imagery, and remains valuable to the contemporary culture as an important element of social integration.

Phonology.—The phonemes of the north Alaska dialects, Barrow in particular, are as follows:

Consonants:								
	p					m		
				v				
			s			n	l	
	t			ɬ	c			
						n^y	l^y	
								r
	k	g	x			ŋ		
	q			γ				
Semivowels:								
			w					
			y					
Vowels:			i			u		
				e	o			
				a				

There are thus 18 consonantal phonemes, two semivocalic, and 5 vocalic phonemes. Length is suprasegmental; stress is nonphonemic.

Of the consonants, the stops, p, t, k, g, and q, are in the main unaspirated. p is bilabial; t is alveolar rather than dental, with some retroflexion; k, the only stop with a corresponding voiced equivalent, is velar, but the point of articulation is drawn back further against the velum than in English; q is uvular and contrasts phonemically with k.

The spirantized series is not distinctive. ɬ is a continuant (tl), x is strongly articulated and velar, γ is a uvularized spirant, sometimes trilled. v is bilabial, unrounded in contrast to w, and voiced.

There is one affricate, c, alveopalatal, unvoiced (tch).

The nasals n^y and ŋ are palatalized and velar respectively. The lateral l^y is palatalized.

r is post-palatal in point of articulation. Some speakers make a uvular trill with wide aperture. It is, however, contrasted with γ, which employs a close aperture.

The vowels are not complex. There is a distinct pattern of vocalic harmony. In unstressed syllables following long vowel with stress, the vocalic quality becomes indeterminate. It is clear, however, that shewa is not phonemic but rather that a harmonic pattern of short vowels is established. e and o are phonemic.

Vowels appear in conjunctive clusters with semivowels and in disjunctive clusters with each other.

Length.—Vowel length has been indicated by orthographic gemination as ii, ee, aa, oo, uu.

Consonants appear as geminate clusters rather than as lengthened forms. Examples are iccavik, tukumminaroaq, etc.

Stress.—Stress is both primary and secondary and nonphonemic. The clustering of morphemic units (agglutination) creates some complexity in stress (Thalbitzer, 1910, pp. 981–983). These general patterns are, however, consistently observable:

1. Stress occurs on any long vowel in open or closed syllable. Examples are: tiŋileráatak; ukúutaq, etc.

2. All vowel clusters are stressed, likewise the first member of a disjunctive cluster. Examples are: tiŋileráwtak; amáwk; taréumiut.

3. Stress falls on any short vowel in a closed syllable, including syllables closed by consonantal gemination. Examples are sakírraq; túttu; kíkíktáaxruk, etc. In such cases, primary stress is accorded either a long vowel or vowel cluster; short vowels assume secondary stress.

4. Stress is in the main recessive. With short vowels and no closed syllables, stress occurs on the initial vowel. In words of some length, barring the presence of long vowel or cluster, the initial syllable and either the penult or ultima may bear stress, this being, in the latter instances, a secondary stress. Examples are: núkaceak; tátarúruq, etc.

HOUSES AND SETTLEMENTS

Although the present study makes no attempt to analyze the complex technology and material culture of the North Alaskan Eskimo or to present any systematic treatment of it, the arrangements of the houses as well as of the surroundings of the village and camp have marked implications for the organization of society. There are also several cultural historical points suggested by the presence, in both ecological settings, of construction features in common, however much the basic dwellings may differ in outward form. Several areas of overlapping may also be noted in the forms of summer shelters; tents, brush shelters, and other temporary dwellings could be the same for both ecological groups. The permanent houses, designating these as the winter quarters, did differ quite markedly in outward form. It is worth remarking that the dome-shaped ice lodge, while known at nuwuk and utkeaaγvik, and sometimes used by these villagers, diffuses neither inland nor farther southward along the coast. Its westernmost point of diffusion may properly be regarded as Barter Island (Kroeber, 1939, p. 24).

Quite apart from the importance of the house in whatever form as a shelter, there were significant attitudes which surround the dwelling and which should be evaluated in order to give proper focus to the relations between house and society. The dwelling was the center of activity for the nuclear family, and while it has been shown that the personnel of such a group might change with varying conditions, the attachment to the house was an emotional one and very strong. For the individuals who resided in it, it was ever a source of refuge and sanctuary. No nonresident entered except by invitation, although once this was given, there was thereafter a greater degree of freedom. Actually, there were well-defined regulations by which houses could be approached and entered by nonresidents. Anyone desiring to enter, for example, shouted into the skylight or called through the passageway. The cultures of the various Eskimo groups are marked by a high degree of sociability, a development no less true of the North Alaskan peoples. But in Alaska, at least, social activities were not centered in the houses, nor were the recreational periods tied into interhouse visiting. These centered rather in the karigi (pl. kariyit), the quasi-ceremonial gathering place. The karigi (qalegi, or kashim, as it is variously designated) was a social hall for men primarily, although women also entered it from time to time, and is seen widely among the Alaskan Eskimo, its distribution ranging from Point Barrow, but not farther to the east, down into southern Alaska. In a general way, it may be said that kinsmen could and did meet in each other's houses; the meeting place for those who were not connected by ties of kinship lay in the ceremonial house. But even kinsmen did not have freedom of one another's houses and visited specifically by invitation. While ownership was not invested in any one individual in the house residents, it is clear that all who lived in it had essentially equal rights to it, there being, however, a few areas within the house the rights to which were limited by age and sex. In summary, the house, even though its location might be changed and the number of those resident in it might vary, was a primary factor in cementing the primary group. The nuclear family can be equated with the household.

The general term for any dwelling is iγłu (pl. iγłut). Specifically, this term refers to a permanent dwelling and thus comes to be applied to the more or less continuously inhabited houses of the tareumiut. An elaborate and complex lexicon exists to describe the many variations in tents, in shelters of various kinds, and the more permanent houses. Similarly, the many terms for the parts of the house and the details of construction types and materials reflect the intimate preoccupation with the habitation (cf. Rausch, 1951, pp. 159–161).

HOUSES OF THE NUUNAMIUT

(Pl. 3, *b*)

The small band of Eskimo which continues to reside in the foothills along the Killik River, moving into Anaktuvuk Pass and the area of Chandler Lake, still makes use of an aboriginal house type. This is the iccellik, so named from the iccuk, a caribou hide used as a cover. It is a portable, tentlike structure made from caribou hides stretched over a willow frame. This type of dwelling is also designated as kaluγvik, i. e. a frame, but this is a general term for any tent in which poles are used. The iccellik is a wholly practical house, warm, fairly spacious, and easily erected and transported. In ground plan, at least in modern times, the house is oval, although in the past it is said to have been round, a fact substantiated by the presence of rings of sod at old campsites. Dwelling size varies, depending on the number of inhabitants, and may run from 10 to 15 feet in length and in some instances 8 to 10 feet in width. The inland Eskimo pattern, followed here in the erection of the iccellik, but also employed to construct a sod house and other variations, involves the placing of four center upright posts, connected at the top by light beams, to which willow withes, usually 2 dozen in number, are joined. The latter, often tied together to effect greater length, radiate out from the central upright posts and are fastened to the ground, either forced into the ground or blocked into position with sod and stones. In the center, on one of the longer sides away from the prevailing wind direction, are set two posts for the door frame. Lacking the heavier uprights, a light willow frame is set up in a dome shape, the willow rods being lashed together at the point where they cross.

When the frame is in position, the skins, 20 to 25 in number, are drawn over it. The skins are scraped on one side only and the hair side is turned outward. Once in position, they may be pinned or sewed together. A principle of insulation is employed in that a second cover, formerly consisting either of skins completely scraped, i. e. with the hair removed, or of skins with the hair side turned inward, is laid over the first in winter. This creates an air cell between the two covers, ensuring additional warmth. This may perhaps be regarded as an extension of the principle used in respect to clothing, two suits being the winter garb and affording the same kind of insulation. The door to the iccellik is usually covered with the skin of the grizzly bear, this being sufficiently heavy as to keep out draughts. It rests against the house with the hair side turned inward. The iccellik usually has a window, the traditional skylight of the Eskimo house. This is most frequently located next to the door, being somewhat higher than the doorframe itself. Formerly, this was made of grizzly bear intestine, sewed together and mounted in place with a frame of wood. Not infrequently, too, the skylight (igalaq) was made from ugruk intestine obtained from the coasts by trade. Among the present killiγmiut, the outer cover of the iccellik is of canvas, although caribou skins still are used for the inner lining, and commercial materials are used for the skylight.

The iccellik remains a wholly satisfactory dwelling in which an average of 10 persons can quite adequately live. The house is draught-proof, being banked at the base with sod, and is capable of being warmed readily; the lamp was formerly used for warmth, although fires were also built in winter in front of the door and a smokehole made above the door. The mention by some sources that the iccellik is covered with snow in winter is apparently incorrect. Snow was applied to sod houses at times, especially if the sod, in being dried out by heat, contracted and let in draughts. Moreover, a snow-covered willow frame was used as a parturition hut. The iccellik itself, however, is sufficiently weathertight as to require no additional insulation (Rausch, 1951, p. 160; Ingstad, 1952, pp. 31–35). In heating today, metal stoves with pipes are used. Formerly, the heating in the iccellik was kept to a minimum and much of the actual cooking done outside.

The general structure of the iccellik, or indeed of any kaluγvik, did not involve an excavation. When the tent was to be erected, the snow was simply cleared away and the dwelling rested on the surface of the ground. This point is worth noting in view of the presence of excavations in some of the nuunamiut habitations.

On the move, the iccellik could be erected in a matter of a few minutes. The poles for the supporting structure were carried by sled or umiak as were the skins which made up the covers and the bedding. If the tent were to be left standing for any period of time, willow branches were cut and laid in the interior along the sides to form the sleeping places. The various items necessary to the maintenance of the household—vessels, weapons, extra clothing, and the like—no particularly elaborate inventory being involved, were also transported with the household. This meant, of course, that in travel a sled or boat was heavily loaded and reduced much of the actual travel to walking by the able-bodied members of the group.

But the tent structures were not the sole habitations of the nuunamiut, even if today there has been principal emphasis on the iccellik. Sod houses were known and employed. These would be located at the chief winter settlements of the various inland bands. In keeping with the emphasis on the hunting of caribou in seasonal drives, each larger grouping had settlements from which the seasonal migratory round was begun and which served as centers for the caribou hunting when it became a concerted group activity. It was these settlements which lent a sense of cohesion to the inland groups and which permits, as has been shown, some designation of these groupings by territory and name. Not all the inland peoples had such semipermanent settlements and it is also true that the settlement itself could move after a period of time as the caribou migration routes themselves shifted. The most elaborate development of such villages, if this term may be applied to them, was in the Noatak, Kobuk, and Selawik regions, those of the areas farther to the east and north becoming considerably less well defined. The archeological investigations of Giddings and others point to the presence of continuous settlements existing over long periods of time, while the naval explorer, Stoney, lists the names of some of these settlements which he visited (cf. Giddings, 1944, 1952; Stoney, 1900, p. 46.) The noataγmiut, for example, according to a man born at the headwaters of the Noatak, had a winter hunting village at piŋalu. Here, the iccellik type of house as well as the semipermanent sod house were employed.

Houses erected at the winter hunting sites formed the base of operations for most nuunamiut. Here they were able to keep extra supplies of food in caches and to store any equipment not immediately needed. The houses themselves were of several types. There were those families who chose to use the iccellik the year round and there were those who built somewhat more elaborate structures of sod. The sod houses were erected on the general principle described above, making use of central posts and a willow branch frame. In the square space left by the four uprights was placed the skylight. A general term for the sod-covered winter house was iivłulik, a complex which might vary considerably in plan and structure. There were those, for example, who chose to remove the skin cover of the iccellik and to place sod over the frame, sometimes covering the entire structure with snow. In spring, the sod could be removed and the frame transported. But in addition several other plans appeared. A double sod house was known, the akilγereik (opposite each other—dual), which consisted of two apartments joined by a central passageway, in the center of which was the door. Two related families or the families of trading partners might share such a house, each family taking one apartment but cooking and eating together. This house likewise could be built up on tent frames, and, indeed, most frequently was, since such double family houses were rarely used for more than one season. A more permanent sod house, suggestive of the coastal dwellings, was the paamerak, a house built to last longer than one winter and usually erected at a more permanent site, such as at a fishing station or in the neighborhood of a caribou stockade. This plan made use of a passageway leading into the house although the more elaborate wooden interiors of the coastal peoples were lacking. Similarly, while an excavation might be made for this type of dwelling, it rarely went to a depth of more than a few inches, sufficient perhaps as to have permitted the removal of a bit of the topsoil in summer before the permafrost was reached. A double paamerak, with a short passage leading from that which connected the two apartments, was also known. A single-room dwelling of sod was known as tawvsiliq.

The permanent sod structures were thus built with a passage and a skylight and had banked areas of sod placed along the side walls for sleeping and reclining. A fireplace was located under the skylight, the gut window being rolled back when fires were built and serving as a smokehole. General heating was done with the stone lamp. Stoney (1900, p. 46) remarks that panes of ice were sometimes used as the skylight. Ingstad (1952, pp. 174–175) obtained additional information on the shape of such houses and differentiates an elongated from a round type and one with the passage along the side rather than in the center. Stoney also noted longer passageways than were described by modern informants and points out that the passage might also be equipped with a skylight, a feature paralleled along the coasts (Stoney, ibid.). It is to be indicated that none of these types were particularly marked in height; 5 feet from floor to ceiling at the highest point of the dome seems reasonable, a feature still to be seen in the modern iccellik. In general, too, the inland houses were smaller than those on the coast. They lacked the spaces off the passage of which the tareumiut made such good use, and they do not seem in any way so carefully finished. In traveling inland and in setting up campsites at fishing stations, the tareumiut also made use of the paamerak and iivłulik.

The nuunamiut camp was differentiated as to season. Thus, a winter camp was known as ukiivik; the spring camp was called upinaksiliivik; the summer settlement, upineriivik. An abandoned campsite, and there were many, was called iniroaq and inigiroaq. To form some impression of the distribution of the nuunamiut in relation to permanent and temporary houses, the case of the ikpikpaŋmiut may serve as an example. This group, broken up into families as indicated, moved up and down the Ikpikpuk River. The permanent base at the headwaters of the Ikpikpuk was located at a point in the foothills. This was known as ikpikpuk and it was here that the paamerat and iivłulit were to be found. A second permanent camp of the ikpikpaŋmiut was at aviulaavik, some 25 miles from the mouth of the Chipp River. It was not impossible for families to own houses in both locations and spend part of the year in each, moving in the meantime and living in the transportable tent. A third campsite, also more or less permanent, was at kaxłeraavik, located at the confluence of streams along the Chipp. Here, too, semipermanent houses were set up. All those who identified themselves with the ikpikpaŋmiut, however, regarded ikpikpuk itself as the home base. This was the point at which the hunt for caribou started and it was here that the principal ceremonial activities took place. Here, too, was the karigi.

The nuunamiut settlement—and from the foregoing it is not possible to give any statement as to how many people might be found in it at any one time, population expanding and contracting with the seasons—was thus made up of some temporary houses, of the tent variety, others seasonal, tent posts covered with sod, and still others semipermanent. The actual population of any such settlement at the height of the caribou drive would probably rarely exceed 200 to 300, making up a maximum of 50 to 100 able-bodied hunters. Indeed, this figure seems exceptional and the general pattern was 30 hunters, all of whom could use the same karigi.

A village thus consisted of the houses as noted and a karigi. Unlike the karigi of the tareumiut, that of the inland Eskimo was a temporary structure. Stoney (1900, p. 72) mentions that at kiŋalik, (cf. map 4) a large dance house was set up and that each man gave

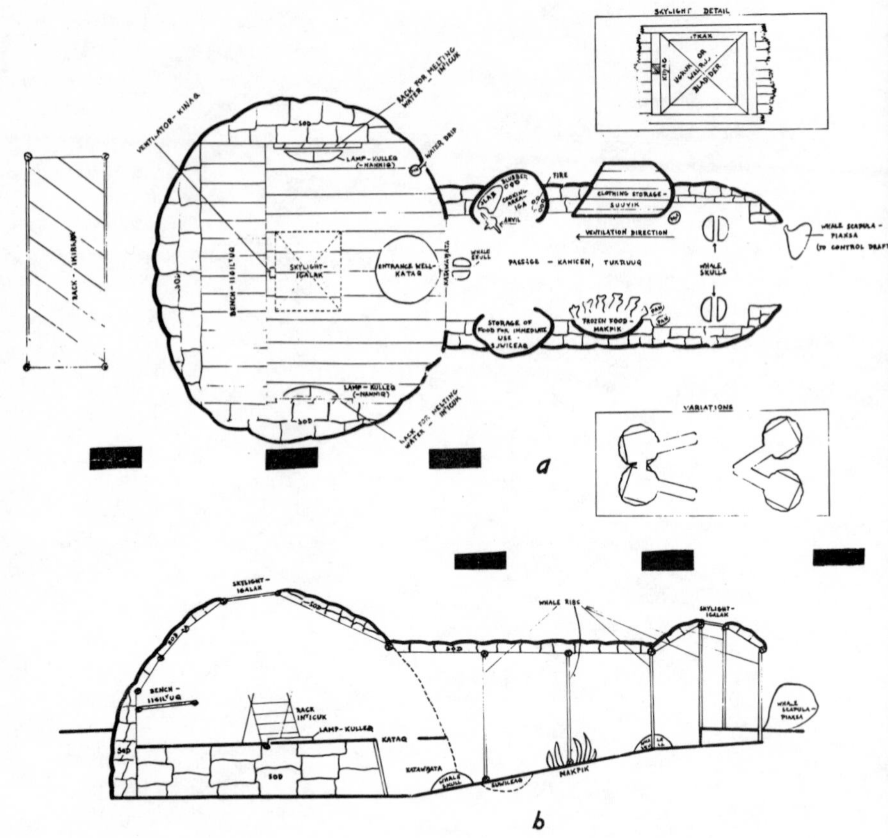

FIGURE 1.—Maritime Eskimo house: *a*, floor plan; *b*, cross section.

several skins for its construction. The karigi of the nuunamiut was merely an elaborated and extended tent made up of willow branches supported on four uprights. A tent passage led to the main door, and the skylight was usually of ice. This type of karigi was also seen at nuwuk and utkeaaγvik, the karigis of these villages being less permanent than those farther to the south. The ceremonial preparations for hunting, the Messenger Feast, as well as an elaborated series of recreational activities took place in the karigi.

The nuunamiut village, if such it may be called, was thus a fairly ephemeral unit. The fact that it could move, and frequently did, caused several marked differences in the choice of dwelling. If a family owned a more or less permanent house, they frequently stored extra food, clothing, and skins in it. As a house, it was inviolable and there was clearly no danger of marauders or trespassers. The houses of the nuunamiut, however, lacked the complex series of household amulets and charms which characterize those of the tareumiut. The village was not so well integrated as that on the coast nor were the houses so well constructed.

HOUSES OF THE TAREUMIUT

(Cf. fig. 1)

The house and settlement along the coast were far more elaborate than in the interior. The village itself had defined locations which were allocated to specific tasks. Paths led through the villages, and around these paths certain definite usages developed. At utkeaaγvik, for example, the paths which ran along the bluffs facing the beach could not be used by pregnant women. If they were to walk on them, they would die in childbirth. The larger towns, such as tikeraaq and utkeaaγvik, were marked by the presence of several kariyit. There were three at utkeaaγvik in 1895, and six or seven at tikeraaq, although only three or four of these were active. One karigi stood at nuwuk but there was another at piγinik which was built and maintained by whaling crews from the nuwuŋmiut. There was, further, one karigi at Wainwright and still another at Icy Cape. Point Lay was not yet existent in 1895. The karigi at tikeraaq was a permanent structure, analogous to the house in construction, and historically related to the ceremonial houses of Cape Prince of Wales and the regions farther to the south. Along the northern sections of the Arctic coast, the karigi was not usually so well developed. An abandoned house, refurnished and expanded somewhat, might serve, but the tendency was to use the tent in much the same manner as the nuunamiut. In any case, the place at which the karigi stood was well defined, the karigi was named, and the men who belonged to it [illegible] it. While the nature of karigi names and the imp

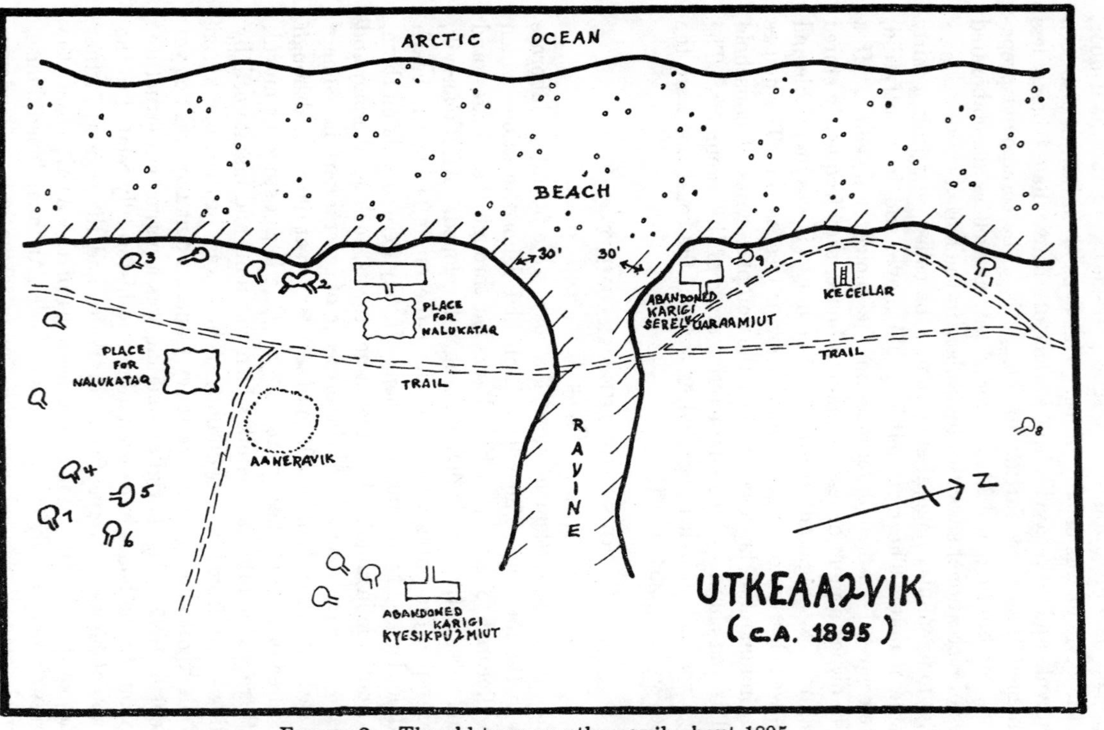

FIGURE 2.—The old town or utkeaaγvik about 1895.

(For explanation, see opposite page.)

community can be reserved for later discussion, suffice it to note that the place for the structure was designated and played an important part in each village. It was a cleared area where dances and the whaling celebrations could be held, where men and women could come to sit in the summer sun and busy themselves at various tasks. The cleared space by the karigi was the aaneravik. Nearby was the shed where the crew leaders, the umealit, kept their whaling umiaks and where work on them and other whaling gear was done. In short, through the karigi a focus was given to the physical arrangement of the village, an element which was not nearly so well defined among the nuunamiut.

The houses in each maritime village were scattered somewhat at random over the village area. All houses were named, either from the owning family, that is, the name of the family head, or from the distinctive charm which the house possessed and was conceived to own. In the accompanying sketch of utkeaaγvik (fig. 2) the general arrangement of houses flanking the beach can be seen. The same pattern was followed in all of the coastal villages. The total impression was one of a series of mounds scattered over a fairly wide area. Unlike the inland houses, those of the coast made use of a fairly marked excavation and were built, at least in terms of the finishing in the interior, with considerable care, employing both driftwood

---

EXPLANATION OF FIGURE 2

The houses which made up the old town of utkeaaγvik are now largely in ruins and were abandoned when the people moved a few hundred yards northward to cluster about the Cape Smythe Whaling Company's installations and the school. Archeological excavations were undertaken by Stefansson in 1912 and later by Rasmussen and Ford. Living informants recall the houses and their residents.

Houses had names which were either descriptive of the house itself or were the names of the family heads. The names of such houses as living residents could recall were as follows (located by number on sketch):

4. uyaloγ------------------- Name of the owner
5. misagmeuγ--------------- "All wet around it", owned by sisau
6. sakan^{y}araamiut----------- "The people who face the sun"
7. kivalekpaak-------------- "Which is on the end (east)", owned by uwiiγuruq
8. avinγaamiut-------------- "People with lots of 'mice.' "

House No. 2 was destroyed by crush ice one winter and a man inside was killed. Two women were said to have starved in house No. 3. When this happened, the houses were abandoned and the corpses were left. In house No. 1 the murder of masagaroak took place (see Customary Law, pp. 114–115).

The village faced westward to the sea. Trails ran along the bluff above the beach. Pregnant women were obliged to use the eastward trail and could not come down to the water lest they die in childbirth.

---

and whalebone. In construction, the maritime house, with its semi-subterranean aspect and its benched areas, shows historical affinities with other house types in Asia and farther south in North America.

There was no well defined sexual division of labor in respect to house construction. When a man decided he wished to build, having collected a sufficient number of whale ribs and skulls, as well as driftwood, he and his wife began the structure. Building was fairly well individualized, although relatives and neighbors might lend a hand. Certainly, there was no defined pattern of cooperation in house building. The children were sent to cut sod and to bring it back to the site. For obvious reasons, houses were built in summer. Even in this case, however, the 5-foot excavation into the permanently frozen ground was long and laborious work. Several days were taken in making the excavation, since the heat of the sun is sufficient to melt only an inch or two of permafrost at a time (pl. 3, *a*).

Once the excavation was completed and the passageway, with its proper slope inward toward the main room of the house arranged, the wooden and bone understructure was begun (pl. 4, *b*). The passage was lined with whale jaws and ribs, and the skull of a whale was placed as a stepping stone into the passage itself. The entrance to the passage was frequently effected through an outer hall which served as a kind of storm porch and which rested on level ground. This was usually 4 to 5 feet square and was made by setting four uprights in the ground and joining them at the top with beams. A skylight was often placed in this outer vestibule to illuminate the passage. From the porch, one stepped down into the passage (kanicen) by means of the whale skull. Here the depth of the passage was about 2 feet and gradually sloped to a full depth of about 5 feet. It terminated under a floor of planking which was part of the iγłu, the central room of the house. The planked flooring made it necessary to come up from the passage through a trapdoor (kataq) into the main chamber. On either side of the trapdoor, as one ascended into the house proper, were stone lamps, the main source of light and heat for the building. The iγłu, the upper room above the passage, was often quite spacious, measurements taken at abandoned houses at nuwuk suggesting as much as 20 feet in diameter. In plan, the room was square, although the banked sod on the outside gave a circular effect. The floor planking was supported on studs which rested on the frozen ground below and which were sometimes carried up so as to make up the walls. The upright posts and the floor planking were sometimes notched and fitted. The roof was arched and cleverly made by running posts across between the sod blocks which were banked up as soon as the planking was put in place. A good house was carefully finished in the interior; the planking was fitted and scraped, and often bleached with human urine.

In the main chamber, opposite the trapdoor in the floor, was a bench which ran the width of the house and which might extend almost halfway across the room from the far wall. This compares with the benched mounds of the houses of the nuunamiut mentioned above. The roof was not entirely finished off, a space being left for the skylight (igalak). This was placed over a frame (itkax) which was fitted into position in the aperture left in the roof. The skylight was made of ugruk or walrus intestine, finely scraped, sections being sewed together, and carefully stretched. It gave an effective, although opaque, window. In heavy weather a cover of planks could be fitted over the skylight. Adjoining the skylight at the rear of the house was a covered well, a few inches in diameter and frequently made of wood, which served as a ventilator. This was the kiŋaq (nostril), through which the outgoing draught could be regulated.

The passageway led to a fairly spacious area under the floor planking. This area did not, however, go to the far wall of the house, since some of the rear planking of the iγlu rested on ground level. The excavation of the house, in short, was not complete. It took in an area under the front part of the house toward the passageway. This room under the kataq was cut into the permafrost and not finished off. It could serve as an extra storage space and if the meat supply were particularly plentiful, extra meat was frozen and stored here. The actual storage places, however, were alcoves cut into the passage itself.

As has been noted, sod was placed in position against the planking and the supports for the passageway as these were being constructed. This meant that the structure was in some measure held in place by the sod. Actually, except the two skylight areas, the entire house was covered with sod. The house was snug, windproof, and wholly effective. It required no additional banking of snow, although if the sod became somewhat soft, water was poured over it. As soon as this froze, the structure was again sound. In the heat of the seal-oil lamp and with the bodily warmth of the inhabitants, the house heated quickly and well.

The passage was flanked with two to four alcoves. These were often sufficiently large as to accommodate sleepers. Those who slept in skins on the floor of the passage rooms were called kaanegimiut, that is, those who inhabit the passageway. The alcove at the right end of the passage toward the house was the iga, the kitchen, or cooking place. It stood near the kataq so that the woman who cooked there could readily reach food up through the circular trapdoor and serve the men inside. In the iga was a smokehole and stones were placed there both as a fireplace and as a support for conical-bottomed pottery vessels. Boiling was done in both these and in wooden vessels by the stone-boiling method. Fuel was oil and blubber, or moss soaked in oil. Wood was rarely used, being too valuable a commodity. When the woman cooked in the iga—the term refers specifically to the place where the fire is made—she was expected to wear clothing especially for the purpose. She changed her boots and donned an apronlike parka with a tail both front and back. This was a purely practical arrangement and prevented oil and soot from being trailed over the house. In cooking, the woman knelt by the iga. When the cooking was done, the woman put her kitchen clothing aside and returned to her usual garments. A meal was cooked once daily—a point likewise true of the nuunamiut—although people ate much more frequently. In the space for the iga were kept all the necessary cooking pots and kitchen equipment.

Opposite the iga, at the left side of the passage, was the place for storage of food needed for immediate consumption. This larder was called suwiceaq and any meat needed for the next day's meal was kept here. Racks were here so that meat taken frozen from the deeper and filled storage places could thaw out. While the iga was most frequently an area flanked with stones, the suwiceaq and its racks were made from whale ribs.

On the left side of the passage as one entered, was a large bin, most frequently made from whale ribs which were placed upright. This was the makpik, the place for food storage. It was usually large enough to hold several tons of meat. The flesh of whales, seals, caribou, the frozen fish, and the ducks soaked in oil, as well as quantities of sea mammal fat, were thrown into the makpik at random. This was not the principal storage place, the ice cellar being reserved for this away from the house proper, but such food as might be needed ahead for several days was kept here. As the supply dropped, as the daily meals were eaten, the men of the house kept the makpik filled with meat. If the supply of meat were very large and extra space for storage were needed, the katawŋata, the space under the floor boards near the kataq, was used. The woman of the household preferred not to have meat here, since it was here that she preferred to keep the skins on which she was sewing and to store some of the extra bedding clothing. The katawŋata was often planked as well so that a useful nook was made available by it. In a sense, being located near the iga, the katawŋata was the woman's area of the house.

Returning to the front of the passageway, a fairly large alcove was usually placed at the right as one entered the passage from the vestibule. This was the suuvik, an area which was also planked and which made a small roomlike cubicle. This was primarily a place for the storage of good furs, the better clothing, and piles of extra skins. It was here that many chose to sleep. It was to this area, too, that people retired for sexual intercourse. When wife exchange took place, the head of the house took the borrowed sexual partner here with some sense of ceremony.

While women went up into the iγłu, the planked upper chamber of the house, they rarely slept there. If so, they slept near the trapdoor, never on the bench or under it. This was a section reserved for men and for the older women who had passed the climacteric. Women might sleep near the lamp, tending it as needed and when engaged in sewing or skin work, might sit in the iγłu near the kataq. Women frequently ate in the katawŋata, as indeed, did men. At any social occasion, as, for example, at a shamanistic seance held in the house, food was passed into the iγłu. Men, during the winter and whaling season, generally went to the karigi with which they were associated, remaining there all day. Wives brought their husbands' food to the karigi. Very old people in the house generally remained in the upper chamber and their meals were reached into them on a trencher. Old men frequently met on the floor of the iγłu to smoke, when tobacco was introduced, lighting their pipes from the lamp with a kukun, a long thin stick which could be reached from the bench over to the lamp or thrust down into the cooking fire. The bench was known as iigil^{y}uq and was often set as high as 3 to 4 feet off the floor, leaving little space between the ceiling wall and the bench itself. People who slept on the bench were referred to as igiilut (pl.), while those who slept under the bench were kaanermiruat. In a sense, both were status terms, as was the reference to those who slept in the hallway. The owner and his honored relatives, i. e., father, uncles, etc., slept on the bench. His mother and sons slept under it, while women and less honored persons slept in the hallway or near the kataq. Such terms were useful in referring to the relations within the household. To say to another that this person is "my igiiluq" implies that he is either a close and revered relative, a partner, or some individual to whom the highest worth is accorded.

As has been noted, the trapdoor, the circular well at the passage end of the iγłu, was flanked by lamps. The tendency was to place them either at each side of the door or to move them to the sides of the house where racks were present for the drying of boots and other items of clothing. A lamp might also be put at the end of the passage under the kataq, by the light of which a woman could do a certain amount of household work. This lamp also lighted the way into the upper chamber and could be set on the whale skull which served as a step into the kataq. If fuel was short, the woman of the house could take the lamp down to the iga and cook with it. This was more usual among the nuunamiut, however, who were not usually so well supplied with fuel as their maritime neighbors. The lamp of the Eskimo, as an adjunct of household furnishing, has been too well described elsewhere to require additional description here. It was known throughout the North Alaskan area as nanniq, although the term "kulleq" was preferred at Point Barrow. The lamp of the area was both of pottery, manufactured locally, and of steatite, reaching the Colville mouth by trade. The lamp was felt vaguely to be sacred, and there were certain taboos which arose in relation to its handling. If a lamp fell, for example, it had to be extinguished before it could be picked up. If this were not done, the person picking up a lighted lamp suffered from nosebleed. The lamp was ignited from the fire by means of a stick, the fuel being seal oil and a moss wick being used.

In the aboriginal culture of both tareumiut and nuunamiut, fires were made with flints which the woman of the house kept in a bag about her neck. These rested in a bed of "Alaska cotton" to keep them dry. The drill was also used in firemaking and was worked against soft woods. Either men or women could make fires and it was to the lamp, rather than to the fire itself, that any religious attitudes were extended.

The household amulets and charms were many and varied. The general term aanaroat was applied to them. As may be seen, charms were given by especially qualified persons—shamans or old people—both to individuals and to the house itself. In case of an illness befalling a family so that several members became ill either in succession or simultaneously, a shaman might prescribe a charm for the house. This could be virtually anything—a mask, a stuffed animal, such as a goose, a whaling charm, a personal charm—and in one recent case, after the advent of the European whalers, a loaf of dried bread. The charm was hung above the kataq. As has been mentioned, the nuunamiut were less inclined to such household amulets.

In the maritime house, where it was quite warm and dry, men, on entering the house, removed their outer clothing and boots and went about in the house barefoot and wearing their trousers. A man who came in from hunting left the game he brought outside the house, entered, and hung up his weapons on the walls of the passageway. Here were hangers of bone and antler for the purpose. Women, too, went bare to the waist inside the house, although they wore a longer trouserlike garment with the feet, in the form of socks or light mukluks, sewed on. Both sexes hung their garments in the suuvik, the boarded room at the right of the passageway after the entrance, as soon as they entered the house. It may be noted that among the nuunamiut, where such elaborate passages and adjacent rooms were lacking, clothing and weapons were hung up in the houses themselves.

Aside from the fact that women could not sleep on the bench and did not generally sleep on the planked floor of the iɣɫu, arrangements were left fairly free. People slept when and where convenient and the arrangements, on the level of daily living, depended pretty much on family composition and on the number of families resident in the house. A man could sleep with his wife in the katawŋata if he chose, using the same coverings, for a time, move up to the bench, or out into the hallway, as the mood took him. Status terms for the various sleeping places did, however, apply, but were limited to formal usage. As may be expected, the nuunamiut lacked these formalities, although the place farthest away from the door was a place of honor.

On rising, the people in the household urinated in a wooden vessel. The urine was stored for use in skin tanning, for wounds, and for washing and cleaning. Members of the household urinated and defecated in the hallway. Human feces were often dried and fed to the dogs. If there were adolescent boys in the household they were urged to arise early and to go out in the open and exercise before eating or urinating. After a few minutes of this, often stripped to the waist, they were permitted to return and urinate. The concept here was, of course, to toughen the boys and make them hardy and indifferent to cold and pain.

Dogs were allowed in the hallway in severe weather. Among the nuunamiut, the short hallway was often especially for the dogs. Generally, however, the dogs were staked outside the house and able to burrow into the snow banks to keep warm. On the whole, dogs were valued as property rather than as pets, but a favorite dog might be allowed into the passageway. Similarly, a bitch with puppies was brought in from the outside.

Among the tareumiut, menstruating women were not secluded outside of the house. They could not, however, come up into the iɣɫu, but remained in the katawŋata and were expected to sleep there. Among the nuunamiut, there was a more marked sense of seclusion for the woman at menstruation. Parturition taboos were likewise somewhat more vigorously enforced. If the group were traveling, the menstruating or pregnant woman was expected to lag behind and might be required to sleep in a special hut of willow branches covered with snow. Among the tareumiut, men left the house at a birth and did not return to it for some time. A menstruating woman was not permitted to change her clothes in the house, or, indeed, during her period.

In a shamanistic seance, the shaman came up into the iɣɫu. He straddled the kataq, his back to the bench and the onlookers, and drummed facing the passageway. His spirit helpers called to him from out of the passageway.

If there were guests in the house, as there sometimes might be, in the form of a man's partners from other localities, of visiting kinsmen, or of qataŋutigiit (q. v.), there was usually a place for them on or under the bench. A partner always got the favored bench place, sharing the bench with other men in the household. Any such guest sat next to the host, lest anyone in the house, visiting or otherwise, attempt to rake up old feuds or to challenge the guest to a contest of strength. When a stranger arrived in a community, attempts were made to determine his identity. If he belonged to a family with which a group in the community was feuding, he might be in for some trouble. The host took on the role of protector in this case and offered a stranger whose identity was established his protection and hospitality. A guest was usually given a plate of his own from which to eat. A tendency in the area was to eat the one communal meal a day from a communal dish, although at nuwuk and utkeaaγvik the tendency to serve food on individual dishes was more characteristic.

When two families shared a house, the heads, usually kinsmen, may have elected to build together. But if the family heads were not kinsmen, as might occur when two men were partners and living in the same community, or when they were members of the same crew and karigi, the pattern was to build one iγłu and to erect a separate passageway for each family. This served to keep both possessions and cooking arrangements separate. But the two families might eat together and share the cooking and their food. This was regarded as an economical and convenient arrangement and was not uncommon. It was worked out frequently between neighbors who had separate houses. If two related families lived together, they used only one entrance and one passageway. If there were two larger families who wished to live together, they might share the passageway, or at least parts of it and build off a branch passage and another iγłu.

All such arrangements had to be formally worked out in advance and there were specific rules governing the establishment of such relationships, especially as between nonkin. It involved the creating of a partnership, in itself a highly formalized procedure.

Definite rules of etiquette applied to entering another's house. Good manners demanded that no one enter a house where he had not been formally invited. Even then, a polite and respectful person would still refuse to enter. It was unthinkable that any one enter a strange house when the owners were away. People, it is said "were afraid to do this," the fear arising from adverse public opinion. As has been remarked, interdining, invitations, feasting, were reserved for the karigi. It was only when a stranger came into the community and could establish himself in one of the recognized ways that he might be invited to a house and allowed to eat and sleep. Actually, if this privilege were extended to nonkin, it is evident that the host extended sexual privileges to the guest as well, offering him a wife or daughter as company for the night. When a shaman held a seance in a house, as was frequently the case in winter, either to demonstrate his powers or to effect a cure, the house owner might then invite others to come in and watch.

Because of the sense of good usage in respect to entering a house, the skylight was always used to summon people or to announce one's presence. If a person had something for sale or trade, he walked up onto the roof of the house and called through the skylight to the inhabitants. A man who had caught a seal or other animal, especially during the winter hunting, was often asked for some of the meat. The people who came to beg some always approached the hunter through his skylight. It is worth noting that such requests were almost never refused, the hunter being unwilling to appear niggardly. A man who was a member of a whaling crew was often called by the umealiq for one or another duty. Again, the call was sent out for him and he was summoned by a messenger calling through his skylight.

Anyone might take over an abandoned house. The relatives of the people who had left it had first claim but if they had no wish for it, it was open property. A house was regarded as abandoned when it had not been lived in for a year and when the owner's possessions were taken away. The abandoning of a house was not infrequent, because of the movement through the area. A man might announce that he was leaving the community and try to give his house to another, expecting a return gift. In leaving, a man might place his property mark on the house. The house then remained his and would not be invaded. The winter houses sometimes collapsed as a result of heavy snow or ice packed up on them. When this happened, it was regarded as a highly disastrous portent and the house was abandoned at once. Nor was it ever entered again. Houses along the coast were sometimes caught in ice which packed too closely against the shore. This is recorded as having occurred at Point Barrow several times. It is an event always remembered and spoken of with some anxiety. If people were trapped inside and killed, no attempt was made to recover the bodies and the people living nearby might likewise abandon their houses.

The house was technically owned by the head of the family, the chief hunter in it. As has been seen, the house sometimes bore his name. But the rights to ownership were never questioned except at the death of the nominal owner. The widow might inherit or at least hold the property in trust for the children. There was, however, no established rule in this matter. The kinsmen of the deceased, brothers or cousins, might simply seize the house and the dead man's property and evict the widow and children. In this instance, the widow might seek aid of her own kinsmen who, if sufficiently strong, might back her claim. If her group were weak, it followed that attempts to dispossess her were more likely to occur.

A man could trade a house and often did. A house was equal to an umiak in value. A house could be given as payment to a shaman. In historic times, a house was often sold for a gun or for whaling gear. It follows that a house was not lightly abandoned. Abandonment, at least among the tareumiut, generally arose when a man left with his family to travel and then failed to return because of accident or trouble with a stranger group. Among the nuunamiut, the sense of house ownership and the emotional attachment to it were not so strong.

Primarily the winter residence, the house, it is true, was left a good part of the time. Old people who resided in it tended to stay at the winter camp through the year. Even here, however, and if the family elected to remain in the coastal village, they rarely lived in the house proper during the summer. The tendency was to erect a tent near the house or at the beach. This created a sense of change and a kind of holiday. It is of interest to note that the pattern is still followed. The tent was a simple conical tent mounted on a frame. Planks were sometimes put on the floor to hold the bedding. In general, there was no tendency toward building a sod substructure for the tent as was the case among the nuunamiut.

Adjacent to the house were the ice cellars (sirilʸuaq). Although quite large and spacious today, the aboriginal cellars were smaller, cut laboriously into the permafrost with bone picks. The cellar was supported with whale ribs and a whale skull placed at the entrance, the roof covered with sod. Virtually every household had its own cellar where meat of all kinds was stored. Men of wealth had larger cellars. As food was needed from the cellar, it was brought in and stored in the makpik. The ice cellar, like the house, was regarded as private property and thus inviolable. People could and did ask for food and it was freely given. The ice cellar is a tareumiut development. The nuunamiut, drying their meat, were not in need of such elaborate storage space and were in any case obliged to take much food with them in the seasonal round. The inland Eskimo cached food in the semipermanent houses which they built.

Another feature in the tareumiut house was the rack (ikirrak). This was made of driftwood and stood in the rear of virtually every winter dwelling. In summer the sled was placed on it, in winter the kayak and umiak. Stored skins, food, any property not immediately needed were thrown up onto the rack. The dog teams were most frequently staked out under it. (Pl. 3, *c*.)

Houses may perhaps serve to point up some of the outstanding differences in way of life between the nuunamiut and tareumiut. It is evident that the maritime settlement had the greater degree of stability with its permanent houses and its other features which served to lend a symbolic focus. Although the nuunamiut, as groups, did not have the same precise organization of their maritime counterpart, the two groups, however different materially, were more alike than different in their societal organization. From the setting of economy and settlement, it is possible to move to a consideration of the social groupings which functioned in each ecological area.

FAMILY AND KINSHIP

INTRODUCTION

In virtually every respect the aboriginal family structure carries through into the present. However much the inroads of modern living have disrupted other aspects of the cultures of the north Alaskan slope, the system of mutual aid, of social control, and of reciprocal obligation inherent in the family remains paramount. Many features have, it is true, fallen into disuse. The charms and amulets which might pass through a family line are of course no longer used, at least overtly, and the collective responsibility with its implications of blood feud which underlay so much of what may be called law is likewise gone. Individualization, so characteristic of western culture, is beginning to make its imprint on the Eskimo family. As yet, however, it has not fully supplanted the aboriginal family institution. Social controls today still rest in the family. There has been no adequate development, among the native population at least, of political institutions, with the result that there is essential lack of interest in the attempts of the Alaska Native Service to effect community organization. So long as the family continues to provide the social cornerstone, no need is felt for institutional surrogates.

There are those who have claimed that Eskimo society is communalistic. To some extent this is true, if the extended family is regarded as the communal or collective element. Any other nonfamilial forms of either sharing or cooperation were, as has been shown, strictly patterned and somewhat limited. Neither the maritime community nor the nomadic band were permanent units; they depended for their existence on the kinship section which lived together, worked together, and moved together forming a collective entity, but there were recognized ties of kinship that went far beyond the local situation. Aboriginally, along the whole Arctic coast of Alaska, from Point Hope to Barter Island and Herschel Island, there were the intertwined threads of recognized kinship.

Here was neither a formalized clan type of society nor a recognition of unilineal descent. This meant, and means, that there was a recognition of bilineal kinship and that in the individual, membership in two different lineages was possible. Sexual relations with those who were designated by a kinship term were rigorously tabooed. Not that the prohibition was enforced in any tangible way, and there were exceptions. But such deviations were few and bore the brunt of unfavorable public opinion. A basic principle of social organization of the cultures in question was to extend, either through the blood tie or through an acceptable substitute for it, the sphere of kinship. It was between such related individuals that the strong bond of cooperation lay. One might argue that cousin marriage was defined as incestuous because it hindered the development of the patterned cooperative institutions, or at least prevented new ones from coming into being. Because of bilateral descent, the individual could count on a wide circle of kin, reckoning both his father's and his mother's kin grouping as his own. Such recognition was extended to the kin of his grandparents as well, although the tie became quite tenuous when pushed further back. Each individual, therefore, had kinship ties with several different groupings. He belonged to the circle in which he happened to be and his economic contributions related to it. His other kindred, however, likewise had a claim on him and he on them. The ultimate definition of kinship lay first in the designation of kin by specific kinship terms, and second, in the obligations incumbent on the individual to succor his kin and to assume responsibility for their actions. Kinship was and is a reality; it was a practical matter in that the blood tie was known and recognized. The individual thus belonged to a nuclear family and then to an extended kin grouping or at least to groupings which reached a point of convergence in himself. And beyond this lay the realm of quasi-kinship, the formalized extensions of the cooperative tie to nonkin.

THE NUCLEAR FAMILY

People who lived together in one house, who worked together, who might move together for inland hunting or trade, and who called each other by kinship terms were ketuuneraareic, a localized family grouping. In practice, this consisted of as many as chose to live together. It might be parents and children, or it might consist of two brothers and their children. A wife's relative or relatives might also be present in the group. They, with the wife herself, represented different lines of descent although good relations were felt to be mandatory among affined kin. As will be seen, however, if a dispute arose, one took the side of one's kin rather than that of one's spouse, presumably placing the offspring, who would belong to both factions, in a dilemma. Because there was no prevailing attitude toward residence, this being arranged in a wholly practical way, the nuclear group was slanted toward either the male or the female branch. Thus, if it were felt expedient, the man, on marriage, might choose to live in his wife's grouping. Or the reverse was true. As nearly as one can judge, there was a fairly even split as to residence, with perhaps some tendency toward a patrilocal and virilocal arrangement. Dependence was placed on needs of the moment. If a family were poor, which might mean that they had only daughters and no active provider, uxorilocal residence was called for. If a son were the only provider to aged parents, residence was patrilocal. Or a married couple simply built a new house in a community, although here again, residence near the family grouping of either the wife or the husband might be a factor. Informal though such an arrangement might be, there was nevertheless a consideration to be met. If a husband had a recognized place in a crew, whether for caribou hunting or whaling, the matter of residence had to be carefully weighed; he would be reluctant to abandon a remunerative connection with a crew or karigi.

There was some further recognition of residence situations. A family which resided with a married son was called aŋayokaareic. If a married child lived with his parents, i. e. in their house, the situation was called ataatak. The basis of these terms will be readily seen: ataata refers to the grandfather, aŋayokaak to the parents, and ketuunarak (from which ketuuneraareic is derived) to one's own children.

While there was thus no specific residence requirement, a man felt himself to be more closely allied to the kin among whom he grew up. However much he might be responsible to other kin in other places, it was to the local group to which his loyalties were naturally first given. This tended to alleviate the situation of dilemma in which the individual might find himself if his relatives, no kin to each other, engaged in a feud or dispute. His role was properly that of peacemaker. An example will point this out:

> uŋaruk's father and uncle were threatened by a man who went so far as to shoot at them both. At this, uŋaruk and his uncle's son, his cousin, agreed to take revenge. They got their guns and went to kill their fathers' attacker. The latter heard that they were coming and was waiting in the hallway of his house with his gun in hand. As the two advanced to engage him, a woman, the aunt of the fathers of the two boys, came between them. The man whom they sought to kill and who had attacked their fathers was cousin to the aunt through another lineal affiliation. She had then very properly taken over the role of peacemaker and did so effectively. The boys and the man settled their difference and no feud was begun.

It is thus readily seen how the ties of kinship operate. They apply not only in respect to the nuclear family but also in respect to a much wider group. The nuclear family consideration is thus technically superseded by the demands of the wider circle of kinship. The question may then justly be asked: what is the ultimate function of the nuclear family? This was a residence unit and an economic unit. In the matter of day-to-day living, in the preparation of food, the making of clothing, and in the procurement of food through hunting, here being a reflection of the well-defined sexual division of labor, it was the nuclear family which came to the fore. In broader aspects, however, such as in mutual interdependence and aid, in assistance in times of stress, and perhaps most important, in the general pattern of basic individual security, it was the wider circle of kin which began to function.

THE EXTENDED FAMILY

The extended family was iilyagiic. These were, for the individual, kin on both the maternal and paternal side. In the final analysis, this was for the individual a circle based wholly on actual relationship. It was not otherwise a formalized institution. There was no family chief, no structuring of power or authority in the group. Mention has already been made of the umealiq, the man of wealth, the boat owner. In keeping his crew, he might be obliged to depend on the contributions which his kin made to him in return for his protection and assistance. While the umealiq might be a recognized leader in the community, it was the community which accorded him his post, rather than the family itself. His function was local and his sphere of influence limited itself to his community and to his post of prestige among the several households making up his kin in the community. Neither were there ceremonial prerogatives associated with the extended kin group. Charms and amulets might be inherited, it is true, as apparently might property marks, but the question here arose as between individuals and not in whole families. The north Alaskan slope appears to differ in this respect from the cultures to the south where a lineage system and a quasi-totemism arise (Lantis, 1946, p. 239).

The bilateral kinship designation and collective responsibility were the underlying elements of the formation of the wider kinship grouping. It was regarded as important, in the socialization process, that a child be taught the names of his grandparents as a means of identifying kin. Children also learned the names and the appropriate kinship designation for all relatives, however distant they might be. There were also means of extending the reciprocal obligations of kinship to nonkin, the result being to create a secondary circle of cooperation. The child was also taught the names of his parents' partners as well as the names of those to whom he stood in a qataŋuutigiit (q.v.) relationship. But regardless of secondary ties, it was to the blood kin that the primary loyalties were directed. The individual was taught to offer aid to his kindred and to support their actions. Kinship was regarded as a sacred trust; one did not joke with one's relatives nor was it necessary to enter into any barter agreements or partnerships with them. A relative would always be of assistance, an arrangement which pointed primarily to the sharing of food and the granting of shelter. Such cooperation between kin did not mean that one could freely use the possessions of his relatives. Property was personal and not held collectively in the kin grouping; food, however, was to be shared. In summary, the individual quickly learned what was incumbent on him as a member of a wide kinship circle and the extent to which he could go in imposing on those who were his blood relatives.

KINSHIP TERMINOLOGY

The uniform social organization of the North Alaskan Eskimo brought the same general type of kinship terminology into being. It is slightly different from that described for other western Eskimo groups. Several influences may have been operative in the formation of the system, a fact which may be substantiated by the presence of a number of specific differentiating factors. There are both general classificatory and generation factors in the system and to a point, sex differentiation is important. The terms which follow are those of the utkeaviŋmiut, and of the anaktuvuŋmiut. There are no fundamental differences between the two sets of terms. The structure of the system is generally uniform throughout the area, but there are local preferences for certain terms. Informants say that some terms have been recent in their development and that others are archaic. Local synonyms are given where available. The following terms are referential and except for designations of such close ties as the parents do not appear in vocative form. The importance of the kinship system in family and household formation and integration is discussed below. Terms are as follows.[6]

LINEAL AND NUCLEAR CONSANGUINES

Third ascending and descending generations, i. e. any relative, regardless of sex, in the generation of the FFF or ChChCh:

amaw

Grandparental generation:

ataata (FF; MF; FFB; MFB; FMB; MMB)
aanna (FM; MM; FFSs; MFSs; FMSs; MMSs)

Affinals may also be so designated (FFSsH; FMSsH; MFSsH; MMSsH by ataata; FFBW; MFBW; FMBW; MMBW by aanna), but this would apply only if coresident with Ego. They would otherwise be sakirrak, aŋaaruk, or asoaγeeik (q.v.).

[6] Abbreviations: F=Father; M=Mother; B=Brother; Ss=Sister; Sb=Sibling; Ch=Child; S=Son; D=Daughter; GCh=Grandchild; H=Husband; W=Wife; o=older; y=younger.

Parental generation:

aapa	(F)		
		aapaŋ	(address)
		aapaγa	(1st person singular poss.)
aaka	(M)		
		aakaŋ	(address)
		aakaγa	(1st person singular poss.)
aŋak	(FB; MB)	("Archaic" term, specifically FB akaakuk)	
aacuk	(FSs; MSs)		

It may be noted that unlike the traditional "Eskimo" system, there are only two terms for the siblings of the parents, rather than four (cf. Spier, 1925, p. 79).

Where there is coresidence with Ego, an "uncle" or "aunt" term is used for such affinals as FSsH and MSsH, FBW, and MBW, respectively. Males affined through the siblings of the parents are otherwise aŋaaruk, while females affined through the brothers of the parents are asoaγeeik. As with the affinals in the grandparental generation, both may be sakirrak, although this term is generally reserved for Ego's and descending generations. A father's cowife may be called akkaγak; a mother's cohusband (not the father), apaarak.

Ego's generation:

aapayax	(oB)	aapaxatuγa—my eldest brother
nuqaceax	(yB)	nuqaaxa—my younger brother
nuqaxłuq	(youngest B)	nuqaxłuγa (1st person poss. superlative, i. e. my youngest brother)
akicceax	(oSs)	
nayaq	(ySs)	
nayakaxtuq	(youngest Ss)	nayakaxtuγa—my youngest sister

First descending generation:

irin^{y}iq	(S)
paniq	(D)

Second descending generation:

tutiq (GCh)—Variants: in^{y}aγootak. Today, tutaaluk is preferred at Barrow; it is a "modern" form. The latter term may apply originally to the B/SsChCh, for which it may still be used. There is no sex differentiation.

Third descending generation:

amaw

CONSANGUINEAL KIN—COLLATERALS

Ego's generation:

There are two terms for parallel cousin.

aŋuutaken—Children of two brothers. This is often rendered referentially in the dual form—aŋuutakatigiik, i. e. Ego and his parallel cousin.

aaxanaken—Children of two sisters. Dual—aaxanakatigiik.

Sibling terms are not used to designate the parallel cousin.

Cross cousins are iilʸoreik, a derivative of iilʸa "of us," that is, a relative. There is no cross cousin marriage. The cross cousin term can vary in that the female cross cousin may be designated as aaγnʸoreik (aγnak—a woman).

These terms are extended. Thus the child of the cross cousin of the parent is also a cross cousin. The child of a parallel cousin of the parent is also a parallel cousin. Ego designates the cousins of the parents by the term which the parent uses and is reciprocally so designated. It follows that neither generation nor the sex of Ego are factors in the designation of collaterals.

The child of a sibling is uyooγo. A variant form is uyuruq. There is no sex differentiation.

The child of a sibling's child is designated by the grandchild term, tutiq (or tutaaluk). This term thus serves to classify relatives in the second descending generation. Similarly, the children of tutiq are amaw.

AFFINAL KIN

Parental generations:

aaparuak	(HF; WF)
aakaruak	(HM; WM)

Ego's generation:

uwii, also winʸi	(H)	
nuleaaq	(W)	Also, aytpaax, "cowife," used to designate the second wife in polygynous unions.

From the point of view of Ego, other affinals are differentiated as to sex but not strictly as to generation. The following terms are encountered:

niŋaw---------- This term applies to any male in Ego's generation and below who is married into the group which is represented by the speaker. The term thus applies to SsH, DH, DDH, in short, the husband of any woman designated as uyooγo or tutiq, or by a sister or daughter term.

ukuwak--------- The female counterpart of niŋaw, applying to any female married into Ego's kinship group into his generation or those below. So designated are BW, SW, SSW, thus the wife of any man designated by a brother, son, nephew, or grandchild term.

sakirrak--------- This term, reflecting no sex differentiation, applies to affinals outside the family of reference. An example is seen in the fact that although Ego is designated as niŋaw by his wife's brother, being thus regarded as affined to the kin grouping of his wife, the wife's brother stands to Ego as his sakirrak. Here is a reflection of the retention of kinship unit of birth;

regardless of residence arrangement, Ego retains his own kinship unit affiliation and is technically not involved in the workings of the kinship grouping of his spouse. The term is reserved in the main for the nuclear familial situation. Thus it does not apply to the spouses of the cousins of the spouse. It serves to designate WB, WSs, WSsH, WBW, HB, HSs, HBW, HSsH, children of WB, WSs, HB, HSs. In ascending generations, the designation also applies to a point. The spouse of a sibling of a parent or grandparent is sakirrak if not coresident with Ego. If coresident, however, aŋaaruk, refers to FFSsH, MFSsH, FMSsH, MMSsH, FSsH, MSsH. Ego is then reciprocally uyooγo or tutiq. The female relative affined in this way, FFBW, MBW, etc. is asoaγeeik.

nuuleriik---------- This term applies to the parent of the child's spouse. It is a general reciprocal referential designation.

STEP- AND ADOPTIVE RELATIONSHIPS

While adoption is an extremely common element in the social organization of the north Alaskan Eskimo, special adoptive terms are not used. An adopted child is referred to as tiguak but is so quickly drawn into the family grouping that consanguineal terms apply to him. The adopted child will use consanguineal terms in reference both to his native and to his adoptive group. His adoptive parents are called by parent terms. His true parents, if living, are sometimes designated by grandparent terms. In such cases, the adopted child is felt to belong to two families, assuming that he has been adopted by nonkin, and derives benefits from both and is theoretically responsible to both.

There are no terms to designate a foster, step-, or "half" relationship. A half-brother is a brother, a wife's child a son or daughter. The half-sibling, under certain circumstances (note below) may be qataŋun.

COMBINED KIN TERMS

The Eskimo language makes full use of the dual number. Reference to persons in formal narrative style, as in myths, folktales, and the like may call forth various dual combinations of kinship terms. The following have been noted:

irinʸereeik-------- Parent, i. e., father or mother, and son.

panigiik----------- Parent and daughter.

tutaaluwiik------- Grandparent and grandchild; any consanguineal relative in the grandparental generation and grandchild. The term tuticareeik was given as an archaic synonym for this compound; it is no longer used but survives in various myths.

FACTORS IN THE SYSTEM

It will be seen that the north Alaskan Eskimo kinship system consists of a series of unmodified terms in which primary emphasis is laid on the nuclear family. Collateral kin are merged as in the cousin designations while sex differentiation applies only in the nuclear situation. Classification by generation operates in the second descending generation and in the third ascending and descending generation. With respect to sibling terms, there is the designation of younger siblings as opposed to the differentiation between oldest and youngest, a phenomenon described for other Eskimo groups and characteristic of an "Eskimo" type system (Lantis, 1946, pp. 235–236; Spier, 1925, p. 79). While there are separate sibling terms, the children of siblings are classified and not specifically designated. There is a single nepotic term.

It is in the affinal designations that the emphasis on the nuclear family is lent perspective. With the exception of parent-in-law terms and the terms which may be applied to the spouses of the parents' siblings in a coresidence situation, there is classificatory designation of affinal kin. There is the general term denoting male "in-law," and a corresponding female one applicable to Ego's generation and below. These terms apply only to the group outside the unit of reference.

There are no implications in the system for either the sororate or levirate. There is some feeling against the marital union of affined kin, and a strong one indeed against union with those defined by the terms reflecting nuclear relationship and consanguine collateral relationship.

The presence of various synonymous terms does not complicate the system. There are apparently some differences in terms between the maritime and nomadic peoples, and between the coastal villages as well. The structure of the system, however, seems constant throughout the area.

An interesting change is at present taking place in the system. Because the family, both nuclear and extended, retains its importance, the kinship terms likewise are still applied. Many today are beginning to call the father by an English term in reference and address, while the father term aapa is being applied to the grandfather specifically, presumably as a point of distinction from the classificatory ataata. The same is beginning to be true of the grandmother-mother terms.

A significant factor in the kinship system was coresidence. Thus it becomes important to define the place of Ego in the system. As may be seen from the affinal terms, it is the factor of residence which provides the basis for designations. It is easily seen why this becomes important, emerging as it does from the economic functions of the household. While the coresident group might consist of representatives from several kin groupings it was, under normal circumstances, fairly well knit and fairly permanent. Kinship designations might be transferred to the coresident affinals, and sibling terms to remoter coresident collaterals, the situation paralleling that of adoption.

COLLECTIVE RESPONSIBILITY

As has been noted, all those who called each other by kinship terms reflecting the consanguineal tie stood in a relationship of cooperation, mutual aid, and were, in the eyes of the society, responsible for each other's actions. Properly speaking, there was no institution of warfare on the Alaskan Arctic slope. There were, however, feuds, some of which were apparently of long duration. These feuds arose between extended families. The society possessed no formal mechanism by which a situation of feuding could be halted. Only the kin groups involved could reach an agreement to cease their activities. This, as has been seen, might occur when a person with relationships in both families acted as a mediator. The general theory behind the collective responsibility incumbent on the members of the family grouping lay in the evaluation of life for life. Feuds arose because of murder and, properly, for no other reason. Retaliation for other offenses took place, of course, but unless a killing was involved, it was a personal matter and did not call forth the joint action of a kin grouping. Indeed, a man's relatives, fearful lest a feud begin, might attempt to dissuade a man from retaliating for an offense. As has been remarked, a man of integrity would often prefer to suffer in silence and take no action against an offender. If he did so, however, continued insults could lead to a killing and to the inexorable involvement of the entire kin grouping into the blood feud. It is said that if a person wished to begin an argument, his course of action was to kill an enemy's dog. This brought a dispute out into the open and might lead to bloodshed. Even here, however, an "honest" man let the matter pass. As a result of the blood revenge concept, there arose in the intergroup situations of the area the sole basis for legal procedure. This might justifiably be termed "customary law," several examples of which are given in the sections which follow. The various instances serve to indicate how the problems involving interfamily quarrels might be resolved.

When a blood feud existed, the normal patterns of cooperation were disrupted. The term for feud was makuruak "disorder." It referred to any kind of disagreement or strife, including domestic argument. Between families feuding there could be no mutual aid of any kind, no sharing of food, no joint undertakings. This so disrupted the normal flow of life that an individual might come before his enemies, often unarmed, saying "kill me!" If they did so, the feud naturally continued. If they did not, however, this might also serve to end the matter. Or, at least, it might end the matter so far as a feud in a single community was concerned. It could readily break out again, however, since other kin in other communities were also involved and could take revenge without reference to what had happened in some other settlement. The feuds are said to have gone on endlessly, being remembered after several generations. A father or mother is said to have instilled hatred for the enemy group in a child. But while such hatreds between kin groupings might go on over long periods, it did not follow that a "shoot on sight" pattern arose. Again, the reservation, the unwillingness to take immediate action, came to be operative. Hatred and enmity might apply, but it did not always result in overt killing. The stranger was in a particularly unfavorable position, another factor which undoubtedly made for solidarity of the local group. The stranger, assuming he came to a settlement where he had no kin, was immediately catechized as to his relationships. He was unwise to give them, since he might conceivably step into a feud situation all unknowingly. The stranger, subject to such rough treatment as being pummeled and having his clothes torn by the residents of the settlement he entered, in any case, would attempt to get the names of house or tent owners in the community. In this way, he might be able to claim relationship and protection, being thus able to establish some connections in the community.

It is readily seen how blood might be shed in an argument. It was the custom to carry two knives, one on each side under the parka. In an argument, the knife could be drawn with either hand. Even a wound might lead to murder in retaliation. The impression is obtained that such killings took place in the heat of the moment. They appear to have been planned less often. Kin groups might agree to meet for "war," called, in this case, anuyuq. In this event each side marshaled as many men as possible, armor was donned, and the one group went forth against the other. Such "battles" seem always to have been indecisive and did not succeed in terminating a lasting feud. Several Barrow families even today carry bitter memories of feuds with groups from the Point Hope area.

Another example of a feud which was averted is the following: Two men wished to be good runners. They became involved in an argument over the matter. "You are slow like an owl," said one. "You think you can move as fast as an ermine," replied the other. As they argued, the father of one of them came out and suggested that they run a race to settle the matter. "Owl" ran ahead of "Ermine" but the latter caught him and threw him to the ground. They wrestled but "Owl" broke away and this time "Ermine" couldn't catch him. "Ermine," speechless with rage, went home and got his bow. "Owl" was warned by others and ran after "Ermine." "What are you going to do?" he asked. "Ermine" replied, "I'm going to kill you right now." "Here I am," said "Owl." At this "Ermine" said, "I forgot myself." "There's no use killing me," said "Owl," "my relatives will make trouble for you," and they were "friends" after that.

Relationships thus existed as between kin which demanded that the individual fight for relatives and avenge them. There was no social mechanism which enforced such vengeance, although a man would obviously suffer if he failed to take any action whatsoever over a long period of time. He was then regarded as unfilial and could be made fun at. But his action might simply involve confronting his enemies to say "Perhaps you will kill me, too." In so acting, the individual was demonstrating the ideal of "patience." He thus took no vengeance but succeeded in "saving face." The chance was very good that the enemies would do nothing. The individual might, indeed, place them in a bad light in public opinion. Only if a man stood in an unprotected position, lacking the backing of his kin group, would he then be in greater danger. This is why the stranger occupied a somewhat precarious place.

The question is worth raising as to the fate of the person who killed a member of his own group. Since it was an intrakin group affair, no such mechanism as a feud would be called for. Extenuating circumstances were considered. This might also be true in the case of interfamily killings, where if the affront were sufficiently grave, the killer was not harmed nor were any of his kin. But within the family a particularly quarrelsome person who might murder a family member was often driven away to starve. Without the cooperation from his kin, this was not unlikely. While such situations have been mentioned, no one could recall a case of murder of one family member by another. When, however, a murder occurs between affined kin, the blood feud again takes place, since marriage is not regarded as creating a situation of collective responsibility between the principals. There is a folktale which reflects this situation:

Five brothers lived together. The oldest was the provider and married a woman who came to live with them. The youngest brother was still a little boy. For some reason, the woman hated this boy and resolved to kill him. She waited until the four older brothers were out hunting. She then murdered her young brother-in-law with her ulu. She hid the body on the rack on the back of the house. The other brothers looked for him for a long time but not until much later did they find the body. The corpse was infested with worms. The brothers now worked out a punishment for the murderous wife. They decided that since the worms had eaten their brother, this should be her fate as well. They suggested a race around a lagoon to see who could run around it the greatest number of times. The woman lagged behind. Her husband caught up to her from behind and threw her into the water. The brothers had attracted the worms in the water by throwing pieces of meat in beforehand. The woman was attacked by the worms who stripped her body of flesh. After a time, only her lungs appeared floating on the surface of the lagoon.

While this tale, which again uses the worm theme, and reflects the morbid fear of worms which these groups had, is clearly folklore, it may serve to indicate that marriage was regarded as no primary bond. Clearly, it was second to blood kinship. Always the mistreated wife could demand and get aid from her kin. To her husband's family she made no appeal and could expect no backing from them. With children, of course, with long time coresidence, this differentiation between the kin groupings of spouses became less well defined.

It has been shown that a person had kinship affiliations in more than one family. He belonged to both a paternal and maternal group. The demands of collective responsibility applied principally to the kin grouping in which he grew up. It was again the factor of coresidence which determined the primary loyalty. However, an adopted child was responsible for the group of his adoption and was regarded as a member of it. Moreover, he was obliged to defend the blood kin, the family grouping out of which he had been adopted. The adoptive relationship extended the demands of responsibility. This was true not only in cases of formal adoption, where a child of one family had been raised by another, but it extended also to the husband of one's mother, if, for instance, the mother had remarried. Such a man was in a sense an adoptive father. The child was thus placed in the position of greater responsibility than the spouse.

As the kinship situation is examined, it is clear that a bilineal organization emerges. There was no formality regarding residence requirements. Patrilocal or matrilocal residence, or separate residence, in fact, depended wholly on expediency. The kinship terminology reflects no bifurcation of paternal and maternal kin. There is, however, some slight evidence that the patrilineal bond was considered somewhat more important. A man was embroiled in dispute because of his kinship affiliations through his mother but it appears that the kin related through the father could make a more forceful plea for assistance, support, and defense. All that this could be said to amount to was that if a choice were involved, the individual sought the kin grouping of his father. Similarly, the stranger, if catechized as to his kinship affiliations, was generally asked first the name of his paternal grandfather. No other evidence of a preference for paternal descent can be cited, neither the matter of inheritance, whether of tangible or supernatural property, nor residence being involved. In summary, the kinship grouping was a perennial source of support.

One was not only safe wherever one had blood relatives, but could also enlist their aid in any enterprise, and could without fear of refusal demand of them food, clothing, lodging, and comforts. In return, one had to be prepared to accord blood kin the same favors. But above all, defense of one's blood kin, vengeance for them, and responsibility for their actions were primary factors which served to effect family integration.

MARRIAGE

The family groupings to which the individual belonged were ideally exogamous. It is evident that a goal in marriage was to extend as far as possible the bonds of mutual aid and cooperation. For this reason, marriage between cousins was not desirable and similarly, there was no levirate or sororate. Cousin marriage is reported as occurring in a few instances; here, however, even the second collateral degree was held improper, such marriages occurring only between relatives of the third collateral degree. But even such marriages were frowned on. It was felt that marriage between blood kin, however remote the tie, produced inferior offspring, individuals who were "not quite human." This seems to be an aboriginal concept and not derived from Euro-American contact. One informant was asked if her own children could marry the children of her brother's daughter, the respective children designating each other by "cousin" terms. She remarked that this "wouldn't look good" and indicated that she felt very strongly against such a union. Indeed, the only circumstances which would justify such a marriage arose when a person found himself alone, lacking the benefits of the nuclear family. Then he might marry a cousin, albeit a distant one, in order to reaffirm family ties.

The feeling was carried further in that the adopted child was subject to the same restrictions in regard to the family of his adoption. Not only were his blood kin prohibited but the adoptive kin as well. Recently a case arose where a family had adopted a boy and girl. They married and their behavior was considered highly scandalous. "It looked terribly bad."

The various towns of the maritime peoples tended toward endogamy. Here again, however, there was no rigid regulation. The nuunamiut, subject essentially to the same regulations of marriage, might tend to endogamy in the extended band. Here, however, the regulations of kinship exogamy on all sides might necessitate going fairly far afield for a wife. It might generally be said that a man married into a family with which he was acquainted. To take a wife from an unknown group was simply to court trouble in that one could never be sure of the industry of the woman, of the reputation of her family, or of any number of possible involvements.

A problem of some interest emerges in respect to the contacts between the nuunamiut and the tareumiut. These, as has been seen, were principally of a trading nature, a mutal interdependence based on the exchange of certain commodities. That there were sexual unions between members of the two groups goes without saying, in view of the exchanges of wives which took place between partners at the great trading sessions. Marriage between the two groups was, however, rare. It occurred sometimes but was, in general, exceptional. And, again, such marriages did not take place unless there was a thorough acquaintance of long standing. A man of the ikpikpaŋmiut, for example, came regularly to piγiniq to trade. While there, he married a woman named tupineraaluq and took her back to the inland country with him. Everyone, it is said, felt sorry for her. She was obliged to adjust to the inland life and to learn new skills. Moreover, she would have to move about all the time. She adjusted well to the inland life, however, and came with her husband back to piγiniq every summer, and visited her family at this time. There are a few other instances of such marriages between the two ecological groups, but it is to be emphasized that such unions were not sought. Each group had its own sets of skills, its own type of adjustment. The result was to keep contacts on the trading level but not to effect any greater degree of intimacy through marriages. As between the two groups there would thus be the relationship of the qataŋun (qataŋuutigiit) but not of actual kinship.

A man did not marry sisters in the accepted polygynous unions, nor could he marry a mother and daughter. There was also the strong feeling that a man could not marry the sister of a deceased wife, nor a woman her dead husband's brother. Two brothers were likewise forbidden to marry two sisters. There is one instance of such marriage recalled today, the case involving marriage between a man and woman whose respective sister and brother also married. This "only happened once" and "it was a terrible thing." In another case, quite recently in Barrow, a woman married the brother of her deceased husband. This was "not right."

No one had ever heard of an incestuous relationship between brother and sister. In only one instance was there recalled an incest situation. A family had adopted a daughter. When the wife died, the daughter remained with her adoptive father as his wife. People said of this man, "He should be ashamed" and of the girl that "she had no pride." While no group action could be taken in such a case, the guilty parties could be made to feel the full force of adverse public opinion. When the girl's adoptive father died, she was claimed by another family in marriage. It is thus clear that there was no lasting stigma in such cases.

In the case of the death of a spouse, particularly of a woman, and there were young children of the union, it was felt that the widow should remain with her husband's group. There was no rule regarding this, but if a woman resided with the family of her husband and had good relations with them she might hold the husband's property in trust for her own children. The husband's family would support her in this. It also happened that the husband's family would seize his property, his house, umiak, or other possessions and simply drive the widow away. In short, there was no rule of prescribed behavior relating to disposition of property or residence following the death of a spouse. A widow might be seized immediately at her husband's death by some man who desired her. This was a kind of marriage by capture, which took place at any time, since a woman who lacked the backing of her kin or of that of her deceased husband was regarded as fair game. An unprotected girl or widow would simply be seized by a man who wanted a wife or an addition to his household. Or it might merely be a matter of rape. A widow with children could generally rely on the support of her dead husband's kin. If, however, she continued to reside with her husband's family, and, marrying again, brought her new husband to live with her among them, there was usually no objection, another worker being welcomed. If a man continually plagued a widow to come with him as his wife, she objecting, and if he raped her or sought to do so several times, as again might well occur, her own kin and that of her dead husband were likely to offer protection and might even kill the man who desired her.

Marriage in these cultures was of course essential. The unmarried man was virtually helpless since he then lacked the work which a woman could provide. It would appear that marriages were more or less permanent, since a couple learned to adjust to each other's ways and a strong bond of affection might arise. But while the state of marriage operated largely in economic terms, and was permanent on this basis, it was defined sexually. As will be seen, when a man and woman had had sexual relations, a state of marriage was considered to have existed between them. The result was to call forth certain kinds of attitudes and behavior reflecting a cooperative situation into which not only the principals concerned, but others as well, might be drawn. The criterion of a permanent marriage was of course coresidence. Divorce was simply the breaking of the residence tie.

But there was a vague sense of marital arrangement, particularly in the case of young people entering marriage for the first time. Parents, especially the women, made the arrangement directly and informally. Such arrangements were frequently made between families in the same community whose members felt that they could agree. A "good" marriage resulted in peaceful relations between the families involved. It was also desirable that marriage within the community or group, should this be a nomadic situation, take place. This kept the closeness of family ties between the principals. There was also a vague feeling that marriage should be patrilocal. Again, however, there was nothing which enforced any of these points. When an agreement was made, the parents of the girl made a gift to the boy—a knife, a harpoon, a parka—while he in turn came to their house to work for them. Such bride service was of short duration, although somewhat formalized, since the boy might merely catch a seal and give it to his prospective parents-in-law. The marriage might be consummated at any time during these proceedings. And once consummated, it was viewed as marriage. There was no demand for chastity or virginity.

It is worth repeating that while there were no definite residence requirements, patrilocal residence was generally preferred. Much, however, depended on the allocation of men. A married couple, if it did not at once choose to build its own house, might move back and forth to the various in-laws. If, for example, a woman's father was dead and she had only younger brothers, her husband would be expected to support her family. Or, if both families were small and there was only the husband to act as chief hunter, there was nothing against bringing the two sets of in-laws together under one roof.

In marriage arrangements, a girl particularly was often reluctant to leave her family for a husband. If so, her parents would attempt to talk her into marriage by saying such things as: "Another girl will take him away from you if you don't go to him"; "His parents will treat you nicely if you marry him";"Look out, some other man will grab you and take you to his house." If a girl refused marriage, and her freedom of choice was clearly recognized, her suitor might marry another. If her own later marriage either failed or ran into difficulties, the parents told her, "You see, you should have married when we wanted you to; now you have made only trouble for yourself." A feeling that the arranged marriages were preferable was strong. This was because the parents selected a partner from a family which they knew and liked. "In-law" troubles were a frequent cause of divorce.

Since chastity was not valued, and premarital sexual relations were usual, and these must be defined as on a temporary, noneconomic level, there was no stigma placed on a fatherless child. Since the father can always be recognized because "the child looks like him," as is still the strong feeling, the illegitimate child created no problem. Indeed, it was often the kin of the father of the child which insisted on claiming the child, rather than the reverse. It meant adding a family member and creating a potential worker for the group. Hence, when an unmarried woman had a child, there were always those who would marry her. Parenthood was desired and reflected status. Hence, if it were known that a woman was not barren, she was desirable. She might then have a choice of marriage partners. The kin grouping of the purported father might urge him to assume his place as the woman's husband and might be very angry if she then refused him.

A girl who was sexually free was not considered too desirable. The feeling appears to have been that she spent too much time with her romantic affairs and too little in "being busy." In short, such a girl was chided for laziness, not for her morals. Hence, a young girl was kept in check so as to meet the ideal of industry. If a girl had several affairs and became pregnant, the family looked at the new-born child to see whom it resembled. The father, if a desirable "catch," was usually allowed to marry her. But this did not always follow. Any man might take her. If she had a reputation of philandering, hence of laziness, she might have some difficulty in getting a husband. But the girl who philandered a good deal and then denied that she did so was considered most reprehensible. Here the feeling against falsehood was strong. Such a girl might be taken by her father and have her mouth cut through the cheeks. Her father then might say, "Now you have a big mouth; tell all the lies you want."

There was room in the society for romantic love. A love match was considered a good risk. Romantic affairs often went on after marriage and there was a definite ideal of female beauty. Men went after beautiful women, so it is said. A woman of beauty might succeed in playing one suitor off against the other. Her family often warned her not to do this, since she then might be seized by an older and stronger man and take a place as a second wife. Indeed, this not infrequently occurred. When a man desired a woman, he might simply seize her, take her to his house, and rely on his kin to see that she neither escaped nor was rescued by her own family. Both single girls and married women were taken in this way. Seizing a woman and keeping her as a wife was nusukaaktuat, "grabbing off a wife." If a single girl was taken, her kin usually let the matter go and permitted her to remain with the abductor. If the abductor were undesirable from the family's point of view, they might complain but there was usually no action. In fact, a family might abet an abductor. If a girl refused to marry, especially a man of the family's choice, they arranged for a kidnaping. Or, if she were abducted, it was said, "This is what she has been wanting."

But such abductions went well beyond marriage since married women were also seized. Sometimes it was merely a matter of rape and no permanent alliance was contemplated. Some men had reputations as "women chasers," although women might likewise attempt to attract men. If anything, the woman was blamed more than the man. It was felt that a busy, modest woman "wouldn't get into trouble." A man who wished sexual relations with a woman solicited them by seizing her belt. She might then agree to a clandestine meeting. Jealousy was frequent and many men felt that they had to "watch their wives." Because sexual rights were in a sense property rights and linked with male status, a cuckolded husband might feel some revenge necessary. His retaliation against his wife's seducer was to rape his wife or to attempt to arrange a meeting with her. A husband and his wife's seducer stood as nuliinuaroak to each other, the sense being that they shared a woman.

The term aŋutawkun, also aŋutawkattigiit, etymologically like that for parallel cousin, was employed in two specific ways. It referred to men, partners, who had exchanged wives. It also designated the men who had been married to the same woman at different times. A synonym was inʸukawtigicuq. Conceptually, this might be a significant relationship, especially since the woman's children by both men would be half-siblings. The men so involved might thus share an interest in the children and in each other. If partners, they would in any case have a common interest and tie.

If a man desired to keep a married woman as his own mate, he generally informed his kin of his intentions. They either agreed to support him or tried to dissuade him. If they did assist him in capturing the wife of another, the woman was simply dragged off and kept in the house or the band of the captor. The abduction of a wife was not a cause of a feud. But the husband could enlist the aid of his kin in getting the woman back and her own kindred could also offer their help. If the ensuing dispute resulted in bloodshed, as was not unlikely, a feud then resulted. A wife was free to return to her husband if she escaped her captor. But it seemingly frequently occurred that the abduction took place with the woman's connivance. If so, and if the husband from whom she was taken knew or suspected it, he might make no effort to recover her. The decision was his to make.

It would be incorrect to assume that wife-capture followed a uniform pattern. The resulting situation might be wholly benign with the result that no bad feelings or enmity arose between the husband who lost his wife and the man who had taken her. It might result in bitter feelings and continued hatred. Witness, for example, the case of the man who found his wife's captor asleep and who tied a dog to his foot, indicating that he had had him at his mercy but had declined the opportunity to kill him. The situation was not formalized and the following possible results can be listed:

1. The man who lost his wife to another and made no effort to force her to return was "honest," "patient," and in no sense a laughing stock. Indeed, if her absence were ignored and she then returned to her husband, his action in allowing her to resume her position as wife was regarded as highly magnanimous and virtuous.

2. Should he decide to let the matter go and not attempt to force a return of his wife, the affronted husband could demand compensation from his wife's abductor. If this were given, the husband relinquished all claim on the woman. If it were not given, the kin grouping was enlisted to effect a recovery of the woman.

When the matter is followed through, any number of possible solutions to the problem of wife loss by abduction arise. For example, if the man who had lost his wife demanded compensation and it was given, it was then inevitable that the two men involved should become friendly. This was because they had conceptually effected a trade. More significantly, however, does the fact emerge that the two shared an interest in children resulting from either union. A factor to be considered here was residence. If a woman were taken from a husband within the community, she might bring her children to her abductor's house. They would then stand in an adoptive relationship to the mother's captor. But they would of course retain ties with their own father. If the abduction took place as between communities, the kindred of the father would be reluctant to let the children go. But children born of the second union were then half-siblings to the children of the first. Since there was no recognition of step or foster relationship, they might extend to the mother's first husband the same term which their half-siblings used, that is, father. Similarly, the children of the first marriage, even if they continued to live with their natural father, the mother being gone, called the mother's second husband by a father term and were obliged to defend this man. This tie was indeed strengthened when children were born of the second union. Thus the term nuliinuroak (nuliinuaroak) which arose between two husbands of one woman reflected not shame or disgrace, but rather a quasi-kinship in which a certain degree of cooperation and mutual aid was implicit. The same term was applied to men living with a woman in a so-called polyandrous situation. In the latter case, there would be no question of actual paternity since the child "always resembles the father."

In these cases, residence was always a factor. If a man living with his wife's kin lost his wife, both he and the kin of the wife would be unwilling to let the children join their mother in her new marriage. Even when no children were involved, however, if a man occupied the position of provider to his wife's family he continued to reside with them. If he remarried, he either brought his new wife to them or left them.

The possibilities described above were all regarded as conceivable in terms of the social structure. It appears that any bad feelings could be alleviated by an exchange. But a wife abductor, often fearing the anger of the former husband, frequently made his decision to leave the community, taking the new wife with him. The absence of formal regulation as well as the impermanence of the marital tie created the great variability in solving the problems which arose. Far from creating an immediate and outright enmity, however, the resulting situations appear to have extended kinship involvements. Both polygyny and nonfraternal and temporary polyandry were possible under the system. The latter was apparently less frequent.

DIVORCE

The precontact cultures did not insist on marriage as a permanent union. Indeed, marriage may be defined only in terms of its economic involvements. In one sense, any sexual union or liaison constituted marriage inasmuch as there were recognized status shifts which arose as a result of sexual relations. More specifically, however, marriage, as a recognized institution, might be said to result when a couple shared the same house and worked together toward the upkeep of the house, each contributing a share of labor to its maintenance. Children, of course, created a basis for stability.

But since marriage must be defined so loosely, divorce likewise cannot be regarded as a formalized mechanism. The pattern in general was that if the couple agreed, shared its labor, had offspring, became recognized as sharing a common social role, the two were married. The same status was accorded to individuals with more than one mate. If, therefore, there was any discord, if a wife were abducted, if either partner chose to leave, divorce was recognized. If a couple disagreed or if a man mistreated his wife, relatives of either partner might urge divorce as a logical course of action. Divorce was not an item of gossip but rather a usual means of solving a problem. In the precontact cultures, it would appear that virtually everyone had been married and was divorced at least once. Here again, however, it becomes difficult to offer an exact definition. Sexual relations did not constitute marriage in the exact social sense but there were other involvements arising from sex. A person may have "played the field" before settling down to a more permanent marital union. Once a couple became used to each other's ways, it was unlikely that divorce would occur.

Since there was no formalized property involvement in marriage, divorce did not entail any redistribution of property. Each partner took his own personal possessions, such as clothing, tools, boats, dogs, or whatever. The matter of the house itself was decided by whatever arrangement had originally been made as to residence. If the couple had built its own house, and several children had arrived, divorce was in any case unlikely. An offended partner who left forfeited rights to a house. This matter can be somewhat complex when it is considered that a husband might leave, move to another place, take another wife, and so settle down elsewhere. His first wife might thus be left with house and property. She, in turn, might marry again. The couple is thus presumably divorced, even though it has made no formal decision on the matter. On the other hand, the husband might then return to take up with his abandoned wife again. He might also retain a wife in another place. By this token, divorce becomes difficult of definition.

If there was a formal disagreement, however, an actual makaruak, the offended partner might leave. He or she often did so on the advice of relatives. In such a case, custody of children was left to the most expedient solution. Children might be given a choice of parent; they might be divided between the separating couple; they might be given out to others in adoption. There was clearly no hard and fast rule.

WIFE LENDING AND WIFE EXCHANGE

It is clear that the marriage bond, while essential to the successful functioning of the culture, was not conceptually a permanent one. It frequently occurred that a man went to trade or on a prolonged hunting expedition and left his wife behind. If he had many relatives about, he could safely leave the woman with them. But if he had few, he might impose on a partner or neighbor, asking him to take the woman in charge. This situation was known as aleupaaktuat. A friend, partner, or neighbor had sexual rights to the woman, a relative of the husband did not. If a man thus went to trade, leaving his wife in a friend's care, he generally had some commission to discharge for the man in return.

Between partners, especially those of long standing and proven friendship, there could be wife exchange on a temporary basis. This was also true of "friends," often as between those who had established a joking relationship. Hospitality might involve wife lending, since such hospitality would be extended in any case only to individuals occupying a special status in relation to a host. Wife exchange on a temporary basis took place only between men who occupied a status of formally defined friendship or partnership. Aside from partners and joking partners, there was no institutionalized friendship. Informal good relations, however, as between men in a whaling crew, in the same karigi, might call wife exchange into being. Men who exchanged wives were aŋutawkattigiit. The two men involved agreed to exchange their wives and did not consult the women involved. A woman was told, "Go over and stay with so and so." The exchange lasted for a few days, the women then returning to their husbands. The return of a woman after an exchange was called allupaareik. The woman was taken to the house of a man to whom she was lent. Among the maritime people sexual relations took place in the suuvik.

The Eskimo of the area deny that such exchanges were economic and insist that they were purely sexual. In wife exchange, the cooperative tie between the men and women involved was enforced. The respective children stood to each other as qataŋuutigiit and, as will be seen, were likewise drawn into a situation of cooperation. Wife exchange was thus always arranged and had no implications of rape or abduction such as were described in the previous section. It was in a sense an exchange of property rights and led to the exchange of other forms of property, hence again to mutual aid. Rape or wife abduction, on the other hand, was wilful violation of property right and it was for this reason that the various mechanisms described might arise.

A wife was lent, as noted, when a man was obliged to be gone from the community for some time. The man to whom he lent his wife might request the same assistance at a later time. When a man's partner visited, assuming he came alone, his host might offer him sexual rights to the wife. If partners came together with their wives, they frequently exchanged wives on a temporary basis. It was felt to be advantageous to do so, since it strengthened the bond of partnership and extended the system of mutual aid to the children of the respective couples.

Sexual trading, wife lending, or wife exchange, was called simmixsuat. The point that it was a sexual matter and not an economic one should be emphasized. It has been said that such exchange might arise of work specializations which each woman commanded. This does not seem to be the case, since in the cooperative situation of community living, work was freely exchanged without reference to sexual privilege.

Women who were exchanged were known as aytpareik. It apparently happened not infrequently that the exchange might be permanent. This would arise out of a matter of preference. Several such instances are recalled.

QATAŊUUTIGIIT [7]

It would be erroneous to assume that the sexual freedom inherent in the cultures of the area was wholly random and uncontrolled.

[7] A paper describing this rather unusual social institution was read at the 1953 meetings of the American Anthropological Association, Tucson, Ariz., December 29, 1953.

Sexual relations carried with them a degree of responsibility and served to create a series of reciprocal obligations not only between the principals concerned but also between the kin of those involved. Even casual sexual affairs had certain consequences, as, for example, in the case of the girl who was "free." Here the failure to exert a degree of control over the situation was disturbing to her kin. Because sexual relations were regarded as rights, and because defined obligations arose from sexual activity, it is clear that a well-defined pattern of behavior arose in connection with sexual affairs and that the involvements of the individual were channeled and predictable. Perhaps in no case is this more precisely defined than in the development of the qataŋuutigiit (dual) relationship.

As one considers the balance between social forms and economic life, it is apparent that the North Alaskan Eskimo sought in every way possible to extend the patterns of economic cooperation. Not only is the kin and household unit founded in cooperation but marriage itself was a device which served to extend the forms of cooperation between otherwise unrelated family groupings. The strong feelings against the levirate, sororate, or cousin marriage may be explained on this basis. But there were also ways of developing lasting relationships between nonkin. An obvious way lay in the ties of crew and karigi, another in partnerships and in joking partnerships, both of which came as close to an idea of blood brotherhood as was possible without some formalistic declaration. And it is further evident that sexual relations provided a clinching point, serving to cement the ties of friendship and mutual aid. Wife exchange was thus not wholly lustful; it had a definite function in the society as a means of extending a cooperative relationship. When sexual relations took place, and when of such intercourse children were engendered, the offspring of the various unions came to occupy a special cooperative relationship to each other. They stood to each other as qataŋuutigiit (sing. qataŋun).

This relationship arose between nonrelatives on the basis of previous sexual relationships. It came about under the following circumstances:

1. If two persons, divorced or widowed, married, each having offspring from the previous marriage, their respective offspring became qataŋuutigiit to each other.
2. When wives were exchanged, the respective children of the two couples who then had engaged in an exchange stood in this relationship.
3. This provides the basic point of definition. From the point of view of Ego, the children of any person with whom his father or mother had previously had sexual relations were his qataŋuutigiit.

The qataŋuutigiit (pl. qataŋuutigiic) were thus not blood relatives. Under most circumstances, they could marry. This would be forbidden in the first instance listed above, where a man and woman marry, each having children. This was then an adoptive situation, the children called each other by sibling terms, and were forbidden to marry. They might extend the relationship here, designating it as nukaxrareik—half-siblings—a term not otherwise used.

Basically, this was a cooperative situation. A child was told that when he went to some other place where there were no kin, he should seek out such and such a person who would aid him. "He is your qataŋun." An individual could, in traveling, always seek out the children of his father's partners, assuming that in the partnership wives had been exchanged, and demand of them assistance and support. It was freely given. It is worth mentioning that here was a basis for forming new partnerships and it is in this respect that partnerships tended to follow along family lines, the two families involved retaining the relationship.

Some examples may serve to point up the importance of the relationship:

1. When taaluq traveled down the coast, he stopped at Kotzebue camping near two houses some distance from town. He was invited into one of the houses where a woman was living. She asked him who his father was and where he came from. He told her. She said, "My children are like your brothers." Then he remembered that his father had told him that he had been married to this woman. After that, in his journeys up and down the coast, he always stopped at that house. The woman's daughters would repair his clothes and chew his boots. He had intercourse with them.

2. A man from Barrow went down to Noatak. The people there were very suspicious of him and tried to kill him. They shut him up in the karigi and gave him no food and prevented his coming out. He had a qataŋun there, however, who got food to him and finally set him free. In escaping from Noatak, the man was lent a sled by his qataŋun. The latter urged him not to return to Noatak but said that if he did so, he would always be given help. The rescuer's mother had once had sexual relations with the father of the man from Barrow.

3. A stranger came to utkeaaγvik from kuvuk (Kobuk). He was accorded the usual treatment reserved for strangers, the men coming out and pummeling him, tearing his clothes, and crying, "hii, hii." His qataŋuutigiit recognized him and pulled him away from the others, bringing him home and caring for him.

As a result of the development of this relationship, it became necessary to recall the former sexual partners, to keep the tie with them alive, and to inform one's children of their whereabouts. The result was a quasi-kinship. While the family loyalties came first, it nevertheless followed that one attempted to give assistance to one's qataŋuutigiit whenever possible. It was an important relationship in other ways, as, for example, in terminating a blood feud. If a sexual arrangement could be worked out between a man and woman in the two feuding factions, the respective children then became qataŋuutigiit to each other and the now existing cooperative relationship forbade further bloodshed.

At present, there is still a strong sense for the relationship. Many who still recognize qataŋuutigiit call them by sibling terms and are close friends with them. As one woman remarks today, however, "You are just talking about your parents' sins when you have this." This statement would indicate, perhaps, that the coordinated patterns of mutual aid are falling away.

ADOPTION

In the qataŋuutigiit relation was seen one means by which the kinship tie could be extended in effect to nonkin. Another such way lay in the adoption of children who were then raised in the household of their adoptive parents, no distinction being made between them and natural children. The patterns of adoption were well worked out and the institution continues to be an important element in the contemporary society.

Either a couple with children or a childless couple could be eligible to adopt. If anything, the former were preferred as adoptive parents, since their success as parents and their kindness would presumably have been demonstrated. The motivation in adoption is clear: not only did adoption extend the kinship circle and hence the bonds of cooperation, but it served also as a kind of insurance; "children take care of you and look after you when you are old." There was no social stigma attached to barrenness but childless individuals or couples might find themselves in dire straits if they lacked the support that children might give.

A woman now living at Barrow has the reputation of being "cruel"—"She is mean to all her relatives and now no one will help her." Although she had children of her own, all are now dead, their deaths, it is said, being directly attributable to her own negligence. Such a woman, even though her husband enjoys a somewhat better reputation than she, could not hope to take children in adoption.

Adoption took place within the extended family, as in the case of a brother adopting the child of a sibling, a parent adopting a child's child, adoption through cousins, and the like. But there was no regulation prescribing this. Adoptions might occur just as frequently between nonrelated groups of kindred. A couple who wished to adopt looked about for available children. Such might be an orphaned child, but it might be the youngest in a large family. Economic stress being what it was, some infanticide was practiced. If in traveling under stress, a woman gave birth to a child, it might have to be left. This was spoken of as "throwing a baby away." Some would say, "Don't throw the baby away—give it to me." There are accounts of individuals who had been adopted in this way and who survived to become men of wealth and position. If a parent were ill, impoverished, or had too many mouths to feed, a solution to the problem was to let a child or two leave in adoption. In such cases, the parent might select the adoptive parents on the basis of their proven worth and kindness.

When an agreement relating to adoption had been reached, there was a sense that the arrangement should be witnessed by competent adults. This prevented a change of heart on the part of the parent who was relinquishing the child and the demand that the child be returned. These informal witnesses served merely to offer a reflection of public opinion that the adoption was legal. The factors in adoption were, as may be surmised, coresidence and support.

When a parent who had relinquished a child demanded it back, he might encounter difficulty. Certainly he would receive no backing of public opinion. Nor would his kin support the demand for a return of the child. Several instances of this kind were described. In one, a couple took a child back after it had been given out in adoption. The child's mother's father felt that a wrong had been done to the adoptive family. When a child was born to his own wife, he insisted, over his wife's objections, that the child be given to the family from whom his grandchild had been taken. In modern times, the sense for this pattern is still present. When a woman who was suffering from tuberculosis was hospitalized, she left her new-born infant with her parents. On her return from the sanatorium, she attempted to get her child back from them. They refused to surrender it and she did not press the matter. A person with a sufficiently aggressive character might force the return of a child given out in adoption. In another modern instance, a baby girl, the mother having died in childbirth, was given in adoption to a family which had only boys. The adoptive parents kept the child for some months and then the father, uncle to the pair, who was about to remarry, demanded the return of the child. He insisted and the adoptive parents gave in, but there has been bad feeling between them since. It would be more frequent, however, that the adoptive parents would refuse to return the child and public opinion would unquestionably back them.

But only in extreme cases, it is said, would the natural parents demand the return of a child given out in adoption. The effects of public opinion are clear; the natural parent who demanded his child back was held guilty of an immoral act. In another such instance, which occurred many years ago, a woman, delivering a child, experienced a protracted and difficult labor. Another woman came to assist her. The parturient's husband stated that if the child was alive, the midwife and her husband might take it as their own.

The child, a son, was delivered and given to the mother's helper. About 2 years later, the natural parents demanded the return of the child. The adoptive parents refused at first but the natural father became so persistent, threatening and bullying, that at last they reluctantly consented. Public opinion was aroused, but no action was taken. The behavior of the natural parents was viewed as particularly offensive because, in taking their child back, they made no payment to the adoptive parents. The couple who thus took their child back then went inland and had an extremely difficult winter. They became so short of food that they were obliged to give their child away again, this time to okumayl^{y}uq and his wife. They became very fond of the boy, who began to call them "father and mother." Somewhat later, however, they encountered an old man who knew the background of the boy. He urged that they return the child to his natural parents again lest okumayl^{y}uq and his wife have misfortunes too. While they were reluctant to do this, they felt that this was the wiser course and so returned the child again to his natural parents. The child's father was thereafter known as a man who "broke his promise."

When a couple desired a child, they might select some family which they admired and ask a child of them. This request might be granted. The father of the family could indicate that the next child would be given out in adoption to the people who requested it. Only families who had proven industry and proper kindness and modesty could qualify for a child. Some people, it is said, were "careless" with their children. Only if families failed to give proper care did the children die. A couple who had children but whose children had then died could not qualify as adoptive parents. The feeling was that if they had taken proper care of their natural offspring, they would have lived. To give them a child in adoption was to take a serious risk.

To be eligible as an adoptive parent, one had to have a good reputation of industry. The natural parents or guardians of the child took care to note that the child could be properly cared for and given food, clothing, and lodging in a dependable way. Similarly, families with reputations as "scolds" could not qualify for adoption of a child.

Adoption was considered to be permanent. The family who had given the child out in adoption relinquished claim to him and could not demand anything of him or of the foster parents. On the other hand, the foster parents might occasionally make a request of the child's natural parents for food or clothing for the child. The natural parents who refused such a request would again suffer from adverse public opinion. The fact that "they had done nothing for their own" and had given their child out in adoption did not relieve them entirely of responsibility.

In the aboriginal culture, if the child's mother had died of some illness, the child was not considered a good adoptive risk. Such children were often not adopted. They became "orphans" and might be shunted about from family to family without ever being taken in as family members under adoption. This pattern suggests a kind of "service" in that the child then might be obliged to work for his keep and was not accorded kinship status. There are several such cases still operative in the village of Barrow and many individuals are living who had this kind of upbringing.

It is also evident that families were reluctant to adopt an older child. Although this occurred, the tendency was to take an infant in adoption and not a child whose loyalties were already fixed. The child who lost his family through death was expected, provided he could do some amount of fending for himself, to attach himself to any of his remaining kin. It is at this level that the role of the "orphan" becomes established in the society. Such an individual was a child too old to be taken in adoption and while his services might be desired, he did not come to occupy a status and role of family member. A family which took such a child in did not call him by kinship terms, nor did he reciprocate. The "orphan" concept provides so marked a basis for folktales, accounts of the "poor" boy who becomes a great hero, that it is evident that the status was a fairly well-established one.

In some instances the "orphan" was sought as a mate for a daughter. This might occur when the family was reluctant to let a daughter go from their household. The orphan boy with no other family commitments might them come in as husband and adopted son.

Sometimes the individual made a choice for himself. In one such instance a boy, apparently well into adolescence, made a connection with a family not related to his own. He became so fond of them and they of him that he left his own parents and went to live with the family of his choice. This was viewed as a true adoption, inasmuch as he employed kinship terms in referring to his foster parents. Having called the daughter of this family "sister," he could not have married her. Now and again he returned to the house of his natural parents and made them gifts of food. For all practical purposes, however, he had severed his ties with his own family.

Thus when a child was adopted, he became a member of the kinship groupings of his adoptive parents and was involved in the pattern of collective responsibility in that relationship. He called his adoptive family by kinship terms and was accepted as a full member of the group with all the rights and obligations incumbent on a blood member. He was, moreover, forbidden from marrying his adoptive kin. A child was told of his adoption but often much later in life. When he was told, it apparently often came as a profound shock and was resisted. It was necessary to inform the adopted individual of his antecedents since he was responsible not only to his family of adoption but was also involved with his genetic kindred. If the latter became involved in a feud, he was likewise obliged to take their side. Many examples were cited by informants of adoptive children who refused to accept the truth of their adoption and who insisted that the "real" parents were the adoptive parents. It might happen that the child enjoyed good relations both with his adoptive parents and his natural parents and might call both by parent terms. More often he called his adoptive parents by parent terms and designated his natural parents by name. There was no exact rule relating to this, however.

It is not to be supposed that adoptions always took place between families in no way connected by ties of kinship. On the contrary, common practice was to give a child in adoption to a kinsman, there being a tendency, in fact, to prefer the choice of a kinsman as foster parent. Thus it is not uncommon for a grandparent, a brother, or a cousin to assume responsibilities for a child. okumayl^{y}uq, for example, adopted his sister's daughter. The sister's husband became involved in an expedition going to trade at Herschel Island. The sister wished to accompany him but had a small daughter whose presence on the trip might have caused delay. She therefore gave the child to okumayl^{y}uq and his wife. He asked her if she wished the child returned. On her indicating that she did not, he took the child as his own. Numerous other instances of such adoption might be cited. kanayuruq's son chooses to live with his mother's brother and calls him "father." Although this has disturbed kanayuruq and his wife, they have agreed that the uncle may keep the boy. On the death of his son-in-law, sikvayuŋgaq took his daughter's two boys in adoption. Although they are his grandchildren, he designates them as his "sons" and does not distinguish them from his other children.

It was generally agreed that the adopted child was "dearer to the heart" than a natural child. One reason given for this was that the adoptive parents so admired the natural parents of the child that deep affection was inevitable. Informants also remarked that there "was no pain in adopting a child." The basic element in this would apparently lie in the fact the adoption had to be justified before the community and the adoptive parents proved worthy of their trust.

It would be difficult to estimate the number of adoptions in relation to the population at large. They were extremely frequent, and it seems safe to say that almost every family was either directly or indirectly involved in the institution. Certainly, this remains true today. There was much adopting between relatives, and the benefits arising from the extension of kinship bonds by the adoption of nonkin were eagerly sought. Children were, and are, much desired and were given out in adoption or abandoned with great reluctance.

ABANDONMENT

Intimately relating to the matter of the family tie was the question of the abandonment of the very young, the aged, and the sick or infirm. This has been treated so frequently for the Arctic Eskimo from the point of view of the outsider that some further mention of it is required here for the purpose of clarification. The economic demands of Arctic life, particularly of travel in the Arctic, might require that one relative be left by the others so that the whole group could survive. As such, abandonment would have been more common among the nuunamiut since the nomadic way of life was much more precarious. On the coasts, settled life as well as provision by way of food storage somewhat minimized the problem.

It is clear that modern inroads have by no means changed attitudes toward this problem. If a relative had to be abandoned, it was "very sad," "a hard decision," but the group might be saved at the expense of one life. The most recent case that anyone can recall took place in 1939, when an old shaman and his wife were left inland to starve. The family head, a son of the old man, was obliged to leave his father and stepmother and go on by team to get food. He was unable to return in time to save his parents. No blame was of course attached to such an action. In fact, the older people often asked to be abandoned if times were hard and faced the prospect of death with equanimity. Captain Brower, who found himself with an old woman on his hands when he had saved her, was extremely puzzled as to what he should do with her. It was strongly felt that a parent would stint on his own food in order to save the life of a child. Similarly, the older people sacrificed their own food to the younger members of a party. In a sense, abandonment revolved around the matter of production. When a person was no longer able to produce, he had no right to expect continued support. This might be given and willingly so, as a filial duty, but in emergencies it was the nonproductive who were sacrificed. This is not to imply a disrespect for the aged. Indeed, the earlier accounts point clearly to the important role of old people in giving counsel and in making decisions.

A new-born baby might be "thrown away." This was quite literally true, since a woman, having gi en birth to a child, and being unable to care for it, simply left it. If the child were named, however, and had been taken along with the group, every attempt might be made to save it. It was rather the unnamed child, the child who was not regarded as a member of the society as yet, who was subject to abandonment. Such infanticide as did occur, and it was rare, considering the desire for children, was not limited to girls. Babies of either sex might be left should the circumstances warrant it.

In the pattern of abandonment, one again encounters the primary loyalty to blood kin. In times of stress, a man could leave his wife and his wife's kin and strike out on his own. If however, he abandoned his own children or his own blood kin, his action was considered most reprehensible. In general, however, a man who saved himself at the expense of a number of others was felt to have acted in a criminal way and might be hunted down by the kin of those he left. The same was true of the use of food, either in caches inland or in cellars on the coast, by those to whom it did not belong. One could take food from a cache or cellar to meet his own needs and was welcome to do so. If, however, he took all the food, causing the starvation of those to whom it belonged, as might occur, he was guilty of murder. If known, a blood feud began.

A woman was less under obligation than was a man to stand by kin. Several instances of starvation are reported where a woman and her children might go to her own parents in times of stress, leaving her husband and his family. One such took place in the piγiniq area. The family needed food. The wife went to her parents at utkeaaγvik, leaving her husband. He in turn walked to Wainwright where he had a brother. Later, when food was again available, the husband, tawyuaq, returned to his wife and the two took up residence together again. This was expected behavior, both on the part of the man's parents-in-law and of his wife. It relates to the fact that one depends on one's own parents and kin regardless of the marital tie. tawyuaq felt no resentment at such treatment. In another instance, a woman was left by her husband when food was short. She had several siblings on whom she could depend. The husband later returned and tried to claim her. Her siblings, however, refused to allow her to return to him. They argued, "He'll do the same thing again to you."

But any case of abandonment was hard. Only in the direst of circumstances would it have taken place. There is the impression that the individual upbraided himself for leaving those dependent on him. When a newborn baby was abandoned, it might have to be torn forcibly from the mother. This suggests that the decision was not an arbitrary one on the part of an individual but a carefully considered group action. It was when an individual left others and so failed them that his action was condemned. In the case of the abandonment of infants, the family might agree to sacrifice a girl child rather than a boy. The economic potential of the boy was considered greater.

The instance of the woman, utaatuq, illustrates fairly well how a problem of abandonment might have been faced. Among the nuunamiut, during the winter travel, utaatuq became a burden to her group. She had an adopted son and was pregnant. A daughter which had been born to her the previous winter had been abandoned. Her husband urged her to abandon the small boy she was carrying also but she steadfastly refused. Because of her pregnancy, she lagged more and more behind the group which, pressed for food, was obliged to travel as rapidly as it could. At last, she could no longer keep up the pace and was left behind, her adopted baby still on her back. She found a likely place to camp and, taking sinew from her sewing kit, made ptarmigan snares and fish lines. She got enough food through the winter although she continued to live on the edge of starvation. At last her baby was born. There was hardly sufficient food for herself and the adopted infant and she found herself unable to nurse the newborn child. Obliged to abandon it, she moved to another camp, locating herself in an abandoned house. Now relieved of the burden of her pregnancy, she lived more adequately the rest of the winter, trapping squirrels (siqsiq), ptarmigan, and fishing. She made clothing from the squirrel skins and used their fat for oil and light. Gradually, she built up some surplus food and was able to survive. In the spring she was found by a hunting party and brought to utkeaaγvik. Here she established contact with her husband and rejoined him.

While a family might caution a girl against marrying a man who had been involved in a case of abandonment, pointing out that such might be her fate, circumstances in such cases were generally recognized as sufficiently pressing as to justify the action. utaatuq herself felt no resentment against her husband for having left her under the circumstances.

Cases of abandonment were much more frequent among the nuunamiut. The reason is clear in view of the more precarious inland life. The settled maritime village generally built up its food surpluses and could last through a lean year. This was not the case among the more nomadic inland peoples who lacked the same facilities for storage of food. Similarly, if the maritime village did become subject to starvation, whole settlements would suffer together. The smaller groups of nuunamiut were thus frequently obliged to make greater concession to the environment. In traveling, for example, as the above instance illustrates, no place could be made for the laggard, especially if dogs were few, as was most frequently the case. One woman of the ikpikpaŋmiut recalls that her mother "threw three babies away," in spite of her own childish protests and tears. It must be said that every attempt was made to save an infant; if the group was large, efforts were made to place it in adoption. While some children were saved in this way, many were left to perish. It is said of the nuunamiut by those of the coasts, "They are just like animals; they let everyone die," a reflection of the fact that some sense of difference between the two ecological groups existed.

In only one instance, as nearly as anyone living can recall, was cannibalism practiced. Several women were left alone. When the mother and sisters of kivigiloak, one of the women, died she ate their flesh and survived. People talked of it, saying that it was regarded as very sad but there was otherwise no stigma attached to the cannibal.

While the rather harrowing tales of abandonment of aged relatives might be strung out at length, it is perhaps sufficient to note that here again the family operated as a unit.

CONCLUSION

The family and kinship situation as it has been described for the North Alaskan Eskimo groups appears on the surface vague. There was little by way of strictly formalized structure. The local situations, the crossing of family lines, the factors of common residence do, however, combine to produce a unit of cooperation and a strong sense for kinship. Of interest in this respect are the patterns by which the bond of kinship can be extended so that even random sexuality becomes a means of reaffirming and developing certain social ties. In summary, the means by which kinship ties could be extended to nonkin were as follows:

1. In the partnership relationship.
2. In the sexual involvements following a broken marriage or wife exchanging giving rise to the qataŋuutigiit relationship.
3. In adoption.

Friendships were not otherwise formalized. There were, of course, economic interrelationships of other types, such as that between crew members and men hunting together. If a more meaningful relationship were desired than that arising from hunting interests, it was necessary to undertake and establish the kind of relationships indicated above. The term iilyonaaruq was used to mean "friend" or more properly, one's "pal," but the term had little meaning unless extended to kinship in one of the above ways.

One can only admire the familial institution of the groups in question. It does not exist because of economic or environmental factors. On the contrary, it makes possible ease of living in a hostile territory. The family was a supple tool, arranging and rearranging itself to meet the needs of the moment and to effect the workings for the common good. Of political structure there was none. Nor indeed, was any necessary. It was the kinship grouping which remained the potent instrument of social control. Blood feuds are gone, but the sharing institution of the family and the inherent collective responsibility still serve to effect integration of North Alaskan Eskimo society.

CUSTOMARY LAW

A yardstick by which to measure social behavior, social controls, and individual responsibility is best provided by an analysis of actions which deviate from the social norm. Even though, like many other primitive groups, the Eskimo of northern Alaska lacked an elaborated system of legal procedures, there was, nonetheless, a strong sense of customary sanctions, resulting in patterned ways of dealing with the deviant. It is clear that the primary mechanism of social control lay in the family, the solidarity of the family being defined and enhanced by the strong sense of collective responsibility. Properly speaking, no crimes could be said to exist; offenses of any kind related to interfamily disputes. These relate almost exclusively to murder. Sorcery, likewise, might be regarded as significant in interfamily quarrels, but this was de facto murder.

The causes for murder were several. Any offense, real or imaginary, by one individual against another might result in bloodshed and so, by the regulation of collective responsibility, involve the families of the two disputants. In the main, however, offenses relating to property would not result in killing. If a man were cheated, if some of his property were stolen, if a piece of property were wantonly destroyed, the injured party had only to air his complaints to the community at large and to allow public opinion to pass on the merits of his claim. His satisfaction thus lay in obtaining a balance of public opinion in his own favor; only in the rarest instances would he seek further retribution.

This can best be illustrated by example: When, at Barrow, there was the general breakup of the reindeer herds and the collapse of the industry, one of the men who had received government training as a herdsman became involved in a dispute with a family which had lost a good many head of deer. Failing to understand the herding system and the governmental policies relating to it, the family, not surprisingly, attached blame to the herdsman. When he proved unable to give them satisfaction, the woman of the family destroyed a umiak belonging to him, cutting the skins with her ulu, and breaking the frame. He might have gone, at this period, to the United States Marshal and demanded retribution. Instead, however, he told anyone in the community who would listen what the woman had done, at the same time pointing up his own virtuous patience in the matter and saying that, although he had been wrongfully treated, he would take no action. Since the reindeer herding was a sore spot at this time, it is doubtful that the herdsman got the community support which he wished. Behavior of this kind may be noted for the earlier culture as well. It was unusual for an offended party, whether the injury were real or fancied, to do more than to destroy property. Nor does the litigation seem to have gone further than to call for a judgment of public opinion. Offenses arising between partners often followed a similar pattern and resulted in the end of the partnership.

The misanthropic person, and it is clear that there were such, who made a practice of taking petty vengeance on others by damaging or destroying their property, was marked for death. In this case, a family involvement was inevitable. Here again is encountered the "bully," the nonconformist personality. How far such an individual could go in violating public opinion was variable and depended on the amount of backing he could get from family, or from such associations as his crew or with the supernatural. A long-suffering community would put up with such an individual over a long period of time, each person being anxious to avoid "trouble" and submitting patiently to his irascible antisocial behavior. At last, however, when his backing became less strong or when his unpleasantness reached a peak, he might be murdered. And here again, public opinion would decide the legitimacy of a claim of vengeance. Not that the community could prevent a feud, but members of families other than the two involved might take occasion to point up to the dead man's kin that the situation was now better for all concerned. It frequently happened that the murderer would present himself unarmed before the family of his victim and invite their vengeance. If they demurred, not killing the murderer on the spot, it would be unusual for them to claim later vengeance. Nor would public opinion support them if they did.

The blood feud was thus not necessarily a perennial thing. When it arose within a community, it could usually be quickly settled and forgotten. More frequently, it would continue between communities, the relatives of a murdered man in other groups or settlements being less concerned with the justification for homicide and more eager to keep the idea of vengeance to the fore. This serves to explain the attitude toward the stranger; he was treated with hostility because of the possibility of his involvement in a remote murder-feud situation. But within the group, the justification of a homicide was important. Even if crime as such could be said not to exist, the recidivist murderer was regarded as a criminal menace. He was put out of the way, not, it must be mentioned, by group action, but rather by being killed by an individual. The fact that the recidivist murderer could occur in the society is explainable only because no one, at the first murder, was willing to take action.

But killings arose less because of antisocial behavior relating to food and personal property than because of sexual involvements. Sexual rights were de facto property rights and it was this area which provided a strong motivation for action. The stolen wife, the disrupted betrothal, the love triangle—all might lead to ultimate homicide. In addition, strife and discord could arise in rape, in the mistreatment of a wife by a husband, or again, in the sexual appetites of the "bully." Adultery, too, was a cause for dispute, particularly if an affair were protracted. Again, however, adultery is less easy to define; a husband might beat an unfaithful wife but it is apparent that he inclined to take no action against her lover unless emotional problems arose to create additional difficulties. The majority of cases collected point to legalistic involvements over sex. Indeed, the Eskimo say of themselves: "It's always the woman who causes the trouble."

The nature of collective responsibility, the solidarity of the family system, and the relations of dispute to the group or community at large are best illustrated by the actual cases. Older informants recall the details of these quite vividly, giving names and specific particulars of events which may have taken place a century and more ago. While a selection such as the following cannot cover all aspects of customary law, sufficient is given to throw the nature of family and community solidarity and interpersonal relations into somewhat sharper perspective. It is apparent that some of these instances have become classic and are recalled for their dramatic appeal, others are more recent.

CASE 1

There was a man at nuwuk named kuwooviq. One winter, he went to Point Hope to trade with his partner there. His wife accompanied him. He visited with his partner, traded, and got his gear ready for the return to nuwuk next day. But when it came time to depart, his wife was missing. He was obliged to postpone his return and began to search for her. He knew that she had not left the town and he feared that she had been abducted. He looked into each house, glancing in through the skylight, peered into the hallways and the iga, but he couldn't find her. At last, his partner, who had been making inquiry, discovered that she had been taken by a man named suuyuq. This suuyuq was aŋatquq and had a large family. The partner informed kuwooviq that this man had three wives already. He advised strongly against doing anything against him. So kuwooviq went back to nuwuk alone.

Through the rest of that winter, his family and the family of his wife urged him to do something. His wife's family, in fact, became quite threatening and insisted that he go down to recover her. In the spring, therefore, he went back to Point Hope by boat, hoping to regain his wife but not knowing how to proceed against the strong suuyuq.

The immediate family of suuyuq consisted of two brothers and a sister, in addition to his three wives, his children, and the wife he had taken from kuwooviq. For many years, he had lived agreeably with his family but when kuwooviq returned to Point Hope that spring, he found that some troubles had begun. suuyuq had raised a girl expressly for the purpose of marrying her to one of his sons. During the previous winter, however, suuyuq's elder brother had taken this girl, while suuyuq was inland hunting caribou, and had married her to his own son. When suuyuq returned, he said nothing. His elder brother's son, however, the one that had been married to the girl, died within a short time of his return and it was generally agreed that suuyuq had killed him with his aŋatkoaq. Thus there was growing trouble between suuyuq and his elder brother. The second brother and the sister took no sides in the dispute but were beginning to be very upset at what was happening in their family.

The feelings in suuyuq's family reached their height when kuwooviq came to Point Hope. He looked into the situation and found that the whole community was very troubled by suuyuq's use of sorcery against his own nephew. kuwooviq's partner urged him not to mix himself up in the affair and to go back to nuwuk. And kuwooviq agreed that this was the best course. As he was ready to leave, however, the younger brother of suuyuq, much troubled by the actions of both his brothers, asked kuwooviq on the side if he might accompany him back to nuwuk. He told kuwooviq that he was really half-brother to suuyuq and that he feared suuyuq's wrath would be turned against himself rather than against the elder brother who was a full brother to suuyuq. He remarked that he felt it best to go away for a time. His name was samaruruq. And kuwooviq agreed to take him back to nuwuk.

On the way, kuwooviq and samaruruq went ashore to hunt a bit. Quite by accident they ran into suuyuq, the sister and her husband. The latter's name was qulliuq. With them were several others, relatives of the group, who had made up a hunting party with them. That morning, before kuwooviq and samaruruq had encountered the party, suuyuq had risen early and, wearing only his trousers, having neither boots nor parka on, had walked up and down in front of his tent. He carried a bow and two arrows and exclaimed again and again: "I wonder what will happen if samaruruq and I shoot at each other." When he had said this several times, he shot his two arrows into a sod bank. This behavior was very shocking to everyone present and no one commented on it.

When kuwooviq and samaruruq ran into the party, they stopped only a moment and then prepared to go on. qulliuq, brother-in-law to samaruruq and suuyuq, troubled by what he had seen suuyuq do that morning, decided to take sides with samaruruq and kuwooviq. As the latter two left, qulliuq and his wife went with them, leaving suuyuq and his party behind. The four started north toward nuwuk, while suuyuq and his group turned south back toward Point Hope. On the way, suuyuq's party decided to stop for fish along the streams and so camped at a fishing place.

Meanwhile, kuwooviq, samaruruq, qulliuq and his wife found evidences of caribou. The three men tracked them and killed a fair number. They therefore camped to make a disposition of the meat they had taken. When their butchering was done, they erected a windbreak and the three men sat down, waiting while qulliuq's wife cooked caribou meat for the three of them. When the meat was ready, qulliuq's wife brought it over to the three men. As she did so, she heard her husband tell her brother and kuwooviq what he had seen suuyuq do, how he had walked up and down, what he had said, and how he had shot his arrows. The woman was unhappy; she had wished to keep the whole matter quiet. She put the food down and, following the usual custom, retired from the men a way to eat by herself. But when the meat was put before them, neither samaruruq nor kuwooviq could eat it at all—they were far too shocked. They sat there just looking at the meat and not touching it. At last samaruruq called his sister over and asked her if it were true that his half-brother suuyuq had shot his arrows into the sod as if it were at him. The sister was silent. He asked her a second time. She was unwilling to answer but since her husband had already told of it, she whispered: "Yes, it's true." She had hoped so much to avoid trouble between all of them. When she indicated that the way her husband had described it was really so, the three men were able to eat.

When they finished eating, samaruruq said to his brother-in-law and to kuwooviq that they should now kill suuyuq. kuwooviq remarked that he had lost his wife to suuyuq and had been unable to get her back and so declared himself in. qulliuq said that he had had enough of suuyuq's troublemaking. So the three men turned back toward Point Hope.

As they went back toward the settlement, they discussed the problem. Both samaruruq and qulliuq pointed out that suuyuq had a large following, consisting of cousins and the children of other brothers. He had supported many of his relatives and it followed that these would stand by to avenge any injury done to him. Moreover, they were very troubled because he was after all a powerful aŋaquq. The three men cut inland and used kuwooviq's umiak to take one of the streams down toward Point Hope. It occurred to samaruruq that suuyuq and his party may have stopped to fish. Hence they took in the various fishing camps on their way. At one, they were told that suuyuq and his group had passed by and were heading for another fishing station nearby. The three men camped nearby, waiting until dark before they made a sally against the camp of suuyuk.

When it was dark, they walked over to the camp. One of the women in the party was having trouble putting her baby to sleep and was walking back and forth with it after the others had retired. Meanwhile, samaruruq was having his own conflict. He was extremely troubled about the necessity for killing his half-brother but he could see no avoiding it in view of what suuyuq had done. On the other hand, he felt that some warning should be given. When he saw the woman walking with her baby, he therefore twanged his bowstring. The woman, recognizing the sound and guessing what was happening, ran into one of the tents to tell the others. But they disregarded her, saying she must have heard something else. Then all went to sleep in the camp.

Meanwhile, the three had discovered which tent was occupied by suuyuq and his wives. When all was quiet, they crept forward to it, carrying their caribou spears and their bows. They lifted the flap of the tent and there was suuyuq asleep. One of the three crept foward into the tent and drove a spear through his body. suuyuq rose, wounded, but still active. He was still active because he was aŋatkuk. The three men tried to hold him down but his strength was so great that he wrenched away from them and ran outdoors. Once outside, he began to run to the beach. The three pursued, shooting arrows at him. Then suuyuq began to backtrack, making his way from the beach toward the tent. One of the three, it is not known which one, had, in planning suuyuq's murder, recalled his great aŋatkoaq and so had prepared a special arrow to counteract his power. As soon as suuyuq came back to the tent, this arrow was shot at him. It struck him just as he reached the flap of his tent and here he fell down and died. Now it is said that suuyuq's shaman power was derived from the polar bear. When the murder was discussed later, all were agreed that if, in running away from his killers, he had been able to get closer to the beach, even though it was considerable distance away, his tuunaraq would have saved him. His mistake was in backtracking.

As soon as the three had committed the murder, they turned inland at once and went north and east as quickly as they could, knowing that they would be marked for vengeance by suuyuq's male relatives.

Although it had turned out that no one really knew who the murderers were, one bit of evidence came to light. When suuyuq had gone inland, he did not take all his wives with him. Two accompanied him, one being the former wife of kuwooviq. When the first man speared suuyuq in the tent, this woman was lying beside him. She had raised her arm and started up and been cut across the forearm by the spear. When the three made sure that kuwooviq's wife was present, they took her along on their inland flight. She left a trail of blood for a short way. Later, as the story was pieced together, the group recalled that the woman had been the wife of kuwooviq, who lived at nuwuk, and that he had started north with samaruruq. Guilt therefore was attributed to both. Later, too, others recalled seeing qulliuq with samaruruq and kuwooviq. When the three fled, the men in suuyuq's party followed them for a way but were outdistanced.

As the three, now with the woman, returned to their camp, they discussed what they should do. kuwooviq was for having them come to nuwuk with him but both samaruruq and qulliuq strongly defended a return to Point Hope, saying that they did not want it said of them that they feared suuyuq's kinsmen. At that, kuwooviq, now reunited with his wife, decided to leave for nuwuk. He did, sett'lng there again, and was never again bothered in the matter of suuyuqir murder or his complicity in it. qulliuq, his wife, and samaruruq now seturned to Point Hope. The case was discussed a good deal but nothing was done about it for some time.

suuyuq had a son, a young man named kunuyuq, recently married for the first time. He was especially bothered by his father's death and felt that he should take steps to avenge him. He began to piece the affair together and gradually came to attach blame to his father's half-brother, samaruruq, and his aunt's husband, qulliuq. He was, however, a bit reluctant to take revenge on people who were allied to him so closely. The next fall, however, the wife of qulliuq, the dead suuyuq's sister, died. qulliuq waited for a time and then remarried. By his dead wife he had a son, kayugaq. He continued to be intimate with his dead wife's half-brother, samaruruq, and the two frequently went hunting together. kayugaq was a boy in his teens and began to join his father and uncle at hunting.

A fairly long period of time passed. Even 10 years later, kunuyuq had taken no steps. In the Point Hope community, factions had arisen over the matter; there were those who felt that suuyuq had got his deserved end, while others, more closely allied with suuyuq by blood, felt that kunuyuq was too infirm of purpose in avenging his father. Meanwhile, qulliuq had two sons by his second wife.

One year, qulliuq, his son kayugaq, his wife, and his two small boys went up to the inland country to hunt and fish. They were gone all summer and planned on returning to Point Hope in the fall. Early storms made their return difficult and at last they were forced to abandon their umiak, the rivers having begun to freeze. They camped, waiting until the ice was solid and then started back by sled. It so happened that their way led them down a river which emptied into the sea some distance north of Point Hope. At the mouth of the river a stranded whale had been reported with the result that a large party had come up from Point Hope to butcher it. In the party was kunuyuq. qulliuq and his party met this group and stayed a moment to watch what was happening in the butchering of the whale.

While qulliuq and his family were still inland, kayugaq had fallen ill. When they returned to the coast, they allowed him to travel in the sled; he had become too weak to walk. The sick boy, kayugaq, was actually very fond of his cousin kunuyuq and the feeling was reciprocated in spite of the bad feelings between qulliuq and kunuyuq. Hence, when the qulliuq party reached the beach, kunuyuq came over to see what was wrong with his cousin. He began to entertain the thought that his illness was perhaps brought about by sorcery for which qulliuq was responsible. This was not likely, since both qulliuq and his second wife were actually very fond of the young man, kayugaq, the wife, indeed, loving him as though he were her own son. But kunuyuq looked at his cousin, turned and stared at qulliuq, and then started off without saying a word. Everyone present began to feel most uneasy.

Now the woman in the party, the second wife of qulliuq, was very strong. She was so strong, in fact, that many men feared her. She began at once to watch her husband to see that no one did any harm to him. When the party from the settlement had finished butchering the whale, qulliuq and his family joined the group for the trek back to Point Hope. His wife urged him to be careful and walked with him behind the others. The men in kunuyuq's group were armed with their bows and they also carried the long knives for whale butchering. qulliuq's wife pointed this out and drew him behind, standing between him and the others. Each time the group rested, the woman sat down by her husband. The whole group had now moved some distance out on the ice-covered ocean, taking the shorter way and avoiding the curving line of the beach. They all paused to rest, loaded with whale meat, some distance out on the ice.

At one such stop, the dogs drawing a sled near to that in which kayugaq was riding began to fight. A whole team was disorganized and the fighting began to spread to other teams. qulliuq's wife started forward to see to her stepson in the sled, fearing that he would be overturned and injured in the melée. Thus, she momentarily forgot her husband.

As she started forward, she heard her husband groan. Someone had stabbed him in the back with a whale butchering knife. She rushed back to him but he was dead. She then turned to protect her stepson. The men in kunuyuq's party, seeing that qulliuq was dead, ran forward to the sled in which kayugaq was lying. The woman tried to head them off fearing that they would attempt to take revenge on kayugaq. She got there to the sled as they did. As she confronted them, the men were a bit uncertain as to what to do. They awaited some signal from kunuyuq. He, however, had sat down at once when qulliuq was killed, and stared ahead of him, not moving. He had no wish to kill his sick cousin, whom he loved.

kayugaq, aided by his stepmother, got up out of the sled and went behind it, protecting himself behind the umiak which was also borne on the sled. An impasse had been reached and the men of kunuyuq's group called to him as he sat some way apart: "What shall we do to him?" kunuyuq failed to answer and sat staring into space, his face troubled and brooding. The men decided to let the matter end there and turned away from kayugaq.

Meanwhile, the two small boys, the sons of qulliuq and his second wife, as soon as they saw their father killed, took to their heels and made for the shore. No one pursued them. When the men left kayugaq, they returned and wrapped up the body of qulliuq. Then one of the men went after the two boys, shouting to them to come back, that nothing would happen to them. So the two small boys returned.

When the party returned to Point Hope, kayugaq, his stepmother, and his two brothers went to their house and shut themselves in, waiting to see what might happen further. The stepmother took care of him and gradually, he began to recover from his illness. After a time, kunuyuq sent food over to their house and everyone knew that the matter was to all intents and purposes settled. When kayugaq was well, he began to hunt again and supported his stepmother and his two half-brothers. He was reputedly an excellent hunter and a good provider.

Sometime later, the wife of kunuyuq had a baby. During the last stages of her pregnancy, she took up residence in the house of kayugaq and his stepmother. Her reason for doing this was that she belonged to an extremely conservative family, one which very carefully observed all taboos and restrictions. Such families felt that good form demanded that a woman, approaching the time of her confinement, should not stay in the same house with her husband. While not everyone was so careful, suuyuq's sons were brought up to observe all such restrictions with great care. kunuyuq selected his cousin, kayugaq, as a person with whom he could leave his wife, not only because kayugaq enjoyed a reputation as an upright person, but also because kunuyuq wished by this means to erase any feelings of hostility which might survive from the murder of kayugaq's father, qulliuq.

Hence, kunuyuq's wife went to kayugaq's house and was welcomed there. kunuyuq himself came to build the snow house in which the birth should take place and the wife, meanwhile, would come to her husband's house and call down into the skylight to tell him of her needs with respect to food, clothing, or the like. The woman had her child in the snow house, but continued on in kayugaq's house, again according to custom, until the resumption of her normal menstrual periods. She continued to have her wants supplied by her husband, kunuyuq.

And then it happened that the woman fell in love with kayugaq. She kept after him all the time, but he resisted her, saying that she was married to his cousin and that this wasn't right. But she would not be put off. She refused to stop in her declarations of love for kayugaq. And at last he was overcome by her wooing and had intercourse with her. She stayed in the house with her child, letting it be known that she was now married to kayugaq. Occasionally, however, she went back to kunuyuq, asking him for food, clothing, or ornaments. He always gave them and never complained of her behavior. "This woman was a liar, lying and cheating all the time."

As some tension began to develop between the cousins again, the woman once came back to kayugaq's house carrying her baby. She had just been over to kunuyuq's house to make a request. kayugaq asked her where she had been. She answered that she had been over to kunuyuq's house and had heard him talking about his cousin. She reported that kunuyuq had said that he was afraid of kayugaq and would have to do something about him. kayugaq sighed and went to bed without saying a word more.

In the morning, he asked the woman what kunuyuq had said. She repeated her story. kayugaq sighed again and said: "Now it will be the same as before." As he said this, his stepmother became frightened and began to follow him about to protect him. One evening, as they were sitting in the house, kayugaq got up and went down into the hallway. His stepmother got up and followed at once but she was too late. kayugaq had taken down his seal spear and killed himself by falling on it. He lay already dead in the hallway of the house.

At once, the community tried to find out why kayugaq had killed himself. The stepmother told what the woman had said. kunuyuq, when he heard this, was grief-stricken. He had been at peace with kayugaq for a long time, in spite of what had happened, and the two had traded and shared together. He heard what his wife had said.

After this, everyone knew that the woman had lied and that she had hoped only to frighten kayugaq and get him to leave the community, taking her with him. When kunuyuq found out what she had done, he turned her out and gave her no further help. He lived a long time and many people knew his story.

CASE 1, SEQUEL

The two small boys, sons of qulliuq by his second wife, were named aneksuaq, the younger, and kayuqtuq, the elder. They grew up largely dependent on the bounty of kunuyuq. The elder boy lived a long time and is still remembered by living people. He died in 1908.

These two boys, when grown, became involved in a murder case. There was a chief at Point Hope named ataŋawraq who had tried to kill one of the two brothers. This was the great ataŋawraq mentioned by Capt. Thomas Brower (cf. "Fifty Years Below Zero," 1942). When ataŋawraq became threatening, the two brothers left Point Hope and took to wintering at Utokok. They would come to Point Hope for the whaling, but would always take great care to avoid ataŋawraq. After a time, they became tired of avoiding the issue, asking themselves: "Why are we like women and forever afraid of ataŋawraq?" They therefore came to Point Hope for the winter. At that, however, they took care to avoid the great umealiq.

During that winter, ataŋawraq was drinking heavily, a concoction made of molasses and flour. When drunk, he was especially vicious and homicidal. One day, he was drinking at home. The brothers decided that they would now take action against him. Taking their guns, they went over to his house. kayuqtuq remained by the skylight of the house, while aneksuaq entered the house through the hallway. As the latter peered up into the house through the kataq, he saw that ataŋawraq had fallen into a stupor. One of his wives was sitting there with him. aneksuaq motioned her out of the way. When she moved, he shot ataŋawraq through the head. When kayuqtuq heard the shots, he ripped off the skylight and fired his rifle inside. Two other men were with him and fired their rifles in also.

The relatives of ataŋawraq then came to get the body and to carry it away for burial. The two brothers came along with the group, standing there, their firearms on their backs. No one menaced them nor made a move to take revenge. The chief ataŋawraq had become so unpleasant with his drinking and his bullying that even his relatives made no move to avenge him. In fact, no one even wanted to carry his body. Hence, there was no fighting over this.

As it happened, both brothers were very popular. That same winter, they themselves began to drink. They made liquor from molasses and flour and were drinking by a fire, looking at an old gun they had found. As they examined it, it discharged and struck aneksuaq in the abdomen. A shaman came to heal him but despite all efforts, he died.

After his death, his brother refused to remain in one place. He went back and forth along the coast, staying for a time at nuwuk and then moving back to Point Hope. He died at Point Hope many years later when he was very old.

Now even though the relatives of ataŋawraq did not take revenge, they did express their delight when aneksuaq was killed by accident. Their general feeling was that his fate was a deserved one.

CASE 2

When people were living at the Point, that is, nuwuk, there was a man up there named uuγuruq. He made an agreement with another man named kinʸaveaq. The latter was going to the east for the purpose of hunting caribou and was taking his family with him. He had a dog with a new litter of puppies and asked uuγuruq to take care of them and of his bitch until his return. After kinʸaveaq had been gone for some time, the dog bit one of uuγuruq's children. Angered, uuγuruq killed the dog.

This uuγuruq had two grown sons, unaliilʸoaq and patiiraniq. Both were good hunters and had the reputation of being good runners. uuγuruq had recently married a woman, ikilʸaakpuk, who had a daughter by a previous marriage. It was this daughter who had been bitten by kinʸaveaq's bitch.

When, at last, kinʸaveaq came back from his hunting "up east," he asked for his dog. The family of uuγuruq said that the dog was dead and offered him another one in its place. This he refused to take, demanding again and again that his own dog be returned to him. The argument continued for some time, kinʸaveaq proving more and more difficult to reason with. When he became more and more violent in his demands, patiiraniq drew his knife and killed him.

At this, uuγuruq, his wife, and sons went back into their house. The relatives of kinʸaveaq came together at once and began to make plans to be avenged on uuγuruq and his sons. As the relatives were assembled, a man from piγiniq, kattik by name, came into the house and listened to their debate. After he had been present for a moment, the others, knowing he was not a relative, demanded of him what he wanted and why he had joined them. He refused to answer and started to leave. As he went out the door, one of the family of kinʸaveaq stabbed him. He was not seriously injured. "What did you do this for?" he cried. "You talk now; why didn't you say something before?" they replied.

Meanwhile, uuγuruq and his family remained in their house awaiting developments. unaliil^{y}oaq, thinking it might be possible to save his father and to end the trouble, decided to kill his brother patiiraniq, thus making it clear to the kin of kin^{y}aveaq that the matter had been settled. He waited until his brother was asleep and then stabbed him in the chest. patiiraniq leaped into the air, struck his head on the roof beam of the house, and fell dead. It was now necessary to get the news of the atoning death over to the other faction. Father and son debated the matter for some time, remaining with the body in the house. At last, unaliil^{y}oaq decided to go over to the house where the people of kin^{y}aveaq were assembled and to try to tell them of his action. His father was against it and attempted to persuade him not to go. But he insisted that this was the best course and started out. He put his arms in his parka and, carrying no weapons, made his way over to the other house. But as he approached, two men of the family of kin^{y}aveaq came out and killed him with their arrows.

uuγuruq now flew into a violent rage. He came out of his house and paced up and down in front of it brandishing a harpoon. After a moment, he went up on the roof of his house and shouted through the skylight that he would harpoon his wife and stepdaughter. When he descended from the roof, mother and daughter escaped through the skylight and ran away. By this means he succeeded in removing them from the fight. They were then spared by the others. uuγuruq now hurled his harpoon through the skylight of the house and leaped in after it, remaining there with the body of his son.

After a time, the kin^{y}aveaq faction began to show impatience. They waited for some days outside the house of uuγuruq but he failed to show himself. He had actually hidden himself in the hallway of the house and barred the entrance. His enemies finally decided to drive him out. They began to pour water into the house through the skylight. Even though uuγuruq's bedding of caribou skins was soaked and the water rose in the hallway, he did not show himself. Later, his stepdaughter brought fresh bedding and dropped it to him through the skylight. The hostile group had momentarily given up trying to drive him out.

The next day but one, uuγuruq took a quick look out of his skylight. A man named ipexsin was waiting and shot an arrow at him. It was impossible to see where the arrow had gone and ipexsin believed that he had struck uuγuruq and killed him. He therefore went up on the house to look into the skylight. uuγuruq, unwounded, was waiting for him to appear. As ipexsin looked into the skylight, uuγuruq killed him with an arrow and his body fell through the skylight into the house.

When this happened, kin^{y}aveaq's group decided to act. They formed a bucket brigade and kept pouring water and dropping chunks of ice into the house through the skylight. They left when the house was pretty well filled. That same day, the stepdaughter brought fresh bedding and food. She received no answer when she called and it became evident that uuγuruq had drowned in the hallway.

The kinsmen of kin^{y}aveaq now decided to recover the bodies in the house. Removing the roof from the hallway, they let the water escape and found the three bodies. The body of uuγuruq was laid out and the procedure customarily associated with the treatment of corpses of murdered men was followed out. The group, however, argued as to who should dissect the corpse. Finally, they demanded of a man named atuktuak that he cut off the joints of the corpse of uuγuruq. atuktuak refused but the group threatened him with death unless he complied with their wishes. He therefore cut the limbs of the corpse off at the joints and stuffed the little fingers of the corpse into the mouth. The bodies of the three men were then cleared away and the matter was at an end.

atuktuak was not a relative of the dead uuγuruq but the two did possess the same charm (oyamitkoaq). At one time, moreover, the families of the two men shared the same house. Since uuγuruq had no other relatives in the community at nuwuk, it was feared that his friend atuktuak might continue the feud. By forcing him to dissect the corpse, the opposing group placed him in a position of complicity in the murder, thus ruling out any chance that he might avenge his dead friend.

CASE 3

The incident described here took place in the 1890's. The groups along the Arctic coast had been in contact with outsiders, the European whalers and Government officials, for a few years. A family from Barrow moved down to Icy Cape. The man of the family was named kanayuk. When they had been for a time at Icy Cape, the wife died. kanayuk was alone but it was not long before he began to look for another woman. At Icy Cape was a man named tagiiluq who had a wife and house there. kanayuk approached the woman and persuaded her to have relations with him. For some time thereafter, kanayuk visited her. tagiiluq, knowing of the affair, was extremely angry. He was unwilling to let his wife go and at the same time he was unsure as to how to deal with kanayuk. He therefore approached his various kinsmen and asked them for advice. One of those to whom he went for counsel was tukumminaroaq, from whom the present account was obtained.

The relatives of tagiiluq had no suggestions to offer. Their general feeling was that as long as no bloodshed was involved and as long as tagiiluq's wife chose to go with kanayuk, they had no obligation in the affair. tagiiluq talked his problem over with anyone who would listen but was unable to come to any conclusion as to his course of action.

One day, tagiiluq came home and found kanayuk there. He pretended to ignore him and lay down on the bench in the house as if to sleep. As he did so, kanayuk took hold of his ankle and dragged him off the bench, exclaiming: "Why don't you let me have this woman?" tagiiluq pushed him away and answered: "The stronger of us will have her." They struggled for a moment and kanayuk was thrown down. Then tagiiluq seized his wife and threw her roughly on the bench. She lay there weeping. And tagiiluq said again: "If we are going to fight over this woman, then perhaps the stronger of us will get her." kanayuk said nothing but left the house.

All that day, kavissuk, tagiiluq's wife, lay on the bench and sobbed. Neither would speak to the other. In the evening, tagiiluq said: "Go to bed now and don't go out of the house." She answered him only with an angry look. By this time, several of tagiiluq's kinsmen had come over, among them tukumminaroaq, who said: "Don't have trouble between you; I will try to help you but if this goes on, one of you will kill the other. You are breaking our hearts. Maybe it would be better if both of you went away from here altogether." Another kinsman of tagiiluq said: "I can't stand it if one of you is going to kill the other; both of you should go away." And after this, the relatives departed and refused to talk either to tagiiluq or to his wife again. They hoped by this means that they could force the couple away from the community and from the troublemaking kanayuk.

In the spring, the crews were assembled for the whaling. tagiiluq joined his usual crew. In the course of the work, ostracism of him or of his wife was forgotten. It seemed, moreover, that the trouble over kanayuk had quieted down. No more was said about it.

In the summer, tagiiluq, kavissuk, the latter's daughter by a previous husband, tukumminaroaq, together with several other people, went to camp inland to hunt caribou. While they were camped there, kavissuk offered tea to her husband. Tea was poured into several cups and the group started to drink. At this point, the group was joined by a man named qaγmuk. He remarked to tagiiluq: "What's the matter with your tea?" They all looked and saw that the tea was unusually black and was bubbling. "Don't drink that," said qaγmuk, "it looks bad." kavissuk said: "I wonder why it got that way; the cup must not have been clean." "Throw it away," qaγmuk said, "we have plenty of water." But kavissuk urged her husband to drink the tea, saying that none should be wasted.

At this point, tukumminaroaq seized the woman by the arm, shouting: "You have put poison in that tea." The group raged at her until she admitted that she had done so, confessing before them all. She said that kanayuk had given her the poison, that he had got it at Barrow from the whalers, and that it was used for poisoning rats aboard the ships. The Barrow Eskimo had only recently begun to use such poisons in catching foxes. kavissuk admitted that she had put three "pills" into her husband's tea.

When this happened, tagiiluq decided that it would be best to get his wife away from the influence of kanayuk. He took her, his step-daughter, and his other children and started up the coast to Wainwright. They traveled in an umiak and were accompanied by several other families. It was not long before kanayuk was noticed in the umiak of one of his brothers. He had three brothers living at Icy Cape. When the group stopped to camp for the night along the coast, tagiiluq complained to the others of feeling ill. Some of the other men stayed with him for a time. He then indicated that he was feeling somewhat better.

When the group was about to break camp in the morning and to go on toward Wainwright, caribou were sighted on the tundra near the beach. The men, tagiiluq included, took their guns and went off after the herds. They went in several directions, some of the men attempting to circle the herds and come at them from the land. Several animals were taken and the men started back, carrying the meat. On the way back, they came across tagiiluq, who had lagged behind. He had fallen to his knees on the tundra. He said that he was deathly ill, that he could not see, and that his stomach was on fire. The men were unable to do anything for him. They rubbed snow on his head and chest but it did no good. They asked him if he could walk back but he said that he was too weak and in too great pain. One man offered to run back to the camp for seal oil, thinking that this might relieve tagiiluq's sufferings.

Several of the men, feeling that nothing could be done for tagiiluq, started to walk back to the camp. kanayuk was among them. When they got back to the camp on the beach, he sought out kavissuk. She gave him something to eat. When he had eaten, he told her what had happened. "You are the one who has caused all this trouble", he told her, "You had better get up there to tagiiluq and see that he is still breathing." And he shoved and pushed her.

The volunteer obtained the oil and, accompanied by a boy, ran back to where tagiiluq was lying. The sick man was rolling about the ground in great agony. The men who remained stood helplessly by. When the oil came, one of the men tried to get tagiiluq to drink it. But his mouth could not be opened; his teeth were clenched and the oil could not be poured in. One of the men took his knife and tried to pry tagiiluq's teeth apart but was unable to do so. When kavissuk arrived, tagiiluq was already dead. The men carried the body, wrapped in canvas, back to the campsite. They decided to return with the body to Icy Cape and not to push on to Wainwright. When they approached the village, they put the body down some distance away and left it there.

tukumminaroaq had been out hunting. When he returned, no one had yet done anything about the body of tagiiluq. As soon as he heard what had happened, he determined to kill kanayuk on the spot. He removed his parka and took out his knife, saying again and again: "My heart is broken." His father, however, the brother of tagiiluq, said, holding him fast: "Let us not have trouble; let this be until we find out what has really happened." Gradually, tukumminaroaq calmed down and taking his team, went out to get the body of tagiiluq. The men who had brought it back had hesitated to bring it into the community for fear that the kinsmen of the dead man would accuse them of having some part in the death.

When the body was brought into the community, it was blue under the eyes and on the lips. It was thus known that the dead man had been poisoned, but no one knew how it had been done. They examined tagiiluq's clothing and found a few raisins. Among them was a little "pill." But they were unable to say whether the murderer was kanayuk or kavissuk. Both denied any knowledge of the crime and neither could be induced to confess.

Shortly thereafter, the Government cutter came. The officials were told of tagiiluq's strange death and investigated. The people were brought out to the ship. Since definite evidence was lacking, no accusations were made but the officials decided to take the woman, kavissuk, away. The stepdaughter of tagiiluq swore that he had been ill for some time. Mother and daughter were taken by the cutter to Barrow and they wintered there. Next spring, they returned to Icy Cape, but by then kanayuk was gone.

kanayuk had an evil reputation even before this event. He had always played roughly and unfairly in the football games. After tagiiluq's death, although all were suspicious of him, his own part in tagiiluq's death was not clear. He had the backing of his three brothers at Icy Cape and it was decided to let the matter rest. In the football game that winter, kanayuk and tukumminaroaq were playing against each other. They wrestled and kanayuk was thrown down. As he got up, he said: "I shall not play unfairly any more." After that, he played to everyone's satisfaction and the trouble ended at this point. He then found another woman to marry and the two camped inland for several years. kavissuk also remarried on her return to Icy Cape and died before kanayuk returned.

CASE 4

The events noted here occurred shortly after Captain Brower had established his station just north of utkeaaγvik.

There was a man named masagaroak who lived to the north of Brower's station. He had the reputation of a drunkard, having learned to distill flour and molasses. One day, he came down from the whaling station and was quite drunk. He made for one of the houses in utkeaaγvik, looking for a woman he knew. The woman was kavenaceaq, wife of a man named pukuk. The couple had an adopted daughter and shared a house with pukuk's brother, uweeguraq, and his family. When masagaroak entered the house shared by these two families, he asked for a drink. Everyone in the house was frightened and the women ran outside. A relative of pukuk, a man named il^{y}uusiγiroak, came in to see what the row was about. masagaroak grabbed him by the hair and banged his head against the posts of the house. As soon as he let go, all ran out of the house, leaving masagaroak alone. When all were outside, they discovered that the baby, the adopted child of pukuk, had been left with masagaroak alone. They feared that he would harm the child but they were all afraid to go into the house while he was there. Actually, he lay down on the floor and fell asleep.

But meanwhile, pukuk and il^{y}uusiγiroak debated what to do. Since incidents like this had happened before, it was decided that it would be best to kill masagaroak. They agreed that pukuk would get masagaroak out of the house and that il^{y}uusiγiroak would kill him when he came outside. pukuk went back inside his own house, awakening masagaroak, who by now docilely agreed to leave. As he stumbled back toward his own house, pukuk followed him at a distance. By the time masagaroak reached the ravine, his head had cleared somewhat and he walked without staggering. At the ravine, he met il^{y}uusiγiroak. The latter said: "Are you masagaroak?" Knowing what was intended, masagaroak began to run. il^{y}uusiγiroak waited a moment and then raised his rifle and shot masagaroak in the back.

This il^{y}uusiγiroak was a shaman of great power. masagaroak had four brothers living in utkeaaγvik. They swore revenge but were fearful of the power of il^{y}uusiγiroak. They did go about saying that they would get their revenge. Some time later, the four were camped with their families at one of the fishing stations. It happened that il^{y}uusiγiroak passed by that place. When he saw them, he came over to them and said: "I hear that you wish to kill me; if you want to do so, kill me now," and he handed them his rifle. They stood looking at him and made no reply. He then picked up his gun and went away. The matter was not mentioned by them after this and the trouble between them was over.

When one of the sisters of masagaroak heard what her brothers had done, of their failure to take advantage of the opportunity for vengeance, she was furious. She went about saying that she would kill ilʸuusiγiroak. But she, too, was afraid of his power and made no attempt against him.

Everyone at utkeaaγvik thought that masagaroak had been justly treated and had got no more than his actions deserved. Opinion was strong against carrying the feud further.

CASE 5

payyaq was a man of the nuunamiut. He was "crazy" and killed many people. He had committed several murders among the inland people. At one time, during a food shortage, he had murdered a whole family and taken their food. Since the family was camped out alone, he was not suspected. On a later occasion, however, he murdered another family, and his activities became known.

A man named tuvłi, despite public opinion, had married two women, a mother and daughter. In the family of tuvłi was also an adolescent girl who had been adopted by the older wife. This girl had been promised as a wife to qiwaq, from whom this narration was obtained. tuvłi had lived at utkeaaγvik with his family and qiwaq had visited them there. He had had sexual relations with the girl but had not yet settled down with her. tuvłi also had had sexual relations with his wife's adopted daughter and was somewhat opposed to her marriage with qiwaq. It was for this reason that he took his two wives and his wife's adopted daughter inland, hoping that qiwaq would marry someone else.

As tuvłi and his family were camped, payyaq arrived. tuvłi himself was out hunting at the time and the three women were in the camp alone. The younger wife was pregnant and was, in fact, just getting ready to enter the birth hut for her confinement when payyaq arrived on the scene. He first went into the tent and murdered the older woman. Then he came out to the birth hut and called the younger wife out. When she came out, he killed her. The adolescent girl, meanwhile, ran away and escaped the killer.

When payyaq had killed the two women, as well as two younger children who were with the group, he sat down to await tuvłi. As soon as the latter arrived, payyaq persuaded him to go to the birth hut, perhaps by saying that the younger wife was having her child. As tuvłi turned, evidently to investigate, payyaq drove an arrow through his back and killed him.

Then payyaq became aware of the girl's tracks leading away from the encampment. He followed them and succeeded in tracking her down. He did not kill her but kept her with him thereafter, marrying-her in effect, in that he demanded work from her and had sexual relations with her. The couple now moved away from the camp where the murders took place and settled down among some others. payyaq kept close guard on his wife to see that she talked to no one.

But it became evident to the others in the encampment that payyaq was not using the heads of the animals he killed. People commented on the fact that caribou heads were piled up near his tent. They then remembered that he had a personal taboo on using the heads of animals for some time after he had killed a person. This was, in fact, a not unusual personal prohibition. Hence, although they recognized that he had taken a human life, they did not know who his victim was. As people began to wonder about it, payyaq became aware of their gossip and left, taking his wife down to utkeaaγvik.

At utkeaaγvik there lived iil^{y}averaq, brother of tuvłi. He had for some time been expecting his brother and his sisters-in-law. He was beginning to be rather concerned at their failure to appear. When payyaq came, bringing with him the adopted daughter of tuvłi's wife, iil^{y}averaq guessed what had happened. Awaiting his opportunity, he finally got the girl alone and learned from her of payyaq's murders. He then attempted to get help against payyaq. He enlisted his own kinsmen but also asked help of others, largely to determine on what kind of community support he could count. He approached qiwaq, for example, to enlist his aid in killing payyaq. qiwaq, although he had lost the girl whom he had desired as his wife, refused to help. The problem arose because payyaq was on the alert. He was a man of tremendous strength and reputedly had considerable supernatural power. He bullied and blustered his way about the community, intimidating everyone, and threatening to kill iil^{y}averaq. The latter, to whom everyone looked to avenge his brother tuvłi, was extremely hesitant to take action. But community sentiment began to build up in favor of iil^{y}averaq. As payyaq became more and more troublesome with his bullying, it was feared that he would do other violence. Although he and his wife spent the winter at utkeaaγvik, it was not until spring that anything definite could be done.

After the spring whaling, nalukataq was held and with it the football game. payyaq played in the game. The men who played with him, led by iil^{y}averaq, knocked him down and trussed him up. Then they picked him up and began to carry him over to the karigi called serel^{y}uaraamiut. As they were carrying him, he began in a loud voice to call to his mother. At this, several of the men in the procession became frightened and ran away, it being known that payyaq's mother was dead. iil^{y}averaq, however, was too far committed to abandon his purpose. He continued to drag payyaq up to the karigi. When they got there, payyaq was laid before the karigi door and iil^{y}averaq cut his throat.

When he had killed payyaq, he went into the karigi and brought out the oil which had drained from the lamp there. This he poured on the dead man's head to allay the supernatural powers of his victim. Then he cut off the little fingers of the corpse and thrust them into its mouth. The other men came to drag the body away.

Even though payyaq had some supporters in the community, no one came to his defense and the matter ended there. The facts about the murder of tuvłi became known. This, together with his unpleasantness in the community, was sufficient to prevent any further retaliatory action. qiwaq thought then of taking over the dead payyaq's wife. He decided against it, however, and the girl married another man.

CASE 6

The present instance was obtained from a man now about 50 years of age. It is illustrative of the concept of blood revenge carried through until fairly recently.

When the informant, Pete, was about 5 years old, he and his family, father, mother, and grandmother, together with another family, camped at Harrison Bay where some other people had already settled. His own and the second family built a sod house with a common entrance and were eating together. While the men and women were working on the new houses in the settlement, Pete went off to play with other boys there. One of the boys, roughly his own age, found a rifle standing inside a sod house nearby. He took the gun and started to play with it. Presently, the boy's brother and Pete joined him and the three went inside a tent nearby to play with the gun. The lad who had taken the gun said: "Lie down on the floor and make like you are a seal and then I will hunt you." Pete answered: "No, you might hurt me." The boy was very angry and said that Pete couldn't play with the gun unless he did as he was told. But Pete refused.

Then the boy gave the gun to his brother and said: "Now I will play like a seal." He lay down on the floor and pretended that his arms were the seal's flippers. "When I come up out of the water, you can shoot me," the boy said. His brother held the gun about a foot away from his head. When the boy said: "Now I am a seal and I am coming up out of the water; shoot me now," his brother pulled the trigger. The bullet entered the boy's head above the right eye and blew the back of his head off. He fell down in a welter of blood. Pete began to cry in fear and ran to the house where his family was living. His grandmother was there. When she saw how disturbed he was, she coaxed him over to her, lifted her parka and let him crawl inside and hide. She patted and comforted him.

Meanwhile, the brother who had done the shooting ran away. Soon, however, he came back. The father of the dead boy had found the body and wanted revenge. He came over, demanding Pete and that he be allowed to kill him. Pete's father put him off, saying that he didn't know where Pete was. The man went away. Later, even when he had seen his son and learned the manner of his other boy's death, he was still far from satisfied. He repeated his desire to kill Pete for revenge. After that, Pete could never go out alone; someone had always to be with him.

Soon the father of the dead boy wished to kill Pete's father. He came over to the house and called in through the skylight for Pete's father to come out. The man had a knife in his hand. Placing it against the breast of Pete's father, he said: "I'm going to kill you." But Pete's father said nothing. He confronted his enemy, staring at him but not moving. At last, the man threw his knife on the ground and turned away. Having made this gesture, it was known that Pete need have no further fear of the dead boy's father and the matter was closed.

CASE 7

There was a man at utkeaaγvik named kayaakpuq who was married to an attractive woman named kallikcuk. Another man, tiguaceak by name, desired this woman even though he had a wife of his own. She responded to his suit and would meet him from time to time. She would pretend that she was menstruating and would leave the community. Some distance away she would join her lover. After a time, kayaakpuq, discovering the affair, got his bow and attempted to kill his rival. tiguaceak, however, was warned by his relatives and carried his own bow. The two men exchanged a volley of arrows but each missed the other. When this duel occurred, kallikcuk left her husband and went to live in the house of tiguaceak as his second wife. From time to time, she would go back to her former husband and have sexual relations with him. People in the community said: "This isn't right; this doesn't seem right."

The man tiguaceak then decided that he had best kill his rival, kayaakpuq, before the latter killed him. He informed his kinsmen about his decision. When his second wife, kallikcuk, heard about this, she told her former husband of tiguaceak's intentions. kayaakpuq said, on hearing of the plan to kill him: "Let me go and stand where he can see me. He can shoot me there; let him kill me." After that, however, the kinsmen of kayaakpuq watched him closely, giving tiguaceak no chance to get at him. They even guarded him while he slept. kayaakpuq would get up in the morning and go to an open place and stand there, waiting for his enemy to come and kill him.

It so happened that the family of kallikcuk sided with the former husband. One of her brothers came each day to stand guard over kayaakpuq. One day, tiguaceak came, an arrow fitted to his bow. kallikcuk's brother walked toward him. Each man had a reserve of about 20 arrows. These they discharged from a distance. At length, tiguaceak succeeded in hitting his opponent in the upper arm. The wounded man came back to where kayaakpuq was standing. kallikcuk's father was present and came forward to assist his wounded son. He drew the arrow from the wound, remarking to kayaakpuq: "Unless you go after him now, you'll always be afraid of him." kayaakpuq did not reply but took his former brother-in-law's bow and remaining arrows and went out, walking slowly through the houses toward tiguaceak. The latter came out again and exchanged arrows with him. At last, an arrow shot by kayaakpuq struck tiguaceak in the ear and he fell dead. It was a long and lucky shot. As he fell, his first wife came out of the house and ran to him. She was a shaman and attempted, by her powers, to get the arrow out. Had she succeeded, she could have sung over him and perhaps restored him to life. But she was menstruating at the time and her powers were hence nullified. kayaakpuq then walked back and forth among the houses in the community, crying in a loud voice: "If any is against me, let him come foward now." But no one took up his challenge and the matter was thus ended. Everyone in the community felt that kayaakpuq had acted "honestly," and his former wife, kallikcuk, now came back to his household.

CASE 8

The following case occurred in the 1870's. An uncle of the informant was indirectly involved in that he accompanied one of his kinsmen when the latter discovered the abduction of his wife.

A kinsman of the informant's father had married several women in succession. His last wife was much younger than he. Although they had lived together for some time, he had no children by her. In the community, utkeaaγvik, was a man who had recently arrived. He was single and looking for a wife. He awaited his chance, having selected the wife of the informant's relative. One day the woman came out of the house on her way to an ice cellar for water. The man seized her, threw her to the ground, and raped her. He then dragged her back into the house in which he was living. So far as public opinion was concerned, she now had become his wife. The man whose wife she had been debated as to his own course of action and called in his relatives to discuss the matter. Since the abductor had kinsmen in the community, his own relatives were reluctant to begin a feud and urged caution.

The ultimate decision was to do nothing. Sometime later, the deprived husband was walking through the community with the uncle of the informant. They came on the abductor of his wife sleeping in the summer sun in a sheltered place. His team was staked nearby The former husband took the lead dog and tied it to his sleeping rival's leg. When the man awoke, he knew at once that the man he had offended had passed by and done this to him. He knew that the man had had the opportunity to kill him and had let it pass.

He then called his own kinsmen and told them of the incident. They passed the story around and all in the community were much impressed with the "honesty" of the husband who had been deprived of his wife. While the abductor kept the woman he had taken, he and the former husband became close friends. They called each other "aŋutawkun," that is, men who have had intercourse with the same woman. Everyone in the community felt obliged to comment on the "honorable" way in which the man had let his wife go.

CASE 9

This incident took place at Wainwright. There was here a man who had recently married. He and his wife had built a house and were living together. Another man in the community went after the woman, making frequent attempts to talk with the woman and to persuade her to have an affair with him. The husband forbade his wife to have anything to do (i. e., sexually) with that man. One day the woman went a little way off from the village in order to dump some trash. Her pursuer waylaid her, threw her on the ground, and attempted to rape her. She was wearing caribou skin trousers. Her attacker ripped them up one leg and was trying to get them off. The woman began to scream. Her husband, hearing her, came running up and threw the attacker off his wife. The two began to wrestle, the husband attempting to strangle the other man. The latter managed to throw him off and struck him in the ribs with his knee. The husband, winded, sat down, and the attacker ran away.

Other men had come to see what was happening. One of them, the brother of the attacker, came over and asked the husband: "What are you going to do?" "I'm going to kill him," was the answer. "Ah, don't do that; he has a wife already; there won't be any more trouble," said the attacker's brother. And he urged the husband to go home and forget the whole thing.

But the offended husband went over to his relatives and talked the matter over with them. He finally reached the decision to do the same thing to the wife of his wife's assailant. His kinsmen urged him to forget the whole thing and watched to see that he had no opportunity to be alone with the other woman. They constantly urged peace between the two men.

But one day the husband whose wife had been attacked was making a sled. He was working outside on a cleared place. The wife of his enemy passed by. He chased after her, knocked her down, and attempted to rape her. He tried to get her belt off and broke it in pulling it. Then he saw that she wore another pair of trousers underneath the first, fastened with another belt. He broke this too, got his hand inside her trousers and touched her vulva. He stopped there and let her get up. Weeping, she went back home.

Her own husband was now enraged. He demanded revenge and started off after the other man. Then the relatives of both sides came together and stopped them both. They talked the matter over with both men and the two finally agreed to let the matter rest. After that, the bad feelings between the two came to an end.

CASE 10

There was a girl at Barrow who became pregnant and was the cause of a fight between two men, each thinking himself the father of her unborn child. In order to settle the issue, they decided to hold a foot race. The first one to reach the girl was to claim her as his wife. Actually, the girl in question was too free in her relations with men. Neither man realized that the other also had had sex relations with her. They ran the race and one of the rivals won. Not until then did they discuss the matter and discover that each had had sexual relations with the girl. Both men went to their respective families and discussed the matter. The two families felt that the girl was too free and raised objections to a marriage. Hence the winner gave up his claim to the girl, leaving her to the loser. He, too, now refused to take her as his wife. The girl, when her child was born, abandoned it, "throwing it away," and later married someone else.

CASE 11

When the informant was young, there was an old woman who stole something from the sled of her family. The old woman was aŋatquq, so they hesitated to take direct action against her. The members of the family looked for the things she had taken and brought them back. The old woman did nothing.

On a later occasion, the family had some caribou legs from which they were planning to get the marrow. The old woman stole these from them. At the time, they were all hunting and camping inland. Even though they shared their food with the old woman, she constantly took advantage of them. When they missed the caribou legs, they decided to plant a trap for the thief. More caribou legs were left lying about in the tent. One member of the family lay down and pretended to be asleep. When the old woman came in, attempting to steal the meat, the family member opened his eyes and exclaimed "ku!" Terribly startled, the old woman left. Nor after that, did she ever disturb the family again.

In such cases, it is said, only the unwary were regarded as safe to rob. When the old woman discovered the watchfulness of the family, she never again bothered them with her stealing.

CASE 12

The great whaler, taakpuq, while his wife was living, had an amazing variety of clothing. Later, however, when she died, he could find no other woman to sew for him and his wardrobe became quite shabby. It was universally recognized, however, that he was a man of great wealth. At one time, he had exchanged his wife for his partner's. He took his partner's wife and went hunting inland. On his return, he reexchanged wives, taking his own wife back from his partner. The two men then settled down for a drinking bout. This took place on the coast below Barrow, at the now abandoned settlement called nuunavak.

taakpuq and his partner quarreled after a while and the latter left. taakpuq camped with his wife at nuunavak and started drinking by himself, quite heavily. His wife became frightened when he began to become quarrelsome and to tax her with her relations with his partner. All the while he held his rifle and continually pointed it at his wife. Later, while he slept, she removed the cartridges from the chamber but neglected to remove the one in the barrel. taakpuq awoke and, drinking again, pointed the rifle at her and fired. The bullet entered her breast and came out her back. She fell down and appeared dead.

At this, taakpuq, realizing that her kin lived nearby, ran away at once and made his way inland. An old woman, camping nearby with her family, went over to investigate the shot and found the woman's body in the sand. At once, she called the shaman, kaγgil^{y}aq. He came immediately, restored the woman to life, and remained with her until she was cured.

As soon as they heard of the shooting, the relatives of taakpuq's wife swore revenge against taakpuq. The woman had a brother, aakivienna, who had been adopted into her family when his own mother had died and when he was about to be abandoned with his mother's body. This man started out at once after taakpuq and although he was able to track him for a long distance, he did not succeed in overtaking him. He was gone for several weeks but was at length obliged to abandon the pursuit. On his return, he found his sister well on the way to recovery. At this, he gave up his idea of vengeance but stated that if his sister died, he would seek out his brother-in-law and kill him. He also got the other members of his sister's and his own group to avenge the woman if she were to suffer further ill effects from the wound. Later, however, taakpuq heard of his wife's recovery. He returned and the two began to live together as man and wife again. No further troubles arose and the matter was dropped. It was only some years later that the woman died of another cause. Everyone knows that the woman was killed by taakpuq but was restored to life by the shaman.

ECONOMY AND SOCIETY

INTRODUCTION

Because the social relationships in the cultures of the Eskimo groupings of the Alaskan Arctic slope are so intimately affected by economic considerations, it becomes virtually impossible to offer separate treatment of the two institutions. There are interrelationships between them which are eclipsed if economy is viewed out of context from social forms or if social life is described without reference to the economic round. But a word of caution is in order—many who have investigated the Eskimo have implied that the economic demands of Arctic life have tended to place great limitations on the social achievements of the Eskimo. Limitations there are, indeed, but the selections made by the North Alaskan Eskimo do not indicate that in fashioning his social institutions, he has been wholly at the mercy of his environment. Society implements the food quest and, conversely, the food quest becomes a factor in the structuring of society. In northern Alaska, it was the family and kinship grouping which underlay the considerations of economy and environment and which was sufficiently pliable as to permit adjustment to inland nomadism or to settled maritime activities in the permanent village. The individual functioned first as a member of a kinship grouping and developed his economic skills and interests in relation to a circle of kindred. Starting with this primary unit, he was then able to extend his activities by forming associations in a series of well defined ways with nonkin. In short, the circle of kinship was broadened by a series of voluntary associations which in their patterning resembled kinship situations and in which the themes of cooperation became paramount. In kinship and in the extensions of kinship patterns to nonkin in specific ways lies the basis of the social system. And it is through such a system that signal success in mastering the environment was achieved. The bugbear of environmental determinism can thus be at once dismissed.

When the aboriginal past is considered, the observer is at once confronted with the problem of differentiating between the two major ecological manifestations. In each he finds a well-defined seasonal economic cycle and a concise patterning of activity. And since the two major groupings coexist and come together only in quite specific ways, he is obliged to bring the differences between nuunamiut and tareumiut always to the fore. Only in the rarest instances does kinship cross the ecological boundary. Within each setting, however, the ties of kinship extend over a wide area so that it was not at all inconceivable for a man of the utkeaviŋmiut to have relatives at tikeraaq, or for an utokaγmiu to recognize ties of kinship with a family of the ikpikpaŋmiut. As nearly as can be judged, the ties of kinship among the whaling villages were restricted to the coastal area of whaling, while the nuunamiut relationships in northern Alaska were reckoned only within the area of the Arctic slope. One could simplify by noting that northern Alaska formed a culture area in which two major tribes with differing economic systems were found. But here were no tribes in the stricter sense of political definition; there was rather a series of coexisting families operating in a pattern of common culture and keeping the concept of the tie of blood to the fore. Kinship was not fictitious; it was bilateral and widely extended. A village or an inland band, as centers of economic activity, had meaning but they lacked formal organization and they ceased to operate as units when the tie of blood, which went so far beyond the confines of the individual community, was infringed upon. The cohesive force was kinship and all economic considerations were secondary to it.

Kinship and economic life together provide the basis for group behavior. The family could not practicably live together in view of the limiting nature of the environment. This, coupled with the fact that there was great freedom of individual choice in economic activity, served to spread family memberships all along the coast or widely within the interior. As a result, nonkindred came together in village and band. Beyond the primary units of kinship, therefore, lay the extrafamilial associations, those dependent on trade and economic partnership, the joint participation in hunting groups, such as in the caribou drive or in the whaling crew, or the quasi-ceremonial and recreational association of the dance house. Beyond the family, these became the forces of societal integration. Social controls were inherent in the family and, by the same token, there was no defined political organization. There were no chiefs as such, no one to direct behavior or to harangue the populace. A man settled where he chose and did as he pleased in respect to forming new social ties or in formulating economic goals. The village or band, unless viewed in the light of its component kinship elements, was most ephemeral. The result was a socioeconomic balance which applied to the entire area.

In the sections which follow, an attempt is made to relate the social and economic institutions of the Alaskan Arctic slope and to present a picture of the aboriginal society in action. When the situation of today is considered, it is evident that although many customs have been changed and many social forms dropped, family and voluntary association continue to function. Even today the balance between economy and society still exists, with the result that the basic cultural orientations have changed but little. The modern scene has witnessed the disappearance of most of those inland bands which once moved over the foothills and has seen the end to those complex patterns of trading and mutual interdependence which once characterized the two groups. This has meant a loss in the richness of the aboriginal setting, but, despite this, the modern natives of the area retain their same general social structure in their coastal villages.

HUMAN ECOLOGY OF THE ALASKAN ARCTIC SLOPE

1. NUUNAMIUT AND TAREUMIUT

The problem of the dual ecological division of the Eskimo is one which has suggested several differing solutions. This dichotomy is by no means limited to the area of northern Alaska, although it is here perhaps best exemplified in view of the existing balance between the two ways of life. One has only to turn to the adjacent Siberian areas to find a close parallel, that of the difference between the reindeer and maritime Chukchi and Koryak, as described by Bogoras, Jochelson, and others. Among the Eskimo proper, the Caribou Eskimo of the Barren Grounds further to the east are distinctive in their orientation toward caribou, although the interrelationships between them and their maritime neighbors are less easily definable (cf. Birket-Smith, 1929). The question of the priority of inland, caribou-hunting adjustments is one which can only be resolved in terms of archeological sequences. Birket-Smith has raised the question either that the maritime and inland life are equally old, or that the tribes of the interior are an outgrowth of maritime existence, or, finally, that the maritime adjustments reflect later movements to the coast from an already settled inland population (Birket-Smith, 1952, p. 12). One suggested solution to this problem lies in the recognition that the inland Eskimo, both of Alaska and of the central regions, by virtue of the culture traits which they share, represent a Proto-Eskimo stage. This widely distributed culture was intruded upon by the patterning of seal and walrus hunting—but not whaling—in the Paleo-Eskimo phase represented in both Ipiutak and Dorset. The impetus for this comes from Asia, as demonstrated in the configurations of culture in the Ipiutak (Collins, 1951; Larsen and Rainey, 1948, pp. 157–161). Whaling represents a specialization developed in the Neo-Eskimo stage at such horizons as the Okvik, Old Bering Sea, Birnirk, and lastly, the Thule (Birket-Smith, 1952, p. 13). The picture is one of substratum culture, characterized by caribou hunting, subjected at the points of its intrusions to the sea to modifications resulting from the diffusion of culture traits from west to east. In the areas away from the sea, the ancient pattern of caribou hunting remained. A recent movement of these peoples to the sea in the central regions creates the Eschato-Eskimo stage, a late, but primitive overlay (ibid., p. 13).

That whale-hunting represents a presumably late development in the face of the continuing existence over a long period of time of caribou hunters seems a reasonable assumption. The investigations of Solecki and Irving north of the Brooks Range and of Giddings to the west would point to the antiquity of inland settlement, a feature further substantiated by the Ipiutak study of Larsen and Rainey. (Cf. Solecki, 1950; W. Irving, 1953; Giddings, 1949, 1952; Larsen and Rainey, 1948; et al.) From an ethnological point of view, a more detailed treatment of the elements of culture in the interior setting is needed, together with a comparison of these data with those from other inland groups. The question of origins is not wholly germane to the present discussion, which proposes to concern itself with interrelationships rather than with comparative differences. It may be sufficient to accept the view that caribou hunting in the setting of inland life is less specialized than the richer existence which is adjusted to whaling.

It is true that several questions are raised when the two patterns are compared. That they may represent different populations is suggested but by no means proved on the basis of available physical evidence (Birket-Smith, 1952, pp. 13–17). Linguistically, the differences are wholly negligible. One language only is represented and the dialect differences between modern Point Hope and Barrow, for example, are more pronounced than between Barrow and the modern killiγmiut. Moreover, however different the modes of life in respect to the food quest, the two patterns do employ essentially the same kinship system and show the same type of social organization. The greatest differences would appear to lie in material culture, a consideration which is not treated in the present study. The nomadic existence for example, required variations in the structure of houses which were of necessity different from those of the coast. The tent and its forms differed from the permanent semisubterranean house of the coastal villager. Similarly, there were some marked differences in clothing and weapons. But, in general, the primary orientations, the basic assumptions and postulates of the culture as manifested in religious attitudes and world view, the concepts of individual goals and responsibilities, were the same for both groups.

In the recent aboriginal past, it is clear that contacts between the two groups were not of long duration. On the formal side, they were limited to the great trading expeditions, when large aggregates of people representing each ecological setting came together at the designated markets. At this type of gathering, the formalized trading partnerships between seaman and landsman arose. There is also the record of the elaborate social and ceremonial event, the Messenger Feast, having taken place between the two groups, or more correctly, between segments of them.

On the less formal side, however, there was a fair amount of individual and family contact. Single families of nuunamiut not infrequently came to the coasts in the summer, camping where they chose, entering into the social life of the coast to a reserved degree. Such a family tended to settle for a month or two at a place where they were already known, at the village of a trading partner, for example, where protection and welcome were assured. The coastal groups also tended to disperse in the summers, spreading out to the inland and spending long periods of time at the fishing camps there. Here, too, there were opportunities for contact with inland families which were also moving about in smaller units at this time. These contacts, never very prolonged, were economic rather than social. They arose on the basis of a trade which was somewhat less formalized than that which took place at the recognized centers. Indeed, they were often a prelude to such more formalized and elaborated trading. It is worth noting that these contacts always took place in the summer, this being the period of free movement and group dispersal.

While the economic interdependence between the nuunamiut and the tareumiut is a point reserved for fuller discussion, the problem of the social balance between them is one about which the people themselves had no doubt. There was a marked reserve between the two, a reflection of the suspicions and fears which the aboriginal society directed toward the stranger, that is, anyone not involved with an in-group either in kinship or established trade or other economic relationships. When trade relations had been established, and continued, as they most frequently did over long periods of time, these expressions of reserve tended to disappear. The reflection of attitudes which each group entertained toward the other is interesting. The nuunamiut, among other things, said of the tareumiut, "They don't know," the inference being that they lacked the proper inland virtues and points of view. Among the tareumiut, the expressions were somewhat stronger, "they live just like the animals; they have no real homes." A person of either setting might express his opinions of the opposite way of life in this off-hand and contemptuous way, but would refer to his own recognized partners in the other group with respect and even deference. Among the maritime North Alaskan Eskimo, the inland peoples were regarded somewhat in the light of simple bumpkins at whom fun was poked. There is, indeed, something of the sailor's attitude toward the landlubber. On one occasion, it was said, a landsman obtained a place in a whaling crew. The umiak was at the edge of an ice lead and the crew were waiting silently for the appearance of a whale. When at last a whale spouted, the crew leaped into their umiak and gave chase. The landsman, not knowing what to do, failed to take his place and was left behind. He shouted to the crew to return for him with the result that the whale was frightened off and lost. But the same tale is told of the seaman who attempts caribou hunting. Some error which he makes causes the caribou to be alerted and to avoid the hunting corral.

While hostilities occurred between groups representing the differing ecological patterns, these being on the level of feuds between families for real or fancied wrongs, it seems apparent that they were not too frequent. The general pattern was one of avoidance of unrecognized people. Thus, if a tareumiut family were engaged in summer travel and encountered a group of nuunamiut, each would tend to steer clear of the other. In time, assuming that the two groups met yearly at essentially the same place, a trade might develop and there might be closer social ties established. But in the normal course of life, assuming no formal bonds of any kind had been established, there was mutual suspicion and distrust. It must be emphasized, however, that this applied to any group of "strangers," however met, or wherever their place of origin. The stranger was always a target of suspicion and often the butt of hostile actions. If a numerically large group met a small one, they might behave with some hostility or viciousness, tearing clothes, wrecking sleds and boats, and becoming extremely abusive. They might also rape or kidnap the women of the smaller or defenseless party. Again, however, this behavior arose in any social context where affirmed ties were lacking and may be interpreted in terms of patterned assertions of status.

Since the contacts between the nuunamiut and tareumiut were almost wholly economic, it follows that marital alliances and consequently kinship ties between the two were virtually nonexistent. But at the same time, it would not be wholly correct to stress the endogamous nature of each setting. There was clearly no demand placed on the individual to avoid ties of this kind with families or persons in the opposite ecological grouping. Marriages, referring here to permanent cohabitation and not to random sexual unions, could and did occur but were most infrequent. The basic reason for this lay in the different kinds of skills which each setting demanded. A nuunamiut man who took a tareumiut woman as a wife was assuming an economic burden rather than a helpmeet, a luxury he could ill afford. But sexual relations between men and women in each setting could and did occur. In the cementing of trading partnerships, for example, there could be temporary wife exchange and the consequent formation of close ties of friendship, the result of which was a virtual kinship situation. Similarly, there was kidnaping of women on both sides. This likewise was apparently not too frequent, but well known. Such stealing or raping of women might result in a feud. Again, however, it might have a salutary effect, the woman being returned and the two families involved using the sexual bond as a means of establishing trading relations.

Marriages which did take place most frequently involved patrilocal residence. The woman left her group and joined that of her husband. Unquestionably, this was because there was greater uniformity in the women's sphere than in the men's. Women in both maritime and inland life learned the skills of cooking, of sewing, and of general household arts, and these, however different they might be in the nomadic as compared with the settled life, stood in sharp contrast to the ability and judgment required for whaling or for the mass hunting of caribou. It is not possible to obtain any picture of the number of women who married out of one setting into another, but when it did occur it was worthy of note. A family is recalled, for example, that lived regularly at piγiniq at Point Barrow. Every summer they were visited by a family of the ikpikpaŋmiut with whom they enjoyed friendly relations. One of the daughters married into this group, left her family, and settled inland with her husband. When her husband's group returned in the summers to piγiniq, the woman complained bitterly of the hardships of inland life and at last her family persuaded her to leave her husband. Her children grew up on the coast but did retain their kinship ties with their father's family, a situation which was viewed as sufficiently unusual as to require comment.

The problem of intermarriage between the two groups is somewhat clouded by the events of recent years. The gradual drop in population of the interior may be attributed to movement to the coastal communities as a result of imposed administrative pressures. At present, many families recognize erstwhile ties with the nuunamiut. The indication is that many intermarriages have recently taken place but that this was not the former pattern.

One of the characteristic aspects of the cultures of the area lay in the freedom of choice which the group accorded to the individual. A person was free to make capital of the skills which he possessed and to select the kind of career which best suited him. No stigma attached to the hunter who, feeling himself unsuited, physically or temperamentally, to a group activity, chose to ignore the communal aspects of hunting. It is true that the attitude existed that the proper activity of a man lay in hunting; there was some intolerance of an individual who devoted all his time to making umiaks, sleds, or weapons for exchange with others. But on the whole, if a man liked only to hunt ducks or only to fish, there was no one to deny him his choice. It may, in fact, be said that the greatest sin was idleness. A man in either setting was free to work as he saw fit, in keeping with his inclinations.

This point is of some significance when it is considered that there were nuunamiut who moved to the coasts and remained there to depend on seal hunting. And similarly, there were men from the tareumiut who, with their families, settled inland and gave themselves over to exclusive caribou hunting. Despite this fact, however, it is to be emphasized that such choices were individual, were not communal, and were not subject to the same degrees of ritualization which the communal effort required. If a hunter chose, he could specialize in this manner and he might involve a small segment of his kinsmen, as well as members of his immediate family. A pattern of this kind is seen in the recent movement of the kivalinermiut from the inland to the coast.

But this does not mean that the line between the two ecological types becomes ill-defined. The tareumiu who chose to devote his activity to the inland regions did not become associated with the nuunamiut groups or drawn into their social activities. Similarly, if a nuunamiut band settled on the coast for a time, it was generally away from a maritime community and the men did not share in the activity of whaling by becoming members of the established whaling crews and all that they implied. In short, regardless of the choice of economic activity, the original affiliations were constant; ties of kinship reached out to claim any individual. If his kin were to be found on the coast, he was, by definition, and regardless of his chosen activity, a tareumiu. And the reverse was equally true. Such choices of economic activity offered a situation which was rather different from that in which casual or seasonal visiting between the two groups took place.

The line between nuunamiut and tareumiut was thus well drawn. Basically one of differences in economy, it served to create a twofold distinction of society. In terms of general culture, except certain marked material differences, the structuring of these two settings was not essentially different. There were the same common understandings, the same general kinship and familial patterns, the same socioeconomic values, and on the whole, the same kinds of ritual behavior, applied differently, it is true, but similar in basic approach and premise. The problem of description of these two groups emerges as one in which the two ways of life are contrasted and in which the mutual interdependence of the two is demonstrated.

2. THE NUUNAMIUT

It has been suggested that the nuunamiut, in the aboriginal setting, were the numerically larger group. Their range was a wide one, easily definable along the northern slopes of the Brooks Range, the foothills, and the adjacent plain, although somewhat attenuated and less easily designated to the west and south. It is in the latter center, the drainages which converge on Hotham Inlet, that the principal remaining nuunamiut are still to be found. Estimating an aboriginal population of 3,000 for the northern and western Alaskan regions, somewhat more than half of this number might have been found north of the Brooks Range. These were the nuunamiut who were most successful in forming a balanced relationship with the maritime whalers and to whom the attention of the present study is primarily directed.

The term nuunamiut, people of the land, or more accurately, "Inland People," is often encountered in its variant form, nunataγmiut, and has sometimes been employed to designate a single tribal division within the area, a contention which is not substantiated. That it is a term carrying with it the connotation of a specific status and reflecting the basic economic adjustment, is indicated clearly by native usage. Conventional reference to any person requires that he be described in terms of his point of origin, either as a member of a grouping whose territory is known and so named, or as nuunamiu or tareumiu, depending on his provenience.

In the interior of northern Alaska were the numerous groups scattered along the watercourses. Each grouping bore the name of the locality or river along which it habitually moved and was united through a general concept of common territory. Not, it must be stated, that such territory was in any sense owned or that trespass by others not of the grouping occasioned of itself hostility or objection; it was simply that groups of individuals, as many as 200 to 300 in number, customarily resided and moved through an area defined by familiarity with its resources and possibilities. These were not kinship groupings, although they might be. Provided that the regulations against sexual unions between close kin were not violated, intragroup marriages could take place. But kinship ties with other groups did exist; indeed, the impression gained of the nuunamiut society is one of fairly widespread bonds of kinship. An individual was free to ally himself with the grouping of his choice but only if he possessed kinship ties with it or had married into it. This larger territorial grouping or aggregate, named for the area which it inhabited, had a primary economic function in that its members acted in concert in the season of the great caribou drives. This in turn implied ceremonial activities centered in the nonkin association of the karigi, the ceremonial houses of which there were usually several in each group and in which concerted hunting activity began.

But if the extended territorial grouping—one hesitates to employ the term "tribe" in view of the wider circles of kinship which cut across territorial boundaries—met periodically for the caribou drives, the nuclear families which made up the grouping were usually dispersed during much of the year. The problem which the individual faced at this point and one which he, with his wife, children, and any other dependent relatives, was entirely free to solve, lay in the choice of the activity to be undertaken when the caribou drive was over. The family head, occupying a position as principal hunter and provider, could elect to go off alone, to camp at a particular place for further hunting, for fishing, or to the coastal areas for trade with tareumiut. When the hunt was over and the skins of the caribou cleaned, the meat dried and cached, most, it is true, did make the trip either to the Colville mouth or over the portages to Hotham Inlet. The groups to the north of the Brooks Range tended to trade along the Colville and to travel down in the summers. But the choice and decision was always a matter for the nuclear kin group. The associations of the yearly round might thus be quite variable. The nuclear family could travel alone; it could associate itself with other families to which it was related by blood; men belonging to a ceremonial house, the karigi, and forming a hunting "crew" could continue to work together. The pattern, in any case, was one of movement and the groups did not remain fixed but dispersed and moved over wide areas.

The result was a kind of nomadism. It is not, however, possible to define movements within a fixed territory in view of the alternative choices which a nuclear family could make. Thus, after the caribou hunting and trading, the family could join other nuunamiut, these not necessarily of the same territorial grouping, and return with them toward the general home ground, pausing to hunt or fish along the way. It could cut out alone, moving up into the mountains for berries, sheep hunting, or further fishing. If it chose, it could associate itself with another grouping for a time, especially if there were kinship ties with them, and remain with them for a year or two. This is not to say that any grouping is ephemeral. It was not, being stabilized and integrated by the presence of the ceremonial associaations. It is indicated, however, that the personnel of a grouping could vary and was in no sense fixed. An additional factor in this respect lay in the unpredictability of the caribou movements. When these changed, shifting to another route or becoming less in number, segments of a grouping, the nuclear familial elements, were free to break away and to select their own manner of livelihood. This implies that the ethnic names—killiγmiut, utokaγmiut, kaŋgianermiut, etc.—have meaning only in a geographical sense and were made up primarily of nuclear families, secondarily of extrakin associations. In general, people returned to the area which they knew best and where they were best acquainted but it is clear that this did not always follow, especially in view of wider circles of kinship.

Because of the vaguely defined nomadic situation, and the fact that there was so much movement of individual families, it may be well to consider a few examples of family composition and to note the seasonal round in which each chose to be involved. The first was given by an old woman now resident in the village of Barrow who had spent most of her life with the nuunamiut and who considered herself an inland Eskimo.

The family elements, which traveled together and when settled occupied one house, were as follows:

1. ŋuyaaruq, the informant, at age 15, i. e. ca. 1895.
2. suŋaarak, her mother; the informant's father was dead.
3. tigutak, older brother.
4. nesuquluq, wife of the older brother, tigutak.
   This couple, after their first child, left the group, settled for a time at neγłiq, and then moved to utkeaaγvik at the invitation of a trading partner. This shift in pattern, taking place about 1895, is clearly a reflection of a changing culture: at this time the nuunamiut were beginning to be attracted to the coast; and economic advantages were being offered by the European whaling companies, such as the Cape Smythe Co., and others. It seems reasonable to assume that this would not have occurred in the aboriginal setting. The name of tigutak is well known at Barrow today in view of his prowess as a whaler.
5. atammaq, younger brother. A child in 1895, this individual later left the group to marry. "He was always getting married and leaving his wives."
6. panigiroaq, older sister.
7. tuxuttaq, her husband.
8. ipaaluq
9. manuluq } Children of panigiroaq and tuxuttaq.
10. aaluq

At one point, therefore, the group consisted of 10 persons, but the older brother left with his wife, and the younger brother appeared only occasionally. Leadership of the family, if such it may be called, but at least the role of principal provider, fell to tuxuttaq, husband of panigiroaq. The reason given for this was that panigiroaq was the oldest of the siblings and since ŋuyaaruq's father was dead, the group was "poor" and required the services of a good hunter. The food quest was thus met by tuxuttaq. This situation lasted for some years, at least until after the birth of aaluq, the last of panigiroaq's children by tuxuttaq. Then the marriage ended in divorce, panigiroaq with her children moving to the coast, while tuxuttaq rejoined the family of his mother, his own father being dead. This marital rift broke the family grouping.

The informant, ŋuyaaruq, married a man from another band and went to live with him and his family. suŋaarak, her mother, accompanied her and stayed with her and her husband for some time, ultimately electing to move to the coast where her son and other daughter were now residing. atammaq ultimately settled at Point Hope and still lives there; the informant has not seen him in many years.

The family situation described here appears fairly typical of the nuunamiut situation of the past, the exception being the general exodus of many of the family members to the coast. In terms of activity and composition while inland, however, it follows the usual nuunamiut pattern. This family unit chose to remain alone for the greater part of the year. When tuxuttaq was its leader and provider, it moved along the central Colville much of the time and was involved a good deal with inland fishing at the established stations. In the spring and sometimes in the fall, they joined others of the group generally known as kaŋgianermiut for the caribou drive. In the winter, they tended to separate from the main grouping, although this depended on how successful the caribou drive had been. If they felt that more food was likely to be needed, they spent the winter at ice fishing along the rivers, while the men went off to hunt caribou individually, the women remaining at the fishing station to tend the nets and freeze the catch. In the spring, they rejoined the other families for the hunt, tuxuttaq being associated with a regular hunting group and having a karigi association. To hunt in this manner, to return to the fishing camps in both summer and winter, required considerable movement. On two occasions while tuxuttaq was still leader of the group they went down the Colville to neγłiq to trade with the tareumiut. This tuxuttaq did not do regularly since he had no established trading partner and was consequently obliged to obtain much of the necessary seal oil by trading with other nuunamiut. In both the spring and fall, the family moved up to the foothills where they rejoined the others.

The periods of the caribou drives were the most active ones for the family. Here the men were engaged in rebuilding the caribou stockades, in stringing lines between the V-shaped posts on which the caribou would entangle their antlers. Here, too, the necessary ceremonial preparations were undertaken; the men engaged in the hunt retiring and making the preparations for the hunt. The impression which is gained is of a gradual meeting of the larger grouping, the individual families straggling into the designated campsite in order to participate in the hunt. When the hunt was over, the women were actively busy with the skinning, with the cutting and drying of meat, and with the many other tasks involved in caring for the catch. The men meanwhile continued to hunt for stragglers when the herds had passed and gave much of their time to the many recreational activities which took place in the karigi. When the spring hunt was over, there was much time for visiting, for gossip, for the arranging of marriages. There was the feast of greeting the caribou, marked by dances, and there was occasionally the elaborate Messenger Feast, invitations being extended from one band to another.

While the pattern of movement of the family in question emerges as one of movement in the central Colville drainage, to the foothills, and occasionally down the Colville to the sea, it is not to be implied that this group was always alone. Sometimes it was, especially during the winter at the fishing station. However, panigiroaq and tuxuttaq had come from the same larger grouping and on several occasions, brothers of tuxuttaq and their families joined them. tuxuttaq's mother remained with them for two summers and then chose to remain with another son since she disliked panigiroaq, a factor which later bore on the latter's separation from tuxuttaq. But even if the family moved alone, there was the general tendency for them to turn up at the same times during the year at the same places. Here they encountered kinsmen and others from their own larger band and might stop with them for several days. If there were caribou in the area, the men of such parties regularly hunted.

The impression is therefore one of a fairly well-defined round in a circumscribed territory. Each family used essentially the same route of travel, being familiar with it and having an extremely clear and detailed conception of the terrain. There was a tendency to avoid land which was less well known and it is this factor which seems paramount in fixing the stability of the groups. But there was the element of choice and it did not follow that the lines of movement were immutably fixed. This meant that the seasonal round of activity was not so well defined for the nuunamiut as it was for the tareumiut whose permanent villages afforded somewhat greater stability.

This family followed the accepted methods of travel since tuxuttaq owned an umiak. The nuunamiut umiak was somewhat larger than the type used by the tareumiut, being covered with from 5 to 6 scraped walrus skins, obtained by trade with the coasts, and as much as 30 feet in length. The usual tareumiut umiak was a smaller craft, covered with 5 to 6 ugruk (bearded seal) skins. The reason for the presence of the larger umiak is evident in that a somewhat greater number of people were obliged to travel in it. A group of 10 persons, such as that described, together with their dogs, a sled, food, clothing, and other gear, needed a large boat for transport along the streams in summer.

In winter, the sled was taken out, the runners frozen—by pouring water over the sled runner and allowing it to freeze—and the umiak mounted on it. Thus—and this was true of virtually all the nuunamiut—if the summer destination were neγłiq, the travel route was by the open stream, the return effected by dog-drawn sled. The greatest problem, and this was ever a source of worry to tuxuttaq, was the shortage of dogs. Always fairly plentiful on the coast, they were harder to raise and train in the inland areas. tuxuttaq never had more than two, and it was a wealthy family that had four. Two dogs were ample to draw a sled with frozen runners on level ground, but the people were obliged to walk, preventing the sled from sliding too fast or from overturning, and helping the dogs up slopes.

In traveling, use was made of a skin tent, the skins being those of the caribou taken in winter, mounted over a frame of willow branches. This differed somewhat from the semipermanent house which was set up at any place where a fairly prolonged stay was proposed. In colder weather, this tent was covered with moss and then with snow. Cooking was done inside the house and there was a smokehole but no skylight. Bedding was arranged around the sides of the tent, often on a banked area, suggesting a benchlike structure. The stone lamp was used with seal oil as fuel. When not in use, the tent was folded up and transported, the willow branches usually being included, especially if they were notched for repeated use. A dozen or so persons could be accommodated in such a tent, which was thus wholly adequate for the average family. There was no use of the ice house by the nuunamiut. They knew of it, as did the tareumiut, and it was the latter which only occasionally employed it.

Turning to another example of nuunamiut group and family composition, a somewhat larger enclave is encountered. This situation can also be roughly dated as 1895.

1. tukumminaroaq, the informant, then an active hunter, but not yet married, aged ca. 17.
2. aaxłuaq, his father
3. ikitkiirak, his mother
4. tiŋuq, younger brother
5. kanayuruq, his youngest brother, then a boy of about 7, who died during the summer of 1896.
6. aakuq, his older sister
7. her husband
8, 9, 10. aakuq's three duaghters, all infants, all of whom died within a short time of each other.

But this did not constitute the whole group. While it is true that these 10 persons shared one tent while on the move and continued to reside together when the semipermanent base was reached at the time of the caribou drives, they customarily traveled and were associated with other relatives. In another tent lived the informant's paternal grandparents; the grandfather also had another wife and four small children by her. A paternal uncle, his wife, and one child made up the remainder of the group in the second tent. This likewise made up a group of 10 persons. These 20 regularly traveled together and made use of 2 umiaks and 6 dogs. They ranged between the coast and the foothills along the Utokak River and may hence be regarded as part of the utokaγmiut.

It was the grandfather who acted as leader for the group. He made the informal decision as to when they should move and where they should go. The informant recalls that one year he wished to remain by the sea, sealing and engaging in caribou hunting on the mainland back of the lagoons to the south of Icy Cape. His fatber, however, wished to return inland for the winter and to wait there for the spring caribou drive. The two households accordingly split up but came together again during the following summer. There was clearly no argument on either side, each being regarded as wholly free to make the decision as to how time should be spent. Because there were several able-bodied men in the two tents, the families were rather well-to-do and were usually well supplied with food. One year, however, they had come up from the coast, joined others with whom they customarily met for caribou hunting, but were unsuccessful in finding caribou. The younger men traveled far afield attempting to locate herds but failed. All winter long, they were short of food and spent the time trapping squirrels, rabbits, and ptarmigan. Several died of starvation, including the nieces of the informant. They were about to move to the coast again when the caribou, for some reason delayed in their movements, were sighted and the hunt went on.

The killik band, the group which continues as the last remnant of the nuunamiut north of the Brooks Range, today offers a picture little different from the foregoing. Even though the trade has disappeared, although many new devices have been introduced, and despite the loss of the older ceremonial patterns, the social composition remains constant. The 60-odd people who make up this unit consist of members of five families, there being much interrelationship in terms of kinship. Today the group remains together pretty much, although when visited by the present writer in 1953, several of the men were off on prolonged expeditions. The more extended residence units have broken down somewhat in that an average of 4 or 5 individuals inhabits each semipermanent house. When, in the fall of 1953, caribou were short, the group moved over to the Chandler Lake region, returning to Anaktuvuk Pass in the late spring of the following year. Several people, however, chose to remain behind at Anaktuvuk Pass during this period.

Examples of the social composition of the inland groups might be extended at length. Sufficient has perhaps been described, however, to demonstrate the type of socioeconomic organization which prevailed. It is evident that the primary functioning unit was the group which chose to remain together because of consanguineal or marital ties. The band, employing the term rather loosely, was not a fixed unit except vaguely, as a sense of common territory might dictate. That kinship cut across territorial lines is demonstrated by an instance such as the following: qiwaq's father was an utokaγmiu, his mother a noataγmiu, that is, from one of the groups along the Noatak River. qiwaq had thus a wide circle of kin on whom he could depend. His mother had come to live in the territory of her husband, with the result that qiwaq could be regarded as of the utokaγmiut. But the father, although he had three sons, felt the group was not sufficiently large to function properly, and adopted a boy from the kaŋgianermiut, thus extending, by implication, qiwaq's circle of kinship claims.

It becomes apparent that on any level beyond the family which moved together as an economic unit, relations could not be regarded as formalized. No family was obliged to attend the caribou drive or to participate in any festival. To be sure, there was the extrakin association of the karigi, involving men not related to each other who hunted together and had evolved a specifically patterned espirit-de-corps. On no level could leadership be said to be fixed. There were clearly no political controls. Men of skill in hunting were in effect men of wealth and might exert considerable informal influence, but again controls rested in the family and were not formalized.

3. THE TAREUMIUT

When a man had been born in one of the villages along the coast, when he counted his kindred as among those in the maritime setting, he was regarded as a seaman. Failing to satisfy these requirements, even if he belonged to a whaling crew and maritime karigi, as might sometimes occur, especially in the last half century, he was still viewed as a nuunamiut (pl. 5, *a*). It is worth noting that the individual may have preferred the inland life and that he may have spent the bulk of his time caribou hunting, but that his backing and cooperative support came only from his kinsfolk at the coast. There were men who were allegedly "afraid of the sea," hazardous and threatening as it was, and who thus preferred to make their living away from it. This attitude even today characterizes many; there is no stigma attached to this fear and a man is free to make his choice of livelihood.

The few maritime villages were never very large, at least, not in the period since the first European contacts. As has been noted, the more remote past was apparently marked by a much larger population and a greater number of active villages. Similarly, there were any number of hamlets scattered along the coasts, quite apart from the population centers, and inhabited by both tareumiut and some nuunamiut. It may be inferred that population expanded and contracted with fluctuations in the food supply. This does not imply that starvation was an omnipresent threat; it apparently was not, although in periods of food shortage there was greater dispersal of the population.

For all of the maritime groups, those from Point Barrow to Point Hope, the seasonal pattern was in essence the same. The whaling season was in the spring, beginning at tikeraaq in early April, and at utkeaaγvik and nuwuk a month later when the whales made their way northward. Through April and into May and sometimes, June, the whaling activities continued. This occupation demanded the time of virtually every member of the community. It was necessary to insure proper ceremonial treatment of the whale, the butchering and storage of meat in the ice cellars, and the maintenance of the numerous social involvements which arose around the whaling. When the whaling was over and the gear cleaned, when the proper social and ceremonial observances had been undergone, there was the summer breakup of the community, analogous to that of the nuunamiut family groups. Here again, the element of choice prevailed, each family or extended kinship unit doing whatever its informal leaders saw fit. Some went inland and hunted caribou, others settled for the summer months at one or another of the fishing camps, still others went to the stations where ducks and geese could be caught. Some men might begin long journeys, undertaking the far trip to Barter Island and to the McKenzie mouth for extended trading. If a whaling crew decided to meet again during the summer for the walrus and ugruk hunting, the men most frequently took their families to a summer station away from the community. Here the women fished, spreading the nets in the streams and carrying on their other domestic tasks, while the men returned to the home community for the walrus hunt. It is not to be implied that the home village was deserted during the summer. Older people usually remained there, as well as young children who were left under grandparental supervision. If a man wished to build an umiak or sled, he might remain in the home village and spend much of the summer working on it.

The walrus movement usually begins in the area with the breakup of the ocean ice in midsummer. The ice is then split into floes which float rapidly northward drawn by winds and currents. Large herds of walrus appear off the coasts of Point Hope by mid-July and may be seen a few days later off Point Barrow. The time of the walrus movement, as is equally true with the appearance of the whales and other migratory animals, is wholly dependent on the action of the ice. If the ice fails to break by August and is still packed in along the beaches and considerable distance out to sea, it is not likely that the walrus season will be a good one. The crews associated with whaling went out together in the summers after the walrus, harpooning them on the floating ice, butchering them at sea on the ice floes, and returning the meat and ivory to the home village. The bearded seal, the ugruk, an animal which does not herd, was harpooned in the course of walrus hunting. Just as taking as many as 15 whales marked a successful whaling season, so also taking 100 or more walrus marked a good summer's catch for each community (pl. 5, *c*).

When the walrus hunting was over, the tareumiut began to make preparations for the trading with the nuunamiut. This might involve a fairly long journey to the Colville delta for the inhabitants of utkeaaγvik and nuwuk, over to the Utokak headwaters and down the Colville or the Noatak for the kuγmiut, or south to Hotham Inlet for the other villages. Trading, an economic endeavor in itself, involved, in the course of the extensive journeys, hunting stops along the way.

With the beginning of the fall, when the first freezes came, most families began to return to the home village, straggling in from whereever they happened to be. The beginning of the winter darkness saw the communities once again with the population stabilized. The late fall was not an actively productive period in terms of economic pursuits. Fish, fowl, and caribou taken during the summer months were stored in the ice cellars along with the whale, ugruk, and walrus from the previous seasons. The population supported itself through the fall and winter with the stored food.

The dark days of winter were largely given over to the various aspects of social and ceremonial activity, with shamanistic seances, and recreational events in the karigis. Hunting was in the main individual and involved sealing at breathing holes on the ice. The hunter spread his nets and returned to them daily to collect the catch. This was often a dangerous undertaking, since the ice might break and the hunter be carried to sea and perish. The search for the breathing holes was frequently time-consuming and involved long walks across the treacherous ice in semidarkness. There are numerous instances of hunters stranded on ice floes, many of whom managed to survive through the winter. Some reached the shores of Siberia, making their way back in the summer, provided they could withstand ill-treatment at the hands of the natives there. A lost hunter was not, at any rate, given up until the following summer, and there were numerous magical means by which his safety could be insured or forms of divination by which it could be determined that he was still alive. The winter seal hunting reaches perhaps the highest degree of specialization in requiring knowledge of the nature of the pack ice and the means of Arctic survival. To go out on the ice under the severest weather conditions imaginable, either for a single day or for several days on end, demanded a high degree of skill, not to mention a highly complex technology. (Rainey, 1947, pp. 235–36; Larsen and Rainey, 1948, p. 27.) Several involved methods for hunting seals along the pack ice were known and employed, ranging from the dangerous occupation of stringing nets through holes under the ice to harpooning at breathing holes when the seals emerged. Methods of decoying the seals were also known and used. Although one might wonder at the attraction of sealing, so hazardous an individual occupation, especially in view of adequate supplies of food obtained in a normal year through spring and summer hunting, it must be noted that seal meat, together with the black skin of the baleen whales, was the preferred food. Moreover, it was considered highly reprehensible for a man to give his entire time to social activity in the winter and to allow the meat in his ice cellar to decrease. Even if the sealing were unsuccessful, a man was expected to continue trying.

During the winter months, polar bear were most frequently encountered on the ice. These animals, often appearing in large numbers, were a source of danger to the hunter, and were themselves hunted (pl. 6, *a*).

If the whaling had been unsuccessful, or if the supply of walrus and caribou fell below the usual seasonal quota, the community might be faced with food shortage in the winter. While this did not happen too frequently, every sixth or seventh year might be marked as a famine year; just as among the nuunamiut, a shift in the routes taken by the caribou could cause severe shortage and privation. Because the diet was exclusively meat, it follows that tremendous quantities were required to support a household through the winter. An adult individual may be expected, even today, in spite of some dietary changes, to eat as much as 7 to 8 pounds of meat per day. In addition, teams of dogs, larger on the coast than in the inland regions, required an equal amount per dog. This would mean that a family of 10, with 8 dogs, would require at least 125 pounds of meat per day.[8] Thus, even though immense supplies of meat were piled up after the whaling and walrus

[8] M. Smith, 1902, p. 116. Smith, who was with the expedition of 1881–83, remarks that one group, made up of several households from Point Barrow (nuwuk), and numbering 30 people, took in a 2½-month period 200 caribou and about 2,000 pounds of fish. When they returned to the community, they had eaten all but 50 caribou and 500 pounds of fish. He estimates the total eaten in this period as 18,500 pounds of meat, or 8¼ pounds per day per man. This is not excessive and in view of the high water content of meat, probably comparable to an average food intake of a person at hard labor in milder latitudes.

hunting especially, and much fish, numerous caribou, as well as waterfowl might be added, the failure of one source of supply could readily mean short rations for the winter. Sealing in the winter thus provided an important secondary source. The fall whaling likewise could be regarded as a secondary source of food supply. When the whales returned at the end of the summer, they were often sighted off Point Barrow and pursued in the open sea. This was, however, an uncertain source of supply and limited to the three northernmost towns.

Through the winter months, while the men engaged in sealing on the ice, the women and children of the communities were active in other areas of food getting. The tomcod (*Boreogadus saida*), a small arctic fish, and one of the few actually taken from the ocean, began to run at Point Hope in January, appearing somewhat later farther to the north. Holes were chopped in the ice and women sat for long periods over them, jigging the fish with snag hooks. If the cod were running well, as many as might fill a bushel basket could be taken in one day. Out of the water, the fish froze at once and were stored and eaten in a frozen state. Although valued as a source of human food, the tomcod were most frequently fed to the dogs. Crabbing in winter was known at Point Hope but not elsewhere along the coast.

By the March equinox, preparations were again under way for the spring whaling, the ice cellars cleaned and made ready for the whale meat, the umiaks covered with new skins, the whaling gear made ready both practically and ceremonially. These preparations, together with the restrictions imposed on members of the various whaling crews, involving activities in the karigis, took up much of the last days of winter. The year might be said to begin again with the launching of the umiaks along the ice leads when the first sign of whales, the presence of the northward-flying snowbirds, was remarked.

From the foregoing summary of the yearly round of activity of the tareumiut, it becomes apparent that the center of daily life, the point from which all economic pursuits began, was the village itself. Common residence, linked with the factor of kinship, served to cement the ties of villagers to each other. But again, the village could not be regarded as a localized kinship grouping; it clearly was not, in that family ties cut across village boundaries in much the same way as was operative among the nuunamiut bands. Marriages occurred both between people of the same village, recognized kinship affording the only barrier to sexual relationships, and between people of different villages. Similarly, the individual was free to exercise choice in the matter of where he resided. A general pattern was to settle where one's kin, either genetic or affined, were the most dependable and where ties of affection developed. A sense of responsibility to one's wife and her kindred might cause a man to settle in the wife's community. Conversely, if a man had parents of younger siblings dependent on him, his wife came to reside in his village. It is to be emphasized that the factor of choice was ever present and no coercion would be exerted on the individual as to where he should reside or where his sphere of activity should lie. Similarly, adoptions took place both within and between villages, widening the kinship circle, but never, so far as is known, did adoptions across the ecological line take place.

Although it may appear that the maritime village was as unformalized as the inland band, there was an integrating factor which was perhaps better developed than among the nuunamiut. This lay in the formalized and established relations between an umealiq, that is, a boat and whaling leader, a so-called boat captain, and his crew. This was a dependent relationship, in that the crew member occupied a social place subordinate to that of the boatowner and leader and was dependent on him for considerable aid, both economic and moral. There was a parallel to this in the nuunamiut situation, where the builder of a stockade, a recognized man of wealth and prowess, tended to direct the hunt and to draw to his leadership the same men year after year. But the nuunamiut lacked the very precise sets of involvements which the tareumiut had developed in respect to the whaling crew. This constellation, with its economic activities, its social relationships, and its ceremonial obligations, was wholly formally conceived. It centered in the ceremonial house, the karigi, existed apart from the kinship tie, thus becoming a primary nonkin association and fundamental in creating an intravillage bond.

The tareumiut family, on the nuclear level, did not differ materially from that described for the inland Eskimo. A house—and as will be seen, houses did differ in arrangement, number of passages and rooms—consisted in the main of a single room in which a closely related group resided. In numbers, this rarely went to more than 10 persons and might frequently be less, consisting at times of only a couple (Ray, 1885 b, p. 38). The head of a household, if such may be designated, was the principal hunter. Although deference was paid to old persons resident in the household, and their wishes consulted, the decisions affecting the yearly round and its course were made by the chief provider. But here again the integrity of the individual was paramount; a coresident member of the household was by no means obliged to undertake any task for which he had no taste, nor would any attempts be made to persuade him to follow the group in any activity.

As among the nuunamiut, family and household composition could change over a period of time. An example or two may suffice to demonstrate this. Thus, when uŋaruk was small, he lived with his parents at utkeaaγvik. In the house were his two brothers and one sister, his father's brother and his wife, a childless couple, and his father's maternal aunt and his maternal grandmother. This made up a household of 10 persons of which uŋaruk's father was chief provider and informal leader. When the father's brother and his wife adopted a child, they left the household and built a house of their own close by. ("The passageways were almost touching each other.") For convenience sake, the father's aunt settled in the new household. uŋaruk's older brother, not yet married, went on a long journey to the east, visiting the mouth of the McKenzie and Herschel Island and was gone for 2 years. When he returned, he moved to Point Hope, where he married and settled. When uŋaruk's grandmother died, the family moved inland for a year, hunting caribou and trading. The sister died on the way. When he, his parents, and his brother returned to utkeaaγvik, they decided not to live in the house which they had previously inhabited. They then decided to move down the coast some distance and so settled at walakpat for several seasons. By this time, uŋaruk was himself old enough to join a whaling crew. He returned to utkeaaγvik, lived with his uncle, and engaged in whaling. When his second brother married, the family, now consisting only of his parents, returned to the home village and also resided with the father's brother. This instance, not at all unusual, reflects the amount of movement even among the tareɪmiut. Although motivations are not wholly clear, as to why, for example, the family declined to return to their abandoned house at utkeaaγvik—it was not a question of family quarrels—both the pattern of movement and the variations in economic pursuits, as well as the changes in household composition, were fairly typical.

Brothers frequently resided together. Provision was generally made for the aged in the household. An old person was free to select the relative with whom he wished to live. This continues to be true at the present time and there are no known instances of an aged relative being denied the right to live where he chose or with whom he wished. Men closely associated in the whaling activity, members of the same crew, might build adjacent houses and share food. But it was always expected that one could reside with relatives and if the claim of relationship could be made, and was generally recognized, demands for food and shelter never went unheeded. There was thus no formal crystallizing of the residence arrangements in villages and in the last analysis, nothing which tied the individual to the community beyond his own choice and desire.

SUMMARY: NUUNAMIUT VS. TAREUMIUT

The attempt has been made in the foregoing to deal with the structural units of the two contrasting aspects of the North Alaskan Eskimo cultures. Granted that the societies are in some measure structurally dependent on the economic round, the units themselves, because of their often ephemeral nature, are not too easily definable. Despite the differences in the food quest, there are certain marked parallels in the social organization. Two basic structural principles emerge in the area. The first lies in kinship, as defined, it will be seen, bilaterally, and the second in patterned voluntary association. These apply in each setting, although the latter becomes somewhat more formalized in the maritime economy. Proceeding from the nuclear family in each case, as making up a functioning economic unit both in the inland setting of the group which travels together and in the village as the household, the aggregate of families makes up the band among the nuunamiut and the village among the tareumiut. In each case, however, the component groupings could and did frequently change. Among the maritime Eskimo, the village became a somewhat more stable unit because of the whaling crews as a factor of social stability and solidarity. The caribou drive of the nuunamiut, while clearly communal, was less demanding of participation by formally associated individuals, although the effect might certainly be the same. Both through the nuunamiut and the tareumiut ran the threads of extended kinship, of genetic, recognized, bilateral relationship, which cut across both band and village lines. In the main, separate and coexistent, the two settings were brought together in formal ways through trading and institutionalized partnerships. This is the structure and the economic setting for it. It remains to determine how the two ecological patterns operated within their respective hemispheres and how each was activated.

PROPERTY, WEALTH, AND STATUS

The North Alaskan Eskimo societies, unlike the groups farther to the east, had a fairly elaborated concept of wealth. In it, influences from the south may perhaps be detected; certainly one of the most elaborated of social occasions among both tareumiut and nuunamiut was the Messenger Feast, a complex series of socioceremonial gift exchanges suggestive of the patterned prestige economy of the North Pacific Coast tribes. Wealth as such provided the basis for social status in the groups in question and must be considered as a prelude to any discussion of the formalized extrakin relationships. The societies were thus structured along the lines of wealth serving to create social distinctions. Property thus became most important and certain formalized usages arose in respect to it. In general, the problem of subsistence could be readily met; indeed, it may be said that the economy of prestige grew out of abundance. The concept of wealth rested primarily in the possession of surplus goods and food and a condition was created whereby the economy of prestige coexisted but was not related to that of subsistence. An examination of the concepts of property and wealth may serve to indicate the ways by which social position and social status of the individual were regulated.

OWNERSHIP

Strictly speaking, the North Alaskan Eskimo lacked a concept of communal property. The house, as has been shown, belonged technically to the builder or to the two family heads who may have cooperated in the building. The concept of real property in any sense was lacking. There was a vague sense of territorial tie, effected by knowledge and experience of the terrain rather than by any sense of rights to it. Usufruct rights to hunting and fishing stations existed, and to a degree this was also true of such property as a dwelling. As has been noted, a house could be sold and often was, but it also could be abandoned and taken over by another person or family. To all practical purposes, a family owned a house jointly. The same was true of the various means of transportation, the sled, the umiak, or the dog team. Members of the family group all had a share in the use of these items, and participated in their manufacture or maintenance. Theoretically, a family head could dispose of his house or any of the means of travel without consulting the other members of the group. That he would do so was most unlikely. Simply on the basis of sharing and use, therefore, the family could be conceived to hold certain kinds of property in common.

As far as a community, whether inland or maritime, went with respect to communalized property, only the ceremonial houses might be regarded as falling into this category. It is true that karigi associations were extrafamilial and that in this sense, the karigi itself became the property of the group which used it. This is worth noting in view of the fact that various unrelated individuals might contribute skins, logs, whalebone, or other construction materials to the erection of a karigi and thus they had an individual share in it. In the nomadic groups, this was more likely the case. Among the tareumiut, however, especially where there were several karigis in the village, they were the possession, in effect, of the whaling crews which met in them, and their maintenance was somewhat individualized in that the crew leaders, as men of wealth and standing in the community, were expected to maintain them. All crew members who used the individual karigi were expected to share in building, cleaning, and repairing the structure. A karigi frequently maintained an umiivik, a shed where the whaling umiaks were stored and repaired, where the new skins were put on prior to the spring whaling. Anyone in the community could do his work there and use the shedlike structure if he wished. Technically, however, the umiivik was the property of the whaling captains of the karigi which maintained it. It is thus clear that any concept of joint holdings was vaguely invested in the family and household and that the concept of community property had not been developed. When individual property is considered, however, a different situation arises.

Personal property was well defined as to age, sex, and social position. Things which fell into the category of individual property, such as clothing, tools, weapons, charms, and songs, were inviolable. An umiak, sled, or house could be used by family members resident together. A kayak, however, was individual property and could not be used by another, even a coresident family member, unless permission to do so were forthcoming from the owner. Lending of personal property was common, the more so since no one wished to appear miserly, but permission had always to be sought.

In the realm of personal property, things which belonged to men were sharply differentiated from those which belonged to women. Game, for example, belonged to the hunter who took it and he was free to dispose of it as he saw fit. The patterns of generosity which were imposed on the individual might mean that he gave away much of the game he had taken, a point particularly true in winter, when individual hunting of seals was the usual occupation. In such cases, meat was given to all who asked for it. But once the hunter had taken the game into the house, or once it was butchered and stored in the cache or ice cellar, it became the property of the woman of the household—that is, of the wife of the hunter, or if he had several, of the chief wife. The woman then had the rights to dispose of the meat as she saw fit. This point is of some importance in strengthening an otherwise ephemeral marriage bond.

Men and women owned their respective clothing, tools, and weapons. Women made and sewed clothing, men made tools, weapons, and utensils, except pottery. A wife made her husband's clothing at his request, while she in turn could ask that he make tools for her. When an item was once made and given, it could never be taken back without the owner's consent. No man, for example, could sell his wife's possessions without her consent. If he went trading without her, she often gave him items to trade and stated the goods she wanted in return. These were always hers and the husband had no rights over them. In case of a marital dispute, a husband might maul and pummel his wife, tearing her clothes and bedding, but not in any way damaging her other property. This is an example of a general pattern of behavior in disputes, the point being that an offended person made attacks on the property of another.

While the lines of ownership were fairly well defined as between the sexes, women could inherit property which fell into the domain of men. At a man's death, for example, the widow continued to hold the house unless she were dispossessed by the husband's kin. Similarly, a widow might fall heir to her husband's kayak, weapons, clothing, and other possessions. If the family owned an umiak, this, too, she might keep and hold in trust for children not yet grown. She might keep such items for trade or hold them against paying a shaman for his services; since an umiak was the customary shaman's fee for a successful cure, a widow might hold a craft against this. Again, however, a widow might be obliged to stave off her husband's relatives in her attempts to keep his property for her own or occasionally for her children's use. The support of her own family might be sufficient to do this. The most usual way out was for her to marry again; if she held property, she was a desirable catch, her industry and efficiency having been proved by the fact that her deceased husband had property to leave. There was hence no prescribed period of mourning nor any restrictions on the age of a woman at marriage.

Sexual rights were property rights in some measure. A prescribed way of cementing certain kinds of social relationships was through wife exchange on a temporary basis. But, in addition, when a man had been cured by a shaman, he might permit the practitioner to have sexual relations with his wife. If the shaman was pleased with the woman, he might desire to keep her. Indeed, by blackmail and threat he might force a husband into relinquishing her. In such cases, the woman was given to the shaman in lieu of other payment.

Possessions were loaned quite freely. Relatives often borrowed from each other, as did close neighbors, and crew mates. Tools and containers were the items most frequently borrowed, particularly the pottery vessels which some women specialized in making. When a person wished to borrow an item from another, he went over to his house and called into the skylight for the desired object. No repayment was involved when the borrowed item was returned.

Important movable possessions were designated by a property mark. These were variable from individual to individual and were not inherited. A man drew up his own mark. There is a suggestion that certain basic patterns of property marks were reflected in family lines (Boas, 1899). The marks were simple designs, made for the most part with three, four, or five strokes. The more elaborated designs described for the Eskimo living farther to the south in Alaska do not appear among the northern peoples (Lantis, 1946, p. 242). Hence, the marks were in no sense decorative or demanding of artistry. The individual worked out his own mark when he felt that he had sufficient possessions to justify it. If a man used the mark V, his son might vary the pattern and employ a combination VI. Marks died out with the individual but could reappear in the same family, just as names might; but there is no evidence of a supernatural tie between the living and the dead with respect to property marks.

Property marks were known as nalunaytak. Some examples of their development at utkeaaγvik are as follows:

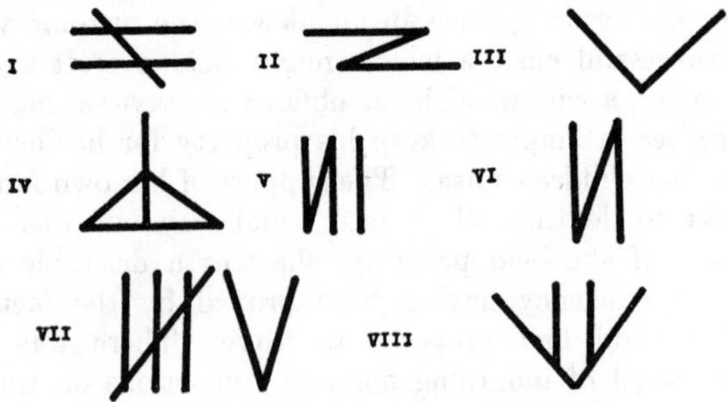

Property marks are still used widely by the peoples of the area. The coastal Eskimo place them on whale bombs and thus succeed in avoiding any dispute as to the crew which took a whale. If several crews succeed in bombing the whale, joint ownership is established and division accordingly made. The marks are also made on other gear—rifles, traps, sleds, and the like. The modern marks have taken on some new features, letters and initials sometimes being used. A recently developed mark is seen in the following:

IX 

In the past, property marks were put on arrows, lances, any gear relating to hunting or trapping, on canoe paddles, or the like. It is said that marks were not put on umiaks or kayaks since these were readily identifiable. The primary function of the mark was to differentiate game taken by different hunters. In the whaling of the past, where several umiaks might converge on the whale, division was regulated as to the owners of the harpoons identified by mark. Similarly in walrus hunting, sealing, and in individual and group caribou hunting by stalking, it was important to identify the owner of the meat taken. In cases of murder, the recognizable weapon was of course a clue to the killer. When a murder occurred, all present assembled and examined the murder weapon, if on hand, for the telltale mark.

Apart from the formal property marks, however, there were ways of indicating ownership of objects which might be found or discovered. A dead seal found on a beach, for example, could belong to the first finder if he chose to claim it. He had merely to erect a small cairn of stones on or near the head of the animal. Anyone who came after would respect the claim and not touch the carcass. The rules applicable to umeaktuat, that is, communal hunting and communal game, were in force in respect to naturally dead animals. Any animal whose carcass was washed up on the beach was treated as though it had been taken in hunting. Thus no individual claim could be made on a dead or stranded whale, walrus, or ugruk. Seals, caribou, and other game not hunted communally belonged to the finder.

WEALTH

The aboriginal culture of both the nomadic and maritime groups permitted no elaboration of social classes. As is evident, the family was the primary source of social control. Extrakin associations were those which were formalized and structured along the lines of partnership, crew memberships, and karigi participation. As has been noted, the nuclear family tended to carry on its economic activities as a unit, often varying its work in relation to the seasonal round as it chose, settling inland or on the sea as the family head decided. A result of this trend was to preclude any development of elaborated political controls and to place the community as a most ephemeral kind of organization. But if social classes were not elaborated, there was at least some sense of them arising out of a wealth-poverty dichotomy. In certain well defined areas, men of wealth emerge as significant leaders. In the maritime communities, the position of wealthy men, related as it was to whaling, was somewhat better defined than among the inland peoples.

A man of wealth was an umealiq, the technical meaning of which is "boatowner", but not all owners of umiaks were umealit (pl.). In both ecological settings, the umealiq held a position of both social and ceremonial importance. On the coasts, he was the head of a whaling crew, he carried on the ceremonials relating to the success in whaling, and, by virtue of his wealth, he extended material support to the men who had joined his banner as crew members. Anyone might own an umiak, but unless he was able to command the respect and loyalty of others who would join him as helpers, and to support them with gifts during the off seasons, he could not be regarded as belonging to this social category. Similarly, among the nuunamiut, the umealiq was the director of the caribou drive and again, by virtue of his wealth, the one to initiate the rituals connected with it. In either setting he was a man to be respected and in relation to the hunt, at least, obeyed. On the coast the umealiq had great prestige in any community but his actual sphere of influence extended only to the men who formally cast their lot in with his. In this sense, he was not a chief or political leader. To a degree, the same was true in the inland setting. And, as may be seen, the position of the umealiq depended wholly on wealth; his prestige arose on the basis of the goods he was able to control.

It is thus evident that the concept of wealth arose in respect to possession of surplus goods. Anyone who was able to command an abundance of surplus goods was eligible to undertake the enlisting of a crew and thereby qualify for the social rank of umealiq. This was never easy, since the goods and surplus involved would demand considerably more than the abilities and skills of any one person could supply. A man might inherit sufficient property to enable him to carry on crew leadership and have the backing of his relatives. When a man had shown considerable skill as a hunter and when he had proved his abilities, his relatives, however remote, might then back him, and the kinship group might then work together in order to amass sufficient goods to permit his assumption of the role of umealiq. In the interior as well as on the coast, a man attracted others to himself and his leadership by proof of skill and ability. Among the nuunamiut, the families would return for the caribou drive to a familiar locality and the same umealiq, the leader who placed the stockade and who, by virtue of his openhandedness, could encourage the same people to return. A family that was not satisfied with the local leader simply went elsewhere. On the coast, an aspiring umealiq was obliged to bid for the services of skilled hunters, persuading them to leave another umealiq and offering them sufficient food and goods to do so. Once a leader had a crew and once he had taken a whale or two, his success was insured.

It is to be emphasized that such social standing was reserved for very few; it might take years of building toward sufficient property to command the services of a crew and one lean year could ruin a good start. The coastal umealiq was thus faced with a gamble. He could support a crew with gifts of objects and food for a season and then find that the whaling was unsuccessful. His status would then be reduced to that of an ordinary hunter and family head; no one would judge him of less social worth, but prestige and the semisacerdotal role of the umealiq would no longer be his. There were, moreover, checks on the building of a surplus. Generosity was a primary virtue and no man could risk a miserly reputation. Thus anyone in the community, whether inland or coastal, could ask aid from a man of wealth and it was never refused. This might mean that the men of wealth would be obliged to support an entire group in times of stress. Here, too, aid was extended to nonkin. The result was to create a bond of community feeling. This was informal, it is true, but there was some sense of the community, be it band or village, being united through the presence of men of wealth.

So much of the folklore of the region deals with the theme of the poor. It is evident from the tales that poverty is considered to stem from the absence of family ties. Indeed, the term for "orphan" (iil^{y}epuk, iil^{y}epaaruk, iil^{y}aaruk) is employed to designate the "poor" person in the sense of lack of wealth. A favorite hero theme in folklore is that of the orphan who makes good either with supernatural aid or through his own prodigious efforts and ends up as a successful umealiq. Those who had a circle of relatives, an established place in crew and karigi, were never regarded as "poor." If there was a man of wealth in the extended circle of relationship, all his relatives stood to benefit through him and extended to him their support and allegiance. One pertinent example of this is seen in the Messenger Feast, where, as in the potlatch situation of the North Pacific Coast, the men who acted as principal hosts depended on the support and backing of their kin in assembling the property to be bestowed on guests.

It is clear that the man who was skilled in all types of hunting would best qualify as an umealiq. His success was proof of his abilities and called forth the allegiance of those less proficient. In addition, there were certain personal qualities which were required of an umealiq. He had to be able to command respect and show abilities as a leader. He had, moreover, to be a shrewd trader and a skillful bargainer, taking advantage of his position so as to increase his wealth. Conversely, he had to be generous and was obliged to avoid any appearance of envy toward others, the temptation toward the latter being sometimes strong, especially when crew members were wooed away by a rival or when another umealiq organized an outstanding Messenger Feast. In his own circle of relationship, the umealiq could be a bully, and apparently often was, badgering his kin to be more cooperative and productive. Since it was to the advantage of the individual to assist his wealthy relative in his aspirations and in the maintenance of his status, he generally tried to agree to any demands. The star of the individual rose with that of his umealiq kinsman.

There is some suggestion of the beginnings of rank as between men of wealth. In the Messenger Feast, for example, the umealit were seated in order depending on prestige and following. There was, however, no associated list of titles and apparently no other elaborated form or protocol. It is conceivable that the concept of ranking based on wealth was in its incipient phases at the time of contact with Europeans by the North Alaskan peoples.

It is evident that there was a certain amount of anxiety associated with wealth. This was perhaps not yet too strong but it is apparent that it was present. A wealthy man feared the envy of the shamans and the evil which they could unleash. Actually, however, the threat of the envious shaman had an effect which militated against the growth of social gradations. No person could thrust himself forward in any activity so as to appear overly skillful. A hunter who took too much of any game, the man who excelled in running or wrestling, was advised to tone his successes down so as not to become the target of malevolent shaman power. Thus the man of wealth never boasted of his success; he was modest, generous, and expected to show dignity and serenity. He was not obliged to conceal his wealth, but at the same time he could not make undue display of it. It was of course there for all to see. The beads which decorated his clothing, his labrets and headband, his personal possessions, such as might be seen in his storage places, ice cellars, caches, or racks, all testified to his affluence. The great umealiq, taakpuq, who lived at utkeaaγvik a half century ago, offers an example of the behavior of a man of wealth. He wore parkas of beautifully matched skins, his labrets were the most expensive, and he wore a headband of green and white beads. The many whales he had taken were indicated by the tattoo marks on his cheeks. He is said to have walked slowly and with great dignity, speaking seldom and then in a measured way, and he was noted for his extreme generosity. He never boasted of his successes, and he sat silently in the karigi while others played games and made sport. His was an ideal character, recalled by all who knew or had seen him. It is said that he could enlist the services of any man in the community.

Wealth thus contrasted with poverty, and, as noted, the person who lacked adequate kin support was regarded as "poor." The same category extended to families where there was inadequate support. Every kinship grouping had its quota of poor relations, families where the head was a bad provider, lazy, or in other ways dependent on his wider circle of relationship and on handouts from successful hunters. It is worth noting, however, that such families did not in the main hold together for very long. A wife would leave a husband who was always unsuccessful in his hunting, and she might send the children away to her own relatives to be raised. The only acceptable activity for men was hunting and it followed that there were men who failed to measure up to the standard and who refused to hunt. Some of these became specialists, manufacturing sleds, umiaks, and other items for trade. This, however, offered an insecure livelihood and the nuclear family with which such a man was involved was regarded as "poor." There are one or two suggestions of sexual deviants in respect to resistance to hunting, and mention is made of several individuals who refused both to hunt and to marry. The aboriginal culture was not receptive to homosexual behavior. In general, the problem did not arise and there was no institutionalized transvestitism. Any one who inclined in such a direction and thus became an economic burden to relatives or spouse was "poor." Even here, however, real poverty, as defined by the culture, implied having no circle of kin on which to depend.

Both the nuunamiut and tareumiut had a patterned method of assisting those who lacked kinship ties in the community. It can readily be understood that the death of a provider, the departure of relatives from the group, or other circumstances could leave a nuclear family in difficult straits. Without kin, there was technically no source of support. Such families, it is true, could ask men of wealth for aid and did so, but it is evident, in view of the emphasis on self-reliance and integrity, that it was painful to do so continually. The community sometimes during the winter held a marelaktutiruat, a social dance at which gifts were given to the poor. These were held in the karigi. Those who had gifts to give to the less fortunate members of the community danced and wound up their dancing with a gift to a selected poor person. These gifts were usually of clothing, tools, and weapons, food being given less formally. This relieved the necessity for begging and could assist a growing boy who lacked the support of male kin in starting a career as a hunter. This solution to the problem of aiding the less fortunate was not regarded as offering charity, and the gifts could be taken without censure for laziness or lack of skill.

Wealth was conceived to exist in expendable surplus of any and all goods. This meant extra food, a full cellar, extra clothing, skins and furs of all kinds, pokes of oil, weapons, utensils, tools, boats, sleds, dogs, and the like. In the 19th century, tobacco and trade beads came to be regarded as wealth and indeed served to create a virtual medium of exchange. The bead particularly, some of which were of Russian, others of English and American manufacture, came to be a kind of monetary unit. Beads were of two main types. There was the more common blue glass bead which was called suŋaaraveak. These were of less value than the beads of green or blue glass, larger than the first and with a white marking in the center. The latter were il^{y}uunminik. The plain blue beads came in assorted sizes and were usually strung on sinew and sewn on clothing or placed on headbands. As a reflection of the value which was placed on such beads in the period in which they first appeared, it can be said that one small blue bead was equal in worth to a single wolverine or wolf skin; skins sufficient for a parka, that is, 5 matched skins, for 4 or 5 blue beads. Similarly, a poke of oil was worth one such bead. But the il^{y}uunminit were worth considerably more. While they might be worn on clothing or headband, the tendency was usually to fasten them to the labrets. An indentation was made into the ivory or bone labret and the bead glued in with seal blood, the most practical adhesive. A pair of such labrets, each containing a bead, was worth an umiak, and, indeed, the umiak was regarded as the most valuable single piece of property.

Since the value of the beads became fixed, it appears that they began to take on value as money. The original beads may have reached both coast and inland from the Hotham Inlet trading, coming up from the south with tobacco and metal vessels. John Simpson mentions the presence of tobacco, beads, flint and steel, as well as metal vessels, well integrated into the nuwuk culture of 1853 (Simpson, 1855, p. 235 passim.), and tobacco was noted by Thomas Simpson (1843) in 1837. It thus appears that all such items had reached northern Alaska before the initial contact with Europeans, probably by the late 18th century. The commercial whalers later brought similar beads for trade with the result that their value inflated and they became commonplace.

The northern peoples began to develop a number of legends relating to the beads and their origin. The general belief at present is that the commoner blue bead came from the south but that those of greater value came across the Arctic coast from Greenland. While archeology might substantiate the latter claim, it is also apparent that such a tale as the following, which proposes an indigenous origin for beads, still gains much popular acceptance.

A young man was walking on the sands of a beach. He saw a hole in the ground and walked down into it. It was never light there, it was dark always. As he walked there, he felt his feet go over some round, pebblelike things. He knelt down in the darkness and felt the round stones with little holes in them. He picked up as many as his bag could hold. It was very heavy. Then he began to walk back. When he returned home, he found that he had been gone for several years and that his parents were now very old. At home, he put his bag down and told where he had been. His mother tried to lift the bag but it was too heavy. Then she opened it and saw all the beads that the young man had collected. The parents said, "This is from a far place and it must be worth a great deal." Then they began trading the beads to the people and were never in want again.

Any person, man or woman, might own beads. They were traded back and forth and a person might work diligently toward the amassing of some. All that he collected were carefully strung on sinew. A general tendency was to make a headband of white sealskin. The goal was to collect sufficient beads as to make a single strand which would circle the head. But only a man of great wealth could hope to own the green and white beads. It is worth noting that strangers to a community, always suspect, and sometimes subjected to various indignities by the residents there, were treated considerably better if they came to the group with fine clothes and beads. Only a man with definite kinship support could hope to show off finery, and there would be hesitation to treat roughly a man of obvious affluence.

It becomes clear that there was a rising preoccupation with wealth and that such social ranking as did exist in the society was in large measure based on wealth. While the umealit might emerge as the important figures in the nomadic or maritime communities, distinctions between people of lesser rank were not well defined. There were the few indigent or unfortunate individuals who could not count on kinship ties for support and who thus made up a class of the poor. But it is also apparent that not everyone aspired to the status of umealiq. This was a position of great responsibility and could be, for some, at least, too demanding. Indeed, it might be more advantageous for a man to join a captain, participate in crew activities, and avoid assuming rank and leadership. By sharing in the products of crew endeavor and by adroit trading, not to mention successful hunting, it was also possible to become quite wealthy. Thus, a man could be regarded as having prestige through wealth even though he was not officially a group leader. Such a man could participate in such economic festivals as the Messenger Feast. It is clear that social standing rested with those who hunted, were successful at it, and had the backing of their kin, and who in turn backed them in the amassing of surplus, the basis of the prestige economy.

But if the lines of social status were vague for men, the lines for women were even less sharply drawn. To a degree, the women found the same kind of status as did their husbands. A wife of an umealiq had with him certain ceremonial functions in respect to whale and caribou hunting. On the coast, it was the wife of the umealiq who offered the fresh water to the whale's snout and voiced the proper words of greeting of the game. A woman who was widowed, who lacked the support of her own or her husband's kin in the community, was regarded as poor. Industry was a primary virtue for women as well as for men; censure lay not so much in failure as in idleness.

COMPETITION AND COOPERATION

Although it may be evident from the foregoing discussion that the Eskimo societies of Northern Alaska possessed both competitive and strongly cooperative aspects, it may be well to risk repetition by pointing up the areas in which each type of behavior was acceptable. In general, one cannot view the culture as basically competitive. There were, it is true, certain situations which called forth competitive attitudes and actions but these are in the main eclipsed by the infinitely stronger demands for cooperative activity.

Competition and the competitive sense arose both between communities and between individuals. There was some feeling for community loyalty and some sense of rivalry between villages or local groupings. This is borne out in the past by the Messenger Feast, an event which was intervillage on the coast, or between nomadic groupings in the interior. In this festival, it is true, the rivalry was conceptually between individuals but the community took a part, assisting the principals, and engaging in the foot races and in the ball game. It was borne out further in the competition over possession of the karigi at the Messenger Feast, the first use of it being accorded to the team which won the foot race. This festival thus involved a competitive situation between groupings in both ecological settings and might also place maritime village against nomadic band on the same basis. When people representing different communities met, the custom was to praise one's home community and to disparage that of another. But although the sense of local loyalty might be fairly well developed, any number of other considerations—family ties, food shortages, new opportunities—caused people to pull up roots and settle elsewhere. Crew and karigi membership, moreover, were demanding of a sense of loyalty far stronger than that arising around mere community awareness. Thus, except for the Messenger Feast, there was scarcely any formal competition between bands and villages.

Within the grouping itself, particularly if there were more than one karigi, a sense of competition arose. This applied especially to the inter-karigi games, such as kick ball, and to the invitations which one karigi extended to another. But while one could boast of one's town or community, no individual would praise his own karigi at the expense of another's. In the main, more attention was given to competition between individuals than between groups. In each karigi on the coast there were several umealit, each commanding the loyalties of a crew. Between such crews, however, there was never a sense of rivalry or competition in whaling. True, the individual umealiq might be furious when a rival captain was more successful than he but in no case could he afford to let his annoyance be seen. On the contrary, he would incline to be more lavish in his praises of his rival's success. In another setting, however, when whaling was past, he might sing insult songs at this rival. This, however, gave rise to a spirit of banter and joking and by no means reaches the same intense proportions as it does among Eskimo farther to the east. In the karigi the separate crews did not vie with each other in games or contests. This was always an individual matter and competition in such things as tests of strength arose as much between crew members in the same boat as between men of different crews.

As between individuals, competition and rivalry were thus fairly well defined and arose under the following circumstances:

1. In the formalized Messenger Feast, where one man tried to outdo the other in the lavishness of his gifts and to establish an individual reputation for great wealth.

2. In sports and games, such as wrestling, in foot racing, tests of strength, singing, story telling, in the kick-ball game, where men vied individually, despite team play, for possession of the ball, and the like. Opportunities for such competitive behavior arose principally in winter when the karigi was open and when the men of the community passed some of their time there at leisure. Men would compete with one another, too, in inventing new games for play in the karigi.

3. In economic pursuits which were individually carried on. Men in winter, for example, would wager as to which one would take the greater number of seals. Economic rivalry between individuals also applied to mastery of various technical skills, one man trying to excel another in the making of an object.

Such competitive behavior had always to be good natured. If a person became angry or showed his spite, others would withdraw and make every effort to avoid carrying on an argument. It may be noted here that this was and is standard behavior relating to tense and unpleasant situations. To do nothing, to withdraw, to stay out of any argument are points reflective of "honesty," and point up the behavioral ideal. Argumentative and quarrelsome persons were ignored. If there were boasting, it was always tinged with good humor; self depreciation actually became a standard form of boasting. In a trading situation, a person who drove too hard a bargain, who acquired the reputation for too forcefully demanding his way, might have difficulty in continuing his trading contacts. People were not free with advice, coming with it only if it were requested. The culture had some difficulty in setting up a role of peacemaker, since it was a task from which all would steer clear if tempers had flared and arguments were in progress. Indeed, the native cultures lacked any mechanism for halting a dispute. The blood feud is a case in point. While people were very careful not to embark on a feud and would do so only with the greatest provocation, the feud, once begun, could not be checked except by the participants themselves. The society at large played no part in them. The emphasis lay on the integrity of the individual, on his freedom of choice, and no attempts would be made even from within his immediate kinship circle to halt an action on which he was determined.

Because there were so few formal checks on the individual, public opinion being perhaps the primary factor in promoting the behavioral ideals, there were those who took advantage of the good will and reluctance of others to take a forceful stand. The bully was not uncommon, the individual who would simply force his way by sheer strength or lung power. One of the ways in which such aggressive behavior could be expressed lay in sexual situations. The seizing of women, the kidnaping of other men's wives, sexual rapacity in general were ways by which an individual could assert himself and so establish a reluctantly accepted role. It is of interest that sexual competition between men afforded a means of achieving status. The end was not so much sexuality as social position. If a person's behavior became too violent and too disruptive of public welfare action was taken. It then became a matter for family groupings in reaching a decision as to how the matter should be handled. If an aggressive individual were killed, his own kin became embroiled and the legal mechanism of the feud was put into motion. On the other hand, if the actions of the individual had become too violent, even his own kin might refrain from exacting vengeance for his murder, even though custom demanded that they make a token display of force. Much of the patterned behavior which may be interpreted in terms of the legal system arose through such instances.

Apart from the special behavioral circumstance noted above, several checks, on competitive actions existed. The most prominent was the anxiety which arose with respect to the shaman. The shaman, it is said, would take action against the man who always won in the foot race. He "hated the hunter who was always good." A man of wealth was obliged to exercise care lest he offend the shamans. In fact, when a man was in any way more successful than others, his relatives would urge him to be careful, to avoid a constant repetition of success, lest the shamans "hate" him. And, in theory, the shaman brought disease to the man who was overly successful in any activity.

Whether the shaman lived up to his ascribed role and actually did feel envy toward the signally successful is of course debatable. It is clear that the shamans would occasionally blackmail a man and threaten him with crippling disease. The point of importance is that the culture made use of the shaman's role as a threat to effect essentially uniform behavior. It was the concept of uniformity which emerged as significant; a man who was always successful in his efforts was not popular. This attitude was instilled in the child as part of the socialization process. The child was expected to be diligent and industrious but not necessarily to excel over his fellows. Indeed, if he did always succeed in excelling, or if he so much as commented on his own abilities or efforts, his parents or relatives regularly said, "What's the matter with you? Are you trying to put your head above everybody else's?"

The result of such indoctrination and public opinion was that competitive situations were minimized. The man who did emerge as a great success in the acquisition of wealth through hunting and crew support, a man such as the famous whaler, taakpuq, compensated for his preeminence by silence, modesty, and particularly, by generosity, always being careful to avoid giving or taking offense. But such was prescribed behavior for everyone.

But it was in forms of cooperation that many of the social forms of North Alaskan Eskimo society were structured. Such cooperative activity, that of hunting together, working together, was inherent in the nuclear family at the first level but extended to the wider kinship circle. It was this bilateral grouping which backed the individual in all situations. The man who was "poor," it will be recalled, was the man without this kinship circle. While every attempt was made to keep the kinship tie to the fore, there were always those social situations where the extended family could not effectively function. The community, for example, owing its existence to patterned economic activities, and lacking any kind of political organization, could continue to exist only by common cooperative agreement. The question arises as to the nature of cooperation and its patterning in nonkin situations. A primary way of handling cooperative activity was to extend to nonrelatives behavior patterns which in essence were the same as those applied to family members. In other words, it became essential to involve nonrelatives into a circle of defined cooperative relationships and so to increase the benefits which were basically those of family membership. This was done in several ways: by adoption, by the recognition of ties arising through quondam sexual relationships, by sexual relationships themselves, as in formalized wife exchanges, by partnerships, by joking partnerships, and by the formal crew and karigi associations. Each of these institutions had the effect of creating close cooperative ties.

But these forms of cooperation, except crew and karigi, were largely conceived by the individual and arranged by him. They had little to do with the community as such, since the ties so formed cut across the lines of community within the two ecological settings and between them throughout the area at large. The community, whether village or band, possessed only an ephemeral solidarity. People settled where the opportunities seemed best, either where there were other relatives or where hunting seemed most favorable. Thus the primary nonkin tie to the community was the cooperative hunting activity. And this, it is evident, inspired loyalty to the crew and karigi first and to the community second. It was an allegiance to an umealiq which provided the motivation to become associated either with a whaling crew or a caribou compound. In a hunting group, whether whaling crew or men associated in the caribou drive, the members cooperated not because of their kinship affiliations but rather because of their skills. Through leadership, centered in the man of wealth, the umealiq, and through common purpose, they developed a strong esprit-de-corps. Not only did such a hunting group cooperate in the hunt itself, each man taking his proper place and performing the task for which he was best qualified, but there was agreement on social and ceremonial activities in which a crew engaged, and on the economic side there was agreement as to how the products of the chase should be divided so that each participant received his due share.

It was in this form of cooperation, division of game, that the profit of crew participation lay. Not only were the hunters allied with a hunting group supported with bribes and gifts from the umealiq, but they stood to build up their own surplus stores of meat by working together and ordering their activity. A formal method of division of game existed. This was known as umeaktuat. The term refers to the concerted activity of a crew working together in an umiak and going out together for the taking of game which could be divided. Game thus fell into two categories: there was the game which was hunted individually and not shared; secondly, there was the game which, communally hunted, was umeaktuat. Actually, the patterns of division still apply at the present time and remain as an important factor in community cohesion. Individually hunted game involved all small animals, seals, birds, fish, and any animals which were trapped. It also included caribou if these were individually hunted, but not caribou hunted by the impound method. Polar bear, mountain sheep, and such rare animals as the occasional porpoise were also regarded as individually hunted game. The hunting involving concerted cooperative activity, that is, umeaktuat, concerned whales, walrus, ugruk, and belugas in the maritime setting, and caribou hunted by an organized group on land.

In such communal hunting, the division of game was equal among the participants. There was also a share made up for the boat, or in the case of caribou, for the stockade itself, both of which reverted to the owner, to the whaling umealiq or to the umealiq who organized the building of a stockade. At the present time, such shares compensate the boatowner for his expenditures of gasoline and for the food which he provides to the crew members who accompany the expedition. In the past, too, this extra share was in some measure a repayment to the umealiq for the amounts he had paid out during the year in gifts and bribes to crew members to insure their continued presence and support. The boatowner also received the heads of walrus with the ivory and was given special parts of the whale, although in this instance, the captain's share had certain ceremonial implications. The umealiq's share, whether of whale or caribou, depending on ecological setting, was also used to feed the community at the feast at the end of the hunting season. It is the latter point which served to effect some further sense of community solidarity, although it was the division between crew members which created an incentive to participate and called forth primary loyalties.

Sufficient has already been described regarding the demand for generosity on the part of any successful hunter. The boatowner was particularly subject to this demand and gave freely of his catch to all who asked some of him. Stinginess was abhorred, as was greediness, and the ideal of generosity was inculcated in the growing youth. When a hunter in winter took seals on the ice, he dragged his catch home. As soon as he had laid his quarry down by the side of his house, anyone in the group could ask for some of it. Similarly, among the nuunamiut, a caribou taken by a hunter, when butchered, was often divided among those who requested some of the meat. People came with wooden pans and asked for small portions, specifying what they wanted. In times of food shortage, it was the successful hunter and his family who might go hungry, since in his generosity he gave away whatever he had at hand. There were those indigent and lazy people who took advantage of this situation and always begged meat. One family is recalled which always asked for meat from the returning hunter and went so far as to store it, a shameful situation, since self-respect demanded that one ask for no more than was immediately needed. When this was discovered—it was an instance which took place at utkeaaγvik some years ago and which is still recalled—as might be predicted, the hunters continued to give food to this family. It is said that if this were to happen today, the leaders in the churches would attempt to appeal to such a family. Formerly, however, there was no way of stopping such flagrant begging except to turn the weight of public opinion against the beggar.

In summary, forms of cooperation in the various communities, apart from the patterned ways of extending kinship situations to nonrelatives, arose principally in respect to hunting practices surrounding crew and karigi activity. The karigi, with its component crews, became a center of mens' work and a focus of nonkin group solidarity. Beyond the umealit, there were no men who could be said to hold public office, and even the boatowners could scarcely be regarded as chiefs. If there were men of age and proven skill in the community, their advice might be heeded, but, again, their abilities to control were wholly informal. Community solidarity, whether among nuunamiut or tareumiut, depended in the main on the cooperative patterns which have been described. Such cooperation, moreover, extended far beyond the limits of the community in many directions.

VOLUNTARY ASSOCIATIONS

One of the more striking aspects of North Alaskan Eskimo life is the emphasis which is accorded genetic relationships. A "poor" man was one who lacked kin and a "stranger" was one who was unable to establish kinship ties in a community to which he happened to come. The question as to how far one may carry the concept of kinship permits no immediate answer in that this was a matter which each nuclear family chose to decide for itself. There was clearly no sense for genealogy: the kinship terminologies did not extend beyond the third lineal ascendant generation and the names of the dead which continually recurred in a family were those held by recently deceased relatives. The kinship situation, although bilateral, had to be practically resolved and resulted in a situation whereby the individual ascribed his loyalties to those with whom he was in closest contact, whether on the maternal or paternal side, or, as the case might be, on both. This does not in any way minimize the widespread sense of relationship; when brothers split apart, choosing different areas in which to live, the fraternal tie continued and the demands of collective responsibility remained incumbent on each. A man likewise retained a close sense of kinship with the offspring of his brother or sister even if these happened to reside in a remote area. But after this, as one moves farther afield among the various collateral relationships, the sense of bond became less well defined. It was a matter of choice for the individual family; in the remoter instances the kinship bond became eclipsed by quasi-kin associations, a situation which prompted the extension of kinship attitudes and behavior toward those who were not genetically related. Certain examples of this tendency have already been demonstrated in the adoptive and qataŋutigiit situations, patterns which served to augment the nuclear family and to extend the means of cooperative dependency to nonkin.

The groups of people in the North Alaskan area moved, as has been seen, over large sections of territory. They were, moreover, free to settle where they chose and to make associations where they chose. Because of the two different ways of economic life, the tendency for the inland individual to remain in the setting of caribou hunting, and conversely, for the maritime whaler to capitalize on the skills which he had amassed on the coast, was strong. Within each setting, however, there was, as has been shown, considerable movement. The primary tie was thus inevitably that of the nuclear family, defined here as the coresident group. Kinship ties in all directions emanated from this unit and it is thus wholly possible to refer to the extended family if it be understood that the circle of relationships would vary with each such nuclear unit. It has been shown that it was the genetic bond which determined the patterning of collective responsibility and that the adopted child was drawn into this web as well. The primary cooperative unit was thus the small group of coresidents whose genetic ties reached out in essence as far as the demands of collective responsibility may have been conceived to operate. Actually, however, this would tend to place the social patterns in a somewhat negative light. As far as the kinship ties were felt to go, however spatially remote, the cooperative bond, the fact that one's relatives could be counted on for aid and support, applied. Within the community, however, and also between communities, there were especially patterned ways of creating cooperative relationships. In effect, there were ways of extending the rights and obligations, except collective responsibility, to nonkindred.

The individual was always free to exercise choice in forming such associations. In certain formal ways, he could ally himself with others in a recognized economic partnership. This was tantamount to friendship; indeed, with one exception, it was the only recognized way of establishing relations with nonkin. The second pattern arose as an intracommunity feature where there were recognized associations between individuals in the cooperative acts relating to hunting, whether in the association of the caribou hunting group or in the whaling crew. In the latter case, however, the membership revolved around the relations between the component individuals and the leader, the umealiq who was able to command respect and so to draw individuals to himself. A secondary feature of the crew association lay in the concept of the men's house, the karigi, which, however important in ceremonial and ritual activities, was basically implemented by the economically derived hunting crews and their leaders.

In summary, partnerships, the added element of the joking relationship between partners, the crew membership, and the karigi institution were the primary voluntary associations, acting in some measure to substitute for the cooperative bonds of kinship.

PARTNERSHIPS

Partnerships were of several different kinds. All had marked social implications and were basically economic, whether related to the structured economy of prestige or intimately connected with subsistence. A man and his partner were known as nʼuuvereyik (dual;

sing. n^{y}uuviq), a term which refers primarily to the relation of trade. Indeed, the most important category of partnership was that which related to trade and exchange, whether between men in the same ecological setting or between nuunamiut and tareumiut. As trade in the latter instance is considered, it is highly significant to remark that the balance which existed between nomad and seaman was made meaningful in the exchange of the commodities in which each group specialized and that such trade was effected almost exclusively by means of the established trading partnerships. There was trade within the same ecological grouping as well and it too was worked out by means of partnerships. These, however, tended to have greater social and recreational functions and led, in many instances, to the formation of formal joking partnerships. Conversely, the trade between nuunamiut and tareumiut was a highly serious business and permitted less latitude for social intercourse.

It may be well to consider first the trading partnerships which formed the sole formal means by which the two ecological groups met. Such partnerships were begun in a simple way. As men (and women) came back to the trading stations year after year, they tended to trade with the same people. As they did so, an informal agreement was first reached. After 3 or 4 years, one individual proposed to the other that they become partners. The relationship now became formalized in that gifts were exchanged between them, such gifts not being equated on the basis of like for like or in terms of the recognized values. A nuunamiu, for example, gave the seaman with whom he had worked out the relationship extra caribou skins, pelts of fox and wolverine, or some other valued article. The tareumiu made gifts in turn. The relationship could be cemented further by wife exchange.

The partnership, once established, meant that the two men, representing different ways of life and livelihood, now stood in a special relation to each other. A seaman might go with his partner to an inland region where he had previously been and the two might hunt together. The partner in such an instance became a guarantor for the stranger. If a man had a partner in any community, he could go there freely and count on the protection of his mate. The various families of nuunamiut who spent the summers on the coast did so because of the relations they had established there with trading partners. In such cases, the visitor would not fall into the category of "stranger" and so be subjected to hostile acts from within the alien community.

Primarily, however, the partnerships which cut across the lines of ecology were for the purpose of the exchange of goods. Each setting supplied the other with needed commodities, the nuunamiut primarily for fuel and food in the form of seal and whale oil, and the tareumiut for caribou skins for clothing. While many other items were also exchanged, these were the most important. A man met his partner once yearly, usually in the summer at the recognized points of trade.

When a person had no partner, he was definitely at a disadvantage in the trading and was obliged to look about in order to find the best bargains. A partner, on the other hand, "always treated you right." There was no bargaining and haggling with partners; each member of the partnership team attempted to extend himself in favor of his partner. When a man had partners whom he knew to be waiting for him at the trading camp, he could take his time in getting there, knowing that the other would hold on to his goods until the two met. If, for any reason, a man could not get to the trading station, he sent a message to his partner by another man as well as a gift for him. The partner was then released from any obligations and was free to trade with others as best he could. When a man in a partnership met another from his partner's community or group, he always asked, "Is my partner coming?" The existence of such a partnership was common knowledge and no one would attempt to break up an existing partnership relation. Usually begun in the way described, such ties might also be inherited by a son or other close relative and so perpetuated after the death of one of the principals. There was thus the tendency for the institution to grow up and continue between family groups.

After greeting his partner and exchanging gossip with him, the trade between the two men, or more, as the case might be, began. The partners unloaded their umiaks, each taking, in an ideal situation, what the other had brought without question. Between partners, every effort was made to the other's benefit. A poke of oil, for example, might go to one's partner for 7 green caribou skins when 5 would be the usual number traded. A good partner, it is said, was always overgenerous.

While most partnerships began in the simple and relatively informal way described, the relationship was frequently more formally instituted. At the trading station, one man might propose to another that they begin a partnership in the following year. Each, having agreed, would then go to work to collect as much wealth as possible. The partnership thus began with a formal exchange which generally exceeded in amount that which might occur in ensuing years. There appears to have been a general tendency for men of like wealth and social position to develop partnerships.

There was no limitation on the number of partners a man might have. A man of wealth and standing could work out relations with 5 or 6, all of whom, of course, aided him in maintaining his position of wealth and enhancing his social position. A less successful man might have only one partner. Such partnerships were extended to the Messenger Feast, since, when a man invited a guest, he most frequently named his trading partner. Partnerships existed both within and outside of the ecological setting and it was thus theoretically possible for a man to extend his sphere of interest and his nonkin relationships over a wide area.

Although an arrangement effected primarily between nonkin, extended collateral relations might sometimes enter into such a partnership agreement, although, of course, this would be limited to one ecological setting. The more distant collaterals, such as cousins, could form partnerships particularly if they lived in different communities. One would not form a partnership with a brother, the theory being that one secured assistance and aid from one's close relatives in any case. In partnerships, just as a man might ask and receive aid from his relatives, so also could he make demands of his partner. Protection and refuge, goods, food, and sexual favors, in the form of wife lending and exchange, were to be had from partners. A partner would not theoretically become embroiled in an interfamily dispute, but any number of instances to the contrary are known. A faithful partner would stand up to assist his mate except against members of his own family if the occasion arose.

When the trading was over, and the partners ready to depart from the trading stations, they might announce to each other what goods they each wished for the next season. A man would do his utmost to meet the request. This pattern is carried to its ultimate conclusion in the Messenger Feast where the partners involved in the host-guest relationship made specific and often impossible requests of each other. It was always a challenge to the partner's, or host's, ingenuity to meet the request made.

Some specific examples of actual partnerships might serve to point up the institution:

1. qiwaq had three partners. They were brothers whom he had met at neγłiq. Their names were piγiniq, paamiu, and tumaacaq. qiwaq began by trading with piγiniq and obtained skins from him. After he had done this for several seasons, the latter suggested that they form a partnership. qiwaq agreed. piγiniq then suggested that his two brothers be included as members of the partnership team. They agreed on this and the three brothers and qiwaq traded amicably for many years. qiwaq brought from the coast such items as ammunition and pokes of seal oil and received caribou skins and wolf pelts in exchange. The four men never quarreled or haggled and they finally reached so ideal an arrangement that they did not even have to state what it was they needed. The three brothers divided what was brought to them and the three pooled their contributions in giving them to qiwaq. It sometimes happened that qiwaq brought items for which the three had no need. If so, they took what they wanted and tried to arrange with others for good bargains. On several occasions, qiwaq

went inland and stayed with the brothers as with his own kin. On two occasions, in fact, he went up the Ikpikpuk River and stayed at piγiniq's camp during the caribou drive. He had sexual relations with piγiniq's wife. qiwaq had no other partners but the three brothers had another man from the coast with whom they traded as well. The three died in an epidemic between 1908 and 1910 and qiwaq ceased going inland after this.

2. tukumminaroaq was living at Icy Cape when he formed a partnership with a man named aaγeaq who lived at utkeaaγvik. This was first a trading partnership and was then extended to the Messenger Feast and to formalized joking relations. aaγeaq took the role as host and sent messages to tukumminaroaq, inviting him by name. He requested of aaγeaq in the Messenger Feast both ugruk skins and .30–30 cartridges. He received enough skins for an umiak cover. Later, he returned the invitation to aaγeaq who requested some mountain-sheep skins and some caribou hides. These were provided. But apart from the formal Messenger Feast, the two did trade in other items and periodically sent each other gifts by others who were traveling up and down the coasts. They met only rarely but continued an active exchange over a period of years through intermediaries. The death of aaγeaq in 1930 terminated the partnership.

3. tukumminaroaq had another partner who lived at Point Hope. With him he did not engage in Messenger Feast activities. His name was in^{y}uaavik. tukumminaroaq got to know this man through a family which had come from Point Hope and settled at Icy Cape when he was still living there. in^{y}uaavik, in fact, was the son-in-law of the family in question. After the two men had traded for some time, it turned out that in^{y}uaavik was dishonest and the partnership was broken off. It came about in this way: in^{y}uaavik sent a message saying that he needed skins for parkas and had whaling bombs to offer for them. He stated that he would give one bomb for two wolf skins. tukumminaroaq sent 10 skins down to him and waited for his five bombs. They failed to appear. Later, he went to Point Hope and asked for his bombs only to find that his partner did not have as many as he had pretended. Only three, in fact, were available. There was no alternative for tukumminaroaq but to demand his skins back. These were given reluctantly and the partnership was dissolved. Such dissolutions of partnerships were not infrequent and could arise at any time either partner was dissatisfied, when "one did not please the other." This was called n^{y}uuverelaaktuat, "breaking a partnership."

4. Partnerships are by no means a thing of the past. They continue still. Two women in the Barrow area are described as still carrying on a partnership. One lives at Meade River, the other at Barrow village. They are said to send each other various items constantly, using the mails and the "cat" train in winter. The Barrow woman sends dry goods, flour, and whale meat. In return, her partner sends berries and pemmican. They are said not to ask each other for goods but to send what they think will be needed and appreciated. The two are "friends" and "can be trusted." At the present time, too, the sense of partnership between the remaining nuunamiut and some of the coastal peoples still remains. kakiin^{y}aq, a killiγmiu, now resident in the Anaktuvuk Pass area, was partners with nusaŋgiin^{y}a, a man living at Barrow village. The trade between the two no longer continues but the sense of partnership is still strong and each refers to the other as "partner."

The ultimate function of the partnership was to extend the process of cooperation beyond the kinship grouping and thus to lend additional stability to the society as a whole. Such partnerships, in cutting across the lines of community and ecology, came to have meaning in providing an easier basis for trade and dependable contacts. One may go so far as to say that the balance which existed between nuunamiut and tareumiut was channeled and effected through the existing partnerships. When new products began to be brought into the coastal villages, when employment and the economy of money were introduced as the result of administration from abroad and missionization, the balance was disrupted. It was no longer necessary for the trade to continue. The result was the decimation of the inland Eskimo.

Within the same ecological setting there were also partnerships. These too were based primarily on trade. But more than this, the partnership was in effect an institutionalized friendship. Indeed, except hunting group association, it was the only means of establishing relationships of duration with nonkin. The member of the partnership went out of his way to be generous and to consider his partner's every request. Tied up with the partnership was the institution of "asking," which, while somewhat less formalized and less well institutionalized than among the Eskimo of the Bering Straits and southward, was nevertheless meaningful. The partner was given whatever he asked for, even if it meant deprivation on the part of the giver.

Partnership was thus both economic and social. The designation n^{y}uuvereyik applied to the economic aspects of the arrangement, specifically to the involved trade. Forming a partnership, however—the concept of the social relationship being implied—was called iil^{y}aliuktuak, literally translated, "making an attachment to one's self." The concept involved is that the partner becomes conceptually a member of an in-group and is identified with it. Such an alliance thus carried over to social relations and extended beyond mere economic considerations. To cement their partnership, the principals might exchange wives or lend wives, the force of the temporary sexual union lending additional force to the bond. Their respective children thus became qataŋuutigiit to each other and a situation closely approaching the kinship tie was achieved. But even if there were no sexual involvements, the partnership was designed to last and in the main did so.

JOKING PARTNERSHIPS

Properly, this relationship should not be viewed as a primary economic one. It was rather an ultimate outgrowth of partnership and was all but removed from the economic realm. Yet, because the joking partners might also be trading partners, and because the joking association might arise in respect to the institution of the Messenger Feast, it may be justifiable to consider the institution here. There were several ways in which an individual could obtain joking partners. In one situation, men who were not related and who grew up together played jokes and made sport together. Two members of the same crew, for example, might behave in this way and employ the pattern of joking in order to indicate their mutual esteem and friendship. This was the least formal kind of joking partnership and had few direct economic implications. When the nature of interpersonal relations of any Eskimo group is considered, it is evident that the general life situation is hemmed in with a great deal of humor. Joking, poking friendly fun, "kidding," making humorous remarks on any and all occasions make up an important aspect of daily life. The joking relationship between individuals was first on this day to day level of humor and meant simply that a person selected some other individual with whom he joked on an essentially equal basis. The term for such a joking partner was iil^{y}aaruq (dual—iil^{y}oreyik) perhaps best translated as "pal."

Such largely informal intracommunity joking partnerships still exist. In one instance which the writer observed, a man who had been absent from Barrow village for some time returned to the community. The son of another man, his joking partner, saw the newcomer and rushed to tell his father, calling excitedly, "Your iil^{y}aaruq is here." The two men greeted each other with much enthusiasm, hugging each other and pummeling each other on the back.

It is to be emphasized that the iil^{y}aaruq relationship was a pattern of friendship that did not cross community lines. It never applied to kindred, indeed, "one does not make fun of one's relatives." Men who hunted together, shared various kinds of experiences, worked together, could develop this kind of relationship merely out of the situation of being thrown together and in terms of the joking which was a pattern inherent in the culture. An umealiq of wealth and power would be unlikely to have such relationships—the dignity which his position demanded would tend to create a degree of social distance between himself and the men with whom he was associated. On an informal level, the joking partnership, like the trading partnership, but intracommunity, involved mutual aid and might result in temporary wife exchange.

But there was a second, more formalized, intercommunity pattern of joking. Here is a suggestion of the insult song situation which is found farther to the east, for indeed, sarcasm, irony, and a certain spiteful humor made their way into the exchanges of songs which characterized this relationship. The partners in this case were iγłuusuuvik, that is, in different places, and the basis of the pattern lay primarily in the sending of songs from one community to another. The relationship generally began in a trading partnership, reached the proportions of a Messenger Feast invitation, and then resulted in song exchange. Actually, in the Messenger Feast, where a wealth display feature is uppermost, the happier trading relations between partners tended to be put aside and the feast itself became characterized by a definite rivalry between principals. Here, friendship was put aside and attention given to the notion of besting one's partner in the display. And in keeping with this, songs of a nature reflecting patterned rivalry were sent from one principal to another.

Quite apart from the formal occasion of the Messenger Feast, however, songs could be sent from one man to another whenever the opportunity for contact arose. If a family from one town or band were going to another, a man in the community which they were leaving would work up a song to send to his partner elsewhere. To send such a song was regarded as clever, humorous, and a test of a man's ingenuity. He attempted insofar as he could to best his joking partner in the exchange, using plays on words, puns, and mild insults. Since the songs became popular, and since a new song, especially one in which the humor was marked, was awaited eagerly by everyone, there was no small amount of acclaim for the composer. As the new song developed, the composer might also invent dance steps to go with it. These, like the song, were imitated by others and both might ultimately find their way into the vast body of dance and song variations which the people possessed. The singer sent his song, with the new dance steps, to his partner by a chance traveler. The latter was carefully coached until he had both letter perfect. But if such a song were sent, the partner was also the recipient of a gift, likewise dispatched by a traveler.

It is clear that the joking partnership was a great source of interest and entertainment to everyone in the community. When a traveler arrived, he announced that he had a song for such and such man. At this, everyone in the community came around to hear it, and the new arrival sang it to the recipient before the assembled community, usually choosing a karigi as the place for the singing. The erstwhile importance of the songs as a recreational outlet is indicated by the fact that they are still remembered and still sung in many cases. The men who sent songs to each other and maintained the song-partner relationship are likewise vividly recalled.

Such an arrangement existed between aapigerak, miligiroak, and sukcaq, men in different communities on the coast who sent songs to each other. The songs are remembered, even though the singers are long since dead. But perhaps the most famous of such partnerships along the Arctic coast was that between kucirrak at utkeaaγvik, annesiraq at Kuk River (Wainwright), and arvaksin^{y}a at tikeraaq (Point Hope). In this case, the first was bested in singing by the latter two, although it was kucirrak who had started the sequence of songs. He had been a shaman and had traded with the two men in the other communities for some time. During this period, the mail was being taken up the coast from Point Hope by an Eskimo driving a dog team. kucirrak took advantage of the mail carrier, teaching him the songs, and having him carry them to his partners in the other two villages. His first song (sayuŋ, pl. sayuutit) was as follows:

kanusik keyaksakimna aylariŋnʸaymannava
I wonder what kind of person he is. He isn't bashful.
pikuwiyakteruuvłu puyuveamnʸunexłuat
He has a lump on his neck. The crab's big legs.
irimawtiŋaγaatit isiviraaktinearikpik
He bends them inwards. He'll stretch them out again.
ikayelura anootit
I'll help you a little.

kucirrak's song, said to be "full of old words," reflects the use of obsolete words in poetic constructions. This was a recognized formal device in songmaking.

From kuk, annesiraq sent back a song in which he made a play on the name kucirrak. The term kucak refers to a bone in the hind quarters of the caribou, and kucirrak, having this element in his name, and also having been a shaman, could not eat, a reflection of a personal taboo, the meat associated with this bone. The song dealt with this theme.

Next, from tikeraaq, arvaksinʸa, who had received the same song as had his partner at kuk, sent the following back to kucirrak at utkeaaγvik:

uvanni aalakesaaktuŋa keevekesaaktuŋa
here he looks here he looks there
niiviksilaaktuŋa puyuweam niumiuksa
He looks to see how good it is. Of the crab the legs.
akunuratigaa aniilʸiraatakamma uveaniuktuŋa
between when I get out I feel happy.
awłaniksimaasuγaw sanipuaniktu aniŋŋan
He gets away. He goes sideways. his grandmother
irimaktuq suuγuruktuktuq tikiitpattin
bent them up he comes against it if he gets to you
irimawtikpattin pikeaksaneyana
if he grabs you try to get away

The sense of rivalry in such singing was strong. The last song was considered better because it used the same theme as the original song and turned it back at the original singer. The song sent back from kuk by annesiraq, while clever, was not so well done in that it failed to tie into the original song of kucirrak.

The joking element of these songs, the allusions to names and to physical characteristics, are at once clear to the audience. The rivalry in singing could thus go on for some time. In the above instance, kucirrak replied to both his joking partners with another song. At last, however, annesiraq sent a song which made use of the shaman songs used by kucirrak. This made the latter so angry that he refused to participate in the exchange any longer. The people thereafter made fun of him and asked him slyly why he no longer sent songs to his partners in the south. This was a case where the songs gradually reached a point where they became more and more insulting with the result that one participant was ultimately obliged to drop out.

Insult singing, while fairly well developed, was not used as a social device for settling formal disputes as was the case among the Eskimo farther to the east. That it was a means of exerting certain social pressures is of course not to be questioned, since such songs and singing took place both within communities and between them. All such songs were sung slowly and with slow, often impromptu, dance steps.

There was another aspect of such singing which had little to do with the formalized joking partner relationship. This occurred within the same community and was also in effect a contest of insult singing. In the karigi, for example, one man might start singing a song at another. Clearly, this was an accepted way in which to indicate hostility and to take out feelings resulting from any grievances. The man to whom the song was directed had to return the song with another. A person's mistakes, his misdeeds, his faults of character were all freely aired. A clever singer could extemporize on the name of his opponent and adroitly pun on it. When one or the other ran out of ideas, or indeed, became so angry that he could no longer continue, the contest ended and the loser, he who had been unable to reply with a suitable song, was the butt of jokes for some time thereafter. "Maybe you won't sing any more; maybe you just better go away" was said to him. In so far as he could, a man was expected to contain himself and not to show resentment or temper in such exchanges. When he became angry, he naturally became the butt of further jokes. The two men who sang in this way were called iivireyik, "two against each other." The impromptu songs, too, became popular and were sung for amusement. Such songs were not usually so well worked out, of course, as those which a man sent over a wide distance and over which he could spend some time in thought.

When a man had an iil^{y}aaruq, a joking partner, in his home community, these two did not sing against each other. Indeed, the joking on this level was good-natured banter and simply reflected the patterned way of behaving toward nonrelatives with whom one stood on a friendly footing. The iil^{y}aaruq relationship also involved mutual aid and assistance at various tasks. Two iil^{y}oreyik would act as partners in the kick-ball game, passing the ball to each other. They worked together and frequently hunted together or were members of the same crew. In the community itself, the joking relationship and all that it implied and involved was a friendship situation. It offered another means by which cooperative endeavor could be extended in yet another direction beyond the kinship circle. A joking situation was the expected behavior between friends. "You must show a man that you are happy and that you will not harm him." The formal singing partnerships, on the other hand, arose between communities and out of the context of the trading relationship.

WOMEN'S PARTNERSHIPS

Women, as has been seen, were free to arrange their own trade without respect to a husband's wishes. By the same token, women developed partnerships of their own, in the main with other women, although a trading relationship between a woman and a man was not unknown. The most frequently established partnerships for women were those with the wives of the husband's trading partner. But since families traveled together to the trading stations, the women were in a position to carry on their own trade and to select those with whom they wished to deal. On the whole, women's partnerships were considerably less involved than those of the men. They did not have the sense of mutal aid and protection which the male accorded to his partner, nor did they have the patterned joking relationships. Women, it is said, wished to be on a friendly footing with their partners and to avoid giving them any offense. The female partners thus regularly gave in to each other and made the trading a friendly social event. Women made friendships in the community and there was interhouse visiting between them. Both within and without the community, however, such friendships were inaugurated by trading.

THE HUNTING GROUP AND THE UMEALIQ

In both the maritime setting and in the inland regions a man was free to associate himself with a hunting group. Indeed, this, as has been demonstrated, was largely the basis of inland organization in that among the nuunamiut, the men who hunted together in the caribou drive made up, with their families, the extended band or section. The same was in large measure true of the maritime village; the economic association of whaling and the whaling crew drew individuals to the community. This hunting group relationship was further centered in the personage of the "captain," the umealiq, who came to serve as a keystone for the activities of intensive hunting and for the ceremonialism associated with it. Such figures, as noted, were the men of wealth and highest social position in the various community groupings.

The umealiq was a boatowner by definition. In any community he was in effect a chief but, as may readily be understood, he lacked any defined authority. Only through the force of his moral character and the prestige which was generally accorded him could he assume a leading role in a community. He did, however, command the loyalty of the men who formed his crew and it was in him that the activity defined as umeaktuat, that is, group hunting with division of the take, centered. An umealiq, although the owner of a boat and the leader of a crew, was defined not so much on these terms as through the fact that a series of recognized relations with members of his crew arose. Other men who had boats could freely enlist the services of others on a momentary basis but unless the relationship were lasting, unless it was affirmed by specific kinds of behavior, the leader was not considered an umealiq.

Whether by the sea or in the inland caribou drive, a hunting group was made up of an average of 8 to 9 men, including the umealiq himself. These men always engaged in the great annual hunt together, be it for whales or caribou. Taking the maritime group as a primary example, since it was in this setting that the crew institution was best elaborated, it is seen that the crew worked together, that the men were frequently iil^{y}aaruq to each other, and that as a crew its activities were centered in a karigi. A whaling crew thus consisted of the members and the captain, but there were other specialities which likewise had to be considered. At sea, the umealiq had no more authority than other members of the crew. The entire procedure of the hunt—where the tents should be placed, the placing of lookouts and the like—was conducted in a wholly democratic manner, every member of the crew having a voice in decisions made by the group at large. If opinion were divided, the umealiq could cast a deciding vote, although it is to be emphasized that this often required tact and good humor on his part. Authority, if any can be said to exist, belonged to the harpooner, the nawligax, who might conceivably be the umealiq but more frequently was not. Because he was experienced and had learned his specialty well, his opinion tended to carry weight with other crew members. The umealiq, apart from his economic role, had ritual and ceremonial duties to perform. He was in effect the priest of the whaling cult.

An umealiq was a "good and honest" man who looked after the interests of his supporting crew. He was usually a skilled hunter, although his skill lay as much in careful bargaining and in playing opposing factions off against each other as it did in other activities. He was at once a diplomat, an orator, and a man of wealth. Some description has already been given of the role of the umealiq in the society. Suffice it to note again that the leader was marked by dignity, modesty, popularity, circumspection, and great wealth. Any man could aspire to the role and, as has been seen, could enlist the support of his kindred to help him achieve it. When the would-be umealiq had acquired his umiak, he began to attempt to enlist the services of other men whom he knew to have skill and experience. This was by no means easy to do. He had to make offers to them to leave the crews with which they were already affiliated. In bidding for their services, he was forced to compete with "captains" of established reputation and standing. The aspirant would also be obliged to leave the crew with which he was already associated and gamble on his getting the necessary personnel. If he failed, he might be left out of the whaling altogether. There were many unskilled men about, it is true, men from the coast who habitually hunted inland, who were "afraid of the sea," and there were often nuunamiut partners who came down in the spring in the hope of getting a share of whale meat, returning inland with it if they were successful. Such men were taken on as "hands," and indeed, failing to find men, the aspirant could take on a woman or two as crew members; but men of experience—the harpooner whose task it was to stab the whale in a vital part, men strong enough to cast lines into the whale, skilled helmsmen and boatmen—were the primary requirement. To work this out, to have the wealth required to establish it, created problems by no means easy of solution.

Unless an aspiring umealiq could do all this and find the necessary skilled men, his was a losing financial gamble. It was hence rare that a man moved into the position of umealiq. A stroke of luck, signal success in one season's whaling, might help, but strong family support was also necessary. The end result was that the office tended to run in certain family lines. A successful hunter might be groomed for the role and in effect inherit the position from a relative. In the aboriginal culture, movement upward to this status was limited and inevitably slow. Moreover, many men, did not want the responsibility. Some changes came about as the result of the intrusion of foreign whaling interests. With new commodities available, with improved weapons, such as bombs, the darting gun, and motor driven boats, there were new opportunities for captains to rise.

The economic interrelationship between an umealiq and his crew was a fixed one. A captain had to support his crew. A crew was thus drawn from men in the home community and from different communities, men who voluntarily allied themselves with a leader in return for economic support. It was thus in no sense a kin group. It conceivably could be, of course, if a man were to enlist all the males from one family as his crew members, but the crew was not conceptually bound together by ties of kinship. Karigi membership and loyalty to the umealiq were the primary factors with the result that crew and karigi membership cut across kinship lines.

Support of a crew by an umealiq involved several elements. Not only did the crew get a share of the game communally taken, such as whales, walrus, ugruk, or caribou, but they were also supplied with clothing, weapons, kayaks, and other useful things. In short, a captain bid for their services, bribed them to come to his boat, and continued to pay them in order to keep them under his banner. There was rivalry between umealit on this basis, the result being that a skilled whaler could choose the captain under whom he wished to serve and play one off against the other by forcing them to raise their bids. Should a captain succeed in enticing a crew member away from another, there was no ill feeling or resentment shown. The attitude was that the crew member had complete freedom of choice to serve in any crew that would set sufficiently high a price on his services. It was thus up to the umealiq to keep his crew satisfied to stay with him. When another attempted to woo one of his crew away by offering a higher bid, he had no alternative but to match or beat his rival's offer. It follows that in order to meet the demands of the men who made up his crew, an umealiq had to have considerable resources. Only through the added loyalty of his kindred could he hope to keep the wealth in hand for such crew support.

The umealiq's profit lay, on the coast at least, in actually getting a whale. The whale was divided, parts going to the boats which assisted in the catch, but since many tons of meat were involved, there was a great deal for the boat credited with the actual taking of the animal. This, together with the lesser share for any "assists," was divided between the crew members, being umeaktuat. But the umealiq received a choice share for himself, in the form of the much desired flippers, and the boat likewise got a share. Even here, however, the umealiq was expected to be generous and to feed the entire community. The whale meat was still sufficient to trade for goods which in turn were passed to crew members for their support. Similarly, the umealiq gave meat to his kindred and insured their continued backing. It can readily be seen, however, that there were ways of losing a following. If in any one year a boat was successful, getting at least one, but often several, whales, all was well, since shares could be arranged all around. But if there were an unsuccessful year, it was a wealthy captain indeed that could stand the burden of keeping a crew and there was the danger of losing crew members to wealthier and more successful leaders. Usually, however, the lean periods—when the whales went far afield as the result of changing ice conditions or were limited in their movements because of an unusual weather sequence—hit every crew alike. It is possible, too, before the intensive whaling of the late 19th century by Europeans, when whalebone and oil were so much in commercial demand, that whales were more abundant. At least, so the modern residents of the area claim.

In the main, a captain attempted to win the loyalty of a crew not only by promises of large shares of whale meat, by continued bribes and gifts, but also because of his own charm and personal magnetism. A popular captain was sure of a following, even in a lean year. This gave the umealiq a further incentive to behave in the ideal way and to meet what the culture defined as good qualities of leadership.

The situation for the nuunamiut was in general similar. The umealiq-karigi association was likewise paramount in all group hunting activity. The impression which is obtained for the inland peoples is one of an individual leader for the local group, or at least one karigi in a settlement rather than several. It is true, however, that when the caribou migration looked promising, several separate groups, each with an umealiq, came together and joined forces in the hunt. A communal caribou drive could involve 8 to 10 men, organized by a leader who brought the men to the crew by the same methods as have been described, that is, by making it worth their while to return to the same encampment and to engage in the communal hunt. The nuunamiut lacked the same degree of skill specialization. It is said, however, that an umealiq was usually an older man, wise in the ways of the caribou and able to predict, on the basis of a lifetime of experience, where the herds would begin to move northward. When several crews were involved in the drive, each with its own umealiq, these leaders would work together informally. In such cases, the men of different crews shared the same karigi, would feast each other, and play games against each other. Among the nuunamiut, too, there was a greater tendency for relationship ties to operate in respect to crew formation. The reason for this was that the men who moved together on the yearly round were often kin and stayed together in the yearly communal hunt.

The general pattern which is described above still operates in that the owner of a boat, today a motor-driven vessel, supplies his crew with ammunition, feeds them while afloat, and buys the fuel for the boat. Among the remaining northern nuunamiut as well, the group association depends on two men, umealit—although they are no longer designated by this term—leaders of the two groups making up the killiγmiut, paneaq and kakiin^{y}aq, who work together and organize the hunt. But ceremonial activities are for the most part gone as is the karigi, the erstwhile ceremonial house. The killiγmiut today make use of a tent in which they occasionally meet for social dancing and feasting, not to mention the social games which are still played. But it is true that in both settings the sense of crew membership and the loyalty of a crew to a leader remain. The crews today may continue to whale together, to organize a caribou hunt together, and to engage together in all those activities which are formally designated as umeaktuat. In short, the structure of the older crew concept is present but stripped of its former religious and ceremonial trappings.

THE KARIGI

The foregoing description of the relations between crew members and umealiq is necessary to the understanding of the association of the ceremonial house or dance house of the area. It was in the karigi that the whaling crew conducted the first of its ceremonial rites before the whaling and it was here that crew and captain came together to treat properly the captured whale. In the inland setting, the ritual activities relating to caribou hunting began in the karigi as well. It was the center of the cults of whale and caribou, and the focus of most social activity taking place between men.

The karigi, listed variously in the literature as the kashim, the kazigi, kazhigi, etc., was a common institution in the cultures of the Alaskan Eskimo. The dialects of the nuwuŋmiut, the utkeaviŋmiut, as well as of the adjacent nuunamiut give karigi, while there are some phonetic variations in other North Alaskan maritime villages. kaligi (Rainey's qalegi) and kaγigi are heard at tikeraaq (Point Hope), but karigi seems phonemically justified for the area (Rainey, 1947, p. 242). The plural is kariyit.

Basically a ceremonial structure, the karigi of northern Alaska was not so elaborately built as was that among the peoples farther to the south. It seems most highly developed at Point Hope, where there were several permanent karigi structures. At utkeaaγvik and nuwuk, the karigi was frequently semipermanent, consisting of a basic structure which might when needed be roofed over with ice blocks and skins. There was, however, a permanent karigi at piγinik which was abandoned in the 1890's. The kariyit at tikeraaq were considerably more elaborate in both construction and furniture than those farther to the north, suggesting that the northern maritime villages offer a marginal development away from a Point Hope center. Point Barrow, indeed, is the northernmost and easternmost coastal development of the institution. It may be regarded as wholly Alaskan. The nuunamiut also had kariyit which were always temporary structures, built as needed at the time of hunting assemblages (pl. 4, *a*). The tendency was to build the karigi on the surface of the ground and to avoid the semisubterranean character which applies farther to the south. Point Hope again, however, did have the semisubterranean karigi, built much like the usual dwelling although larger and with a shorter hall.

The karigi was a center for whaling and caribou hunting ceremonialism, it served as a focus for the Messenger Feast, and it was a place where the men of the community could come together. Women were not barred from it and it seems to have no character of a secret society house, or of the ethnographically defined bachelor house or men's house as such, a feature which is somewhat more elaborated among the groups farther to the south in Alaska (Lantis, 1947, pp. 104–107; Nelson, 1899, p. 286 ff.).

Dr. Simpson, visiting at nuwuk in the early 1850's, describes the karigi at nuwuk, noting that there were two, one in process of being abandoned, and that there were three at utkeaaγvik. The largest, he relates, was at nuwuk, measuring 18 feet by 14 feet and consisting of upright planks chinked with moss. The roof was higher than that of the dwellings; there was no interior bench of planks but rather a low seat which ran around the four sides. A short entrance passageway and a skylight made up the added features. The house, he relates, was on high ground and not sodded over (J. Simpson, 1855, p. 259). Simpson calls this a public building, owned by wealthy men, and devoted to the use of men for working, loafing, and dancing. He points out that women joined in as well.

The present writer obtained a detailed description of one at utkeaaγvik which was abandoned in 1890. Here the structure was made from blocks of ice placed on a permanent foundation of sod. It, too, was rectangular in floor plan, and fairly long and narrow, ca. 15 feet by 35 feet. The door was placed on one of the long sides in the center and had a short passageway or storm porch leading into it. This, too, was made from blocks of ice. There were windows and skylights in the structure, clear ice being spaced at intervals to admit light. The roof was of skins, later of canvas and sailcloth. The skins, supplied by the umealit, were stretched across beams laid across on the tops of the ice walls. These were also held in place with blocks of ice. There was a skylight, sections of translucent gut being sewed into the skins of the roof covers. The sides of the karigi were banked with snow. Obviously a temporary structure, this type of karigi suggests an inland development, the ice blocks being used with sod and willow beams to make the karigi of the nuunamiut. On the other hand, the karigi described by Simpson suggests the type of structure used at Point Hope. It may well be that in the extreme north of the area, at Point Barrow, the tendency was to make use of two types, each drawn from a separate area.

At tikeraaq, the karigi was essentially square and semisubterranean. It was made with a planking of driftwood much in the manner of the usual dwelling, although the karigi was considerably larger, ca. 20 feet by 20 feet. A sunken entrance passage led to the upper chamber, access to which was through a well, the usual circular hole cut into the floor (kataq). The passage, unlike that of the dwelling, had no side rooms leading from it (Rainey, 1947, p. 242). The kataq and sunken passageway do not seem to characterize either the inland regions or the villages farther to the north of Point Hope.

Stoney mentions a large dance house being built at kigalik, on the Ikpikpuk River. He does not describe it but mentions that the men contributed skins for its construction (Stoney, 1900, p. 72).

Since the type of structure was thus somewhat variable, it follows that internal arrangements would also differ. The kariyit at tikeraaq had the bench around three sides of the structure, and the men who belonged to the karigi had their special seating places. This was also true farther to the north, where, in the rectangular buildings, men sat and slept on the benches which ran around the sides, and each man kept his own special place. At Point Hope, oil lamps flanked the kataq, while farther to the north and inland they were placed in both niches in the walls and on the floor.

The most distinctive feature of the karigi, one which reinforces its character as a ceremonial house, was the presence of any number of charms (aanaroat) on the walls, on the floor, hanging from the roof beams, etc. There were several classes of these, the greatest specialization of them being in the kariyit at Point Hope. In general, each karigi had its own special charms which were tied up with the whaling and other sea mammal hunting. The tikeraγmiut recall that the karigi known as kaaγmaktuq made use of a carved whale, and a sea bird which was stuffed. The jaws of the whale could be manipulated with strings and the wings of the bird likewise moved. These charms were important in the whaling ceremonial. Carved human figures in umiaks and kayaks were also present as part of the charm array.[9] Each karigi throughout the area had its own special charms. These were known as aanaroat and also as qulugukłut. When a woman brought food into the karigi, she set the platter before each charm before offering it to the men present.

The karigi was not used in summer. The umiivik, a skin tent or windbreak, was then set up and men congregated there. In winter, when the members of the community had returned from their summer and fall round, there was a formal opening of the karigi. The ceremonial season could then be said to be getting under way. The karigi was a center of ritualism, it is true, but it was also the primary

---

[9] A point also described by Rainey (1947, p. 248). He notes also the principal charms for the other tikeraaq kariyit.

winter recreational area. When the Messenger Feast took place, the activities centered in the karigi and it was here that the invited guests slept. Prior to their opening in winter, there were recognized procedures to be followed. The members of the house cleaned out the passageways, went out to cut the blocks of ice should these be necessary, and refurbished and cleaned the charms, frequently washing them in urine in order to ensure successful hunting for the coming seasons. The clear ice for the making of skylights and windows had to be obtained. Even at tikeraaq, clear ice was used to make the skylight both of the karigi itself and that of the entrance hallway. At Point Hope, for example, there was a special pond where the clear ice was always obtained. The men who belonged to the karigi went out in a group, followed by the boys, the latter carrying food. When they arrived at the pond, all ate, the ice was then cut, and when it was loaded on a sled, the remainder of the food was thrown into the pond, given, it is said, to the tuunaraq who resided there. Parallel patterns are mentioned for the opening of the kariyit in other settlements.

Properly speaking, there was no established sense of ownership in the karigi. A person was associated with it through his membership in a crew and his tie with the umealiq who led his crew. This meant that in a technical sense, the captains who led crews from out of a particular karigi were its owners; they at least supplied the materials for the construction and maintenance of the structure. Because the position of umealiq tended to pass on in certain family lines with wealth, there was likewise a tendency for the karigi to become associated with certain families. The point of ownership obviously cannot be pushed too far. A man was a member of a karigi by virtue of his association with a hunting group. True, he might make the tie with both hunting group and karigi through some male relative, as, for example, a boy who took a place in the crew in which his father or brother was active. But if he changed his allegiance to an umealiq, he also changed his karigi, assuming that he allied himself with a man from a different group. The result was that karigi memberships tended to be fixed but were not actually so instituted.

The karigi bore a name. In the case of the inland groups where one karigi to a section existed, the name was generally that of the locality. On the coast, however, it was somewhat better defined. The three historic kariyit at utkeaaγvik, for example, bore the following names:

1. wallaraq—"in another direction." The people associated with the structure were designated as the wallaraamiut. This karigi was located at the head of the ravine, southeast of the settlement proper.

2. qilullaraq—"on the land side." The people were known as the

qilullaraamiut. This was located on the bluff just south of modern Barrow village.

3. serel^{y}uuaraq—"at the ice cellars." serel^{y}uaraamiut were the members. This karigi was located on the beach just north of the ravine.

The karigi situation, with its memberships and its function as an integrating force in the community, was somewhat better developed at Point Hope. Here, although the community was generally small, there were six or seven karigi organizations at the beginning of the 19th century. Toward the end of the century, however, only two of these were active. They were named kaaγmaktuq and uŋaasiksikaq. Indeed, these remained significant long after the institution had disappeared farther to the north.

There was a sense of membership in the karigi determined by birth and by crew association. In the north, a boy went to the same karigi as his father, entering group activities at the age of 12 onwards, "when he was strong enough to shoot a bow." It was not required that he stay with this group, since, as has been seen, the membership in a crew and hunting group could break down any equation between karigi association and family. Membership could readily be changed at utkeaaγvik and nuwuk. Rainey remarks that at tikeraaq a man was expected to join the group of his relatives and apparently to stay there. This would place membership on the level of the family tie but in view of the role played by the umealiq and the fact that the crew together carried on ceremonial life as a unit, karigi ties seem to rest in the hunting group and to be worked out without regard to relationship. Marriage, moreover, was not a factor in the association.

Some detail relating to the karigi function at tikeraaq may be obtained from the following verbatim account which describes the experiences of okumayl^{y}uq, who as a young man lived in that village and was associated with the kaγmaktuγmiut:

> It was toward fall and they were going to open up the karigi when we came back to the village. My stepfather's mother told me that it was time I went with the other boys to the karigi and helped. She told me to get some food because they always ate when they went to the pond to get the clear ice for a window. When we came home, we put the ice in the skylight frame. Then there was an umealiq who brought a big lamp and put it up in the middle of the floor. Some men asked me if I would be one of the four boys who stayed all night in the karigi to take care of the lamp. I was afraid, but I had to do it. They told me that we had to keep awake all night and watch the lamp, making sure that it didn't go out. In the morning, they said, we would be sent muktuk(whale skin) to eat. So all night long we sat there and kept watching the lamp. Next morning, the umealiq came back and we first heard a noise in the hallway. Then a stick with meat on it came up through the kataq. We all grabbed for it, but we knocked it off the stick and it fell back through the kataq. The umealiq put it on the stick again and this time one boy got it. Then three other umealit came,

each with meat. When we had eaten, they came into the karigi, looked at the lamp and thanked us (kuyanaq) for taking care of it.

Shortly after this, the people in the karigi got a whale and they brought in a lot of muktuk and meat. They pushed back the boards in the karigi roof and dropped the meat in on the floor. Soon everyone came and there was a full karigi. It was warm and the men took their parkas off. All the men in the different crews were there. The only women were the wives of the four umealit, each of them sitting behind a lamp and tending it. Then the food was divided between the men—the women didn't get any. When we had all eaten, the men of the other karigi, uŋaasiksikaq, came by and ate some food with us. Then we all went over there and they fed us. At night, the women went home and the captains and the men lay down and slept. Every day, as long as they feasted for the whale, they stayed in the karigi.

My grandmother's husband belonged to the uŋaasiksikaγmiut. One day she told me that my karigi would be invited by her husband's for a special feast. She advised me to bring muktuk on a stick over to the other karigi. When I got there, I found my friend (iilʸaaruq) and I gave him some of the meat I carried. In the other karigi, I saw all the meat and muktuk, piled up. On the ends of the meat was a seagull and a raven. They were flapping their wings and acting just as if they were alive. My iilʸaaruq asked me to sit down by him. He was the son of my stepfather (hence qataŋun). The men then stood up and left us younger boys sitting there. They told us to eat as quickly as we could. In the back were women, each holding a little bucket, the kind they used to give water to the whale. They told us that when we had eaten, we should get up and get out quickly. The last one out would have the water in the buckets poured all over him. I started to eat but my knife was dull. I hurried but I was only half done when a boy got up and left. They kept going out and still I was eating. At last, not swallowing my last mouthful, I rushed away. I was the last but one and that boy got wet. Then a few days later, we invited the other karigi and did the same thing all over again. That is how I got started in the karigi.

While the karigi does not wholly meet the definition of a men's house, the behavior associated with it indicates that it was a meeting place for the men and a recreation hall. A resident of a community, member of a crew, called the karigi his own and went there to while away time and to engage in the winter activities, both ceremonial and social. Indeed, a man spent all his days there, whenever he had leisure, and might even choose to sleep there, although this was not the usual custom. The men who stayed in the karigi remained for days on end. Their wives cooked food at home and brought it over to the karigi in pans and trenchers to feed their husbands. If he were not otherwise engaged, such as in the winter sealing, the man left his house on awakening and went over to the karigi. His wife brought food at times during the day, usually in quantity, so that it could be shared with the other men. The man then came home at the end of the day to sleep. This pattern was followed throughout the winter, "until the days get longer," when some other economic activities demanded the individual's time. But in the dark months, full attention could be given to the karigi and the social events taking place there.

The recreational aspects of the culture, in so far as they related to the domain of the men, centered in the karigi. The instance given above, that of a contest between boys in the karigi and interkarigi visiting, is only one of a host of similar events. Games in the karigi were called karigiiraktuat. There were many such, reflecting the elaboration by the Eskimo of games of all kinds. Not only were tales told, songs practiced, and new social songs composed, but many formal and informal games were developed. Tales were an important factor in the socialization process, offering as they did information as to such practical circumstances as getting lost and finding one's way again, and providing knowledge of the basic lore of the group, the world view, and idealized behavior. Informal games involved the famous string figures, the cat's cradle (ayaraq). These were begun in the fall, "when the days are short," and they were practiced until the winter solstice, when agerulerravik shines, that is, Venus. The string figures always began with tutaŋwaceak, the figure in which a man pretends to take out his intestines and make string figures from them. The men then had a kind of contest to see how many figures and associated songs each knew. The impression is clear that the man who was most resourceful in inventing new games and, new contests of strength or endurance was welcomed in the karigi. The men sat about until one suddenly came up with a new game. All played until they were tired of it and then a new game was begun.

Among the games played in the karigi were shooting contests. Small bits of wood were hung from the rafters and the assembled men shot at them with miniature bows and arrows. The pieces of wood represented ptarmigans. The object was not only to hit the bit of wood but to make the arrow stick into it. If a man made a successful hit, he was expected to bring food for all present. Some men, when they made a hit, "ran out and brought back meat right away." The extra food which a man's wife brought to him in the karigi was often reserved for the purpose of distribution as the result of some such game.

Other games involved hoop tossing, a kick ball, played within the karigi itself, a game of "take-away," played with mittens on a string, and a variant of horseshoes, ivory sticks thrown against a stake. The last is a gambling game, called kiputaktuat, and is still popular. The foreign whalers introduced cards and dice, which quite early took on great popularity. Indeed, there is a suggestion that cards reached the area originally from the Russians and were known at the time of first direct contact. Poker and similar games have been known to the oldest living residents of the area since earliest childhood. All such games were reserved for winter. There was no strong feeling about such recreational forms in the summer; people say that it was simply not done because the personnel of each community was scattered about, busy on the economic round, and there was no time.

Important as an aspect of karigi recreation were contests of strength and endurance, wrestling, the object being to throw the opponent off his feet, and weight lifting. There were jumping contests, chinning on a bar, contests of so-called "Indian wrestling," and the like. Actually, the sense of rivalry between kariyit extended to such exercises. One invited the members of another over as guests and spent the time in such games and contests. The contests were over any feature of moment or interest. Men would sing, for example, to see who could sing the most songs, vie in knowledge of the cat's cradle variations (pl. 9), test newcomers to see how many names they had, and all would engage in contests on an interkarigi basis. One team would line its members up in the karigi and the men, barefoot, would do a standing broad-jump. The other team, the guests, would then do the same. The team which had the man who jumped the greatest distance won. If the guests were winners, they were free to begin another "stunt," introducing their own, and perhaps new, game. If the hosts won, they had this privilege. These became contests of endurance and resourcefulness, inasmuch as the idea was to stay in the winner's position as long as possible without losing the privilege of starting a new activity. It is said that men would leave, go home to sleep, and then return to join in the same game. If a strong man, a member of a karigi, were away at home and his abilities needed, men would go fetch him. The guest karigi group could not leave until they had bested their hosts in something. In one such contest, as now recalled by a participant, the guest group was constantly beaten in every new game that the hosts proposed. At last, one of the guests succeeded in walking on his elbows. None of the hosts could match this and the guests were able to retire. This was wholly friendly rivalry but the karigi members went to great lengths to succeed in besting their rivals from another group. In the karigi itself, much time and practice were given to working out new stunts.

Everyone at utkeaaγvik remembers nasaayeluq for his amusing antics in the karigi in winter. He had had charms which were worn about his calves and there was a food taboo associated with them. He violated the taboo, and one day, out hunting, he was caught and lost in a storm and his feet were frozen. They were amputated just at the place where he wore his charms. After this he wore knee pads and ran and jumped about in the karigi on his knees. His agility was said to be amazing. One of the endurance contests in the karigi, among such things as holding the breath the longest, standing on the hands without moving, and the like, was to leap up, catch at a ring in the ceiling posts and hang there by one finger as long as possible. nasaayeluq made a prodigious leap, caught the ring, and easily won. Another man lost a bet over this and became very angry, claiming that nasaayeluq had cheated by having no feet.[10]

Games were also played outside the karigi but always in association with it. These were called iilʸakawtuat. In these, one karigi played against another. If there were several karigi, each fielded a team and all played against each other. The kick-ball game which began inside the karigi frequently went outside as the confines of the small structure proved too narrow. The rival kariyit would then turn up as teams and the game was on. The "take away" game could also go outside and last for a long time. It was, in effect, a variant of the kick-ball, the object in this game being to see who could hold and control the ball or such an object as mittens the longest. A man who made off with the mittens generally came back and fed the karigi. He gave a few morsels of meat but in so doing, preserved the fiction that he had given clothing to all who participated in the game.

When there was intercommunity play, as in kick ball or foot racing associated with the Messenger Feast, or on a less formal scale, karigi affiliations were forgotten. The home community got a team together from all the kariyit. The point was that the men in one karigi acted as hosts in the Messenger Feast, the umealit associated with the karigi extending the invitations, not, it must be emphasized, as representative of their karigi but rather of themselves personally. They then selected any men from any karigi to represent them in the foot races and ball games. The karigi association was thus momentarily eclipsed.

Actually, these karigi contests were important in several ways. Not only did they produce a sense of community cohesion but they offered the ways by which the young men attaining adulthood could be selected as crew members. When a youth distinguished himself by racing, by his endurance on the football field—misnomer, since there was no field, the game being played over a several mile area—an umealiq would make a bid for his services and enlist him in a crew. The tendency was for the umealit in his family karigi, that to which his male relatives tended to belong, to make the strongest appeal to him. It was this, too, which kept karigi membership fixed for certain families. A boy was thus first associated with a karigi as an athlete, then as a crew member.

---

[10] This kind of humor is very close to our own. Another very funny tale is told about nasaayeluq. He wished to marry a woman with a bald spot. She refused him, saying "No, you have no feet." He replied, "Ah, go home and comb your hair."

In the interkarigi contests, or indeed, within the group itself, a feeling of general good will was held to exist. To show anger, although some did, was to be a "spoil-sport." A definite concept of sportsmanship existed, although it was phrased as "being happy." Good manners, and indeed, the whole culture pattern in this respect demanded that one ignore the poor loser. If he persisted, the weapon of the insult song could be turned against him.

Throughout the winter, social dances were held in the kariyit. At this time, women came in and danced and sang with the men. Women, in fact, were never barred from the karigi unless they were menstruating or unless the solemn preparations for whaling were being carried on. They came in regularly with food for their menfolk and often stayed to watch the games and would now and again join in. At dances, however, the women had a better defined part in the activities. Social dances were of several different kinds. Dances specifically limited to the men, called owamiit, involved the dramatic imitation of game. Here the dancer was free to evolve his own patterns. A high degree of acclaim surrounded the successful dancer. Women's dances were more stereotyped in that they followed set patterns and allowed no variations. In these, several women danced together or a chorus of women sat on the floor, sang, and made motions with the hands. These were called oyyuttuk or uyut. Certain of the well-known and popular songs had their own dances. They began in a standard way, with conventional steps, and then changed as the dancers worked out variations. These were called sayyuq, sometimes designated as "motion dances," in which one to three persons participated. A conventional dance, such as that sometimes performed during the Messenger Feast, involved the men dancing in front, the women placed behind them and also dancing. This type was called anayuuk. Dance steps were quite involved as, indeed, is music and song. Dancing regularly took place to the accompaniment of a group of singers, 6 or 7 men, often in company with women who sat behind them. The singers used drums of the conventional tambourine type. The variations in musical style and pattern remain wholly remarkable, reflective of a highly evolved musical system (pl. 7).

Women also participated in karigi activities in the Messenger Feast. During this activity, two women were selected as leaders of the women's section and both served in inviting other women to come to the special women's dances which were held at times during the celebration. These two were called oyukaktuk.

When a Messenger Feast was held, the kariyit in any maritime community, if there were more than one, took turns sponsoring it. The karigi of the principal host was the one chosen as a center of festivities. Actually, men in the community arranged a feast apart from karigi association and participated jointly. This meant that the Messenger Feast could cut across lines of karigi affiliation, a point already noted in respect to selection of foot racers, ball players, and the like.

The karigi was thus a primary social center of the winter festival season. It was the focus of all community recreation, of the sports, games, and dances so dear to the Eskimo everywhere. But it is specifically an Alaskan development and in the cultures in question it had the important function of serving to weld together the interests and in-group consciousness of the community. This does not suggest the important ritual and ceremonial functions of the karigi, a point yet to be considered in relation to the festivities of preparation for whaling and the caribou drive.

In summary, the individual belonged to a family unit which consisted of his nuclear group and his extended circle of kin. He had nonkin associations with trading partners, friends in his joking partners, relations to an umealiq in his crew membership, and he was tied, by virtue of this last, to a karigi. It was in the latter categories, those of friendship, hunting group, and karigi, that he was bound to a community and came to identify himself as a nuunamiu or tareumiu. It is to be stressed that these associations were voluntary, that the individual was free to make a choice regarding them, and that there could be, and was, some shifting of membership and association, as, for example, when a man elected to serve under a new captain and might accordingly change his karigi affiliation. Kinship, with its rights and obligations, was not a voluntary aspect of the society. Here the individual was bound to his kindred and obligated to them, as they indeed, were to him.

TRADE

An exchange of commodities took place yearly between the various groups of the coast and the peoples of the inland. From each village and from each inland section came family groups who proceeded to their customary trading place each summer (cf. Stefansson, 1914 a). Here the men met their partners and effected an exchange of goods which were of value both as items affording prestige to the owner and trader and as elements important in the subsistence economy of both ecological settings. The primary contact between nuunamiut and tareumiut was on the basis of such trade. The result was to create a balance and an economic interdependence between the two which lent a high degree of stability to the respective societies. Out of the trade had grown the voluntary association of the partnership, in itself a cooperative institution and an arrangement by which a mechanism for intergroup stability was created.

Apart from the trading relations between the two ecologies, the patterns of exchange were established within the respective groups as well. In a community, whether inland or on the sea, trading and exchange were recognized ways of channeling certain kinds of interpersonal relations. The nature of the partnership association was such that exchanges could be effected without haggling and through the accepted device of "asking" one's partner for something, a wish which in the main he sought to fulfill. If a man lacked partners, he was at the disadvantage of having to declare his goods and to dispose of them by the recognized means of calling for bids. It is possible to see the beginnings of partnerships and of the concepts associated with exchange and wealth in the patterning of trade on this less formal level. Before considering the trading expeditions with their elaborate involvements, it may be well to examine exchange and its patterning when no partners were involved. In the main, this was less well formalized, unstructured, and nonselective in the sense of being open between individuals in all categories and circumstances.

OPEN TRADE

A distinction has already been made between the economic array that related to subsistence and that which was regarded as wealth and which accordingly created a basis for prestige. Generosity, as expressed by such leaders in the community as the umealit, by the successful hunter, or as among kindred, was in the main a reflection of the subsistence level. The family, viewed as a cooperative unit, and involving demands which one kinsman could make on another, worked together for subsistence and further contributed wealth to maintain an umealiq, thereby gaining prestige benefits. The men allied to an umealiq, dependent on him for support, also assisted him. Within the family group and within the crew and hunting segment, there was considerable movement of property. But this was not formal and, in general, it reflected a return of favor for favor. In this sense, there was a trade involved, but it obviously was not conceived as such, however much such economic loyalties and contributions to family and crew served to stabilize these institutions.

An exchange of commodities, whether for subsistence or prestige, was always taking place. Among both nuunamiut and tareumiut, there were those men who had obtained surplus quantities of goods from their partners in the interecology trade and who then traded this surplus to others in the home community. This is significant because it meant that commodities which were not produced but which were required by a group were available to those who had not engaged in trading with those from the opposite ecological setting. If a person had such goods of which he wished to dispose (assuming that he did not make them available to kindred or to his social partners, his iil^{y}aarut), there were defined ways in which he made these goods available to others. In short, an actual exchange was demanded outside of the intimate circle of kin and crew and one did not have trading partners within the home community. Trading partnerships as such arose only between groupings, either between the ecological settings themselves or between men in different inland sections and in different maritime villages.

At times, too, the seller might repent and return to the buyer demanding the return of his goods. Public opinion in this case favored the buyer. All such demands, whether on the part of buyer or seller, might lead to dispute and trouble and involve one person's being bullied by another. The following illustrations may serve to point up the dispute situation:

A man named in^{y}uveroak bought a wolverine skin from another man. The seller then wanted its return but in^{y}uveroak refused to return it, saying that he needed it. The seller persisted and the buyer became very angry. He cut the wolverine skin up into pieces and returned the small bits to the original owner. It is said that people were on his side up to this time but after the skin had been ruined, it was felt that he had done a bad thing. Behind his back, he was called sikume, "the cutter," and there was considerable reluctance to trade with him thereafter.

A second instance relates to the more modern situation:

Thomas Brower began his trading post on the north side of the lagoon at Barrow village. A man named kiŋaktak had a blue fox skin for which Brower gave him a lantern and five gallons of kerosene. Later, kiŋaktak made another purchase at the trading post and demanded it free, saying that he had received too little for his fox skin. Brower himself, wise in the Eskimo ways, gave him what he asked. kiŋaktak thereafter suffered in reputation and no one would trade with him in the home community.

When a man had an item which he wished to dispose of for gain, he sent a member of his family from house to house. He attempted to canvass the entire community, a call being made at each house. A son, daughter, or wife would make the round, stopping by the entrance of each house or, in the maritime village, calling into the skylight, and state that such and such an object was available. The people in the house, if interested, bid for it, making a definite offer. The seller then went to the next house and repeated his cry. The bids were noted, and, having received several, the seller then went back and attempted to bargain, trying to get the bids raised. By playing one bidder off against the other, the seller might get a fairly high price. It was viewed as an exciting game. In the heat of the bidding, some might go too high. In this case, they might, if they won out and received the item, say that they had bid too much and ask the seller to take back his goods. The seller might then agree and start the process all over again. But it seems to have been more frequent that the buyer paid the seller, received the item purchased, and repented at leisure. There would be some community censure of the individual or family which constantly reneged on such an auction agreement. But even after considerable time, when an individual, for example, discovered that he had no actual use for an item bought, he might go back to the seller and state that he wished to return it. The seller either returned his payment and took his original possession back or he returned some of the price to the buyer. An "honest" seller, it is said, would realize that he had taken too much and set some of the purchase price aside for return to the buyer should he request it.

When an item was so purchased, the kindred of the buyer, either those in his own household or in the same community, might tell him that he had paid too much. The buyer might be troubled over this but at the same time reluctant to demand a return on his payment. If he did so, he might get a popular reputation as a miser and penny-pincher and others would refuse to sell other things to him. A prospective seller, once he had his bidders lined up, might be told of one of them—"Don't sell to him; he'll want his payment back." At the same time, the concept of avoiding trouble, of not putting one's self in a position where argument or dispute might arise, became extremely important. In general, the view was taken that it was better by far to lose out in a transaction than to acquire a quarrelsome reputation.

On a somewhat less formalized basis, too, there was trade and sale of items which were turned out by skilled artisans. In a community, there were always a few who possessed special abilities at handicrafts and who then traded off the objects they made. Some individuals, indeed, rarely more than one or two in any community, would devote their entire time to such manufacture. There was some stigma attached to such a role, since it was felt keenly that proper behavior for a man was to hunt. But again, such activity was viewed as legitimate and it was only when there was refusal to work that stronger censure arose. Thus when an individual began to develop manual skills in one or another direction, he might make capital of them. One man at utkeaaγvik, for example, sikvayuŋgaq, made only sleds and umiaks and never left the community to hunt.

When a person desired the services of the skilled artisan, he worked a contractual agreement with him. When the finished article was delivered, payment was made, usually involving some extra gift for the worker. The contractor then asked the maker—Are you satisfied? If the artisan then chose to ask for something additional, it was generally freely given. In the main, however, the skilled workman, who engaged professionally in such manufacture, was content to take what was offered him. Were he to become too demanding, he would lose his patronage. When a hunter desired an umiak made, for example, he generally supplied the materials and paid the artisan for the labor. Pay was customarily in food, although other items, such as skins, oil, clothing, or the like, might enter into the arrangement. The few such skilled workmen, it is said, were able to maintain themselves and their families by their labor.

Certain women likewise had economic specialties. They were free to enter into agreements with other women and to do work for them for a price. This might be true in bootmaking, cutting out clothes, and in such work as tanning. If one woman had an item for trade which another desired, the latter might work for her in order to obtain it.

There were no slaves.

Economic specializations thus involved a situation of exchange. Individuals made for themselves the things they needed but would occasionally be required to depend on some skilled workman and in effect paid him for his services.

Pay to a workman, the objects traded about within a community, as well as those which might be exchanged between individuals in different communities in the same ecological setting were often made up of items that had come to the community by the more elaborated means of structured trade. When a man traded in his own community by the method of offering to the highest bidder, the object which he took in return could be virtually anything except food. A contracting workman could take food and it was in this respect that some stigma attached to him. It was considered shameful to be put in the position of buying food, although to do so was not unknown. In a community, one could ask for food of any successful hunter and in accord with the patterns of generosity, it was freely given. But to buy food was a tacit admission of one's own failure. It could happen that a hunter had been successful in trapping and had skins available for trade but had been unsuccessful in sealing. In this case, he might be forced to buy extra food. If he did so, his associates often said to him that he should be ashamed. The stock answer was—"We'll see who runs out of food first." A man who bought food generally set portions of it aside and had his wife cook meals for all the men of his karigi. In this way he could escape the shame. The situation arose not infrequently in winter when stores ran down and the winter hunting proved less successful than anticipated.

In all such situations, the pattern was in essence the same. In house-to-house trading, in pay to a workman, in obtaining food by trade, the process of bidding came into operation. While there was no economic unit, goods came to have fairly standardized value. Beads and tobacco, for instance, were highly valued and beaded labrets or a bunch of tobacco leaves were worth an umiak. A poke of seal oil was worth five green caribou skins, one wolf skin, one fox skin, while a wolverine skin was worth two. Overbidding, therefore, was not a real problem since the value of articles was established. The impression gained is that trading and selling were significant in establishing certain kinds of social relations. It also had its aspects of humor and amusement. In all such situations, there were those who chronically overbid, becoming excited at the prospect of engaging in a trading situation. Some fun was had at their expense and they earned the reputation of karawtawraktuat, "those who overbid." A man who demanded some of his payment back was called aŋiruksiruaq, this being a term of blame and applying only to "greedy" people. Persons who traded with each other were akuuviksuat, the force of the term implying that here was exchange without formal partnership.

STRUCTURED TRADE

(Maps 2, 3)

The organized trade which took place between the peoples of the inland and those of the coast marked a major event of the year. In winter, the peoples were to be found in their permanent or semi-permanent communities engaged in ceremonial and recreational activities; spring saw them capitalizing on their principal food-gathering activity, whaling or caribou hunting; and the summer brought them together at various points for trade. Summer, in short, was the period when the peoples were on the move and when vast stretches of territory were covered.

But although there was considerable movement, the families in each community had their preferred round and tended to make the same trip each year and to engage in essentially the same activities as had characterized the year previous. The end point of such travel was the emporium, the point at which they met their partners, traded, and so returned to the home community. In general, it is possible to work out the patterning of movement throughout the Arctic slope and to note the kinds of contact each community had. This may be summarized as follows:

The people of nuwuk and utkeaaγvik traveled along the Arctic coast to the mouth of the Colville. Here they met the tulugaγmiut, the kaγmalliγmiut, the killiγmiut, and the kupiγmiut, not, it must be understood, en masse, but rather representatives from these groups who had come for the trade. The place of meeting was neγłiq, located on one of the western mouths of the Colville Delta (Stefansson, 1914 a, pp. 4–5). This was not a permanent center and was active only for the two or three weeks of the year during which the trading took place. A second emporium, somewhat further removed to the east, was Oliktuk Point, a less frequently attended center where partners from Barter and Herschel Islands were met.

The kuγmiut, those who live at the present village of Wainwright, did not go to neγłiq for the trading. They, like all other tareumiut, went south to the Kobuk, traveling down the Utokak River, portaging over to the Noatak, and so down to Hotham Inlet to kiŋaliq (modern Kotzebue). They also traded with the utokaγmiut at the trading station at the mouth of the Utokak on the kasegaluk lagoon. Their principal contact was thus with the utokaγmiut, the kaŋgianermiut, the noataγmiut, and the kovuŋmiut. Many of the kuγmiut did not go the entire way to Hotham Inlet and contented themselves with proceeding down the Kuk River as far as kaŋic, a point on the head-waters where they met partners from the koluguraγmiut and the

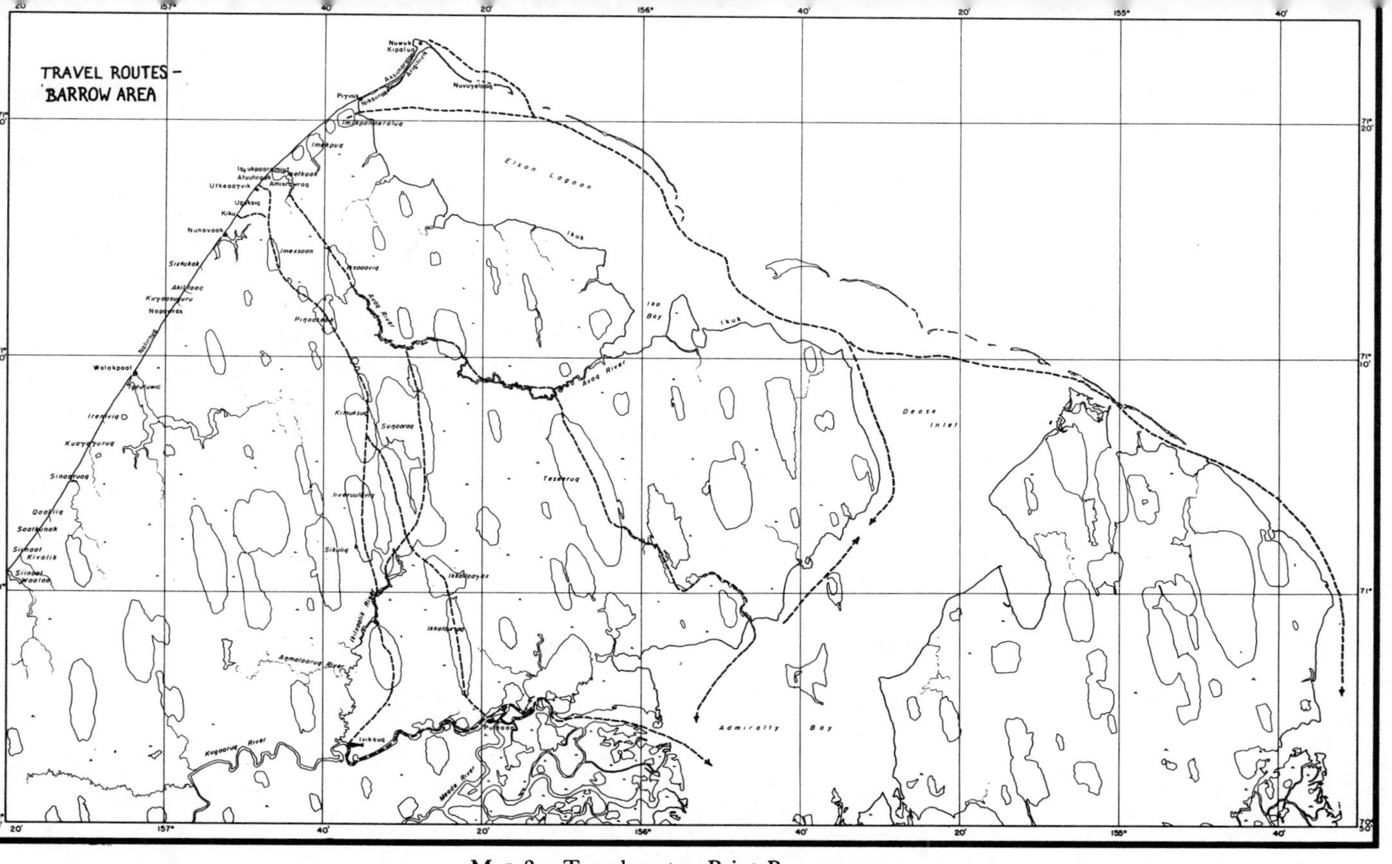

MAP 2.—Travel routes, Point Barrow area.

kaŋgianermiut. The kayaakserevinmiut, those of Icy Cape, followed the same course, taking the route via the Utokak to kiŋaliq.

For the tikeraγmiut, the route was somewhat easier. They went by the coast to Hotham Inlet directly or had the alternative of working inland to the Noatak and so down this river to the trading center. (See map 3.)

At kiŋaliq, another great trading emporium comparable to neγłiq on the Colville, existed. This was visited by the river peoples of the western ranges, the noataγmiut, the kovuŋmiut, the selawiŋmiut, and many of the so-called Malemiut peoples from farther to the south. There are those who came from as far away as the Bering Straits, the Diomede Islands, King Island, as well as Cape Prince of Wales. Metal vessels, tobacco, trade beads, knives, and many other items of European manufacture came up to the northern coasts by these peoples and through the center at Hotham Inlet.

Trade, in short, was the factor which brought tremendously widely separated people together and which promoted the spread of ideas and culture elements from one center to another.

Because much of the background for the present study was laid among the utkeaviŋmiut, attention is necessarily given to the center at neγłiq on the Colville. As may be seen, the nuunamiut who traded here were chiefly from the central Brooks provinces; those to the west tended to go to Hotham Inlet. Similarly, neγłiq was a point at which trade goods of aboriginal manufacture, notably stone lamps, came in from the east. This is in contrast to kiŋaliq, where European goods entered long before actual contact with Europeans themselves. It is worth noting, however, that the Colville was the great avenue of trade for northern Alaska and that the utkeaviŋmiut and nuwuŋmiut got such items as knives and beads from neγłiq rather than from the coasts to the south. Such objects reached the Colville mouth after passing along the river itself. In short, the nuunamiut were the trading intermediaries. If, however, attention is given preponderantly to the Colville center, it is to be understood that the pattern of trade, the involvements of travel to the trading center, and the goods exchanged were in essence the same for both the center on the Arctic Sea and that on Hotham Inlet. Of the two, kiŋaliq was probably the larger center and involved a greater number of traders. Moreover, it was a point of permanent habitations.

The appearance of a trading center was everywhere the same. The people had come by prearrangement and would gather to await their partners, those from the opposite ecological setting. They unloaded their umiaks, set up their tents, the nuunamiut favoring the iccellik, the tareumiut the conical skin-covered kaluγvik. The tents were set up in rows, those from each community or grouping tending to congregate in one place. The umiaks were drawn up on the bank, turned over to dry, and the goods for trade cached under them or placed on racks which might be especially built. In a few cases, families built a paameraq as a summer dwelling at the trading center. This was not generally done, however, unless they remained for a longer period and fished nearby.

The numbers of those who came to the trading centers tended to vary from year to year. It is to be stressed that the majority of those who came were nuunamiut, since it is evident that these were more dependent on trading than were their neighbors from the coast. At neɣłiq, in a peak year, it would apparently not be unusual to find as many as 600 people present, although 400–500 would perhaps be a more normal figure. As has been stated, a roughly similar number might be found at utokak, on the Utokak River mouth, while kiŋaliq had a somewhat larger assemblage. The numbers of those who came to Oliktuk Point were small, as they were also at piɣinik near Point Barrow, where the ikpikpaŋmiut tended to come for the summer to trade and hunt ducks.

These, then, were the points at which the inland Eskimo of northern Alaska met those from the sea. The involvements of trade marked the high point of the summer's activity, and the expeditions were begun as soon as the period of intense economic productivity was over.

The nuunamiut, having completed their spring caribou drives, prepared the caribou meat for their own use and stored it, and having scraped the hides and dried them—they were not tanned—set out in their large umiaks as soon as the ice conditions permitted. They were generally ready to move by early June, when the streams began to flow, although the trading did not actually take place until early August. Since the caribou drives were over before the coastal whaling, the inland groups had adequate time to arrive at the rendezvous.

The tareumiut, too, as soon as the whaling celebrations (nalukataq) were over, began their trading journeys. Like their inland neighbors, they tended to make use of the fresh-water streams as avenues of travel. This was because, on the northern fringes at least, the ocean ice had not generally receded by late June, the time when their own trading expeditions began. The Point Barrow people, especially, were obliged to use the inland routes, although the sea route was generally possible in early summer from Point Hope southward. If by chance the northern seas were open, a quick trip could be made with the result that many might wait in the hope that the ice had receded off shore.

The general pattern of travel to the trading centers and return was the same for both groups. Travel was in family groups which con-

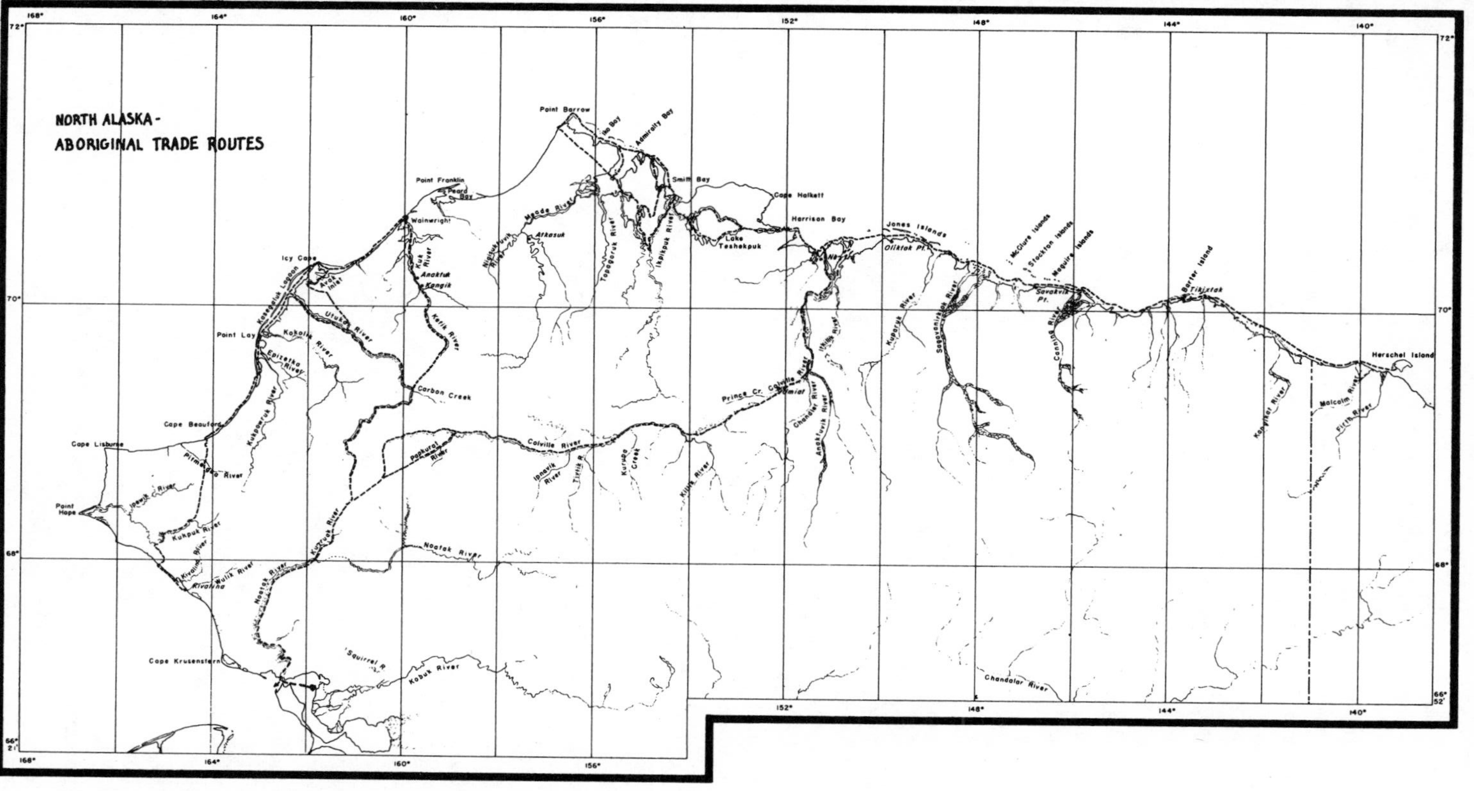

MAP 3.—Aboriginal trade routes, North Alaska.

sisted of one or two umiaks, the families breaking off from the main village or section. The way taken by each family was quite regularly the same each year, attempts being made to avoid any unfamiliar areas. (See map 3.)

Both inland and maritime Eskimo also followed the same methods in traveling. The umiak and sled were the means of transportation. A general pattern was to load the umiak as full as possible with the goods to be traded, leaving small space for passengers, camping gear, such as tents and food, and the sled which rested on the cargo. Dogs regularly accompanied the party. A general practice was to pull the loaded umiak upstream rather than to paddle it, and the dogs were regularly used for this purpose. Indeed, if the load were heavy, the family tended to walk and to draw the umiak behind them. This was an arduous undertaking, in view of the marshy character of the ground and the shallowness of some of the watercourses. Should the group encounter frozen areas, the sled could be brought down and the umiak mounted on it, the dogs again being used to draw the vehicle. If there were no current to contend with, such as in the tundra lakes which formed so vital a series of links in the trade route, the umiak rode more easily and could be paddled. Similarly, if the sea were used, the vessels stayed fairly close into shore and it was possible to paddle and to move more rapidly. Since some of those who went to the trading centers chose to remain out of the home community until the fall freeze, the sled was necessary as a means of return. The method of travel, the alternation of sled and umiak, as circumstances demanded, was thus well worked out and wholly efficient.

The preparations for trading were elaborate and went on for the entire year. "Extras," traded items obtained within the home community, virtually any and all surplus goods not otherwise expended were reserved for one's partner. Basically, the items which were traded between nuunamiut and tareumiut were two—seal and whale oil and caribou hides. These were vital to the economy of each setting and, all things being equal, could not be obtained in sufficient quantity in the native setting. The inland Eskimo required the pokes of oil not only as an added and highly important increment in their food supply, but it formed the basis of the all-important fuel. Indeed, the question of oil as a source of fuel for the nuunamiut raises some significant questions as to the cultural position of this group. If whaling and sea mammal hunting represent a late specialization, which they apparently do, it follows that the inland Eskimo must have originally obtained their oil as the result of a balanced sea and land hunting economy analogous to that farther to the east. This being the case, the historic nuunamiut pattern, entirely removed

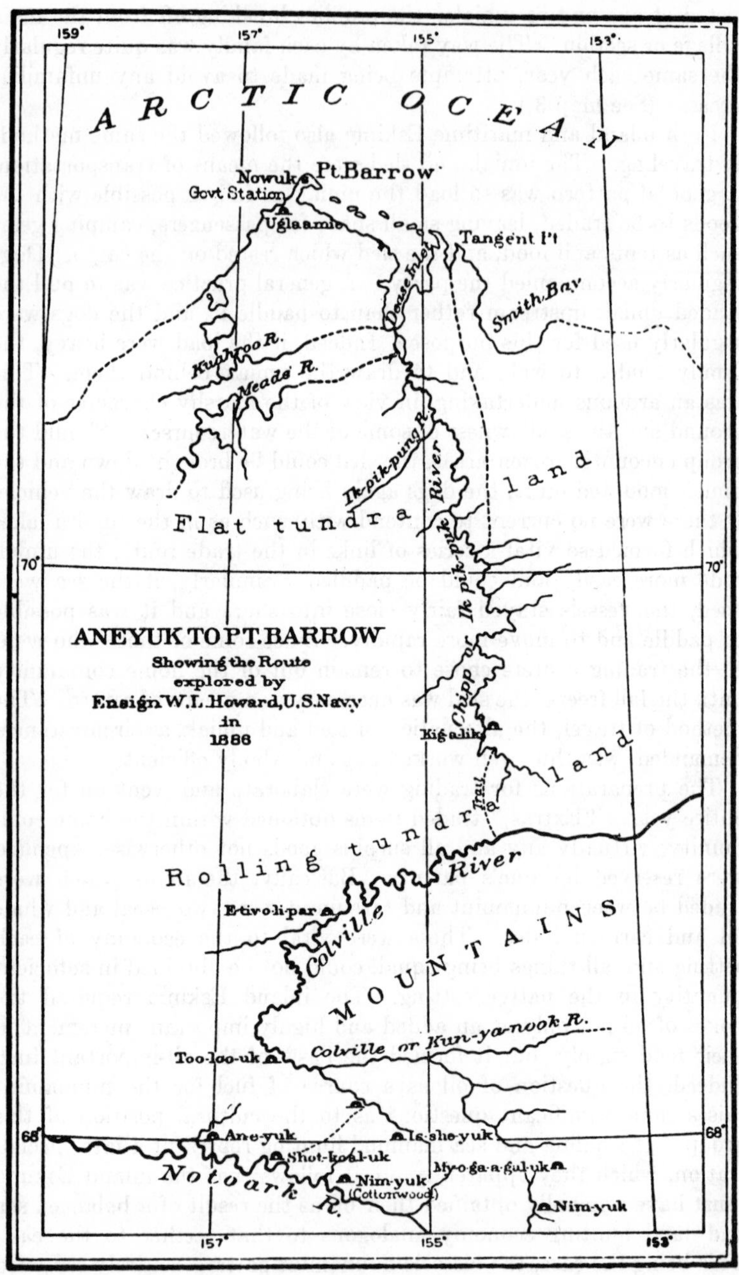

MAP 4.

(For legend, see opposite page.)

from the sea, is as much a specialization in respect to inland adjustments as is the sea pattern.

The tareumiut were slightly less dependent on the trade than were the nuunamiut. The caribou skins which they obtained in exchange were, it is true, the principal material from which clothing and bedding were made. They did, however, have some access to caribou and were able themselves to obtain skins in fair numbers. Moreover, they did engage in some inland trapping so that other commodities, such as wolf and fox pelts, were also available to them. But if their subsistence economy was somewhat less intimately involved, the great numbers of caribou skins which they obtained by trade counted as wealth and in this sense, they derived an incentive to continue the trade. As is noted elsewhere, when these prestige items were outweighed by others which were introduced by outsiders, the trade collapsed, much to the detriment of the inland peoples.

But the basic trade of caribou skins for oil pokes was in turn outweighed by the trade in items affording prestige and wealth. It was this which became significant in maintaining the trade and which culminated in such elaborate festivals of exchange which took place between communities.

The amount of goods which were traded must be regarded as considerable and it is true that each principal devoted much time throughout the year toward the accumulation of goods. The nuunamiut came with umiaks fully loaded with caribou hides. These were packed into bundles, about thirty hides to each, and loaded into the vessel carefully so as to provide proper ballast. It was not unusual for a single umiak to carry as many as twenty such bundles, the catch of a single hunter, and a load of from 500 to 600 hides. A man could take such hides for a relative or associate as well and act as agent for him in the trading. Similarly, the peoples of the coasts loaded their umiaks with sealskin pokes filled with oil, a single umiak carrying as many as fifty such together with numerous other items.

But in addition to the basic items of caribou skins and oil, other goods were numerous. Omitting for the moment such objects of European manufacture which had begun to reach the area by the early 19th century—metal tools and containers, tobacco, beads, muskets (of the early Hudson Bay Company manufacture)—each

---

Map 4.—Route taken by Naval Expedition, 1886 (Stoney, 1900). The route followed by the naval expedition to the Point Barrow area from the south by land is of interest in showing the conventional Eskimo route. Portages led from the Noatak to the Colville; a further portage to the Ikpikpuk provided an avenue to the north. While the residents of Point Hope (tikeraaq) generally traded at Hotham Inlet, some made their way to neγliq via the Noatak and Colville.

setting was able to assemble a formidable array. Trade goods may be listed as follows:

1. From inland to the sea: Green caribou hides were the basic item, the tanned being worth considerably more. Pelts of all kinds including wolf, fox (in five varieties), wolverine, sheepskins, and more rarely, musk-ox hair. The wolverine was especially desired because of its water shedding qualities and was used as a "face-piece," i. e. a ruff on the parka hood. The musk-ox hair was formerly obtained in the area by hunting. No living individuals, however, can recall seeing the animal and point out that the hair was traded from the McKenzie mouth in historic times. It is inferred that the musk ox is recently extinct on the Arctic slope (cf. Skarland, MS., quoted by Rausch, 1951). The hair was used for the manufacture of twine. But there were other items. Sheep horn, used for wedges, lance-heads, and dippers, reached the coast by trade as did caribou sinew, a product extensively employed for cordage and thread. Legs of the caribou, with skin and hair left on, were regarded as a valuable item. The skin of the caribou leg was used for the making of the tops of boots, sinew was obtained from the leg, and the bones were cracked for marrow, a favorite food, indeed, with the back fat, the preferred part of the caribou. Pitch, for use as glue, objects of wood and stone, manufactured items, such as mittens, and some foods, particularly pemmican and berries, made up other important contributions from the inland.

2. From the coast to the interior: As stated, the basic item was oil, representing the greatest quantity of maritime goods. But in addition, there were numbers of seal and ugruk skins, used for boots, and boat covers. Walrus skins, too, were traded in for this purpose, since the nuunamiut used a larger umiak and frequently employed a walrus skin cover. Rope made from walrus hides was an important element, as well as pottery, finished wooden vessels, stone and slate for dart points, some finished clothing, and bags. The latter were often the seal flipper bag used for water storage and water thawing. (A hunter frequently carried such a bag under his parka. It was filled with ice or snow and the body heat thawed the water for drinking.) Ivory was traded inland also, as were logs of driftwood, and now and again, umiak and kayak frames.

Although these were the principal items of exchange, the list is by no means exhausted. Virtually any item was a legitimate trade object. Some food, for example, made its way across the ecological boundaries. Again, the feeling was present that to trade for food was reprehensible, but since each setting had its own specialties, this attitude was in some measure obviated. Pemmican and berries, nuunamiut staples, were traded for muktuk, the black skin and epidermal fat of the baleen whales. The latter was highly prized as food and large pieces of it were brought in from the coasts. It could also be used as fuel. The pattern with respect to food was less concerned with formal exchange. It was used to cement good relations between partners and when given as a gift, the notion of trading for food was avoided. It was in effect a trade but since food was given for food and not for other items, the transaction was not regarded as trading, but rather as gift exchange. Weapons were generally not traded, although they could be, and the materials for their manufacture were. Slate, ivory, and stone were brought in from the coasts and traded for caribou and moose antler, and for sheep and musk-ox horn. Each man was expected to be able to manufacture his own tools and weapons for himself and for his dependent family members.

Trade, as has been suggested, was structured around the formal partnership relationship. There were some discrepancies in the balance of trade between coast and interior in that goods from the sea did command a higher price. This was settled by an arrangement which permitted several nuunamiut to share one partner. Even in this case, however, there was the recognition of one chief partner and of several more distant ones.

When the family groups from each setting embarked on their trading expeditions, the umiaks frequently went together at least for part of the way. Dr. Simpson, describing a departure of traders from nuwuk in 1854, mentions that 14 boats, heavily laden, and carrying 74 people, left on July 3, arrived 4 days later at Dease Inlet, and so pushed on to neγłiq (Simpson, 1855, p. 264). A prompt arrival at the trading station was important since to be there when the trading began meant an ability to make selections and to command the greatest variety of goods. Hence, although families might start out from the home community together, some were outdistanced by others eager for an earlier arrival. Groups would camp at designated places along the way, stopping overnight and traveling during the day. It is said that there were those who merely pretended to camp for the night. As soon as the others were settled and asleep, they broke camp and left, paddling furiously in the hope of reaching the trading station first. The same was true of the two settings in this respect. Eagerness to arrive at the trading center was tied up with absence of formal partnerships. If a person lacked a regular partner, he was at the disadvantage of having to barter. A man with dependable partners could afford to take his time, knowing that they would wait for him and save their goods for him.

Even when a man had trading partners, however, he was not obliged to give all his trade to them. Having satisfied the amenities of the relationship, he could, if he had additional goods, trade them with others. When the umiaks were unloaded at the trading station, there was a display situation, the goods being placed out so that all could see. The traders then walked about, eyeing the goods and attempting to make bargains with the seller. This could take place in addition to the formal demands of trading partnership and it could happen that an individual had a number of trading negotiations going on at the same time. The pattern of open trading which has been described as taking place within a community between nonpartners was followed in the interecology trade as well. A situation of such exchange could proceed like the following:

A seaman has a poke of oil he wishes to trade. He takes it in hand and walks about, crying that he wishes to trade with someone. At once, several nuunamiut come to him and begin to make offers. The first bids three skins for the poke. This is refused. Another bids four, another five. The owner of the oil poke then turns back to the first man who has bid three, asking him if he wishes to raise his bid. The man may well do so and the poke may go for six or seven skins.

As in the open trading in the home community, practice demanded that the first bidder always be given the privilege of raising his bid. The seller was obliged by custom to return to him and to inform him what the intervening offers had been. The practice remains true today and a seller who fails to do this is "dishonest."

Because the maritime people had the greater variety of goods and because their products were of greater necessity to the inland setting, they were in a position to control the situation and to initiate the bidding for articles among the inland traders. Barter tended to raise the price and the men from the coastal villages attempted to control the situation by getting as many bids as possible. Much the same attitudes prevailed in the intergroup trading as applied in the local community. There were those who always overbid and there were the same general attitudes expressed toward proper behavior. A case in point is noted in the following:

A man at neγliq took a poke of oil and sold it to the highest bidder, obtaining six skins for it. Another trader then offered seven after the arrangement for six had been completed. The seller then went to the original buyer and demanded that they return each other's goods. The buyer refused. An argument followed and the buyer took the poke and ripped it with his knife, letting the oil waste on the ground. "Take it back," he is remembered as saying. The original seller left at once without saying a word. He was not, of course, obliged to return the six skins he had received, but it is clear that had he done so, he would have been less liable to blame. Here again it was well to avoid a reputation of being dissatisfied with a bargain once made.

In trading, each man was independent. Men traded with men, women with women. Each person was free to make his own decisions and to trade the products of his labor as he saw fit. Husbands and wives did not consult each other in the trading arrangements they made. Family groups separated, in fact, each going his own way to drive the best bargains possible.

When partners had traded, if one still had goods remaining, the other would assist him in disposing of his property.

The trading ventures lasted for several days and no definite period was set aside for it. When the last of the traders had arrived and everyone had traded to his own satisfaction and had disposed of the property brought, the season was over. A general tendency was to hold games and dances after the trading. Every trading station devoted several days to recreational events. Nuunamiut and tareumiut did not mix in the dancing; it was rather that one group danced for the other. The ball game was played between the two and there were foot races, contests of strength, and singing. At neɣɫiq, piɣinik, utokak, noatak, piŋalu, and the other centers, a Messenger Feast frequently climaxed the trading. This, of course, was between umealit, lesser people looking on and sharing in the food and festivities if not in the gift exchange on a lesser scale.

Families made their own arrangements to depart. If the trading was completed by early August, eight to ten weeks of freedom remained before the darkness set in and before the start of the winter festivities. The usual tendency was to embark on some chosen activity. Some of the seamen, for example, might return quickly to the home community in order to share in the walrus hunting. Frequently, they left their families at a fishing station and returned for them as soon as the first freeze began and the ground was sufficiently hard to be traversed with a sled. Men of both settings might move inland for caribou hunting. A family could return slowly, pausing to fish, to hunt caribou, but remaining together as a unit. In all such cases, the catch, whether of caribou or fish, was cached and the men of the family would return for it when sleds could be negotiated.

The inland Eskimo followed essentially the same pattern, moving slowly back to the home base. Many came to the coasts after the trade was over, either to continue trading, as some did, especially with those who had not made the trading trip, or to hunt ducks and geese. The ikpikpaŋmiut, nuunamiut of the Ikpikpuk River, regularly came to piɣinik as has been noted. They traded there and then remained at the duck camp. "They were very friendly people; everybody was glad to see them."

The situation described here thus involved the lively trade in the summers at the various centers of the Arctic Slope. There were those, however, who went further afield and made contact with other Eskimo groups both to the far south and the east. The contacts at Oliktuk Point with the peoples of Barter and Herschel Islands have already been mentioned, as well as the fact that this area was a source of steatite lamps. "Greenland beads" are also mentioned as coming from this source. From the south, several Siberian products reached the north Alaskan groups. In the period before European contact, an important Siberian contribution was the reindeer skin, spotted or variegated ones being particularly preferred for clothing by men of status and rank. With the advent of European contact, however, and the introduction of metals and tobacco, an added incentive to the southern trade was provided. Much of this, it is true, took place at Hotham Inlet. In the nineteenth century, many of these items reached the northern coast through the nuunamiut who traded along the Colville. Indeed, it was not unusual for a nuunamiut family to trade at Hotham Inlet one summer and then to move up to neγłiq the following summer to dispose of goods acquired in the south. This meant that many inland Eskimo had partners in both great centers and made the trip between them regularly. Because the tikeraγmiut had regular access to kiŋaliq at Hotham Inlet, they received many goods of European manufacture in advance of their neighbors farther to the north. This promoted an intensification of partnerships in the setting of the tareumiut and there were regularly four or five individuals from utkeaaγvik who made the trip to Point Hope in winter by dog team. Having established trading partnerships there, they were able to make capital of them by returning with highly desired items—beads, tobacco, and metal vessels particularly. Those who traveled in winter for trading were known as piroaaktuat. European objects thus reached the Point Barrow-Wainwright area from two sources—via the Colville through the Noatak-Colville route to neγłiq, and by winter trade through Point Hope.

After direct European contact, trade was doubly intensified. The Euro-American whalers introduced new products which increased the volume of trade, especially since furs were a desired commodity. But the exchange began to decline by 1900 with the introduction of the domesticated reindeer and with the establishment of administrative centers on the coasts. The economy of money broke down the necessity for trade and it was the nuunamiut who suffered accordingly. They had no alternative but to move to the coasts. Many did, but found their numbers decreasing as the result of susceptibility to new diseases.

But trade, formulated in partnership, and founded on the exchange of goods between peoples with different economic systems and a consequent mutual interdependence, was basic to the social stability of the peoples of the region. There were no tribes; community solidarity was conceived in terms of hunting group memberships rather than in terms of community loyalty as such. The family was bound together by the kinship tie within the community and beyond it. But the ties of genetic relationship reached beyond the community within the single ecological setting. There were unquestionably few kinship ties between the two ecological groups. There was at least the situation of quasi-kinship, the fact that there were types of behavior associated with sexual exchanges which resulted in a cooperative relationship. But if there were actual genetic ties which cut across ecological lines, the choice was to forget them and to stress the partnership relationship founded in concepts of trade and interdependence. A social balance was effected through trade which worked to the benefit of all.

THE MESSENGER FEAST (kimŋic)

Without question, the most elaborate socioceremonial occasion in the culture of the Eskimos of northern Alaska was the so-called Messenger Feast or Messenger Dance. This was the principal social event of the year. It is to be contrasted with the principal religious event of the year, the Whaling Feast and the Caribou Feast. The Messenger Feast had actually few, if any, religious implications and is ceremonial in the sense that the activities were patterned in an elaborate and complex way. The basis for the Messenger Feast was the enhancing of individual social status, or more specifically, the status of umealit, men who owned boats and headed whaling crews. By association, all the residents of a particular community stood to gain by the activities of these men of wealth and status. Thus community prestige related to the Messenger Feast and those participating by assisting the umealit also stood to gain by the gift exchange involved in the feast. The significance of this festival cannot be underestimated; for communities that lacked formalized political controls, the Messenger Feast served as an integrating element, one which enforced the otherwise vague sense of community solidarity.

Basically, the feast lay in the invitation of the umealit of one community by those of another to attend and to engage in an economic exchange. Such invitations were extended at various times by all the communities up and down the Arctic slope. The village of utkeaaγvik held such feasts with nuwuk, at the point, with Wainwright, and with Icy Cape. To the east, invitations were likewise extended to Barter Island and to the Colville River settlements. There is no doubt that when these festivals were held, an opportunity existed to reenforce ties of kinship and friendship between the villages involved. One result was to establish a sense of solidarity and cultural uniformity between the communities of the region. No village could afford to hold such a festival every year. If the group felt able to command the economic outlay involved, the umealit would invite those of another village of their selection. The village selected for invitation was chosen in large measure on the basis of existing trade and joking partner relations between principals in the respective communities. When, in the early 1900's, Barrow (utkeaaγvik) invited the people from the Colville River area, the feast ended in tragedy. It was on the return trip of the latter people that they were struck by a measles epidemic and were wiped out, dying on the way amidst the gifts they had received. The feast was rarely extended as far south as Point Hope, since this community had such festival relationships with Cape Prince of Wales and other communities to the south. In 1911, an elaborate feast was held at Barrow, the guests being from Icy Cape. Barrow again invited nuwuk in the winter of 1913–14, and the last feast was held at Wainwright, the guests being from Barrow, in 1914–15.

As nearly as can be judged, the Messenger Feast travels no farther east than Barter Island and the mouth of the Colville. It has been described, however, for the Eskimo groups around the Alaskan coasts, such as at Nunivak Island, etc. (cf. Lantis, 1946). The entire pattern of the festival, the elaborate economic exchange involved, and the implications for social status are suggestive of the Northwest Coast potlatch. Of interest, and a point for further research, is the analysis of the diffusion of such ideas from a central Northwest Coast location to the Eskimo of this northern area.

The Messenger Feast was regularly held in winter, usually after the shamanistic festivals of December. The period of early and mid-January is a slack time in which few economic pursuits were carried on, either at the present time or in the past. The winter period, in which the majority of community members were present, was the time for concerted social activity.

As noted above, the feast was social rather than religious. There are one or two religious suggestions which apply to the festival. The umealit, owners of boats and crew leaders, were those who officiated at the festival and who acted as principal hosts. By definition, of course, such men had the greatest wealth in the community and were, by virtue of their continuing gift giving, able to command the loyalty of their respective crews. Since the community was divided, among other ways, along the lines of whaling-crew membership, and since each crew had its respective ceremonial house (karigi), it follows that the Messenger Feast served to implement the socioreligious solidarity of the whaling crew. Likewise, certain restrictions and prohibitions applied to those who participated as leaders in the Messenger Feast. Elements of the feast may be listed in order. (Data refer to Point Barrow, i. e. nuwuk and utkeaaγvik.)

1. The umealiq who conceived of the feast and who determined the guests was the principal host. The chief who directed it tended to weigh the matter carefully over a period of years, gradually laying by a surplus of goods. The umealiq enlisted the aid of his crew. When he felt that sufficient goods were on hand, he broached the matter to other crew leaders and obtained their support. These men then assumed the role of secondary hosts and also obtained the support of

their respective crews in bringing together a large supply of surplus goods. Not only was food amassed in quantity, but also were clothing, skins, pokes of oil, kayaks and umiaks, sleds, dogs, and the like. The women of the various households involved would spend considerable time in preparation, in sewing, in tanning skins, etc. It is to be remembered that the aboriginal community was fairly small in population. A result was that virtually every community member was sooner or later called in to assist in the preparations.

Informants recall the case of maaniksaq, an umealiq of great wealth. Having enlisted the support of the other crew leaders in the community, he issued a statement to each family head indicating how much that family should contribute. If a householder was uncooperative, or attempted to reduce the amount of his contribution, he was threatened by maaniksaq and his lieutenants and forced to comply. It is clear that by working through the crew leaders, this principal was able to enlist the support and contributions of the entire community. Nor would this have been difficult. Since the community at large gained in social prestige through the feast, it is apparent that public pressures would have served to effect wholehearted community cooperation.

2. The economic preparations for the feast having been completed, there remained the matter of the formal invitation. Two kinds of participants to set the machinery of the festival into motion were selected by the principal and secondary hosts. The first to be selected were the messengers themselves. These, the kiviexsuat, from whom the festival takes its name, were older men of dignity and stature in the community, but not hosts. Two messengers were generally chosen. Each was obliged to learn a series of messages to be brought to leading men in the community which was to be invited.

Since the festival involved a foot race and a racing contest between the guest and host community, each principal selected a runner (paaktuat—foot racers) to represent him. This was done at a dance held for the purpose in the karigi of the chief host. The young men of the community assembled there and began to dance, actually rehearsing the particular steps of the messenger festival dances. As they danced, the chief host came forward and danced at the side of a selected young man, one with a good reputation as a runner. After this, the other crew leaders, the secondary hosts, made their selection of a runner in the same way. These young men would later go out to meet the guests and the foot race would be held. They each received a new suit of clothing from their sponsors as well as other gifts.

3. The messengers had now been selected. They met with the hosts in the karigi and were given wooden staffs. These were paddle-shaped sticks, variable in length, with a feather attached

at the end. Across the stick were painted red marks, each for an individual principal guest invited by the respective hosts. Informants disagree as to the marks painted. Some say that the sticks were merely marked with horizontal lines, each one to represent an invited guest, and hence a mnemonic device and badge for the messenger. Others note that the particular property marks, the specific possession of each invited guest, were painted or carved on the messenger's staff. As noted, each messenger was expected to commit to memory the particular message for the invited guest.

4. The principal guests were likewise usually umealit in their home community. The general tendency was to invite men of essentially equal rank. Between them and the prospective hosts there was usually a specific relationship of partnership. While this might involve either a trading partnership or a joking partnership, there was often merely a general understanding that a person from one community would regularly invite some specific individual from the other community. Thus aside from the two types of partnership noted above, there was the third, applying specifically to invitations to the Messenger Feast. Such individuals stood to each other as kiimik, that is, Messenger Feast partners, or more exactly, perhaps, an alternating host and guest relationship. Secondary guests were akpatet. One sent to one's kiimik a specific message via the selected two messengers. To each messenger the same set of messages were given by the various hosts. These were couched in formal language and often were given at considerable length. They involved songs as well as a formal statement of invitation. And they were concluded by a listing of the items which the host expected to receive from his guest. Often, too, they included a listing of what the host expected to confer in return. The messengers were expected to be letter perfect in their recitation to the guests. Hence, they were drilled again and again by the principal hosts. Some days before the dance was expected to begin, the messengers were sped on their way. They traveled in teams, separately, each one driving a dog sled belonging to a principal host. As their badges of status, they carried the painted sticks.

5. At the village of the host, the messengers were sped on their way by means of a special dance. This was a "round dance," a central pole having been erected at the open dance place outside of the karigi of the chief host. As the people danced, the principal hosts approached them and, selecting one man, caught him by throwing a rope about his neck, He was led about the central pole in a sunwise direction several times. He was then taken into the karigi and seated across from the door at the side of the box drum which was used especially for this festival. He was thus selected as the drummer for the dances to follow. His was a special post of honor and for his services

as drummer he was allowed the best food, always being free to state what it was he wished to eat. His food was supplied by the principal hosts. He was also given new clothing and was now expected to remain in the karigi beside the drum until the festival was over.

6. While these activities were being carried out, the young men selected as runners were urged to practice. It was generally the rule that about 20 such young men and boys, usually unmarried individuals, were chosen. Daily they ran out into the tundra for about 5 miles and back again. It was said that they ran to piγinik and back, or down the beach from utkeaaγvik to the area now occupied by the "monument," a distance of some 10 miles. They were urged to practice running so that they would not be beaten. Meanwhile, to the preparations were added the costumes. The members of the crews of the various hosts prepared their dance clothes and brought them to the karigi in readiness for the dancing. Involved here were the best looking parkas, long mittens, and a feather headdress. The latter consisted of a band of matched skins from which feathers were suspended. Women also prepared for the dancing. The dancers lined up in the karigi, men in front, the women behind them. Two young couples, known for their dancing ability, were selected to head each end of the line. They were given particularly elaborate mittens made of polar bear skin which were very long and which came well up over the forearm. The dance was practiced a few times by the home villagers, the men in line facing the door, and engaging in the "jump"dance of the Messenger Feast, the women dancing behind them. (It may be mentioned that while the associations and gift giving of the feast have fallen by the way, the modern Christmas and New Year dances at Barrow follow the old Messenger Feast pattern.)

7. Attention is given elsewhere to the structure and nature of the karigi. As noted above, this structure, devoted particularly to the social and ceremonial activities of the respective whaling crews, is in effect a men's house. utkeaaγvik had three such kariyit at one time and they have also been described for the adjacent villages. The karigi was a permanent structure which paralleled the dwelling in general architecture. For the Messenger Feast, however, the karigi of the host group usually built a special house. This was also called a karigi. Reference to the karigi here in relation to the Messenger Dance refers especially to this building. This structure was generally made of snow blocks set up in a line to form a rectangular building some 40 to 50 feet long. Skins were stretched over the roof and a central skylight was added. Theoretically, the building was the property of the whaling crew, although it was felt to belong to the individual umealiq. He at least owned the skins making up the roof,

which was sometimes supported by whale ribs or wooden planks. The karigi stood all year and was important in the various whaling feasts and preparation. Following the advent of the European whalers, the roofs of the buildings were made of canvas, and sailcloth curtains were used at the door and inside as well. The structure possessed a single door, covered with a caribou skin or canvas curtain. This was placed in the center of one of the long sides of the building. Although the door often faced east, there was apparently no regulation demanding this, or that the building be lined north and south. Opposite the door was a central post with a series of smaller posts paralleling it. This set off the stage for the drummer, as well as a place for the retirement of the returning messengers. Skin curtains were placed for the latter. The great box drum (kalluγaq) was hung from the central pole (pl. 8, *b*). In use, it was swung from side to side and struck by the drummer on the bottom. By the early 1900's, some of the kariyit had ceased to function. In 1911, a dance house was erected for the festival and set up against the Alaska Native Service school.

8. The goods making up the contributions to the guests were also assembled at this time. All the food and other materials destined for distribution were brought together and placed near the houses of the principal hosts to be brought later to the karigi. One can imagine the tremendous excitement associated with collecting the goods. The amount of property assembled was indeed amazing. Not only was there food in great quantity, various cuts of meat, but scores of skins, boats, sleds, clothing, and in more modern times, guns, tobacco, flour, canned goods, and the like. It seems safe to note that the advent of the European whalers with their trade goods lent an added impetus to the Messenger Feast, the new items allowing so much more latitude for distribution and largesse.

9. With the preparations now in order, the drummer selected, the runners to compete, the costuming in order, and the goods collected, the karigi was made ready and the guests awaited. The messengers, meanwhile, had proceeded to the village of the guests. When they came within sight of the community, they halted their teams and remained waiting until they were seen by the people. As soon as they were sighted, the village to be invited, recognizing the staffs and what they portended, came out in a body to greet them. They were then formally invited to the village, and having arrived, announced first the names of those for whom they carried messages. They were then taken to the karigi of the man who was specifically named by the chief host of the inviting village. When all named were assembled, the messengers delivered their formal speeches, sang the songs associated with them, and stated to each guest the

amount of property involved in the invitation. The guests named then replied in kind, stating their own demands, and indicating what they would exchange in return for the items given. The guest had freedom in this respect. As an invited guest, he stood to profit more by the transaction. He was free to make demands on his host and was himself not obliged to comply in every detail with the items which his host demanded of him. Not until he stood in the position of host, presumably at some later time, would he necessarily have to meet the demands of his kiimik. Following the formal reception of the messengers at the village of the guests, the men invited selected runners, amassed whatever they could by way of bestowable property, arranged for teams and men to help them transport their gifts back, and so prepared to set out.

10. If for any reason the invited guest could not come to the village of his hosts, he could name another man of essentially the same status to substitute for himself. Lacking such a man, he could name a woman who then went as his representative. Should either of these be impossible to find, he was free to name a dog who could go in his place and receive his gifts for him and in turn make gifts in his name. The dog was brought on a leash.

11. The guests now began to make their way to the village of the hosts. Accompanying them were the messengers who now bore return messages. In deference to the latter, they were permitted to ride in their dog sleds; the guests, however, were obliged to walk and lead their teams. The trip might thus take considerable time, involving the distances between Barrow and such villages as those at Barter Island or Icy Cape. The guests, thus proceeding on foot, camped for brief periods along the way. As they stopped, the runners and helpers engaged with them in a dance practice, the jump dance of the feast to come, while the runners also practiced running. The group made its way to a point nearby the village of the hosts where it pitched camp and waited. Since it was generally known how long the messengers would be on the way, their return was anticipated. As soon as the guests had camped, the messengers made their way directly back to the karigi of festivities. They came in directly, entering the karigi, and made their way back to the rear of the structure, seating themselves behind the caribou-skin curtains near the drum. Taking their sticks, they raised them so that the marks appeared one at a time above the curtain. As each mark appeared, the messengers alternated in indicating the names of the men who were coming. As they spoke the assembled people moved back and forth and lined up facing the drum, the men to the front, the women behind. At this time, the messengers merely gave the names of the invited guests, without stating whether the guest was actually coming or had sent a substitute.

Nor did they indicate how extensive the entourage of the individual guest might be. The guest was free, of course, to bring his retainers, usually members of his own family, in whatever number he chose. The host was obliged to be prepared for any emergency, to feed and bestow gifts on any number, and of course, it was vital to his position and prestige that he do so, having the reserves at hand to meet any unforeseen situation.

12. Having made their announcements, the messengers came out from behind the curtain and joined the dance which had been proceeding during their detailing of the names of guests. When the dance was over, the messengers went to sit silently in a corner of the karigi, pretended anger, and could not be induced to talk further. The various principal hosts went to them, one by one, to induce them to speak. They turned away, however, with angry looks. It was not until the chief host came to speak with them that they could be persuaded to talk. They then heaped abuse on the chief host, saying that he had sent them on a fool's errand, and that they had not been well received in the guests' village. Custom demanded that they be treated jokingly in the other village, and their elaborated messages deprecated. The pattern appears to have taken a turn such as the following: If the prospective host relayed in his message that he had umiaks and sleds for his intended guests, the guests were expected to laugh and point out that the intended host was niggardly and poor and could never afford such gifts. The messengers were upbraided for undertaking so foolish an errand for so penurious a host. The messengers now repeated this back to the chief host and upbraided him in turn for having so deceived them. This was a signal for the chief host and the men associated with him as principals to pretend insult and to indicate that they would double the amount of their intended gifts.

But the messengers could not yet pretend to be placated. Still making angry faces, they continued to sit in the corner. The chief host ordered the caribou skin curtain taken down and announced—"Now we can begin," and called for everyone to be happy. The various people in the karigi, men and women alike, now go over to the messengers and try to cheer them, making jokes and trying to make them laugh. In whispers the messengers were asked who was coming, what they were bringing, how many were coming with them, etc. In whispers, the messengers gave the answers. These were relayed to the chief hosts, who were supposed to feign utter indifference as to the number of people they would ultimately have to entertain.

13. During this procedure, the runners selected by the hosts were preparing for the foot race. Each of the runners, the number being usually about 20, took a long stick, his own height in length, and fastened to it a pound or two of boiled meat. The runners then

assembled in the karigi, following the announcements and byplay of the messengers, and danced. This dance was to the accompaniment of the swinging box drum, presided over by the man chosen as drummer. Following this, the hosts made sure of the amount of food available, and all retired to await the beginning of festivities on the following day.

14. The messengers had meanwhile made the hosts aware of the individual demands of the guests. The concern here was food, since the guest could request any kind of food from his host. The host, in turn, was obliged to meet the demand. Men vied with one another in imagining the rarest, most costly kinds of food. Should the host be unable to supply the demand, he was subject to ridicule. As nearly as can be judged, this rarely happened, since the demands, although often extremely difficult to meet, were usually within reason. The host made it a point of honor to comply with his guests' desires. Actually, too, the host had considerable time in which to prepare for the guest, since at the close of the feast, the host, whose role at the next meeting will be reversed, told his guest what he expected to get the next time they met. There is unquestionably a reflection here of the elaborated values which were placed on food.

Some examples of these food requests are the following: In one of the feasts in which Barrow had invited the Wainwright people a man from the latter village demanded of his host that he be given the supply of canned goods which Captain Brower, then in charge of the whaling station, had in his store. The host entered into negotiations with Brower and met his guest's demand. Neither he nor Brower ever told what the price for this entire supply had been but it is recalled that the man was in debt to the storekeeper for some time thereafter. In another case, the guest insisted that while eating, he should look at the back fat of a male caribou which was to be hung up before him in the karigi. It so happened that the caribou had for some time roamed inland at some distance and had been rare among the maritime Eskimo. The host went from person to person in the community, asking for the back fat of a male caribou. Finally he located a man who had a few caribou in his ice cellar. Knowing why the demand was made, the owner of the caribou fat drove a hard bargain. The host finally got the desired piece at the cost of a new rifle and a box of ammunition, and, it is said, thought himself lucky to get off at this price. By meeting such requests, the host established his reputation as a man of wealth, resource, and merited high social status.

15. With the guests now camped some distance from the community, and after such time as they had rested, the feast was set to begin with the summoning of the guests through the foot racers. The young men who had prepared the stick and the meat now, at the

beginning of the second day, ran out to the encampment of the guests. The host village assembled and began a jump dance as the young men, twenty or so in number, carrying their sticks with the meat attached, ran from the village. Two dog teams followed them as they ran to the guests' camp. When all were out of sight, the dance ceased and and the host villagers waited for the runners to return. The guests could camp at any point they chose away from the village of their hosts. This was often a few miles. For their camp, the guests had erected a snow house, large enough to accommodate them all, and roofed with skins. When the runners from the host community appeared, the guests came out of their lodge to meet them, standing formally in a line, the principal guests in the center. The runners came up to them, forming their own line and waiting until all had assembled.

16. When the runners from the host village had all drawn up, they formed a line at right angles to the line of guests. Each runner, representing a host, now jumped over to the guest invited by the man he represented. He stood before him and, calling him by name, offered him the stick with the meat. When each guest named had taken his meat, the group stood aside and the runners from the host village were invited into the snow house erected by the guests. They sat down on the floor of the structure and the guests, facing the runners, ate a few mouthfuls of the meat which had been offered. Each guest then offered the meat to the runners to eat and each runner also engaged in the ritual eating of a few mouthfuls. This exchange was marked by certain verbal formalisms, the guest, for example, saying to the runner—"Take some meat; you must be hungry." The guests now replaced the remainder of the meat on the sticks and returned it to the runners. As they did so, another ritualized jump dance began, and dancing with the feet together in a series of jump steps, the group moved out of the snow house.

17. The guests were now at liberty to change their names. This was done specifically for the Messenger Feast, a man taking on a special nickname by which he would be known throughout the course of the feast to follow. This new name was announced to the runner, and at the same time a formal repetition of the desires of the guests with respect to food, special gifts, and the like, was made. When these statements had been made, the foot race was ready to begin.

18. A marked formalism arose with respect to the foot race. The race itself was run from the encampment of the guests to the karigi in the host community where the festivities were to be held. Because of the nature of the proceedings, a handicap was accorded to the runners representing the guests. The race itself was run between the two men representing respectively the host and the guest. The guest's runner started off first, the host runner following him a few moments

later. As the runner's aim was merely to win against another individual, there was no sense of team activity. The course led directly back to the karigi in the host village. The runner on the side of the hosts ran directly into the karigi if he won against his opponent. The guest runner, however, had to circle the karigi once and kick a stick suspended from a pole near the door. It was for this reason that a slight start was given to the runners on the side of the guests. If a runner saw himself beaten on the way and believed himself unable to overtake his opponent, he simply stopped and waited for the teams which came up behind the runners to carry him on. If a guest runner won, he remained standing outside of the karigi, while the runner on the host side, if the winner, was permitted to enter the karigi and to take his place near the drum. In the latter case, the runner returned his stick with the meat attached to the host he represented.

As the race started from the camp of the guests, the latter waited until the runners were out of sight. They then followed by team, carrying their baggage, and picking up the runners who may have given up the race along the way.

19. In the host village, when all the races had been won, the arrival of the guests was signaled by the man at the kalluγaq. His drum, swung from a central pole in the karigi, was swung during the initial proceedings in a sunwise direction. If the race was won by the runners from his own side, a majority of races won by one side or the other constituting a win, he continued to swing his drum in this direction. If, however, the race was won by the guests, he changed the swing of the drum to a countersunwise direction. This was further a sign that the guests, when they arrived, might take possession of the karigi. When all the runners arrived and the winning side was determined, preparation was made for the formal reception of the guests following behind.

The runners on the side of the guests were queried formally as to the requests of the men they represented. From the runners of either side a formal announcement of this was forthcoming. At the same time, the assumed name of the guest was announced. This took the form of a statement that a person of such and such name, giving the nickname, expected to receive the items named. While, as has been indicated, the host was aware of the demands of his guest, he might be suddenly confronted with a wholly unexpected demand. It was a tribute to his status and resourcefulness to be able to comply. Frequently, this involved a rush on the part of the host to meet the request. He might, as noted, be obliged to go further into debt to someone in the community able to supply the item desired.

20. Some time after the completion of the race, the guests, riding slowly in the teams, came into sight. The small boys of the com-

munity now ran out to greet them, running out to the sleds and racing back ahead of the approaching guests. When the guests came into the community, they drew up some distance from the karigi and staked their teams, awaiting developments. The runners representing them then seated themselves near the door of the hosts' karigi and food was offered to them. The host runners, congregated inside, were likewise offered food. If a runner on the host side had given up the race, he could not enter the karigi until the race was over. He generally remained in the house of some friend or relative and only now came forward to join the others.

21. Now was the time for the reception of the guests themselves. The principal hosts came out of the karigi wearing the ceremonial garments of the feast, long bearskin mittens, a feathered headdress, and rich parkas of matched skins. They approached the guests standing by their dog teams, each man holding a bow with an arrow taut against the string. They came slowly over to the guests, feigning anger, and making threatening gestures with their weapons. No sign of recognition of the guests was given. Some of the guests might at this point have donned masks, or at least special headdresses representing various animals. The principal hosts looked closely at each man and then backed away. As they did so, they shot the arrows over the heads of the guests.

This was a signal for the dancers assembled in the karigi to come out and begin a dance toward the waiting guests. In full costume, and forming two lines, they approached the guests, dancing to the accompaniment of the kalluγaq within the karigi. The dancers circled the guests and then withdrew again to the karigi. When all were inside, the guests, in a group, walked slowly to the structure. The dancers had meanwhile seated themselves in a line, the men facing the door on the side of the kalluγaq, the women facing them with their backs to the door. The drummer, having now ceased his drumming, let the drum down to the floor and seated himself on it. Before him he placed a package, representing the first of the gifts to the guests. This was a token gift, containing small, but choice, portions of meat, some ammunition, tobacco, or beads, or some other article of value. The package was wrapped in a skin, usually a caribou hide, carefully tanned. This gift was the offer of the initiating host to the principal guest. Near it, on each side of the drum, the other hosts had placed similar packages. These were lined up, one by each seated man.

The guests now entered the karigi and stood ranged along the wall. Each host now named the guest whom he specifically had invited, taking care to observe any assumed nickname, and, calling him forward, offered him formally a choice cut of meat and the small gift package. This procedure began with the man who had initiated the feast, who first called his special guest. As soon as the first gift had been conferred, the drummer raised the kalluγaq again and began a slow rhythm. This was a signal for the other seated men to pick up tambourines and to begin a series of songs associated with the feast. As they sang, and as the conferring of the gifts was completed, the guests retired to their teams, filing out of the karigi. The singers continued to sing, while the guests, depositing their gifts, brought back similar wrapped packages from their sleds. With these, they now danced into the karigi, moving up and down between the line of seated men and women. The music stopped while the guests in turn gave their gifts to their respective hosts. No food was offered by the guests to the hosts. This ceremony completed, the music began again and the hosts and guests danced together.

The guests now returned to their sleds. After a time the hosts, having briefly continued to dance the usual jump dance of the feast, left in order, principal host first, followed by the men in the order of their arranging the feast, and went out to the sleds of the guests. The principal host then stated formally, "Not enough is yet given." He offered to his guest a second wrapped package, containing much the same type of gift as the first. Each man in order then gave a similar skin-wrapped gift to his guest. The guests reciprocated with similar gifts of their own. When this had been done, the hosts withdrew in order of giving the gifts. The principal host waited at the door of the karigi and, as each man returned to the karigi after the exchange with the guests, he questioned him formally, asking, "What did that man say to you?" The inevitable answer came back, "Nothing." The leader then remarked, "Not enough is yet given," and taking another package, he returned to the guests, giving another gift, and receiving yet another in exchange. He was followed in the same procedure by the other hosts. This was done four times. When the last of the gifts had been exchanged, the chief host made the formal announcement, "Now that is all," and the host group retired back to the karigi.

If the runners representing the guests had won the foot race, they came to take formal possession of the karigi. The guests left the place where they had hitched their teams and danced into the karigi, while the hosts retired. If the host team had won, it was not necessary for the latter to give up the dance house, although the guests would in any case be quartered there. If the hosts had won the foot race, they left the guests to wait outside the karigi for a time before formally inviting them to enter. In case the guests won, they were free to enter the structure whenever they chose after the initial interchange of gifts. Activities now came to a halt, the guests resting in the karigi, the hosts dispersing to their respective homes.

22. On the third day, festivities began with a dance started by the guests in the karigi. This was again the special jump dance of the feast, accompanied by the beating of the kalluγaq. When the guests started to dance, the hosts began to assemble and entered the karigi. Then followed a series of dances between the various secondary attendants of each group. The men who had run against each other in the foot races now danced together, as well as the men who had led the dog teams for each side. Between these men there was also a gift exchange, the gifts being small packages of skin-wrapped meat, tobacco, etc. The hosts with their principal guests came forward to dance again. Here was the opportunity for the hosts to exhibit their generosity and to give some display of their own affluence. Beginning with the principal host, gifts were given to all from either side who had had some connection with the arrangements. The principal hosts gave gifts of skins, pokes of oil, tobacco, beads, labrets, weapons, and the like to the dancers, runners, drummer, and to the drivers of the dog teams. Any who came with the guests, that is, their kinsmen, trading or joking partners, received gifts from the first host and in turn from the men who agreed to initiate the feast with him.

But attention was now directed to the principal guests themselves, the men who had been invited by name and for whom the messages were intended. Following the random bestowal of gifts on all present, the guests left to take again their station by their staked teams. The gifts destined for these men were now brought into the karigi and placed before the box drum. This was unquestionably the most dramatic part of the feast. Here were displayed goods in remarkable quantity and size. Skins, pokes of oil, weapons, all in quantity, as well as sleds, kayaks, and even umiaks were brought in. An assemblage of property, the amount and variety of which increased with the advent of the whalers, was piled high in the karigi. The impression obtained is of the entire community congregated to see the amazing display of goods, of excited expressions at the amount, and of openly avowed admiration of the men of such wealth.

The hosts involved in the conferring of these gifts ran one by one from the karigi out to where the guests were waiting. As each called his guest by name, the two ran back to the dance house, "racing," but with the guest drawing slightly behind. When both entered the karigi, they were obliged to kick at an inflated bladder suspended some feet above the floor near the door. They put the feet together and jumped, hitting the bladder with both feet. The host then made a formal presentation of the great gifts which he had for his guest.

As the name of the guest was called, the drummer, sitting at the kalluγaq, struck the drum four times. When the gifts were presented to the guest, he was given, at the last, the food which he had demanded. He sat near his pile of gifts in the karigi and proceeded to eat what was given him, or at least as much of it as he could. Whatever he failed to eat was taken along with the rest of the presents.

The gifts were given to the guest all at once. When his name was called and the drum sounded, he came forward with his host and the latter indicated to him the gifts which were his. As noted, some of these he had requested, others were given him as a reflection of the generosity of his host.

23. The conferring of the gifts was concluded with a dance, again to the accompaniment of the kalluγaq. The tempo now changed, however, and a slow measured dance was the result. In this dance, women played a part, each dancing behind a man. All sang a series of songs related to this aspect of the Messenger Feast. At this dance, the previous idea of alternating dances between hosts and guests had been abandoned and the two groups danced together.

When this was concluded, the hosts presented their guests with sticks, small wands each with a red mark on it. The guests and hosts selected another man, indicating the selection by giving him the stick, to represent them in the soccer game of the next day. Again about 20 young men were chosen by each side. The choice was made from among the men of one's own group.

It may be imagined that much time was consumed in the display and bestowal of gifts. Following the formalities of the day, the guests and hosts could now devote the remainder of the time to informal visiting, gossip, etc. The third day was concluded with social dances and the gifts received were brought out to where the guests had stationed their teams. The guests again retired to the karigi, the hosts back to their homes.

24. The fourth and last day of the feast involved a kick-ball game between the teams which had been chosen by the guests and hosts. The formal gift giving was now at an end. The guests began to dance in the morning and the members of the host community gradually assembled and joined them. After a time, the young men chosen to play the game met on the beach and the football was thrown to them. Here was the usual game of the Eskimo, a kick-ball variant, played with a baleen-filled skin. The game was not played in a definite court, nor were there goals. One team simply kept the ball as long as possible, dribbling it, and passing it from one to the other. The side lost which first gave up. This was played most of the day up and down the beach. At last, the guests signaled that it was time to go. The soccer players came together, raised their hands in the air,

palms touching each other, while the players for the guests remarked, "Next time you will come to us."

25. The principal guests and hosts now went back to the karigi for a final dance. Here, a formalistic pattern again emerges. After dancing the slow dances of the previous day, guests and hosts filed out of the karigi. The hosts took their places at the side of the door; the guests filed out and assembled some distance away in the direction of their sleds. Now from within the karigi came two men (uluweaktuat—bowmen) in disguise. They carried bows with arrows taut against the bow strings and wore loon-bill masks and hoods (pl. 1, *b*). They danced a jump dance around both groups, first between the two groups, then around the guests, then around the hosts. As they completed the dance, they discharged arrows over the heads of the hosts. This was the signal for the departure. The guests mounted their sleds, now loaded with gifts they had received, and departed. The people of the home village stood by to watch them off. At the final dance, the guests had been told by the hosts what the latter expected from them the next time a dance of this kind was held. The host stated his desires, indicating as well what he thought he might like to eat, to see, or to sit on.

26. The final dance of the fourth day was known as "coming out of the dance hall." It was said that if the masked bowmen broke their strings in the course of their dance or in shooting over the crowd, they would die. There is a recollection of a bowman breaking his string as he danced. The people were said to have been terribly shocked. The man himself died the following summer.

When the guests had departed, the skins were removed from the roof of the karigi and the walls were renovated. It was thus made ready for the preparations for the spring whaling. There seems to have been no special rededication of the structure at this time. There is rather the reflection of a concept of a transition in the character of the building. The skins were scraped, the drum removed, and the building cleaned out. After this, the karigi again became the domain of the whalers. This took place, of course, only in the event that the regular whaling karigi was used for the Messenger Feast. One especially built for the purpose was simply dismantled.

A specific instance of behavior associated with the Messenger Feast was recalled by contemporary residents of the Barrow community. In a festival in which Wainwright invited men from Barrow (utkeaaγvik), kanayuq of Wainwright invited a man from Barrow named simiγiroak. As part of the message forwarded to simiγiroak by kanayuq, his kiimik, songs were sent. These were frequently composed for the occasion by the prospective host and formed part of the message which was carried by the man selected as messenger.

Dance steps were often especially created for the particular songs. Part of the training of the messenger was the drilling in the new songs as well as the verbal messages. kanayuq, on the occasion in question, had created several special songs. simiγroak, in turn, made a song which he brought with him to Wainwright. This he sang, dancing with the men who accompanied him, in the karigi at Wainwright. It was a reflection of the requests he made to kanayuq. The song is still recalled:

kanukuvaŋa
My condition

kapiŋaytpiq
How am I?

kanayuq
May kanayuq

okuqaaniŋmun
My skins for clothing

kavili awramu
My wolverine skins

uneatkamikimisuak
The smallness of my sled

The song refers to his own requests both for wolverine and other skins for clothing and he indicates that his sled is not big enough to carry all the things which he wishes to take back with him. Later, when simiγiroak was invited to Icy Cape by another man, he sang the same song to his host there. It is also recalled that simiγiroak changed his name when invited to the feast, as, indeed, did kanayuq when he came to Barrow as a guest. The names which they assumed are no longer recalled. One informant stated that the names chosen were secondary names, conferred in childhood and reflecting a dead ancestor, but not otherwise used. Others stated that special Messenger Feast nicknames were selected. The latter situation was said to apply between joking partners who might stand as kiimik to each other in the feast.

As between men in the kiimik relationship, a joking partnership thus might also exist. The humor, especially in making ostensibly impossible requests of one's kiimik, is not to be overlooked. Indeed, even when no messenger festival was under way, the sending of songs to men with whom one alternated in the guest-host relationship was usual and humorous. The Messenger Feast, however, did not primarily involve the joking partnership, a feature reserved for other, less formal occasions; it was simply that the various partnerships might in some measure overlap. An exchange of songs was usual, even where no Messenger Feast was involved, a reflection, too, of the social value placed on songmaking. Such songs are not to be confused with the more ritualized, magical songs developed for some specific purpose. Thus, tarrak, who acted as principal host with maaniksaq, had a song to compel the runners for the opposition to slow down.

CONCLUSION

The primary purpose of the Messenger Feast was an economic exchange. In this sense, it was social rather than religious, although any number of ritualistic elements are discernible in the patterning of behavior associated with it. As mentioned above, there is much in the feast suggestive of the potlatch exchanges of the aboriginal Northwest Coast. It seems most probable, in view of the distribution of the festival, that the feast is indeed a rephrasing of the basic potlatch idea. In general, however, the tone of the Northwest Coast culture is lost. It is true that a man of substance in the community stood to enhance his social status by his participation in the feast, and it is also evident that he depended for support in it on the good will and assistance of his followers. There is no concept of the staggering rise in the exchange of surplus goods that characterizes the area farther to the south. But that there was the concept of validation of status and the opportunity to achieve the highest social rank that Alaskan Eskimo society provided indicate a marked parallel to the Northwest Coast idea.

The Messenger Feast reflects a preoccupation with property and wealth in the North Alaskan cultures. Such gifts as were bestowed were not of course lost. At the next feast, the host became the guest and stood to regain his property. But aside from these considerations, the social aspects of the festival are to be emphasized. It was in the Messenger Feast that a chance for contact with other communities arose, something which unquestionably had its reflection in the growth of an extended aboriginal trade. Through such contacts, ties with other villages were reaffirmed, and trading, as well as feasting partnerships, formed. The village as a whole was remembered for its generosity and largesse and each community sought to enhance its reputation in this direction. In this respect, despite the ties of kinship which cut across the village community, the Messenger Feast had a decidedly integrating effect in creating a solid community front and a sense of in-group solidarity. The kinship groups and the whaling-crew grouping were unquestionably factors which might tend to draw a community apart, or at least make its cohesiveness somewhat ephemeral. It was in such an institution as the Messenger Feast, on the one hand, and in the distribution of meat by a whaling crew following a successful hunt on the other, that the sense of community was brought to the fore. And, except for the occasional feuds between families, either inside or outside of the community, a development like the Messenger Feast provided lasting contacts and a sense of cultural uniformity between the peoples of the Alaskan Arctic slope.

So far as is known, the Messenger Feast has not been described elsewhere for the culture of the Barrow Eskimo. As noted, the festival does not appear to have spread to the Eskimo farther to the east, and the Barrow area may accordingly be regarded as the ultimate point of the distribution of it. The Point Barrow Expedition of 1881–83 was aware of the feast but the reports contain no data on it. Both Murdoch and Lieutenant Ray mention an invitation extended to the latter. Murdoch's statement may be worth quoting:

"We never heard of any such elaborate 'donation parties' as are described at Norton Sound and the Yukon Region, where a man 'saves up his property for years' to distribute it among his guests" (Dall, 1870). A festival, however, was held at nuwuk in June 1883, which apparently resembled the second kind described by Dall. Two men came down from nuwuk to invite Lieutenant Ray and Captain Herendeen, telling them what presents they were expected to bring. Unfortunately, it was considered that too much was asked and the invitation was declined. The messengers carried "notched sticks" (Murdoch, 1892, pp. 373–375).

It is evident that had Ray and Herendeen accepted the invitation, they would have received much more property than they had been obliged to give. The guests gave gifts, it is true, but the burden of giving lay with the host. In this case, it is possible that the nuwuk people were attempting to exploit the white men and to obtain considerably more than would have been asked of an Eskimo guest.

Murdoch mentions three kariyit at utkeaaγvik and two at nuwuk. He lists them as kudyigi, although he refers to Simpson's earlier karigi. No detailed description is given, except to note that the building was broader than it was long, with a central ridgepole and a sloping roof. He does not mention the fact that the karigi was built of ice blocks, but does record the fact that the walls were banked with sod. He also records the presence of a clear ice window, suggesting the ice construction, but does not mention the skylight. Murdoch also notes that the structure might accommodate 60 people, according to a description he received from Lieutenant Ray. This points to the fact that the karigi was much larger than the dwellings. Murdoch further points out that the karigi was not used in winter except on the occasion of dances, games, and "conjuring ceremonies." This seems generally true, since the structure became a sleeping place for men during the whaling activities. That it was not used for guests as Murdoch claims seems unfounded in view of the fact that the visitors in the feast described had the building for their own use (ibid., pp. 79–80).

THE INDIVIDUAL AND THE LIFE CYCLE

INTRODUCTION

Attention has been given to the various social units which made up the cultures of the Alaskan Arctic slope. Through them moved the individual, occupying a series of statuses in relation to the society at large. When the individual is followed through the course of his life, the nature of the social units is lent perspective. In the individual the meeting place between family and community, between kin group and mode of life, and between the various kinds of extra-familial association is found. It is thus possible to determine the place of the various life crises and to obtain some concept of underlying values in answer to the question—what constituted an ideal person? The present section proposes to deal with the individual in his various roles from birth to death and to lay particular emphasis on the socialization process—the techniques by which the individual was made one with the society.

PREGNANCY

A woman was regarded as pregnant when the menstrual cycle was interrupted. Nine moons were then reckoned from the time of the cessation of the menses. It is said that the early stages of pregnancy could be readily ascertained since a woman's eyes became shadowed, and her lips and breasts "turned kind of blue." As soon as the pregnancy was further along, the weight and size of the woman was judged and these led to the prediction of the sex of the unborn child. It is said that a woman gets thinner before the birth of a boy but gains weight before a girl is born.

Some abortion was practiced, but no contraception was known. A woman desiring an abortion continually pressed on the fundus of the uterus with both hands or leaped down from a high place. She might also press her body against sharp rocks. There is a suggestion of coitus interruptus. Contraception was otherwise magical. A woman who did not want children could borrow a belt from a barren woman and wear it. Some old women knew songs to prevent conception and sang them over a woman's belt. This was sometimes requested, but often it might be done from sheer malice on the part of the old woman. It is said that if a woman got such a belt, either one which had been sung over or from a barren woman, and then conceived, her delivery would be extremely difficult. A girl was told always to avoid the belt of another woman, not to touch it and certainly not to wear it. As noted elsewhere, a man solicited sexual intercourse by touching a woman's belt.

It may be mentioned that the people of the area today have no means of contraception. No birth-control advice is given out by the native service hospital. One man who has lived elsewhere in Alaska is reputed to practice birth control. Informants were agreed that it was very necessary. There are said to be more children now. This is, of course, true and probably relates to the better health care in certain directions. At least, more infants appear to survive.

There were, of course, any number of beliefs relating to pregnancy and a series of associated prohibitions. Unless these were followed, harm might result for either mother or child. A child would be lazy if the mother rested or slept apart from the prescribed bedtime. The pregnant woman could not walk backward out from a house lest she have a breech delivery. There was a bit of countermagic here. If a woman had to leave a house backward, she said aloud, "If a child is born, it won't be turned around." A pot or vessel could not be put over the head of a pregnant woman. If it were, she would not be able to deliver the placenta. If a woman put a bag into another bag, the child would be born with a caul. No special attitudes toward a caul could be elicited, however. It was not a bad omen. If a pregnant woman kept her arms in her parka all the time, the child might be born without arms. One woman was described who kept one arm inside the parka during pregnancy. And, indeed, her child was born with one arm under the flesh of its chest. The old concept, common to so many people, that a pregnant woman should not make cordage appears here. This would delay the delivery and might result in strangulation of the child from the umbilical cord. The father was also well advised to refrain from net making and tying knots. There appears to have been no other particular restriction on the father.

Sexual intercourse was permissible during pregnancy. It was not viewed as harmful to the child nor as affecting the child in any way. Even in the advanced stages of pregnancy, the husband might effect penetration from behind his wife in contrast to the usual superior position.

There was no elaboration of theories relating to conception. Because aborted fetuses had been seen, a general homunculus idea was prevalent. The child was formed "very tiny—a little dwarf," in the body of the mother. "It comes out when it is ready." There was likewise no particular theory as to how the child was related to the respective parents. A child was felt to resemble its father more than its mother, but the seed of both combined to create the child. It was said of a child, "He is just like his father," and the judgment was made on the basis of appearance, manners, actions, the walk, and the like. As among ourselves, people gathered to see a newborn child and pointed out resemblances to the father, the grandfather, the mother, and other relatives. If a child was lazy, it was because his father, grandfathers, or mother, had been the same. If a grandfather was a great whaler, it was said of the child that he would also excel in whaling or some other activity for which the grandfather was famous.

There was no particular magic used to determine the sex of an unborn child. At least, there seems to have been none which the parents themselves could perform. A woman might repeat, "This is a boy," in order to have a boy baby, but, as noted, size and weight were regarded as factors in prediction of sex. But if a family felt strongly about the matter, the services of a shaman could be enlisted. By his songs, he could change the sex of a child in the womb. Generally, a family preferred that the first child be a girl. When older, she could assist in the care of her younger siblings. Boys, however, seem to have been otherwise preferred. When a family wished a boy, for example, a shaman might say, "This child was born a girl, but I changed it to a boy." Others were also said to have the power to change the sex of a child either before or after birth.

When a woman married and had a child before the 9-month period, so that the husband could not have been the father, some ill feeling might arise. The husband might search for the natural father, which he could do, of course, by noting the appearance of the child. He might then insist that his wife leave him and marry the natural father. On the other hand, he might be glad of the child and wish to keep it.

BIRTH

Birth took place in a special parturition lodge, a snow house which was erected for the purpose by the father of the child or, if he were absent, by one of his relatives. This parturition hut was known as the aanigutyak or apuutyak. The woman went thither when she began to labor. If the group were traveling, as among the nomadic groups generally, the people stopped and hastily erected the structure, waiting while the woman delivered. The apuutyak was small, large enough only for the woman and an assistant. It was lined inside with moss and was covered outside with dog feces which were collected for the purpose by the husband. No data could be had on why the latter was done. The moss was arranged so that the woman could kneel on it. It was here that the baby would be placed. Moss had been collected before the birth by the woman and her husband and dried over the oil lamp. It was then sacked and used in the birth hut as well as for diapering the child.

The woman delivered the child in a kneeling position, often hanging from the roof of the birth hut by a strap or beam. There was no special class of midwives, the woman's mother, mother-in-law, grandmother, or some other female relative usually rendering aid and receiving the child. The female assistant was generally one who had some experience with childbirth. Before delivery, people in the house might untie knots, thus aiding the ease of birth.

All birth magic, except possibly for the shamanistic activities designed to determine the sex of a child, was aimed at easing delivery. A busy woman was thought to make herself strong so as to have an easy birth, as well as preventing laziness in her child. She might also have worn a strap about her body so as to prevent the fetus from becoming too large.

The parturient was potentially dangerous, to herself as well as to the community. During pregnancy and birth, she should avoid other pregnant women. She wore old clothes during the pregnancy which were discarded when she returned from the birth hut with her child. Birth was particularly in the domain of women. No man assisted at birth or entered the birth hut. The husband might stand outside, or, if the husband were away from the community, a relative, either his or the woman's, waited during the birth. The husband could engage in no activities during the delivery process. He was obliged to remain in the house or tent and if he came out, he was to stand by the birth hut. Although a shaman lost his power if he came into contact with a pregnant woman (or one menstruating), he might assist in the birth. This he did by singing, usually at the house of the parturient. He could help his own wife in the same way, but he could do nothing to aid his child. A shaman, in fact, was considered to lose his power if he attempted to treat his own children.

The child was delivered, laid on a bed of moss in the birth hut, and the assistant waited for the expulsion of the placenta. When delivery was completed, the assistant cut the cord with her ulu and tied it. Skins were at hand to wrap the placenta. This was done at once with the cutting of the cord. It was taken out and buried. No woman dared look at it lest her eyes become weak. While no definite information could be obtained, it would appear that if the placenta were not properly treated, and thus eaten by dogs or other animals, the results would be harmful to the child.

After birth, the woman was under restrictions for 4 days, if the child were a girl, 5 if it were a boy. During this time she remained in the birth hut and was subject to food taboos. These were especially true if the child was a boy, less so, if a girl. The concept was to eat only those foods which might have a beneficial effect on the child. Meat from animals whose characteristics were not admired was avoided. Thus, one woman is described as having eaten only the wings of ducks in order to make the child a good runner and paddler. Her son later won a kayak race in the games played after trading at neγeliq, beating out a man of great reputation as a paddler. But there were other taboos similar to those imposed on women when menstruating. The mother could not eat raw meat or blood.

For 2 days, the newborn child was not nursed, the mother waiting until the voiding of the colostrum. The baby's mouth was washed out and the baby was given water with a little oil warmed in the mouth. At 2 days, nursing began. The newborn child was not washed. The mother put it in her parka, frequently licking it clean and rubbing it down. The baby was immediately diapered with moss and caribou skins.

When, after 4 or 5 days, the mother returned to the household, she discarded her old clothes, donned new ones, and the taboos to which she was committed were lifted. At this point, the child might be said to be accepted as a member of the household and family groupings. It was then named, taking the names of various deceased relatives.

If the economic circumstances were such that the child had to be abandoned, it was not named but taken at once from the mother and tossed aside near the birth hut. This was, as has been stated, a family decision, the wishes of the mother being frequently overridden. It was the woman's mother-in-law who most frequently came into the birth hut and took the abandoned child away from the mother. But when the child received its names and was returned to the household, it was a member of the group. Then only the most extreme circumstances would warrant its abandonment. If the family were pressed, it was regarded as better to give the child out in adoption than to allow it to perish. Indeed, even when it was agreed that the child be given out in adoption, the natural mother kept it for a time, she being the only one who could effectively nurse and care for it. Once weaned, it could more readily be given away.

There were, it is true, a number of restrictions which applied to the parturient woman. In general, these were conceived to protect both mother and child. Such magic as there was met this end. There was no surgery associated with birth, except the cutting of the navel cord. There were no attempts at manipulation of the fetus in case of a difficult delivery, although some old women were reputedly skilled at turning the baby in case of a breech delivery. If the placenta failed to follow, there was no action taken, no attempts being made to pull on the cord. In a difficult delivery the old woman assisting might bear down on the woman's uterus, clasping her body from behind and dragging her weight against it. If labor were prolonged, a shaman was hired to sing, but there was no other known technique. There was no Caesarean type of surgery, either on a living woman or posthumously. Shamans never performed autopsies, as in some adjacent cultures.

Some of the women living at present in the area, who have given birth to children both at the hospital and by the older method, are agreed in preferring the aboriginal way. They claim that delivery while prone, as in a hospital bed, is far more painful, since the uterus presses on the spine. There is probably little doubt that the method was a successful one. The isolation of the child in the birth hut reduced the possibilities of contagion from others. Only if the birth were difficult was the culture at a loss, having developed no techniques to meet unusual situations. Infant mortality was high, but it seemingly arose from postnatal care rather than from birth itself. Not that this was not adequate; exposure, food shortages, the failure of mother's milk, were factors enough even without the introduction of such European diseases as the common cold, measles, and tuberculosis.

INFANCY

"A happy home likes children; people who could not agree threw babies away." There is no question that babies were welcomed, that maternal devotion was a strong theme in the culture. A woman was expected to want children, to care for them, and to give them affection. There is little doubt that a childless woman suffered. Apart from the economic potential of a child, and quite apart from the fact that the family groupings welcomed a new member, the women of the household were delighted to have children about. Even in adoption and in step relationships, the maternal development was vividly defined. "You love your children; you kiss them and hold them all the time."

The child was, and is, carried in the mother's parka. It was not cradled or bound, having considerable freedom of motion in the roomy parka. Mothers went to their daily tasks carrying the child. Indoors, the child was released and set on skins. The mother always attempted to keep the child warm.

The child was nursed when it cried. There was no scheduling of feeding times. In traveling, as among the nomadic groups, which might be resumed within 4 or 5 days after birth, the child was fed at the mother's breast whenever it cried. Among the maritime groups, where the mother might be busy about the house, the child was fed at the times most convenient to the mother. However, "it is sad to hear a child cry," and it may be inferred that the child was given the breast as it demanded. The child had only mother's milk until the age of about 1 year. Shortly before this, it was introduced to more solid foods, being given broths and premasticated meat. Water was also given shortly before the child was a year old. It was at this time that the child was given out in adoption, if it were so planned. If the mother's milk supply failed, the child was sometimes given to another woman to wet-nurse, but more often, reliance was placed on broths and premasticated food. It was here that the child might suffer, and the mortality seems highest among such. Weaning was a gradual process. Children might nurse until 4 or 5 years old, even though they had been introduced to other foods at the age of about 1 year. A mother might nurse two children of different ages at once. Some twin births have been reported but no special attitudes toward them appear to have arisen. One of the twins might be abandoned.

It would thus appear that the weaning process was a very gradual one and extremely easy for the child. An older child was not rejected by the mother in favor of a younger. Indeed, it is still true that the eldest child is the one to whom the greatest degree of affection is given. Sibling rivalry in relation to breast feeding could not of course be wholly averted. When an older child was of necessity displaced by several younger siblings, he often showed temper in the form of tantrums. These were usually ignored. Today, women put salt or pepper on their breasts to keep an older child away, although today nursing at so late an age as 2 is most unusual. There was no attempt to shame a child away from the breast; his desires and tantrums were overlooked and he presumably quickly saw that he got nowhere with them. By 4 or 5, in any case, the child was out at play a good deal. Up to this time, he enjoyed a warm and intimate contact with his mother, not only at her breast, but being carried in the parka.

But if weaning was a long and gradual process, toilet training was effected while the child was unusually young. While there was no punishment involved, the child was taught to control bladder and bowel processes while still an infant. At the age of 2 to 3 months, the mother set him over one of the wooden vessels used to collect the household urine and held him there until the sphincter muscles relaxed. She usually blew gently on the child's head as she held him. Bladder control was not especially differentiated from anal control. The process of blowing on the head evidently served to establish the response. The child was diapered while young and while carried in the mother's parka. Soft caribou skins covered a layer of moss which was periodically changed. Later, when the child began to walk, he was fitted with "training pants," as they are still called, a legginglike garment from which the child's buttocks protrude. Today these are made from cast-off clothing and worn by the child about the house. They appear to be aboriginal, however. The child quickly learned to avoid wetting or soiling himself. One can see an environmental reason for such early toilet training. It would be distinctly dangerous to be out with wet clothing in cold weather. If a child had an "accident," however, he was not punished. The mechanism of shaming a child was not used. There was no punishment for the chronic bed wetter. This is true today. With the fairly serene home situation, and the absence of punishments, one might assume that the toilet training adjustment, however early, was not a highly traumatic feature.

The child slept with his mother, or parents, as the case might be. He was nursed as he wished in the parents' sleeping area. As soon as the parents were able, following the birth of a child, they resumed sexual intercourse. Women complained that their husbands were too demanding following the birth of a child. The child was not barred from the parents' bed during intercourse. Women were said to like to continue to nurse as long as possible. A younger child generally took the place of an older sibling in the mother's or parents' bed. The older sibling in this case was relegated to a place with a grandmother or older female relative. The importance of these older women in child raising and care cannot be underestimated. The older women presumably had leisure to give to the child, while the mother did not. Again and again one encounters the grandmother as a source of protection and affection. As is so frequently the case in many cultures, the grandmother plays an important role in the socialization process. The grandfather, too, was important, especially for boys. Because there was always some older relative present either in the house or the nomadic tent, the child was not wanting in affection and was not rejected. The older siblings were always interested in the younger, while grandmothers, aunts, and others, looked after children. It was this development which apparently curbed any sense of rejection and minimized any pattern of sibling rivalry.

In the old culture, because the child was not confined, he began to sit up at the age of about 8 months. Shortly thereafter, he began to crawl about the house or tent. This was a prized stage of life so far as the parents were concerned. And it was at this point, too, that the father began to take a genuine interest in the child. The child was not forced into either walking or talking. He walked at about a year or more, began to talk slightly later. The relatives held out their hands to make the child come walking to them. They also repeated certain words for the child as it began to talk. A slower child was not forced into any activity; he was allowed to develop much as he could.

Infancy, then, was a period of freedom for the individual. He was allowed to suck, chew, move, much as he chose. He was warmly welcomed by all his kin, not rejected at any point, and clearly made to feel one with the family grouping. There were for boys, however, certain rigors in the social environment. When the north wind blew, an infant boy might be placed outdoors for a time naked. This was felt to make the child hardy and to enable him to take his place as a man at a later time. The north wind was male, the south wind female. This was not done to girls. Physical strength was prized. An infant might be told by his grandfather, as soon as he was able to talk, how he should develop his strength and excel in feats of physical prowess.

CHILDHOOD

One may define childhood as the period from walking, talking, and a degree of independence until puberty. There were no status terms in the language—a general word for child, it is true, but the various stages of development were not especially designated. One of the characteristic criteria of childhood as against infancy was the beginning of sex differentiation. Part of the socialization process was the dichotomizing of girls' and boys' activities. In the main, this related to the beginnings of work. Girls remained with the mother, and were introduced gradually to such tasks as cooking, sewing, gathering wood, and bringing water. Boys, on the other hand, watched the activities of the men, learning to butcher, to accompany their fathers or older male relatives in boats and sleds. Boys were not usually introduced to hunting until after puberty, however. Beginning by about age 10, they might go along as spectators on a hunt and do menial chores for the hunters.

As soon as a child was capable of reasoning and being reasoned with, certain instructions were given him in an informal way. He was taught the names of all his kin, of his qataŋuutigiit, his parents' partners, and the like. These, he was told, would always "help him." Similarly, he was made to feel disapproval if he were unduly noisy in the house or tent. This was rationalized in that unexpected noises disturbed the game all around and would drive it away. As a result, and this was presumably enforced by parental attitudes, the child learned to speak softly. Even today, children are accustomed to whisper in conversing with adults and to remain quiet. The child was expected to obey all older people, and fell into this regimen fairly readily. In keeping with the ideal of hardiness being instilled in boys, no boy could eat except when the family meals were ready. Two meals a day being the general practice, a boy became accustomed to eating morning and late afternoon. He should avoid broth once the infant stage was passed, since this was conceived to stretch his stomach and make him greedy and unable to withstand privation. "You get hungry too quick if you eat too often" was apparently an oft repeated maxim. Boys who wanted to eat during the day were told, "Are you going to eat all the time if you go hunting?" Girls were allowed more food than boys. It was the boy who had to live up to the role of provider, of feeding others at the expense of his own wants. And since this was a virtue, it was repeated and demonstrated in various ways. Girls, too, were taught generosity. They were taught to offer food freely and gladly, with respect for the food and for the person to whom it was given. Food could never be tossed to another person. This was the height of bad manners and was regarded as treating someone else "just like a dog."

The individual was presented with something of a dilemma in his social development. On the one hand, he was urged to be hardy and to excel in the tasks he undertook. On the other, however, he was urged to be circumspect, to hold himself back, and not to show off his excellence in one or another activity. Boasting and other forms of immodest behavior were anathema. There have already been described the various ways in which the individual suppressed himself and was in turn suppressed by the society. The good runner, for example, dared not win too often. It is at this point that an ideal of behavior emerges. It would be clearly indicated that the individual should excel, but not at the expense of others. His abilities and talents would be quickly seen but it was desirable that he suppress them. In his own abilities, however, he was permitted to develop a reserve of confidence, being aware and content that he could meet new situations and conquer them. The child, particularly the boy, worked toward the ideal of individual integrity and was discouraged from seeking approbation from others. This was, in a sense, the goal of socialization and education and in childhood were instilled the traits of personality making for individual security, dignity, and ability. The child who pushed himself forward was quickly checked by an older person. "Your head is coming up above the others" was warning enough.

The individual was thus taught to depend on his own reserves and to look for merited support from his kin. He was not shamed into conformity nor was he punished either by a physical means or by withdrawal of affection. It was made clear to him that certain actions deserved approval while others did not. His chance for success lay in himself with family support. If he failed to measure up to the standard, he might discover that he could get his way by shouting down any opposition. Here was the bully who might achieve a degree of material success, but who could never hope for a devoted following from kin, friends, or partners. There was no social mechanism by which such behavior could be curbed and it is clear that there was no special pattern of bullying. Such people were "just hard to get along with." A child was encouraged to agree with others and to avoid making scenes or forcing his way through social situations. The child could show temper and might have tantrums. In this case, the parent might take him home and would give every evidence of unconcern. It may be assumed that bullying, either by a child or by an individual who doubted his own abilities, provided a culturally accepted mode of behavior for the unadjusted individual. Shamanism was the other course open to such a person. As is suggested elsewhere in this study, the successful individual, he who excelled in production and hunting, who had the full backing of his kin, had no call to become a shaman. He would, moreover, be inclined to give in to the wishes of others.

But in the aboriginal culture, every individual was in some measure in control of the supernatural. The infant was given names and charms, either by shamans or older relatives. In childhood, the stock of charms owned by the individual might be increased. Through the awareness of the supernatural, the child was made subject to other kinds of controls.

The child was encouraged to work hard and to avoid laziness at all costs. Industriousness was the prime virtue in both men and women. With industry arises the ideal of cooperation and generosity. The educative process was aimed, however informally, at instilling all these values in the individual. It succeeded in a remarkable way. It produced an individual capable of living in the cooperative situation demanded by the social and natural environment. Under the socializing agency of the family, there was a high degree of personal security, one which is by no means lost today.

It can by no means be supposed that life for the child was secure but yet austere. Changing situations might create periods of hardship and privation and it is true that the child was expected to work when he could. But at the same time, there were innumerable recreational outlets open to the child. He was free and encouraged to share in these. The present study has not given full attention to the game complex among the groups in question. There were games, often with associated songs, for both children and adults. One cannot help being impressed by the endless variety of games. There were games for boys and girls, group games, group songs, sports, and many toys. Of the latter, balls, made of deerskin stuffed with baleen or mountain sheep horn shavings, tops made of bone or ivory and whipped, and dolls were prominent. The bull roarer appears as a child's toy and there were the innumerable string figures, each with an appropriate song.

The group games played by children were many. A few examples are given here:

1. sixłikpayuu. The children formed a line, while the two strongest sat opposite each other. As each child passed between them, the leaders pulled at him, the stronger drawing him to his side. The game ended when the children were divided, the side having the greater number being the winner. A song was sung during the game. It was:

sixłikpayuu
sik atuu mikayu mikaa
siyuuk siyuuk siyuuk

2. Tug of war. This game was common to children and also played by adults. The two leaders locked hands, while the teams lined up behind, each with his arms around the person in front.

3. Old woman. This was a children's game, involving someone who was "it" playing the old woman. She pretended to be blind, and set up a number of "bags" containing her possessions. These she guarded, while the children came to steal them. The "old woman" pretended to be asleep. When she missed her possessions, she came accusing the others. Another "old woman" has the stolen property and the two work up sides and struggle over the items. In this game there was a good deal of word play and exchange.

4. Getting water. Lines were made in the snow to form a "road." Someone was selected to be a "devil" to guard the road. As the children walked down single file along the road, the "devil" tried to get them out of line and off the road. If one were off the road, he was out of the game.

5. Hunting. Girls tied antlers to their heads while boys tried to track them down and pretended to shoot them.

The child was prevented from hearing gossip. This was in keeping with the pattern of thinking well of others and of being agreeable. The child himself was discouraged from talking about his playmates. The "tattletale" was made to feel disapproval both from age-mates and from parents and elders. Truth was a virtue. Those who exaggerated or told falsehoods "would never be believed again." This attitude is an important one and carries into the present.

In summary, and still true, the child after infancy becomes subject to more rigorous controls. He learns by processes of imitation and by guidance by members of his family grouping. By the time he has reached the age of ability to reason, his role is established. The careful differentiation between men's and women's spheres of activity is impressed on the child and he begins to fulfill the expected sexual role, taking on more and more responsibility for work, and developing new skills as he moves toward puberty.

PUBERTY

The puberty situation for girls was somewhat more rigorous, being tied up with the first menstruation. There was no special series of rites for boys, although a transition from childhood to adolescence, and by extension, to adulthood, was defined by the change in clothing and by the perforations made to hold the labrets. Among boys, the initial change was marked by new garments. These were given to the boy when his voice began to change. As a child, he had worn long trousers to which a sock was sewn. Over the feet were worn boots. As an adult, the qalliik, the short trousers, which came to just below the knee, were worn. The child's female relatives made the new garments but they were conferred by a father or grandfather. Fun was poked at a boy when his voice changed and it was said, "You'll be getting married pretty soon now." There was clearly a recognition of status change. When the voice changed, the boy was treated as an adult. Should he fall back into his childhood ways, it was said, "You have brains enough not to do that now."

At this stage of life the boy was often enlisted as a runner. He was told to practice running and endurance. The introduction to such communal festivities as the Messenger Feast was effected by men who invited various boys to represent them as runners. At the same time, advice was given as to how to run. In a race, for example, the boy was told not to look behind except under the raised arm, lest he lose. Similarly, the child, who had up to now been kept away from shamanistic activities, unless of course, he were ill, was permitted to attend the seances. But the parents often told the child not to learn the songs which the shaman sang. Were he to do so, he might well become imbued with shaman's power. The office was not a desired one.

It is clear that the shift from childhood to adolescence was not formalized. It involved merely the assumption of greater responsibility on the part of the boy and his being included gradually in adult activities. When his clothing was changed, he was permitted to share in hunting and whaling, not yet as a fully fledged participant, but as an observer and apprentice. This was considered to form a vital part of his education.

The end of the vague adolescence period was signalized for boys by the piercing of the lower lip for labrets. This was an individual matter, there being no group initiation. A father or male guardian decided that the boy was ready and enlisted the services of a man who was skilled in making the cuts. This was not a shaman nor was he paid for the service. The man who performed the operation was skilled at doing it quickly and "making a straight cut." The boy put his hands over his ears and lay back against the knees of the cutter. The latter pressed his knees on the boy's hands against his head, holding the head and hands tightly between his knees. He then called the boy by name. If the boy didn't answer, it was a sign that he couldn't hear, and it was at this point that the cut was made. A piece of wood was put inside the mouth and a chisellike knife of stone was driven down quickly through the flesh just under each corner of the mouth. The boy did not cry out. He was expected to say that the operation was not painful. The blood was wiped away and the wounds washed in urine which was taken into the mouth and expelled through the cuts. At this point, the labrets were introduced.

Labrets were of three kinds. A small round labret, an inch or less in diameter, called tuutak, was worn first. This was a conventionally worn labret, not regarded as too valuable. Men might wear these for "every day," but changed to more expensive ones on festive occasions. A man of wealth wore only the more expensive. Before the operation, a boy was told to make his own labrets. He made the tuutak, although more costly ones might be given him as gifts. The labret "buttoned" into the cut and was put in and left at once. During the early stages of wearing, it was taken out and cleaned, a smooth shaft was run through the wounds, and the wound treated with urine. More expensive lip plugs were of two kinds. The first was an oblong labret called simmeak, running to perhaps 1½ or 2 inches in length. The most expensive was the aŋmaloak, a round labret "about the size of a dollar," into which a bead had been glued. Some of the pairs of the latter actually had names and were of great value. Even a single one might be traded for an umiak or a whole wolverine skin. The three grades of labrets were all valuable and all might be used in trading. After the lip plugs had been introduced, they were rarely removed. Men wore them in all activities. Only an umealiq of note would wear the aŋmaloak. It is said that styles changed frequently with the result that men were often employed in making them for themselves at leisure moments.

When a boy donned the labrets, it was a sign that his childhood and adolescence were passed. He could now marry. He was free to find sexual partners where he could. As nearly as can be judged, there was little or no homosexual activity. A boy formed a brief attachment or two before settling down to life as a married man. It is clear that there was no group initiation of boys, either into the lore of the group, into a place in a whaling crew, or into a karigi. The wearing of the labret signalized a transition into adulthood but it was an individual matter. No attempt was made to establish a formal bond of initiation between boys of the same age group. There were no recognized age classes.

Girls were subject to restrictions at the first menstrual period. This was for them a situation corresponding to the wearing of a labret by boys. Like the boy, the girl, as she began to mature—a condition observed by the growth of her breasts—was allowed to change from the garments of childhood, essentially the same for both sexes, into those of adulthood. Somewhere between childhood and puberty, the girl was tattooed. Informants disagree on this point. Some of the older women were asked about their tattoo marks, since virtually all women over 65 have them. Some remarked that they were tattooed as small children, and that it was done because they wanted it as a beauty mark. Others say that they were tattooed as part of the puberty rite and that the mark reflected marriageability. The latter explanation seems the more correct one and it is possible that the function of female tattooing was beginning to be lost even in the childhood of older women alive today.

The tattoo mark consisted of a series of closely drawn parallel lines extending from the center of the lower lip to the base of the chin. After a time, the lines drew together with the result that most women had a tattoo ranging from ¾ to 1 inch from lower lip to chin. The tattooing was done by an older woman, often a relative, and like the piercing of the boy for labrets, was quite informally done. It is said that a girl would plead to be tattooed. She might be warned that if she were, men would rape her. This too suggests that the mark was a sign of eligibility for marriage. When it was agreed that she be tattooed, the girl sat down, raised her chin, and another woman, working with needle and thread which had been drawn through the soot of the oil lamp, pulled the thread through the flesh of the area. Girls were not expected to show the same indifference to pain as boys. It is said that they complained long after of the soreness of their chins.

The first menstruation was the critical one, although any menstruating woman was potentially dangerous both to herself and the community. There was no menstrual lodge, although sometimes a girl would be obliged to retire to the birth hut, especially if some man in the house were out whaling. But the girl was mostly confined to the house, as indeed, were all menstruating women. At the first menstruation, the period of seclusion was 5 days. The girl wore a special hood of caribou skin which covered her eyes. It was felt that if she looked at light, her eyes would be harmed. She could only look down and was not supposed to gaze out on the world. When she had to urinate, another woman guided her to a place some distance from the house, since she could not, of course, mix her urine with that used by the household. She was also subject to various food restrictions. She could not touch raw or bloody meat, let alone eat it. She had to drink water from a special vessel of her own, usually made of wood, which was kept for subsequent menstrual periods. The girl could not work on any game. Even if she touched it, the hunter would lose his skill and could never again be successful in catching the particular animal which she touched. Likewise, were she to touch a weapon, it was rendered useless and would never again kill game. Similarly, the shaman lost his power if he came into contact with the menstruating woman and particularly with the girl who was menstruating for the first time.

The pattern associated with the girl's first menstruation is of course to be expected in view of the attitudes of all adjacent peoples. It is only remarkable that the girl was confined for so short a period. And too, once the first menstrual period passed, she was not subject to further restrictions. There was no idea that she had to observe certain prohibitions for a year thereafter, nor was she otherwise secluded. Not only is the absence of an elaborate puberty ceremony for girls to be associated with the marginal position of the cultures in question, but the demands of life made prolonged seclusion and prohibition impractical. In subsequent menstrual periods much the same restrictions applied. The woman should avoid raw and bloody meat but she could touch it. In short, she was not prevented from working. She wore a deerskin napkin lined with moss. She could sleep with her husband but she could not remove her clothes during her period. She had only to be careful that the menstrual discharge did not contact weapons, men, shamans, and the like. She urinated away from the house. There was of course a taboo on sexual intercourse during menstruation. After her period, a woman generally changed her clothes and might reserve old clothes for the menstrual period.

When the first period was passed, a girl was regarded as adult. She was now tattooed and presumably had mastered the skills which lay in the domain of women. She was now free to marry. As noted, she might be reluctant to do this. If she did not marry at once, she had to be careful lest some man seize her, rape her, and take her to his house. It was advisable that she marry as soon as her menses began.

SEXUAL BEHAVIOR

The boy and girl, having passed puberty, were thus eligible for marriage. There were no well-defined restrictions as to sexual behavior; a girl, as noted, was not expected to remain chaste. The child saw others in the household engaging in sexual relations and there were hence no secrets from him. Should he ask where a new sibling came from, he was told at once that it came out of the mother's body.

This is quite in contrast to the situation today, where under Euro-American influence, the frankness relating to sexual matters has vanished. The child was not curbed in his sexual pursuits. He was not prevented from masturbation, nor is he at present. Indeed, the writer has observed mothers masturbating an infant to quiet it. Heterosexual experimentation in late childhood was apparently not unusual.

Boys and girls, around the age of puberty, might go off together on excursions away from the community and engage in sexual relations. While this was permissible, a girl was urged to avoid promiscuity, since this might complicate the system of mutual obligations between families which could arise from sexual ties. In general, it was felt that young people, while free to play the field for a time, should settle down in a quasi-permanent marital relationship. In this way, good relations between families were effected. There was nothing against trial marriage, however, and frequently the first marriage or two ended in divorce. It is clear that there was a certain amount of competition among older people for the younger eligible ones. Older men might seek young girls as second wives, and girls were warned by their families that this might happen if they refused to marry when it was possible to do so. Young men might also be sought as husbands by older women. Many such marriages are recalled. An older person might use the threat of magic to blackmail a younger one into marriage. Even a very old woman might be on the lookout for a young man as a husband. Her interest lay not in the sexual relationship, nor even in any prestige goals, but rather in gaining a provider. Since old women, who had passed the climacteric, were viewed as possessing supernatural power, a young man might be drawn into a relationship with one quite against his will. There was nothing against his taking a second wife or finding sexual outlets elsewhere.

There were, however, certain ideals in sex relationships and in marriage partners. A family preferred to arrange a marriage, since it could then depend on the good will of the other group. Hence such features as bride service developed. One woman recalls that her husband came to the family while she was still very small. He remained in the house, working his way, assisting her father in hunting. When she passed her period of puberty, he was then accepted as her husband and the marriage was consummated. She had not wanted to marry this individual, but both her mother and grandmother directed her to do so. A person could have certain values which a mate might be expected to meet. Not the least of these was a demand for affection, there being a fairly strong sense of romance in the culture. "Love," as such, was not idealized but romantic attachments were formed on the basis of physical beauty such as large eyes. Regularity of features was also important. This was true of men also, a person with some prominent physical feature being considered ludicrous. Too beautiful a face was considered a bad risk. Such girls were "stingy"; "They won't feed anyone." But a woman had to be judged on a series of personal traits, rather than on beauty alone. She was expected to keep herself neat and to be industrious. Other physical features were not regarded as too significant. The breasts were not important in sex play, nor were the buttocks or thighs. An attractive person, man or woman, ran to an average. He should not be "too fat, too thin, too tall, too short; you look at them and see that they look just right. Then you know that you can marry them."

Sexuality was fairly well stereotyped. Sexual intercourse was regarded as an end in itself and there was little interest in sexual variations. Sexual perversion as such was not disturbing but sufficiently unusual to require comment. One man is described as having had intercourse with dogs. This was unusual behavior but was treated in a matter of fact way. The few Indians (itkiyyiq) with whom the North Alaskan peoples came into contact were said to be the offspring of a man and a dog named asanu. Older people apparently accepted the tale as a fact but there was no feeling of contempt expressed toward the Indians. They were, in fact, "very good people." There is no evidence of homosexual behavior of any kind. One might expect that with the rather rigid definition of sexual roles there might be some transvestitism. The only case which in any way suggests the berdache was that of an old man who likes "to cook, clean, and scrub." He did not, however, wear women's clothes and apparently hunted like other men. "He just liked to be busy all the time." A woman was mentioned who always hunted and attempted to join a men's crew. Although she was not permitted to do this, she caught seals at breathing holes in winter. This angered a shaman, who crippled her; she froze to death as a result. Another suggestion of homosexual behavior arises in that "many men say they wish they had been born women." The woman's lot was regarded as generally easier. But some women were also said to have wished they had been men. When a person had such wishes, he might request that his name be given to a child of the opposite sex after his death. The idea of transvestitism or of homosexuality was clearly not shocking to informants but was instead fairly amusing. All were agreed that shamans never were transvestites. One person was described as a hermaphrodite but this was "because he acted funny," not, as nearly as can be judged, because of physical evidence.

Sexuality thus involved heterosexual relations. There was some sex play prior to sexual intercourse, such as kissing and biting, but beyond the genitalia, there were no well-defined erogenous zones. The breasts and buttocks, as noted above, were not important in sex play. During the sex act, the couples lay prone, the male in a superior position, and the partners might bite each other in the fleshy part of the neck. In the house, women customarily went about naked from the waist up, as did men. Clothing was removed for sexual intercourse.

But despite the fact that sexual relations were definitely patterned, few variations being permitted, or indeed, thought of, sexual behavior might go to extremes in rape and violence. A man who raped a woman seized her by the belt and threw her down. As he held her, he generally ripped off her trousers or cut them with his knife. A man who seized and held a woman's belt was soliciting sexual intercourse. If a woman objected, she might scream and draw her kin to her rescue. Women, on the other hand, had no such device; they could ask a man or could, of course, convey their desires in more subtle ways.

The individual was raised, as may be seen, in a fairly secure family situation. He was expected to repress resentments and to avoid showing his feelings. Those who succeeded in maintaining this behavioral pattern were regarded as "honest and patient," two virtues which are again and again extolled. In certain situations, however, the pattern of repression was broken and passions flared out in often violent ways. Violence was frequently directed toward the shaman, particularly toward strangers, and likewise in sexual behavior. Sexuality appears to have been at times a release from tensions, not so much in sexual satisfaction itself as in the violence of preparation for the sex act.

In general there appears to have been little coquettishness in the culture, an element which may be anticipated in keeping with the absence of vicarious sexuality. Dress, either in the past, or today, was not viewed as a means of provoking sexual desires. "People want to be comfortable, not pretty." In keeping with the desire to attain a mean, clothing was regarded as best which used conservatively matched skins. Today, in the trade-goods parkas which women wear, the design elements should be neither too large nor too small, and there should be an element of white in the design. Small designs on cloth are reserved for little girls. Design elements on the sleeves and collars of parka covers need not be matched with those of the body of the parka itself.

The patterns of behavior relating to the selection of a mate have already been discussed. Family arrangement, capture, and mutual agreement were the ways by which a mate was chosen. There were, however, certain expected behavioral forms. A girl who was modest and "bashful" was a good risk as a wife. One that was forward might lead the husband into difficulties. An unmarried girl, past puberty, stayed with her female relatives, going out alone only under the most exceptional circumstances. The fear of rape or capture, since an unattended girl was fair game for any man, resulted in the ideal situation of marital arrangement. Opposing this, however, were the excursions undertaken by young people in which sexual relations might play a part. Families seeking to arrange a marriage could do so formally but there was also an informal way. The two groups might agree to summer at a fishing camp or to go off to the trading together. They would then throw the young man and young woman together and soon begin to treat them as a married couple.

There was little by way of instruction of any kind given either to the boy or to the girl before marriage. It was understood that the skills acquired during the socialization process were applicable to adult life. Boys were encouraged to be good workers and providers; girls learned to keep a house in order. An unmarried girl made her own clothes which were covertly inspected by prospective mothers-in-law. A careless seamstress was judged as lazy and undesirable. It frequently happened that a girl was taken aside by an older female relative before marriage and shown the things which a hunter needed. A good wife was expected to keep all clothing in order, food ready, and all hunting gear except weapons properly arranged. But there was little or no mention of sexual practices or expectations. If a boy and girl were known to be engaged in a sexual relationship, some gossip might arise. On the whole, however, sex was commonplace. There was no sense of artistry in it nor was it felt necessary to explain to the young person anything relating to the sexual mores.

Prior to marriage, and this remains true today, there was no attempt between a betrothed couple to work out future plans. They might discuss residence arrangements, although this was a family decision primarily. There was no attempt at intellectual intimacy and no overt sign of affection. No person could relate his own aims, ambitions, or hopes to another. This was done neither with a spouse nor with a relative. The closest tie which might exist was with one's friends, that is, partners or joking partners. In short, a young couple did not discuss their marriage beforehand and settled domestic problems as they arose.

MARITAL BEHAVIOR

Intimacy between husband and wife was thus sexual and not on an intellectual level. One reason for this undoubtedly lies in the fact that the marriage bond was secondary to the bond of blood kinship. As the married couple engendered offspring, the tie between them became stronger. The marital bond, too, was enforced by economic considerations—the fact that the couple made up a team and depended on each other for material support. As several women were asked: "What do you and your husband talk about?" the answer was inevitably, "We don't say anything; we don't talk about anything." This was quite accurate. The husband came home for meals, ate in silence, and left at once to do this or that task or to join his mates in the karigi. Women, on the other hand, went to work at their tasks, often with other women, a group frequently pooling its labor and gossiping at the same time. And, with a few exceptions, this pattern of living is still followed.

The culture made no provision for expressing "feelings." No one could feel free to indicate to others that he might be out of sorts. This was true in all interpersonal relationships. People talked, and still do so, of weather, hunting, food. There was no attempt to evaluate situations or to pass judgment on them. This was likewise true as between husband and wife.

In the family, a unit larger than the husband-wife team must be considered. The house or tent owner generally made family decisions. These were never formal, however, and the family or household head could be dissuaded from his project if enough of the kin group felt strongly against it. As noted elsewhere, the person was free to make his own decisions often without reference to the family or household at large. If the family decided to spend a summer at fishing, while one member chose to remain at home, no pressure was put on the latter to change his mind. This was also true as between husband and wife. In trading, in traveling here and there in the economic round, the wife might choose not to come. A husband might force her to come with him, but would not be likely to do so. After marriage, a wife, living with the family of the husband, might elect to go back to her own kin for a time. There was no objection. She might stay for a long period and if this met with the husband's approval, the marriage might simply end in a permanent separation or divorce.

Only when a wife was obviously miserable and sought to get away again and again was the ire of the husband aroused. In this case, he could force her return. If the woman's kin felt that he was justified, as they well might, unless he reputedly abused her, they would assist him in returning her. The husband might in such an instance hamstring the wife to prevent her running off.

A husband and wife agreed on child rearing without question. There is little doubt that the same methods were used in generation after generation.

The henpecked husband was rare. If a woman became a shrew, the husband ripped her clothes. If she were a scold, he could rip her cheeks open from the corners of her mouth. These were very rare cases. If a woman were inclined to shrewishness and her husband condoned it, relatives of the pair might interfere and point out that the two were not making a good marriage. These kinds of sanctions were evidently sufficient to keep a degree of conformity to the marital ideals.

If there were a great discrepancy between the ages of the marital partners, as, for instance, in the case of young man marrying an old woman, it was felt not "to look nice." It frequently occurred, however. The feeling was that the purpose of marriage was in some measure defeated. The young man was advised to get away from the older woman since she could bear him no children. Such a union might adopt a child. The children of the older partner from another marriage, and there were usually such, often resented a young stepfather. Here was a source of some dissatisfaction and discord. As has been shown, such marriages were often the result of blackmail, of magical threats directed against a young person. Indeed, when a young person was unwilling to marry, the family might ask an old person to pretend that he or she wished the young man or woman in marriage. This usually forced the issue. The general feeling was that people of the same age should marry. Both then benefited by the offspring, who were responsible for the parents in their old age. Marriage between two people of the same general age provided a better link between the families involved.

There was a certain amount of marital jealousy. A husband or wife might resent attentions given by other men and women to their spouse. If a spouse were unfaithful, his kin might advise him to be careful and not to become the butt of gossip. "Why do you want to make your wife mad?" A jealous husband might tear his wife's clothes.

In the main, if there were children, and if there were good relations between the family units involved in the marriage, the union lasted. If a man took a second wife, there was no objection from the first, however much she might complain at a husband's casual affairs. The two wives settled down amicably enough, sharing the work.

There was likewise no apparent discord in the rare polyandrous union. The woman in this case was called tapicciga, "doubler." It is to be remembered that a man could not marry sisters, nor could polyandry be fraternal. It is worth repeating that feelings against this were extremely strong. In one remembered instance, a woman was widowed and went to live in another place. She later married a man who proved to be her first husband's brother. People then called the wife tapicciga. The husband, puzzled, then learned what he had done. He committed suicide by hanging himself. Other things being equal, however, marriage lasted. Those who shifted from mate to mate were apparently the exceptions.

OLD AGE

There was no particular attitude relating to old men. When a man became too old to hunt, he more or less retired. He could remain indoors as he chose. Some continued to go to the karigi, others remained at home, resting on the bench in the house. The old men busied themselves with various tasks, making nets, carving ivory, searching for ivory washed up along the beaches. They might be in demand as storytellers, drummers, or singers. Like old men everywhere, the Eskimo oldsters wearied others with tales of their youth. Old age in men was apparently not related to sexual decline but rather to economic productivity. Some old men capitalized on youthful skills, making kayaks, umiak frames, and sleds, as well as weapons, for others.

In the case of old women, the transition was somewhat more dramatically marked. The cessation of the menses was regarded as the period of transition into old age. The old woman was as active as she chose, the work habits of a lifetime probably being too well engrained to ignore. She could also have sexual relations. But the old woman was regarded as endowed with rather pronounced supernatural powers. If women became shamans, they usually did so following the climacteric. The wife of a shaman, too, although she might have ignored her husband's profession up to this time, or at least might not have participated in it in any way, might now at this stage of life take an active part in her husband's activities. She might learn to handle the drum and to dance in the shamanistic seances. But even if not especially classed as shamans, old women had dangerous powers. These they could use to their own advantage, causing illness and death of those who offended them. The revenge technique of cutting a piece from an enemy's parka, unknown to him, which, if undiscovered, caused sickness and death, was reputedly a favorite trick of the spiteful old woman. But an old woman could also be friendly and could use her powers to the advantage of others, particularly of children. She gave a name and a charm to the children of her choosing. In this way, she could insure success for the child, preventing his illness or death.

Because of the work demands placed on younger women, the old woman often became the custodian of children. Most informants today still recall the affectionate grandmother. A child might seek refuge and protection with his grandmother rather than with his mother. As is so often the case in societies where the work load is so well defined, the grandmother, and to a lesser extent, the grandfather, become guardians of the young. This was clearly true of the Eskimo of the area in question. The grandparents thus became important to the child in the socialization process. The child was given the name of a deceased grandparent in most instances. When this was done, the child was told that his actions resembled the ways of the grandparent whose name he bore. Often he would attempt to emulate these actions. The result was that the grandparent became a model in death as well as in life.

Old women also busied themselves about the house or camp. When their place as cook in the household had been taken by a younger woman, they continued to sew, to make bags, to gather feathers and willows for bedding, and the like. A very old woman usually remained indoors and rarely moved about. This was also true of the very old men. In the nomadic situation, when old people became too infirm, they were abandoned. When tobacco was introduced, old women particularly took to it avidly. Old women remained under the platform in the house, smoking. It is of interest that this carries into the present; the writer has interviewed several very old women who slept under the bed of a child and child-in-law, remaining there throughout the day on a bed of skins, and smoking a pipe.

Old people sometimes got the reputation of being querulous and unhappy. Ideal behavior, however, was for the oldster to remain silent and uncomplaining.

DEATH

There was, and still is, some fear of the dead. Neither ghosts nor souls were too well defined, but the uneasy notion that something might return was present. Death could occur from natural causes, although the malevolence of a shaman was always worth considering. At death, a shaman might be summoned, not to perform an autopsy, as in some adjacent cultures, but to ask the dead body what the cause of death had been. The dead often answered.

If a person died of an illness in the house, the body was removed through the skylight and taken away. Among the nomadic Eskimo, the body was left and the group traveled on. In each case, however, a series of taboos arose. The maritime groups were obliged to remain in the house for a brief period, for 4 days if the deceased were a woman, 5 days if a man. Similarly, among the nomadic groups, no one could hunt for 4 days if a woman died, 5, if a man. The mourning period, was known as naaciiruat. No one was permitted to visit the bereaved family, except, as among the coastal groups, to call in through the skylight of the house. The family could not change its clothing during the mourning period. No one in the group could sew, lest the ghost be drawn back into the house. Among the nomadic groups, when a person was abandoned to death, the group which traveled on observed the same mourning restrictions.

The body was wrapped, carried out some distance from the community, and laid on the ground. Coffins and graves came after European contact. There were no markers and the body was never revisited. There was no concern at the thought of wolves or foxes eating the corpse. The personal possessions were laid out with the corpse. Less personal ones, such as boats, extra clothing which had never been worn, dogs, and the like, were claimed by the kin. They might go to a widow or they might, as noted, be taken from her and her children by her husband's kin. Or the latter might hold such property in trust for the children of the deceased. Personal possessions included the deceased's weapons, used clothing, ornaments, and the like. A man could make a will. Some did so and the expressed wishes relating to property disposition were generally honored. As the corpse was carried out to the area where it was to be left, a man walked behind brandishing a knife. He was called "the cutter," his action was "cutting," kivłuktuat; it is said that he frightened away the spirit of the dead—"he's cutting the death so it won't return."

There were few other elaborate actions surrounding a death. The family might throw clothing away at the close of a mourning period. There was the feeling that the immediately personal possessions of the deceased should be avoided. Hence they were left with the body. The house was not abandoned, although it is said that no one today can live in the house where Captain Brower lived; his ghost is still about. In general, while death created an interruption of the normal routine of life, and created some uneasiness, the Eskimo of the area did not have a hysterical dread of death or a notion of contamination by it. The latter idea could possibly survive in the custom of the changing of clothing by family members, but even in the aboriginal culture this was not always done.

CONCLUSION

Having taken the individual from birth through life to death, the pattern of a fairly stable personality type emerges. There was little marked individualism. Freedom of choice was balanced by a meaningful integration into the family system. The person was agreeable, self-effacing, dignified, and industrious, yet withal had a fund of good humor and a strong drive to fit himself into the cooperative pattern of communal living.

THE SUPERNATURAL

INTRODUCTION

Like other Arctic peoples, the Eskimo of the North Alaskan region had not developed a particularly complex cosmology. Speculation regarding the universe and natural phenomena was not an important feature in the culture. Nor, although some rather involved conceptualizations relative to the nature of human and animal souls existed, was there an elaborate eschatology. Indeed, much of the universe lay in folklore and did not play a significant role in what might be termed religious behavior. But although the culture lacked any concept of a hierarchy of spirits, it is not to be implied that the groups of the area or, in fact, any of the Eskimo from Siberia to Greenland, were either irreligious or indifferent to the defined supernatural world. Within the limits of cultural definition, religious attitudes played an extremely significant part. Given a definition of the supernatural, both individual and group goals relating to it reflect an attempt to exert control. And indeed, it is in respect to the control of the supernatural that the bulk of religious behavior arises. Such behavior lay in acts which had to be performed by the individual in control of the supernatural by especially endowed and trained persons, the shamans, and in ceremonials conducted by the group for general communal good. But absolute control, by means of formula and ritual, was not always possible. This was especially true in the relations between men and the animal source of food. A basic concept in religious practice was that the animals of the surrounding Arctic were endowed with the ability to reason, to talk, and to react much in the same manner as men. Animals were conceived to allow themselves to be taken by men, a belief generally common to the American and Asiatic sub-Arctic and Arctic hunting cultures. If offended, if confronted with a set of circumstances that were displeasing, if insulted, maligned, or mistreated in any way, the animal would withdraw its presence to the detriment of human survival. Much of what might be termed religion thus lay in attempts to placate, cajole, compel, or otherwise to influence the animal in question. It followed that men were obliged to avoid creating those situations which might prove offensive or hateful to the animals. The economic aspects of aboriginal religious practice cannot thus be ignored, and it is evident that virtually every act of the individual had some supernatural implications.

Shamanism offered another aspect of religious behavior reflecting the relation of man to the external universe. As will be seen, every individual had power of some sort, some ability to exert a degree of control by ostensibly magical means over a variety of situations. The shaman, however, had a greater degree of such power and so enjoyed a far greater intimacy with the supernatural world than did the layman. In the work of the shaman, not only in such aspects as curing and doctoring, but also in the performance of acts necessary to the good of the group, there was established, as will be seen, a dramatic and meaningful rapport with the supernatural. The shamanistic seance was unquestionably a real and vital experience for all who saw it.

In ceremonialism, the North Alaskan Eskimo appear to have been less well prepared than were their neighbors to the south. Two main feasts were developed, both of which appear to relate historically to other areas and had economic as well as social and religious implications. Since the northern Alaskan cultures were primarily concerned with whaling, it is to be expected that a cult of the whale should have an important place. The Whale Feast and its inland counterpart, the festival for caribou, involving both preparations made prior to whaling and the caribou drive and rituals to receive the captured animals, were the principal communal religious rites. Next in importance was the Messenger Feast. This was more socially oriented and less religious in content. It involved a series of socioeconomic exchanges reminiscent of the wealth preoccupation of the southern Alaskan peoples. Although it was a social festival, as has been seen, it had a series of complex ceremonies accompanying it and was not wholly divorced from the realm of the supernatural.

But religious practice was in the main individually conceived. Emphasis on religion lay in the solution of problems of immediate concern. It is perhaps for this reason that the contemporary Eskimo have apparently no intimate involvement in Christianity. The modern church as a social force has significance, but it has not been wholly effective in eradicating the sense of the close relation to nature which the aboriginal Eskimo felt. It is clear that the native religion had none of the dualistic quality of the European religious systems. The associated concepts were in the main magical; punishment, that is misfortune and starvation, were the inevitable results of an act on the part of the individual. Such an act was chiefly a violation of one of the rules of the natural order. But more frequent was the concept that the individual himself was at the mercy of various hostile forces. However much the individual sought to effect control over the natural order, he often proved incapable of doing so. Hostile enemies, unconscious violation of prohibitions, particularly with respect to eating, and a host of other possibilities made one's physical as well as spiritual existence quite hazardous. And here is the rationale underlying the presence of the shaman; he (or she), above all others, could exert a degree of controling power to permit events to proceed more smoothly.

The ways in which the Eskimo solved the problem of the relation of man to nature are most numerous. The general patterning of religious, ceremonial, and ritual behavior, as well as the attitudes, values, and beliefs surrounding the supernatural, are both complex and involved. The view of the universe, the problem of the definition of the human soul, the questions of compulsive power, the relations to the world of the animals attest that while here is a religious development of a nonliterate people, the resulting institutions are far from primeval.

COSMIC VIEW

The attitude toward the universe as reflected in aboriginal North Alaskan Eskimo beliefs is largely encompassed in myth and folktale. Much of this has parallels and connections across the Arctic and is found distributed among Asiatic as well as American Indian groups. Folklore, for example, stresses the Raven (tulugaak) as the creator of the world. This may be recognized as related to the cycle of Raven myths common to northwestern North America and as part of the general pattern of trickster myths. Raven, however, was not regarded in any special way. The anthropomorphic character of Raven appears in several of the myths collected at Barrow. It was related that the first missionaries at Barrow told of the creation according to the Biblical account. Many people, it was said, refused to accept this and were reported as having said—"Very well, God made the world, but Raven made it first." It does not appear that there was at any time identification of the Raven with the Christian God, as may occur in other cultures. Raven is described as having brought the land up from the water, as differentiating night from day, and is often viewed as the first man. He is not, however, regarded as necessarily ancestral to the North Alaskan Eskimo.

The world itself is flat according to the Eskimo concept. It rests on four wooden pillars, one at each cardinal point. Lost hunters were said to have fallen off the edge of the world. The concept of an underworld is mentioned in a number of sources, sometimes as the abode of the dead (cf. Birket-Smith, 1936, p. 161, et al.). No mention of this was obtained from the contemporary people. From several informants was obtained the account of the wiivaksaat, "those who come around again," the "strangers in the sky." These are discussed below in greater detail but are mentioned here since they may suggest the concept of the "world above" which has been recorded for the Greenland Eskimo. No other details could be had on the nether or upper worlds.

According to the older cosmology, the sun and moon rest on the rainbow. The common Eskimo tale of the "Man in the Moon" appears in the area as well. The moon is considered male, the sun female. The tale goes that they were once husband and wife. They argued over the weather. The man wanted the weather cold, the woman wanted it warm. The man took a knife and cut off the woman's breast. She left and went up into the sky by the rainbow. Although her husband followed, it was always too warm where she was. Sometimes he tries to get at her and then the moon and the sun are visible at the same time. When the sun shines red, it is the woman's breast bleeding. No mention was obtained of the control of game by the moon man.

There are no tales extant relating to a solar eclipse. Lunar eclipses, however, have been observed and call forth a few explanations. At this time, the moon wishes dogs and travel gear and reaches down among men to get them. The dogs are hidden, snowshoes, sleds, and other travel gear put away at this time. If a dog is out in the lunar eclipse, it will die.

The stars were well known by name and there were a few tales concerning them. They were only rarely used for navigation. Nor were they important in land travel. At sea, if one could see the stars, it followed that the coastline was either visible or easily reached. In a storm on land or sea, the stars, being often invisible, were of no aid. Hence at sea, direction was determined by the ground swell, on land by wind direction and the detailed knowledge of place geography which every hunter has. The morning star bore the proper name sivolliik, the evening star aaguruk. The Pleiades were known as the hunters. Mars was called kayaktuq, the red fox. Another tale concerning Mars was that there was a white fox and a red fox fighting over a single foxhole. The Dipper was called an animal with a horn, possibly a narwhal, mention of which survives in the folklore.

In general, the aurora borealis was feared. To some extent, the uneasiness occasioned by it survives. Children were told to go into the house when the lights appeared. The phenomenon was personified and the child was told that it would take his head to use for a football. Adults likewise were frightened by the aurora. It was believed to bring headache and pains in the neck. One turned one's back to it and waved a knife behind one to ward off the influence. Songs were also sung to prevent harm from the aurora.

In the main, darkness does not appear to have been disturbing. During the months of darkness, people settled down for the winter ceremonial season. Shamanistic seances were held at this time as well as the Messenger Feast. Aside from ice sealing, it was a slack season but did not occasion anxiety. Today, as in the past, children play out in the darkness and there is much visiting and such social activities as dances, song fests, and general recreational events.

In general, there was little interest in the more remote celestial bodies and, clearly, little or no curiosity about other lands and peoples. This attitude is reflected in religion and in supernatural beliefs. Speculation for its own sake, at least of the kind which went beyond the confines of the immediate world, gave rise to little interest. Far more important were the things in the world at hand. It was the area of settlement and the problems in it that were of primary concern. Although in the course of travels a man might go a great distance, he seemed to have acquired a knowledge of virtually all the terrain over which he had gone. He could draw maps of it, describe it to others, and quickly familiarize himself with the many names of places which were inevitably given. But he did not interest himself in what lay beyond. In religious attitudes, it was this world which was of importance and concern.

DWARFS, MERMEN, MONSTERS, AND OTHER SUPERNATURAL BEINGS

Coexistent with man were numerous beings of various kinds and classes. In the main, although such beings shared the terrain with men, and might in some cases depend, as men did, on the surrounding fauna for their food, theirs and the human world touched only rarely. When it did so, it often resulted in human misfortune. Some of these classes of supernaturals were left strictly alone, others might be capricious and hostile, and hence create problems for humans, and still others had to be placated. Some of these supernaturals might work to human advantage if approached with due respect and a proper sense of supplication. Others would exact vengeance on man if certain kinds of prohibitions were violated.

The western Eskimo appear not to have developed the rather elaborate views, found in the central and eastern regions, of a race of elder beings, those often referred to as the *tornait*. The term, however, is cognate with tunarat, which in North Alaska refers specifically to the powers of the shaman. There are one or two suggestions in the folklore but the emphasis is generally placed elsewhere. Dwarfs and giants played a prominent role in the folk beliefs. The former were particularly significant and might occasionally work mischief.

The belief in such dwarfs is by no means lost at present and these troll-like creatures are seen from time to time.

Dwarfs (in^{y}uarolliq; in^{y}uakolligawrak, "little people") are described as being one foot high. One can never touch them, although many have tried. Their tracks always lead to the sea and then they disappear. They dress like the Eskimo, wearing little parkas and skin trousers made from caribou and sealskins. Their houses are under the ground. They speak Eskimo, but when they are seen, they make noises like a wolf. If rocks or other missiles are thrown at them, they disappear. When people come in from the sea, landing on the beach, the dwarfs are often heard singing and making wolf noises. They do not hurt people generally.

There are numerous descriptions of the dwarf people still extant. The view of them generally suggests that they are small Eskimo, having much the same kind of life. No particular supernatural power is ascribed to them. A few descriptions of the dwarfs may be in order:

1. A party returning from walrus hunting saw a dwarf under an upturned umiak on the beach. They ran after it but it was gone. Its tracks led to the sea but no one had seen it move across the beach.

2. There was a man living on the north side of the lagoon at Barrow (Browerville) who knew such a dwarf. Once the latter came and challenged him to a race. They ran along the shore for a way and the human won. The dwarf was furious and tried to kill him. But the human killed him. He took the head and kept it and it has been seen by a good many people. If a dwarf is killed, the slayer should always take the head. This prevents the relatives of the dwarf from seeking revenge.

3. Out near Umiat, where the tundra begins to bank, a family had camped. While they were there, a dwarf and his wife came over and asked for bone needles. They were given some and prepared to leave. The human wanted to accompany them and see their camp. The dwarf said not to follow him since the others in his camp would kill the humans with their strong bows. The humans did follow their footprints in the snow for a time but then they disappeared.

4. Once, when Barrow had a reindeer herd, a herdsman at saŋmaleak, the lagoon, was challenged to a race by a dwarf. The dwarf lived on the north side of the lagoon. As his weapon he carried a piece of ivory which was sharp on both ends. The dwarf and the man agreed to race but the man insisted that the dwarf run on the south side of the lagoon, while he would run on the north. Since the north side was straight and the south side irregular, the human won easily. The dwarf was very angry and tried to kill the man with his ivory weapon. The man drew an arrow and killed the dwarf. He took the head and kept if for all to see. It was "like an owl's head." It is still there and some people see it when they go up to the lagoon.

5. Of interest is a variant on the above. It was given by another informant. There was a man at saŋmaleak who became a trading partner with a dwarf. They met from time to time. The dwarf had a long ivory staff pointed at both ends. They raced around the lagoon, the human running the straight side, the dwarf the crooked. When the man won, the dwarf, angry at losing, tried to kill

him with his ivory staff. He threw it and missed. The man picked it up and threw it back, killing the dwarf. The head is still there for all to see. It was like "the head of a goose."

6. On Saturday, September 6, 1952, a dwarf was seen on the beach just below the town of Barrow. Several boys saw the apparition, and all vouched for it. A little man, about one foot high, was seen at the base of the bluff on the beach. He was wearing a caribou skin parka with a wolverine hood. The time was late afternoon. The boys gave chase but the dwarf vanished.

7. At Wainwright, on August 15, 1952, a fire was sighted some distance down the beach. Everyone in the community was accounted for, hence the presence of the fire was extremely puzzling. Rev. Wartes, the Presbyterian missionary, happened to be in the community at the time and flew down the beach to determine the source of the fire. No one was sighted and no explanation for the fire has as yet been given. A general consensus is that dwarfs were camping on the beach and it was their fire which was sighted.

Aside from the dwarfs, giants were also a part of the local terrain. They had no special powers, were simply "big men." The view was that the giant lived alone. Such giants were not necessarily supernatural and it was felt that humans grew to a gigantic size if they lived alone. If a person alone got lost, remaining away from the others for many years, he would turn into such a giant. They were regarded as timid and avoided contact with other men.

But although such dwarfs and giants might be regarded as inhabitants of a supernatural world, their powers, as has been stated, were not particularly different from those of men. In the main, they avoided humans and there was little contact between themselves and human affairs. The concept of what may here be called mermen gives an introduction to beings of a somewhat different sort, forms which likewise inhabited the Eskimo terrain but which had to be treated with great care and circumspection lest misfortune befall those who came into contact with them. Such mermen were seen only in the wintertime during the winter sealing. As the hunter has spread his nets under the ice, he knows from experience the size and type of seal he has caught simply from the behavior of the animal. When the ivory clinkers on the net sound, indicating that a seal has been taken, the hunter draws the net in. But before the net is drawn up on the ice, the hunter should take great care to touch the captured seal. If it has long hair and if the skin of the face feels like human skin, he must unhesitatingly let the quarry go. Before he does so, he may name a sea animal which he wishes to capture—whale, walrus, ugruk, or whatever. The merman will send him this game. If, however, the merman is not released, the hunter will die.

Such mermen have the body of a seal and the face and hair of a human. Pressed for an accurate description, the informants agree that this being appears only in winter on the ice in the dark. Hence, it is not known whether the being is male or female. One informant reports that when young he was told, "Watch out in winter over the seal net. Do not be afraid if you get a person instead of a seal." The danger for the hunter lay in bringing the merman up onto the ice. If he were afraid and ran away, leaving his capture on the ice, he would surely die. Within the last few years, it was related, a man had caught one at nuwuk. He left it on the ice and ran away in fear. He died the following spring. The merman was thus malignant only if the regulations relating to him were broken. It was generally felt that he allowed himself to be taken in order to do his captor the favor of sending him other sea game. He never spoke to the hunter and simply disappeared back into the water. It was customary to ask the merman for an ugruk rather than for other game. When the merman made his gift, after being released, it was well not to keep it but to give it away. Thus, if the hunter asked for an ugruk, often saying to the merman—"Come back as an ugruk," the first ugruk thereafter caught would differ somewhat from the usual type. Its liver, instead of being lobed, would be whole and solid. It was not, therefore, a true ugruk. The hunter might ask for a whale next spring after an encounter with a merman. He would get it but might become ill if he were to eat any of the meat. Hence, only the smaller sea mammals were requested. It was further stated that if only a small seal were asked of the merman, the hunter would get a great many. The first he was obliged to give away, the others he might keep.

There was no special term for the merman. It was referred to as in^{y}uq, a person. After one is caught, it never again allows itself to be taken.

There were different kinds of supernaturals which inhabited the world of the Arctic. Some of these were merely animals of unusual shape or form, others were beings which "created" themselves because of actions on the part of men. An example, referred to below, is the caribou skull, breastbone, and spine, which flies through the air after the taboo-violating hunter. The various supernaturals of this kind are as follows:

1. amixsak. The term refers to any covering of skin, such as the skin covers over an umiak or kayak. This is a vengeful spirit of the walrus. In walrus hunting, it is customary to butcher the carcasses on the ice. If the meat cannot all be transported, some of it may have to be abandoned. In the past, should this occur, the walrus had to be given fresh water to drink, and the skin had to be dissected. If the skin were left on the ice, it would later sink, and the skin itself became a vengeful monster, the amixsak. It came up under an umiak and reaching its flippers over the gunwales, pulled the boat under. If the skin covering the flippers were removed, the danger was avoided.

2. The dog of the walrus. If a dog is seen with a walrus herd, the herd is to be avoided. The dog will always run around the resting herd in a circle. It is not a dog at all, but a great serpentlike being who protects the walrus by encircling

them. At a distance, the serpent gives the appearance of a dog. It is never seen without walrus.

3. kukuweaq. This is the ten-legged polar bear. Young men were told: "If you see five men standing together, and it looks like they are wearing sheepskin parkas, don't go to them. That is the polar bear with ten legs." Such animals have been taken by the Barrow people, according to popular belief. One man, coming face to face with such a bear on the ice, stabbed out its eyes with his harpoon. He then began to run home, seeking out the crevasses in the ice so that the monsterc ould not follow him. The bear remained stuck in one such crevasses. The man then speared the bear to death. It is said that this bear lacked shoulder bones in its legs, except in the hind pair. It was huge, its ears being a man's span apart.

In addition to those listed above, there were also animals in the sea which were feared because they might assume monstrous shapes. Mention was obtained of a giant fish but no detail was forthcoming. The narwhal is also mentioned in folklore and is regarded as a supernatural being. In general, the same is true of octopi and there is mention of a giant squid.

In general, the treatment of animals required special respect. Should this not be given, the animal returned in one form or another to haunt his slayer. The general practice was to remove the head of the game. If this were done, the spirit escaped and vengeance need not be feared. The following tale is an example of the prevailing attitude:

Not long ago, a man and his wife were out on the ice. The man shot a polar bear. He went up to the carcass and decided not to do anything with it. He needed a flap for his door, however, and took a square of skin from the bear's back. Two years later, he saw another bear. It had a black square spot on its back instead of the usual white hair. It began to pursue him and he shot it. It fell down just like the bear he had shot previously. This time he took the meat home. When the skin was removed, it was found that the square of skin on the back was missing in the pelt. They ate some of the meat but it made them deathly ill and they were obliged to throw the rest of it away, not even giving it to the dogs. Captain Brower, it is said, took the skin and sent it to a museum. If the man had taken the bear's head off, it would not have pursued him later.

The caribou requires special treatment. If the breastbone is eaten, it should be accompanied by the meat from the ribs. Unless this is done, the caribou skull, with breastbone, ribs, and spine, will come flying through the air in pursuit. This monster also pursued the braggart. There was a man who recently remarked, "I don't know what kind of animal I haven't caught." There was a shaman present when he said this. The latter remarked: "Now maybe you'll see the caribou skeleton come at you." Sure enough, when the man was out hunting some time later, the caribou skull came flying at him. He ran from it but it caught up to him. Then it whistled and went away. The man returned to the community, told what he had seen, became ill, and died soon after.

If the walrus is taken in the manner described above and must be abandoned, the marrowbones and edible cartilage should be removed and brought along. If this is not done, and if the head is not removed, the walrus will exact vengeance.

Other supernaturals, such as ghosts and spirits, are reserved for discussion below. The foregoing section, however, suggests the important religious preoccupation, that of the proper treatment of game. It is clear that the attitude toward game, involving treatment with respect, addressing the slain animal, and the like, relates to the fear that the game may go away and not allow itself to be caught. This is unquestionably a more important consideration than the vengeance taken by an animal on a willful violator or despoiler.

RELATION TO ANIMALS

As noted above, animals were felt to have the ability to reason, talk, and in general, behave like men. Through their kindness to man and because of bribes, cajolery, and magic, they allowed themselves to be taken. Animals became offended and remained away when certain taboos were violated. In relation to the food quest, Eskimo religion was intensely practical. Religion on this level dealt with (1) power and ritual to make the animals come, and (2) proper treatment, to avoid giving offense to the spirit of the animal.

Although animal motivations conceptually reflect an anthropomorphism and are thus essentially the same as human goals, the spirit of an animal was "different" from that of a human. An animal did not object to being killed, so long as proper and respectful treatment was forthcoming on the part of the slayer. If offended, the released animal spirit told the other animals what had happened and the game remained away. A close rapport with such animal spirits existed, especially with those from the land. It was in this area that the shaman found his power, and the tunarak, the "helping spirits" of the shaman, were of course derived from the animal world.

One of the primary points of definition of the animal world, so far as the North Alaskan Eskimo were concerned, lay in the conceptual dichotomy between land and sea. Basically, this implies that the products of these respective spheres should be kept separate. The underlying theory appears to have been that animals of the land are repulsive to those of the sea and the reverse. But the Eskimo of Barrow and adjacent Alaskan regions have not evolved the elaborate seasonal dichotomy of some of the groups farther to the east (cf. Boas, 1888, 1907; Weyer, 1932, p. 349 seq.). The concept is there, to be sure, but in considerably attenuated form. Nor is there in the area the elaborated ceremonial relating to the goddess of the sea, the Sedna myth, which is found among the central groups. But at least there is the idea that some circumspection is necessary in bringing things of the sea together with those of the land. Barrow examples are: A woman engaged in working caribou skin clothing must not touch a seal; before hunting caribou in the spring, the body must be washed of seal grease accumulated during the winter; the body must be washed again, and new clothes worn, before going out whaling in April, thus getting rid of the scent of caribou; weapons which are used at hunting caribou should not be used at sea—the reverse, it is worth mentioning, is not true. The elaboration of the taboo system in relation to land versus sea products appears to stop with the Copper Eskimo. Thus Jenness records that the latter group may eat both land and sea game at the same time (Jenness, 1922, p. 188 seq.). This was also true at Barrow. However, should these foods from different sources be eaten at the same time, the partaker should wash his hands between "courses." Thus, if the person was eating caribou and turned next to seal, the hands should be washed. Failure to do this might have two results—the eater might become ill himself; the respective animals might be offended.

Should these prohibitions have been violated, it was essential that the cause of misfortune be averted and the wrong undone. Here was one of the important functions of the shaman, determining who had broken the customary taboo. And here, too, was the development of the mechanism of confession. The person who had broken the taboo, the result manifesting itself either in illness to the person himself or in starvation for the community, simply confessed his wrong, either publicly, or to the shaman. The imposition by the shaman of particular food taboos for that person was usually sufficient to remove the sickness or misfortune. Of interest in this respect were confessions apparently of a compulsive nature.

But there were of course numerous other food taboos, not only those which related to the difference between land and sea. Anyone going out whaling, for example, was warned to avoid eating shortribs of seal. These were hateful to the whale and the animal would not allow itself to be taken. Similarly, while caribou could be taken out on the ice and eaten, bread, when it was introduced, was regarded as frightening to whales and other sea mammals. It was also said that if one ate bread out on the ice or at sea, one developed a stye in the eye. People who might cook for the karigi, and this was frequently done, had to wash their hands before bringing the food into the building. If they failed to, they became ill. Each animal, as will be seen, had its own set of taboos and restrictions. Those that were most elaborately developed concerned the animals that were most important to the food supply—whales, caribou, seal, and walrus.

Despite the vague attention to a land-sea dichotomy, there was a sense of certain land animals being related to or having counterparts in those of the sea. Thus the wolf was equated with killer whale. While the voraciousness of both might suggest the connection, it is said that the wolf, if game is plentiful, will eat only the tongue of animals he has killed. The killer whale, in preying on the small, black, humpback whale, reputedly does the same thing. The caribou has its maritime counterpart in the small black whale as well. Both are said to be able to transform their shapes. No other such relation exists, as nearly as can be determined. The polar bear and the brown bear, for example, are hostile to each other; the latter is reputedly stronger and more spiritually dangerous. Great shaman power, especially curing power, in keeping with the widespread development of the bear cult in Asia and America, was obtained from the brown bear. But despite the connection between the wolf and the sea in the shape of the killer whale, wolf power could be negated by the use of sea water. This was hateful to the wolf in his land form.

Animals may, and frequently do, talk to men. When they do, they push the skin of their face back. A humanlike face appears which speaks. Even dogs, although they have no souls and no spirit power, can do this. It was reported that recently a man at Barrow was forcing his dogs on and beating them. The leader pushed his skin back, turned, and asked—"Why do you beat us so hard"? The man is alleged to have fainted at this. When the shamanistic candidate was out alone, "practicing his songs," his helpers, the tunarak, were alleged to come to him in their natural form and speak to him in this way.

Young hunters were given advice by the older and more experienced men. They were told never to catch an animal that was unfamiliar to which a name could not be given. If they did, the animal might "pull the skin of its head back like a parka hood" and talk to them. A tale told to young hunters, ostensibly to instill the necessary quality of respect for the animals of the surrounding area, was the following:

There was a boy who caught a snipe in a trap. He didn't want it. He plucked off all its feathers and let it go. Later, he tried again and again to get a seal but was never successful. Once he was sitting by the seal's blowhole and he heard a voice calling up to him from under the ice. Frightened, he made out the words: "When you plucked me, you made me suffer; now I won't let you get any seal." The boy sat for a long time, unable to move. Then he plunged his spear into the aalluq (seal's blowhole) and when he pulled it out, there was the snipe, caught in the line. He let the bird go and after that, he was able to catch seals.

A second tale, likewise told to young men when they began to hunt, was this one:

A man was hunting seals. He heard two of them talking. One said to the other: "Go over to where that man sits and come up through the aalluq." But the other said: "No, he will catch me and when he does, he will drag me home and bump my head on the ice." But the first said: "His wife will be sharpening her ulu all the time; why don't you go over there"? They stopped talking and the second came up through the blowhole and the man caught it. On the way home, he was careful not to bump its head on the ice. At home he told his wife to give the seal a drink of fresh water. He made her sharpen her ulu carefully and advised her not to stir the seal meat in the pot. After that, the man and his wife were careful to observe this way of treating seals and he was able to catch a great many.

In a third tale, formerly often told to the young hunter, the common theme of the animal offering its assistance to the hunter is repeated. It was said that if a man were not a successful hunter, the animals might come to him and tell him what to do. If he followed their advice, he could become successful. The tale follows:

There was a man who was a poor hunter. He tried and tried and never caught anything. One day, he was out stalking some caribou but was unable to get close to them. Suddenly, a caribou came running toward him, pursued by a wolf. The caribou came to him and drawing back the skin of its face, said: "Hide me." The man stood between the wolf and the caribou. The wolf approached the man, and pushing back the skin of its head, said: "Go away; let me take that caribou." The man became frightened and ran away. At this, the caribou ran to the nearby lagoon and turned into a small humpbacked whale. The wolf leaped into the water also and became a killer whale and the two swam about in the water. So the man gave no protection to the caribou when it was asked for and he never became successful after that. He should have listened to what the caribou had to say.

Because of the elaborately evolved series of restrictions and taboos relating to the animal world, it may be well to list them and to demonstrate the views toward the respective animals which were held by the aboriginal North Alaskan Eskimo. The whale is not included here in view of the somewhat more complex series of rituals pertaining to the whaling cult for which a separate section is reserved.

LAND ANIMALS

1. *The fox.*—Five types of foxes are designated. They are: (a) The red fox, kayaktuq; (b) the cross fox, kenrak; (c) the white fox, ciriganeak; (d) the blue fox, kenraktunuq; (e) the silver fox, kerenektaq. It was the red fox which was regarded as the most cunning of all the animals. The red fox can approach close to humans, knowing that his intelligence will keep him safe, and it is the red fox which will avoid a trap. It takes a most resourceful hunter to get the red fox.

In the aboriginal culture, the foxes were hunted by means of traps between December and April. After the first thaw, the season was regarded as over. Only five of each kind of fox could be taken at a time. The theory was that five skins were sufficient for a parka of matched skins and the fox was offended if more than five of his kind were killed. A daily take, i. e., five animals, was called mitkosaaxaret, five skins for a parka.

When a hunter went out to inspect his fox traps, ice deadfalls being used, he brought with him objects to appease the spirit of the fox. If a female fox were taken, a needle and an ivory thimble were tied to the carcass. If the fox were male, a man's knife was tied to it. The fox spirit remained until the head was cut off. This was done at home where the skinning took place. From the tundra, the frozen carcass, with the offerings tied to it, was brought back by dog sled. The knife, or thimble and needle, was kept with the carcass until it thawed sufficiently for skinning. When the head was cut off, the offerings were removed and the hunter remarked to the fox spirit: "You better come back again." When the spirit left, it told the other foxes that knives, needles, and thimbles were there for the foxes and they had only to go over and get them. If the hunter failed to remove the fox's head, the spirit would remain about and cause illness and misfortune. The hunter would, moreover, not get other foxes.

Fox meat could be eaten freely, although it was frequently a personal taboo. There were no other restrictions applying to foxes.

2. *The wolf.*—Wolves were treated in much the same way as foxes. Only five traps could be set at a time. Wolves were taken with traps—the ice deadfall mentioned above, a noose and trigger set in stones, willow branch traps, and the like. When traps were set for either foxes or wolves, songs might be sung over the traps at the time they were baited. Not everyone owned such songs but they seem to have been fairly common. An ingenious method for catching the wolf was by means of frozen baleen. The baleen, sharpened and cut to a length of about 6 inches, was bent and frozen inside a piece of suet. When the wolf ate the bait, the baleen, thawing out in the animal's stomach, would spring back into place and stab the animal. Willow was also treated in the same way, although baleen was regarded as more efficient. Such a device was called isiiviroaq. When the wolf swallowed one, his tracks were followed and the carcass found.

When a wolf was taken, the carcass was treated in the same manner as the fox, with offerings of needles and thimbles, if the wolf were female; a knife, if male. The wolf, amawk, was regarded as spiritually more dangerous than the fox. In the aboriginal culture, very few would dare eat the meat of the wolf. When the head was removed, the body was left on the tundra, the hunter often brandishing a knife much in the same manner as at a human death in order to drive the wolf spirit away. Taking a wolf, moreover, gave rise to food taboos. The hunter was expected to eat cold, uncooked food for 4 days after taking a wolf, if female; for 5 days, if the wolf were male. This food taboo did not apply when foxes were caught. The wolf spirit was asked to return and to tell the other wolves of the good treatment he had received.

3. The wolverine, kaavik.—While this animal was particularly desired for the skin, of which parka ruffs were made, it was not easily come by in the area. Some wolverines were hunted by means of traps to the south. The take was limited to five at a time but there appear to have been no other restrictions. Most wolverine pelts were obtained from other groups by trade. The importance of limiting the number of animals, foxes, wolves, wolverines, and the like, taken at a single time is illustrated by the following tale:

There was an unsuccessful hunter. He traveled inland, bringing with him a poke of oil for purposes of trading. At a trading point, he met with two men who offered him five wolf skins for his oil poke. He related to them that he was not successful as a hunter and asked their advice. They advised him to set his traps facing the sun. When he had taken five wolves and five wolverine, he was told he should face his traps toward the north and so not get any more game. He did as he was told and was successful. He got five of each animal, wolf and wolverine, but wanted more. He continued to allow his traps to face the sun. After a time, he returned to them to see what had been caught. He found nothing but was pulled irresistably toward the traps he had set and was himself caught in them. Thus he died, caught in his own traps. And this, it is said, is why one does not take more than five of each animal.

4. The lynx, n^{y}uutuyuq.—There appear to have been no restrictions on either the lynx or the mountain sheep. Both, it is said, were once taken in greater numbers than today.

5. Caribou, tuttu.—Since the caribou were so vital a source of food for the inland Eskimo, and were not unimportant among the maritime groups either, it is not surprising that a series of elaborated taboos should have arisen regarding them. In general, maritime people engaged in hunting caribou observed the same restrictions as did those more intimately concerned with them. As has been noted, weapons which were specifically for the caribou should not be used at sea. However, a maritime hunter, proceeding inland along the water courses, was free to use his sealing weapons for caribou. The specific lance designed for the caribou, whether it was made of the os penis of the walrus, of stone, or whatever material, could only be used for caribou hunting. There was no limit on the number of caribou which could be taken at one time or in one season. The principal restrictions lay in the ways in which caribou carcasses had to be treated.

When men went out specifically for caribou, either individually or as a crew, effecting communal drives, children were obliged to stay in the house. They could not walk directly on the floor but had to stay on winter skins of caribou which were stretched out on the floor. The child was obliged to be quiet lest the caribou be driven away. The restriction was not lifted until the hunting was declared officially over and the legs broken for marrow. The period of restriction usually was in spring, in March and early April.

In the communal drives, sleds were generally taken into the tundra to bring back the caribou meat. These were brought out in fair numbers, each being capable of carrying about 20 caribou carcasses. The runners were iced and the sled could be drawn by one or two dogs, aided by the hunter. Sinew was laid along the runner actually made of ice. When the caribou were taken in large numbers, each man went to work to load his sled or sleds, the division of game being made between the hunters. For purposes of transport, the carcasses were disemboweled and the entrails carefully cleaned. The carcasses were laid crosswise on the sled, alternating the heads. Before starting back to the community, the heads were bent upward so that they froze in an upright position and did not strike the ground. If this were to happen, the caribou would be offended. If the group were camped out on the tundra when the sled load reached the home community or campsite, the intestines were put to one side, the leg bones disarticulated and laid carefully to the side of the house, and the meat butchered and put away. Not until the hunt was officially over could the leg bones be broken for the marrow. During this time, children were restricted and confined to the house. When a sled load had been deposited, the hunters might return for more game.

When it was decided that no more caribou would be hunted, other activities now being planned, the leg bones were cracked for the marrow and children were released from the restrictions imposed on them. The antlers were cut off the heads at this time as well and used for various purposes. Awls, spearheads for the caribou, and mitiŋiu, the baleen and antler strainers used to clean out an ice hole before sealing or fishing, were made from them. After the leg bones had been cracked and the marrow taken, no one could hunt caribou until after some other activity, such as whaling, walrus hunting, or the like, had been undertaken. Caribou hunting later in the year was pretty much an individual task.

Mention has already been made of the pursuit by the skeleton of the caribou of those who had given offense to the animal.

6. The brown bear.—With the red fox, the brown bear was reputed to be among the most intelligent of animals, endowed with great power. It was felt that the brown bear should not be shot either with arrows, or later, with a gun after it had been introduced. If a man had a brown bear in his trap, his proper course was to draw his knife and to fight the bear singlehanded. If, in doing this, he were mauled and bitten, another person should take the skin of the bear and wrap the injured man in it. If this were done, he would recover quickly from his wounds. It is related that one man, having caught a bear in a trap he had set, shot it, but succeeded only in wounding it. The bear, dragging the trap, went after the man and wounded him badly, mauling and biting him. He then succeeded in shooting the bear dead. He went back to his house but no one would go out and skin the bear so that the wounded man could be wrapped in the skin. He died of his bites shortly thereafter. It was regarded as exceedingly unwise to talk of the brown bear unnecessarily. Wherever he might be, the bear would hear and take his revenge on those disrespectful to him. Actually, this attitude was carried over to all animals. Particularly one should not say, "I am not afraid of the brown bear." If this were done, the bear was sure to attack and have his revenge. Shaman power was, of course, particularly allied to the brown bear and was curing power for the most part. Although no one at Barrow today claims shaman power, it is said that a man who died a few years ago had a particular affinity for the brown bear. When he died and was being buried in the Presbyterian Church, a bear came walking into the community. This was extremely unusual, since the brown bear is out of place as far north as Barrow. The meat of the brown bear could not be eaten by women. A man who ate this meat had to refrain from sexual intercourse for 4 to 5 days depending on the sex of the bear, whose flesh had to be cooked at the place where it was caught. One did not bring the flesh home nor butcher the bear except where it had been taken. When men ate of the flesh of the brown bear, old clothes had to be worn. Violation of any of these restrictions inevitably resulted in sickness. This was the most terrifying of all the animals. The attitudes surrounding it reflect the circum-polar attitude toward the bear and the presence of a shamanistic bear cult.

7. *Lemmings, ground squirrels, and other rodents.*—The Arctic rodents were not a primary source of food. The inland Eskimo, however, did often eat rodents when other food was scarce. If this were done, the pot in which the flesh was cooked could never be used for anything else. Some shaman power came from the rodents, particularly from the ground squirrel, and the dried and stuffed bodies of these animals were often used as personal charms. Children would sometimes dig out the burrows of the various rodents in order to get at the collected seeds, which, it may be mentioned, is the only native vegetable food known to the Eskimo of Barrow and adjacent regions. If this were done, the child was warned not to take the entire store,

but to leave half for the rodent family. Children learned songs to sing to appease the mother rodent when this was done.

8. Birds.—While technically classed with game from the land, and unquestionably of some economic importance both in the past and at present, the various birds appear to have played no part in the system of ritual prohibitions. Birds of all kinds, ducks, geese, owls, and a host of others, were taken in a variety of ways. Despite the elaboration of Raven mythology, there was apparently no particularly special attitude toward this bird. As nearly as can be ascertained, no hunting taboos relating to birds and no special treatment of them or their eggs existed.

As a further reflection of the land-sea dichotomy, the bones of all animals taken from the land had to be treated in special ways at certain times. Before the spring whaling and before people were free to go out on the ice with umiak and whaling gear, peace had to be made with the land animals. This was done by assembling as many bones as possible of land animals taken during the previous summer, fall, and winter, and burning them. Until this was done, at the edge of the pack ice on the beach, the land animals would be offended and communicate their displeasure to those of the sea. In principle, this had the final effect of releasing the hunters from the taboos imposed during the caribou hunting season, since the attitude applied particularly to the caribou, and paved the way for a new manner of life with its associated and different taboos.

SEA ANIMALS

In general, all sea animals, or more exactly, sea mammals, were offered a cup of fresh, cold water after they had been brought into the community. This was usually the task of the wife of the hunter. A special pot was used for this purpose. It was made of either pottery or wood and kept in the karigi. The woman who needed it would go to the edifice to obtain it, pour water on the face and nostrils of the captured sea animal, and return the pot to its place. As with land animals, when there was a change of seasonal activity, when maritime hunting was dropped in favor of hunting on land, the bones of seals, particularly, were collected by the family and burned. At this time, cold fresh water was again offered to them. This again released the family from the prohibitions associated with the sea and paved the way for land activities. As has been indicated, there were also the changes in weapons, in clothing, the ritual washing, and the like in connection with this transition.

Excepting the whale, the attitudes and behavior associated with sea mammals and other game from the sea and water were as follows:

1. The polar bear.—The polar bear was less powerful than the brown bear both spiritually and physically. As noted, the two were hostile to each other. They were reconciled at one point only—the would-be successful wrestler wore a charm from a brown bear on his right arm, one from the polar bear on his left. This is not to imply that the polar bear was conceptually weak. On the contrary, he likewise had great spiritual power but in essence it was not shaman power; it did not transfer to humans. There was no limit on the number of polar bears that could be taken. They were usually harpooned. It was necessary to cut off the bear's head to release the spirit and to give the animal fresh water. The flesh of the polar bear was always divided and in a joking manner. As soon as the hunters brought the carcass of the bear to the beach, the word was passed along from house to house. All rushed out to get a piece, bringing a knife and a container. The bear was hacked to pieces on the spot and each one took a section. There was considerable play on this occasion, blood being spattered over clothes and on faces. The hunter who had taken the bear held onto the hind leg while the villagers cut up the bear. When the bear had been cut to pieces, the hunter kept his joint and took it home. The bear was not previously skinned. Each one who took a piece tried to get some of the bearskin also. If large enough, this was made into mittens, if small, a piece was sewed to the mittens. If two men had taken the bear together, each held a hind leg. For the rest of the carcass there was a general free-for-all, the strongest emerging with the largest pieces. Bear (naanuk) was thus not divisible among a crew but belonged technically to the hunter who had taken it. Informants give no reason for the behavior associated with the polar bear division. It was the only occasion on which such joking rivalry in respect to game took place. It presumably reflects an attitude toward the polar bear which is borne out in the behavior toward it. It was denied that this brought additional bears or in any way appeased the bear. In any case, the hunter had previously released the spirit of the bear and had formally asked it to return. Beyond the offering of water, there was nothing else given to the polar bear.

The behavior described, while it has fallen into disuse, may persist in one form. When the first polar bear was taken at Barrow in the summer of 1952, the hunter kept the skin for himself. He went around to various neighbors and friends, however, and gave them the meat, keeping only a small portion of one hind leg for himself.

Returning to the aboriginal past, if a polar bear wandered into the community, it was killed and cut to pieces at once. The behavior associated with division when the bear was brought in may be a carry-over from this notion, that the bear was treated as an enemy and intruder. As is known, a stranger entering the community would have his clothes ripped off, and be pummeled about by the inhabitants. Any connection, however, cannot be ascertained.

2. Seals.—As stated elsewhere, the various smaller seals were individually hunted, the ugruk, the bearded or barbed seal, was divided among the crew which took it. All types of seals were given fresh water to drink when their carcasses were brought to the community. In addition, and this related particularly to the smaller seals, mittens might be put on the flippers as an offering and to induce the seal to return. The seal, reporting in spirit form to its fellows, would say: "Those people gave me water to drink and gave me mittens; they have those things there for you too." For the seals particularly, it was most important that water be given. While mentioned above as extended to the polar bear, it was not so essential that this animal be so treated.

Associated with the seal were certain omens and related phenomena. Mention is made above of the concept of the merman that is so closely associated with the sealing in winter and may be taken at the seal's blowhole. Seals might talk to men, as some of the tales recorded above indicate, but on the whole, the seal, of whatever kind, existed for the benefit of man and had only to be "treated right" in order to be made to return. It was said in the past that if the hunters saw an ugruk lying on the ice and it could be noticed that the animal's nose was running, the mucus making a rope down to the ice, then by no means should that animal be caught. If he was caught, the hands of the hunters would stick to the rope as they pulled the animal onto the umiak and they would be pulled down into the water and drown. There was a way by which the right place to put down a seal net in the spring sealing could be determined. The nets were set up and often left overnight so that the seal when caught would drown. In order to place the net, the hunter ran from the beach toward the edge of the ice, carrying his two nets. He held his breath as he ran. When he could no longer run and hold his breath, he had reached the place where the net was to be lowered. Similarly, when the marker attached to the net was down, indicating the presence of a seal in the net, the hunter could not draw the seal in at once. Again there was a small ritual. The hunter pulled once, then twice more, and one final pull drew the seal in. This is a reflection of an act being performed four times. Unless this were done, the seal would be offended. There was no preferred way to kill a seal, although an attempt was made, for purely practical reasons, to keep the blood from being lost. Hence, seals were often knocked on the head or strangled if caught alive. The larger ugruk had to be harpooned.

3. Walrus (*ayvuq*).—The walrus was regarded as one of the most intelligent of the sea mammals but was "careless." In contrast to the shy beluga, for example, the walrus would not pay attention to an approaching boat, relying on his "dog" (q. v.) and thinking that the boat was another walrus. It is said that it is this very carelessness which made the walrus a dangerous adversary. Red was a color hateful to the walrus and polar bear. Both were said to attack if they saw this color. The hunters often talked to the walrus while engaged in hunting it. When a herd had been disturbed on the ice, the walrus had to be persuaded to let the boat pass. An example is the following, narrated by an old man:

When I was young, my father took me walrus hunting in an umiak. We shot some walrus on the ice. The others were swimming around us and wouldn't let the boat pass. By their swimming, they kept the boat from moving. My father talked to them—"My father is old. He is listening at home, and if you endanger us, my old father will starve." After he said that, the walrus swam away from the boat and let us go. One walrus near the boat made a lot of noise talking to the others. When he finished, they all went away. My grandfather sat in a little kayak near the house while we were out on the sea hunting. He listened all the time. He heard my father talking to the walrus and he scolded the children playing there for making so much noise that he couldn't hear. He heard what my father said and he heard what the walrus said to the other walrus. As he sat there, he heard drumming all the time. He knew if people were having a dance in other towns or if the aŋatqut were busy. He could hear everything.

The walrus were likewise credited especially with power to hear at a distance. Young hunters were strongly advised against saying such things as "I am not afraid of the walrus; nothing will happen to me when we go out hunting." This was to court disaster, since the walrus would avenge themselves on such carelessness. There were songs for walrus in fairly common use. Walrus hunters had special cries which were used to signal the shore on returning from a successful hunt. Walrus were offered fresh water. This was often done by the hunter himself, since the butchering of the huge animals usually took place on the spot where the animals were killed. As today, the meat was transported back after butchering.

4. Killer whale (*aaxlu*).—The killer whale was greatly feared and never hunted. When sighted, it was addressed formally: "We are your friends; we are glad to see you." This was so that "the killer whale won't hurt us." No one dared spear a killer whale. If it were done, the animal always remembered and came back to get his revenge. One case, still talked of at Barrow, was that of a man who drove a harpoon into a killer whale. He was in a kayak at the time and made his way to the ice. He was able to get ashore in time to avoid the animal but each time thereafter that he tried to launch his kayak, the killer whale was waiting for him. At last he did not dare go out in a boat again. He was forced to abandon the sea altogether.

And so it was that the killer whale was carefully left undisturbed. If it were bothered by anyone, it always sought revenge and was reputed to wait for years for the opportunity. Nor is this attitude lost today. In August 1952, two young men were drowned when their outboard motor propeller struck a log or some other object in the sea. It was said by a good many that one of the boys had once fired his rifle at a killer whale and this was the result.

If a man saw an ugruk being eaten or captured by the killer whale, he could call out, asking for half. The killer whale would leave the half of the carcass on the beach.

5. The beluga (*kilʸelluaq, sisuaq*).—The beluga was harpooned in shallow water with a special stone lance. They were taken in spring at the edge of the ice. Like other sea mammals, they were offered fresh water and the hunter said: "Tell the others about us." The beluga was reputedly timid and cautious. In approaching the beluga, one was required to be very quiet and to whisper if talking were necessary. Any loud noise would drive the beluga away. There appear to have been no special prohibitions associated with the beluga.

6. Fish.—There should be no hair on a fish net. If the fish sees human hair or animal hair woven into a fish net or line, he is repelled. It is said that the fish is afraid because it thinks that human heads are close by and he will not then allow himself to be caught. When tomcod are caught with a hook and line, the fisherman should not put them into his snow shirt. Putting any game or fish into the snow shirt was called puxłuktuat. Tomcod must be put into a sack and carried. Failure to do so drives the cod away.

As noted, there is little or no sea fishing. Fishing was reserved for the inland waterways and lakes. No other prohibitions could be elicited. Fish reputedly did not fear noise.

Other game from the sea appears not to have been especially treated. There were a few other animals but their appearance was most rare. Octopi (nipiccak) were known but rarely seen and not eaten. Nor was there any series of tales or beliefs concerning the jellyfish. The narwhal exists in mythology but does not appear in the Bering waters. Dolphins and porpoises have been reported and are caught occasionally. Whale, seal, and walrus were the animals of greatest importance and it was around them that the largest body of myth and belief circulated.

Sufficient examples have perhaps been shown to demonstrate the conceptual intimacy between man and the denizens of the animal world. As noted, some occasions in which the relationship to animals was felt to exist required the aid of the shaman. In the main, however, the individual was responsible for maintaining his good standing with animals. Should he fail to meet the necessary requirements, should he neglect the prohibitions, then not only he, but often his family and the community as well, might be made to suffer. Some degree of control over the animals could be exerted through the compelling songs, but even these were not sufficient if respect and proper treatment were omitted.

Some attention to the nature of the song is in order.

SONGS

Songs were known as attuu (pl. aatuutit). This term referred to any kind of song, whether magical or social. It is to be remembered that Eskimo music is highly developed, despite the paucity of musical instruments, and the song is an extremely important social and recreational outlet even in the contemporary culture. The social songs passed from individual to individual. While they might be composed for a particular purpose, such as for a particular dance, or for an individual, as in the case of the host at the Messenger Feast sending a song to his guest, or merely sung at the inspiration of an individual with new accompanying dance steps invented at the same time, such social songs were generally common property. A way to some acclaim and prestige was to be a good singer and to be clever at new compositions. Such songs as these, however, important though they may have been to recreation, were not "owned" songs and had no magical implications.

It was the song that underlay virtually all compulsive magic that the North Alaskan Eskimo practiced. In general, these songs had the effect of controlling game and weather. There were songs that could be owned by anyone for these purposes but there were also the songs that were the particular property of shamans. The latter reflected the rapport between the shaman and his helping spirits. Shamans, however, had other songs in common with laymen.

Such supernatural songs were regarded as property. They were both inherited and purchased. An elaborately evolved series of songs of all kinds existed. Thus there were songs for virtually every act associated with hunting, with boat using, with house raising, with new clothing, with charms, and the like. It was not always regarded as necessary to have a song in order to perform a certain act but unquestionably the song gave a far greater chance of success. When a song was inherited, it was taught by a parent to his child. Any person might own a song of any kind, women not being restricted. Since, however, hunting was men's work, women did not usually know hunting formulas. There was a tendency for the song to pass along in a family line, if not from parent to child, then at least to a younger sibling or to a collateral relative. A family might thus own a song in common and any member was free to sing it. For this reason, there was a slight tendency for the shaman's songs to pass from relative to relative. The office of the shaman, while not strictly hereditary, tended to restrict itself to certain families, the shaman father often teaching his arts and songs to a son or even a daughter.

But songs could also be sold. The price was variable. Of cases reported, one man bought a song which enabled him to attract caribou for six caribou skins. A not uncommon price was a poke of oil, several beads, or a pair of labrets, and in cases where a particular song was much in demand by the buyer, the price might go up to a kayak. For the most part, these were hunting and weather songs. The purchaser, having struck his bargain, went out with the owner and the two sat together until the song had been learned. The seller had then no right to sing the song again, in fact, it is said, "he couldn't ever remember it again." A song which was the common property of a family could also be sold by the individual members. After selling, the song lost its efficacy so far as the original owner was concerned. By this process, however, a song might be known by several people of different families.

Songs were principally for hunting and weather. When a man baited a trap, for example, there were various songs associated with each step. There were songs for attracting game of all kinds, both from land and sea. Unquestionably, the most important song cycle of the area was that associated with whaling. Men who had a song for a particular purpose might be invited to sing it when the need for it arose. The singer was usually not paid for this service but was expected to do it for the communal good. All weather phenomena were subject to control by songs. The singer could change the direction of the wind, cause the ice to move in or out, bring storms, and the like. A particularly malignant shaman was generally blamed for an adverse change in the weather. Anyone, however, who owned a weather song might sing it for his own purposes. An old woman reports that when she was a girl, she had gone out with another young woman to pick berries. A wind came up and it began to snow. The girls were becoming frightened, being unable to make their way back through the blizzard. Suddenly, the weather cleared and they came back safely. When they returned, they found that the husband of the informant's aunt had been singing a weather song for their benefit and by changing the direction of the storm, had saved them. This song was later taught to the informant by her uncle. She refused to sing the song for the ethnographer on the grounds that the summer weather was pleasant and there was no need to call up a wind. Other examples of weather songs were given (cf. shamanistic activities).

There is no doubt that although supernatural songs were had in large numbers, it was dangerous to use them or to apply the power which they contained. The statement was frequently made that a father, mother, grandmother, or some other relative warned the young person against using songs and learning them. One reason for this was that to become interested in songs attracted the dark powers associated with shamanism and to bring the shamanistic calling on one's self. Because the shaman was feared and unpopular, it was well to avoid anything which brought the individual up against the more intimate realm of the supernatural. A person who became a shaman did not always wish to become so; not infrequently he was called into the office simply because he was unable to resist the urging of the tunarak. An informant relates that his grandfather was urged by his mother not to have such songs. He stayed away from them and "was a good hunter anyway; he could still catch anything." And it was often reported: "I didn't want to fool with those songs."

A song could take the place of an amulet or charm and was often associated with an amulet. This suggests that there were "personal" songs which had the general effect of promoting the well-being of the individual. Such songs, or charms, or songs and charms associated, were generally given by an older person to a younger. The following is a case in point: Two boys who had grown up together and who were associated with the same karigi, but were otherwise not related, were selected by an old woman to receive identical charms. To each, she gave the same song. One, when lost on the tundra, sang his personal song and at once found his way again. The other was once eager to catch up with a man on the tundra who was driving a team some miles ahead. He found that he couldn't signal the man he was pursuing and instead sang his personal song. The result was that the other's sled broke and he could be overtaken. The man was at a loss to know how his sled, which he had just checked over, had broken and the singer did not tell him.

But when a song was sung, regardless of what it was, or for whatever purpose, the singer was placed under restrictions. He generally had to observe a special food taboo for 4 or 5 days after singing the song. The type of food tabooed depended on the nature of the song itself and on whatever foods were conceptually related to the song. Failure to observe this regulation resulted in illness to the singer. It was this attitude which appears to have produced the anxiety associated with the song.

There was no limit to the number of songs which an individual might have. One man is described as having six songs. They were: (1) for whales, (2) for caribou fawns, (3) for causing an animal to be weak and lose its strength, (4) for curing, (5) for ptarmigans, (6) for putting people to sleep. Nor was the man in question a shaman. While it is true that he used a tambourine in singing, he did not resort to the shamanistic seance and to the legerdemain associated with shamanism. The fact that he did not make capital of a trancelike state and did not pretend to have powers other than those produced by the songs would suggest that, while spiritually powerful, he was not classed as an aŋatquq. Presumably, after singing each song, the man had to observe restrictions of various kinds for the stipulated period.

It is not to be implied that the songs of the shaman were any different from those used by laymen. They might, it is true, call forth powers which a layman was reluctant to deal with, but there appears to have been no essential difference in kind of song. Thus a shaman might have a sickness-producing song but so might anyone else. Curing songs, too, were not limited to the shaman's office, as the example above attests. There was no doubt that the shaman was freer in his use of songs and, because of the spirit powers associated with him, was less reluctant to use them.

All such supernatural songs had to be learned from someone else. They could not be composed, as was the case with the social and recreational songs. It was said that a man might pretend to have such songs and would sing them but if they brought no result, it was clear that they were either "made up" or had not been sung right. It was in this respect that the failure of the song could be explained. The most important aspect was that the song had to be letter perfect; it had no compulsive value unless it were. It was said of the songs that they were "true," that they were in existence even before the shamans came.

Since the singing of such supernatural songs was a purely individual matter, and since the songs themselves were individually owned and could not be transmitted except to a family member or a buyer, the actual performance was not highly formalized. One result has been to keep alive the sense of power associated with the song. There seems little doubt that despite the inroads of Christianity on the culture, the belief in the efficacy of the song remains. In engaging with the Barrow Eskimo in walrus hunting, the writer heard an old man softly singing a song for the walrus. For the same reason, it becomes difficult to elicit the songs themselves. Two examples were collected and are listed under shamanistic activities (see pp. 316–317). Difficulties were at once encountered when informants were asked for such songs. Some denied ever having such songs. One man professed to have a song which broke things at a distance. When asked for it, he replied, logically enough, "Why should I sing that song? I'm not mad at anybody." The writer paid five dollars for the songs that are mentioned below. Presumably, these songs are now his property and only he has the right to sing them, or, at least, they will be efficacious only when sung by the writer. Other informants, after giving the details of songs, would, when pressed for the songs themselves, say they had forgotten them. It would thus appear that the attitudes toward songs remain.

It would be difficult to compile a list of the purposes for which songs were employed. Hunting and weather, as noted, were two of the most important considerations in magic singing, but curing, bringing sickness, causing sleep, breaking objects, finding lost objects, and many others were controlled by singing. One informant reported that he had in his youth engaged as a runner in the Messenger Feast. As he ran the race, he found his legs getting weaker and weaker and at last he could no longer run on and so lost the race. When he returned, he found that his father had been singing to make him lose the race. His father, of course, had done this in order to protect him, fearing the anger of the shamans who were the deadly enemies of a successful racer. There was also the concept of love magic, again related to the song. The case was mentioned of a man at Barrow who customarily sang songs for people who desired some other person. He was given a gift for his services if the songs proved successful. Another case is that of a hunchbacked man who wanted to marry a girl who was working at the Native Service school. She constantly refused him. At last, he bought a song which compelled her to think of him when he sang it. Finally, she gave in and married him. They had no children, and when he died she married another man and had children.

There were songs which were used in feuds in order to weaken the enemy. The tale is told of a feud between a group from Point Barrow and one from Point Hope. The group from the south came well armed, wearing wood and horn armor and carrying clubs and slings. At length, after attacks on both sides, the tikeraγmiut (those from Point Hope) were isolated on a sandspit and beseiged. A woman at Barrow was nursing a child and was singing lullabies to it. She could see the enemy from where she sat. Then she began to sing a song to weaken the enemy. She sang—"How great a fighter is your grandfather!" When she sang this, the Point Hope group became weak and was unable to stand off the attack. Their leader was paralyzed and when it was seen that he could not move or lift his weapons, the others lost heart and were killed.

The supernatural song was sung with a slow, measured rhythm. A hunting song would often imitate the sound of the animal hunted. Such songs differed markedly from the sprightly rhythms of the social and recreational songs.

Closely allied with the song was the amulet or charm. Here again, a complex series of patterns emerges.

CHARMS AND AMULETS

There were different classes of charms. Some were purely personal and, as such, individual property. These were aanaroak or oyamitkoak. There were also household amulets and a complex series of charms which were placed in boats and which generally related to whaling. Charms were also used in association with the stone lamp of the household. Special charms, known as aaroraq, were placed by the door of the household. The primary purpose of all such charms was to compel success in some undertaking. It was this idea which appears fundamental rather than that of warding off malign or hostile influences.

The personal charm, individually owned, might be anything relating to the surroundings. There were carved figures of men, seals, whales, wolves, and any number of animals, made from ivory or bone. But there were also the stuffed bodies of small animals, such as lemmings, squirrels, and small birds. Sometimes only the head and skin of a small animal was used as a charm. Ermine skins were regarded as a good charm. Of the larger animals, the teeth and claws might be used. Thus ugruk claws, polar bear teeth, seal teeth, the feet, parts of the skin, and the like, might be used. Sometimes the nose of an animal made up the charm. The charms were either sewed on the clothing directly or were placed in skin bags and tied under the clothing or sewed there. Charms were worn on the sleeves of the parka and across the back.

Charms might be owned by anyone. There was no limit to the number of charms which could be owned at the same time, although practical considerations, since each charm, to be effective, necessitated the establishment of a food taboo, limited the number. While people of all ages and of every status had charms, they were felt to be particularly efficacious for children. When a child was born, an attempt was made at once to secure a charm for it. This was often a small bird, stuffed, which might be worn by the child for a time and then discarded.

An amulet was obtained from another person. The general feeling appears to have been that the older a person became, the less his need for an amulet. Old women, for example, a status defined in terms of reaching the climacteric, often passed their charms on to younger people, usually to relatives. Because old women were regarded as having special powers, they often worked out a charm for an individual. The same appears true of old men, although it is evident that they did not achieve the same degree of supernatural power as did women past the menopause. Shamans also might provide a charm. An old person or a shaman was simply asked to give one to a child and might be paid for the service rendered. Like songs, charms were reputed to come from great antiquity. Theoretically, this meant that no new charms could be created. In practice, however, this was not true. If a person found an unusual stone, a piece of bone or ivory on the beach, he might either carve it or simply sew it up into a bag and wear it. Moreover, if he were to do this, he was properly advised to ask a shaman about it and to receive from him the associated food taboos.

In case of illness which had been cured by the activities of a shaman, the final act of the shaman in curing was to give the patient a charm and a food taboo with it. This implied that the illness would never return. It was only in this sense that the amulet served to ward off a return of illness. The child, too, was protected by the amulet.

If a person found a piece of ivory and desired a charm from it, he was free to carve it himself. If he elected to carve the figure of a sea animal, he was advised to refrain from eating food from the land for a season. The reverse was likewise true. It was always advisable to consult the shaman in such cases, however.

When a charm was given, food taboos were likewise imposed. The shaman or old person who gave the charm stated what foods the person receiving it should thereafter avoid. The following is an example: A man brought his son to a shaman to obtain a personal charm for him. The shaman gave the boy an amulet carved as a wolf's head in ivory. The shaman said that the boy should thereafter avoid eating the flesh of the female walrus and the shortribs of the female ugruk. It was not prohibited for the boy to eat the flesh of the male of these animals. It may be noted that here is again a reflection of the land-sea dichotomy: wolf power is adversely affected by certain things derived from the sea. Such special taboos applied throughout life.

In order to obtain charms, most people went to an older relative. The shaman could be approached for this but it more frequently occurred that the shaman gave a charm after he had effected a cure. The shaman regularly made charms for his own children, the only service he could perform for them. One shaman at Barrow in the past regularly supplied children with charms. When a charm was requested of him, he would ask the parent for a trade bead. When this rather expensive item was given, the shaman swallowed it, sang and drummed, and in a moment coughed the bead up on the drum. There was always a cord strung through the perforation in the bead and it could then be hung on the child's clothing. The trick of swallowing an unstrung bead and then coughing it up as strung was of course completely mystifying and lent great efficacy to the charm. The shaman demanded a bead for his own services. Beads were not usually charms but might be. In another case, a shaman cured a man by using the bead which was the patient's personal charm. He removed it from the patient's neck, caused him to swallow it, and then recovered it from the man's feces. The shaman cleaned it and returned it to its place on the patient's neck. As soon as the bead was replaced, the man became well at once. The man was advised to refrain from eating the marrow from the female caribou.

It was well not to ask a shaman for a charm unless one were "sure of him." Out of spite, he might give the wrong instructions. Moreover, he might demand a high price for his services and any failure to meet his demands could result in illness. An older relative was considered more trustworthy.

When a charm and the associated food taboo were given, a song might also be included. Amulets, like songs, had compulsive power. Some were for success in hunting, in racing or wrestling, to make wealth come to one, and the like. The amulet, if it had an associated song, was doubly efficacious. There were those who by adulthood had not collected any amulets. They might, however, get songs without the charm. The effect was regarded as the same; food taboos were imposed with the song as well.

If a man wished to be a good runner, he might ask the family of a successful runner who had recently died for the dead man's charms. He might also take some of the hair of the dead man and wear this in a bag under his clothes. A charm might also be made by the would-be whaler from the hair of the corpse of a successful whaler. This was the only instance of mutilation of corpses recorded. The wrestler wore bear teeth as charms, using the canines of the brown bear and the polar bear on each side. This presumably lent strength to his arms. There were various hunting charms, the amulet itself, with the song, having an affinity for the game which was being hunted and compelling them to come and be caught.

The question arises as to violations in respect to food taboos associated with charms. When a person became so ill as to summon the shaman, one of the first questions raised by the practitioner was with respect to the foods eaten by the sick person. And from this the shaman often made his diagnosis and cure. But because of the economic uncertainties which might arise, it was not inconceivable that an individual, having only the tabooed food at hand, and no other, might be forced to eat it to keep alive. An out was permitted. The individual could do several things to ward off harmful effects: (1) He could rub the forbidden food over his body. (2) He could hang the tabooed meat outside for a time and allow it to drain. (3) A mitten could be stuffed into the collar of one's parka, hand side outward, and the food eaten with no ill effects. In the latter case, it was felt that the harmful essence of the food would go into the mitten. When the person had finished, he took the mitten and shook it out outside of the house so as to cast away the harmful essence.

One informant related that he, as a boy, had been given a wolf charm by an old woman. He was forbidden to eat whale meat. But since whale meat is so prized a food, and since it forms so vital a staple, the informant never followed the taboo. He simply put a mitten in his parka collar and never became ill.

There was no secret to a food taboo in connection with a charm. Moreover, since it was regarded as very bad manners to refuse food, a person might maliciously be offered his tabooed food to eat. This was a dangerous practice, however, particularly so for the evil man who gave another food which he knew to be prohibited to him. The guest could take the food, eat it, and then go to a shaman. The latter could transfer the illness to the malicious giver. A case was reported where one woman had given another food which she knew to be tabooed to her. A shaman sang over the woman who had eaten the tabooed food and the giver of the food became ill and died. A person who became ill because he had eaten food prohibited to him without observing the precautions noted above was called agila^{ly}uktuak. When a food taboo had been carefully observed for a time, the person on whom it was imposed might try a bit of the forbidden food. While technically the taboo lasted for a lifetime, in practice it was of short duration and the person built up an "immunity" after a time.

Charms were inherited. Any relative could inherit, whether male or female. If for any reason a charm was not wanted, since its efficacy was doubted or the taboos associated with it were too onerous, it was buried under the house and abandoned. If no one wanted a particular charm from a dead man, it was left with the corpse.

But in addition to the personal amulets which have been described, there were those associated with the household and the whaling umiak. The latter are reserved for description under whaling; the household charms, however, merit fuller attention here. The most important household amulet was the aaroraq, that placed over the subterranean entrance of the house. This was generally a round stone, described as about the size of a man's fist, and perforated. Not every house had one and no details could be obtained as to how a house acquired one. The purpose of the charm was to work to the good of the house and all in it. It was particularly related to curing, first as a means of keeping illness from the house and second, as a nonshamanistic curing agent. When a member of the household became ill, the aaroraq was taken down from its place above the door descending into the hall and was rubbed over the affected parts of the sick person. Actually, this charm gave rise to a small curing ceremonial in which the activities associated with curing were communal rather than the individualistic ones performed by the shaman. A group of relatives and neighbors assembled outside the house and a fire was built for them there by the members of the household in which the sickness appeared. The group standing outside, known as taaktaktuat, began to sing. The songs were not of the social type, nor were there any words in them. Meaningless syllables were uttered by a leader and the group followed. Inside the house, the patient was rubbed with the aaroraq and the members of the household likewise sang. If the patient improved, it was felt that the force of sickness had been driven away and the group was dismissed. If he failed to improve, there was no recourse but to the shaman. Should illness occur in the house in summer, a model of a boat was made, touched to the patient and to the aaroraq, and set adrift in the sea. It bore the illness away with it. It is worth mentioning that the North Alaskan Eskimo never caught colds, so it is related, until the foreign whalers came. When they did, colds were a serious illness. Little boats were then made to carry the colds back to the intruders who brought them.

The aaroraq was the property of the house, not of anyone in the house, and as such could not be removed. If the house was rebuilt, the same site was used. This was not true of the houses which did not own such an amulet. Charms were also placed next to the lamps in the house. These were of stone, bone, ivory, and other materials. Because the lamp had mystic properties, these charms served to keep it in order and "happy" in the household. To a degree, the lamp was personified and was in effect a tutelary guardian of the house. Dolls, so-called, or human figures made of wood and bone, were usually hung on the walls near the lamps. Another lamp charm was the uppermost vertebra of a seal. The concept was that the lamp essence accompanied the seal hunters and enabled them to make a successful catch. This was called nikpaakturak and served as well to notify the group in the house of the hunter's successs. When a man had taken a seal, the bit of bone fell down from the wall. The doll by the lamp, like other general charms, was aanaroak. It is of interest that when wheaten bread was introduced from abroad, it was not popular as food but was instead used as a household charm. Pieces of bread were hung up on the roof beams as a means of protecting the house and those in it. One informant recalls the humor of this situation. When a man eagerly sought a piece of bread as a household charm, it was sometimes said to him, "Why don't you eat it instead of hanging it up—it will do more good that way?"

NAMES

Like songs and amulets, names had a marked supernatural significance to the aboriginal culture. Basically, there was no elaborated belief in life after death. There were ghosts and souls, to be sure, and there were several ways of dealing with them. But the ghost was an ephemeral thing; it had no continued reality. Because the name was regarded as so vital a part of the individual, and is still so regarded, it is impossible to describe the complex of names and naming except in terms of the supernatural. Names tended to be inherited, passing directly from parent to child, from relative to relative, or even from friend to friend. A general, although vague, concept of reincarnation existed. In short, there was the idea, which to some extent continues to exist, that the dead are absorbed into the living. The tangible link between the living and the dead lay with the name. To placate the dead, it became essential that the proper series of names be given to a child.

The name (aatuq; pl. aatkic) was given to the individual shortly after birth. It is not known whether the mother of the child actually gave the child a name after delivery in the parturition hut. It is, however, conceivable that she waited through the 4- or 5-day period of seclusion and that the child was formally named only when mother and child returned to the household. Any relative could name the child; several names, in fact, were usually given. In any case, the child was given the name of either a recently deceased relative or close associate of the family.

When a person died, it was conceived that the soul or essence wandered about. The absence of an elaborated view of life after death permits neither a concise definition of the soul nor more than a vague concept of where the soul went and how it acted in the world of the dead. It was generally stated that the essence of the dead "hangs around" and in a vague and rather weak way might intrude in the affairs of the living to the extent that it sought to call attention to itself. When an unexplained noise was heard either in the house or outside of it, when an object fell without apparent cause, when a voice was heard calling out on the tundra, such were regarded as manifestations of the dead. At any of these occurrences, water, and later, tobacco and water, were thrown out the front door of the house for the wandering spirit. Similarly, when one's ears buzzed or hummed, it was the spirit of a dead person attempting to communicate. These spirits were not especially feared, but if ignored they might bring illness. The principal way to placate them was to give their name to a newborn child. When this was done, they were absorbed into the child and so reappeared in the living.

There was no limit to the number of names which a child might get. Each one, moreover, represented a deceased person. Nor did the question ever arise as to the presence of several souls in a single individual. The point appears to have been that the essence of the dead person was somehow dissolved in the newborn child. While the child might take on some of the character, some of the likes and dislikes, of the person or persons whose names he bore, no further speculation arose, either as to conflicts between the souls now ostensibly resident in the child, or as to the nature of the process of reincarnation. Even though a child had several names, and had thus absorbed several dead people, he still had his own soul which in turn related to the name he used throughout life. The essence or soul of a deceased person was a single entity, not a conceptually composite one. Only in a very vague way did the characteristics of a dead person whose name the child bore reappear. Thus, if a family had lost a member, and a child, not a member of the group, received the name of the deceased, the family customarily gave the child the things of which the dead person had been fond. Thereafter, they "loved that child," since in him their own lost kin continued to live.

Every attempt was made to take proper care in naming a child. The point was that the child was spiritually weak and subject to harm by a soul "trying to get in." Such a soul might cause the child to cry constantly. If this happened, and the child cried frequently, it was decided that some soul was trying to get in. As nearly as can be ascertained, there was no attempt made to divine whose soul it was that caused the difficulty. The child was simply given the name of a recently deceased person and if it then cried less frequently, it was regarded as evidence that the soul had entered the child when the name was bestowed. An informant reported that when his first child was born, he took his wife and baby and went inland to hunt caribou. They traveled by umiak and as they traveled, the baby cried all the time. There seemed no way of making the child stop. They then remembered that an old woman had died recently. They called the child by the old woman's name and it stopped crying at once. Later, when they returned to the community, they told the woman's son. He was very pleased and, not being a relative of the family, gave frequent presents to the child who bore his mother's name.

The dead might appear in a dream to the parents of a child, asking that their name be given. Or it was often sufficient that one dream about a dead person. If so, it was a sign that the name of the dead should be given to someone living. This practice is far from gone at Barrow and in adjacent communities. The writer's interpreter related that for three nights running she had dreamed of a man who had drowned. The man's name, in English, was Dan. She had recently borne a child whom she had named Barrow. He had cried a good deal in the hospital just after birth and she decided to follow her dream and add the name Dan to the others he had received.

Her child stopped crying at once when he received the new name. The woman now feels that she may have acted too soon. Her son, Barrow Dan, is unable to sing a note or carry a tune. Had she let him cry a bit more, she feels, he might have developed a singing voice. (A child which cried became a good singer.) However, when she named the child after the deceased, she no longer dreamed of the dead man. This incident further indicates that the name did not have to be an Eskimo one. Another informant, a man, received a woman's name along with his other names. Later, when he thought about his names, he humorously asked his parents, "Where is the tattoo mark on my chin?"

But a soul, in attempting to enter a child, would often cause illness and death to the child. When a family, a man and wife, had a series of either stillborn children or children who died shortly after birth, steps had to be taken. There were several ways of handling this problem. One was to adopt a child and keep it. If it lived, the children born to the couple thereafter would also live. Another method was to take a child immediately after birth, when its previous siblings had all died, and give it out in adoption. Again, children born thereafter would survive. But still another way of handling the situation was to call a shaman to give a name to the newborn child. He found a proper name and then children which might thereafter be born would also live. There was a man at Barrow named piŋuusuruk. He was not a shaman but was skilled in finding proper names for children. In one case, he was called in by a family whose children had not survived and who now had an infant girl. He called the child nawnareen^{y}a, a dog's name, and she survived. There are several individuals living at present who bear dogs' names. The name was given under the circumstances described. It was stated that in this case it was not the name which was important, but rather the power of the man, or shaman, who gave the name. Remembering that dogs had no souls, however, it is possible to note how such a name might serve to end a series of names which had proved unfortunate.

Within the last century, when a child, for whatever reason, was given the name of a dead person, a bit of tobacco was placed on the child's neck. This was to draw the soul of the dead to the child and permit it to enter easily. In the remote past, other offerings were made. What they were is no longer remembered.

Although a person might thus have a good many names, he was generally called by the first one which had been given. This name accompanied the individual throughout life. Unless it proved unfortunate for some reason, it was not changed. There was no concept of changing one's name either at puberty or marriage. If a man was ill, he might, when recovered, call himself by one of his other names. This, however, was his own choice. The men in the Messenger Feast who changed their names did so for only a short time. Often, however, they used one of their other names or a nickname. Nicknames were fairly common in the area but were apparently not in such common use as among Eskimo groups elsewhere. If a person were given a nickname, he might be called it by his relatives and friends, and by his joking partners. It was regarded as bad manners for any other person, not intimately connected with the individual, to use his nickname. As stated, a man went by one name. His other names were not generally known but there was no concept of keeping them secret. Children, in fact, would play a game in which the idea was to see who had the most names.

When the name of a child was changed because it cried too much, it was generally called by the new name. If a person disliked his name, he was free to call himself by one of the other names given him. While there was a general sense of names belonging to men as against those which were women's names, no linguistic device was used to indicate a difference. Nor was there any feeling against calling a boy by a woman's name or the reverse. One such instance has been noted above. In another, a man at Barrow named his son by his own mother's name. This was accepted practice and occasioned no comment.

An example of names which a member of the group might have is the following:

ipaaluq iriceelega awktellik nan^{y}eeluk

The third and fourth names might have originally been nicknames. awktellik refers to a strawberry birthmark; nan^{y}eeluk means "jumps on one leg." These characterizations did not apply to the individual so named and appear to have been names which passed on to him. Many names are not meaningful, as, for example, the first two. The man in question was always known as ipaaluq. Four names were the usual number for each individual. It is clear, however, that there was no insistence on this. Some have only 2, others as many as 6 or 7. It is the name by which the person is known that is of primary importance. And, indeed, one does not refer to people except by name. Unless the names of the principals in a tale are known, the tale itself is valueless. Informants were always careful to supply the name of the person under discussion.

Families themselves were not named, although the group might sometimes be referred to by the name of the leader or wealthy member of the group. Children were told the names of their grandparents as a means of identifying relationships. In reference, a child was designated not infrequently by the kinship term applied to the deceased whose name he bore. Thus, if a stranger inquired in a household, saying, "Whose child is that?", the mother of the child might answer, "That is my grandfather's father (amaw)." The stranger is able to identify the situation at once, knowing the child to belong to the woman addressed, and having received the child's name, is able at once to determine who is related to whom in the household situation and what the antecedents of the family are. Similarly, a child might be asked, "Who are you?" The child, giving its name, answers, "I am my grandmother," thereby again informing the stranger of his background and family. For a child, the learning of names not only in his own community but throughout the various communities along the Arctic coast, formed an important part of a process of education. Names are thus quite important as a means of identifying kinship relationships and it is clear that there could be no teknonymy. Given names of ancestors have today become surnames.

The connection between the name and the charm, or the name and the song, has already been mentioned. When an older person gave a charm, and with it the necessary food restrictions, a name might also be given. This again was the name of a dead person. In this case, the new name was not necessarily a replacement for the name of common use, nor in receiving a charm was the name always changed or a new one given. If the children in a family had died, the help of an old person might be sought. For a survivor, the old person made a charm and often gave a song. A new name was regarded as incidental to the song and the charm in this case.

GHOSTS AND SOULS

The soul, or essence, of the deceased was called ilitkosiq. A ghost was ilitkosixluk or aliuqtuq. In general, the soul departs when the deceased's name is conferred on a child. While there appears to have been no concept of multiple souls, ghosts and related phenomena were occasionally seen. In the main, these seem not to have been regarded as human. Many of the concepts allied with the ghosts are perhaps recent. There is a fairly extensive lore with respect to ghosts, but in general there is a view that when one has an unusual psychic experience, it may derive from the tunarak, the helping spirits which call the shaman and are his familiars. Thus, the event is told of a young woman, who, during the summer, was camped down the coast while the men in her family were ugruk hunting. She was about to go to sleep in a tent when she heard her name called by a voice which she recognized to be that of a friend at Barrow. She was terrified and became ill. She related to a shaman what had happened and was cured. This was not held to be the voice of the friend, but rather of some spirit which had imitated the friend's voice. And this is the usual behavior associated with the experience of an unusual nature—the person who underwent the experience inevitably became ill. If he failed to tell what he had seen or heard, he would die. The experience had to be confessed to the shaman, who could then effect a cure.

In another instance, so it was related, there was, recently, a whaling crew camped out on the ice in the spring. The crew had gone to the boat leaving one man behind to attend to some chores. He was about to go to sleep in a tent on the ice when the bottom of the tent bellied as if from wind—but it was not windy. The man heard a voice calling his name. He saw nothing but the voice seemed next to his ear. He told no one what had happened. Later, he became weak and ill and was dying. At the last he related his experience but then it was too late to save him. In short, the experience must be related. People who received calls of this kind might become shamans if they listened to the voices and followed them. If they resisted, they had to tell a shaman to withdraw the effect of the call of the spirit. Presumably, the instance here was one such.

Many other cases of this kind might be listed. In one, a boy was out tending to the reindeer when the Barrow community had a herd. He saw a head coming toward him. It seemed a human head with a wolf ruff around it. It came close to him and disappeared. He was horribly frightened and ran back to town telling of what he had seen. Another such case of a disembodied head being seen supposedly occurred at the Pass. Noises were heard and a man went out to investigate when all the people in the community were accounted for. He suddenly saw rise up before him a great, round, shining face. It was much larger than a human head but the features were human. The phantom could not be explained. Whenever such things are seen, they are the ominous harbingers of sickness and death.

Ghosts of the dead specifically warned of their presence by buzzing in a person's ear. Noises and calls also marked their presence. There were two principal ways of placating a ghost. This was done by throwing cold water against the door of a house and by hanging a tobacco leaf upon it. A second way involved the process of naming for the deceased as has been described. The dead might also appear in dreams and again could be laid by attaching the name of the dead to a child.

Some reflection of the fear of the dead appears in the ways in which a corpse was disposed of. A dead body was removed through the skylight of the house and brought out to the tundra where it was simply left. As the group moved out to dispose of a body, a man walked behind, brandishing a knife. This was to prevent an early return of the soul. Similarly, those in the house were under restrictions for 4 days, if the deceased were a woman, 5, if a man. During the mourning period, called naaciruat, no one in the house could sew lest the spirit be drawn back into the house. Similarly, no noise could be made, lest the ghost find its way back more easily. The removal of a corpse through the skylight suggests a similar practice on each side of the Pacific. The practice was followed, it was said, because the doorway and hall were hard to negotiate. However, the skylight was immediately covered again with the pane of gut when the corpse was taken out.

DREAMS AND PORTENTS

The dream was not too significant a part of the supernatural as conceived by the North Alaskan Eskimo. When a person had a dream, it was a sign that his soul was wandering about. If the dream was a good one, it should be told to others. When a member of a whaling crew had a good dream, he told the owner of the boat about it before embarking. If his dream was bad, he told no one and might even remain away from the whaling. Dreams could be a cause of illness, since the wandering soul was often entrapped and kept from returning to the body. In this case, the shaman might entice the soul back and so effect a cure.

Dreams had meaning for the future. If a person dreamed of the moon, it meant that someone would die. Dreams of noises were also regarded as harbingers of death. People are careful not to tell of a bad dream—a fact which is still true—since the evil portended by the dream may then become realized. If a person dreamed a good dream of another person, he went at once to tell him of it. When a tragedy occurs, a drowning, an airplane accident, or the like, there usually appears someone to say that he had dreamed about it beforehand.

When a person's toe hurts, or the eye twitches, it is a sign of success in hunting. A hurting toe can also mean that strangers are coming to visit.

Such concepts do not appear to have been elaborated. Even at present, however, there is reluctance to tell one's dreams unless they portend something especially good.

MASKS

As a final note to this section on the supernatural, the mention of masks should be made. These were never too important in the North Alaskan Eskimo areas, nor did they reach the same degree of elaboration as in the southern areas. The masks which were used were principally dance masks. There may have been a concept of supernatural impersonation but certainly it is not well developed. A suggestion of this appears in the dances associated with the whaling feasts, where masked men visited the houses and frightened children, asking for something from the householder, usually a bit of moss for a lamp wick. The masks worn were called axrellik, they and the dancers together were axrelliktuat, and the dancers in the ceremonial were specifically known as axraligiic. The mask was a simple wooden face mask with slits for eyes and mouth. Murdoch (1892, pp. 365–370) describes some of this type (his figs. 366, 368, 369).

An older type of mask, at least according to modern informants, was the sakimmak. It was this one which had wings, an attached gorget, and to which various figures might be attached. Often the mask had boards protruding from it suggestive of the whale's flippers. On these were painted whales, walrus, and other sea mammals. Such seem to have been worn by the umealiq in the procession of axraligiic.

Whether there was impersonation here, or whether, as has been suggested under the treatment of the whaling cult, these masks suggest a secret society situation in the karigi, cannot now be said.

In the Messenger Feast, a fillet or headband made from a loonskin or from the head and feathers of a raven was worn. This was a costume, however, rather than a mask as such (pl. 1, *b*).

The snow goggles of the Eskimo were listed by informants as a mask. They were called akaatuk.

SUMMARY

Because situations were so largely controlled by songs and the magic inherent in them, there was little beyond the institution of the compulsive song that was highly formalized. Songs, charms, and names were three vital features to what might be called the religion of the North Alaskan Eskimo. When other aspects are encountered, they are of considerably less significance. These three features, with shamanism and the necessary ceremonial, associated with a development such as the cult of the whale, were fundamental. These institutionalized aspects of religion had the effect of minimizing other less well formalized features such as an attention to world view and cosmology or to an eschatology. The Eskimo of the Alaskan Arctic slope had capitalized on the song as a means of achieving the desired result. This they had developed more elaborately than had Eskimo groups farther to the south in Alaska. Hence, divination, omens, and similar phenomena were of much less significance. No attempt was made, for example, to predict weather; since the desired weather could be sung for, it was hardly necessary. No attempts were made to predict success in one or another undertaking. Here again, the individual had a degree of control in the songs which either he or another knew. It is true that there were casual connections between various actions and events but one had only to avoid an act to prevent an undesirable event from occurring. Thus one became ill if he saw or heard a spirit and did not tell of it, he got a nosebleed if he picked up a lamp which had fallen while lit, and other forms of illness might come from failing to observe the necessary prohibitions and restrictions. In general, however, these and like developments were overshadowed by the control which the individual could exert over specific situations. If he could not effect the desired result alone, he could rely on an older relative to assist him, as in the case of giving charms, or, as a last recourse, there was the shaman.

A few instances arise where attempts are made to determine the unknown. When a man was lost at sea, for example, the family would wish to know if he were still living. His mukluks, were hung up from the roof beam of the house, the wife or some other person first having smoothed out the linings of the mukluks, whether of caribou skin or baleen shavings. The group then slept. On awaking, they felt in the man's boots. If the lining were at all disturbed, that is, pushed back or no longer smooth, it was a sign that the missing man was still alive. This was repeated until the mukluks showed no sign of change. Then it was known that the hunter was dead and not moving about any more. But if a family were really concerned, the shaman would be asked to go out to look for him. This he did either in a trancelike state, his own spirit leaving his body, or he obtained the answer from his familiars.

Another aspect of supernatural concepts which should be given further attention is that relating to other means of establishing controls over situations. Such power was best developed in the shaman, who, apart from the compulsive songs and the familiars which he had, had developed other power. Shamans could reach out and take what they wished, according to several accounts. But again, this power was not restricted to the shaman. Here arises the complex body of folklore relating to the worms, without mention of which no account of North Alaskan supernaturalism would be complete. Worms were a source of fear and horror. Some of this attitude was carried over to animal parasites, but in general, it was the earthworm which occasioned such feelings. It was told that anyone could develop great power from the worms if he were willing to undergo a horrible experience. If a man, traveling alone on the tundra, came to a hummock and turned over the earth, finding the depression alive with worms, he could use them to his advantage. This he did by baring his arm and inserting it among the worms. After a moment, he took it out again and would find that the flesh had been eaten off. He then replaced his arm into the worms and when he removed it a second time, the flesh would be returned. After this experience, he could reach out with his arm and take whatever he wished from any distance. He could make game come to him, he could reach out to the houses of other people and take their possessions, and he could even cause illness and death by reaching up from under the ground and stealing the hearts of people. Many shamans were reputed to have undergone this experience. When it was related, the informant became extremely uncomfortable and remarked, "This scares me when I think about it." The earthworms were called kupillerok. The threadworms which appeared in fish (iŋilik) were also to be feared. The part of the fish into which they had bored had to be thrown away. These worms, it is said, if swallowed, will eat a person from within.

Sufficient has perhaps been given as to suggest the major religious preoccupations of the Eskimo of the area in question. The above, so far as can be ascertained, reflects the aboriginal religious emphasis. There is one aspect of religious attitude and belief, however, which requires treatment and which is somewhat difficult to place. It is that of the "Strangers in the Sky," the wiivaksat, "those who come around again." To anyone familiar with the history of the Indian of the United States, much of what is described for these visitations suggests a messianic cult. Informants are agreed that the development of this notion reached a high point just before the advent of the whalers from abroad. If this is true, the concept may have arisen because of the diffusion of possibly Christian ideas from some other area, possibly from some point of Russian or other European contact. Much of what is told relating to the belief does not coincide with aboriginal religious concept. Undoubtedly, further attention should be given to the concept.

THE WIIVAKSAT—STRANGERS IN THE SKY

The term wiivaksat, wiivaksaat, means literally, "those who go around and come back to the place where they started." Another term used to designate them was aŋin^{y}eric, "strangers." The basic idea was that these were the dead who would return "some day." When they came back, they would bring everything needed for a comfortable life; one would have only to ask them and anything one wanted would be given. The idea was also expressed that the dead circled around the world and then returned to the land of the living.

There is no agreement as to the meaning of the concept. Some say that the way the dead behave was ordained by Raven. After death, a soul flies about the world and then returns, entering the body of a living person when the latter bears the name of the dead. This concept would of course be wholly aboriginal. Engrafted onto it, however, appears the idea of a time, a kind of millennium, when the dead would return, bringing with them the things that men needed. It is this aspect which is clearly not aboriginal and which suggests an attitude of revivalism and messianic cult. One associated feature, mentioned by several informants, was that the dead would come back as they had been in life, not in the form of souls to enter a living body when a name was conferred. "Your father will come back; he will not be old, but will be young again" was a statement made to a girl of 15, who, as a great grandmother, still recalls it today and still awaits the event.

Another informant, age 68, recalls that his grandfather's father mentioned the "strangers." He said that when he died he would come back again, not old, but as a young man, and he would live over again. He said that he would be happy when he did so because he had never killed a man.

Another informant reports that when she was a child, the family traveled inland. They met some people from kuvuk, the kuvuŋmiut, who told them that "strangers are coming—we can follow them and we won't have to bring anything; they will have everything for us."

Still another tells of her mother and her family who were traveling down from nuwuk to Barrow. For some reason, she lagged behind and pitched a tent by herself and stayed there briefly to "look at some work." Once she was coming back to the tent and heard voices overhead, speaking in a strange language. She was frightened and fell down, hiding between the ridges of drifting snow. After a moment the voices were gone and she went back to her tent and heard of them no more. When she told of her experience, it was agreed that she had heard the wiivaksat passing overhead.

Other examples might be given at length. They are essentially alike: "It was said that strangers were coming; they brought everything for us and we had only to ask for it." And it was agreed, too, that this took place "just before the first missionaries came." Many are today agreed that what was meant was the coming of the mission and Christianity.

It appears that there was the development of a cult related to the concept of the "strangers" which must have arisen in the 1870's and 1880's, at the time when contacts with the outside began to be more numerous. Apparently, too, there was the view that the wiivaksat were coming at any time. It is said that children were cautioned to be quiet lest they disturb the "strangers." There is also mention of the fact that the shamans were bitterly opposed to the idea and worked hard against it. As one informant remarked, "It was not the shamans who did this [i. e., introduced the idea of the wiivaksat];

they were always mean and against the Christians and did nothing to help them. They were always against anyone who helped the poor people." Another said, "There were shamans who fought with the people over it."

In general, the "strangers" appear to have been identified as the dead. They would return and bring abundance with them. If it is correctly assumed that the concept was a recent one—and this would be borne out by the disagreements on the part of informants over this point, such disagreements never occurring at other questions—then here is presumably the evidence for the beginning of a messianic cult in the Barrow area. Perhaps the entrance of trade goods, metal, beads, tobacco, and the like prior to the first contact with Europeans brought with it ideas which were somehow made meaningful to the culture. On the other hand, a development such as this may have been a reflection of reaction against the power of the shamanistic class; with such fragmentary evidence, and with the lack of corroborative materials from adjacent areas, it becomes impossible to say.

SHAMANISM

In the aboriginal culture of northern Alaska, the principal religious practitioners were the shamans (aŋatquq, pl. aŋatqut). These were both men and women whose activities related primarily to curing and doctoring. They were also concerned with finding lost articles, foretelling the future (although with little of what might be called divination), reviving or speaking to the dead, and locating missing people, and there is a suggestion of such activities as bringing game, controlling weather, as well as of malevolent work which might be viewed as black magic or murder. Another important function was to provide charms for people desiring them. They also established taboos for the individual, usually relating to the charms which they furnished and to hunting activities, and they determined those who had violated any customary practice such as might impair communal good. There are no significant differences in the pattern as between the nuunamiut and tareumiut.

The shaman in general worked as an individual. There were no shamanistic societies; on the contrary, rivalry between shamans tended to exist. Occasionally the shaman had an assistant or helper. In such cases, the person involved was an apprentice. In a few instances, there is a mention of a husband-wife team, the two working together.

For the average individual, there is no doubt that the shaman provided a tangible link with the supernatural. On the one hand, the shaman stood as a buffer between ordinary men and the realm of spiritual power; the shaman was present to be called in at times of sickness and so fulfilled the role of healer and physician. But on the other hand, the presence of the shaman was productive of fear and anxiety. The practitioner could not only relieve sickness, he could also bring it. One never knew at which point his personage might be offended so as to call forth his vengeance. He could, moreover, bring illness so as to cure and profit from it. Under the circumstances, it is hardly surprising that shamanism should have died out with the advent of the Christian missionaries. Not that Christianity is necesssarily a force in such communities as Barrow, or Point Hope, but it has served to relieve in some measure the anxiety-producing tensions which were caused by the presence of the shaman in the community. These tensions, it would appear, far outweighed the security which a shaman might have afforded. Although the formalized office of the shaman is gone, there are unquestionably still present the attitudes which in the aboriginal culture brought the institution into being. No one today would deny the erstwhile power of the shaman or question the reality of the activities in which he engaged. If such denial does occur, it is usually uneasy.

The various discussions of shamanism among the Eskimo and other Arctic peoples imply a dichotomy between shaman and layman. That this existed there is no question. As the data are considered, however, it is clear that a line of social cleavage is most difficult to draw. In some measure, every Eskimo of the aboriginal Alaskan Arctic slope was a shaman. He or she, at least, had a certain amount of power which could be used to advantage in one or another set of circumstances. The various songs, the charms, and skills which effected magical compulsion in this or that area, such as in bringing game, in controlling weather, even in curing, applied to shamans and nonshamans alike. Such powers as were regarded as inherent in the shaman were therefore in a sense general, open to any who chose to make capital of them. This general power, available to all, was suuŋan, a term which merely denotes power in the general sense, and it could be obtained in various ways. It lay in songs, in charms, and to some extent, in names, all of which had to be acquired in some manner. Such power came to the individual through inheritance or purchase, since songs and charms, specifically, were salable commodities and could pass through family lines by inheritance. Shamans had such power together with everyone else. They might merely have more of it, and there was, moreover, a suggestion of the concept of the guardian spirit in respect to shamans.

One difference, then, between the shaman and nonshaman lay in the degree of power. Informants note frequently, "That man had six songs, but he was not an aŋatquq; he didn't have enough." But more than this, there was the concept of a special class of shamanistic power—the tunarak. This reflected rapport on the part of the shaman with a particular type of spirit, which in the North Alaskan area was conceptually animal, although some natural phenomena, such as fire, might also be a source. As nearly as can be judged, no other supernatural beings, dwarfs, giants, monsters, or the like, were sources of shamanistic power. Such power implied that the shaman either had such an animal as his guardian or familiar, or that from time to time he actually became the animal in question, or both. tunarak, animal power specifically, was the factor which distinguished the shaman from others. Such power appears to be linked with land animals, reflecting in some measure the concept of a land-sea dichotomy. Thus power coming from walrus, seal, or whale, or even polar bear, although this is questionable, was seldom encountered. It was rather that power arose particularly in association with brown bear, wolf, and fox. Bird power, from the ptarmigan, as well as power from lemmings and ground squirrels was also known. However, because wolf and killer whale were equated, the latter being the sea equivalent of the wolf, the wolf shaman might appeal to the killer whale. At that, however, the wolf shaman was offended and his power nullified if salt water, that is, sea water, were used against him. Sea water was regarded as hateful to the wolf. Brown bear and polar bear were not equated and were regarded, in fact, as enemies. There was no specific mention of polar-bear power, but there were were-bears, men who might assume the form of either the polar bear or the brown bear, never both. Caribou and mountain sheep seem not to have been sources for power, nor were dogs, of course, since the latter lack souls. Mention of power emanating from insects, such as bees and mosquitoes, was not encountered, although bees were often used as charms.

It was generally agreed that one "could not always tell" who was a shaman. Unquestionably, there were those who claimed to be shamans but who lacked the necessary intimate rapport with an animal spirit. "Other shamans could always tell" is the general consensus. The charms of the shaman were no different from those of other people. Charms which have been noted for the shaman include the skin and head of a loon; a weasel, stuffed and dried; a box containing insects; or a wide variety of other acceptable aanaroat. It could not be said, therefore, that there was any shamanistic badge. A shaman was to be recognized as such when he "begins his aŋatkoaq," that is, when he demonstrates the necessary qualities of frenzied or hysterical behavior.

Much has been written concerning the hysterical types of behavior associated with shamanism in the cultures of the Arctic. It has been generally agreed that the neurotic, possibly schizoid, individual is given some social acclaim and latitude for his aberrant state. The imperfectly understood phenomenon of the so-called "Arctic hysteria," whatever its environmental or cultural causes, is unquestionably a factor in shamanism and in the molding of the would-be shamanistic practioner. It appears true that the unbalanced, neurotic, hysterical, or even psychotic personality, however these attitudes and states are defined, was the one who seemed destined for the office of shaman. It is to be emphasized, however, that the aboriginal cultures of the North Alaskan area called forth such types of behavior, created circumstances which induced them, and, to a point, rewarded them when they appeared. And, indeed, this seems true of the Arctic cultures in general (see Aberle, 1952).

Rarely did a person consciously seek the position of shaman. If he did, the probability is that such an office was held by father, mother, grandparent, uncle, or some other member of the family group. A shaman might select his own successor, not necessarily a relative, and prevail on him to undertake the period of training and apprenticeship. Not infrequently, this was a man traveling alone and dependent on his own resources. In such cases, the person would often hear his name called. Were he reluctant to assume the power, he might resist, not answering. Were he to answer, however, the power would be his. It is said that a man to whom the power came might begin to act abnormally, seeking to kill himself, behaving in a frenzied and wild manner. When, for example, the shaman pisiktaaraq was beginning to develop his aŋatkoaq, he felt compelled by his tunarak to drive knives into his body. Later, when his power was recognized and his status as a shaman assured, he ceased this activity. As indicated in the examples of shamanistic activity which follow, the borderline between a socially accepted shamanistic vocation and forms of paranoid schizophrenia was thin indeed. A person who, in youth, was given to what might loosely be termed schizoid behavior was often selected by a shaman as his apprentice. He might resist and try to withstand the demands of the shaman. Unless he was a relative of the shaman, he was expected to pay the shaman during his apprenticeship; not, it must be added, for the services of the shaman in instructing him, but rather for the songs which he was supposed to be purchasing. As part of the process of instruction, the various techniques associated with the office were imparted: legerdemain, ventriloquism, and the like. It is said that the shaman would select as his successor only "someone he could teach." Fred Gordon, who visited Barter Island, was selected by a shaman to be his successor. Although he resisted, he reluctantly went out with the shaman to observe his aŋatkoaq. When the two returned, Fred was badly shaken and was thereafter unable to avoid periods of trance and ecstasy. He failed to follow up his training and so was not recognized as a full-fledged shaman. It is agreed that he could have been one had he wished.

Formalized instruction, although important, was not, however, wholly necessary to the office of aŋatquq. A person who had been traveling alone, or who might otherwise feel the compulsion to undertake the shamanistic role, could develop his powers without instruction. Many evidently succeeded in working out their own forms of public magic involving such features as swallowing and regurgitation, or their own skills at a new sleight-of-hand variation. Hence, although formal training might occur along family lines or in the event that a particular shaman picked a likely candidate as his successor, it was not so formalized an institution as to call forth in every case some specialized training. The element of individual psychological compulsion was clearly uppermost. It is also agreed that the power "seems to run in certain families."

The shaman alesuuraq received no formal instruction. He was traveling with his brother-in-law along the Utokok River after caribou. The two men came to a tributary stream with a steep bank on each side. At this time alesuuraq was becoming aŋatquq but was unaware of it. The two men split up, the brother-in-law walking on the top of the bank while alesuuraq took the course along the stream. The brother-in-law failed to meet him at the designated spot and retraced his steps along the stream. At length, he came across alesuuraq who had his hands tied behind him with his belt. So tightly were his hands and arms bound that the brother-in-law had a difficult time releasing them. Afterward, alesuuraq was barely conscious, and it was known that the tunarak had bound his hands. After this, alesuuraq began to take on the ways of the shaman and to practice.

When a man became a shaman, he made his own drum and kept it always. He also made his own sticks for the purpose of head or foot lifting, the method by which the life or death of a sick person could be determined. This was the only form of divination or scrying known to the culture. If a shaman made songs, these remained his own and were an ever-present source of power. At shamanistic seances, there might be those present who knew the songs of the practitioner and would sing them with him as he put on his demonstration of power. In such cases, the singers themselves might lapse into a trancelike state.

But socially, the shamans did not form a group apart. They acted like others and were concerned with the usual tasks of living. The male shaman hunted, joined a whaling crew, not necessarily as a leader, since this depended on success and on physical prowess and skill. The female shamans were likewise engaged as the other women. The shaman had no special badge of office, clothing, or other adornment. It is said that when not engaged in the tasks of his office, he "was just like anybody else." The shaman, therefore, could not be considered a community leader simply by virtue of his calling. If he were wealthy, he had the usual status accorded to the man of wealth. Lantis points out that the Nunivak shamans were often poor, unskilled men, and not infrequently physically or even mentally handicapped (Lantis, 1946, p. 201). From what can be gathered regarding the northern Alaskan, this also seems to be true, the point being that for the otherwise unsuccessful, here lay a means of attaining prestige.

Shamans had no special sacerdotal functions in relation to either the Whale or Caribou Festival or the Messenger Feast, the principal ceremonial affairs celebrated by the Eskimo of the Alaskan Arctic slope. If they participated, it was as other men. But they did have a definite place in the society in relation to the tasks outlined above. And in the winter months they came into their own. It was at this time, through December and January, during the sunless period, that the shamans were most active. It was now that they held their seances, assembling people in the house to show off their powers. Involved in the seances were such features as speaking with a corpse, shaking the house or tent, bringing in the voices of the familiar spirits, being released from bonds by the spirit helper, flying through the air, and the like. At this time, the shaman would have himself bound. The group, seated in the darkened house, would hear him fly up through the skylight of the house, hear his voice on the roof, and after a period of silence, hear him return. He often claimed to have visited some other village, and told of events there, what people were doing, and the like. The lights would then be turned on and the shaman would be present, bound as before. In the winter months, too, were the shamanistic contests, when shamans would unleash their power against each other. There is no doubt that to see a shaman, seated in a semidarkened house, wrestle with hostile powers sent by a rival was a dramatic and terrifying experience. And clearly, it was by means of such seances that the shamans were able to keep attention focused on themselves. It was asserted that in this period two shamans might meet, being outwardly friendly, while all the while their tunarat were engaged in a bitter struggle. It may be noted that one of the terms for November, or, at least, for one of the last moons, was kiyeevilwik—"the time when the shamans get busy."

While there was no special clothing associated with the shaman, it is true that much of his activity centered in the tambourine and the songs he knew (pl. 7, *b*). Any activity on his part was prefaced by a series of songs and the beating of the drum. After singing for a time, the shaman would lapse into a trancelike state, undergoing a kind of autohypnosis which not infrequently transferred itself to the attending audience. As has been mentioned, it was the songs more than any other feature which characterized the shaman. The various feats of legerdemain might be performed by anyone. Various people, indeed, knew "tricks" which they could use from time to time. One man, for example, is described as having a blue bead which he could roll across the floor and it would then return to him. Another man knew a trick by which, in drumming, he held his drum out and tobacco leaves appeared on it. The drum of course was not the exclusive property of the shaman; it was used in social dances and for social singing as well. The shaman's drum was said to be somewhat larger than others. Anyone skilled in drumming was free to practice. Male shamans, it is true, did use the drum, but it appears that the female group did not. The latter, too, were less skilled in legerdemain and ventriloquism. If the shamans were a husband-wife team, the woman might then handle the drum. The feeling appears to have been strong, however, that such a woman should have passed the climacteric. The trance state did apply to both sexes, and women, as well as men, learned to induce it with singing.

In a few instances, male shamans are described as wearing a headband of bleached sealskin from which a little bag containing a special charm was suspended. This type of headband, with charms attached, however, appeared among other people as well. There was no sense either of shamanistic initiation, such as the death and resurrection theme which appears elsewhere, or the idea, encountered in Siberia, that the shaman wears old clothes.

In addition to the seances described above, the shaman might be called on at any time to effect a cure. When a family member was ill (the various recognized types of illness being discussed below), the shaman of the patient's choice, or the "family doctor" was summoned. The feeling appears to have been strong that a shaman in the in-group, that is, either in the household itself or in the community, was safe and would exert himself in behalf of the sick man. There was, however, a vague tendency for shamans to "specialize" in treating certain kinds of sickness. Thus, one shaman is decribed as being especially good in treating wounds. It is true that the idea of specialization seems not to have occurred to the native peoples in respect to attitudes toward shamans; it was rather that a shaman of known powers was preferred to one whose tunarak was questionable.

Illness arose from two primary causes. The first, and most important, was soul loss. The causes for this were: (1) the soul was taken from the body by a malevolent shaman; (2) the soul wandered in dreams and failed to return; (3) the soul wandered because of the breaking of a restriction. The soul, ilitkosiq, was often identified with the heart, and the attitude existed that the shaman could pull the heart away. Young people were always warned never to sleep on the stomach, as evil shamans went abroad underground and reached up and removed the heart, causing sickness. Similarly, young people were advised against yawning loudly and gaping. If they did so, they were told, shamans and the dread spiritual forces clustered around them would say, "He's tired of living; let us take his soul." A shaman could be paid to bring harm to another by stealing his heart or soul.

Also, the soul wandered in dreams. A dream, therefore, could be the cause of illness, if in the dream world some event occurred which prevented its returning to the owner. Hence, if a person fell ill following some vivid dream of this kind, he related it to the shaman whom he employed to cure him. The shaman then sought to entice the soul back to the patient. But a more significant cause of disease than the latter was the infringement on or violation of a prohibition. For the most part, these were personal prohibitions imposed by a shaman. When a person was given a charm, either inheriting it or purchasing it, he took on with it certain restrictions. These were, for the most part, food taboos and were usually fairly limited. Some examples are: "The aŋatquq said not to eat any of the meat from the saddle of the female walrus." "He said not to eat any of the marrow from the hind legs of caribou." But there were more serious violations also. In the aboriginal culture, when a person ate foods which were not spiritually compatible as, for example, caribou and wolf meat, or whale and any meat from a land animal, his soul would be offended and wander off.

The second basic cause of disease related directly to shamanistic malevolence. This was the familiar phenomen of intrusion, the belief that some object, usually invisible to all but the shaman, was driven into the patient's body by a hostile shaman. Another shaman had then to be employed to extract the cause of illness for all to see. Among the North Alaskan Eskimo, this was a far less frequent cause of sickness than the concept of soul loss.

When a man was ill, he usually waited for a time before summoning a shaman, trying any ways of curing or remedies that were at hand. When the case proved stubborn, the patient often being in extremis, the shaman was summoned. He either worked in the house of the patient, or, if it appeared that a larger audience could be commanded, in the karigi. If he did his work in the house, he most often had the patient laid out on the floor boards. He then walked about the patient, examining him from all angles. Then he might touch the patient about the spot where the "pain" lay. He licked his hands, then rubbed them over the painful area. Some shamans blew on the affected part, occasionally sucking at it tentatively at first if the case was diagnosed as one of intrusion. With duck wings, the shaman might sweep the affected area. When these preparations were completed, the shaman began to sing.

He stood over the kataq, the round door which was located in the floor of the house, straddling it, his feet either firmly planted or kneeling. Then he began to talk with his familiar. He stood with his back to the room, facing the door in the floor. The people assembled in the house could hear the voices of his spirit helpers coming from the hall. Then he lifted his tambourine before his face and began to sing. The tambourine, it is said, was just a bit smaller than the trapdoor itself. The shaman would sing for some time. Sometimes, in the course of his singing, he threw mittens belonging to the patient or to any of his kin, tied to a cord, into the hallway and struggled to make them return. Here, the concept was that the mittens would go out to seize the errant soul. Another method was to place the tambourine on his head after singing and lapse into a trance. At this point, the shaman might announce that his own soul was leaving his body to fetch that of the patient. The trance followed. Such a trancelike state might last indefinitely, often for several days. During this time, no one present dared go into the hallway, and no one entered the house. At the end of the trance, the shaman moaned a little, and as he moved, it was said, "His soul is coming back now." On coming out of his trance, the shaman drummed again and made a formal announcement to the effect that he had succeeded in restoring the soul, or was having a hard time getting it back from whatever being had it.

Undoubtedly, the sight of a shaman at work in the house was fraught with drama and terror. All are agreed that "he was a devil," "he acted like crazy." The shaman stripped to the waist, sang his measured songs, often gradually stepping up the tempo to a frenzied pitch. He perspired freely, his eyeballs turned inward, and his performance was punctuated by the voices of his familiars, with their wolf howls, their bear growls, or other sounds coming in from the hall. His pounding and stamping shook the floor of the house and, working in darkness or semidarkness as he often did, the effect must have been wholly dramatic. Certainly, the contrast between the frenzied singing and moving of the shaman and his sudden lapse into a wholly silent, trancelike state was striking. Even while he was in a trance, however, his spirits continued to speak from the dark hall.

Still another method employed in relation to disease was to lift the head or feet of the patient. After singing, the shaman took a special stick which he placed under the feet of the sick man. These he lifted. As he did so, he might ask his powers if the patient were going to be well, and the "yes" or "no" answer was returned from under the floor. Frequently, too, if the patient's feet were found to be "light," that is, easily lifted, recovery was predicted. Similarly, the shaman lifted the patient's head. To do this, he tied a string about the patient's head and attached it to his stick. He lifted it in the same way. But if the head were "light" it foretold death. Should the portents have indicated the death of the sick man, the shaman then proceeded to develop a series of defenses. He instructed the patient and his family in the procedure they should follow. Sometimes this was an imposition of silence, that no one in the house could talk or make noise for a certain period, usually 4 to 5 days. Or else the shaman banned some food to the members of the household. The concept was that if the food taboo were violated during the period of illness, either the patient or someone close to him, that is, in the household, would die.

If, by his divination, the shaman foresaw the death of the patient and felt he could take no measures to counteract it, he left the house and abandoned the case. He was not paid in this case.

This activity, coupled with weather forecasting, was about as close as the North Alaskan shaman came to an actual divination. There were those, however, not accorded the status of aŋatquq, who could also perform in this manner. One old woman at Point Hope was said to be highly skilled in the lifting of the patient's limbs with the sticks and was even able to cure by this means. She was not, however, a recognized aŋatquq. For such services, she was always paid.

If the shaman decided to perform in the karigi, his activities were carried out in essentially the same way. Here, he placed a curtain before the door of the structure. His spirit voices spoke from behind it.

The successful shaman was paid for his services. There are varying accounts as to how much the shaman was paid, but it seems safe to say that several factors were involved in payment. The fact that no one wished to appear niggardly undoubtedly played a part in the contribution to the shaman. Further, the shaman, knowing in general what a family's resources were, could gage his demand accordingly. Failure to meet it meant, of course, that the disease which had just been banished might now return. In general, the shaman was paid "something which he could use all winter." The man who wished to establish his reputation for generosity and gratitude might, however, give the shaman all his possessions. Some, it is said, gave extra clothing, boats, ammunition, dogs, and the like. An acceptable payment was the offering of a wife or a daughter as a sexual partner. As the various payments to shamans are compared, however, it seems that extremes were avoided. An average payment for a successful cure was an umiak, which, in terms of the aboriginal culture, represented a handsome fee. If a shaman were unsuccessful in his efforts, he was theoretically not paid. However, it is to be recalled that the shaman was a dangerous force in the community and it was fitting to keep his good will. Hence, the shaman, even when the patient died, was offered something—a new parka, a puppy. If the gift were refused, the shaman was regarded as "honest."

This would imply that the shaman, by virtue of his fear-producing role, might be rich. Surprisingly, this was not always the case. As has been indicated, shamans were not always successful in other pursuits, such as hunting, and might be forced to depend solely on their field of specialization for a livelihood. And this in itself was often defeating, since people feared particularly a shaman whose activities were limited to his craft. Unable to compete with others in manifesting skills, such shamans were often regarded as querulous and misanthropic. And, indeed, in this is reflected a degree of social control which the community at large was able to exert over the shaman. The uncooperative and quarrelsome man, even if a shaman, was particularly suspect, was avoided, and ran the risk of being killed by the relative of some person recently deceased, on the ground that his malevolence caused the death.

Malevolence and hostility, as conceived by the community, were by no means confined to those classed as shamans. An interesting series of scapegoat techniques was developed in keeping with the patterns of enmity. Old women, for example, were often suspect and, indeed, made themselves so. An old woman, one who had passed the climacteric, and hence was believed to have developed certain special powers, was often feared. A special term existed for the power which old women were believed to have, ilisiicuk. This was sickness-bringing power, and the pattern developed much in the same way as in the witchcraft cases of European fame. Such an old woman might go about and tell someone, "someone whom she hated," that he would become ill. Illness usually followed. And here, in fact, was an "out" for the shaman. The diagnosis in curing might involve the statement "there is an old woman making this man sick." The shaman then would lapse into a trance and seek to discover the culprit. In this respect there arises another parallel to the witchcraft lore of Western culture in that the accused person might compulsively confess. The shaman sought the guilty person much in the same way as if he were looking for a lost article or a thief. He might make all suspects tread on his drum. The guilty would break the drumhead. Or, having found the culprit in spirit, the shaman would ask for a public confession. When confronted with the words, "You are making so and so sick," it was not unexpected that confession might follow. After the confession, moreover, the family of the sick person might demand an indemnity and might not kill the old person. The same behavior was also attributed to old men, although to a lesser extent. A case is described of an old man at nuwuk who had said to two women, "Your babies will die." The babies did die, and the women's husbands killed the old man without question. All knew of it, it is said, and no attempt at vengeance was made by the old man's relatives. While it seems true that the shaman was a "scapegoat" in that hostile attitudes might be directed toward him, and that he might be regarded as responsible for the ills of a family or community, the shaman himself could discover a target and could redirect community hostility. It was probably a fairly safe practice, especially since the economic unproductiveness of the old people made them fair game.

Actually, the mechanism of confession in Eskimo culture is an interesting one and not restricted to older people. A person could confess and thereby relieve his own anxieties. In the aboriginal culture, the pattern seems to have been fairly well developed. With the advent of the whalers from abroad, however, the mechanisms of confession were lost. The shaman was the principal functionary in the process. He called the people together, either into a house or to a karigi, and might make accusations to force confession. This was done in such cases as that given above, for theft, and also to ward off any undue misfortune in the community. Thus, if meat were scarce, a person might voluntarily confess to the violation of a prohibition. The shaman, by imposing other restrictions, or by enforcing the old ones, could set the matter right. In this respect, the shaman might work for communal good. The matter of confession, especially in relation to food taboos, suggests the patterns described by Boas and others in relation to the Sedna myth (Boas, 1888, pp. 592–593). It was interesting that no ramifications of this myth, or the tale in any form of the goddess of the sea, could be tracked down in the area.

Although a man could employ a shaman to steal the soul of an enemy or to shoot magic spears, arrows, or darts into him, this practice was presumably rare. Informants mention its occurrence but no cases could be recalled where this actually had happened. Much more frequent was the employment of a shaman to inhibit success on the part of another. Between whaling captains, for example, there was considerable rivalry, and living informants recall the anger of one captain against another more successful. Nor, indeed, is this feeling lost today. Hence, one captain could employ a shaman to sing and drum in order to drive whales away from his rival's boat. And the same rivalry could extend to other activities. There were special songs to deflect the aim of the hunter, to drive game of any kind away as well as to make them appear, and to bring general misfortune. But such songs were not, as has been shown, the exclusive property of the shaman. These were songs which might belong to anyone, and were inherited and purchased. Again, the shaman "had more of such songs."

Thus shamanism raises the whole problem of hostility and interpersonal tension in the culture. It would appear that the less skillful, the more misanthropic, the aggressive type of personality found its outlet in shamanism. The songs, too, which reflect aggressive tendencies might serve the nonshaman in this direction. All are agreed that the jealousy, hatred, and ill will resident in the community centered in the person of the shaman, man or woman. There were certain things which the shaman hated and which would inevitably call forth his wrath in the form of sickness and misfortune. The hunter who was always successful was a fair target for the hatred of the shaman. The man who was credited with many whales or walruses or the hunter who got many caribou could attribute any sudden lack of success, or his illness, to shamanistic malevolence. When a hunter out on an expedition became ill, he always blamed the malefic influence of a shaman. In such cases, he always turned home at once and employed his local shaman to remove the influence or to find out who the responsible party might be. If the guilty shaman could be divined, he was often paid to remove his spell and the hunter might return to the field. Similarly, the shaman was said to hate a good runner, and there existed a whole series of songs designed to make a runner lose a race. As late as 1914, when the last Messenger Feast took place, the foot race was won by a man from Barrow. It is recalled that his mother took him aside and warned him not to race again lest he incur the hatred of the shamans. Such was apparently frequent advice. It appears that the attitude is explainable in terms of the modesty and uniformity which the culture demanded. Any form of exceptional behavior was frowned on. Unquestionably, too, the shaman existed as a force to stabilize this attitude and to produce conformity to the norm.

A shaman who had hatred toward an individual might act in several different ways. In order to kill the person, he might cut a small piece from the garment worn by the object of his wrath. If this were discovered, the person merely had to throw the garment away and the spell was broken. If not discovered, the person would sicken and die. There is today, it is said, an old woman at Wainwright who still resorts to this practice against those whom she dislikes. Another method, and this was more restricted to the shaman, was to send out the mittens on a string. They seized the soul of the victim and removed it, and illness followed. A shaman could also produce illness in a house by holding a handful of hair and shaking his fist into the doorway of his enemies' house. Eskimo views toward what the shaman does when he captures a soul are not well defined, "He had it in himself"; "He keeps it." Unquestionably, the most effective method of bringing sickness and misfortune, and the one most easily publicized, was the song. The shaman who sang, in his own house, out on the tundra, or in the karigi made it plain that evil was in store for someone.

There is no doubt that the shaman's life was fraught with danger. He ran the constant risk of being killed by vengeful relatives. It was regarded as good practice to stay away from a shaman who bewitched one. Always this task was relegated to one's kin. But, it is repeatedly said, it was exceedingly difficult to kill a shaman. His supernatural guardians kept him from harm and he himself had miraculous recuperative powers.

But apart from the character of the shaman as a curer and as an ostensibly vengeful and malevolent personality, there were certain well-defined functions of the shaman in the community. When a particularly valued article was lost, for example, the loser would often summon the shaman. He recovered it, either by forcing a confession from a thief or by sending his spirit helpers out to look for it. If the article was recovered, the shaman was again paid for his services, although not, of course, as much as when he had effected a cure. Actually, the same method was employed when a person, hunting or engaged in some other expedition was lost and failed to return. Attempts were made by the shaman to locate him and to draw him back to the community. Among the specific cases of shamanism which follow appears a detailed example of this type of activity on the part of the shaman. Similarly, the shaman might attempt to make the lost article appear, often using the magic mittens to fetch it.

As has been noted, divination was not an essential part of shamanistic function. The shaman might predict good for some individual, as related in one of the following cases, or he might employ practices which suggest divination in predicting the recovery of a sick person. But the emphasis lay not so much in divination as in actual magical control. Thus, game was compelled to come by the force of the songs which were sung, and, similarly, weather was controlled by singing. Again, however, these were not limited to the shaman, since anyone with such songs could sing them as the occasion demanded.

Another function of the shaman was to deal with the recently dead. Particularly powerful shamans were often able to restore the soul even after it had completely departed the body and the spark of life was extinguished. Here is perhaps a reflection of culturally induced mental states, catatonic or otherwise, which presumably might appear in any member of the community. Often, too, after death, the shaman might speak with a corpse. An instance of this kind was witnessed by an informant living today at Barrow. He related that a man had died at nuwuk and that a shaman had been attempting to cure him but failed. When the man died, the shaman said to the corpse, "Who is it that has killed you?" The corpse answered, giving the name of another shaman nearby. Here was the signal for the family of the deceased to take action, but, as the informant put it, "they were afraid."

As has been mentioned, amulets and charms (aanaroak) were obtained from the shaman. This is not entirely true, since occasions did arise where a charm was purchased from another, and such amulets, like songs, might also be inherited. Frequently, a shaman might be summoned to make a charm for a newborn child. He was paid something for this and prescribed at the same time the food prohibitions which accompanied the charm. These would presumably accompany the owner of the charm throughout life.

A question which always arises with respect to the shaman is the extent to which he believed in his own powers. All informants are agreed that there were pretenders, people who wished to be shamans and knew the lore and the sleight of hand but who did not have tunarak. The man with the true helping spirit, the man to whom the power had actually come, whose "life had been taken" by another shaman, was regarded as genuine. He underwent a course of instruction from his guardian and familiar spirit and he was taught songs and tricks by his shaman mentor. It is not known how long the period of instruction lasted, although it is generally agreed that it was a long time and probably varied depending on the circumstances of each shaman. Certainly the impression obtained is that shamans were essentially older people; a young person, while he might be a candidate, was not regarded as sufficiently versed in his craft to practice at length or to compete with others more mature. One learns of young shamans practicing, that is, going out alone on the tundra and singing and presumably finding rapport with their spirit helpers. One such young man was said to go out a great distance and sing. Even then, however, the sound of his voice would reach the community. The shaman had a bag of tricks and was evidently clever in inventing new ones. These involved swallowing and regurgitation, as for example, in the cases which follow, the man who tied knots in strings held in the mouth, tricks with drums, ventriloquism, as presumably speaking to the spirits clustered in the hall of a house, and general legerdemain. In the latter class appeared such problems, to the people at least, as the knife through the body, a trick mastered by most shamans. Vomiting blood, bleeding from nonexistent wounds, and the whole dramatic procedure of the seance belong with the shaman's trade.

But when it is remembered that the shaman's presence was essential to certain community activities and that the shaman was a source of fear and awe, it is hardly difficult to understand the underlying motivations. The shaman could ward off forces of malevolence in the community. He was himself an essentially "unbalanced" personality and in his ecstatic state, the line between fantasy and reality was undoubtedly stretched pretty thin. And since, too, the total experience of both shaman and layman was limited to and lay in the institution of shamanism, it is not difficult to accept the fact that the shaman was probably sincere. There is no doubt that the institution was perpetuated since it did so effectively serve to channelize hostile and aggressive behavior.

Shamanism as an institution in the area was of the ecstatic type. It could hardly be regarded as possessional shamanism, however. In general, the shaman coexisted with his tunarak; he did not become them in the main. It is true that there are tales of shamans becoming bears, and the case is described below of the shaman with the wolf familiar who, in dancing, seemed to have wolf legs. In changing his shape, however, the shaman was still himself. His behavior, while often frenzied and wild, was in the main controlled. If his spirit were wolf, he might, it is true, howl like a wolf, but the familiar would answer him from nearby. There was the tacit recognition that the shaman controlled his spirits. There was no conception of the reverse being true. Conceptually, the tunarak was always with the shaman. He was often seen conversing with his familiar, and there is the suggestion, made by a number of other Eskimo observers, that a shaman's language consisted of archaic forms (Weyer, 1932, p. 435). No examples of this, except in songs, could be secured.

It is interesting that the concept of the shamanistic spirit still survives in Christianity. The various missionaries have employed the term tunarak to designate the devil, Satan, and other evil powers. This attitude has been carried over to today in the Christian church and the rationalization is present that the devil inspired the old shamans. By the same reasoning, the Christian missionary is not a shaman, nor, actually, is he regarded as having spiritual power, at least analogous to that of the shamans of the aboriginal culture.

Another pertinent question with respect to shamans is that of their number. This is somewhat difficult to answer, there being no statements available. One of the factors which make it a problem is the thin line separating those with certain spiritual endowments from those with an actual tunarak. Thus a curer might be summoned who knew curing songs but was not a shaman. And it is again true that each person had some kind of spiritual specialty. That not every household had a shaman is quite clear, and it also is evident that the shaman might live alone, either by choice or because others feared living with the powers which he had. Among the inland Eskimo, shamans were, if anything, more numerous than among the maritime groups. At least, data recorded with respect to inland life point out that a shaman often traveled with a small band. Judging from the living conditions as described for the aboriginal culture on the coast, and allowing for one hundred to one hundred and fifty people in a community, it seems safe to say that one in twenty to twenty-five was a shaman (Weyer, 1932, p. 435 seq.). Hence, at Barrow, in, let us say, 1875–80, there were five to six individuals reputedly active shamans and a somewhat lesser number, perhaps three to four, at piγiniq and nuwuk. It is to be remembered that these were not always present in the community. Like other men, they traveled about with their families, went inland for the hunting and fishing, or camped down the beach away from the settlement in the summer time. Active shamans would come together in the winter ceremonial season, although in an informal way.

When living with others in the community, the shaman always had to guard against threats to his power. Certain elements did curb his effectiveness. The presence of a menstruating woman, for example, was dangerous to him. She was expected to avoid him. The same was true of a woman who had just given birth. They were, in any case, expected to stay in the birth hut or menstrual lodge. It was actually this fact which prevented women from becoming as powerful as men in shamanism. A case (see p. 119) is described where a female shaman attempted to revive her slain husband. She was unsuccessful because she was menstruating and had no power at the time. Children also were a source of annoyance to the shaman; they were not allowed to bother him with talk.

There was some feeling that the power of the successful shaman lived on after his death. The great shaman ipexsin had the power to reach out, extending his arm, and could seize things. He was alleged to have obtained all his food in this way. After his death, his spirit wandered about and continued to pull things. Children, particularly, were dragged about by his spirit.

In conclusion, it may be noted in how far shamanism was a vital, although not highly formalized, institution in the cultures of the North Alaskan Eskimo. As a person the shaman was not popular. Many who were called to this position—those by chance alone out on the tundra who heard the voices of the tunarak and who were approached by a shaman to take over his office—resisted. Good advice was, "Stay away from the shaman; don't get friendly with him, don't hear his songs or he'll take your life and give you the shaman's life."

EXAMPLES OF SHAMANISTIC BEHAVIOR

The foregoing discussion of shamanism would scarcely be complete without some attention to the details of shamanistic behavior. The ecstatic, hysterical, or compulsive acts associated with the office are best illustrated by example. Unquestionably, some of the cases recorded here may be ascribed to the realm of the folktale and have reached modern times only by hearsay. Others are actually witnessed events. In either case, however, the reality of the shamanistic experience is not subject to question. Even if the shaman is no longer an accepted public official, the recollection of his acts is still strong. The following examples of shamanistic activity will serve in some measure to point up the nature of the institution and indicate some of the psychological as well as social factors relating to the pattern.

1. There was one man at Barrow who had talked to the polar bear. He had been sealing out on the ice and was attacked by a bear. The bear bit and clawed

him. After he said, "Stop, you hurt me too much," the bear left him and went away. When the man returned home, he became aŋatquq. He took the claws and teeth of the polar bear. Sometimes he wore the claws, sometimes the teeth. He growled like the polar bear. Everyone knew that his power and his songs came from the bear.

2. At Herschel Island there was a woman who had bear power. Once, when she visited people at Umiat, she changed her shape to a brown bear and walked all the way. It was noticed that when she started out walking, she would stop now and again to rest. Each time she stopped, she looked more like a bear. At last, she turned into a bear altogether. When she came back from Umiat her husband was afraid of her. He loved his two children, a boy and a girl. To protect them from their mother, he killed them with his knife. When the woman came back, she took the knife from her husband and brought her two children to life again.

3. There was an aŋatquq trying to kill another man. The man's family hired another aŋatquq to make him well again. The latter saw the little spear which had been driven into the patient to make him sick and die. He came to the house, began to beat his drum, standing astraddle over the entrance hole at the end of the passage. He acted "like a devil." After a while, he took mittens, tied them together and threw them toward the sick man. Then, of their own accord, they moved away from the patient. The shaman who was causing the illness from far away looked into a tub of water and saw his opponent using the gloves to cure the patient. He tried to stop the mittens from moving, but his power was not sufficiently great. The mittens pulled the little spear out from the man's body and he became well again. As payment, he gave all he had to the shaman who cured him—his clothes, his umiak, his stored food, etc. He kept only the clothes on his back, his house, and his gun and ammunition.

4. There was a young man who was trained to be an aŋatquq by his mother who had great power. He married and settled inland with his wife. Every day he went out alone to practice his songs and his animal noises. They could hear him everywhere.

5. If a man, not necessarily a shaman, had power in hunting, he could use it at any time to his own advantage. A shaman, however, could sing for his food and it would come to him. It might come to him even from another person's ice cellar. Most shamans, however, went hunting like other men. If a man had no success, particularly in inland hunting after caribou, there were special songs which might make the caribou come. People who owned such songs were "like shamans." One man had several such songs. He put his arms in his parka and then put one sleeve ahead and sang through it. This made the caribou come to him and he could shoot them at his leisure. The caribou ran toward the sleeve,

The songs, obtained by a man from his father, are as follows:

I. pisiksigaa manŋa
my bow I carry with me
saagava qaymattna paŋaaligicli
they come to me in a run [caribou]
magoowoo magoowoowoo
[Wolf's growl]
alivakvimnilyu u u u
from strength
sanivakvimnilyu u u
with strength

ya ya ya
ya xa xa xaŋaaγa
yuyuaxaman a
ayexiyya γa γa
ya ya γa xaŋaaγa
[Archaic language and meaningless syllables]

II. Song to hit caribou once they have assembled:
nawkuoxowoo iγinavigu kaareroaxaa
ayyiiyaxaa xaaŋaa
[Repeat above once.]
setkugaaxaaγa ayiiyaxaaxaaγaa
tutkumii tuneaaktuk xaaŋaa tokuaagun
aayiiya yaŋeaxiyaa aaŋaaγaa xaŋaaγa
Free translation: It makes the arrow to strike where the animals will die [caribou]. I don't miss with it.

6. One shaman had a piece of mastodon tusk about as long as a man's forefinger. It was carved and had three strings run through holes in it. The shaman placed it on the tambourine, then picked it up and swallowed it. Then he vomited it up on the tambourine. When he threw it up, the strings were knotted. He swallowed it and threw it up again; the strings were untied. The informant was a small boy at the time this was done. He watched the shaman and saw the ivory come out on the tambourine. The shaman took the drum and held it toward him. The informant picked up the ivory and felt it. Then he gave it back to the shaman, who swallowed it again. Again the informant picked up the ivory. "Does it feel different?" asked the shaman. "No," he said. His mother and father were nearby. His mother pushed him and shoved him out of the house. She was quite worried. She said, "You made a bad mistake when you said it doesn't feel different. Now he'll do something to us." His father said, "Try to do something now that will please that aŋatquq; don't go bothering him." The informant was quite anxious over it for some time, but the shaman didn't do anything.

7. Several people were in a house at Barrow. They were visited by a shaman. He said, "Let me pull each of you. The man I cannot pull will be the first to get sick." The shaman had a rope in front of him. He tied it to each person in turn. Then he stood in the passage below the floor of the house and pulled on the rope. While he pulled, he kept talking to himself and to people who weren't there. The informant was in the house with his mother. She said, "You are next." He was afraid but tied the rope around himself. The shaman began to pull. The boy was pulled to the edge of the flooring in the house. He saw that the shaman had pulled up his trousers and that his legs were bare. The shaman was pulling at the rope with his legs, not with his arms. One man was there who couldn't be pulled. He did get sick some time later.

8. A group was seated in a house and a shaman joined them. He took off his parka and sat naked from the waist up. He said to the people, "I will show you something." He put two lamps on the floor and sat between them. Then he began to sing. After a while he said, "I shall make feathers come from my arm." He put his arms akimbo and as the people watched, from the bare upper arm came a redness. After a few moments black marks appeared on the red mark on the skin. Real feathers grew from the place, about as long as a man's thumb.

9. Children were always told, "Don't go around too much where the aŋatquq is working: don't make fun of him." There was once a boy at Barrow who did make fun of some shamans. They were the shamans who wore a special kind of

labret, which looked like a walrus tusk. This boy made as if he had such labrets and followed a shaman around. The shamans agreed to make the sticks which the boy was using to imitate the shaman's labret cleave to the boy. They worked magic. The boy was unable to open his mouth and died. The shamans took the body and it is said that they buried it near the lagoon at piγiniq. People are looking for it to this day but the body has never been found.

10. The shaman atoktuak, whom Captain Brower called "Shoo-fly," could drive a knife through his body. He used a snow knife and drove it into his chest so that it came out the other side. When he removed the knife, there were no wounds to show where the knife had entered.

11. Three families from Barrow went to Canada. While they were there, they wondered how things were at Barrow. They called a shaman from among the local people and asked him to fly to Barrow to see how things there were getting along. The shaman had them tie him up tight, his arms behind him, his legs to his neck. Then he blew out the lamp. They heard the sound of wings above the house where they were, and all was quiet. After a while, they heard the wings again and the voice of the shaman, saying, "I have returned." They lit the lamp, untying the shaman. He told them that he had flown to Barrow. Then he gave the names of people who lived there, he described the ravine and the houses around it. He drew a map on the floor showing the various houses and gave their names and the names of the people who lived in them. He said that all was well with the people there. This same shaman had power over whales. The whalers always gave him gifts before whaling and were successful always.

12. There was a man who was not a shaman although he knew many songs associated with shamanism. When still a young man, he had lived at Wainwright and was in contact with a powerful shaman there. This aŋatquq said, "I am going to take your life and give you the life of the aŋatquq." He made him sit down by him in the house. The shaman put his head between his knees and went into a trance. The young man felt the same influence working on him. He began to fall forward and felt his eyes turning inward. But he grabbed at his ankles and kept himself from "going out." He did not lapse into a trance. Then the shaman said, "Hold up your hands and open your fingers." He held his open hands before the shaman but only seven fingers would open up—the others remained tight against his palm. The shaman said, "Open up your other fingers." But try though he would, only one more would come up. The shaman said, "Now you are going out for the winter hunting. You will take eight wolves. When you have taken that many, come back to me and I will take away your life and give you the aŋatquq's life." The young man went out after caribou and was gone a long time. When he had taken seven wolves, he became frightened and tried to avoid taking another. He turned back and drove toward the settlement. Suddenly his dogs stopped. Sticking up in the snow, he saw an ear. He dug around it and found the eighth wolf. He realized that the shaman's prophecy was fulfilled. But when he got back, the shaman had died and the young man did not have to become a shaman.

13. Once when the informant and his family were camped for the winter, there came another man and stayed with them for a while. He began to be more and more nervous. Finally, he said, "Get me a flint blade, as wide as your hand and twice as long" (whaling lance head). They gave him one of these. As he took it, he became tense and his eyes rolled. He took off his parka and shirt and sat naked in the house. He began to talk to himself. Suddenly, he plunged the blade into his chest and worked it into his breast bone. Blood spurted out from between his fingers. He pushed the whole blade into his breastbone, working it in gradually until it disappeared. Then he fell forward

as if dead, remaining in a trancelike state for some time. At last he came to his senses, got up and left the house. It was noted that he had a red mark on his chest but that there was no wound. Only his hands were covered with blood. When he left the house in the place where he had been sitting the lance head was found. He was not otherwise injured.

14. Several shamans had the ability to drive a knife through their bodies without injury to themselves. One indeed, was a woman. She lived at the coal mine. Her father was a Russian, her mother Eskimo. Her mother had been a shaman. She knew this art but none other. Hence, she was not regarded as a true aŋatquq.

15. Shamans were often apparently mortally wounded but survived the wounds, frequently without showing more than a mark on the flesh where the wound had been. In a feud between some people at Barrow with others inland, some of the representatives of each party met in the mountains were they had gone to hunt sheep. This was in the area to the south of Umiat. A shaman was also there representing the maritime group. One of the other faction, a little man, shot him in the back. He fell and rolled down the mountain, leaving a trail of blood behind. When the man who had shot him came down, he passed a few tents where people were camped. Near one tent was the man he had shot. He was presently joined by seven of his kinsmen. They stood and looked at the little man for a long time. No one said a word. Then the shaman he had shot said, "Have you tobacco; have you flint and steel?" The little man reached over his pouch and his fire-making equipment. Still, he said nothing. The shaman said, "It is good that you have these things. If you hadn't, it might have been different." And they let the little man go. He said that he could see the bullet hole in the shaman's wrist where the bullet had gone through after passing through his body. On his body, however, there was no mark at all. The informant remarked, "I don't know if they could really do these things, but it seems like they could."

16. There was a shaman living on the beach at Barrow. He had a female dog which he especially liked. His spirit was wolf and he danced in wolf-skin trousers. When he did so, it seemed as if his feet became the feet of the wolf and his wolf-skin pants looked just like the skin and fur of a wolf. He lived all alone in a sod house with a roof entrance. One day a man came by and was attacked by his bitch and severely bitten. He ran away but came back again and shot the shaman's dog. His whole family got sick and died within a year.

17. When the informant relating this instance was about 25, just before he was married, he went up the coast, traveling with his dogs. He was just seeing the country. He came to a place where relatives of his were. They were the nephew of his mother's grandmother and the wife of this man. The informant called them "uncle" and "aunt." He stopped with them and they fed him. Then he decided to go on. "No," they said, "you have to stay here and we will find things out for you." So he stayed another night. That night, the old man, who was a shaman, took his drum and beat it and sang, while the old lady danced. She danced a long time. Then she said, "There is going to be good weather tomorrow." Then she and her husband changed places. She drummed and sang, while the old man danced. After a long while, he said, "You are going to have a good life; good things will happen to you and you will live a long time." Next day, the informant went away. "Now," he says, "what that old couple told me came true; the weather was good and I haven't had a bad time in my life."

18. Mental illness (hysteria) with associations of shamanistic ecstasy: There was a man who went insane not too long ago. He lived near Wainwright up the coast and a little inland from the town. When winter came he and his family

didn't have enough food. They even ate their dogs. Then the man decided to go to Wainwright and get food. He took a tiny sled and dragged it behind him; he was very weak. After a while, he lost his way in the dark. He camped near some old abandoned houses but he was afraid to go into them. He built a snow house and slept there. While he was asleep, he heard his name being called. In his half-sleep, he answered, "Yes." Then he awoke and was alone. He was horribly afraid and went on to Wainwright. He sat all trembling in the informant's house and related what had happened to him. "Something is now touching me, it has its hand on my back," he said. "Something has stuck its finger up my rectum," he cried. He went to the fire and picked up the burning ashes in his hands, pouring them into his parka by the handfulls. He dropped his trousers and rubbed kerosene into his anus. "They still touch me," he yelled. Then he began to scream and wouldn't stop. After a moment of this he said, "There is my father-in-law's face looking down at me; he is looking in, he is looking in." The man's father-in-law had been a great shaman. He turned away from the skylight so that the face couldn't look at him but it appeared on the other side of the room, still looking at him. He screamed "aw, aw" and fell into a faint. After that, he couldn't do anything. He just sat around and wouldn't talk and wouldn't answer when people talked to him. He just sat staring. But every once in a while he said that things were touching him. In the spring, he was sent out from Wainwright to the A. N. S. doctors. They took him to Morningside, and he stayed there 2 years. At last they sent him back on the *North Star*. For a while he was all right. But one day he was carrying a large piece of driftwood and something grabbed it from behind and he couldn't go on. After that, he couldn't work any more and he said that things were touching him. They sent him to the hospital again and he died there.

19. The informant's uncle had not been a shaman originally. When Stefansson came, it was the father, rather than the uncle, who sang him the songs associated with shamanism. Or at least, he gave him a few; he refused to give them all because he was really afraid to sing them. Now the uncle lived at Barter Island and the informant went up there to see him. When he arrived, the uncle's wife was insane. She yelled all the time and had visions. She said that great numbers of caribou were coming and that people were there behind them, driving them. The informant stayed 3 days and during that time, the aunt didn't sleep at all; she just yelled about the caribou she could see. The uncle said, "I'm going to cure that woman." He had the informant get him several weasel skins. He made songs over them and laid them all over his wife. Next year, when the informant returned to Barter Island, the woman was cured. The uncle had meanwhile established his reputation as a shaman and people were coming to him to be cured. The uncle had acquired his power from the weasel.

20. An informant related the case experienced by her husband. Before his marriage, he had visited Canada and had camped with some Eskimo living there. Among them was a shaman. He was old and wanted to pass his power on to someone else. He selected a young man from Barrow whom he wished to instruct. The young man had accompanied the woman's husband. He was a Christian and had no belief in the powers of the shaman. However, he consented to go along with the shaman's ideas and was skeptical of the whole business. He went out with the shaman on the tundra and the two of them spent some days alone. At last, however, the young man became terribly frightened. He refused to go out again and wouldn't have anything more to do with the shaman. "It was as if some of the tunarak of the shaman rubbed off on him," she said. The young man would never tell what had happened between himself and the shaman when they were alone.

21. A woman who was camping with a group at Brower's Ranch recalled that she had been a bear. Her husband had recently died and while the other women were sitting with her, offering condolences, she felt the urge of the bear power. She took the skin of the brown bear on which she regularly slept and, placing it over her head, walked back and forth. She repeated again and again that she was a bear and would turn into a bear. But she didn't.

22. An inland family had a daughter whom the shaman crippled through his drumming. He broke the bones in her back because she refused to marry the shaman's son. The proposal for his son had been made by the shaman in person to the family. On the whole, the family was willing but an uncle of the girl objected. The family agreed with his objections and vetoed the marriage. In revenge, the shaman began drumming. The family made no attempt to take revenge on the shaman.

23. The informant's grandmother grieved so much over the death of her only son that she attempted to commit suicide by hanging. Before she died, however, she was saved by her daughter who cut her down. Her son's death was "harder" because he died away from home. It was recognized that something "evil" came from the shaman. The family had a daughter whom the shaman wanted to marry. She refused and was backed up by her family. The shaman took his revenge against the family. When the son, the brother of the girl, and his wife were out hunting, he lost his pipe. The shaman found it and "did something to it." When the young couple were camping, the shaman came and said, "I have found your pipe." The young man was glad to have his pipe back. Both husband and wife began smoking from it again and became sick and died. If they had known that the pipe had been tampered with, they would have made a new one. No one knows what poison was in there that made the young couple die. The sister of the man, the girl who had refused the shaman, also got sick and died within a few days. There was nothing that anyone could do to help them.

24. An informant relates that her older sister and older brother were killed by a shaman. He drummed, singing, although he was not among them at the time. They died after a few days. The shaman was angry because the girl had refused to marry his son. Another shaman diagnosed the cause of death.

25. There was a shaman hunting caribou. He got his toe caught in a trap out on the tundra. He could not get out even though he was a shaman. (A fact regarded as highly amusing.) After a time, he called for his mittens to come to him. They came to him across the tundra and freed him. His toe was frozen and was amputated.

26. There was a man at nuwuk who became sick because he had offended a shaman. As it happened, he did not know that the shaman, whose name was umigłu, was really the cause of his sickness. Hence, he hired him to effect a cure. The family of the sick man paid the shaman, umigłu, but the patient failed to improve. He was getting sicker all the time and it seemed as if he would die. The reason that the patient was sick was that umigłu had shot a lot of little wooden spears into his body. Not until the family got another shaman to work on the sick man was this found out. The second shaman, more powerful than the first, drummed and sang. Then he put his mouth against the sick man's body and coughed up a little wooden spear. It transferred itself from the body of the patient into the shaman's mouth. "Here," he said, "This is what is making you sick." The second shaman now knew who had sent the little spear. He went over to umigłu and said: "Here, I return your spear to you; you better not do that again. Next time the spear will turn on you and you will die." The man who was sick now was well and the second shaman protected him. The

family paid an umiak to him. The evil shaman, umigłu, was obliged to return the payments he had received from the family.

27. There was a man at Barrow who had six special curing songs. He had gotten them from his relatives, although it is said that he bought one or two from a shaman. He was not a shaman himself although he could cure. He did not use a tambourine. In curing, he put his parka on backward, with the hood in front. He made the patient lie down and began to sing into his parka hood. When he had sung for a time, he would blow into the patient's armpits. He was very good as a curer and was paid for his services. But he did not have the true shamanistic power.

28. A shaman could staunch the flow of blood. There was a man at nuwuk who was making an umiak. He was working with an adz. It slipped and he cut his leg very badly. It was bleeding very much and his wife tried to stop the flow of blood. She was unable to do it. Finally, the man sent her to utkeaaγvik for a shaman who was a specialist in such matters. She walked down the beach 10 miles or so. Finally she returned with the shaman. The man was weak from loss of blood and was holding his leg to keep it from bleeding more. The shaman took his drum, sang over the wound and talked over it. When he was done, just a little scratch was left on the skin; there was no wound at all. They paid him two seal pokes full of oil for his services.

29. Shamans used a special kind of magic poison to kill people. They could treat arrows and other weapons so that these poisons would work and the weapons would always be effective. Actual vegetable poisons were unknown. A case of the shamanistic poison is the following: There was a man at piγinik who married a woman from Wainwright. She had a brother who was lame. When the family went down to Wainwright, they stayed with the woman's brother. Now the couple had a son who had grown to be a young man and was starting to learn to hunt. He asked his lame uncle if he might borrow his bow to hunt caribou. The uncle refused. The boy borrowed a bow from another man and was successful in getting some caribou. He gave the meat to the man from whom he had borrowed the bow and arrows. The uncle was furious because he had not been given any of the meat and in his violence killed the boy. The news traveled up to piγinik and the relatives of the boy's father decided to take action. They hired a shaman. He took arrows and started working on them, singing over them. He gave them back to their owners and said that bodies touched by these arrows would swell up. The shaman took a snipe's crop and placed the arrows in it while he worked over them. The piγinik group came down to Wainwright and took after the boy's uncle. He lined up his supporters and there was a battle. The piγinik people touched their enemies with the arrows. They all went into their houses and never came out again. The besiegers circled the houses and shouted, "Come out and fight." An old man said, "They can't come out—they are all swelled up." And all the people touched by the poisoned arrows died. Among them was the murderous uncle.

30. An inland family had moved to the coast bringing berries with them. The son in the family got a polar bear. Shamans warned him that no member of the family should eat things from the land for a time. The informant and his sister ate some of the berries they had with them. She got sick at once. Her mouth dried up and she was unable to swallow. Her mother blew into her mouth again and again. While it relieved the pain she felt, it did nothing to cure her. So the mother tried another means. She lit two fires on the ground and had the girl walk back and forth between them. This made her sweat. Then the mother took a duck feather and rubbed water on her throat. After

that, she could drink a little water. Now there was an old shaman who was traveling along the beach where they were camped. He said that he would cure her and that all he wanted was some tobacco. He made her lie down, blew on her neck and licked it for a long time. Then he sang over the neck. Then he licked it again. Part of this time, the girl fainted. He said, "You will be able to eat well tomorrow." She lay exhausted after the shaman finished with her He stayed with the family that night. In the morning, she was hungry and ate and was completely cured. No one in her family had any tobacco to pay the shaman but the mother gave him two caribou skins and he was content. He went away after that.

31. After the establishment of the whaling station, some liquor was available. A man named taakpuq, a great whaler, had gone with his wife inland. He was drunk and shot her dead. As it happened, there was a shaman nearby. He came quickly, breathed over her, and sang and drummed, and she was well and alive again. Her wound was closed by the shaman. Her brothers heard what taakpuq had done and wanted to kill him. Since she had been revived by the shaman, however, and was not seriously injured, they let the matter go. They did, however urge her to leave taakpuq.

32. Shamans sometimes recovered lost articles. They were called in particularly when an article was stolen. At piγinik, there was a man who had stolen an ice saw. The owner had put it under the cover of his sled and when he looked for it, it was gone. He was convinced that someone had stolen it. So he decided to employ a shaman to help him recover it. The shaman went into a house, made all the men come into the house. He had them sit around the floor in a row. Then he had each man in turn come to the middle of the floor and stand on his tambourine. The one who broke his tambourine, he said, would be the thief. Each man took his turn. The cover of the tambourine remained intact as each one stood on it. At last there were two men left. The last man said to the other, "I have that saw at home; I just borrowed it and meant to bring it back." The man to whom he told this pointed him out to the shaman. The man didn't stand on the drum and break it. He returned the saw and gave something to the shaman. The shaman was also paid by the owner of the saw. He received three caribou skins. After the shaman had them for a while, he decided that he was not entitled to them. Besides, the father of the owner of the saw had recently died and everyone had pity for him. So the shaman returned the caribou skins.

33. There was a shaman at Wainwright named kovanna. He married a woman with a daughter by a previous marriage. When they had been married for some time the daughter, ayranna, became ill and was close to death. Her mother told her stepfather, the shaman, that if he could cure her, he might take her as his wife. He succeeded in curing her, and, although he made no demand on her at the time, let it be understood that she was to become his wife. At a later time, the girl's mother separated from kovanna and went with her daughter to Barrow. After they had been there for some time, the mother died. The shaman, kovanna, then came from Wainwright to claim ayranna. She was afraid of him at first because of his power but he overcame her fears and succeeded in marrying her. It was agreed that this was right, that the shaman was in effect taking his fee. Even though kovanna was at the time quite old, the girl lived with him and the two settled at nuwuk. When he died, she married a younger man named isawvaq and lived with him for many years. They had only one child.

34. There were two shamans who had the same-sounding name. There was a tall man named uweeruraq and a short one named uweeyuraq. They shared

their fees and were very rich. Sometimes they worked on a sick person together. In some cases, they would demand only sexual relations with the women they cured or with the female relatives of their patients.

35. On the Noatak River lived the shaman inʸaxłuuraq who had power from the loon and used a loon head as his aanaroak. On one occasion, he went hunting with a number of people and the loons kept coming to him. Nor at this time did he fully realize that he was aŋatquq. Later he developed his powers and became well known, so much so that he was widely feared. Fear prompted his murder and a group of men shot him, took the body away, and dropped it into a pond and covered it with sod. Later, the killers were hunting in the same area and they saw a loon swimming in the pond. When they had driven some caribou into the pond and killed them, the loon began eating the flesh of the dead caribou. Meanwhile, the other shamans in the area began to be curious about the missing inʸaxłuuraq and set out to find him. They put their tunarat together and discovered that he had become a loon. They went to the pond where his body was, recovered it, and restored him to life. He then settled at sisoaliq, near Point Hope, and continued to inspire great fear because of his unusual powers.

36. In a shamanistic seance, a shaman was bound and a hatchet put between his feet. The lights in the house were then extinguished and the assembled group heard the rushing sound of wings. These seemed to fly away and then return. At this, the lights were put on again and the shaman was seen, still bound, but the hatchet between his feet had blood on it. He then took his drum, sang, and conversed with his tunarat in the hallway.

37. There was a female shaman at Point Hope named kuuturuq. She was extremely vindictive and able to bring crippling diseases. In this way, she destroyed several people. One of them was a very successful hunter, a man named samarun. When kuuturuq was insulted by this man, she, aided by other shamans, crippled him and he was never able to hunt again. She weakened his bones so that he could not walk. At Point Hope, also, there was a blind female shaman. She was traveling in her spirit power when she met kuuturuq. The latter's power was so strong that she killed her blind rival. The woman died in her house. Her relatives assembled and placed the blind woman's aanaroat on her. Through their power she was restored to life. She then swore vengeance on kuuturuq and arranged it so that the latter's power would return to her own family. At this, kuuturuq's children began to die and one by one they perished. There was nothing that kuuturuq could do to prevent it.

38. There was an old shaman at nuwuk who had the loon and fire as his tunarat. His daughter was traveling with a group which was going up to neγliq to trade. She called the attention of the group to a fire which always appeared in the distance behind them at night. This was her father, following them from his house at nuwuk but traveling in his power. His name was amawroaq.

39. When qiwak was a small boy (ca. 8 years old) his father was out on the ice. The ice broke and took him away. It was in the fall and the father didn't return until the spring whaling.

There were two families going to Point Hope. The head of the other family, a man named kaleak, told young qiwaq that if anything happened to the latter's father that he, kaleak, could be depended on to help. At Point Hope, the ice was not yet thick. Several of the men went off to get seal. They were unsuccessful and went back to shore, leaving qiwaq's father alone out on the ice. He took a seal and was dragging it back across the ice when he noticed that the ice had shifted and that he was cut off from shore. He found a breathing hole in the ice and dropped his net again, waiting to see if he could get in touch with the people on shore. Meanwhile, he got another seal. He then started to walk along the ice, in view of the shore, until he could come opposite the place where his family and the others had camped. With him he took a seal net to rest on and some pieces of meat which he cut from the dead seals. He called to shore again and again but he was too far out to be sighted. He took the tobacco pouch which he carried and carefully tied it to his sleeve. His pipe he strung around his neck. He sat on the ice, smoking, waiting to be sighted. One of his hands got numb.

qiwaq meanwhile went to kaleak to get help. The latter sent after a shaman who lived at Point Hope. The father's sister had a song which made the south wind blow. She sang it and the ice was blown into the shore. They thought that qiwaq's father, axooceak, might be able to make his way to the shore. But the wind veered off and ice moved out again. Several of the people walked the beach to see if they could spot the missing man on the ice but they missed him. Meanwhile, the shamans began their work.

Now axooceak walked about to find a safe place to spend the next few days, thinking that he could get back when the ice moved again. But it was hopeless. The offshore rift remained. Meanwhile, the pack on which he was stranded was constantly moving. He was already a considerable distance away from shore. He thus realized that there was no hope of his being found and he gave himself up to dying out on the ice. He looked for a hollow in the ice where he could rest. There he laid his seal net, and his three seal spears he stood on the ice outside his shelter. Meanwhile the days grew shorter and at last the light was gone. Once he looked at his seal spears. They had moved and he thought that a fox was about. And while he sat there, his boot started to work itself off. He caught it before it worked off his foot and pulled it back on.

Now this was the shaman who was trying to get him back. The aŋatquq was moving his spears and had nearly pulled the boot off his foot. In a house, the shaman was pulling. He stamped in the hallway to draw the father's soul to the hallway of the house. He had the family in the house cover the skylight, put a rope across, and he had the floor covered with canvas and skins. He brought in a bitch with puppies and dragged them across the floor. Out on the ice, the lost man could smell a dog's smell.

As the days passed, axooceak could no longer walk. His legs and feet had swelled badly. He could barely crawl from his ice shelter. He saw three men coming toward him. He crawled out to them, telling them to go away, that he couldn't do a thing for them, that he had no food himself. Carefully, he had preserved the pieces of raw seal which he had taken with him originally. The men whom he saw disappeared. When they were gone, he remained in his shelter all winter. When at last the sun again began to appear and the days to get longer, he crawled from his shelter, very weak, unable to walk. He crawled along the ice with the sun. Finally he got to thin ice and saw that the wind was blowing from the south. In his weakened state, he thought he saw a stretch of water moving wildly. Then he noticed a log caught in the crushed ice along the shore and realized that what he thought to be rough water was really blowing sand. Ashore at last, he tried to get his bearings. He decided to move south into the wind. After a while, stumbling, crawling along, he caught sight of a mast. And, crossing a little frozen stream, he found himself at Point Lay.

At Point Lay, he had relatives—cousins. His family, now following kaleak, had moved northward shortly before. He came to the houses, thinking of how he could reach his family. Actually, following his disappearance, there had been some trouble at Point Hope. His wife, qiwaq's mother, had accused another man, saying, "You killed my husband." She had tried to get her brothers-in-law to take revenge on this man, piwak, who had been along on the ill-fated sealing expedition. The wife persisted but the others would not agree to kill piwak. Because bad feelings were growing, kaleak had taken the family, consisting of qiwaq, his mother, the accuser, the father's sister, and some smaller children, away back up the coast. They had come from Point Hope to Point Lay, stayed there for a time, nad then moved farther northward toward Wainwright. They were slow in getting up from Point Hope to Point Lay, having been overtaken by a storm and circled into their own tracks. At Point Lay, times were hard. The ice had been uncertain, and had broken unseasonably. Hence, the winter sealing was affected. kaleak debated the matter and decided not to push farther to the north but to go back to Point Lay, where in spite of the tension created by the accusation on the part of axooceak's wife, there was at least sufficient food. Hence, a few days' travel out of Point Lay, kaleak turned back, taking a short overland journey to avoid Point Lay and to return to Point Hope. When axooceak appeared in Point Lay, he was not aware of this, thinking his family had headed northward. Happily, however, he learned, from another traveler, of their decision to return to Point Hope.

At Point Lay, axooceak had fallen exhausted before one of the houses. The people rushed out and called his relative. His cousins, and an uncle who was living there, came for him and took him to their house. He was given food, some seal meat and oil, and was provided with a large pouch of tobacco by his uncle—the pouch being made of a membrane from a caribou heart. The wives of his cousins quickly made him a new pair of boots. In a few days he had recovered from his winter out on the ice. He then decided, having learned of his family's whereabouts, to go after them at Point Hope. Because of the food shortage at Point Lay, his relatives could only provide him with oil to take along. They did lend him a team and he joined in with several other men and their families who were going, as well, to Point Hope. On the way, the men hunted ptarmigan. The ice closed in again, and it was found possible to hunt seals. With another man, axooceak took seals. All the group ate, camping to cook the seal meat. The man with whom he hunted on the ice was named masagaroak, a man who was later murdered at Barrow (cf. Case 4, pp. 114–115). The next day, they started off again for Point Hope. axooceak walked ahead of the team, while another man drove it. At last they reached wiivak, a place near Point Hope. He sat down with masagaroak and the two finished the seal meat they had. They then smoked together. After a while, they went over to one of the houses at wiivak to see if there was any more food there.

They entered a house, passing a woman in the hallway. The man in the house was silent for a time but then informed them that they had also been short of food. He offered them water and hung up their mukluks to dry. The water was meanwhile being melted by the women. After a while, masagaroak said, "We are getting no water here—let us have our boots." They ran out of the house. As they passed the woman in the hallway, they remarked that she had melted no water. axooceak's belief was that the couple was thinking of killing him for the tobacco he carried. Water they obtained from a nearby spring. Having rejoined their travel group, they related what had happened to them. Another man with them, aakpalik, was very angry at this and stopped to spring the traps set by the people at wiivak as they passed along by them. The people had been getting foxes.

From wiivak they went on, stopping that night on the ice. axooceak was afraid but they persuaded him that they would not leave him. In the morning, they saw polar bear tracks nearby. Then they went on to neearamiut, a little village between wiivak and Point Hope. They stopped, looked into the hallway of a house and saw a dog team there. An old woman came out and called, "You are axooceak." He left his companions and went into the house. Another old woman there said, "His wife will be glad to have her husband back again." Her own husband, in fact, had been lost on the ice. The people in that house had caught a seal and there were two ribs left. These they offered to axooceak but he said, "Don't bother about me." He stayed on in the house for a day, drying his boots and letting the others have all the tobacco from him that they wanted. The man in the house got a seal and there was enough to eat. Now, niŋiyuk, the man of the house, said, "Don't go to Point Hope during the daytime; hide around—go into town when it is dark." And axooceak saw that this was good advice. This was because people were afraid of a man lost on the ice who returned.

At last he reached Point Hope. The others went into town but axooceak stayed behind. He waited until night and then went to the house where his wife was and called in the skylight to her. He said, "I am alive." As soon as they heard his voice, all in the house came out to see him. His wife was so surprised that she couldn't leave with the others. She just stayed in the house looking for her belt. She couldn't find it and she called over to her aunt that her husband was back. Her belt was on her trousers all the time—that's how excited she was! Then all went back into the house.

axooceak sat down in the house by the stone lamp without removing his clothes. qiwaq and the other children just stood around, looking at him. For 4 days, their father left his clothes on. He didn't take his parka off, or his mukluks, or any part of his clothing until 4 days later.

Now they called in the shaman who had acted for them the first time. He told axooceak of all the things he had done to get him returned. He told of trying to drag him away from the ice with ropes and with the bitch and her puppies. And he related how he had stamped in the hallway. Then he asked if axooceak had seen anything out on the ice. He said that he had seen three spirit men whom he had told to go away, that he couldn't assist them in any way. He told of how his boot had started to come off. The shaman then said that if he hadn't pulled his boot back on again, he would have come in from the ice at once and not been obliged to spend all the winter out there abandoned. The shaman asked for a poke of oil for bringing him back from the ice and this was paid to him.

This shaman was a man of great power. His son had died and he had wondered whether to revive him. He decided not to, being afraid to do so. It was, however, recognized that he had great power.

THE TREATMENT OF DISEASE

Although the shaman was summoned to treat disease and illness, there were many instances of sickness which conceptually did not require shamanistic intervention and treatment. There was some variation in respect to the determination of disease situations which the shaman might cure. As has been noted, other curers than shamans might function from time to time and be paid for their services. Much of doctoring, however, related to a series of home remedies in which the shaman played no part. It would hence appear that the shaman was called only when the disease appeared mortal or when other remedies failed. Unquestionably, there was a marked psychosomatic character to disease situations among the Eskimo. It is known that some shamans were remarkably effective as curers. In following the matter through, it was discovered that many illnesses did not warrant the services of the shaman. Those which did were concerned principally with pains of unknown origin, those occurring in the joints, in the body cavity, or the head. If the illness appeared mortal, the shaman might then be summoned, often not so much to cure as to determine the agent in the illness. There was something of the concept that death was an unnatural state, that it would not occur were it not for the malevolent workings of an enemy. And this, of course, the shaman was well able to determine.

There was virtually no pharmacopoeia among the North Alaskan Eskimo. No plants were used as medicines, no teas brewed; there was no attempt to develop even magical potions. The group had no poisons, or, at least, no vegetable poisons. Aconite was not known, but it does appear in other Alaskan cultures. Although there were magic poisons concocted by shamans, these were purely spiritual. The only Eskimo way of causing death similar to poisoning that was known at Barrow is as follows: A soup is made of the gut of a very fat reindeer or caribou; the partaker drinks the soup very hot and takes cold water right after it; the result is that the fat hardens and the person strangles. There is mention of such cases by a number of informants. It is said that one man did not believe in this method and so tried it. A bowl of hot water was kept ready for him. When the fat began to harden, he, in great pain, drank the hot water and so saved himself. The poisons attributed to shamans relate to food in that the malevolent shaman prepares a bit of food for his victim, singing over it beforehand. He offers it to the victim, who eats it. If he eats it all, he is safe; if he eats only part of it, it will poison him and he will die. Polar bear liver was also regarded as a poison.

The most common home treatment involved the use of blubber for many different kinds of illness. Blubber is mentioned as having been used in the following cases:

(1) Nosebleed was fairly frequent, and was caused perhaps by some dietary deficiencies. It is still common. It was said that if a stone lamp fell through the doorway and remained lit, it should not be picked up at once; if it were, the person involved would bleed from the nose. The procedure was to extinguish the lamp first and allow it to cool before picking it up. A person suffering from nosebleed had strips of blubber made, which were pushed up the nostrils and allowed to stay until the blood had clotted.

(2) A child with diaper rash was treated with blubber.

(3) Boils were not lanced but were drawn with a poultice of fine caribou hair and blubber. The lancing of boils was introduced by the foreign whalers, as was the poultice of brown soap and sugar still in use today. Mucus also was used in the treatment of boils.

(4) Blubber was put on burns.

In common use also was human urine. This was carefully saved, each person in the household voiding each morning in a wooden tub.

Urine was used principally for wounds. If a person had a cut finger, he placed the finger for a time in the tub of urine. Any cut was treated in this manner. When the labret holes on a boy had been cut, the wounds were treated with urine, as well as the ears which were notched for the earrings. Urine, of course, was principally saved for tanning.

Bloodletting was also common. For any persistent ache, blood was let. A persistent headache involved a cut on the temple and blood was allowed to flow. The skin was usually pinched between two blocks of wood and the cut made. A special stone knife was used. This was chisel shaped, fairly sharp, and quite long. Bleeding was also performed for aches in the joints, presumably rheumatism and arthritis. Blood was rarely let from the trunk, then only for backache. People were never bled for toothache or for other pains in the trunk. It is said that this is "dangerous." In such cases the shaman was summoned. The shaman did not bleed the patient, for anyone was able to do this.

Nor was the shaman called in to treat broken bones. Again, anyone might attempt to set the bone and to wrap the injured part. The broken bone was set with pieces of wood or whalebone and wrapped with caribou skin.

Caribou skin, hair, and blubber were also used in wrapping more severe wounds. If the flow of blood could not be staunched, the shaman was summoned. Some shamans had skill in making wounds disappear. Most were credited with being able to reduce the size of a wound.

In cases of strain or sprain, heat might be applied. There was no institution of sweating in the culture, however. A man with a sore back might simply lie against hot stones for the relief afforded. If the trouble proved persistent, the shaman was called in.

Constipation was said to be uncommon. If it developed, there were one or two remedies employed before the shaman was brought in. A constipated person might drink oil for a few days. One informant related the case of his uncle, who having eaten too many fish heads and eyes, became constipated. He made himself an ivory "spoon" and spooned out the hard feces from his rectum. This proved sufficient. If the case proved persistent, the shaman was called. He performed as usual, there being no massage known. A few persons were reported to have died from constipation. For diarrhea, fat was eaten.

An aching tooth might be knocked out with a chisel. However, severe toothache, earache, body and joint pains generally involved shamanistic activity.

There was no tattooing for curing.

In birth, no special techniques were used. A woman who had difficulty in expelling either the fetus or the placenta was worked over by other women or her husband. The pressure was placed at the fundus of the uterus. No other method was employed. It was related that the mother of an illegitimate child at Barrow delivered in the spring of 1952. She did not go to the hospital. This method was applied to her.

Beyond bleeding, there was no surgery of any kind. There was no concept of autopsy, except that the shaman might ask the deceased of what he had died.

Lantis' comment on doctoring at Nunivak applies to Barrow as well:

> Doctoring was the weakest sector of the culture. (People) were adequately fed, clothed, housed, had plenty of recreation, interesting and varied craft work, no oppressive caste system . . ., free competition, allowing any man to rise socially and economically by his own industry and skill. In the case of illness and accidents, however, the people could not care for themselves; they had to turn to the shaman. Yet they did not regard him as their benefactor. They feared him and resented his superior power over the supernatural. [Lantis, 1946, p. 203.]

THE CULTS

The patterning of religious behavior in the two ecological settings, however similar in fundamental outlook and premises, such as in shamanism, in the attitudes toward nature, and in mythology, began to diverge somewhat sharply in respect to group activities associated with the major economic preoccupations. The most important communal religious festivals were those associated with whaling on the coasts and with the caribou drives in the interior. The economic differences between the two are given added weight when the religious patterns are compared. Indeed, these come to underlie the basic conceptual definition of tareumiut as compared with nuunamiut. Because the whale occupied first place in the hunting of the coastal Eskimo while the caribou ranked first in the hunting in the inland regions, and because the rituals, the social events, and the economic implications associated with each are so complex, it is well to contrast the cult of the whale with that of the caribou.

A man from the coast might, it is true, hunt caribou, and he did observe certain ritual practices and express certain religious attitudes in respect to such hunting. But in no sense was he so involved in the elaborated ceremonial that the nuunamiut regularly employed in the wholesale hunting of herds. There was always ritual in hunting and care always had to be taken lest the game be offended and withhold themselves. But the nuunamiut caribou drive was especially characterized by group ritual and prohibition applicable once yearly. In this sense the cult of the caribou applied to the annual drive and the ritual behavior associated with it. It became, in effect, a world renewal rite. Similarly, the details of the whaling cult were lost to the nuunamiut. They had developed among the coastal peoples and reflect an elaborated complex of ideas which, although similar in kind to those arising around the caribou, were evaluated differently. The settled economy of the whalers, in fact, permitted a much more elaborate series of patterns than that which arose among the nomadic inland groups. Just as in the interior, however, the whaling marked the start of the year's activities to which the winter ceremonials formed a fitting prelude.

The two major religious patterns were in essence group activities which brought forth all the attitudes which apply in the realm of Eskimo religion. More than this, they provided the means by which nonkin solidarity could be effected and group cohesion achieved. The ritual unit was the hunting group, the voluntary association of men assembled under the leadership of an umealiq and connected with a karigi. Distinctions of rank and wealth arise in that the umealit, defined as social leaders with prestige derived from wealth, took on the religious role of greeting whale or caribou and in officiating at the appropriate ceremonies. Hence, karigi membership and hunting group association were lent added meaning through the ritual necessary to successful fulfillment of economic goals.

THE CULT OF THE WHALE

Among the peoples of the coasts, the activities of the winter—shamanistic seances, karigi games, social events—were marked by the constant emphasis on the coming whaling season in the spring and by the expression of hopes for its success. The karigi was the center of crew activities and it was here that each crew member came during the winter not only to engage in the sports and games which the karigi afforded, but also to give proper thought to the solemn duties of the whaler. While the men of each crew played their games, spent their leisure making tools, carving, or engaging in other useful tasks, their umealiq was involved in some aspect of ceremonial activity relating to whaling. He prepared the banners and other regalia which the crew would need, he got out the whaling charms, and he would confer with the shamans to insure that the proper procedures were followed. During the winter, much time was given to talking of whales and whaling and the old men told tales of whaling and the experiences of the past.

As soon as the daylight returned, although some of the men went out to the tundra to take a few random caribou, the whaling preparations became intensified. The umealit were making sure of their crews and were seeing that each man was given gifts, whether of meat or other items; and they had begun to think of the more practical problems involved, such as where to place the whaling camp, and where the most favorable location for the umiak might be, factors necessitating examination of ice conditions and some prediction as to where leads might form. By early March, the men of the Arctic coast had put aside virtually every other work and were devoting themselves wholly to preparation.

The getting out of the gear took some time. Every weapon, the harpoons, the lances, and the floats, had to be carefully cleaned and assembled in the kariyit. The whale could not be approached except by those wearing new clothes which had not been contaminated by contact with any animal, that is, had not previously been used in hunting. Moreover, the umiak required a complete new cover of ugruk hides. This work, the making of new clothing and the sewing of a new umiak cover, was done by the women, wives of the crew members, under the supervision of the wife of the umealiq. Each woman made new clothes for her husband. The umiak frame was stripped of its old cover and washed with urine. To make the umiak cover, as well as for their general sewing, the women made use of the umiivik, a shedlike structure which each karigi built. It was a rectangular shed, made of ice blocks and covered with skins, heated and lighted by lamps. Each umealiq associated with an individual karigi brought his umiak frame here in order to have the new cover made for it. The umealit of any one karigi cooperated in building the umiivik, supplying the skins for the roof, while the crew members cut the blocks of ice for the walls. The umiivik was a temporary structure, not too different from the late 19th century kariyit at nuwuk and utkeaaγvik.

While the women were engaged in making the umiak cover, the members of the crew to which it belonged remained in their karigi and were quiet. After the cover was in place on the frame, they could have no sexual relations and slept in the karigi rather than at home. When the cover was finished, the wives of the crew members who had made it sat quietly until the wife of the umealiq fed them. She cooked food at home, and brought it first to the crew in the karigi and then to the women in the umiivik. All ate to signalize the completion of the boat and its readiness for the sea. At tikeraaq these preparations were made after the snow birds had been sighted and when the first of the whales, usually a beluga, was sighted in the ice leads. Farther north on the coast, the signs were somewhat less specific. A careful watch was kept on the ice leads and the length of day. When the April conditions were right, the crews retired to the kariyit. Here they underwent 4 days of preparation before going out to the leads, setting the camp up on the ice, and awaiting the appearance of the whales.

Once the crew had retired to the karigi, they got out the new clothing their wives had made and put it on. This was of caribou skin on the inner layer with an outer parka of caribou or sealskin. While the outer garments were made of scraped skins, the inner suit was softened but not scraped, fat and sinew being left on. This was water resistant and gave added protection during the long vigils in the intense cold by the ice leads. If a double suit of caribou skins was worn, both were left unscraped and untrimmed. Later, when the whaling was over, the crewman's wife could clean the skin clothing and it could be worn for any occasion, although never again for whaling.

For the 4-day period during which the men sat in the karigi before going out to the ice, there was great solemnity. No levity was permitted, no sexual relations, and the men were expected to sit quietly, thinking about whales. From time to time, their wives came to the karigi with cooked food. It was likely that a food taboo would have been imposed on the members of one crew either by an experienced whaler, a shaman, or the umealiq himself. There were men who owned special whaling songs; one of these in effect became the spiritual adviser to the crew. Frequently this was a shaman, although it need not have been. Any person who owned such songs and had sufficient whaling experience might qualify as the kaakłiq, the magician for the group. As the men sat in the karigi, this individual sang his songs to attract the whale and to make capture easier. Such songs might prevent the harpoon from slipping and the lines from fouling, and make the weather serene and the whale weak. The kaakłiq was often an old man, well past his active strength, whose presence in the umiak was nevertheless considered indispensable. Food taboos imposed on crew members were varied and depended on the inspiration of the kaakłiq. In later days, bread was a common food taboo, although such foods as the heart of the female seal, caribou marrow, the liver of the male ugruk, and the like, might be prohibited. One crew was forbidden to chew ice, another to drink cold water in the karigi. Violation of the taboo ruined any chance of success and could also result in accident or in illness for the violator.

The wife of the umealiq, meanwhile, was engaged in certain rites surrounding the umiak which was to be used in the whaling. She had hired an old woman to make her the special mittens which the wife of an umealiq regularly wore. These were long mittens which came halfway up the forearm and had a ruff of wolf fur around them, and were frequently decorated with weasel-skin tassels. She and her husband, the umealiq, had previously obtained the wooden vessel with which water was to be offered to the whale. This was a wooden cylinder onto which a bottom was fitted. It was usually made by a craftsman whose work specialty this was and who knew the songs to initiate such a vessel. When he fitted the bottom, he came to the karigi and sang while the crew members watched silently. A new vessel and new mittens were obtained each year, as were the boots of the umealiq himself, marked with white stitching so as to record the number of whales he had taken. While the men sat contemplatively in the karigi, the umealiq's wife took one of the greater floats associated with whaling to the umiivik. She dragged this on a sled, together with the wooden vessel, and entered the umiivik. She laid the float in the umiak, singing her own whaling songs, and passed around the craft itself. Then she poured fresh water on the umiak, predicting success for the whaling venture.

When the 4-day period had elapsed, the crew members came out from the karigi. As they were about to leave, they donned their new clothes. The crew left the karigi as the sun of the fourth day was setting. They filed slowly out of the building, the older members exhorting the younger, "Don't get tired." Indeed, much of the 4-day period of seclusion was spent singing the proper songs and in listening to the advice given by the kaakłiq, directed especially to the young men who were engaging in whaling for the first time. Such statements as the following were regularly made: "Walk on the sand and on the ice; try to be the first one to get to the water. Always be busy. Clean the frost off from the roof of your hallway. If you don't do this, the whale will see your laziness."

During the 4-day period, the restrictions were especially onerous for the umealiq. Like the members of his crew, he was obliged to refrain from sexual relations, and the restrictions applied to him for a longer period than for his crew. If his wife were menstruating, her place had to be taken by another, and no menstruating woman could enter the house of a man engaged in whaling. She spent her period in the ice lodge which served as parturition and menstrual lodge on those occasions when ritual demanded that a man avoid women in such condition. It was also essential that the umealiq have his ice cellar cleaned of meat, particularly the flesh of any whales previously taken. This did not apply to the meat which was apportioned to the boat and which was considered to belong specifically to the boat. Nor were the members of the crew under the same obligation, being able to keep a store of whale meat on hand from previous seasons. On the day of departure for the ice leads, the umealiq saw to it that the whale meat which was apportioned to him personally was removed. If too much were left, it was simply given away raw to the men in the crew, their wives coming for it, or it was distributed to the community at large. A portion was reserved for the household of the umealiq and it was ceremonially cooked by the man's wife. When she began to cook the meat, the younger boys of the community, those not yet allied with a whaling crew, came and stood over the smokehole of the iga at the umealiq's house. They let lines down into the house with sticks attached. The sticks were driftwood chips which the umealiq's wife would later use in the ceremonial of greeting the whale. She took these and tied pieces of meat in their place.

It was regarded as desirable that the crew associated with a particular umealiq eat all the meat which he had left in his cellar. His wife therefore cooked as much of it as she could, boiling it in pans, and brought it over to the karigi where the crew was assembled. When she had completed giving meat to the boys, these went to the karigi, stood outside and began to sing. As the umealiq's wife came with her pans of boiled muktuk, they attempted to seize some of it for themselves as she entered the karigi. This bit of play marked a social event for the young men of the community and permitted them some degree of sport and horseplay. Actually, the feeding of boys, a pattern so common in the society, had the effect of drawing them somewhat more intimately into the activity of whaling and served to define their status exactly. The boys regularly ran to the karigi of which fathers and other older male relatives were crew members. Although the boys were permitted some mischievous play, the crew in the karigi remained solemn and were instructed to keep their minds on the whale. When the last of the muktuk had been brought in the umealiq's wife signalized it by turning over a pan, and the crew was then ready to leave the karigi.

If an umealiq had not used up all of his past year's whale meat in this distribution, he invited people to come for it and so effected a distribution of it through the community. It was thought better if the crew itself could eat all the muktuk supplied by their captain rather than that some of it be given away. An umealiq attempted either to divide his remaining share among his crew or to spread it evenly through the village. Of the meat supplied by the umealiq's wife to the crew, none could be left. A case is known, at the karigi called the qilullaraamiut, where one crew took 10 whales in a single season. So great was the supply of meat remaining that the umealit of this karigi gave portions of meat in large quantities to other crews in other kariyit. Although it was not usual to single out other crews in other kariyit for favors of this sort, the qilullaraamiut were successful again and it was held that the procedure was a correct one.

At sundown, when the meat had been eaten, the crew left the karigi, the captain in the lead, and went to the house of their leader. The umealiq entered the house, while the crew stood on the rooftop and called to him through the skylight. The harpooner asked for his lances and the various crewmen called for their lines with the attached seal floats. One by one, these items were brought out by the wife of the umealiq. The leader himself came out of the house bearing the charms necessary to the whaling. The group was now ready to depart for the whaling camp out on the ice. From the captain's house they went to the umiivik and obtained the boat. They loaded their gear into it, the charms being placed last, and, each taking hold of the gunwale, they began to run to the sea. The gang of boys followed, shouting encouragement and asking for parts of the captured whale.

While at the present time there is still the feeling that the ice cellar should be emptied, dogs are often used to transport the gear out onto the ice. This was never done in the past. Each crew formerly carried its own umiak and no dogs were permitted out on the ice during the whaling season. These, it was held, would be offensive to the whale. The crew members had also cleansed themselves, a fact indicated by the wearing of the new clothing, and there was a token removal of the essence of the last animal taken. If the hunter had last hunted caribou, it was necessary that the essence of the caribou which still clung to him be removed by washing. This would otherwise be offensive to the whale. Each crew member had also donned a new pair of mukluks. Only one pair was permitted to each man, and the boots could not be changed while the whaling was in progress.

The crew now ran to the edge of the ice which was packed along the shore, usually a distance of several hundred yards. At the point where the sea ice began the umiak was set down, the keel resting on the ice. The umealiq then laid his box of charms near the boat and sat down by it. All the men now got into the boat which was resting some distance from the ice lead, and taking paddles, pretended to paddle rapidly and vigorously. The harpooner in the bow, having previously wet his lance in the sea, made as if to lance a whale. The umealiq, meanwhile, sang songs, as did the kaakłiq. When this episode was over, the crew left the boat, picked it up again, and advanced to the open water. The boat was again set down at the edge of the ice lead, the gear arranged, pokes, lines, harpoons, and lances being put in their proper places, and lastly, the box containing the whaling charms. The umiak was then set on the water, great care being taken to see that the prow entered the water first, and the umealiq entered it followed by the crew (pl. 5, *a*).

Once in the water, the boat was paddled slowly toward the north, the direction in which the whales would swim. The umealiq sat in the center of the craft, singing the songs which would attract the whale. After a time, the crew returned to the place on the ice where they had elected to set up their camp. Here, at the edge of the ice, windbreaks were set up but no tents. No fires were allowed and there could be no cooking while the whaling was in progress. The men slept in snatches and were constantly alert, ready to move if a whale were sighted. Eating was done silently and sparingly. Proper observance of both personal and group food taboos was highly necessary and carefully followed. The umealiq could not allow the whale to see him eat. He could not, in eating, face the direction from which the whales were coming, the south, and he was to feed himself carefully, with his face covered with his parka hood, the food being handed to him under his shirt.

The restrictions imposed on the crew members and especially on the umealiq continued to apply to the wife of the umealiq as well. When the crew had picked up the umiak after the initial stop at the edge of the ice, the umealiq followed behind singing his special songs. He in turn was followed by his wife, she wearing her special mittens and carrying the wooden pot with which fresh water would be poured on the whale. When the umiak was launched into the water, the wife of the umealiq continued to stand at the place where the launching took place. When the boat left, she turned and walked back to her house. She had meanwhile given to her husband the left-hand mitten she wore and her belt. These formed a mystic tie to the land and reflected the activity which she must now carry on. Her consequent behavior at home reflected on the ultimate success of the expedition.

She sat quietly in the house, refraining from work of any kind, lest the whale be made harder to catch. If she were active, the whale, it was felt, would also become active. If she used a knife, the lines on the whale would be severed. Other women in the household—a daughter, a cowife, theoretically subordinate to the umealiq's first, or principal, wife—would cut food for her and would make the trip out to the whaling camp with buckets of meat for the crew. A general pattern was for the crew to employ a boy to keep them supplied with water and to meet the woman who came bringing food. The umealiq's wife was also under prohibition with respect to foods. The taboos which applied to the crew were incumbent on her also. She could not eat food from the land, such as caribou or fish, nor could she eat whale meat while the crew was out. To a lesser degree, the same restrictions applied to the wives of all the crew members. They could not sew, lest by this action the whale be made to foul the lines and escape. They could make no noises, such as chopping wood, or clapping the hands together. Noises were said to frighten off the whale with the result that the whole community became quiet when the several crews were out. Children were warned not to make unnecessary noise.

If the wife of the umealiq were to menstruate, she was obliged to take off her charms, usually in the shape of a whale flipper in bone or ivory, or the ravenskin flag she wore about her neck, and retire to the menstrual hut.

When the news came that the crew had taken a whale, a runner was sent from the boat to the house of the umealiq and the news was given first to the umealiq's wife. She waited quietly in the house until the runner appeared.

WHALING CHARMS AND SONGS

While there were many charms for whaling, each umealiq, each harpooner, each man, an aŋatquq, perhaps who acted as kaakliq, had his own particular sets. Most frequently these were kept in a wooden box which had a cover and was shaped like a whale. These charms were for the boat and were necessary to the success of the whaling expedition. They were in the main personal charms, the property of the umealiq or the other principals, and are not to be identified with the charms which hung in the karigi and which were the special property of the karigi itself. These were the kulugugłuq and although they also made for whaling success, being sacred objects in themselves, they were left in the karigi. The charms owned by the umealiq fell in the general category of personal aanaroak. The box in which they were kept was marked with soot and grease, a mark being made for each whale taken by the owner. While the umiak was at sea, the box was placed under the gunwale at the bow.

The charms were numerous. One inventory which was obtained showed the box to contain the following: a beetle in a small wooden box, one stuffed raven skin, several pieces of baleen cut into the forms of whales, walrus, and seals, a piece of fossil ivory. The contents of other such boxes were variable. A charm might also be fastened directly to the prow of the umiak. This might be a ravenskin, a stuffed lemming, ermine tails, and in one case, a wolf's head carved of ivory. Such charms were obtained by the umealiq from his shamanistic advisers, his kaakłiq, and might also be inherited. When not in use, the charms were kept in the roof beams of the house of the umealiq, and taken down only in the spring when they were needed for whaling. One important whaling charm, owned by taakpuq, the great whaler of piγinik, was the hair of a dead whaler of fame. This was an aanaroak of the class relating to the dead. It was also kept in a box shaped like a whale. Murdoch mentions several other charms—two wolf skulls, the axis vertebra of a seal, and many feathers in association with a ravenskin (Murdoch, 1892, pp. 274–275).

There were also the personal charms of each crew member. These were their own property and were acquired in the usual ways. The umealiq, however, had special personal charms in addition to those which were placed in the box in the umiak. The nawligax, too, the harpooner, wore special personal whaling charms. Both this principal and the umealiq wore beaded headbands or fillets from which were suspended figures of whales cut in ivory and stone. Murdoch mentions the teeth and skins of mountain sheep among other amulets (ibid., 1892, p. 275). Trade beads, especially the green and white ones known as il^{y}uuminiq, came to be valued as whaling charms.

An important amulet associated with the umealiq was a ravenskin. This the man wore on his back, the wings hanging over each shoulder and tied together at the tips. This skin is not to be confused with the stuffed ravenskins which might make up the charms placed in the box. It was, in effect, a badge of office and had ceremonial functions while the umiak was at sea. The wife of an umealiq, sitting at home during the expedition, also wore such a skin. When a whale was lanced and killed and was being towed in, kept afloat by the inflated seal pokes, the umealiq removed his outer parka and placed the ravenskin over his inner shirt, then replaced his outer parka. When the ice was reached, he took the ravenskin out again and placed it on the edge of the ice until the distribution of meat was over. The skin was worn again when the flippers of the whale, the umealiq's special share, were brought to the house in which he lived. Finally, the skin was worn again at the social festival celebrating the successful hunt—the nalukataq. In short, the skin was worn by the umealiq each time a special function relating to the whale was undertaken, such as in the hunting, following the killing of the whale, at the distribution of the meat, when the meat was taken to the ice cellars, and at nalukataq. It was removed when the whale was cut and at the actual butchering of the carcass.

At sea both the umealiq and the harpooner wore soot marks on their faces. Soot from the stone lamp and grease were mixed on a stone or slate palette and marks were put on the faces of these principals, the marks signifying the number of whales they had taken in previous seasons. These were marks which started at the corners of the mouth and ran toward the lobe of the ear, each single dot representing a whale. Both he and the harpooner could also make soot; each member of the crew could also use this form of decoration. The principals in the whaling crew regularly used some device to indicate the whales they had taken. The umealiq could, as has been remarked, have stitches in white up the sides of his boots, each stitch representing a whale. Both he and the harpooner could also make such marks on any of their property. One man is remembered who inlaid a piece of ivory on the lid of his workbox each time he harpooned a whale. Such marks, it is worth noting, were made only when the individual umealiq or harpooner was actually credited with the whale. It is always said that eight boats share in the taking of a whale, and it is true that other umiaks came to the assistance of any which had a line into a whale, and received a share of the meat for this aid. This was, however, an "assist" and it was the boat which first harpooned and lanced the whale which received credit for the take. The principals in that boat were then entitled to a mark. Those who merely assisted were not. Only the umealiq and the nawligax were free to wear such marks and they might, if their status were sufficiently high, tattoo these marks on their faces. Members of the crew could indicate their own not inconsiderable status in the community by use of the sooted eyelids.

Whaling charms had a compulsive effect, serving to bring the whale close to the boat, to make the animal more tractable and amenable to harpooning, to prevent the lines from slipping and fouling, and the like. The theory with respect to the whale was that the whale soul passed into another animal when the whale was killed. Hence, any irregularity of procedure was offensive to the whale. The animal was thought to be able to see from afar the preparations which were being made, and of course to allow himself to be taken by men. The associated behavior was therefore both to placate the whale and to compel his presence by magical means. Charms had the latter effect but the factor of compulsion was perhaps more fully enunciated in the songs which were associated with the charms or, independent of charms, were regarded as individual property.

The singing of such songs was in part a function of the umealiq. Generally, the kaakłiq, the older, more experienced whaler, sang the proper songs as well. It was this individual who was especially hired by the umealiq, who, it will be recalled, imposed the food taboos on the crew, and who might, although not necessarily, be a shaman. The kaakłiq was, in effect, the owner of special whaling songs which he had acquired by inheritance or purchase. His reputation for these songs was well known and his services were in high demand. An umealiq could hire such a man, supporting him, in effect, and allow him a place in the boat. Several umealit could use the same kaakłiq and pass him from one umiak to another. The harpooner, nawligax, whose position depended on skill rather than on magical abilities, regularly had songs which he sang over his harpoon. When the boat was resting prow forward on the edge of the ice, the harpooner stood by, his harpoons resting on a forked stick in the bow, ready to get into the boat at a moment's notice. When the whale sounded near the boat, as he frequently might in the narrow ice lead, the harpooner leaped into the boat and threw his harpoon at once, freeing the line and letting the floats into the water at once. All the while he might be singing. He had songs for the harpoons, the lances, the lines, and for the floats. Songs were also had by members of the crew, and any man who had a whaling song was free and welcome to sing it. While division of labor in the whaling umiak was pretty much relegated to the umealiq, the harpooner, and the kaakliq, there might also be a man who regularly acted as helmsman and took the stern paddle. Special songs for the position in the helm also applied. The umealiq frequently took the helm himself; he seems never to have been nawligax.

Songs were sung during all stages of the whaling. Murdoch (1892, p. 274) mentions the group of men who sat in a semicircle on the ice and sang in order to effect favorable weather. This was apparently a usual procedure prior to embarking. Songs to open the ice leads, to prevent them from closing, for favorable winds were also known. There were the songs designed to attract the whale. These were sung by whoever owned them. The harpooner usually had songs to keep the whale from spinning or moving away. When the whale was killed, there were songs to keep the floats attached to the whale, and the helmsman generally sang to insure a safe passage back to the ice. When floats were attached to a wounded whale, there were further sets of songs to control the whale. Once the dead whale was brought back to the ice, no further songs were needed; the compelling magic had had its effect.

TAKING THE WHALE

To lend continuity to the account of whaling, some further mention of the methods employed in whaling is in order. Murdoch points out that the opportunities for taking a whale were never fully exploited. Rather than comb the open leads, the whalers lay in wait for whales at the edge of the ice. By so doing, they failed to reach as many whales as they might otherwise have done (Murdoch, 1892, p. 276). The same writer comments on the inadequacies of the whaling gear, pointing out that the harpoons were not so well developed as those for other animals. Murdoch expresses the opinion that since the whale is surrounded by archaic ceremony to a far greater extent than is any other animal, the hunting of it likewise requires weapons of an archaic type (ibid., pp. 243–244). This may be true to a degree, but, on the whole, the methods of whaling appear to have been quite adequate.

The harpoons were the familiar toggle-headed variety, the head fitted to a line and the shaft able to work free. The function of the harpoon was to secure the floats and to bleed the whale. The line permitted the umiak to come in close so that the whale could be lanced. When a boat engaged a whale, the animal was approached as silently as possible. From the prow the harpooner, waiting until the boat was as close to a surfacing whale as could be managed, let his harpoon go, raising it from the wooden, ivory, or bone crotch in which it rested, and throwing with all his strength. He twisted the harpoon slightly so that the head would turn in the body of the animal. As he threw, he sang his songs. Once one line was secured in the whale's body, an attempt was made to secure other lines. The seal floats on each line, usually two or three in number, served to make the wounded whale surface again. When the animal did so, the skill of the crew members and of the helmsman were taxed to the utmost. The umiak had to be maneuvered so that the whale could be approached from the side. It was a dangerous occupation at best and there was little hope of survival should the umiak be capsized. Once the craft was close to the whale, the lance, with its stone or slate head locked into a shaft with a bone wedge, had to be used to advantage. The whale had to be stabbed in some vital organ, preferably the heart or kidneys. The harpooner thrust his lance again and again in the effort to kill the whale. For an average-size whale, one running 30 to 35 tons, and a corresponding number of feet in length, two lines and one lance were regarded as sufficient. The crewmen held the lines and drew the umiak near the whale. When the whale was dead, it tended to turn over and was kept afloat by means of the floats which were fastened to the carcass.

An ideal situation occurred when two boats came together, one on each side of the whale. The seal floats would then be fastened equally and the animal could be lanced from each side. In such cases, each boat claimed half of the whale and each umealiq and harpooner had the right to claim a whale kill. When a boat engaged the whale alone, any boats in the vicinity could come to its assistance. The meat was then divided, although only the first boat had the right to claim the whale.

The principal danger lay in a "spinning" whale. If the quarry fouled up the lines and surfaced under the umiak, tragedy could result for the crew. An attempt was made to gage the behavior of the whale and to predict where it would surface. Skill and experience counted heavily in such cases. There were songs to control the surfacing and sounding of the whale as well. Charms, too, were made for this purpose. Most boats had two pieces of baleen, cut into the shape of whales, hung on either side of the prow. These served to compel the whale to follow an even course.

If a harpoon were not well placed, it could come loose and the backlash of the line could endanger the boat. The songs of the harpooner prevented this. Similarly, his songs over the lance aided in locating a vital spot. Both the umealiq and the harpooner spat into the water when the whale was harpooned so the songs would go down to reach the animal. When the harpooner had laid his first harpoon, he remarked "The whale will come back again," a compelling formula which made the whale surface.

The umiak which took credit for the whale managed the towing back to shore. The umealiq fastened a harpoon to the lip of the whale and the towing lines were strung out from this. Each boat which took part in the killing aided in the towing, contributing floats to keep the carcass buoyant. The procession was led by the boat which took credit for the whale. The carcass was towed to the ice, a place being selected where it could be readily pulled ashore. This meant that the ice had to be firm, or a point chosen where there was solid ground. As soon as the community saw the boats returning, the children spread the news excitedly and the whole village turned out to watch and to aid in getting the whale ashore. As previously stated, a formal notice of the catch, however, had to be given the wife of the umealiq, a runner from the crew being dispatched to tell her that a whale had been taken by her husband's boat. Her activities in respect to greeting the whale then had to begin. The dead whale was hauled up onto the shore or ice, as the case might be, by the combined efforts of the community. Lines were carried to the shore and all present, men, women, and children, exerted themselves to the utmost to pull, in a kind of tug-of-war maneuver, the carcass to the shore. When the whale had been beached, it was at once marked for cutting and division. The ceremonial of greeting the whale went on as well.

GREETING THE WHALE

The function of the wife of the umealiq in creating a mystic bond between the home community and the crew at sea has already been noted. She was seated silently in the house all the time that the crew was out on the ice. She had donned the special clothing that marked her status, she had painted her face with soot and grease in the same manner as the harpooner and her husband (or, according to some, from the corner of the eye to the temple rather than from the mouth to the lobe of the ear), and she had been subject to numerous restrictions. Not only could she not sew, she was also prohibited from entering an ice cellar or, indeed, from stooping when she entered a house. Were she to do so, the whale would be lost under the ice. She could not touch the heads of game once the crew had departed and was obliged to wait until she could touch the head of the captured whale. The soot mixture with which she marked the faces of the harpooner and the umealiq—tuqurmiutaq—she could not wipe off her hands. In summary, the wife of an umealiq lived up to a well-defined role and in this capacity she held an important ceremonial position.

As soon as the dead whale reached the place at which it would be dragged ashore, the umealiq drew out the ravenskin he now had under his parka and placed it on the ice. This was a signal for the runner from the crew, a man especially selected before the expedition began, to start his activity. He had previously cut the tip of the flipper of the whale—the right flipper if only one boat received credit for the capture. The runner then started across the ice toward the village, carrying the flipper tip. He ran as fast as possible, not speaking to anyone on the way, and stopped at last at the house of the umealiq. The community at large, of course, had turned out of their houses and stood watching the towing of the dead whale and speculating as to its size from the flipper part which the runner carried. Once the man reached the umealiq's house, he mounted the roof and waved the flipper tip over the skylight. On seeing this, the wife of the umealiq came out of her house and invited the runner to come in.

The two went into the house together and each ate a piece of the flipper. People peered into the skylight and peeked into the hallway as the two sat eating the raw muktuk. The tremendous curiosity as to the expedition, the adventure of the hunt, and the size of the whale had to remain unsatisfied until later. The runner, having eaten with the umealiq's wife, broke his silence to remark, "Let us go." The woman took down the wooden vessel and, carrying it, followed the runner out of the house. The two went back to the sea, followed by the joyous crowd of villagers. When the group arrived at the place selected for butchering, they pulled the whale ashore.

As soon as this was completed, the solemn moment had arrived when a formal greeting had to be bestowed on the whale. The wife of the umealiq took back from her husband her left mitten and her belt. Using an ax or a long-handled ulu, she began to cut off the snout of the whale. She made her cuts so as to include the snout, the eyes, and the blowhole. As soon as she had severed this section from the carcass, with the help of the crew, the crew stood it upright on the ice, the snout pointing upward. The umealiq's wife next took the wooden vessel which she had brought with her, and, taking a seal flipper pouch from under her parka, she poured fresh water into the vessel. She poured this water first on the snout itself, then on the blowhole of the whale, remarking as she did so, "It is good that you are come to us." Now the umealiq himself came forward. Taking the vessel from his wife, he also poured fresh water on the snout of the whale, remarking as he poured, "Here is water; you will want to drink. Next spring come back to our boat." The wives of members of the crew then came forward and thanked the whale for allowing himself to be taken, saying "kuyanaq" (Thanks!). The umealiq now addressed the whale further, likewise offering a word of thanks, and concluded by saying, "It is good that you have wished to come and live with us."

The whale, having now been made a member of the community, was ready for butchering. Everyone present, which unquestionably meant every person in the community, began to cut away at the muktuk, the black skin which was so highly prized a delicacy. As soon as they had taken as much as their containers would hold, they left to store their share. This was an informal arrangement by which everyone in the village received some meat, indeed, as much as he could carry himself—no dogs were allowed on the ice at this time. This reflected the generosity of the crew and the umealiq. The actual division of the meat was a crew matter and was worked out between the crews of the boats which assisted. The people who had helped themselves to the meat were careful not to touch the flippers of the whale. These, together with the heart, constituted the preferred parts of the whale and fell to the boatowner as his share. They were removed first, together with the skin and the flesh under and behind the flipper. After this, the division between members of the crew of the boat credited with the whale took place followed by a division for the crews of boats which assisted. If two boats were directly involved in the kill, each umealiq received one flipper. The ranking captain, however, he of the greatest prestige and wealth, received the bladder of the whale. This he kept as an amulet in his house. It was dried and shredded and hung up in the main room of the house. Similarly, the small digital bone at the end of the whale flipper was reserved for use as a whaling charm.

The captured whale was umeaktuat, that is, game divided between participating crew members. In the main, division was no problem, and theoretically, at least, it was so worked out as to insure each man a suitable share. Trouble, if it arose, came as the result of divisions between crews, one umealiq taking the view that his crew had had a greater part in the capture than the first boat would admit. Moreover, some crew members would claim special shares, and their insistence might lead to dispute and occasionally to bloodshed and murder. An umealiq of stature, although he carried no formal authority, could halt such disputes simply by the force of his personality. A general practice in the division of meat was to butcher the whale, set aside the meat by boats, and allow the boat crews themselves to make the division. Each crew member received muktuk, meat, sections of the internal organs, bone, and baleen. When baleen carried a price, it was more carefully divided.

After the whale was divided, the crew might leave for another hunt, especially if whales were still in the offing and the leads were still open. The hunting season lasted anywhere from 2 weeks to 2 months, although a 2-month season was rare. The actual length of the season depended on the stability of the winds which permitted the ice leads to remain open. If the winds drove the ice inshore, the leads would close and the whaling season would be regarded as over. If a crew left again after the butchering, the umealiq's wife accompanied them as before, then returned to the inactivity of the house. Other women would see to her share and its disposal.

Once a whale was taken, the community became a beehive of activity. Remembering that a single whale represented literally tons of meat, it follows that the community was engaged in bringing the meat to the ice cellars, cutting it, distributing it, and eating it. In the houses, women were cooking; tremendous quantities were eaten. Sleds were taken down to the butchering site and the meat was loaded and dragged back to the houses. Dogs could be used for this purpose, although there seems to have been some feeling against allowing dogs on the ice during whaling. If the butchering took place on shore, this attitude seems not to have prevailed. An "old-fashioned" view, it is said, was that dogs should not eat whale or lick the blood on the ice. Ashore, they could be fed the viscera.

With each whale taken, the same procedure of greeting and distribution was followed. At last, however, the leads closed and the hunting was regarded as over. The crew returned to the home village in triumph if they had taken a whale, but wholly dejected if they had failed.

A successful captain was now in the position of having to feast the community. He had allowed the members of the community to help themselves to muktuk when the whale was first brought ashore, but now his position demanded that he extend himself and that he give food to all. This was cooked food and the women of his household were kept busy boiling it in great quantity. The men assembled in the kariyit and the women brought them cooked whale meat. The women themselves ate in their own homes. There was interhouse visiting, but the pattern of dining together out of the context of the karigi had not developed. To some degree, the social conventions were dispensed with in that people could freely enter the house of the successful umealiq, obtain food, and go away again. Such visits were specifically to ask for, and receive, cooked pieces of the flipper muktuk, the choice parts of the whale, which were the captain's share.

The successful umealiq paid off his obligations when he had taken a whale. Indeed, having feasted the community and seen that his crew was properly provided with meat, there was little left for the umealiq himself. His wealth began to increase only when he took a second whale. He had obligations to those who had been of assistance in any aspect of the preparation for whaling. These included any aŋatqut who may have helped with magic and songs, the kaakłiq, the artisans who made such items as the special mittens, the pot, or the like. The amount of wealth needed to meet these expenses was considerable and the umealiq might be forced to fall back on the continued support of his immediate kindred, particularly if he had taken only one whale.

Following the distribution of the meat, the crew returned to the karigi for additional social events.

CLOSE OF THE WHALING SEASON

Whaling was formally terminated with a spring festival, marked by gorging of food and numerous social events. When a whale was taken, the crew members might meet in the karigi briefly before setting out again, holding a brief social dance in which the taking of the whale was dramatized and the situation recreated. But since the duration of the open offshore leads was hardly predictable, a crew went out again and again, bringing back as many whales as possible, or at least taking a part in their capture. As long as the whales were coming in and the butchering was in progress, people in the village were busy in getting the meat cut and stored. The impression is gained that people ate, slept in snatches, and worked extremely hard setting the meat in order. At last, however, the leads broke and the season for whaling was formally declared over.

The tons of meat were placed in the ice cellars and frozen. The formal close of the whaling season was marked by two final patterns which tended to reflect social rather than religious usage. The whales had been greeted, the proper magic had insured the success of the venture, and the ritual aspects had thus been properly discharged. The first social event was a series of dances which involved the entire community. The principals were the crewmen who had been successful; the remainder of the village merely stood by, observed the festivities, and were fed at the expense of the successful crew. Members of the crew each contributed portions of whale meat, removing it in a now frozen state from their ice cellars, and piling it up in the karigi. The men in the crew put on clothes with the fur outside and donned dance masks and gorgets. The masks, made of wood, were small, just fitting over the face, and they were kept in the karigi except for this occasion. The men put up their parka hoods when they danced, first in the karigi itself, then through the town. From the karigi, they went from house to house, engaging in a stomp dance with no musical accompaniment.

The children in each household were told to sit in the hallway. The masked figures with their shaggy parkas went into each house as far as the center of the hallway. The harpooner came first, and the umealiq followed in the rear. The first man to come into the hallway blew to make a whistling sound. The children were, of course, terrified. One informant recalls that as a child he rushed screaming up through the kataq into the house and took refuge under his grandmother's parka when the apparitions appeared. When the crew were assembled in the hallway, the harpooner went to the kataq, thrust his head up into the house and asked for some moss to use as a lampwick. This was given to him by the people in the house and he placed it in a bag he carried at his side. The dancers then left. Next they circled the house and called through the skylight, inviting those present to a dance and feast of whale meat. The masked dancers were called axrelliktuat.

One might look here for elements suggestive of a secret society, made up perhaps of the members of a whaling crew or karigi. This aspect has been subjected to comment by some students of the

Alaskan Eskimo, but nowhere is the evidence clear (cf. Birket-Smith, 1953; Nelson, 1899; Lantis, 1947). The use of masks, the frightening of children, the suggestions of impersonation, and the use of special costumes would suggest that the crew, acting in this instance as a unit, had certain secret activities. This is borne out further by the fact that women were excluded from the karigi when the men were donning their masks and engaging in the initial dancing there. If such a secret association existed, it is only in respect to the axrelliktuat that it can be supposed. There was clearly no idea, however, that the identity of the dancers should remain unknown to the community. Moreover, once the invitation to the karigi feasting had been given, the people left their houses and came to the festival at once. When the dancers returned, they took off their masks and joined in the feast.

The meat contributed by each member of the crew was placed in the karigi and allowed to thaw. Only when it was thawed would the dance begin and the masked figures extend their invitations. While the meat was thawing in the karigi, young men associated with it by ties of kinship were asked to come to supervise it. They slept in the karigi, keeping the temperature up with lamps the trimming of which was their assigned duty. They remained at this task until the dance began, often engaging in a good deal of horseplay, pushing the meat into each other's faces and smearing each other with blubber. The umealiq of the crew giving the feast was also on hand. If the rough play between the boys got out of hand and tempers flared, he would urge them to quiet down and keep peace.

The dance and feast were social and involved a great deal of fun and play. The people in the community gorged themselves on the whale meat and muktuk, pausing to sing and dance. On the whole, the ceremonial aspects had been put aside, although food was offered to the charms in the karigi and the whalers would occasionally make such pious ejaculations as "Let us get another whale like this one."

The communities of Point Barrow, nuwuk and utkeaaγvik, although they stressed the spring whaling season, also put out boats in the fall. There is a suggestion that tikeraaq, long ago, did the same (Rainey, 1947, p. 263). At this time the boats went out on the open sea and whaling was somewhat more difficult because of the immense distances which had to be traversed out to the pack ice many miles offshore. Preparations for the fall whaling were not so ceremonially marked as they were in the spring. Indeed, the same restrictions as, for example, those imposed on the wife of the umealiq, did not apply. A whale which was taken on the open sea was towed back and the same process of greeting was involved, and the ceremonial charms and songs were also necessary. After the fall whaling, assuming that it had been successful, the dance and feast described above, the axrelliktuat, was held. There was, however, no nalukataq, this being the specific spring festival.

NALUKATAQ

Feasting in the manner described went on for several days, especially if several crews had taken whales. When all had eaten their fill, preparations were made for the outdoor feast of nalukataq. The men from each karigi met on the beaches and prepared for games and contests. There was usually a series of activities, beginning with competitive games and culminating in the blanket-toss, the nalukataq itself.

In the spring festival the functioning unit ceased to be the crew by itself and became the karigi, the crews in each karigi coming together to carry on the festival. Each karigi had its special place where it held its activities. This was the mannixsak, an open place located by traditional usage. At the village of utkeaaγvik these were in the neighborhood of the kariyit themselves, although at tikeraaq they were located down the spit from the village. The members of the karigi met in that building after the last of the boats had returned from the whaling and after the distribution of the meat and the axrelliktuat. It is worth noting that if a crew were to return well in advance of the others, the men did not usually go to the karigi but waited until all of the karigi membership was assembled. The place where they waited was a small karigilike structure, a tent which was placed at the mannixsak. This was called the ukuutak. Here members of returned crews sat until all the other crews had returned and had finished their tasks.

The first day of nalukataq was marked by contests and games of various kinds. The members of the karigi met in their building and started festivities by a foot race to the mannixsak. When they were all assembled at this site, the umealit of the karigi ordered their umiaks brought. These were set up on edge to form a windbreak, the whaling paddles being used to prop them. On his umiak, each umealiq placed his ravenskin as a kind of banner. Flags, designed for this purpose by the boatowner, are used in this connection today. No substantiation was found for Rainey's statement that the arrangement of umiaks depended on the type of charm owned by the umealit. (Rainey, 1947, p. 262). The umealit in a karigi also set up the tripods for the blanket-toss. These were whale ribs set up as tripods in the mannixsak. Four were set up.

When these preparations were completed, the men from one karigi came over to the place of the other. They began by initiating contests and games. Contests of strength, such as lifting weights, feats of endurance, and wrestling, marked the first stages of the festival.

The karigi games of the winter season were repeated at this time. They culminated in the foot races between members of the different kariyit, each karigi selecting its best runners as its representatives in this. The latter part of the day was given over to kick-ball (ayuktaaktuat, also axerawraaktuat), the favorite group game, which was so avidly played.

In the evening, the umealit gathered before the assembled community and gave away muktuk. There were slight differences in the way this was done as between the peoples of Point Hope and Point Barrow. In the latter area, the umealiq did this merely as gift giving, having previously paid the people to whom he owed favors. At Point Hope, however, it took place on the second day after whaling and was a means by which the debts of the umealiq were paid. In general, the pattern was the same. It was a means by which the umealiq emphasized his position in the community and stressed his characteristics of generosity and openhandedness. Similarly, at Point Hope the emphasis on mourning, by offering meat at the places on the tundra where the bodies of the recently dead lay covered with snow blocks, was not practiced at Point Barrow.

The nalukataq feasting went into the second day much in the same way. There were again games, tugs-of-war and the kick-ball. The feast culminated in the blanket-toss on the third or fourth day, the length of the festival depending on community whim and on any other economic demands which might be made. If only one or two whales had been taken by the villagers, the festivities were cut short. If many were taken, a separate nalukataq could be held for each whale. Properly, all contests and participation in them were limited to the crew members who had been successful.

The blanket-toss took place at the mannixsak. The four tripods came into use at this time. Walrus-hide lines were strung between them and a blanket of walrus hide was placed over them. The crew first tossed the captain in the blanket and others followed in turn. The idea was to stand erect and maintain balance while being tossed. It was a very funny occasion when a person who was being tossed went head over heels in the blanket. The crew, holding the edges of the blanket and the ropes, would toss all the harder in order to make the person in the blanket fall. A skilled man or woman could easily stand upright and then the attempt was made to be tossed higher and higher (pl. 6, *b*).

People were tossed in order of rank. First came the umealiq of a successful crew. His crew said, "Come, aarviγil^{y}iq," the term meaning "owner of the whale," applying to the umealiq and to the members of his family. The term is still used in this connection. The harpooner was the next one tossed, then the umealiq's wife. Finally, each of the crew members took his turn. After this, any person who wished to try was free to do so and the tossing continued for some time. The community gathered around and joked, laughing and commenting on those being tossed.

The nalukataq, with its distribution of food, its feasting, and its merrymaking, can be seen as primarily a social occasion. The supernatural begins to fall away when the whale was greeted and when the meat, cut and distributed, was stored in the cellars. Actually, the tenor of the supernatural still remained. It was held that the merrymaking was for the benefit of the whale, "to let the whale know we are happy." In a sense, too, it was a victory celebration.

In the final analysis, it can readily be seen that the same general attitudes applied to the whale as they did to other animals. There was the concept that the whale allowed itself to be taken, had to be placated with proper treatment and the right kinds of avoidances, and had to be invited to return. Since the whale was so vital to the food supply, it is hardly surprising that the basic concepts of religion and ritual should be magnified and elaborated when the whale was encountered. Shamanism did not play a part in the cult of the whale, except in so far as every man was a shaman, knowing certain songs to compel a desired result. If an umealiq used an aŋatquq, it was because the latter had special whale magic, weather controls, or the like. Unless a shaman went as kaakłiq, he went as a member of the crew or other actor. In such cases, he was a crew member not because he was a shaman but rather because of his demonstrated skill as a whaler. It is said again, of course, that the shamans "hated" a successful whaler and attempted to make trouble for him.

In respect to the problem of envy and jealousy toward the successful whaling captain, there were ways in which such hostile attitudes could be channeled. His enemy could cut off the very tip of the snout of the whale taken by the umealiq and a tiny piece from the tips of the flukes. If these were hidden away, the crew of this captain would never take another whale. Lack of whaling success might inspire the umealiq to seek out the services of a shaman who could discover the missing parts. To prevent such sorcery, many umealit took these parts off the whale and hid them away. An unusual case of envy is worth noting. There was a man at utkeaaγvik, himself a successful whaler as attested by his tattoo marks and the stitches in his boots. When other umealit got whales, he became furious and came down to the ice, stamping his feet in rage. He ignored his rivals for a time and would not speak to them. Such behavior was regarded as sufficiently unusual as to be quite amusing.

The historical relations of the cult of the whale have been treated at some length in studies by others (cf. Lantis, 1938, 1947, etc.). There are numerous elements in the North Alaskan whale cult which justify comparison with other areas, particularly those of Alaska. The place of the karigi in North Alaska affords one such example and it would clearly be of value to trace the relationships of this structure somewhat more fully, especially when its somewhat attenuated nature in the Barrow area is considered. In the main, however, the various elements, the boat launching, the attention to the bladder of the whale, whaling songs and charms, and the like suggest the whale ceremonialism farther to the south. The emphasis on whaling among the coastal peoples places this institution at the keystone of the ceremonial activities.

THE CULT OF THE CARIBOU

In the attitudes which the various groups of nuunamiut expressed toward the caribou, some of the same practices and concepts arise as were applicable to the whale on the coast. On the whole, however, the caribou cult was not so elaborately developed. Many of the practices described for the individual hunting of these animals were projected to the group and continued to apply in a somewhat more elaborated and communal way. The nuunamiut shared essentially the same philosophy regarding the caribou and all animals as did the tareumiut. There was the notion that the animals allowed themselves to be killed and that great care must be taken not to offend them.

Caribou hunting, with its corrals and its drives, took place seasonally when done on a communal basis. Just as on the coasts the activities led to whaling in the spring, so also among the peoples of the inland, attention was directed to the preparation for the caribou hunts at this season. The term "umealiq," referring to the boatowner and commander of a crew, was also used by the nuunamiut. Similarly, there were kariyit and the crew-karigi association arose. On the whole, these concepts were not nearly so well elaborated. The inland sections, bands, or simply, nuclear family groups were not so well tied to the community or to the consciousness of community as were the coastal groups. The somewhat ephemeral nature of the sections and the fact that people north of the Brooks Range could move over the whole Colville Valley and frequently did so, did not create the same degree of structural stability as in the maritime situation. This is not to imply that crew and karigi were not significant units. The umealit were the men who organized the hunt, who set up the in^{y}uksut, and who, by virtue of their abilities and kills, not to mention generosity, were able to attract men to themselves and thus to build up the integrated hunting group. As on the coast, this group cut across family lines and so represented a primary nonkin association. But in ritual there was not the same high degree of specialization, any more than there were specialties in respect to hunting tasks. There was no one to assume the role of the harpooner, for example, nor were the activities of the wife of the umealiq so circumscribed with ritual.

Because the site for settlements varied with each group, the members of the various nuunamiut sections came into contact with the others in the same grouping with only random regularity. The decision to do so was up to the heads of nuclear families, the hunters who were elected to engage in one or another activity. If there were an agreed-upon campsite, several families might congregate, especially if there were a man known for his skill in managing the communal hunt. The men thus became members of his group and a pattern was evolved analogous to that on the coasts.

The groups came together after the fall hunting and fishing and there were occasions when many wintered together. Certain sites, such as piŋalu on the Noatak River, tivłu on the Tivłik River, and places above Hotham Inlet and the mouth of the Noatak were points of winter congregation. Another such site was at kigalik on the Ikpikpuk River. Here fairly large assemblages might meet. The activities of the winter at such locations followed the patterns which applied on the coasts. There were many recreational aspects and amusements, and ceremonialism at this period was much tied up with shamanism. Fall and early spring caribou drives necessitated that the people be ready to move at any time and fairly quickly. While this to some extent interfered with any elaboration of caribou ceremonial, the proper rites were carried on in the late winter, just before the early spring hunts. The patterns of ritual behavior associated with the main caribou drive differed in degree rather than in kind from the whaling ceremonials. For this reason, a brief listing of the elements making up the caribou cult are in order.

Although there were sometimes large assemblages of people along the foothill areas through which the caribou came, the few towns noted above offering a case in point, the hunting groups were forced to split off so as to control as many animals as possible during the migrations. At the hunting camp, there was generally erected a temporary karigi, the base of ceremonial activity. Each hunting group—a term probably preferable in this instance to the maritime "crew"—had its shaman who functioned to call the caribou. The men who organized the hunting group—one or several, hence, the umealit—paid the shaman for this service. Taboos operated, both in respect to the members of the hunting group itself and to the community at large. These applied before, during, and after the hunt. There were charms and songs. The former were not associated with the karigi but were always individual property, efficacious for the caribou. Lastly there were the ceremonies of greeting the caribou and of finishing off the hunt.

The ritual role was assumed by the shamans, not by the umealit. Throughout the winter, besides their other activities, the shamans had sung the songs to call the caribou. While this went on, the shaman might also walk about searching for caribou tracks and droppings. If he found them, he could sing over them, thereby compelling the caribou to come. The men sat solemnly by while such singing was in progress although they might also sing. If one man owned special songs for the calling of the caribou, he was free to sing them.

When the hunting groups broke away from the main assemblage, they turned to the hunting grounds where the umealit had their permanent corrals. At the campsite, they built a temporary karigi, each man contributing skins for its construction. It was large enough to accommodate the men of one or two hunting groups and their leaders. The ritual of the inland karigi involved first a 4-day period of continence. The men who were to hunt left their tents to sleep in the karigi, not leaving it for this period. Their wives brought them food. They were to think of caribou during this period and to avoid sexual intercourse, this being offensive to the caribou. The shaman, one at least being found in each hunting group, sang his songs and drummed. On the fourth day, the men departed for the hunt. The departure was usually so timed as to coincide with the arrival of the herds; scouts might be sent out to watch at the points where the caribou customarily came through. In the karigi, the men of the hunting party had assembled their weapons, the light lances with which the caribou were speared either in the water or in corrals, the lines which were to be strung up on which the caribou might entangle their horns, while kayaks, if these were needed, were placed on racks outside the karigi. All such implements and materials were sung over.

The people in the community who were not directly involved in the hunt, women and children, sat quietly in their tents or shelters. The women did some cooking inside the dwellings and brought the food to the men. Children were cautioned against making unnecessary noise lest the caribou hear it from afar. There could be no sewing, no making of cordage, no cutting of meat with a knife, lest the caribou escape. Lieutenant Stoney, visiting in the area in 1883–86, comments on his annoyance at being unable to cut meat with a knife and being forced to use a saw (Stoney, 1900, p. 38). Although the restrictions applied for 4 days in theory, actually the period of inactivity might last somewhat longer. This was because the group might wait until the herds had passed by to the north. When the last stragglers had passed, the hunters might follow them, occasionally circling ahead to effect a corral or water drive and then following again.

The men at the late-winter or early-spring hunt wore new clothes. The weapons were washed and scraped. The kayaks, if such were used, were not given a new cover, nor were umiaks, if it was possible to use them. The new clothing was of caribou skins.

An umealiq of some stature might own a corral, or at least, have a recognized place where he erected one. When the division of meat after the hunt took place, a portion was given to the corral itself. This meant that the corral required the placing of the in^{y}uksut, the posts, piles of brush, or scarecrows which stretched out in a fanwise direction from the impound. When these were put up, before the hunt, if the route were predictable, the same corral being used over and over again, or at especially selected places when the migration varied, there were special sets of songs which were sung with the placing of each.

The hunt itself, involving as it did the wholesale slaughter of caribou, went on for as long as contact could be maintained with the herds. The carcasses were piled up where they were taken. Practices in respect to the treatment of the carcasses varied somewhat from group to group. If sled packing were necessary, some groups bent the heads upward and allowed them to freeze in this position. Some of the groups, however, insisted that the heads had to be cut off the body. This was generally done only at the communal hunt. The men and women who had followed them cut off the heads as soon as possible, placing them as a pile apart from the carcasses. If this were not done at this time, it was said, the caribou would suffer. Actually, when the heads were severed, a formula was repeated. The cutter said "Come back to us again." Formal greeting followed this pattern.

Division of the meat followed the usual pattern of umeaktuat. Each member of the hunting party received a share of the meat, including viscera, marrow bones, hides, and meat for drying. The prized back fat as well as the marrow bones could be given in larger proportion to the umealiq. He, however, received no special share or part, except as his wealth and prestige demanded; it was not in the main a ceremonial division.

After the division, the meat was stripped for drying, the leg bones cracked for marrow, and the hides packed for trading. There were social festivities in which some ceremonial took place. The first meat eaten from the newly hunted herd was cooked in a pottery vessel outdoors. It was passed into the karigi through the skylight.

Social occasions after the hunt might mean the return of the hunting party to the main assemblage. The entire section could meet at any point agreed upon. Here each party reviewed the hunt, cached the meat taken, and might engage in various forms of exchange, suggestive of the Messenger Feast. The leaders of the hunting parties, as umealit, might feast each other. There were the usual games and amusements, and occasionally the blanket-toss although this was not a special feature of the caribou hunting and had probably been derived from the coast. After such festivals, at which much meat was eaten, distributed, and displayed, the umealit gave gifts to the men who had served with them. Also, obligations had to be paid off to the shamans who had sung for the caribou. A final ceremony was the thanking of the caribou. The heads were addressed by the leaders and the shamans, and a message of thanks as well as an invitation to return were given.

In short, although the patterns characteristic of the treatment of the whale on the coasts are in some measure repeated in these ceremonials, the caribou drives and their associated ritual were by no means so elaborated. The fact that the caribou migrations were so variable, that several might take place in a season, especially if the herds broke and moved as smaller groups, meant that the seasonal nature of the migrations was scarcely so predictable as was the advent of the whales to the coasts. Moreover, the caribou movements determined the ways in which the people would assemble. This placed ceremonial on an individual level and it was up to the family head to refrain from offending the caribou, to see that the proper rituals were carried on. If a larger aggregation of people were possible, as at the campsites mentioned, there was more latitude for ceremonialism associated with the caribou. On the whole, however, the nature of the hunting prevented the growth of the elaborate patterns which the maritime Eskimo displayed.

CULTURE CHANGE

The present section concerns itself with the problems of social change that the North Alaskan Eskimo have undergone since the initial contact with Europeans. Of necessity the bulk of the data which follow is drawn from the community of Barrow where some unusual changes have taken place as a result of the naval installation and the increasing influx of money into the community. In other towns, acculturation has perhaps been more gradual, although the influences from the United States Office of Indian Affairs, in the form of education, grants to the indigent, old-age assistance, and the like, have promoted changes as well. On the religious side, the people have been subjected to a fairly intense campaign of missionization, with the result that the older religious patterns, in their formalized structure, at least, have fallen by the way. Actual social change has affected three areas: (1) material culture; (2) economic organization; and (3) religious organization. Despite evident concern on the part of the Alaska Native Service over the economic situation, and the fear that social changes as, for example, in family structure, might occur, there is clearly no evidence that this is taking place or will take place. The aboriginal family is still the basic unit of society and it has successfully resisted any inroads; it remains the superbly functioning unit of cooperation that it has ever been.

At the present writing, the United States Navy has closed its petroleum operations in the Barrow and Umiat areas. This has caused unemployment and the withdrawal of the money which the Barrow Eskimo had been making. But since the men who had been employed by the Navy had been spending much of their money on meat, purchased from those who continued to hunt, thus resulting in the distribution of money through the community, the problem which arises is not wholly serious. Neither the hunting skills nor the basic integrative force of society—the family system—has been lost. Luxury products may, it is true, have to be forfeited, but even though there may be some hardship, the continuing moral and social stability prevent disorganization, both of the social groupings and of the individual. And this is the point which is so frequently forgotten by those who deplore what they choose to call the "exploitation" of the Eskimo. This writer finds no cause for concern; the society is stable, the people are adjusted to it and happy in it.

In the process of acculturation, it must not be forgotten that there are still remnants of nuunamiut and that the maritime-nomadic ecological division still persists. The Killik band, those in the area of Anaktuvuk Pass, are still present, much to the concern of the Alaska Native Service, since no health or educational facilities can be provided them. This group is closer to the aboriginal life, being wholly dependent on hunting, and receiving little by way of luxury goods from the outside. Sources of money to this group are quite limited, being dependent on wolf bounty or old-age assistance.

As between the two ecological types, the former intercourse is gone. Partnerships have broken down since the supplies of textiles rather than caribou skins relieve the necessity for trade. This places the remaining nuunamiut in a dilemma inasmuch as they do not get their complement of oil and blubber which was formerly available to them by trade. One result of this has been to decimate the inland population, most of whom have moved to the coasts. The remaining groups are two—those in the Kobuk Valley, whose maritime orientation was toward Kotzebue and Hotham Inlet and hence away from the North Alaskan coasts, and those in the Killik-Anaktuvuk area. Of the latter, no more than 60 people, in 5 families, remain. Factors of interest in inland hunting, familiarity with the local terrain, and continuing family ties appear to be operative in keeping these groups intact.

Returning to the coastal areas, while it is true that the greatest degree of acculturation has occurred at Barrow, other settlements have likewise been drawn through changing patterns of culture (pl. 2, *b*, *c*). The four settlements, Barrow itself, Wainwright, Point Lay, and Point Hope, still constitute the basic centers of whaling interest, although Point Lay is less favorably situated for whaling and more inclined to take advantage of the caribou hunting along the watercourses. It must not be forgotten that acculturation began long ago, and, indeed, it may be said to have started with the introduction of tobacco, metal articles, and other European items derived indirectly from the Russians. Thomas Simpson and others refer to the trade of the early 19th century, and erroneously thought of the nuunamiut as the Russians themselves (T. Simpson, 1843; J. Simpson, 1855; Stefansson, 1914 a, etc.). It seems evident that the inland people, trading along the rivers with those of the coasts, brought trade items of European origin to the Arctic coasts, having obtained them at the great center at Hotham Inlet. Such items arrived here from the coasts farther to the south, the people of Cape Prince of Wales evidently being early middlemen.

Shortly after Beechey's voyage, this trade began to intensify, with the result that material changes took place on a far wider scale.

J. Simpson, at Point Barrow, mentions guns, and it was not long after the 1850's that the Eskimo of the coasts adopted the European whaling gear, with darting guns and bombs. At the time of the visit of Murdoch and Ray, such items were already in extensive use. Introduction of material elements, not excluding tobacco and trade beads, began to accelerate through the late 19th century, and with the introduction of the schools and the churches, and with the increasing contacts, material development began to change rapidly. Not the least of these features were the patterns surrounding the introduction of domesticated reindeer, and even of new methods of dog traction. Granted that material culture changed, the impact of such contacts on the social institutions was less pronounced. As has been pointed out, religion became modified, perhaps less because of the appeal of Christianity and the success of the individual missionaries, than because shamanism as a source of anxiety and threat was proscribed.

In summary, social changes took place and are continuing to do so. As long as the family system remains intact, however, the future remains a bright one. It may be well to summarize the developments of the impact of Europeanization on the culture of the area and to consider principally the economic and religious changes that were effected. For such a summary, Barrow may be used as a primary example, although with the exception of the naval activities, the other towns felt an essentially similar impact. At that, however, the naval personnel recruitment drew in families from any of the communities, including those inland.

SOURCES OF MONEY (1888–1948)

Money, as such, was introduced into the Barrow community sometime after the establishment of the various trading posts and whaling stations. The whalers and traders of the late nineteenth and early twentieth centuries paid those working for them in goods. It was actually not until the development of Alaska Native Service interest and the rise of the great market for fox furs that money came into the Barrow community to any extent.

This community appears to have reached a peak of whaling activity around 1900. At this time the population of the village was fairly large and most men were either directly or indirectly associated with the whaling industry. Capt. Charles D. Brower devoted much time during this period toward encouraging a beginning in salable native crafts. He was not entirely successful in doing so, a possible reflection of the lack of interest on the part of the North Alaska Eskimo in native arts. After 1905, he urged the making of baleen basketry, which, while not an aboriginal art, was nevertheless suited to the transfer of techniques from the earlier baleen netting. The latter skill was at the time almost gone, only a few older men having knowledge of it. Under Brower's influence, basketry of this type was made by a few individuals. Later, with A. N. S. interest, it was exported for sale.

It was only in a period of depression, however, that such native crafts began to take hold. Baleen was selling well until 1915–16. At this time, the market fell off, baleen dropped to $1 per pound, then to 50 and 25 cents. With the demand gone, the community appears to have been hard hit on the luxury side, inasmuch as trade goods could no longer be obtained.

Beginning with the end of World War I, however, a new economic activity was discovered. This took the form of the sale of foxskins and for the next 12 or 13 years the community wealth, in terms of money, increased. The price of furs went up beginning by 1920, and for the next decade much activity was devoted to fur trapping. This, in turn, was paralleled by an increase in the reindeer industry. White fox furs during the decade of the 20's went for $50; a blue fox went for considerably more, as much as $100 being paid for a single pelt. The writer has been told by one successful fox hunter that he earned $8,000 in 1927, as compared with his present Arcon salary of $5,000. Such earnings were apparently not unusual. It was at this time that larger boats were introduced into the community, paid for by the residents themselves, and that the native stores had their beginnings.

The failure of the fur market may probably be attributed to the 1929 depression, although some Barrow residents deny this, claiming that the recognition of the Union of Soviet Socialist Republics in 1933 created a new competitive situation and that the import of Siberian furs ruined the local market. Be this as it may, the Barrow furs were no longer in demand after 1931; the market had slipped considerably, driving the price down to $5 or less a pelt.

After 1930, many former fur trappers turned to other activities. Money now became short, and the residents of the village were driven back to the land. A few continued to trap and to earn a modest living from it, but most were obliged to return to the basic dependence on sea mammals and to "live off the land."

It was in this period, 1930–46, that one may note the carryover of the aboriginal patterns of cooperation and interpersonal dependence. More so than in a time of prosperity, the community sense of in-group consciousness appears to have developed. Those who did engage in hunting were obliged by custom to share their catch—seal, walrus, caribou, or any other game—with the less fortunate members of the community. But while this factor of sharing operated between nonkin, the economic circumstances of the period furthered the aboriginal family system as a cooperative institution.

Families worked together and extended their joint efforts to the benefit of the community at large. The return to the aboriginal social patterns at a time of economic stress appears to have lent to the family system a force which it still possesses. As may be seen, however, the cooperative arrangement between nonkin in the community tends to break down with the addition of new wealth.

In the 30's and early 40's, however, a marked sense of community solidarity comes to the fore. The reduced economic circumstances of the period created a dependence on driftwood for fuel, and a return, in some instances, to the use of blubber as a heating and lighting agent. Unsuccessful hunters or family heads less skilled at hunting would gather driftwood to exchange with the more successful for food. Little help appears to have come from outside during this period. The A. N. S. aided to some extent, but the church appears to have taken a more dominant role. One outgrowth of the reduced economy was the organization of the community council, a body which continues to operate and to work in concert with the native service administration. The church and council cooperated in the regulation of community affairs. As it was, however, the individual families, working individually and cooperatively in the community, served as the basic front against the inroads of economic depression.

The picture of the Barrow community during the period in question is not too greatly different from that of the Eskimo of precontact days. True, as the result of the introduction of Euro-American commodities and trade goods, certain hardships were faced by those who had become used to innovation as the result of the introduction of money. In itself, however, as regards both survival and an adjusted community, this was not serious. The integrating effect of the social institutions serves to promote a balance between individuals. The Barrow Eskimo have not yet come so far as to have lost touch with their strongly unifying social institutions.

It was into this setting of economic depression that the Naval Petroleum Base IV was introduced. While the survey and explorations for petroleum which began in 1944 are so well documented as to require no elaboration here, it may suffice to point up some of the features of the employment of Barrow residents by both the United States Navy and later by the Arctic Contractors. The possibilities of Eskimo labor at the Pet IV Base were considered in 1946. There was no question as to the desirability of obtaining Eskimo labor, but the factor of the health problem was seriously to be considered. The high rate of tuberculosis among the residents of the Barrow community created several serious administrative questions. There was no question that the inhabitants of Barrow would be able to assume tasks requiring a high degree of manual skill. This was proved by the fact that such organizations as did operate at Barrow and which did hire native labor had obtained markedly satisfactory results. The manual skill and dexterity of the Eskimo are too well known to require further comment here and the Eskimo, as an ethnic group, have been able to transfer skills drawn from the aboriginal setting to modern technology with ease. Many Barrow residents had gone southward to Fairbanks and other points during the war years and had learned various skilled trades, while the few jobs that did exist at Barrow, such as with the Native Service School and Hospital, the Wien Airlines, Alaska Communication System, and the like were successfully held by native laborers. The community council did appeal to Arcon for employment. With A. N. S. selection and aid, Barrow residents were chosen to work at the naval installation, were examined for tuberculosis, and hired.

Commander Roberts, late of the Barrow area, comments that 35 Eskimo were at first taken on as laborers in July 1946 (Roberts, 1952). Later this number was increased to 80, among whom were several women, employed as seamstresses. From 1946 to 1952, the number of Eskimo employed at the Pet IV Base has averaged between 75 and 80, the work being in large measure seasonal and with seasonal layoffs. The health problem, sanitation, and the like have been considered by the naval and Arctic Contractors officials, and attempts have been made to remedy the situation from time to time. The fact that the Eskimo, not only those from Barrow, but those who have come from other settlements, such as Wainwright, Point Lay, etc., to take advantage of the employment opportunities, are paid at the prevailing Alaska wage indicates that a new source for money has been found. The dissemination of cash throughout the Barrow community has made for a series of recent changes in material adjustment. It has meant that a situation comparable to that enjoyed by the community during the fur boom has been recreated.

The fact that the Barrow residents are employed at the naval installation work mostly a 63-hour week, with time and one-half for overtime over 40 hours, and that they are paid standard skilled and semiskilled wages, accounts for the rise of a new cash economy. This is correlated with the decline in the native arts and crafts and the development of new services, such as the motion-picture theaters, the coffee shops, stores, and other luxuries. Since the community has a population of 1,050 and since as much as one-tenth of this population is employed for at least part of the year, the force of the new economy is at once apparent. Virtually every family profits either directly or because of the dissemination of cash by wage-earning residents.

It is just this point which has caused so many well-meaning individuals and organizations such concern. The largely experimental nature of the petroleum installation implies that it cannot exist permanently and it may at some time be deemed expedient to curtail operations. When this happens, or, indeed, if it happens, it is felt that a high degree of disorganization and hardship in the community is inevitable. Is the result predictable on the basis of the experience of the social scientist? If the present source of cash were to vanish, certain readjustments would unquestionably have to be made. Those purveyng services would be hard hit. However, the community has weathered several such storms before and has come through successfully. The recognition of factors of social integration, in this case those of the basic cooperative family, aids in pointing up the core of contemporary Barrow Eskimo society. It would appear that only if the family system is disrupted will community disorganization on a large scale occur. For, despite the cash economy, the social organization of the aboriginal Eskimo is still the potent force. The series of benign interrelations between individuals within the family setting can be made effective in promoting the cooperative effort again to "live off the land" should the necessity arise. To be sure, members of a group, once accustomed to the advantages of the outboard motor, the washing machine, mail-order luxuries and the like, may find life more burdensome if these are removed or curtailed. However, as long as mutual interdependence can be kept to the fore, it is unlikely that such deprivation will bring dire consequences with it. This point emerges more clearly perhaps in the analysis of the social and familial relationships.

An example of the failure of a well-meaning administration to comprehend the Eskimo problem appears in the ill-advised economic solution, mentioned above, of the reindeer. As a problem in applied anthropology, the reindeer emerges as a predictable mistake. It may be stated at the outset that while the inland groups of Eskimo might adjust more satisfactorily to the transhumance associated with the herding of the reindeer, this was scarcely a solution to the maritime Eskimo. As is known, some Eskimo have adjusted successfully to the reindeer economy, or did so at least for a fairly long period of time. At Barrow, the development of the reindeer pattern correlates with the decline of the whalebone industry, that is to say, beginning about 1915. Reindeer had been introduced into Alaska in 1898. It is not necessary here to consider again the rather exaggerated hopes of those engaged in the introduction of the animal. It was felt that here was not only a new source of meat, but an opportunity to exploit the otherwise barren and unfertile areas of Alaska. Further, an attempt to offer the Alaskan natives a new source of food and clothing was also involved, not to mention, for the tundra peoples at least, a new means of transportation. Presumably, the reindeer could replace the dog as a transport animal. Since the Siberian natives have used the reindeer for transport and since the Lapps have successfully broken the reindeer to the sled, this animal, feeding itself on tundra moss as it does, was conceptually ideal for Alaskan native life. Superficially, the idea seems excellent; the carnivorous dog, which makes such heavy inroads on the human food supply, could successfully be replaced.

There were those Barrow residents who, when the reindeer was introduced, devoted themselves to the raising of the animal. The development of community herds at Barrow and Wainwright might reflect a successful beginning. But it was found very difficult to interest young men in taking the time to become herdsmen and to undergo the 4 years of apprenticeship away from the family situation. Since the herd must move inland in search of pasture, the herdsman must move with it. And because, too, the animals become intractable during the summer rutting season, and incline to stampede because of the insect pest, much time must be given to rounding up strays. From the point of view of the individual resident of the Barrow community, herding means isolation. The support offered by family contacts and the social intercourse of community life strongly detract from any ambition in this pursuit.

The entire project at Barrow was fraught with disappointment for those engaged in the industry. Not only was there lack of interest because of the personal isolation which herding entailed, but there was also a series of mishaps associated with herding. Lantis (1950 a) remarks that wolves decimated the herds. While this was unquestionably a factor, hoof and mouth disease was a far greater danger. Barrow and Wainwright got into difficulties over their communal herds. The latter community lacks the whaling in the fall. While the Barrow residents were engaged in whaling, the herds became mixed. When roundup was finally effected, following a disastrous stampede in the mid-20's, Barrow recovered only a fraction of its herd. One herdsman estimates that only 3,500 out of 20,000 were recovered. The depression of 1929 also killed interest in herding, since no market was found for the meat or hides. By 1930, the price of a dressed carcass went from $5.00 to $2.00, and at last the market died away altogether. Basically, however, the long period of training necessary to the herdsman, the type of life implied in herding, and the subsequent insecurities associated with the industry were in conflict with the demands of family and society. Wild fragments of the once great Barrow herds are still sighted occasionally on the tundra, but there is no question that the reindeer industry is incompatible with the sedentary economic and social life of the Barrow people. Some factionalism and ill feeling has grown up between individuals concerned in Barrow and as between Barrow and Wainwright over the ultimate failure of the industry.

The Barrow community thus failed to capitalize on the reindeer and realized little from it in terms of money or capital.

SEASONAL ACTIVITIES

At the present time, the year's activities may be said to begin in mid-April. By this time, the days are again long and it is possible to start the spring whaling. This is the first major economic activity of the year, and preparation for it, i. e., refurnishing of boats, collecting and cleaning of gear, etc., occupies the final weeks in March. The spring whaling continues until approximately June 1.

From June 1 on, some attention is devoted to sealing. This is often done on the basis of cooperative crew activity, the whaling boats being devoted to tracing the various seals, principal of which at this time is the ugruk (*Erignathus barbatus*). Spotted and hair seals may also be taken during this period, although it is to be emphasized that there is no particular time for these smaller game. The spotted seal are taken in some numbers to the east of Barrow along the deltas of various rivers. Smaller seals are taken throughout the year wherever they are found and are often individually hunted. Unless a crew agrees beforehand as to how the game will be divided, the smaller seals are the property of the individual hunter. The ugruk, however, is divided according to custom and is regarded as are larger mammals such as the whale or walrus.

Sealing continues throughout July. By July 1, however, there is some breakup of the community—actually there is less now than formerly because of naval employment—and individual families may go out for the summer months to fish camps or to the "ducking station" near the Pet IV Base for the bird shooting and some other hunting (pl. 4, *c*).

By July, there is considerable diversity in activity. Not only are there fishing and duck-hunting opportunities but hunting on a more intensive scale is also possible with the arrival of the caribou and walrus. The caribou have for some years now pushed down across the tundra and foraged along the coast. This has made hunting of them much easier since it is possible for a crew to direct their boats in the direction of the caribou herds and to load the meat and bring it back to the community with ease. While the caribou herds move rather rapidly, remaining on the coast rarely for more than a week at a time, they can be obtained in very large numbers. As a result, caribou hunting is an intense activity during the fairly short season. Men engage in the hunting of the caribou and may leave the community for a time to follow the herds and to take as much meat as possible. Caribou hunting has thus been intensified by the maritime peoples in recent years. The carcasses are butchered on the spot, and the meat and hides transported back to the community for storage.

At the same time, with the breaking of the pack ice along the shores, the walrus herds come into view, moving along the current northward, their herds resting on the broken floes. Here again, crew activity comes into play, the walrus being shot as they sleep on the ice. Butchered on the floes, the meat is brought back to the community. Boats may go considerable distances, 50 to 100 miles into the ocean, for these animals (pl. 5, *c*).

By August, the walrus supply is pretty well exhausted, the herds having moved away, and the caribou also become less. Duck hunting continues as does fishing. In fact, during August and early September, the fishing activities are stepped up. The fish camps along the inland rivers become centers of activity. Much of the fishing done during the summer is relegated to women, a woman, with her children, leaving her husband at home in the community while she engages in this activity. The family pitches a tent on a selected watercourse and so engages in fishing, putting out nets across streams, etc. The fish is split and dried or simply frozen in an ice cellar built for the purpose at the fishing station. By August and early September, the husband may go for his family and the fish they have taken. The long gill nets described by Murdoch are still in use, although the materials from which they were made have changed (Murdoch, 1882, p. 284). Formerly, baleen netting was usual. Commercial netting is used today, although cord nets are still made locally. Net making is done by men. The various species of whitefish are obtained in considerable quantity. In the summer of 1952, women bringing back as much as 1,500 pounds of fish to the community for storage was not unusual. Fish are loaded in the launches at the river fishing stations and brought back. Netting and ice fishing continue much of the year, an apparent carryover from aboriginal days. It is not an intensive activity until summer, however. Other fish than the whitefish are also taken, most of them in the summer months. On the coast the ocean cod or tomcod (*Boreogadus saida*) may be taken in winter. This is done through the ice with jigs.

Because of the freedom in choice of activity, there is no hard and fast rule demanding that a man (or woman) be limited to a certain kind of work. Each member of the community is free to make his own choice. A family may thus spend the entire summer season fishing. Although women may fish, there is nothing to prevent men from doing so also should they choose. It often happens that a family will fish one summer, spend the next between fishing and various kinds of hunting and the third at hunting alone. This makes for some variation in the pattern of existence.

Duck hunting parallels the fishing season. Here again, a family is free to hunt as it chooses and has the right to set up a summer tent at the shooting station. The men hunt the ducks, shooting them—they are rarely trapped or snared, although this is not unknown—and the women prepare them for storage. Duck hunting is for the most part the activity of older people since it lacks the strenuousness of the chase for larger game. Both ducks and fish are valuable not only as food for the family taking them but they may be traded or sold. This is one of the features which helps disseminate cash throughout the community. For fish particularly, the Native Store acts as an agent, and pays cash for fish and other game.

Formerly, duck eggs were sought. This is no longer done. If bird's eggs are found on the tundra, the hunter may eat them raw or boil them. There is no longer any effort directed to searching for duck eggs. The same is true of owl hunting and owl eggs. While formerly these were sought, there is no longer any interest in them.

With the onset of colder weather late in August, preparations for the fall whaling are undertaken. The beginning of this season is rather unpredictable and has varied rather markedly over the past few years. In 1926, whales were taken at Barrow early in August. More recently, the community has waited until September and even October before beginning this activity. Fall whaling is limited to Barrow. The people at Wainwright and Point Hope, although they engage in spring whaling, have not developed the fall activity. It is actually somewhat different from the whaling in spring. In the latter case, the long stretch of ice from the beach to the open water must be traversed, and there is marked dependence on the dog teams and sled travel. In the fall, however, boats may take off directly from the beach since as yet the winter ice has not closed in. Although slush ice may form along the beaches in late September, the sea has been known to remain open as late as December. As a result of contact with the whalers, the Barrow Eskimo have adopted modern methods of whaling. The darting gun, bombs, lines, etc., reflect modern whaling techniques. The activity is still dangerous, however, since the 30-foot boats are scarcely adequate for the great whales of these waters. The past few years have seen something of a decline in the whaling success. In 1952 there was a total failure in both seasons; lack of adequate boats had caused failure in the fall of 1951. One whaler remarked that his boat would not carry the necessary amount of gasoline together with the crew. He had killed a whale, estimated at 80 tons, in the fall of 1951, other boats having turned away before he had engaged the animal. Since he was some hours from shore, being about 100 miles from Point Barrow itself, he had no alternative but to abandon the whale. The attitude of the man in question was of itself interesting. As he related his misadventure and told of his having to cast the whale off because of his low fuel supply, tears came to his eyes and he remarked bitterly that the other boats had given up too soon. This is a reflection of the continuation of the basic economic interest in the whale. While it was around whaling that the former ceremonial life centered, today, although the ceremonies are gone, the activity is still of paramount interest. Whaling was without question the major preoccupation of the past, and of all hunting at present it is whaling which holds first place.

When the late fall winds begin to pile up the young ice along the shore, the intensive activity of the summer and early fall comes to an end. One of the tasks of November and December is the cutting of ice for storage as drinking water. It is to be remembered that the Barrow area is a virtual desert in the geographical sense and that water is always a problem. Fresh-water ice is obtained from the lakes and streams as the winter freeze begins. Blocks are cut, ranging in size from 8 to 18 inches, are transported back to the community by dog team, and stored in the ice cellars. An attempt is made to obtain sufficient ice to make drinking water, as well as some water for washing and other purposes for several months to come. The amount of ice packed actually depends on the size of the local ice cellar. If a householder has a sufficiently large cellar, he may attempt to store a considerable surplus of ice blocks. These, too, have an economic value and may, if there are extra on hand, be sold.

With winter, concerted activity comes to an end. Today, of course, many men in the community are employed and continue to work at the naval installation. In normal times, however, winter is the period of greatest freedom for the community. In the aboriginal period, winter was the sacred season and it was then that the shamanistic activities and much of the social and ceremonial life was carried on. There is a survival of this at the present time inasmuch as native dances, visiting, and various community-sponsored recreational activities, such as the school and church programs, are held.

The various economic pursuits by no means come to a standstill in winter. It is true, however, that the work undertaken to fulfill the needs of the food quest is in large measure individual. Throughout the dark days men may go out sealing on the pack ice, searching for blowholes in the ice and netting the smaller seals. This may continue throughout the winter at the option of the individual hunter. In

November, men who have been inland either trapping or in search of caribou generally return home. A few families may leave the community during the winter in order to fish on the inland ice. This is again the common method of stretching nets across holes in the ice and obtaining the various whitefish. The sites visited at this time are the same stations or camps which are used in summer. Actually, not many families leave the community in winter; the various social activities offer a strong incentive to remain. There is some further gathering of ice in January and February. During the winter period, a few men may travel out some distances with dog teams to lay a string of trap lines. Since the decrease in the value of furs, however, fewer individuals have been doing this. This is rather arduous work, necessitating as it does a constant return to the traps.

The yearly activities at Barrow may be reviewed as follows:

Month:	Economic activity [1]
January	Sealing (individual, at ice holes) (−) Trapping (−)
February	Individual sealing at ice holes (−) Trapping (−) Caribou hunting (−)
March	Individual sealing (−) Trapping (−); caribou (−) Preparation for whaling
April	Whaling (+) Duck hunting (−), caribou (−)
May	Whaling (+) Sealing, ugruk, etc. (−) Duck hunting (−); fishing (inland) (−)
June	Whaling (−) Sealing in open water (+) Duck hunting and fishing (+)
July	Sealing in open water (+) Walrus hunting (July 15) (+) Caribou hunting (+); duck hunting and fishing (+)
August	Sealing in open water, walrus, caribou (+) Trapping (−) Duck hunting and fishing (+)
September	Sealing in open water, walrus, caribou (−) Trapping (−) Duck hunting and fishing (−); whaling (−, +?)
October	Whaling (+); other sea game, i. e., beluga (−) Caribou (−); polar bear (−) Seal netting (−)
November	Seal netting (+) Caribou, trapping, etc. (−)
December	Seal netting (individual, at ice holes) (+) Caribou, trapping, etc. (—)

[1] (—)=Minor activity.
+)=Activity intensified.

FOOD

There has been considerable by way of speculation regarding the diet of the Eskimo both past and present. This has been particularly true of the Arctic Eskimo groups who, in their aboriginal life, made virtually no use of vegetable foods. At the present time, even though money has come into the community and it has been possible to purchase somewhat more by way of the foods prevalent in the United States at large, the Barrow Eskimo have not exploited this innovation and have preferred to concentrate on what remains essentially an aboriginal diet. A question which is frequently asked, "Is this diet adequate?" can be answered only by pointing out that the present Eskimo, if free of the scourge of tuberculosis, is a remarkably healthy and long-lived specimen. It appears, further, that the basic diet of meat and the associated oils contains the necessary complement of nutritional elements.

Food thus remains significantly meat. The economy has not been so modified as to create a change in the basic dependence on the products of the chase. Modern living has introduced luxury items in respect to food, but it has neither succeeded in offering adequate substitutes for the meat staple nor caused a basic change in dietary likes and dislikes. It is said that a grown man will eat 6 to 7 pounds of meat and oil a day, a fact borne out by observation of the contemporary situation. Modern foods, added to the meat diet, consist principally of flour, sugar, tea, and/or coffee. Other items, such as fruits, pastries, canned goods, and the like, are luxuries and are so regarded. A family which earns a fair amount of cash may add variety to its table by purchases of imported food but continues to regard the meat diet as basic.

One growing variation in the dietary pattern is the tendency toward eating one meal per day which consists of imported food, possibly crackers, tinned meat, or tinned fish. This has been a recent development, however, and appears to depend on the influx of cash to the community. Another possible reflection of this is the use by mothers of the various kinds of canned milk for small children. In some measure, this has been impressed on the women of the community by the school, church, and hospital.

But if all such changes may be regarded as recent, it follows that the aboriginal diet is still in force. Various foods drawn from the adjacent surroundings, hunted throughout the year and stored in the natural ice compartments in the permafrost, form the basic diet. The meats used are as follows: whale, all seals, beluga, walrus, polar bear, fish, the various waterfowl, caribou, and not infrequently, wolf, fox, and sometimes dog. Unquestionably, the sea mammals and caribou are most important. Other animals have been eaten in the past, such as lemmings, owls, etc., but there is no longer any necessity for resorting to such food.

Of the sea mammals, the whale is by far the most preferred food. The whale skin and outer blubber, the so-called muktuk is a prime delicacy. This may be eaten raw and may be boiled. Some of the European whalers—Hopson particularly, but also Brower, Smith, and others—developed a means of pickling muktuk which is still fondly remembered. It is said that the true pickling art has been lost, although a few treat the muktuk in this way.

As stated previously, in spring the whale is dragged to the edge of the ice and butchered. All crews engaged in the pursuit of the whale are entitled to a share. The crew which actually is credited with the taking of the whale, that is, having sighted it and having the first harpoon in it, receives for division the especially favored tongue, heart, and kidneys of the animal. The butchering involves the cutting of blocks of meat weighing 200 to 300 pounds. These are carried to the various ice cellars and deposited for freezing and future use. One interesting feature of the whaling is the continuing custom of opening the house of the whaleboat's captain to the community, if the hunt is successful. All may come and be served portions of the meat. These are taken home to be eaten.

Virtually all parts of the animals taken are used, and skins of the caribou, ivory from the walrus, pelts of the polar bear, and the like are carefully kept for sale. The meat is reserved either for human consumption or for the dogs. In the case of the latter, the important means of winter transportation it is to be remembered, much meat must be utilized. A grown dog will eat as much as a man. This implies that the parts of game not destined for human consumption will serve as dog food. A place is thus found for the use of entrails and other less palatable portions.

The Barrow Eskimo, like other Arctic peoples, have been able to exploit the animals which they hunt to the fullest. Preferred meats, aside from the whale, are principally the various seals and the caribou. Walrus is somewhat less desirable. These four classes of animals, however, for the Barrow people, form the staple foods. All can be obtained in sufficient quantity to insure a dependable food supply. Thus, although no whales were taken in 1952, sufficient walrus and caribou were had to permit the group to carry on through the winter of 1952–53. The basic staples were augmented somewhat by the meat of bears, which were plentiful in the fall of 1952, and the flesh of the various seals. In addition, fish was obtained in sufficiently large quantities to offer an additional food supply. Similarly, various waterfowl were obtained.

The meat of larger game is butchered in chunks for the most part and frozen in the ice cellars. When needed for food, it may simply be boiled with the blubber. It is here, actually, that the basic dietary needs of the Eskimo are met, as the blubber, the layer of insulating fat which is found on sea mammals principally, is rich in numerous nutritional elements. Boiling is the usual method of preparation, equal sections of flesh and blubber being consigned to the pot. It is only since the advent of the commercial oil stove, a commodity recently purchased through the various mail-order houses by many families, that roasting is possible. Even then, the time-honored methods of preparation still come to the fore, and boiled meat is the most preferred. Various methods of preparation and cooking survive from the aboriginal past and continue to be of importance.

It may be well to consider the various ways in which food is prepared and eaten. With few exceptions, the aboriginal fare is still followed.

(1) *Whale.*—Choicer portions are boiled alone and may be eaten with raw muktuk. Whale meat and oil, apart from such favored sections as the heart, kidneys, and tongue, are boiled together. Sufficient oil is obtained from the whale to allow its use in cooking with food other than whale. Caribou, for example, may be cooked with this oil. The whale blubber is stored raw and taken as needed, since boiling before use is said to cause the material to turn rancid. Whale entrails may be chopped into blubber and eaten raw. Meat is said to get sweet if stored with muktuk for 5 or 6 days in the house. The mixture must be regularly stirred and then placed outside to cool. Mention is made elsewhere of the generosity incumbent on the umealiq whose boat takes a whale. He feeds the community, cooking up tongue, kidney, heart, and portions of the intestines with muktuk. Members of the community who partake of the feast at the boat-owners' houses proceed from house to house, eating equally from the portion of each umealiq. Today, when a whale has been taken, fresh muktuk is cooked out on the ice in oil cans, being boiled in salt water, and shares of meat are given to all who assist in butchering the whale.

(2) *Seals.*—The choice portions are the heart, liver, and shortribs. Seals, particularly the ugruk, being rich in fat, are butchered so as to free the blubber layer. The meat is boiled with salt—formerly it was boiled in sea water—and cooked sufficiently long as to "have the middle part red," rare meat being desired. The liver is fried. Seal meat is strung and dried. It is eaten dipped in oil. Many today make ground seal meat and fry the patties. Seal intestines are peeled and hacked in blubber with anulu; the resulting mixture is eaten raw. The brain might be boiled in the head. Eyes are also eaten. Seal

stomachs are eaten, but also they may be dried and used to store oil. Other organs, such as the spleen and lungs, are discarded and served as dog food.

(3) *Walrus.*—The heart, liver, and ribs are eaten. The brain may be eaten raw. Walrus is less highly regarded, and much of the carcass is reserved as dog food. The flesh of the flippers and shoulders is sewn into the skin and allowed to ferment. This is later boiled. Walrus kidneys are also prized as human food. Walrus, unlike seal and whale meat, cannot be eaten frozen. The meat may be put in a barrel with the skin left on and the blubber untouched. The hair, after a time, is easily plucked off and the skin is eaten. Walrus is a tougher meat than that of other sea mammals.

(4) *Belugas.*—While this does not have the same degree of palatability as whale, nor is it treated with the same ceremony, the flesh is eaten, the choicer parts, such as the major organs, are saved, and the meat is boiled.

(5) *Caribou.*—The caribou lacks blubber. It is, however, a desired meat. A caribou carcass runs on the average to 200 pounds, much of which is waste. The saddle, rack, and haunches are preserved as food, being stored in ice cellars. The legs of the animal are kept and cracked for the marrow. Soups are made from the bones and meat. Boiling is the common method of preparation. A common dish, the basis of which is caribou, is akuutuq, sometimes called in the area "Eskimo ice cream." The fat is taken, heated, and chunks of meat introduced. The cook stirs the mixture with her hand, beginning when it is lukewarm, and beating the fat until it becomes "white." Two hours of preparation and beating are required. Only enough is made for immediate eating. A variant of this recipe is caribou fat, whale oil, and berries, the latter obtained from the inland regions by trade. Another dish involving caribou marrow and fat is pacexsut. Marrow and fat are boiled together and then allowed to freeze in a caribou paunch. (It may be mentioned that caribou droppings were saved for fuel and were collected off the tundra for this purpose and sacked. Such droppings also served as dog food, being mixed with oil. Humans would eat this in an emergency.)

(6) *Wolves and foxes; bears.*—Wolf and fox were eaten with relish, the meat being boiled. These are less frequently eaten today. Polar bear and brown bear are eaten both raw and boiled. Of the polar bear, the liver is carefully avoided. Presumably too rich in vitamin A, it is regarded as "poison"—"it makes your hair fall out." The same is said to be true of wolf and dog liver.

(7) *Dogs.*—The inland Eskimo raised dogs for food and parkas. They were eaten when still in the puppy stage, boiled, and the skin preserved for clothing. The maritime groups were less inclined to

eat dog, but had no strong feeling against it. The dog was economically too valuable to form a dietary staple.

(*8*) *Moose.*—These animals, obtained in the inland only, are valued as food. Particularly is the moose antler prized, being used as tool handles, harness snaps, and as wedges.

(*9*) *Rodents.*—Rabbits are trapped inland and eaten. This formerly was true also of ground squirrels. Weasels, ermines, wolverines, and apparently, lemmings are not eaten, although hunted for their pelts. Rabbits and squirrels are skinned and boiled.

(*10*) *Birds.*—Geese are sometimes roasted with the feathers on. Feathers today are used for mattresses and pillows. The various ducks, of which so many varieties were taken, are cleaned and plucked and often stored in oil. Other methods of storage involved drying and freezing. Fowl are boiled, dipped in oil, and then a soup made of them. Two or three ducks might be cut up in a soup. Today, rice, imported of course, may be added to the soup. Ptarmigans are treated in much the same way as ducks. The owl was eaten, having been cleaned out, plucked, and boiled into a soup. Owl oil was formerly used for cooking. The owl may at one time have been popular as food, but it is no longer so. The village name, utkeaaγvik, refers to the "place where owls were hunted." The owl is said to have white meat but to be very tough, "like lemming." Owl wings were used for sweeping and dusting, for arrow fletching, and for costume trimming. Loons were also eaten, but they were hunted more for masks, made from the loon bills, than for the flesh. Rain parkas were made from loon and duck skins.

(*11*) *Fish.*—Most fish, obtained inland, are frozen and eaten raw in the frozen state. This is still a common meal. Eulachon are obtained from the surf. They were cooked for oil. The cods are taken for their liver. A "bonehead" liver is set in a vessel until it dissolves into oil, and this is drunk with no other food.

As stated, there were no vegetable foods, with the possible exception of berries. These were never frequent along the coasts, and were obtainable only by trade from the south. Berries were pounded with fat to make a pemmican. It is said that willow leaves were sometimes put in soups. No other utilization of plants could be traced. Mushrooms, for example, were feared. They were called aareγarenniq, "hard on the hands," and to touch them was to be poisoned and to have the hands wither.

MEALS

In the aboriginal culture, two meals a day were frequent, but this was scarcely definite. A woman cooked at home in the morning or again later in the day. Food which was not eaten at this time was left, and anyone in the household might eat it as he chose at any time.

There was no feeling that a family in a household should assemble for a mealtime. While boys were discouraged from eating too much, there were snacks between meals in which most would participate. Frozen fish was one such between-meal food. Another food of this type was seal blood. The seal was killed on the ice and the blood allowed to form in a pool and freeze. It was then picked out and could either be made into a broth and eaten or could be sucked in its frozen state. Sometimes oil was added to the blood and frozen; people cut off a piece and walked about chewing it.

Today the prevailing pattern of three meals has been adopted. A fairly typical menu for a day might be the following:

Breakfast, the time varying with the season: Biscuits or cornflakes, canned milk, bread, coffee, in virtually any combination.

Lunch: Frozen fish or meat, coffee or tea. Also canned meats, such as corned beef, sardines, etc.

Dinner: Boiled meat, consisting of any of the items listed above. This is the large meal of the day.

Much of the pattern of meals has been subject to changes brought about by employment by the naval installation at Barrow. Where the head of the family is not employed by the contractors, the program of meals might vary considerably.

FAMILY AND BUDGETS

Today, with the introduction of money, budgets of families differ according to income. Those who are employed, as at the naval installation, bring home cash and are obliged to depend on the native store as a source of food, or they may buy meat from the men who are still actively engaged in hunting. With the spreading of money throughout the community, however, all have in some measure benefited and are to some extent dependent on the goods and food which are imported.

Considering a few family situations as to monetary outlay for food, clothing, and other items, one finds the following:

The most important item to be considered in a family budget is food. One woman states that for a family of five, $30 to $40 a week is spent in the purchase of staples, such as bread, milk, fruit juices, canned foods (Spam and corned beef, sardines), and the like. If it runs short of hunted meat, the family estimates that it must spend about $900 for a 3-month period. This would be particularly true of the winter months and does not include fuel. Another woman maintained that her family of five spent only about $50 a month for staples, not including meat. Such items would be purchased at the Native Store, or at the various other groceries which have been developed since the arrival of the Arctic Contractors. This family bought, for example, butter, shortening, flour, and sugar; their staples included flour, salt, tea, sugar, coffee, dried fruits, onions, and soap. This family stretched its purchases and felt that $50 a month was a fair estimate. Since, however, no family makes a careful budget, it is difficult to check the accuracy of the estimate. Some are said to like clothing better than food; as a result, they invite themselves to the houses of others for meals. This suggests the breakdown of the older pattern.

Second in importance in family disbursements is heating. As much fuel as possible is bought with extra money, according to one woman. Since a drum of stove oil, 50 gallons, is priced at $37, the outlay is considerable. A family in a 3-room frame house will use roughly 5 gallons of oil a day. Coal can be purchased at $2.10 a sack, coming as it does from the Meade River. Wood, which is gathered, is also used. Blubber mixed with dry sod is still important as fuel. Pitch has been sent to Barrow, where a severe fuel shortage has always existed, but it is not practical, since one must travel "three dog-team days" to get it.

Clothing is third in importance in a family budget. The local stores supply dry goods, but at a high rate. Mail ordering is common, but actually little is saved by this means since ordering is so frequently done via airmail and air freight rates must be paid. One woman orders her needs as to dry goods and other forms of clothing in the spring and in the Christmas season. A main order about twice a year is common practice, although some order throughout the year.

These are the principal expenditures. Money is also spent by a family for entertainment, such as at the motion-picture houses of which there are two at Barrow. The family keeps its money at home, or often the head of the family carries it about. With employment, the Federal and Alaska income taxes create a problem for many. Property taxes are also involved, despite the absence of defined land tenure. Few people use the banks in Alaska cities, although encouraged to do so as a saving measure. At present, some families are concerned about fire and casualty insurance, although little is done in this direction.

SUMMARY OF MODERN ECONOMIC LIFE

With the advent of money and the changes in distance, some aspects of the society of the town of Barrow have become considerably modified. Modern conveniences, appliances, washing machines, outboard motors, and the like make their way into the community, as does a change in food patterns and habits. Important though such changes are, they have not yet succeeded in disrupting the older spirit of cooperation and of the family tie. The institutional change has been gradual and is hardly traumatic for the community inhabitants. Despite the presence of an elected community council, the town is still not politically structured or defined. The family unit adjusts with ease to the inroads of modernity in economic affairs.

CHRISTIANITY

The American and European whalers, who established posts at Barrow in the mid-1880's and who continued their activities in the area until the whalebone industry began to decline, were without doubt the most powerful acculturative force. From 1854 on, as Murdoch notes, there appears to have been no season in which some boat did not come to Barrow in the summer months (Murdoch, 1892, pp. 51–55). The voyage of the *Plover*, between 1852 and 1854, involved the wintering of this vessel at Barrow and the reports of Commander Maguire, as well as the excellent ethnographic observations of Dr. John Simpson (1855). When the *Blossom's* barge arrived in 1826, presumably the first contact between Europeans and the North Alaskan Eskimo, and when Thomas Simpson arrived in 1837, the natives were already in possession of trade goods from the south or Siberia. These included metals, possibly tea, and certainly tobacco (Murdoch, ibid.; T. Simpson, 1843). The intensive whaling of the period from 1855 to 1885 culminated in the establishment of whaling stations along the Arctic coast, the principal of which was that at Barrow, on what is today the "Brower side" (Brower, 1942, passim). While the details of social change brought about by such contacts between the Eskimo and Europeans may be reserved for scrutiny elsewhere, it is clear that the whalers, themselves rough and lawless men, had little to offer to the native culture. Of material things there were bread, flour, tea, coffee, spirits (this becoming a great problem in the early stages of contact, although it is not today), sugar, and other foods. Metal objects were available in quantity before the visits of Murdoch and Ray, whaling bombs being already in use before 1880, and in Murdoch's day, at least, the rifle was common and had begun to replace other hunting weapons. The introduction of objects from abroad, whether for utility or prestige, seemingly did little to effect an overt change in the native society. It is perhaps true that an institution such as the Messenger Feast might be bolstered by the fact that added goods could now be distributed and that wealth came to take on a somewhat greater significance. On the whole, however, the initial changes seem to have touched the material culture and not to have affected the social institutions. Murdoch was struck by the conservatism of the groups he encountered and mentions the tenacity of the aboriginal culture (Murdoch, 1892, p. 54).

Many of the foreign whalers formed attachments with Eskimo women, some of the unions, in fact, being permanent. One result today is the presence of a high degree of Caucasian admixture among the population. European surnames have likewise persisted. But it seems that the whalers made no attempt to bring about any social changes. They seem to have been content to adjust to the native manner of living. If there was any mention by them of Christianity, it clearly does not survive except possibly in the beliefs relating to the "strangers," the wiivaksat (see pp. 296–297).

Missionization appears to have begun with the intensive missionary activity, particularly by the Protestant churches, in Alaska in the 1890's. The agreements reached by the Federal Council of Churches had the effect of dividing Alaska into zones of missionary influence, divisions which are still in operation. The Barrow area fell to the Presbyterians and remains a Presbyterian mission to this day. Wainwright and the Pass region have also been converted by the Presbyterian church. In the Wainwright area is an ordained Presbyterian minister who is an Eskimo, the Rev. Roy Amagoak. He preaches in Eskimo and has begun a translation of the New Testament into Eskimo, having so far completed Mark and The Acts. The Rev. W. Wartes acts as moderator for the entire district. In 1951–52, the addition to the old church at Barrow was begun. Plans were made to dedicate this building on Easter Sunday, 1953. Thus the Eskimo of northern Alaska, at Barrow, Wainwright, and in the interior nearby Meade River and Anaktuvuk, are members of the Presbyterian church. Point Hope and Point Lay fall into an Anglican area.

Under the circumstances, the individual has little choice as to his church affiliation. The modern Barrow people who have gone to Fairbanks and other cities in Alaska profess themselves to be much attracted by the various "holiness" cults, such as the pentecostalist Assemblies of God. This, they say, is a "friendly" church and they are made to "feel at home."

The interest of the present report lies in the reception by the groups of Christianity. The question may be justly raised as to the role that it plays as an integrative social and religious force. There are many individuals now living who still recall the coming of the missionary in the early 1890's. A Reverend Mr. Stevenson came first, as preacher, teacher, and medical missionary. He set himself up on the "Brower side" at Barrow and attempted to begin English instruction. He is said to have prayed in public, several informants recalling this. No baptisms were performed for some time.

It was said that the mission at first failed to attract much attention. When the missionary went on his knees in public and offered prayers with his eyes closed, this was regarded as the most amusing thing to strike the community in a long while. As the missionary prayed, several young men walked around and around him. One was said to have picked his pockets. The novelty of this performance evidently wore off after a while, and when the missionary introduced hymn singing, he found himself a center of attraction. The high degree of interest in music, together with the Eskimo skill in music, unquestionably was the factor in winning people over. An old woman recalls that when she was a girl, shortly after her first menstruation, she went to a church "sing" with friends. At first she was much afraid of going, but when she heard the music she was quite pleased with it and decided to attend the church sings. There were three groups of singers and she was assigned to one. She enjoyed it immensely and from that day she has continued to sing the hymns she learned.

The Reverend Mr. Marsh, who came next as a medical missionary and preacher, organized the church somewhat more formally. He began to acquire some knowledge of Eskimo, which pleased a good many. He is said to have been a very stern man, and to have made a number of enemies as a result. The first baptisms were performed by him about the late 1890's. Although people were said to have spat at him a few times, he apparently got his message over. When he prayed, his eyes closed, some touched him on the nose and upper lip—the grossest of Eskimo insults. Marsh, after a year or two, was able to communicate, and he talked of Jesus' death and resurrection. This, it was related, came as a great surprise, and the concept was related to that of the wiivaksat, about whom the people had been talking at some length. The growth of the belief in the "strangers" appears to have antedated by a few years Christianity in the Barrow area. As noted elsewhere, it is difficult to say whether this is an aboriginal concept. Under Marsh, Eskimo hymns, translated into Eskimo by missionaries in Canada, were introduced. These were very popular and continue to be so today.

The first two missionaries were described as saying all the time, "Obey God and Jesus; don't steal; don't talk lies." This struck the members of the group as rather inane, particularly since stealing in the aborginal culture was virtually unknown and no self-respecting individual would think of telling a falsehood. In general, among the older generation at least, this desire to maintain accuracy in all statements still holds true. One informant recalled particularly that the missionaries were against liquor. She maintains that she still cannot understand why this should be so.

The success of the mission appears to have hinged on several factors. Certain material benefits were conferred, such as food, clothing, and medical attention. The people appear to have liked the sociability which the mission provided and the songs which were sung. In a sense, here was a complex grafted onto an aboriginal pattern of singing both religious and secular songs. The missionaries were also identified with the wiivaksat, the strangers who were said to be coming. Here patently, was a fulfillment of native prophecy. And since the gift of prophecy was prized, or, at least, the individual who could correctly foretell the future was accorded prestige, the missionaries were regarded as men of truth and veracity. They predicted that the people would suffer diseases, as indeed they did in the measles and influenza epidemics and in the present prevalence of tuberculosis. One informant recalls that the missionaries predicted that there would be much metal, many things in cans, that many white people would come, that people would have abundance and would waste it. All this has come true. It follows that if this is true, then all else that the missionary said is also true. This attitude has seemingly accounted for unquestioning acceptance of the Christian dogmas.

But above all else the mission was successful because it effectively undermined the power of the shamans. The shamans were, as has been shown, a constant source of anxiety and fear. When a new doctrine was advanced which overcame the shamans, it was accepted readily. One way in which this was effectively done was by the medical facilities offered through the mission. It was no longer necessary to go to a shaman for illness and it was no longer necessary to observe a series of onerous taboos which he might impose. Further, the medical missionary demanded no pay, whereas a shaman by blackmail and threats could take most of a man's property away. As soon as this was known and as soon as a glimmering of Christian doctrine was understood, the power of the shamans was broken. They did little about it, being individual practitioners and not an organized group. Some shamans, it was said, reviled the missionaries and tried to get people to stay away from their influence, but their opposition seems to have been short lived. This did not mean that shamanism died out. The last of the shamans at Barrow was still practicing in 1935. He retired then, and died in 1939, starving to death while on an inland hunting trip. There is said to be an old woman at Wainwright who is a shaman still. But it is clear that the shamanistic cult as such was no longer popular after the advent of Christianity and that the anxieties occasioned by the presence of the shaman were in large measure relieved.

As nearly as can be judged from conversations with Barrow residents, Christianity is meaningful. Even the oldest have grasped the concept of immortality and of salvation. The aboriginal concept of "sin," that is, punishment for the violation of a prohibition, could quickly be allied with the sin-guilt complex of Christianity. When to these basic concepts are added the social opportunity afforded by church membership, the men's and women's organizations, the young people's groups, and the like, the pattern becomes clear. The church is not without its opportunities for individual prestige. Being Presbyterian, the ordination of presbyters has importance. The church leaders become, in effect, leaders in the community. Although wealth and whaling and other hunting success still have a vital relation to the prestige system, the church has arisen as another outlet for individual and social expression.

It is not to be implied that Christianity is universally successful in the Barrow community. There are backsliders and there are those who find social opportunities elsewhere. The Barrow church has 219 families, with 392 members as such. There are 430 in the Sunday School. There are 17 presbyters, or about one to 25 members. Three are said not to function. Six new presbyters were ordained in 1951–52.

The Presbyterian church in the Barrow area is very much of an active concern. The congregation itself pays about half of the cost of upkeep and maintenance, and the group is fast moving away from the status of a mission and is about to become an autonomous congregation. As in similar churches in the United States, various organizations operate within the congregation at large. These include a choir, a young people's society, made up of young married people of the 20- to 35-year age group, the Sunday School with its teachers, and various other organizations.

Christianity has effected several changes in older patterns. It has attemped to stabilize and legalize marriage. It has changed the mortuary customs by introducing burial and a funeral service. In paying particular attention to children, both in the Sunday School, in infant baptism, and in burial for children, an important factor considering the high infant mortality rate, it has effected changes in the status of the child over against the older culture.

The Presbyterian church built the hospital at Barrow, turning it over to the Alaska Native Service in 1930.

Certain difficulties appear to arise in respect to the presbyter system. Several of the highly placed men are reputedly eager to demand punishment for "sins" of all kinds, and are willing to subject church members to the various degrees of banishment and excommunication. The incumbent minister remarks that there is much self-castigation and regret over "sins" committed. The result is at times a kind of spiritual austerity. The present writer lacked the time to investigate fully these attitudes. In a more elaborated study of acculturation in the group, the role of Christianity should unquestionably be more fully explored. In it, as among so many other groups, one should expect to find a carryover of ideas from the aboriginal past.

FOLKLORE

The tales which follow offer a very few examples of the vast body of oral literature which the Eskimo everywhere possess. It is of interest to note the presence at Barrow, and in the general North Alaskan slope area, of tales which are so common to the American Indian and which have connections as well in Asia. In working with Eskimo informants of the older generation today, one cannot avoid hearing much of the involved folklore which was so dear to the older culture. Anyone who has worked with the Eskimo has had this experience. The present study made no systematic attempt to collect folklore, although in one instance, in a tale published elsewhere, so many versions were offered that a brief study was undertaken of the distribution of the plot (Spencer and Carter, 1954).

The folktale had great entertainment value in the older culture. There were rewards for the successful storyteller, however informal they may have been. The idea was "to get the story right." If a raconteur deviated as much as by a word in his recital, his skill was considered dubious indeed. Among the older living people, this attitude still prevails. The writer might ask for a story, only to be told, "I know only part of it; I cannot tell it." When pressed for as much as he knew, the informant would answer, "But that wouldn't be right; I can't give you the whole story." This was true, of course, not only of folktales, but of any fact on which the informant was questioned. The sense of personal integrity is so strong that unless a man feels he can be accurate, he prefers to keep silent.

In telling a story, the speaker could hold his audience spellbound by his skill. He acted out the parts of the characters and his mimicry was applauded as much as the tale itself. Even today it remains an interesting experience to be told a tale. The speaker allows himself to be carried away by the drama he recounts. He will go through all the actions of, let us say, arising from sleep, dressing, riding in a kayak, spearing, harpooning, and the like. He shows how the various animals, always central figures in a tale, act, and he will imitate their cries.

Tales were told in winter. Not that there was any prohibition against telling them in summer; there was merely no opportunity to do so, nor the leisure for it. In winter the people assembled in a house or in the karigi and several men told tales. There was often a notion of a contest in storytelling, the tellers seeking to outdo each other, not in the number of stories they could make up, but rather in the number of stories they knew. No one tired of hearing the same tale recounted. Indeed, it was in this way that the stories took their verbatim character. As the men settled down for their winter sports and games in the karigi, they often played and worked hard. Later, after they had eaten and sat about resting, a few might sing. Others played at less strenuous games, such as dice or string figures. Always with these there were songs. But at last, someone might begin to tell a tale. Work stopped, as well as other play, and the group gathered around the narrator. Women might come in to hear the story, and children as well. When the story was over, it was always said, "You can't leave it standing on one leg." This meant that the speaker had to tell another tale, and sometimes several more. Custom demanded that one tell at least two stories at one time.

While the stories in the folklore of the group were often concerned with the supernatural, with monsters and ghosts, with intimate relations to the animal world, neither the telling of tales nor the tales themselves were regarded as in any way supernatural. Aside from the customs associated with narration, there were no prohibitions on recounting a folktale.

Even from the small sample collected here, it is obvious that a great many themes appear. A variant of the magic flight is encountered, the raven mythology so common to northwest North America appears, as well as numerous other common motifs. For the present purposes, however, it may suffice to say that folktales had great entertainment value, and played a significant part in the whole process of recreation which the culture developed.

Although there were no special taboos relating to folklore, it would be wrong to state that these tales had only entertainment value. It is evident that they were believed. Even today, some of the older people find difficulty in reconciling the creation of the world by Raven with the Christian concepts given them by the church. And since, too, the group has no interest in a tale in which the setting is not given, an added basis for credence is given. Thus, in keeping with the detailed knowledge of the terrain which every individual had, the storyteller had to place his tale with great exactness. One is told: "This is a true story, because it happened right here at the lagoon called malekpik."

The folktales follow in translation.

The Folktales

THE CREATION

Men say that the world was made by tuluŋixiraq, the Raven. He is a man and he has a raven's bill on his head. The ground came up from the water. It was brought up by tuluŋixiraq who appeared on the water. He speared down into the water and brought up the land and fixed it into place. The first land was a plot of ground, just a little bit bigger than a house. There was a family that had a house there. There was a man and his wife and their little son. This was tuluŋixiraq. One day he saw a round thing, a kind of bladder, hanging up over his parents' bed. He wanted to play with it and he asked his father for it again and again. Each time his father said: "No, you can't have it." But the boy begged so much that finally his father gave in. While he was playing with that round thing, he accidentally broke it. Now up to that time, it had always been dark. But now it began to grow light. The father said: "We had better have it night, too, not just daylight all the time." So he grabbed the round bladder before the little boy could break it further. And that is how day and night began.

Now the father had a kayak. He said: "There is other land far away; how can we reach it?" Then tuluŋixiraq asked his father to let him go to that other land. But his father said: "No, you had better not go; there is danger there." But at last he agreed to let the boy go. And tuluŋixiraq paddled a long time over the sea. Finally, his kayak came to a place in the sea where some land was bobbing up and down on the surface of the water. First it would rise up above the surface and then it would sink again. The raven boy was afraid and slowed up. When he came close, the land sank down. As he watched, the land came up again. Now he carried his spear along with him in the kayak. When the land came up again, he speared it and held fast to the lead rope. This fixed the land firmly and it stopped bobbing up and down. Then tuluŋixiraq got out of his kayak and walked around on the surface of the land. The place where this was done is called Umiat, the landing place (Colville River, 69°30′ N., 152°16′ W.) even to this day. Because there is high ground there, the raven boy was able to walk about. After the land became fixed in place, the sea began to move away and there was dry ground all around. And so it is because of tuluŋixiraq that people are able to live in the world.

Note: It is readily seen that this tale, even though obtainable in fragmentary form, suggests the fairly common Earth-Diver myth (Boas, 1916, p. 581, ff.). The use of the spear is suggestive and may parallel the Japanese creation tale as recorded in the Kojiki. The initial section relating to the origins of light, and the Raven-transformer's part in bringing it in being, has also been recorded widely (cf. Boas, 1916, pp. 60, 641). A variant of this motif, involving also the element of supernatural conception, is the following.

THE ORIGIN OF LIGHT

In the early times, there was only darkness; there was no light at all. At the edge of the sea a woman lived with her father. One time she went out to get some water. As she was scraping the snow, she saw a feather floating toward her. She opened her mouth and the feather floated in and she swallowed it. From that time she was pregnant.

Then she had a baby. It's mouth was a raven's bill. The woman tried hard to find toys for her child. In her father's house was hanging a bladder that was blown up. This belonged to the woman's father. Now the baby, whose name was tulugaak (Raven), pointed at it and cried for it. The woman did not wish to give it to him but he cried and cried. At last she gave in and took the bladder down from the wall and let the baby play with it. But in playing with it, he broke it. Immediately, it began to get light. Now there was light in the world, and darkness, too.

When the woman's father came home, he scolded his daughter for taking the bladder down from the wall and giving it to the child. And when it was light, tulugaak had disappeared.

THE MAGIC LAMP

There were two old women living together at piɣiniq. They wanted to cook meat but their lamp went out and they had no more oil. One of them, when the lamp went out, said a curse and threw the lamp out of the door. She cried: "Go get some oil for yourself!" After a while, she went out to find the lamp but it was gone. Those two old ladies went all over, looking for that lamp. After a time, they looked out at the ocean and saw the black spot far away. It came closer and closer. And at last, it came to the edge of the beach. It was a whale with a lamp riding on its shoulders. It was their lamp. And when the whale came to the beach, the two old women danced for joy and sang:

suvti inʸuan tipakeevatiiguk taleoligurua
áyyee áyyee
áyyiq áyyiq áyyiq
siŋitkayawmeariŋmaa

After they danced, they cut blubber off from the whale. They brought it home and filled the lamp with oil. And they cooked and got warm in the house after the lamp got the whale.

THE SPIDER

There was an orphan boy. Sometimes he became a cooking pot (utkusik); sometimes he became a needle case (uyamik). This boy was going after a woman who didn't want to get married. Several men were trying to possess her but she refused them all. Once she was sitting in her house. She heard something rolling over the roof; it rolled over her skylight. She went outside and found a pot rolling along. Since she liked it, she took it in and began cooking in it. The pot on the fire made a noise as if it were boiling. Night came. Suddenly, the pot became a man and got into bed with her and had her.

Now this orphan boy could also turn himself into a bird. He wanted the woman to get onto his back and to fly with him to his house. Although she tried to resist, he won her over and she flew away with him and became his wife. He flew with her over the mountains. On his back she flew. He told her to keep her eyes closed while flying and not to open them until they came down. When he stopped flying, they were high up on a mountain.

While the woman lived up there on the mountain, she cried all the time. She cried so much that the tears wet the front of her parka. It became so wet that all the hair came off. Now once while she was crying, a little woman came to her. She told the orphan's wife to get a piece of sinew and to work it to its greatest possible length, working it, braiding it, and curing it so as to make it just as long as she could. Every once in a while, while she was doing this, the little woman came back to see how things were getting along. When the work was finished, the dwarf woman asked her if she wanted to go home. The sinew was now just as long as she could make it. The little woman told her to close her eyes and to wrap the sinew around her. If she did this, the woman said, she could go down the mountain. She wrapped the sinew around and with her eyes closed went down to the foot of the mountain. When she came to the bottom, there was the little woman again. She asked in which direction her home lay. The little woman pointed the way and the orphan's wife left for home.

This little woman was the spider (pilirayuraq). This is why she gave the sinew to braid and this is why, even today, no one likes the little spider to be killed; it always helps people.

NAKKAYAQ AND HIS SISTER

Two orphan children were living on a bluff near the sea. They lived there far away, all alone. They had a hard time with their food; there was no meat. Finally, the brother nakkayaq decided to take his sister away from there. The days were getting longer so they decided to go to utkeaaγvik, that is, Barrow. They started out without taking any food along. On the soles of their mukluks they had only reindeer (caribou) skin. After they had gone a little way, they met a lady who called them. She was a big, tall woman. She said: "What will you do?" They said: We are going on to utkeaaγvik." The lady tried to make them come to live with her in her house but they wanted to go on. So then she licked her fingers and wet the soles of their mukluks. And she gave them a large piece of muktuk to eat along the way. She told them that when they stopped for the night, they should not take the muktuk inside the shelter where they were staying, but should instead leave it outside covered with snow. And this is what they did. In the mornings, when they came to dig the meat out from under the snow, it was the same size as before. It looked as though they had never cut a piece off of it. Their boots, too, never got wet or wore out.

Finally, after they had walked a long time, they came to utkeaaγvik. At the ravine there, they came across the houses. They started across the ravine and came to a house they liked. They thought that they would like to go in and live with the people there. But they were afraid, not knowing the people. But they went up on the house and looked into the skylight. Inside, they saw an old man and an old woman. Now when they saw these two old people, the brother and the sister were unhappy and afraid. While they watched, the old people took a corpse and put it in the middle of the floor. It was the corpse of their only daughter. The two children came down from the roof and peered into the doorway of the house. When the couple began to dress the body in new clothes, nakkayaq's sister thought: "I wish I could have some of those new clothes." It happened that the old woman knew what she was thinking and she said: "If you will help us, I can make better clothes for you than these." When the old woman said this, the boy nakkayaq, said: "I can help you." And the old people said: "Come in, come in, we are not afraid of you." The boy started down the doorstep, down into the hall of the house. Suddenly, he was gone. But in a moment, a polar bear came squeezing its way up through the kataq. When the bear got up into the house, he rolled around the floor and lay down next to the body of the dead girl.

The sister of the boy and the old couple put the corpse on the back of the polar bear. Several times the bear got up from the floor, shook himself, and lay down again. When he had done this several times, the dead body began to come to life. At last the bear became nakkayaq again and the dead girl returned to life. After that, they all lived together and the girl who had been dead treated them very well.

At last nakkayaq became a man. When he grew up, he liked to act like a polar bear. He rolled around on the ground and swam in the lagoon. One day several young men and one old man were going out to sea after walrus. The young men made fun of nakkayaq, saying: "You act like a polar bear all the time." The old man who was with them said: "Don't make fun of him; he really can be a polar bear if he wants to." As they went, the water was so smooth; there was hardly a ripple in it. As they paddled in their umiak over the smooth sea, they made jokes and sang. Then came the polar bear, sticking his head up out of the water. He pulled on the edge of the boat and capsized it. The old man he took in his arms and swam to shore with him, putting him safely aground. But the young men were all drowned.

THE HEADBAND

An old lady lived by the sea with her orphaned grandson. There was a rich man in that place who took care of them, doing what he could to feed them. He gave the old lady all that he could. This rich man had a son, a young man. The orphan boy who lived with his grandmother was mistreated by the other boys, but the rich man's son took care of him and protected him.

Now these people had settled on a beach near where a river came to the sea. They went out on the tundra to hunt caribou. After some time, several men went out and failed to come back. Other men went after them, but they, too, did not return. The son of the rich man decided that he would go to look for them. And he went out into the tundra but did not come back. He had gone up the river. Although all waited for his return, he stayed away. The orphan boy asked the rich man, the missing boy's father, if he could borrow a kayak and go to look for the one who was gone as well as for those who had gone before him. When he talked the matter over with his grandmother, she urged him to start looking for the people who had disappeared. But the rich man refused to lend him a kayak and said: "You are like my own son; in you my son returns to me. I cannot let you go." But again the boy talked the trouble over with his grandmother. She went to the rich man and persuaded him to let the orphan boy go. The rich man said: "Wait! I will make a kayak just right and then you can go." When he had built the kayak, the orphan boy asked for arrows. They were given to him and he said that he was ready.

But before he started out, the rich man called him aside and gave him new clothes and beads for a headband. The rich man said: "An orphan will always return to his home. When you come back, the people will know you by the beads in this headband. Wear them always."

Then the boy left. He traveled up the river in his kayak. Over the river he saw a blackbird flying toward him. He watched to see what this raven would do. Then, as the bird flew nearer, the boy aimed an arrow at the raven, saying: "This is the bird that keeps the men from coming home." The bird flew nearer, dipping up and down over the surface of the water. He shot an arrow and hit the bird; it fell down into the water. He paddled over to it, picked it up and put it in his kayak. Now it was the custom to hunt seals in that river. Just then, in front of him, he saw a seal swimming. He said: "This is the seal that never lets the hunters come back." And he shot the seal. He did nothing to it. He just picked it up and put it into his kayak.

After he had been gone for some time, the people said: "The poor boy doesn't come back; he'll never come back any more. He is not so strong as the other men who went up the river before him."

But the boy paddled on up the river. After a time, he came to a place where there were willows. And there were all the kayaks of the men who had gone up there ahead of him; some were old and some were new. When he came ashore, he arranged his kayak so that he could get into it easily and start quickly down the river if he had to. Then he took his arrows, his bow, his spear with the ugruk bladder float, the raven, and the seal and began walking along the bank of the river.

On a raised place on the bank, he saw a small house, very old and much discolored with smoke. He went to the house and looked into the skylight. No one was there. So he decided to enter and cook meat there. As he came in, he noticed that over the doorway was a brown bearskin. Inside, a fire was going. So he sat down by the fire and prepared to cook himself some food.

Suddenly, a man entered through the doorway. This man's mouth was so big; it was as if it were cut from ear to ear. The man said: "Pahá! If you don't give me something, I'll eat you." The orphan boy threw the raven to the man and said: "Here, you can have this." The monster took the bird and went away. When the man was gone, the boy took his knife and cut the seal in half. Soon the monster returned and said the same thing again. The boy threw half of the seal to him and again he went away. Now the boy began to cut meat from the seal. But again the monster appeard and again he said: "Pahá! If you don't give me something, I'll eat you." So the boy threw the rest of the seal to him. But now he had nothing further to give. He had only the spear with the bladder poke. Soon the monster returned again and again he asked for something. "I'll give you my spear," said the boy, and hurled the harpoon at the monster, piercing his chest. The monster pulled the spear out and fled. The orphan boy ran after him but found him hard to follow; he was unable to see in which direction the monster had gone.

After a while, he walked to a high place where there were many houses. One of these was set off to one side and it was to this one that he went, treading softly, so that the people inside would not hear his footsteps. Two old women were sitting inside the house. In he went and killed them both. He took one of them and put her in bed as if she were sleeping. The other body he hid in the house, taking its clothes. He put the old woman's clothes on and got into bed with the first corpse. Quietly, he waited until someone came in. He did not know where the monster had gone but he did know that he was wounded. Soon he heard footsteps coming to the house. A man came in. The orphan boy acted just like an old lady; he got up out of bed and squatted down near the fire. The man asked the two old women to come and cure their only hunter. The two old women were doctors and had power to cure. The boy acted just like an old woman, saying "ayya." He got up and followed the man outside.

When they came outside, the man was joined by his partner. They stood on each side of the boy and took his arms. The first man said: "This doesn't feel like an old lady's arm; it is like the arm of a younger person, a boy or a woman." At this the boy was frightened and his skin turned hard and his arm felt and seemed like the arm of an old woman. So the men took him to the karigi. All the people of the town were there. In the middle of the floor was lying the monster, the man with the huge mouth, complaining of a pain in the chest.

Now the boy saw that when he had thrown his spear, the harpoon head had detached itself in the monster's chest and the cords and the bladder were all tangled around. When the monster had pulled out the spear, he had removed the shaft only. But no one, except the orphan boy, was able to see the cords and the bladder float. So the boy, using the voice of an old woman, told the people to turn out the lights. And he asked that all the people in the town be present in the karigi. He told them to begin singing. While they were singing, the boy worked in the dark. He began untangling the cords. Taking his knife, he cut his harpoon head out and let the monster die. Then he cut off his clothes, those that had belonged to the old woman he had killed, and, rolling up his cords and taking his ugruk bladder, he began running away as fast as he could. He began to run in the direction of his kayak.

Soon all the people started to run after him. As they ran, they turned into foxes and wolves. Closer and closer they came. From his headband he took a bead and threw it on the ground. He said to the ground: "I'm giving you a bead to protect me." Then he lay down and all the foxes and wolves ran past him. They sat down, sniffing the ground, unable to find him. Two of the people had become brown bears. They called to the others that they would find him. But they looked around and were unsuccessful. "Let the foxes find this orphan boy," they said. As the boy lay on the ground, he saw the eyes of the fox, winking at him. "So don't let them find me," pleaded the boy. And the fox said to the others: "No, I can't find him."

After a while, the boy started up again, making his way to his kayak. This time, the people saw him again and began to pursue him. Again they turned into different kinds of animals, foxes, wolves, and bears. As he ran on to his kayak, they came closer and closer. For a second time he threw his bead to the ground and hid and they were unable to see him. Then the brown bears said for the others to make medicine man's work (aŋatkoak) in order to find his hiding place. They all sat down and began to sing and the same fox was again set after him. The orphan boy saw the eyes of the fox looking into his own. "Don't let them find me; I will bring you a piece of blubber and leave it on the tundra for you." So the fox went back and told the others that he was unable to find the boy. At last the people gave up and started back to their village.

Now the orphan boy was able to reach his kayak. He got in and started off on the water. As soon as he started, all the people, again taking shapes like animals, foxes, wolves, and bears, ran after him. But he was already in the water. From the shore the brown bears called to him and urged him to come back to talk to them. He refused. The bears pulled up a willow tree and cried: "This is what we'll do to you if you come to us again." The boy threw his spear at them, holding fast to the cord and pulling it back to the kayak again. Then he paddled off toward home.

He came to his home at dark and waited until all the people were assembled in the karigi. He walked toward it, slowly so that the people would be unable to hear his footsteps. As he came into the hallway of the karigi, he heard the people talking about him. The rich man said: "Why did that poor orphan boy go away? He was not so strong as the others who went up there." But another man said: "Sometimes it is the poor boys who come back home even if they are not so strong. People are not all the same." He heard a third man say: "It's too bad we let that poor boy go. I used to like to see him working out of doors." And then the boy went into the karigi.

He walked into the house, taking the rope off his arms and throwing his spear on the floor. On the head of the harpoon was still a piece of the flesh of the monster he had killed. "Here," he said, "there is still a piece of skin from the man who would not let the people go." The rich man took the boy and his grandmother to live with him in his own home. And after that, people could safely go hunting up there, up the river.

But then there was the fox to whom the boy had promised a piece of blubber. He forgot all about it and didn't bring the blubber as he had promised. Not long after this the boy got sick and the doctor, even though the rich man paid him well, could not make him well again. Then the sick boy remembered his promise to the fox. The rich man took the blubber out to the tundra and only then did the boy get well.

After that, this poor boy became a great hunter. He married the daughter of the rich man. And there was yet another rich man who also had a daughter. One evening she came into the boy's house and said: "My father wants you to marry me." The first rich man, the father of the boy's wife, said: "Why didn't you ask him when he was poor?" But the second rich man's wife came and asked him to marry her daughter. And the daughter too, came again and again. So finally, he gave in and married the second girl as well. Thus the boy who had been poor and an orphan got two rich wives.

Note: In the tale above is an interesting variation of the theme of the Magic Flight. While scarcely unexpected among the Eskimo of northern Alaska, it is of interest to note how it has been incorporated into the plot here, virtually as a secondary element.

THE WOLF BOY

There were a man, a woman, and their child living alone in a place by the sea. One day the woman went out to get water. She got lost and wandered away, going farther and farther from her husband and their house. At last her husband started out to look for her. He searched a long time but was unable to find her trail. Season after season he looked for his wife. At last he found her far away and together they started back to their house.

Now while they were gone, wolves had come to the house and had found the little boy there. This is what wolves will always do when there is a child left alone in a house. These wolves took care of the child and raised him.

When the man and the woman came back, they found their house. A young man was living there. But he looked like a wolf and his clothing resembled the skin of a wolf. The couple came up to him and said: "You are our son." But he was unable to talk and he rushed at them biting wildly. He failed to recognize even his own parents and tried to kill them. Sadly the couple went away and left him there alone.

THE STORY OF QAAWEIŁUQ

There was once a boy whose name was qaaweiłuq. He was partly bald. His parents had died and he lived with his uncle. This uncle was very fond of him because he liked to work all the time. Once, in the winter time, he went to the river to get water. They had been camped on the river and had built a snow house at the place from which they got their water. The boy went to the hole cut into the ice and dropped his dipper down into the water. Each time he did so, however, the water receded and he could bring none up. So when he found he could get no water, he started off home.

When he reached the house, he sat down facing his uncle. He laid the dipper on the floor at his side and stretched himself out. His uncle said: "Now why do you do that? You shouldn't get angry while you are working." The boy replied: "I am angry because I cannot get the water out of the hole." His uncle said: "Those who are quick to anger only get into great trouble." Again qaaweiłuq went out to get water. This time the water stayed level and did not recede. So he filled his pail and went home.

Some time later, he went to the east to get wood. He grabbed at a piece of wood, but it moved away before he could take hold of it. Each time he reached at it, it escaped him. Even the pieces of wood which lay under the snow somehow escaped him. He got no wood and returned home. As before, he lay on the floor and was sad. And his uncle talked to him again: "Don't feel badly if things don't work out." He began to tell his uncle how the wood eluded him. His uncle replied with the same words: "You should not become angry when you are working." But he did not go out after wood again.

Summer came. It was warm again and qaaweiłuq lay in the place where the warmth of the sun could reach him and began to think to himself: "I'll just go over there to the river and see what I find." So he walked over there. As he approached, he heard the sound of laughter, but it was not such a sound as would be made by people. And he couldn't see where the noise was coming from. There was a low place where the bank came down to a level near the river. There he saw a number of young girls playing. They had taken off their clothes and had laid them together on the bank and were playing near the water. Concealing himself, qaaweiłuq began to creep toward them on the ground. Before long, one of the girls noticed him and stared in his direction, trying to make out what he was. He looked at her as well. He observed that she was both old and young; her face was like an old woman's, but her body was that of a young girl. She called to the others: "Someone has found out that we are here; someone is watching us." But the others replied: "No one will find us here; there are no people around." And they paid no attention. Meanwhile, qaaweiłuq crawled to where their clothes were piled up, and the girl who had first seen him called a warning. At this, he got up quickly and ran to their clothes, reaching them first and grabbing all of them. Three of the girls came over to him and begged for their clothes. They stooped down and begged him again and again. The girl who had seen him first was there. She said: "Give me mine," and pointed to the ones which were hers. He handed them to her; she put them on and at once flew away as a brand goose. The other two asked for their clothes, but he refused to give them. They said: "We won't fly away; we'll remain as people when we put on our clothes." So he gave them their clothes.

As they put their clothes on, they said: "When you were working, did you see what happened to you?" And he remembered the water and the wood. The two girls said: "We are the ones who ran away from you; one of us was the water you couldn't get and one of us was the wood." Now they promised not to run away again. And they reassured him again and said: "Now that we have our clothes, we can build a house together on that bank over there on that high place and we can all live together. This is what we will do." After he had given the clothes to one girl, he waited until she had them on and then he gave the other hers. When they were both dressed, they said: "We are sorry for you; we won't run away from you now."

The three of them then walked up to the high place on the bank where they had decided to build a house. Up in that place were a great many holes where the squirrels made their burrows. The girls said: "Sit by us, back to back with us." But qaaweiłuq said: "Come home to me and stay with me at my uncle's." But the girls refused. So he sat down with them as they requested. After a time, they said: "Look!" And he looked and found that they had built a house and that before it they had placed a rack. On the rack were all the things that he needed: kayaks, clothing, weapons, and all the rest. And the inside of the house was ready too.

The two girls were much better looking and they worked harder than any of the girls around his uncle's place. Always he tried to persuade them to come to his uncle's with him but they always refused. "Any time you want, you can take food to your uncle and he can come here and get anything he wants from us." But they would never leave the place where they were living.

And after a while, too, the first girl, the one who had flown away as a brand goose, came back and lived with them too. Now the two girls who had married qaaweiłuq were really animals. The first was a squirrel, the second was a ptarmigan. And whenever he went away, as to his uncle's, they drew him back to the house on the cliff with their thoughts. Whenever the brand goose was afraid, they reassured her by telling her that qaaweiłuq was coming.

And after a while, too, the uncle learned of his nephew's marriage and of his three wives. He saw, too, that his nephew's wives were better looking and much more industrious than were the girls of his own people. qaaweiłuq continued to work hard. He went out and got loads of caribou meat and gave much of it to his uncle's people. He even gave them meat with the skins on. He traded with his uncle's people, getting blubber from them after their whaling and trading caribou meat for it. At last he told his wives that he wished to go whaling with the other men. They said that he should not do this, that something would happen to him. They urged him to continue trading for blubber and oil and not go out on the sea. But he insisted and went over to his uncle's people and joined a whaling crew. He told his wives that he was going to get a share of the meat.

It so happened that there were other men who had become envious of qaaweiłuq because of his three wives. They wanted to get them away from him but they were afraid of his uncle. A number of men thought of different ways of getting qaaweiłuq out of the way. South of where he and his three wives lived there was another river. The young people of his uncle's town were going there to play games. They invited qaaweiłuq, planning to push him from a high cliff into the river. He arrived there and saw the others enjoying themselves and having a good time at that place. His wives told him: "Don't go over there; there is just trouble for you over there." But he went over to join the people. For a while he stood and watched what they were doing. The people were playing side by side in two teams. One team would hold a plank out over the river at the top of the cliff while the people on the other team would walk one by one out to the end of the plank. Each one took his turn, walking out on the plank until he became afraid of the height and turned back. When qaaweiłuq finally went up to the people, each team said: "Be on our side! Be on our side!" Finally he joined up with a team and took his turn walking out on the plank. He was not afraid because he wore a charm of duck feathers around his neck.

It so happened that the people had planned that when he took his turn, he would be dropped from the cliff. The men would then race away and the ones who ran the fastest would get his wives. So qaaweiłuq walked to the end of the plank. The people upset him and let him fall. But because of his charm, he did not fall. Instead, he floated through the air like a piece of down. At the bottom, his squirrel wife was waiting and ran with him to their house.

Meanwhile, all the men began to run toward qaaweiłuq's house. One man, the fastest runner, got there first. He was thinking that he would take the best woman for himself. He rushed up to the house and ran inside. There, seated with his three wives, was qaaweiłuq. Sweating from his hard run, the man just came in and sat down on the floor. He was unable to say anything. qaaweiłuq turned to his three wives and said: "These men have come, too; they have come to see us. Let us give them something to eat." And all the people came in, one by one, and got some food. Then they left and went back to their own houses without saying anything.

But qaaweiłuq still thought of going whaling. It became spring. His three wives said: "No, you must not go; we would rather see you trade for blubber. We cannot help you out on the sea." This made him very angry and he beat the three of them and went off to the water's edge to the whaling camp. He went with a boat and joined a crew. He did not join the crew and boat of his uncle. In the boat he sat next to the steersman and next to him sat a young boy. All the boats went after a whale. His boat could not approach the whale, although it tried again and again. At this, qaaweiłuq became angry and said: "Why don't we get any nearer to the whale?" The boy next to him said: "Why don't you go after the whale all by yourself?" At that, all the crew faced him and shouted: "Get the whale yourself!" He replied, ashamed, that he did not know how to whale. But they forced him and made a place for him in the bow of the umiak. He held the harpoon and the line with its three seal pokes attached. At length, the steersman neared the whale and the time was ready for the harpooning. qaaweiłuq let the harpoon go and struck the whale cleanly. The crew drew up on the line and the umiak was towed by the whale. As they did this, they reached down and stealthily fastened the line to qaaweiłuq's ankles. Suddenly, they cast off and he was pulled overboard. As they did this, all the other umiaks turned back and gave up the whale. As the canoes reached the edge of the ice, the men leaped ashore and raced toward qaaweiłuq's house to get his wives.

The first one to get there saw the women in the house, one standing near the door, the other two near the skylight of the house. As he ran close, he saw a ptarmigan and a brand goose fly up from the skylight and he saw a squirrel run into the doorway. Suddenly, as he watched, the house was gone. There was only the bank on which the house had stood, run through with squirrel burrows.

Meanwhile, the ptarmigan and the goose flew to the sea and the squirrel, too, ran through the underground burrows to the beach. But they couldn't find their husband and they searched for him all spring and into the summer.

Now when qaaweiłuq found himself on the back of the whale, he didn't know what to do. He closed his eyes. Suddenly, all was quiet. He opened his eyes and found himself on a sandspit with the water pushing him back and forth He got up and saw the whale on the beach and found the rope bound to his ankles. He dried his clothes and began to look around. But he didn't know where he was. He found himself on a river at the sea but he was unable to recognize the place. After a while, he began to build a house. When he had a place to live, he made weapons and caught some caribou. He made himself new clothes and all summer long he lived from the caribou he caught. There was also the meat from the beached whale. He could get water from the river and he had plenty of food and good clothes. At last, when the sea was covered with ice, he stopped his hunting. He turned his attention to the river. He made nets and hooks and chopped a hole in the ice. He fished at the hole and got grayling and other fish. And he made a place to store them.

Now as he fished, he looked down into the hole in the ice and down there in the water he saw a large grayling that he was unable to catch. Finally, he put his arm inside his parka and reached out underneath down into the hole in the ice. He was able to grab the fish by its fin and to pull it up. As he got it to the surface, it turned into a young woman. As soon as she was out of the water, she began to dance. He brought her home and she was dancing all the way. But when she came into the house, she began to work. She worked hard, but from time to time, she would stop and dance again. Even when she was sewing, she would stop to dance. She never said anything.

Meanwhile, his three wives never stopped looking for him. At last, after much time and searching, they found him by the river in a far place. They saw his house there by the mouth of the river. The three came to the house and looked into the skylight. Inside they saw the woman sewing. After a time, she put her sewing down and began to dance. Then she stopped and went back to sew again. It was moonlight. After a time, they heard a voice, singing out on the ice of the sea, far away and very faint. It came louder and louder. "Perhaps it is qaaweiłuq," they said. And they decided to walk out on the ice to see. As they came near the voice, they hid in the shadow of an ice ridge. Among themselves they said: "If he is half bald when he takes his parka hood down, then he is our husband." He walked toward them, dragging a seal. Close by them, he drew back his parka hood. They saw it was he, his half-bald head shiny in the moonlight.

Then they followed him back to the beach and to the house. When he came home, he called in the skylight for the woman to come out and to give the seal a drink. She came out, put her cup down and began to dance. The three other wives then decided that they would wait until the man went hunting again and that they would then talk to the woman in the house. So they stayed there, trying to keep warm. And they waited until their husband left the house and went hunting again.

When they went into the house, the woman was very glad to see them. They had planned that when they had eaten, they would grab the other woman and put her into the water. So when they had eaten, they grabbed her. She was dancing and kept on dancing even while they held her. They dragged her along the ice and pushed her into the hole, headfirst. As soon as her forehead touched the water, she slipped from their hands and they saw the grayling swimming in the water. They then agreed among themselves that they would go back to the house and wait. If their husband came home with a seal, they decided they would not come out of the house with water. After a time he came, dragging a seal behind him. They heard his footsteps and his call for water. He called several times but no one came. He called for the grayling woman again and again. Finally, angered, he began to scold: "My first wives were not like you." And the women inside knew for certain that this was their husband.

Then he came rushing into the house. The brand goose, afraid, flew up through the skylight and away. The other two remained behind. One wife hid herself but the other confronted him. He saw who it was and fell down fainting in the passage of the house. The one who was hiding pulled him up into the house onto the floor. He said: "If you hadn't grabbed me, I would have died." Then he told them: "I don't know where I am staying." And he related how he had been thrown from the boat by the whaling crew. He told them how sad he had been at being so long away from his home and that he would gladly have gone back to his uncle's people but that he did not know the way. The two women told him that he had gone whaling against their advice and that this was why all the misfortune had come to him. "We looked all summer and winter for you and now we have found you," they said. "Your uncle's place, if you want to see it, is far away." He begged them to take him there. After that, they traveled all winter and into the summer, going season after season, for many years. Finally, they arrived at the uncle's village. There were only a few houses left standing and all the people were very old. After that, people said of qaaweiłuq only that he had a brand goose, a squirrel, a ptarmigan, and a grayling for his wives.

KAYAKTUQ, THE RED FOX

There was a boy lying unconscious on the sand. Finally he rose up and began to walk on the beach. After he had gone a way, he saw a red fox walking beside him. The boy did not know where he was. At last he came to a place at the mouth of a river. There he began to build a house and make preparations for fishing. But he did not know who he was or who his people were. He began to fish and caught a great many different kinds of fish. From time to time the red fox would come and the boy would feed him, giving him fish to eat. Once while he was fishing, the red fox came close. The boy seized it and began pounding its nose on the ground. The fox raised its head, the skin of its face folded back, and the fox's face became the face of a man. The fox told him that to the north, some distance up the coast, there were many people. And down the coast, too, southward, there were also many people living. The fox said: "Even farther to the south, on the coast, there live a man and his wife. They have a daughter with no husband." And the fox wanted to take him there.

So they started off to the nearest people. These people lived in a village with a karigi. The karigi had a skylight made from a block of ice. All day long, the people stayed in their karigi. Before they reached the village, the fox said: "Let me go ahead; you wait here. I will come back here and tell you what is going on." The boy agreed. The fox walked up to the karigi and looked into the skylight. He called the people to come out, but they refused to come out until dark. At dusk, a man came out. The red fox said: "There are people coming, many more than you; they will kill you all. You had better take your people and go away."

Now the man was very frightened. He ran at once back into the karigi and announced: "This is the first time that an animal has talked to me. We had better do what he says and go away from this place because there are those coming who will make war on us and will kill us all. Let us leave at once." The people were all afraid and went home at once to get ready to leave.

Then the fox came and fetched the boy. He said: "The people are now all gone; we can go to that village and stay there." And when they arrived, the fox told the boy to pick out the best place he could find. The two stayed together. In the evenings, the fox would sing so that the south wind would blow. It blew and began to thaw out the snow. By evening, it would be all wet. But by morning it would freeze up again. The people who had run away from that village had taken so few things with them that they were not ready for the changing weather. In a short while they had all frozen to death.

From then on the red fox and the boy lived together. Again the fox told him of the couple with the unmarried daughter. He said: "If you want that girl, go and get her." So they walked down to where those people were living. The boy walked up to the skylight of the house to make someone come out. A girl came out and the fox knew that she was the daughter of the house. As she stood there, the fox asked her to marry the two sons of a rich man. "How can they be so rich as to send a red fox?" thought the girl. She said she would go in and ask her father. When her father came out, the fox said the same things to him. "My daughter can do what she wants," said the father. But meanwhile he was thinking: "How rich those two men must be to send a red fox to tell us!" He told his daughter to follow the fox. But the fox asked the father to hitch up his team and to take the girl along. They came back to the village which the people had left. Now the girl saw only the young man. She saw no one else at all in the houses around there. She married the young man but she knew that the fox had lied.

When the boy and the girl married, the fox went to live someplace else. He went back to the parents of the girl. He said: "There is no need for you to concern yourselves about her; she has everything she needs and wants." And he told them that she had much more than her parents. Every time the fox came by that way he told the father of the girl: "Your daughter has plenty; she has much more than you have here."

And since that time, the red foxes know how to make tricks against people and to fool them.

THE BLIND MAN AND THE LOON [11]

There is a lagoon of fresh water to the east of utkeaaγvik (Barrow) which is known as malekpik. Once there lived here a boy named tiptan. He was blind and lived with his grandmother all alone. The boy could not hunt and he and his grandmother were starving. In the wintertime a bear came and sniffed around their house. At last the bear walked up to the top of the house and thrust his nose into the skylight. The grandmother took the blind boy's bow and two arrows and, putting them into his hands, told him to shoot in the direction of the skylight. tiptan did so and struck the bear. He heard it groan and roll down

[11] For a fuller version of this tale, as well as an analysis of its distribution, see R. F. Spencer and W. K. Carter (1954).

off the rooftop. But the wicked grandmother insisted that the arrows had not hit the bear. "You hit the itkax," she said (itkax—the wooden frame of the skylight). But the boy insisted that he had hit the bear and the grandmother continued to deny it. The grandmother gave the boy only poor rotten meat with worms in it. For herself she kept the good rich meat of the bear. All winter long, the grandmother lived off the bear's flesh, while tiptan went hungry.

At last, summer came. tiptan was sitting in the summer sun by the house. His grandmother had gone away to gather wood. Suddenly, he heard his name called and a voice saying, "tiptan, come!" Slowly, he made his way over to the shores of the lagoon. He felt his hand grasped by that of another person. It was a loon who had called him and who took him by the hand. The loon said: "Put your arms about my neck and I will dive with you into the lagoon." He did so and the loon took him down to the bottom. At last, he could no longer breathe and struggled back to the surface. He found he could see the light. The loon took him on its back again and dived with him once more. When he came up, he could see still more. When he had dived with the loon four times, he came up and he could see better than he could before he became blind. And when his sight was restored, the person who had taken his hand was gone. No one was there; in the distance, he saw a loon flying away.

Now tiptan returned to his house. His grandmother still had not returned. He noticed the skin and the bones of the bear he had killed. He became very angry and planned to take revenge on his grandmother. When she returned, he said: "I will eat the bear meat and you can have the meat with the worms in it." Seeing that tiptan had recovered his sight, the grandmother became most frightened and said nothing. Next morning, the boy took his harpoon and said to his grandmother: "There are belugas swimming near the beach. I am going to spear one. I want you to come with me and hold the line for me." When they came to the beach, several belugas were swimming past. The boy who had been blind harpooned one. Suddenly he fastened the line of the harpoon to his grandmother's wrists. As the beluga swam away, the old woman was dragged into the sea. As she and the beluga disappeared, a killer whale was seen following them. The killer whale killed the beluga and tangled himself up in the harpoon lines. As he swam away, he dragged the old woman with him. Today the killer whale has a hump on his back. This is the old lady, whom her grandson used as a seal poke.

THE TALE OF MAXWOŊAW

There was a town where there were many houses together. Outside of this place a mother and her son were living together all by themselves. One day the son got married to one of the girls from that village. When they had been married for several years, they had a baby boy. They named the boy maxwoŋaw. In those days, the men never went out to empty the chamber pots; this was women's work. One night, the wife went out to empty the pot. Her husband waited for a while for her to return. After a time he started out to look for her but he couldn't find her anywhere. Finally, he went over to the village to see if she was with her parents. But she wasn't there either and he told the people in the village that she was missing. So all began to search for her but to no avail. In the morning, they found the chamber pot where she had emptied it but saw no sign of her. The husband attempted to locate her tracks. He circled several times around the house but saw nothing. Again on the next day he looked for the tracks of his wife. This time he found a track some distance from the house. It appeared as though something had been dragged through the snow. It looked like the drag marks left by someone's legs. This track led toward the inland country. But this was all that he saw; he could find nothing else.

Now when he came back to the house, his mother told him to go up to the trees and to cut a branch which he could use as a staff. There were some willows growing near where they lived and the man went to them and selected a branch and took it home. His old mother took it into the house and began to work on it. She made some singing over it and she took a little bag and tied it to the end of the stick. Now she told her son to take this stick and to stand it up outside the house so it would not fall down. He did so, burying the end into the snow and pouring water over it so that it would freeze in tight. In the morning, his mother told him to go to see if the stick was still standing. But the stick had fallen down and was pointing in the direction of the tracks he had seen. And the ice around the base of the stick was broken up. When he told his mother about this, she told him to do this again, putting the stick firmly in the ground so that it wouldn't fall down. And she advised him to be careful so that the little sack on the end would not be knocked off. He placed the stick deeper in the snow, stepping on the snow around it to pack it in and pouring water over the base so as to freeze it in solid. But the next morning, the stick had fallen down again, the ice was broken up around it, and the stick lay pointing in the direction of the tracks. When he came again into the house and told his mother what had happened, she said that someone had taken his wife away in the direction in which the fallen stick pointed. Then she said to her son: "If you go in the direction that the stick has fallen, you must make a pair of water boots and a pair of snow boots." She took the skin of a seal and made a bag to fit on his back. Next she got the boots ready and some dried fish. And she made him ready to go, giving him the fish, the bag with the two pairs of boots in it, and placing the staff in his hand. She told him that if he didn't know in which direction to go, he should stand the stick up as before and go to sleep. He would know the proper direction when he awoke.

So the man started from his house and walked. His boots never got wet, nor did they wear out. Each time he stopped, he ate some of the dried fish and replaced it in the bag his mother made for him. When he took the fish out again, there was just as much as before. And his boots, placed in the bag when not in use, never wore out. When he lost his way, he placed the stick upright, went to sleep, and in the morning the stick had fallen down, pointing in the direction he should go. For two winters and two summers he traveled in this way. In summer, he put on the water boots but they never got wet. In winter, he wore the snow boots.

Now soon after the man had left in search of his wife, his mother, the old lady, who was taking care of the boy, maxwoŋaw, died. One day, as the baby was left alone, there came wolves to the house. One looked into the skylight of the house and saw the little boy all alone there with the corpse of his grandmother. The wolf went in and fed the baby, changing his shape to that of a man. And when the baby had been fed, the wolf left, changing back into his wolf form again. After that, the wolf came daily and kept the baby alive by feeding him.

Now the man who was looking for his wife came at last to a river. When he arrived there, he put his stick up and went to sleep. He did not know in which direction he should go. Next morning, the stick had fallen down and was pointing to the edge of the river. He paused and walked along the bank. As he walked, there were clouds which came up over the river and it became darker and darker. At length, he reached a place on the river bank where some people had settled and built their houses. The people of this village were playing football; it was in the autumn. As he looked at the houses, he noted that he could see no land behind them, only water. He concluded that he had reached the edge of the sea. And when he saw the houses and the village, he decided to remain where he was, waiting until it grew dark. He thought: "I'll just remain here where I am and when it is dark, I'll travel through the village, stopping only long enough to ask the people what they have seen." When it grew darker, he began to walk toward the people and their village. As he walked, he remembered that his wife was a fast runner and that, at home, when they had football, she was always taking part in the racing. He recalled how fond she was of all games. It so happened that the people saw him before he came to the village and they ran out to meet him. When they came close, he looked to see who was the fastest runner. It was a woman who was running the fastest. Behind her came two young men but they were unable to overtake her. As they came up to him he saw the family resemblance and noted that they were a sister and two brothers. Each man took his arm and they led him home to the house of their parents.

When they came back to the village, they entered the house. Inside was the father and mother, as well as a younger brother. The father said: "You are a fine looking man. It will be a pity if that man over there sees you. He always kills strangers." After they had eaten, a little man came into the house. At once he said: "Oh, you people have a stranger with you." He left again at once. The family was troubled and said that the little man acted as a spy for the man who killed strangers. He went about daily, reporting the presence of newcomers to the village. Then the man who killed the strangers would come to seek them out. When the little man had gone, the father of the house asked his wife to bring from the hallway something that had a little bag in it. When the woman brought the little bag in, she put a pan on the floor and began to unwrap the thing she had brought in. Inside was a small object wrapped in skins. This she put in the pan. "Now," she said, "if you can catch this little thing inside this pan, you must swallow it. Then you cannot be hurt by the man who kills strangers. The guest picked the pan up. As he did so, the small wrapped object began running about in the pan. He tried to catch it but couldn't get hold of it. The object never ran over the edge of the pan; it remained only in the center. The woman told him to catch it and to swallow it right away. But each time he put out his hand to get hold of it, it eluded him. It seemed to get livelier all the time. But after several tries, and after watching it for a time, the object seemed to become slower in its movements and he was able to grasp it. As soon as he held it, he put it inside of his mouth. He was surprised that he could feel nothing and could taste nothing. But as he swallowed, it seemed to him that he had swallowed something.

When he had done this, two men came to the house. They said that there was another man who wanted the stranger to come over right away to his place. Then they left, but after a little while they returned and repeated their message. When, each time, they called down through the skylight, the stranger told them to come into the house and they could then all leave together to visit the man who had called him. But they remained outside. Now actually, these two men were also people that the man who killed strangers wanted to kill.

The father of the family said to the stranger, the man who had been searching for his wife: "Perhaps you have nothing that you can carry along with you; what will you do, when they start to do something to you?" The stranger answered: "If you won't be afraid, I'll try something." And he told the old couple to tie a snow knife on each of his arms. After they had tied one on each of his arms, he called the two men again. This time they came to the house and stood by the doorway. He said to them: "Do not be frightened if I must do something; if you are afraid, I'll kill you both when I attack that man." Then he got down on his belly by the doorway and lay there. As they watched, he turned into a polar bear and got bigger all the time. He said: "If you look at me now, as I am becoming a polar bear, take the strings off the knife on my left arm." As he said this, he looked at the two men standing by the doorway. They began to argue with each other as to which one should untie the strings. Both were afraid. But at last they approached the polar bear together and, as they touched the bear's foreleg to take the snow knife off, the bear became a man again. The two old people said: "When that man over there wants to kill people, he turns himself into a giant worm; he circles around the house, getting bigger and bigger, and swallows the person whole." The father of the house said that he believed that if the stranger could become a polar bear, he could beat the worm.

So the stranger, the two men who had come for him, and the two brothers of the house started off. The youngest brother wished to accompany them. He was just a little boy but he began to look around the house to find his father's icepick to take with him. He was looking for something to strike the man with. He was thinking that he could help the stranger and that when the wicked man turned himself into a worm, he could stab him with the icepick. He looked all over but he couldn't find his father's pick and so he stayed at home.

At last the group approached the house of the man who killed strangers. They entered it and saw a big man sitting there. He had a bench which went all around his house. He told them to go over to the other side and to sit on the bench. The five men, the stranger, the two men who had called, and the two brothers, sat down as the man asked them, seating themselves across from him. When they were seated, the big man took a curtain and hung it up so that he was behind it and they could not see him. When he was concealed behind the curtain, the stranger told the young men to help him with the snow knives on his arm as before. After the young men did this, he went to the middle of the floor, turning his back to the curtain and facing the bench where the young men sat. But he kept his eye on the corner of the curtain. Finally, he saw a long worm go out and begin to circle the house. The worm was long and had a hard shell, and its head was shaped like the head of a nail. When the young men saw this, they began to make a loud noise. The two brothers said: "Every time any people come, this worm eats them up." And they began to wail. The stranger told them to be quiet and not make so much noise but they were frightened, too much afraid to stop. They kept right on making noise. Meanwhile, the stranger had become a polar bear. As the worm continued circling the house, the bear began to move. "Something is going to happen," he said. As the worm was about to circle the house again, the bear ran up, and drawing the knife off its right foreleg, cut the worm in half. The worm had grown bigger and bigger all the time. As it was cut in half, half drew back, splashing blood all over. But while they were still watching, the other half, the head and mouth end, ran around the house again. The bear rushed at this part and cut it in half again.

Now the people who were behind the curtain with the worm man began to talk. They said: "The worm is already dead." They took down the curtain. The man who was a polar bear resumed his human form and sat down with the others. He had won. Now when the worm was dead, all the people were happy. They said that the wicked man was dead and that although they had all always wished to kill him, they had not dared to do so. In the house were many women which the worm man had taken from others. He had often taken the shape of a duck when he went about and had abducted women. Even from that same village he had taken women. He seized all those who were good looking. And whenever he got any news of strangers, he sent the little man around to spy on them and then, in his worm form, he killed them. The stranger then asked if there were any other partners of the worm man. "There is only the little man," they said. And the stranger called him over and killed him. "Are there any more?" he asked. "No, you have killed them both," the people said, "we are glad that you killed them both." Then they all went over to the place where the women taken by the worm man were gathered. And among them the stranger found his wife. He learned from her that the wicked man had taken her away, having seized her from the air while in his duck form. He then asked the other women who their husbands were. And the men all began taking their wives home. After this, the stranger and his wife continued living in that village; they lived there several years.

Now while they were there, the son they had left behind had become a young man. He had been raised by wolves. He never learned to hunt because the wolf brought him food daily. Every time people came there, this boy, maxwoŋaw, killed them because he believed that they had taken away his parents when he was small. He became like a wolf too.

In the other village, the parents began to think of their son, maxwoŋaw. They wondered if he were dead or still living and decided to go back and to look for him. So they got ready to go back. The father of the house first visited by the man told his daughter to go back with them. She too became the wife of maxwoŋaw's father. They walked away. The two women walked much faster than the man; in fact, he could hardly keep up with them. They traveled the same way and it took them 2 years. After this time, they saw their house. As they approached, they saw the wolf come out of the house and start running away. The mother of the boy said: "Maybe the wolf has eaten our son and has started living in the house." But when they came close to the house, a big young man came out. His hood was up but they could see his ears clearly and they were just like the ears of a wolf.

Then they looked at the village nearby. It was deserted. The young man had frightened off all the people through his close ties with wolves. As the young man started out from his house, he carried a bow and arrows, the arrow drawn taut on the bowstring. When he came close, the man said: "We are your father and mother and you are our son. Here is your mother; I have brought her back." But the young man replied: "You are fooling me. Everyone who comes here says the same thing so as to keep me from killing them. You are lying so that I shall not kill you." But the man said: "You are indeed my son; I have brought your mother home." The young man said: "If you are truly my father, you will have to say my name. If you cannot say my name, I will kill you." The father answered back: "You are my true son and your name is maxwoŋaw." When he was thus called by name, he broke his bow and cracked his arrows across his knee. Then he put his arms under his parka and began to walk back to the house. His parents, with his father's second wife, followed him back. They could guess that his grandmother was dead and they thought that the house would be filthy inside. But actually, it was cleaner than any house they had ever seen. The family now sat down together and maxwoŋaw began to tell all that had happened since his grandmother had died. He said that a person had come in and begun to take care of him. This person, he said, had no knife or arrows but had brought fresh deer meat every day. This was the wolf, who killed a deer each time it hunted. And it happened that it was a female wolf.

When maxwoŋaw was thus reunited with his parents, he no longer had need of the wolf. It never came back. And his father taught him to hunt and he became a great hunter. Later he married several wives and was very rich. And the people came back to live in the village.

THE GIANT

There is the story of the giant who lived at nuwuk. He was the biggest man all around and he lived in a great big house. He laughed all the time but he beat everybody up and everyone was afraid of him.

Now there were two orphan boys who also lived there. For some reason that big man hated them. Whenever he would meet them, he would grab them, one by one, and pulling his pants down, would rub their faces in his anus, sometimes defecating on them. Then he would laugh and let them go. These two poor boys were at their wits' end; they didn't know what to do. Sadly they wandered around the place, avoiding the giant. At last, a man took pity on them; he asked them why they had such sad faces. At first they wouldn't tell him. Then they said that they were mistreated by that giant. Every time he saw them that big man mistreated them. The man said: "I will help you; I feel sorry for you." And he made them little bows out of bone, carefully fitted together, and backed with sinew. And he made them sharp, stone-tipped arrows. Then he said: "You must learn to hide these under your parkas so no one can see them and you must practice with them."

Every day, the boys tried shooting with their arrows. The man said finally: "Now try shooting your arrows against this dried ugruk skin." They tried it and were able to shoot their arrows through the skin. "That is enough," said the good man, "Now you can do it." And he told them that when the giant grabbed them again, they should shoot him right in the rectum with their arrows.

They went away and the giant saw them. He laughed and grabbed them, dropping his trousers down as he did so. He took the first boy and rubbed his face in his anus. The other stood by. As soon as his brother was free, he grabbed his little bow from under his parka, fitted an arrow, and shot the big man in the anus. The giant fell down, screaming with pain. The other boy pulled his bow out and shot the giant in the chest. He died, and the boys went away.

Now the man who had been so good to the two orphan boys adopted them. Nor did the family of the giant try to do anything to them. Everyone felt that they had done right in getting their revenge on him for his bad ways.

This giant's house is still standing at nuwuk. And he had another house at piγinik, too. He was a very rich and strong man but he always treated everyone so mean.

THE POOR BOY AND THE TWO UMEALIT

And there is the story of the group of people who lived by a river. Among them there were two umealit. And in their village there was the karigi to which all the people came. Here the good hunters fed the people who did not have enough to eat. Across the river, away from the village, there was a poor old woman who lived with her poor orphaned grandson. Now one of these umealiq had two sons and it was his habit to care for the old woman and her poor grandson. The second umealiq had goods and much wealth and he also had four sons and one daughter. He didn't care at all about that old woman and her poor grandson.

The orphan boy, as soon as he got up in the morning, used to go over to the karigi and would wait there. The wife of the first umealiq would give him food which she brought there. The poor boy grew up and was able to help his grandmother. Then when his work was done around the house, he would go over to the karigi and wait for food. This he would bring home. And that is the way he and his grandmother kept alive. But the wife of the second umealiq never gave him any food, even when she would bring it to the karigi. She didn't bother about him at all.

After a time, the orphan boy wanted to join the others in hunting. But he had no weapons. While the boys of his own age hunted, he just stood and watched. There was no one to make the weapons for him. So he continued to depend on the karigi for his food.

His grandmother gave him as an aanaroaq the tissue from the underside of dried blubber. She sewed this on his parka. And she also gave him the tail from a squirrelskin as his aanaroak. He knew what his aanaroat were because his grandmother taught him.

Now one night he was going home from the karigi when the second umealiq called to him and said: "Hey, iilʸonaaruq (a term of familiar address, used only with reference to a close friend; the umealiq pretends affection for the boy) the boys your age are out hunting. Why don't you go out with them instead of begging food in the karigi here?" The orphan boy gave no answer but thought to himself that he had no bow, no arrows, and no harpoon, and that he was unable to make them. And he got up and started off toward his house. But the umealiq said: "Wait!" He opened his tool bag and gave the boy a flint knife The orphan thanked him and left.

When he arrived home, he showed the knife to his grandmother and told her what the second umealiq said. "I am so glad to have this knife." he said. Then he asked his grandmother if she knew how to set snares for ptarmigan. In answer, she picked up the willow rushes off the floor and showed him how to set the snares with sinew. Still he held his knife; he liked it so much. "Now you can set ptarmigan snares for yourself; you see how it's done," his grandmother told him. Then she braided sinew and made five snares for the boy. Then he asked her what part of the ground was best for setting the snares. She said: "In the willows where no one has walked." And after she gave him the snares, she went to sleep.

But the boy stayed up and went out of the house and watched the stars, waiting until morning. While the whole village was still asleep, the boy walked upriver. He walked along by the willows, looking for a good place. At last, he came to a spot where there was a tributary stream flowing into the river. He went up this a way and began setting his traps, each one in a different place. As he worked, he saw ptarmigan tracks. When he finished setting his last snare, it was already nightfall. On the way back, he watched carefully where he went, studying the way because he had never been away from the village before.

When he arrived home, his grandmother asked him if he had set his traps. He told her that he had and then went over to the karigi to get their food. Now it was in the springtime and food was scarce. As soon as he arrived at the karigi, however, the first umealiq gave him food. And the second umealiq asked him what he had been doing all day. He answered that he had been walking around, not doing much of anything. And after he had eaten, he took some food and went home to his grandmother. He was tired and fell fast asleep. But he arose in the middle of the night and went out to look at the stars, impatient for morning and the chance to inspect his traps.

As soon as it began to be light, he started and reached his first snare. All the snares had ptarmigan in them. He brought them home at once. Then his grandmother cooked three of them, and, observing the ritual of the boy's first game, took them over to the karigi to distribute them. Two she kept for herself and her grandson. In the karigi, she told the people what her grandson had done. Then she went home.

The next day, the orphan boy went again to inspect his snares. Again he had taken five ptarmigan. When he brought them home, he asked his grandmother how it was that men trapped foxes. But his grandmother said that she did not know how to do this because her husband was dead. All she could remember was that he made use of rocks.

The next day, the snares again had taken five ptarmigan. But now the orphan boy cached these in the snow and went on walking up the river. Near the bank he found some rocks. As he looked at them, it seemed to him as if someone had put them there. There were five rocks together, placed in a circle with a big rock over the top. The orphan boy lifted the big rock off and inside the circle was a piece of old wood with a smaller piece on it. And he realized that this was a fox trap. He sat down to study how it was made. He saw that one put bait on the long piece of wood and that the big rock would fall when the bait was touched. He took his blubber aanaroaq and used it as bait. It was night when he finished. No one had taught him how to set a trap but he learned all by himself.

Walking home in the dark, he found his ptarmigan. When he reached his house, his grandmother said: "Now you can feed us." And then he went over to the karigi. The second umealiq, who was already there, said: "Now I wonder why my iilʸonaaruq didn't come here all day." So the poor boy told about his snares. Then the first umealiq fed him again and he went home.

Early next morning, he went out again. There were his ptarmigan, five of them. These he cached and went on to the fox trap. There was a fox in the trap. He took the fox, set the trap again and left. And this time it was still daylight. When he returned to the village, he saw a man standing outside, waiting for him. Now, according to custom, the boy had done everything right. He had skinned the fox, had taken its head off, and had cached the meat. He was carrying the head and skin back with him. As he got back to the village, he saw that the man waiting for him was the second umealiq, the one who called him his iilʸonaaruq. The umealiq walked up to him. He snatched the skin of the fox from the boy's hands, tore it to bits, and threw it away. Then he left. The boy went home to his grandmother and told her what had happened. But she said nothing. They both then went to sleep.

Next day, he began again. Again the snares had ptarmigan and the trap had another fox. He skinned it and returned with the skin. And again he met the second umealiq. And again the man snatched the skin and tore it to shreds. When the boy reported this to his grandmother, she remained silent.

Now this happened five times. And all the time, the boy's grandmother said nothing. The boy was not sure what he should do. But when he got five foxes, his grandmother told him to move the trap. So the next day, he moved his trap and went home. On the following day, he had caught a red fox. But the second umealiq was again waiting outside the village. He seized the red fox skin and ripped it to pieces and went away. Nor did the boy's grandmother have anything to say about it when he told her. And this happened five times with red foxes. When he had caught his fifth red fox, the orphan boy again moved his trap. And the next day he found that he had caught a blue fox. He got five blue foxes in a row but each day the second umealiq was waiting for him and each day the man snatched and ruined the skins and threw them away. And still the poor boy's grandmother said no word about it. At the end of five days, he moved his trap again and reset it. He moved his trap and he changed the opening in the trap. Now he took a cross fox. He was tired and sad at what the second umealiq was doing to him but he did not know what to do. He had no other way go going to his own house. There was nothing else he could do. Although he was eager to show his grandmother the skin of the cross fox, he knew that the man would be waiting for him and would destroy the skin he had with him. And indeed, the man was there, the skin of the cross fox was seized and ruined, and when the poor boy told his grandmother what had happened, she refused to say a word against the man who had done this.

Word of this was getting out in the village. The first umealiq heard of it and he would have liked to do something to protect the boy. But as he had only two sons, and as the second umealiq had four, the first felt unable to interfere. The orphan boy would go early to bed and would rise early so that he could visit his snares and trap. Always he got five ptarmigan and always he got one fox. He was getting the cross fox. He took five of them, skinned them, cached their meat. Always as he went on his way homeward across the river, the second umealiq took and destroyed the skins.

And then he got a silver fox. The man was waiting near his house and ruined the silver fox skin. Even though he tried to make his grandmother angry by telling her what the umealiq had done, she remained quiet. Next day, the same thing happened to the second silver fox skin and to the three silver fox skins which he took thereafter. But the grandmother said not a word.

Then he reset his trap. As he approached the trap, he thought: "I wonder what my trap will have in it this time." When he got there, he found that he had taken a wolverine. He started homeward with the skin. This time he really wanted to show it to his grandmother. But the man who called him iil[y]onaaruq was waiting. He looked closely to see what kind of skin the poor boy was carrying. And he grabbed the wolverine skin and tore it to bits. The orphan told his grandmother that he had lost the skin of the wolverine just as he lost the foxskins. But she remained silent.

And each time, the poor boy went over to the karigi for his food. The first umealiq wanted to help him but there was no way to take sides against the man who destroyed the skins. So he could only keep on feeding the poor boy. And again, the boy took five wolverine skins in succession, losing them to the waiting umealiq. Then he reset his trap again.

"What will I get this time?" he wondered. He found, when he reached the trap, that he had taken a wolf. It was dead. Again the man was waiting as the boy came home. He saw the skin of the wolf and grabbed it and tore it to pieces. Still his grandmother kept silent when told what the man was doing to him. Next day he recovered his ptarmigan and found another wolf at his trap. And he lost the wolfskins to the fury of the second umealiq. And still his grandmother said nothing. The grandmother was grateful to the second umealiq because he had provided the knife which had made their food possible. That is why she was silent. She did not feel that she could speak out against this man.

On the day that he took the fifth wolf, he sat for a long time wondering if he should set his trap again. Finally, he decided to do so. He moved the trap, reset it, and started to walk away. But he had not gone far when he found his trap before him, the opening pointing toward him. He turned in another direction, but the trap followed him and came to rest before him. All evening this happened, the trap following his every movement, and coming to stop in front of him with the opening pointed at him. He stopped each time but when he changed his direction, the trap moved again. He didn't know what to do. Then he paused, thinking that no one would mourn for him; he was an orphan, with no kin. So he walked right into the trap. The upper part of his body was caught in the trap. He was locked in place by the trap and stayed that way all night. He listened for someone to come. but he heard no sound at all.

Soon it was morning again. After a while, he heard two men talking: "I wonder where that thing is that the umealiq wanted us to get." But the orphan boy did not understand what it was they were talking about. They never said what the thing was that the umealiq sent them for. And the voices came closer, saying the same thing. After a while, one said: "This must be it." And they lifted up the top of the trap and there was the orphan boy. They lifted him to his feet but he was weak from being in the trap. They worked on his arms and legs, rubbing them, and told him that the umealiq had sent them after him. But he did not recognize the two men. Looking at them, he saw that they wore the masks of wolves, the nose of the wolf being on their foreheads. Their faces were human but they were dressed in wolfskins. The men told him that they had come to rescue him and to take him somewhere. The orphan boy replied that he didn't want to go somewhere unless he could tell his grandmother that he was going away. But the men said: "Our umealiq has sent us and has asked us to take you to him." The poor orphan said again that he would go nowhere without letting his grandmother know. But the men took the boy's arms and pushed him and said that their umealiq really wanted him to come.

There was nothing he could do and he started off with them. As they walked, the men told him that when their umealiq had seen him he could go back to his grandmother.

And after a while the men let his arms go and walked ahead of him. He walked by himself. But the two men walked so fast that he was unable to keep up with them. Then they would stop and wait for him. When he came up to them, they would go on again. Finally, one of the men asked him why he always lagged behind. The boy made no reply. One of the men then stamped with his feet together on the snow, making footprints. He told the boy to stand in the footprints and face away. The man stepped behind him and the poor boy heard something drop. He looked and saw that his wooden bucket and ladle had fallen into the snow. One man said: "When you were small, you drank from the bucket instead of from the ladle." Then they started off again and this time the boy was able to keep up with them. But after a time he lagged behind again.

Again the men waited for him to catch up. This time the second man made footprints in the snow and had the boy stand in them. When he stepped behind the boy, again something was heard to drop. The poor boy looked back and saw the willow broom which was used for the floor, old and mixed up with caribou hair. And the second man told the boy that he had stayed in bed too late in the morning. This time he kept up with the two men and was able to go even faster than they.

Now the two men said: "Our place is not far away; it is just up the river from the place you have been trapping." They went up the river farther. "Now you will see our houses," the men said. At last they came to a bend in the river. The poor boy could see no houses and he began to feel that the men had lied to him. He walked faster and kept on. A hill came down by the river. The two men said that their house was on that hill. But he saw no house; he saw only a small mound. The two men said to the boy that they were going to run a race up to their house. They told the poor boy to try to beat them, running hard so as to get to their house before they did. They stood side by side and began their race. While they ran, the orphan boy was first even with them, but then he began to gain on them and overtook them, winning the race and getting first to the top of the hill. He stopped at a hole in the ground and wondered how he could get in. The two men caught up to him when he stopped and both of them ran on into the hole. Soon he stood alone on the outside. Then he heard someone walk up out of the hole. It was the two men again. This time they had fox masks, with the fox noses appearing in the center of their foreheads.

The two men asked him to come in, saying that their umealiq had asked for him. But he just stood there, saying that the hole was so small that he didn't know how to get in. The men went away but in a moment he heard footsteps again and there they were, asking him to enter. "I can't get into that little hole," he said. The men told him to enter feet first. This he tried and he found that he could enter the hole without any trouble. He looked up and found himself in the hallway of an igłu. Looking around, he saw the kataq there and along the hallway he saw ropes suspended, decked with the skins of all kinds of foxes, wolves, and wolverines.

Then he decided to go up through the kataq into the house. There he saw many people sitting. On one side there sat a very old man. This old man had the nose of a brown bear in the middle of his forehead. And when the orphan boy looked closely, he saw that the brown bear's nose was really part of the man's forehead. The old man asked the poor boy to sit down by him. He did so and then noticed, on the opposite side, a very old woman. A seagull was sitting in the room above the kataq, while over in a corner there sat a raven. Soon the orphan discovered the two men who had conducted him there; they sat in a place together with their fox noses on their heads. Other people were sitting there. Some had wolf noses, some had wolverine noses. And all those people sat there together.

While they were sitting there, the old man said that they had better give their guest some food. At this, the seagull descended to the floor of the room by the kataq, took a hook, and began to prepare it. Suddenly, the poor boy noticed that there was water in the kataq. He saw it and he heard it splashing and sloshing around. The seagull dropped his line through the kataq and began to fish. He began to pull many tomcod into the room. At this, the old couple advised the boy to get ready to grab the fish, saying that the others would grab for them as soon as the seagull had finished. "If you are not quick enough," they told him, "you will get no food." Then the seagull finished and went back to his place. All present grabbed for the food. The old man told him again to get some too. The orphan boy reached down between the legs of the people in front and grabbed a tomcod. Then he went back to his place and began to eat it. As he looked up, he saw that all the others had finished eating and were looking at him. He was afraid but said nothing. Then after a while, he remarked that he better begin to start out for home.

But the old man said: "No, you stay here with us a while; I want these others to show you something. You stay here tonight and then tomorrow you can set out for home." Then the old man called to the others to come. The raven came from his perch in the corner and sat on the side of the house in the middle. He began making a hole in the side of the house. Then the raven called to the boy to come over to look through the hole. He did so and saw all kinds of animals through the hole. When he saw these, the raven told him that whenever he was hungry, he could take any one of them for his meat. Then, when he had showed him the animals, the raven told the orphan boy to go back and take his place again.

Meanwhile, since it was spring, the people back in the poor boy's village were having a hard time getting food. But the first umealiq, he with the two sons, went out daily with his boys and were able to get something. Since they were all good hunters, they brought some food back every day and gave it to the people in the karigi.

Now when the raven had showed the poor boy the animals, the old lady got up and went over and stayed with the kataq. She had a stick with a hook at one end; she reached down through the kataq and pulled something up from within the hallway. She pulled a corpse up, one that was wrapped in an old canoe cover. Then she took the ropes off the wrappings and all present looked to see what she had. There was the corpse of a young woman wearing pretty clothes. The poor boy thought to himself: "She must be the daughter of some umealiq. Wrapped up with her in the canoe skins were the pelts of wolverines, wolves, and foxes. Then the old woman got up and walked around the corpse. She came near the head and kicked it. Then she walked around by the feet of the corpse and kicked them. Then she went back to the head and kicked at it again. And then again she kicked the feet. Suddenly, they all heard a noise from the corpse and the old woman came back around to the head. The young woman sat up and began to look around. They asked her: "Did you know you were sick and died?" "Yes," she said. Then the old woman said: "Would you rather marry this poor, orphan boy or be dead again?" The girl said that she did not want to be dead again and that she would marry the orphan boy. When she said this, and as the boy watched, the old lady touched the girl on the body and she died again. Then the old woman wrapped the corpse back up in the canoe cover and pushed it through the kataq into the hallway.

Now the old man said that they were through showing him things and they all must sleep. "You will sleep beside me," said the old man. Then all present went to sleep. After they had been sleeping a while, the old couple woke the poor boy up and told him that he had been left behind, that all the others had left. The boy looked around and saw that the house was empty except for the old couple and himself. The old man told him to shut his eyes and go out through the small entrance. In a moment, he was standing above ground.

As soon as he reached the open, he thought how worried his grandmother must be. He remembered too, that as he passed through the passageway, all the skins which had been hanging there were gone. So then he started running toward home. He came to where his trap was and saw that the trap had moved again. But his wolfskin was still there. He left it behind and started running toward the home village. As he approached, he wondered if the man who called him iil^{y}onaaruq was still waiting for him outside the house. But the man was not there. Then he came up to his house. Inside, he found his grandmother sitting alone and grieving. She looked up and saw him. She was crying; she thought that he had gone away for good. She looked up and saw him. Then she asked him what he had been doing. So he told her that he had just been traveling around, that he hadn't been doing much of anything.

After a time, he went as usual to the karigi for his food. There he found the man who called him iil^{y}onaaruq. This umealiq pretended to be glad to see him and asked him why he had been away for these days. And the orphan boy answered that he had just been walking around, looking at his snares and traps. Now food was scarce but the people weren't too worried. The first umealiq and his sons always got meat and brought it back to the karigi and the wife of this man always prepared it. And then, too, the orphan boy had always been getting ptarmigan and bringing that back to the karigi. So all had been eating all right. But now the second umealiq persisted and kept on asking where the orphan boy had been. But the boy refused to tell him anything.

Then the boy and the other young men remained in the karigi and started to play games and have a good time. Now the old woman he had seen, the one who brought the corpse up through the kataq with the hook, had told him never to forget what he had seen there. And the boy remembered. So when the young men started to play games in the karigi, the orphan boy said that they better light up some lamps. When he asked for lamps, the two sons of the first umeealiq got up and went to their house and brought back some lamps. They put them on the floor and lit them. And they put one of the lamps in the middle of the floor. This was the custom in those days. And all the young men were all playing, even after all the rest of the people in the village had gone to bed.

Then the orphan boy sat down. He put his arms by his sides and started thinking of the seagull he had seen. He reached down and got a hook for fishing. Suddenly, the kataq of the karigi was full of water, splashing and sloshing around. The water rose right to the level of the kataq. The sons of the first umealiq were frightened and said that if they knew that this was going to happen, they would never have brought a lamp from their parents' house. Now the gull had told the orphan boy that he could fish like this in any kind of water. So he dropped his hook in and started fishing. He brought in many tomcod. Then, because food was scarce, he invited the other young men to share in the catch. He told the others: "This is the thing which I found out when I was away those nights."

When they had eaten, the poor boy thought of the old woman and of her stick with the hook on it, and of how she had pulled the corpse through the kataq. He took such a stick and reached into the kataq, down into the hallway of the karigi. He thought to himself: "The man who calls himself my iil^{y}onaaruq will now be fast asleep." Then he reached out and started pulling. After a while, he pulled in the second umealiq. The man was hooked by the nose and he had no clothes on at all. The poor boy shook him by the shoulder. "Hey, iil^{y}onaaruq!" he said, "Why are you sleeping here in the karigi and why have you no clothes on?" The umealiq got up frightened, ran down through the kataq, and fled home. Then he told the other boys to go on playing their games.

Then after a while, the poor boy took his cane again. And again he pulled the umealiq out of his house by the nose. And he said: "You, my iil^{y}onaaruq, why do you sleep here without any clothes on?" And by now the boys who were with him in the karigi began to get pretty frightened.

Then the orphan boy said that he was going home to sleep. He shared the only bedding with grandmother in their poor house. In the morning, he woke up and stayed around. He decided not to go out and look at his traps.

But the man who called him iil^{y}onaaruq—he woke up with a swollen nose! He didn't know what was the matter with his nose and he was beginning to be pretty scared of that orphan boy.

And the boy stayed around all day. He didn't hunt at all. Then in the evening, he told his grandmother to go over to the house of the second umealiq and ask him for his daughter. "I want her for my wife," he said. The old woman, his grandmother, said: "How will you take care of a wife; we are so poor"; and she begged him not to do this thing. But the orphan boy kept on telling her to go over there and ask for his daughter anyway. She kept on begging him not to make her go over there. But the boy told her to ask the girl and her father. He said that if the girl refused to come, it would be all right, but that his grandmother should try to make her come. So the old lady crossed the river and went to the house of the second umealiq.

She came up into the hallway, went up to the kataq and put one leg on the floor of the igłu. "Why did you come here?" asked the umealiq. "You must be hungry, too, because we all need food; I have none here," he said. Now the old lady was scared to come into the house. That was why she put only one leg on the floor and kept the other foot in the hallway under the kataq. The umealiq thought that she was going to ask for food but she said: „kuxsin^{y}aaruq (this was the poor boy's name) wants your daughter to be his wife; I have come to get her." The umealiq was angry at this and told the girl to throw the old lady out. But the old lady said that she was going anyway and ran away.

After she went home, she told her grandson what had happened, that the umealiq had asked his daughter to throw her out. And she said, too, that the girl had started to throw her out of that house. The poor boy said: "Well, that's all right with me." And then he thanked his grandmother for trying.

Then he asked his grandmother to go to the house of the first umealiq and to ask him for his daughter. But the grandmother said that these were the only people who cared for them and that if she went to ask them, she would offend them. "Then we will lose our only friends." But the old lady allowed herself to be persuaded and went off to the house of the first umealiq. She sat in the same way by the kataq. The umealiq asked her if she were hungry. She answered that her grandson wasn't thinking of food but that he wanted the man's daughter for his wife. At this, the umealiq bowed his head and stopped talking. And the old woman said that she didn't know how her poor grandson could take care of a wife. The umealiq thought for a while, then he looked at the old lady and at his daughter and said: "Sometimes it is the poor boys who become the great hunters." He said that when his sons hunted, they often needed help and that if his daughter married this orphan boy, her brothers would have someone to go with them and help them. The old woman was trembling, but when the umealiq said this, she was again at ease. The man kept talking to his daughter, telling her that the poor boy would be able to help them some day. Then he told his daughter to go along with the old woman. The grandmother wondered if the girl would come. As she walked back to her house, she turned back to look, and there was the girl following her.

The boy saw the girl come into the house. He saw that she wasn't unhappy. The old woman slept and the couple stayed up and talked, enjoying each other's company because they had known each other for a long time. Then the boy went to bed. Before he did so he said to the girl that she should now go home because he and his grandmother had only the one set of bedding. And he told her to come there whenever she liked. The umealiq expected that his daughter would stay there but in the morning, he looked, seeing that his daughter had returned and had spent the night at home. After that, she often spent the day with the orphan boy and his grandmother but at night she always returned to her father's house to sleep.

Now the orphan boy, kuxsinʸaaruq, stayed at home; he did not go out with his snares and traps. And after a while there was not enough food for all those in the village. The hunters brought only small amounts to the karigi. So one day, when the girl was visiting with them, the orphan boy asked her to go to her father and to borrow his bow and all the arrows she could get. He said that he wished to get food and to share it with the needy. He told the girl to instruct her parents to give away all the food they had on hand and to reserve only enough for one day. So the girl told her father what her husband, the orphan boy, had said. At this, the umealiq began to worry, saying to himself: "What shall we do? Suppose we give all our food away and then this orphan boy comes home with nothing?" And he told this to his wife. They he said: "If I give our food away, and then if the orphan boy comes home with nothing, I shall kill myself." Then he gave his bow and arrows to his daughter. She brought them back to the boy's house, staying with him a while after his grandmother slept. And then she went home again.

Early the next morning, the orphan boy went out to hunt. When he came to the hill where the underground house was, he began to run. Then he thought of the raven who had showed him all the animals through the hole in the house. When he reached the top of the hill, he began to look around. On the other side of the hill, he saw a vapor coming up out of the ground. Looking closely, he could see through the vapor and observed a herd of caribou through it on the far side. And even though this orphan boy had never hunted, he shot his arrows at the caribou. When he started down the hill, the caribou came up the hill to meet him. He began to shoot them with the bow and shot until all his arrows were gone. Then when he stopped shooting, the caribou went away.

Next, the orphan boy selected the fat carcasses, taking those so that there would be meat for all. Then when he took the fat carcasses, he began to divide up the rest. He made portions for as many houses as there were in the village. If he left out the house of the man who called him iilʸonaaruq, there would be 10 caribou for each house. Now there was just one fawn left over. This he decided to give to the second umealiq. All day long he worked on the meat. At night he was finished. He looked at himself and found that he was covered with blood.

When he reached home, his wife was with the grandmother. The old woman looked at the boy and saw him all covered with blood, his boots all bloody. Then he told her that he had enough caribou for each house but that for his iilʸonaaruq he had only a small fawn. And she believed him because she saw all the blood. So the orphan boy told his grandmother to tell the umealiq, his wife's father, that he had 10 caribou for each house in the village. And the umealiq believed him too and thanked him. He told the people to go out and get their shares of the meat. And all the people were surprised at what the orphan boy had done.

Now when the second umealiq heard of this, he told his daughter to go to the orphan's house and to help the other girl out. The boy, his grandmother, and his wife were sitting in their house when they heard someone coming in. And this was something new, because no one ever visited them. It was the daughter of the man who called the boy his iilʸonaaruq. They said: "What is it you want?" And she said that her father had sent her to help out with the meat. The orphan boy looked at her when she first came in but then he looked away. Then he turned to his grandmother and said: "Throw her out of the house." And the girl started to leave slowly. Then the orphan boy turned to his wife and told her that they would go to get the meat in the morning, using her father's team to do so. Then she went home to her parents' house.

Early the next morning, she started for her husband's house. From every house she passed, there came a man to ask if it was really true that there was meat for everyone. When she arrived at her husband's house, there were other men there who also asked if there was food. The second umealiq was the last to come. He came up to the orphan boy's house and asked through the skylight: "Can I have meat?" The orphan boy replied that he had saved a fawn for him. The umealiq said it was enough and thanked the boy. Then he asked if there were many caribou where the boy had been. The orphan replied that he had seen only the one herd and had not looked for any more. It had happened, on the previous evening, when the boy's catch was announced, that the second umealiq had sent his four sons out to look for the meat. But they had been unable to see it.

The orphan boy and his wife went out to get the meat. They divided it, giving enough for both their households. Then all went and got their shares of the meat. Meanwhile the sons of the second umealiq spotted the caribou herd. They followed it for a long way but they were unable to catch up with it. And every day, the people of the village went out and hauled their meat. When everyone had brought his meat in, the father of the girl gave her some extra bedding. After that, the girl moved into the house of the orphan and they were married. And she stayed with him and his grandmother. The couple slept on the skins her father had given her.

Then the young men played in the karigi and the orphan boy stayed up with them. One night, he told the others to get a lamp so they could have games. And again, the two sons of the first umealiq went over to their parents' house to get the lamp. They set it up in the middle of the karigi. Then the boy put his hands at his sides and bowed his head. Then he took a staff with a hook at the end and reached into the kataq. And he pulled out the dead body wrapped in the umiak cover—the same corpse the old woman had pulled up. He took the ropes off, started circling the body just as the old woman had done, and kicked at the head and feet. The dead girl then sat up and the orphan boy asked her if she recognized him. "Yes," she said. Then he said that the people in the other house—the animal people—had planned it so that they two should marry. But, as he went on to say, he had already married. "If you want to marry one of the sons, the oldest boy, of the umealiq who is my friend, you can and it's all right with me," he told her. He said that if she did not want to marry, he would send her back to the dead. But the girl stood up and the orphan boy took the canoe cover and the foxskins and wolfskins that were wrapped with the body and pushed them all back into the kataq and they were gone.

And when the young men in the karigi saw what had happened and what the orphan boy was able to do, they looked at him with great fear and respect.

When the poor boy was ready to leave, he told the girl to come with him over to the first umealiq's house. He said that if she wished to go back to her parents when she had married this boy, she might do so. Now the eldest son of the first umealiq was at home asleep. He awoke and saw the girl standing beside him. He noticed her clothes, new, neat, and clean, but of course he could not know who she was. And the boy's parents were glad, even though they didn't recognize the girl.

Then after a while, the orphan boy asked his own wife to ask her father and her brothers to come over and help him build a new house. He said that he needed a much bigger house so that he would be able to feed all the people that came there. He would be able to give food to anyone that asked him. So his father and brothers-in-law came over and helped him build a big house. And all the young people of the village were welcome there and they could go over and get food there any time they wanted to. The orphan boy and his wife were always glad to share their food. And after a time, they had all kinds of furs, boots, skins, and beads. And people no longer called him the poor boy; they called him kuxsin^{y}aaruq, the great hunter.

Now the second umealiq, the man who had called him his iil^{y}onaaruq, sent his daughter over to help. When she got there, she went into the new house. But when the boy saw her, he told his grandmother to shove her out of his house.

Now as for the eldest son of the first umealiq, the man who married the girl who had come from the dead—he and his parents discovered he had married the only daughter of a great umealiq of the tareumiut. As soon as the river froze, the father sent his son and his daughter-in-law down to the sea. It had happened that when the girl was sick and had died, her parents wrapped her body in an umiak cover and had placed it on a rack. Every once in a while, they would go out and look at the wrapped body on the rack, but they never noticed that it had changed. And when the girl and her husband came down the river, the people of her village came out and watched them coming. Then the girl showed her husband where her parents' house stood. And there were her parents. They were much surprised to see a girl that looked so much like their dead daughter. But then she called them father and mother. She and her husband came in and spent the night with her parents. In the morning, her parents went out and looked at the rack. They opened the canoe cover and looked inside. And they found only the skins. Then they asked their daughter how it was that she came alive again and she told them the whole story. Then she told them of the orphan boy who had brought her alive again and of her marriage. She talked about the village of her husband and the things they did there. After they had stayed some time, her father told her and her husband to go back to her husband's people but to come back whenever they wished. And after that, the couple went back and forth, visiting with their parents.

And later, kuxsinʸaaruq, he who had been an orphan, grew very rich and had all that he ever needed. And he became the umealiq in his own village.

THE WOMAN WHO MISTREATED THE CARIBOU

There was a married couple living close by some other people in a village. After a while, they left to go hunting by themselves far away. Now the man was a skilled hunter. He came to the place where there were many caribou and he killed many of them. At other times he had hunted seals; he could hunt both on land and sea. And his wife never wasted any meat. She always went after his catch and brought it back and treated it right. She always gave water to animals from the sea and she was careful about the caribou.

When the couple went to the far place and the man hunted, killing many caribou, the wife stored the meat, dried it, and put the skins up on the rack. And the man, when he had killed caribou, took the sinew and the skins and sent his wife after the meat. He did his hunting in summer mostly and got enough meat for the year. Usually he took just enough. This year, the couple moved far away from the others and settled where there were some old houses where people had lived long before. And he hunted as before and both he and his wife were busy.

Pretty soon, the woman got tired of the hard work she had. She was wearied with the mosquitoes and she stopped looking forward to the summer. She began to hope that her husband would come home with nothing. Then she saw an old wooden bucket which the people who had once lived in that place had thrown away. This was on a day when her husband had killed a caribou right nearby. And it occurred to her that her husband had not yet cut the head off the caribou. She thought to herself that if she were to put the discarded bucket on the caribou's head, her husband might then not be so successful. She did this.

Before she had done this thing, her husband had not had to go far away from their camp at all. He hunted the caribou right there and killed them. He got them quickly. But the next day the man had to go some distance before he could find them. And each day after that, he had to go farther and farther away to find the caribou. And then one day he came home with nothing. This time the caribou were just too far away. It was getting to be near winter and he stopped getting game. He told his wife that if this kept up, they would starve through the winter. He tried hunting again and again, but he got nothing.

At last, toward spring, food was very low. The woman ate with her husband when he returned, but otherwise, she ate nothing all day. Then the food was at last gone. Then they ate sinew and the sealskins they had been storing. And both became very weak.

The hunter began to wonder why there was no game. In his weakness, he could scarcely walk, although he tried every day to find game. Soon he had to use a staff to support him but still he got nothing.

One day, as he staggered along trying to find game, he saw something black moving, somehow stumbling over the tundra. He started to it but it was hard to overtake. And when he came near, he heard a sound, "haw!" (usual exclamation of tiredness or weakness). It had gone dark and he thought that this was another person. This person must also be suffering from hunger was his thought. He approached nearer and again he heard the sound, "haw!". When he got nearer, he thought he could see a caribou. Then he came in front of it and saw that it was a caribou with a wooden bucket over its head. The caribou was talking to itself: "haw! Who will take this bucket off my head? aaaaah, haw!"

The man went up and put his hand on the bucket. He took it off and the caribou saw him. After it was removed, the caribou talked to the man. It said that the man had saved him. "Even though this is what your wife did to me," said the caribou, "all kinds of game will come to you now." Then he told the man to start looking for caribou.

It wasn't long before the man came on a herd. Because he was so weak, he took only one animal from the herd. He took the back fat and the haunch and started back to where his camp was. And as he walked by, he came on other caribou feeding. At home, his wife saw the meat and began at once to cook it and soon they were eating.

Then the man asked his wife if she had done anything to some caribou he had once killed. And she confessed to putting the caribou's head in the old bucket before the caribou's head had been properly cut off. She had intended going back to release the head, she said, but she never did. And she promised never to do this again because of the suffering she had made. Her husband asked her why she did this thing. Then she confessed to her own fatigue and her wish to stop her husband from catching so much game.

The two of them then started off to recover the rest of the caribou meat. While the wife was carrying the rest of the meat home, the man took another caribou. As he walked back and forth, he kept passing the caribou which had its head in the bucket. It was feeding nearby and paid no attention to him. After a while, the man's strength returned and he began to get more and more caribou. Nothing was wasted and all was brought to the camp.

Then in the summer, the man and his wife moved down the river a way and began to get ugruk at the seashore. The single caribou followed them down there but in the fall he went away. Now this couple had no children and each continued to work hard. After the woman put away the meat, she worked on the skins and sinew. She had learned to be afraid of being hungry. Always after that, the man and his wife had enough food.

THE WORM

There was a worm that was about as long as a canvas tent. It crawled on the ground. And this is the story about it.

There were people living in a village by the sea. Among them, there was an umealiq. He had a son and a daughter. Some time before, the daughter had married a man of the nuunamiut and had gone to live inland with his people. In that village by the sea there lived also an old woman. She was aŋatquq. She lived with her son who was a man of great size and strength. And these people by the sea hunted seals and whales. In summer, they went inland to hunt the caribou there and to trade with the nuunamiut. In winter, they stayed in their village where they had one karigi. Whenever the men had finished hunting, they went to the karigi. They would sit there and their wives would cook and bring them food. And this is what that village was like.

Now to this karigi there came customarily the umealiq and the son of that old woman aŋatquq. The people were always a bit afraid of that big strong man. When the men were not hunting, they played games in the karigi and sometimes they played football. One winter, the daughter of the umealiq and her husband, the nuunamiu, came to spend time in her father's village. This nuunamiu was not a strong man. He was, in fact, kind of weak and he couldn't run fast. All the time in that village of the tareumiut, he hunted with his wife's brother. He wasn't good at sealing at all but once in a while, he would get a seal. And when they finished hunting for the day, they all went to sit in the karigi.

Now the big man, the son of the aŋatquq, whenever any person in the village got a seal and the food was brought in and served in the common platter in the karigi, grappled with any person who tried to get the choice flipper parts of the seal and seized them for himself. The first time the man of the nuunamiut saw this, he was mad but he didn't say anything. Then later, he went to his father-in-law's house and told the man what this son of the aŋatquq had done and how angry it made him. But the umealiq answered that they had stood this for a long time, because everyone was afraid of the man's great strength and of his mother's power. He said there was nothing they could do.

The two brothers-in-law continued to hunt together. They went out for seal on the new ice. And when their day of hunting was over, they would wait for the other men and all would come off the ice together. This was because it was necessary to see that everyone came off the new ice safely. They still do this today. While they were waiting for the others, the nuunamiu discovered that the son of the aŋatquq, if he failed to get a seal, would simply snatch one from another man and take it for himself. When they came home, the nuunamiu again complained to his father-in-law. But he said that no one could do anything against that son of the old woman aŋatquq.

In the evening, at the karigi, always the big man grabbed the choice flipper parts for himself. It made no difference if an old man or a young man had this piece; always it was snatched away by the aŋatquq's son. Whenever this happened, the nuunamiu would complain to the umealiq, his father-in-law. But the umealiq always told him not to worry about it.

And in the ball games, the son of the aŋatquq always did well but the nuunamiu was a poor kicker.

Then one day, as they hunted, the aŋatquq's son got no seals. He stole one away from another man. The nuunamiu was angry but he did nothing. After a time, he too got a seal. He brought it home and while his wife was giving it water, he told her to hurry and cook it and bring it over to the karigi. Then he changed his clothes and went over there. They had been sitting there a while when in came the son of the aŋatquq. The wife of the nuunamiu brought in the cooked meat and all started to eat. While the wife was watching, the aŋatquq's son grabbed the seal flippers off the platter. At this, the nuunamiu snatched the flippers out of his hand. He expected to have to fight at once but the big man just sat there and ate no more. Other women also began to bring in food they had cooked but the aŋatquq's son continued to sit and eat nothing. Then after a while, he got up and went away.

When the nuunamiu snatched the flipper parts away from the big man, all in the karigi were surprised. The brother-in-law of the nuunamiu went home at once to tell his father, saying how angry that aŋatquq's son must have been, not eating at all. Then the nuunamiu came home too. His father-in-law said that he had done something for which he would be very sorry. And they all told him how that old woman aŋatquq kept a polar bear as a watchdog, keeping it chained in the hallway of her house. No one ever sees it, they said, but it is there. But then the nuunamiu said that if trouble was going to start, it would be of concern only to himself; he did not want to involve the others in it.

Next day, they went out to hunt seals again. The brothers-in-law each got seals and then waited for the others. This time too, the son of the aŋatquq got no seal and, as usual, he stole one away from another man. He was dragging it behind him across the ice. The nuunamiu saw this and began to look for a piece of ice about the same size as the seal. When he found one, he made a hole in it and pulled it along. When he came up to the big man, he quietly exchanged the seal for the piece of ice he had and returned the seal to the man who had taken it.

When they reached the house, the brother-in-law told his father, the umealiq, what had happened and how angry the son of the aŋatquq would be when he found that he had been dragging a piece of ice. Then, when they had changed their clothes, the two brothers-in-law went over to the karigi. And this time, axsuq, for that was the name of the aŋatquq's son, didn't come at all. When they went home, the umealiq's son told him that axsuq hadn't appeared that evening. And now the umealiq really began to be frightened.

Just as they were going to sleep, someone came over to the house and yelled down the skylight, saying that axsuq was inviting the nuunamiu to go hunting with him on the next day and to play some games with him. The nuunamiu replied: "I'll be right here." And he told the others not to interfere. He said that he was sorry for the poor people and that was why he did as he did. All were very frightened but the nuunamiu was not. And they were all worried because he wasn't afraid. They thought, too, that he wasn't too strong and was a poor runner. So they all told him to make a strong spear. So he sat up making a heavy harpoon. Even so, the men in the house felt it was scarcely enough to go against axsuq, the aŋatquq's son. In the morning, when the spear was finished, someone called in to say that axsuq was waiting.

And when the nuunamiu went out, there was axsuq standing in the place where they played football. The brother-in-law came along but the nuunamiu said for him to stand aside and not to do anything when something started. Now axsuq had a bow and some arrows, so the nuunamiu went back into the house and got a bow, too. They stood and faced each other for a long time. Neither said anything. Then axsuq went back to his own house and began to call something. It was the bear that they used for a dog. And the bear came out, an old yellow polar bear. And axsuq stood by the doorway of his house and said to the bear: "There is the man for you to fight." And the bear started for him. But the nuunamiu, when the bear came at him, just stepped aside. As the bear moved past him, he stabbed it in the arm with his spear. The spear went through and into the bear's side. The polar bear fell over and died.

Then axsuq came forward with his bow. He pulled the arrow back but the nunnamiu was too quick and discharged his arrow first, hitting axsuq. Although axsuq was wounded, he was so strong that he kept on shooting. But he got weaker and weaker and his arrows lost their force. The nuunamiu shot again and killed the bully axsuq. When axsuq was dead, the nuunamiu came forward and called loudly: "Let all who want to take axsuq's part come and fight with me." No one came. But there was one man who ran away from the village secretly to tell axsuq's brother.

That day, the people didn't go hunting. The men all stayed to watch the fight. They saw that the nuunamiu could really move faster than he had pretended. When axsuq was dead, someone went to tell the old woman, his mother. She came out of the house now carrying her aŋatquq's stick and she yelled at the nuunamiu. He ran up and snatched the stick out of her hands. At that, she went back into her house. Now the nuunamiu began to wonder if he should kill the old woman, too. He felt that if he did so, she wouldn't stay dead, being aŋatquq. But he also felt very sorry for her, seeing that he had killed her only son and source of support. But when he came home again, he learned from his father-in-law, the umealiq, that axsuq had a brother who lived inland. This brother, he was told, was also aŋatquq and possessed a huge worm. This worm ate people and the man would send it against persons he hated.

Toward morning, a man came running from inland, telling how axsuq's brother had heard of the killing and was starting down to the coast with his worm, looking for revenge. All morning, the people waited. Along about noon, they heard the sound of snow crunching. They could see axsuq's brother coming up the hill with his worm. And the worm was crawling and crunching the snow.

But before all this happened, the nuunamiu was still thinking about axsuq's mother and feeling sorry for her. He thought about her so much that he couldn't sleep. After a long time, he decided that it would be best if he were to go and kill the old woman. So he got up from his bed and went out into the night. In the dark, he came slowly into the house. He looked for axsuq's wife but he couldn't see her. Then he saw the old woman lying on the bed. He went up to her and shook her but she was cold and stiff. She was dead. Then he realized that in taking her stick, he had killed her.

Now when the brother of the dead man came with his worm, he brought many of his people with him. They all followed the worm and had come to see the worm eat the man. And the nuunamiu waited at the place where he had killed axsuq and the bear. He warned his brother-in-law not to interfere. Now the worm came up the hill and over into the village. Its master came right with it. Then the man said: "There is the man, standing there; he is the man you are to eat." The worm crawled into the open place. It opened its great mouth and raised the front of its body off the ground. It came closer and closer. But when it lunged at the nuunamiu to eat him, he just stepped aside. At once, the worm attacked with its tail but the man stepped over it. The worm did it again and again but each time the man stepped aside.

As he did so, he noticed the joints of the worm on its body. They seemed thin. Otherwise, the worm's body was as hard as a rock and no spear could stab through. After the man had jumped back and forth a while, he took his spear and stabbed the worm between its joints. It began to bleed but still it came on. But the nuunamiu continued to escape. He stabbed again and again. And at last the worm weakened. From the cuts in its joints began to fall human hones. And as axsuq's brother and all the people watched, the worm died. And when the worm died, the power of axsuq's brother was gone.

Now this brother was a big bully, just like axsuq. He would force his people to give him skins and meat. If they refused, he would send his worm after them. But now this worm was dead and he began to be very frightened. He went up to the nuunamiu and said that he would give him all the things that he had if only he might live. The nuunamiu said: "If I hear of you taking things from people again, I shall come and kill you." And axsuq's brother promised. Then he and his people started back inland. But the nuunamiu warned him again.

Back in the karigi, everyone was afraid of the nuunamiu and what he might do. But he told them all that he meant only kindness to everyone and would help them. And everyone was happy. No one ever heard again of any trouble from axsuq's brother. All the people were very grateful and they thanked this man of the nuunamiu. And when caribou hunting time came again, he took his wife and they went back inland.

In the old times, there were many such worms and other things. But they say that men like this good man killed them all off. That is why we do not see them around today.

THE DOG WIFE

There was an old woman who lived with her grandson in the village of tikeraaq (Point Hope). In that same village there lived an umealiq and his two wives. The old woman and her grandson never left; they stayed in the village both summer and winter. As soon as her grandson was old enough, his grandmother took him to the karigi so that he could get food there. Every day he came to the karigi for food.

Now when he had been doing this for a long time, the umealiq, he with the two wives, told him that he was old enough to hunt. "Why do you hang around here all the time?" he asked the boy. "All you do is beg; you should work, even if you have to go out and gather sea worms." But he did nothing and continued to beg his food at the karigi. He stayed with the young men there and when the older people left, he joined the young men in their games.

But once, while the young men were playing, the boy went out into the night and walked around, not doing much of anything. Then he saw a light and realized that it was the skylight of a house he had never seen before. He started over to the strange house and went in. Inside, he saw a woman sewing by the light of a lamp. He saw that this woman wore good clothes but they were made from a spotted kind of skin he had never seen before. The woman saw him and asked him to come in. So he came up into the house and joined her. Then the woman put her parka on and went out, returning in a moment with a platter full of strange meat. She invited the boy to eat. He did so, liking the meat very much, even though he had never eaten meat like it before. He didn't know what kind of meat it was.

After they had eaten, the woman told the boy that he was going to stay there with her. She told him that he could sleep there with her. She said that he could go home the next day. Now the woman was attractive and when she told him to undress and get into bed with her, he agreed, even though he felt a bit afraid. And so they slept together that night.

In the middle of the night, the woman awakened him and pushed him out of the bed. "You must go now," she said. "If they find you here in the morning, it will be bad for you." Then she told him to come again the next night at the same time. So he got up, went out as fast as he could, and slept the rest of the night at his grandmother's house.

In the morning, his grandmother woke him up and sent him over to the karigi for his food. When he got there, the umealiq said: "You are late; you must have something to tell about." But the orphan boy said nothing. Then the others took it up and all questioned him as to where he had been. Still he refused to answer. All day he stayed in the karigi. He kept on thinking of the woman he had been with. When it was dark, he waited a while and then went over to her house. And again he found her doing work by the light of the lamp. When he came in, she gave him meat as before. Again they went to bed together. In the middle of the night she woke him up and pushed him out. He was half asleep and found it hard to get up but she insisted. So he went home to his grandmother's house and finished his sleep there.

In the morning, his grandmother awakened him and again sent him over to the karigi for his food. This time again the umealiq was full of questions. He said: "You might even have a woman somewhere around." But the orphan boy said nothing. That night, when the boy returned to the woman in the strange house, he was treated as before. When she woke him up in the middle of the night to send him home, he tried to stay but again she forced him out. Next morning, the boy was again late at the karigi. But he kept on refusing to answer the umealiq's questions. But that night, when he went back to his wife again, the umealiq followed him when he left the karigi.

As he came up to his wife's house, the umealiq stopped him and asked him if he had a wife. "Yes, I have a wife now," said the orphan boy and told the umealiq where she was. Then the rich man asked him if he would be willing to exchange wives for the night, offering his two wives for the boy's one. The boy agreed and pointed out the place where the woman's house was. But the boy told the umealiq that his wife would ask whoever was sleeping with her to leave in the middle of the night. "If she tells you this," he said, "you stay there and do not go." So when they had agreed to exchange wives, each one left to go to the other's place.

Now the boy had never been to the house of that umealiq. When he got there, he found the two wives in bed, sleeping. He told them that he had exchanged with their husband for one night. Then they made room for him in the bed.

The orphan boy knew that if the umealiq did not leave the woman's house when he was told, he would never again come back. He stayed all night with the man's wives, but the umealiq did not return. In the morning, he went back to the karigi as usual but the umealiq did not come there. They waited for him all day but he never appeared. That night, the orphan went over to the house of the umealiq and took possession of it. He kept the man's two wives as his own and used the man's property. After that, he became a great whaler and umealiq in tikeraaq. And the people around there never knew where that man had gone. They never saw him again.

This orphan boy had had a female dog. She was pregnant and she died. They took the dog's carcass out on the ice. Then that dog returned as a woman. So in reality that woman was a dog and had been the boy's dog wife.

THE MAN WHO MARRIED THE POLAR BEAR WOMAN

There were people of the nuunamiut. They were many in one place. Among them, was a couple with just one son. This boy hunted well and the couple was well-to-do. The people had settled on the bank of a river. On the east side of the river, not far away, was a high hill. When the young men of the settlement hunted, they always hunted to the west, away from the hill. But the son of the couple always hunted alone and always went to the east, in the direction of the hill. In winter, this young man brought in all his meat, racking it and caching it in his racks behind the house where he lived with his old parents.

One day, as he returned from hunting, his parents told him that he was too old to be without a wife. "We are not strong any more," they said. "It is time that you got married and brought a woman home to help around the house." The boy did not answer. After a while, his mother got a girl from another family and brought her to their house. But the young man refused even to look at her. Each day, the mother brought a different girl but the son never even glanced at them. Soon there were no more girls left and the mother stopped in her efforts to make her son marry. Every day the boy hunted. He brought back much meat, even in winter. But otherwise he was very shy in front of other people. He never went to the karigi even if his mother brought food to the men there. And when the other men went off on the summer hunt, the boy would go in another direction to hunt alone. And everyone wondered why he was so good at hunting by himself.

Over the hill, in the place where he liked to hunt, the boy built himself an iɣlugawraq, a small sod house. Here he put up racks to dry his meat. When the hunting time came, he usually lived in his little house, cooking for himself on a fireplace under the skylight. He usually kept the skylight open in the summer.

One night, when he was alone in his little house, he heard a noise in the hallway of his sod house. He looked and saw a white dog there. Using caribou fat, he coaxed it into the house. Then he heard a noise again and there was a girl looking into the house. She said that she wanted her dog. He told her to come in and get the dog herself. But she stayed in the hallway and asked him again for her dog. But the boy told her again to come in. She was afraid, but after a while, she decided to enter the house. The young man offered her food. She sat down in the house and ate. He then told her that he was single and that he was alone with his old parents. He described how his mother had been trying to marry him off but he didn't like the girls she had shown him. Then the stranger consented to marry him if his parents raised no objection.

And the reason for this was that the boy liked the girl's dog so much. He fed it, even cutting up its meat for it. And the dog liked the boy too. The couple decided to spend the night together in the little sod house and to go back to his people the next day. They ate more and the boy noticed that both the dog and the girl liked the caribou fat much better than the meat.

Next day, they decided to start out for home. The man got his meat ready for packing. His own pack was so heavy that he could scarcely lift it. He fixed a lighter pack for his wife. As she lifted hers, she said that it was too light and asked him for a heavier burden. So he added more meat from his own pack. Now they carried packs of the same size but the girl carried hers much more easily than did the boy. On the way back they camped two nights and arrived the third day. They approached the hill by the river and the boy told his wife that the village lay on the other side.

When they arrived, the boy's mother was waiting for him outside their house. She called in to tell his father that he was bringing a woman with him and the father came out to see. The parents came over to the girl, wondering who she was and why the couple had the white dog with them. As soon as they came to the house, the parents welcomed the girl. "Where did you find her?" they asked. They stood outside talking until the father invited them in. Then they got food ready and all ate. Again the girl and her dog hardly touched the meat but ate only the carbibou fat. And the man told of his adventures and of how he had met the girl. And the two settled down in the house of the boy's parents.

Now the girl was a good, strong worker. She did all the work around the house but she would never take food to the karigi, leaving this work for her mother-in-law. All winter the couple stayed in the village and everyone wondered who she was. The dog grew up and was big and strong. When the man went hunting, he took the dog with him and the dog helped him carry caribou meat. Next summer, as was his custom, the boy went off alone to hunt. When he had taken caribou, he sent for his wife and she came to help him carry the meat in. She remained very strong.

After a while, the girl became pregnant. Soon she gave birth to a baby boy. And the grandparents were very happy and proud of their grandson but they gave him no aanaroat. The young man, the father of the baby, did have an aanaroaq. This was made from the puffball which is called "old smoke" (puyualuq). It was covered with skin and the young man wore it around his neck under his parka. Now this baby boy seemed hardly normal because he grew so fast. Soon he was walking around.

Next summer, the young man and his wife went away for the hunting, leaving the baby with its grandmother and grandfather. Even when the water froze, the young man and his wife were still away and the grandparents were feeding the baby. Then the grandmother remarked that the baby and its mother liked the caribou fat even better than the meat.

And when the couple returned, the wife fed her husband. Then she lay down on the bed and said nothing. "What is the matter with you?" her husband asked. But she refused to tell him. He thought that she was acting very strange. Then she got up and left the house. He followed her, asking her again what the matter was. She explained that she was tired, having worked too hard that day. Then she came back into the house and went out again, this time carrying her baby. She had taken the chamber pot out to empty it. But she didn't return. After a while, the young man began to worry and went out to find her. Both she and the baby were gone. He went back and told his parents. All of them looked into each house in the village but they were unable to find her. The young man began to circle the village. At last, he came on his wife's tracks leading to the sea. And when he had located her tracks, he returned home, dressed himself and took his bow. Then he went off, following his wife's tracks.

When it became dark, he stopped and camped. Next morning, he set off again, following his wife's tracks. In the daylight, he came across the place where his wife had camped for the night. From the tracks he could tell that the baby too had walked part of the time. Soon he came to the ice and the tracks left the land and followed the ice out from the shore. And at last he came to the open sea. The tracks led directly into the water and he lost them. So he sat down on the edge of the ice by the sea and began to think. He decided to sit there as long as he could. In his grief, he didn't care whether he got back to the land or not. He put his hands inside his parka. He began to weep, saying that he didn't care if he lived or died. And as he was sitting there, grieving and weeping, he heard a splash. Looking up, he saw a polar bear come out of the water and put its paws just alongside his feet as he sat there on the ice. The bear remained in that position, looking into his face. Then the bear rolled the skin back from its head and he was looking at the face of his wife.

His wife told him to go back to his parents. "I have gone home to my own people," she said. But the young man refused to return; he just sat there. The bear came up on the ice and the young man stood up by the bear. Then she dived into the water and was gone. He watched her swimming under the water. Then she emerged again and said: "The people with whom I stay are not good at all." But the young man insisted on coming with her. Soon many bears came up from the water. With the others, the man saw his own son, also a bear. And the bears all came up on the ice where the man was. Then the polar bear wife became a woman again. She explained that she had parents and two brothers living in that place. And she said that there were those of the people with whom she lived who always killed any stranger or outsider. There was one person who was particularly mean. But still, her husband insisted on going with her. Then he looked up and saw the houses on the beach, houses which had been invisible to him before.[12]

The wife said that they two would wait until it was dark and then proceed to the village. She said that the person who was especially hard on strangers was afraid of her parents and her two brothers but that it would be better if they were not seen. So as soon as it was dark, they ran to the village. They came to the house where the family of his wife lived and entered it. In the passageway, the bearskins hung on ropes. Two of them were old and yellow. Hanging there, too, was a spear just like that used by humans. It had a rope on it and seal pokes.

[12] Animals, like men, have houses, but no human being can see them unless he is granted the ability to do so. Animals, too, can remove their skins just as a human removes his parka. When they do so, they become human in form.

Inside the house were two old persons, sitting side by side at the end of the room. Near them sat a young man.

Now the father began to talk. He said that he had sent his daughter to marry among the nuunamiut and he asked her why she returned. The daughter answered that she knew that the boy's mother complained of her fondness for caribou fat. This made her angry, she said, and she wished to escape her husband and had tried to elude him but had failed. Then her father told the young man, his son-in-law, that there was this one person who hated strangers and always killed them. Any stranger who came by was killed by him and there was no one who could vanquish him. The woman's father went on to say that this person had a helper who came around each night, looking for strangers in each house. When he saw any, he reported their presence to his master.

Then the woman's oldest brother entered the house. He brought his wife with him and together they were carrying a big platter of good seal meat. All sat and ate. The young man noticed that all present ate a good deal but that they tended to leave the meat and to eat much blubber and fat. After they had eaten, they sat around. Then they heard a noise in the passageway and a person came in. He raised his head through the kataq and peered at them. When he saw the young man of the nuunamiut, he looked at him a long time without saying a word. Then, just as silently, he left. Now this person who hated outsiders and killed them was named aŋusilʸuq. The woman's father said: "This is aŋusilʸuq's servant." And he went on to say that next day aŋusilʸuq would come and want to fight him.

Now the oldest son of the family said that he liked his sister's husband and that he and his brother would aid him against aŋusilʸuq. They reported that aŋusilʸuq usually did things a certain way. He had a big ivory ball that he regularly killed strangers with, and if this failed he had others which he used. He also had other strange weapons he could use.

In the morning, while the young man of the nuunamiut still slept, all got up ahead of him. They awakened him and told him to get up and eat. Then someone came to the house and called down the skylight, saying that aŋusilʸuq wanted his aŋutawkun [13] to start this fight. The man from the nuunamiut was a bit concerned at this, thinking that his wife had been previously married to aŋusilʸuq. But the woman's father said that this man had always been trying to get the girl but had never succeeded. After they had eaten, the girl's two brothers followed their brother-in-law outside. They did not put on their bearskins but came as humans. And in the village, people had heard of the presence of the stranger. The men stayed home from hunting that day; everyone stayed around to watch the fight.

Now the young man from the nuunamiut and his two brothers-in-law started out walking. They came to two small hills. Between those two hills stood aŋusilʸuq, tossing and kicking his big ivory ball. He came over to the stranger and said: "I want to play with you." And the man looked at the ball and saw that it was made of ice and ivory and covered with blood, the blood of many animals and humans. They faced each other. "When you get ready to kick the ball, kick fast," said aŋusilʸuq, "it will kill you if you aren't fast enough." The man's father-in-law said to pay close attention because the ball moved so swiftly when aŋusilʸuq kicked it. At first, aŋusilʸuq did not kick the ball. He turned his back to it and walked around a bit. Then he suddenly turned and let fly. The ball went off like an arrow. But the nuunamiu stepped aside before

---

[13] aŋutawkun, term of address used by men when they have had sexual relations with the same woman.

it hit him. Now no one ever knew just how strong this young man of the nuunamiut could be. He always hunted alone but he carried huge packs of meat all by himself over long distances.

Then aŋusilʸuq, having watched the nuunamiu step aside, told him to kick the ball back. The ball was terribly heavy. He dribbled the ball back to where he could kick it. Next he built up a pile of snow and put the ball on top of it. Then he used all his strength to kick it. It flew like an arrow over the head of aŋusilʸuq, hit the ground behind him and broke into pieces. The brothers-in-law said: "Now come home with us." And their father said: "Well, you have won this time. It is good that you have broken his ball. But he will try again tomorrow." As they started away, aŋusilʸuq said nothing. Then they came home and sat there. The wife of the nuunamiu was very frightened.

That night, after they had food, there came again the man who peered at them with head in the kataq. Next day, after they had eaten, they heard someone come to the house and call in through the skylight: "aŋusilʸuq wants to hunt seals with you." And they knew that aŋusilʸuq was proposing a game to see who could catch the first seal. But the nuunamiu had no spear and also he had lived his life inland so that he had no skill in sealing. But his father-in-law told him to dress in the old yellow parka he had seen in the hallway. He said that aŋusilʸuq would be wearing the same thing. When he started out, his two brothers-in-law accompanied him, explaining to him what would happen. They said that aŋusilʸuq and he would dive at the same time into the water. They told him that aŋusilʸuq would stop to do something in the water but that the man should not stop but should go right on. It so happened that the man's father-in-law could catch a seal faster than any of those other bears. In lending his son-in-law his skin, he was making sure that he would win. Then the two brothers helped him get the skin on. It was big, and at first he couldn't get used to the head. But they helped him and they showed him and he learned to be a bear even before he left the hallway of the house.

The three of them went out. There at the edge of the water stood aŋusilʸuq. All of them were bears now. When he came to the edge of the water, he said that he was ready. As they dived in, he saw something white but he didn't pause to see what it was. He went right on, saw a seal, killed it, and brought it up on the ice. And he came up before aŋusilʸuq did. Again he won. Then he went home with his brothers-in-law and they helped him take off the bearskin.

Now this aŋusilʸuq had a big house. In it he kept the wives of all the men whom he had killed. When the man came back to his father-in-law's house, they said that aŋusilʸuq would try again the next day. On the next morning, after they had eaten, someone called in through the skylight that aŋusilʸuq wanted his aŋutawkun to come to the karigi. The father-in-law said that aŋusilʸuq would now be wearing another kind of parka. He told his son-in-law to take with him the spear which was hanging in the hallway. This was the spear which the nuunamiu's father-in-law had made when he was a young man. And again, his brothers-in-law went with him to the karigi. The three of them walked past the big house of aŋusilʸuq.

When they arrived at the karigi, all the men in the village were watching and waiting there. This aŋusilʸuq had not yet come. The young man was carrying the spear which his father-in-law had loaned him. He had it in his hand but no one looked at it and all acted as if he weren't carrying anything, just as though it weren't there at all. Then they sat down at the end of the karigi. Then the brothers-in-law started to tell the nuunamiu what he would see. "The middle door will open," they said, "much water will start coming in. In the water will be a herd of walrus and the biggest walrus will be aŋusilʸuq. You must spear him and then the two of you will fight. No one knows what will happen then." The people were beginning to be frightened and got up, one by one, and left. But the brothers stayed to be at the side of their brother-in-law.

The door opened and from the middle of the floor came water. In the water were many walrus, all bellowing. In the middle of the herd was a huge walrus. "Use the spear!" said the brothers. And no one could see that spear. Then the younger brother left, followed by the older, leaving the nuunamiu alone to fight the walrus. The biggest walrus looked at the young man who was now left alone in the karigi. The man got his spear ready and as the walrus rose, he speared it. Then the walrus submerged. The man tried to hold the rope but it was pulled from his hands. As soon as the rope was gone, the floor rose back and the water fell. The nuunamiu waited a moment but nothing happened and he made his way homeward.

When he reached home, he found his wife full of grief. She was lying face downward on the bed. Joyously, she rose and greated him. All were very happy. Then his father-in-law said that he had passed the worst test but that they still didn't know how it went with aŋusilʸuq. At this moment, someone called in through the skylight that aŋusilʸuq was very sick. After a while, they called in again that he was rolling around the floor of his house in agony. At this, the nuunamiu felt very sorry. He considered all of aŋusilʸuq's wives and how they would be left without a provider if their husband died. So he went to see his rival. He went without telling his father-in-law. He went up to aŋusilʸuq's house, following the rope through the hallway and saw that it led up through the kataq of the house. Inside, he saw his rival rolling around the floor in great pain. He could see the spearhead in his chest with the rope leading from it. And all the man's wives sat about the room and didn't know what to do. The nuunamiu thought to himself: "All these women will be hungry if this man dies." Then he called to them: "Put the light out." He came up into the house and with his knife he removed the head of the harpoon. "You can put the light on now," he said.

Then aŋusilʸuq was free of pain. He asked him how he felt. "I feel much better now," said the man. And he thanked the nuunamiu for helping him. Then the nuunamiu came home. He took the harpoon head and the ropes with him. When he reached his father-in-law's house, he replaced the head of the spear on its shaft and hung it back in place in the passage. This spear was invisible to all but members of that family. When he came back into the house, he said that aŋusilʸuq would now live. And for many days afterward, no word was heard from aŋusilʸuq.

Then one day, some time later, the helper of aŋusilʸuq came again and called, saying that aŋusilʸuq wanted to see which of them could stay under the water the longer, he or his aŋutawkun. And again the nuunamiu's father-in-law lent him his polar bear skin. His brothers-in-law went again to help him get the skin on. When they got outside, aŋusilʸuq was waiting at the edge of the water, this time in the form of a huge polar bear. At the water, the nuunamiu thought to himself that this man continued his wicked ways, even though he had saved his life. This time he resolved to kill him. Then he remembered the puffball that he wore as an aanaroaq.

When they two got ready to dive, they agreed that the man who came up first would be the loser. The young man thought: "Now I will try something." He stayed under the water awhile. Then, when he could hold his breath no longer, he faced the ice and took out his aanaroaq, put it in his mouth, and started blowing all around him in the water. He kept doing this for a long time and then decided that he had waited long enough. So he came up out on the ice. There was no sign of aŋusil^{y}uq. He waited around a while but no one came. A heavy fog began to come up on the ice. The people who had come to watch began to get tired and one by one, they started off for home. The nuunamiu, too, got tired of waiting and left to go home. When he arrived, all were in bed. Next day, the helper called in through the skylight and said that aŋusil^{y}uq had not come home. They waited at home for a while but still there was no word of aŋusil^{y}uq. Then the young man began again to think of the wives of this man and how they would be left without a provider. He went out to look. But it was so foggy for many days that it was hard to see. Then the young man took his aanaroaq and sucked in the air, thus making the fog vanish.

Then, after a few days, aŋusil^{y}uq returned home, all skin and bones. In the great fog, he had nothing to eat. Then he realized that the young man was to blame for the presence of the fog and he became much afraid of him. He was so frightened that he decided henceforward to leave him alone. And when he had his strength back, he said nothing to him again.

After a while, the nuunamiu's father-in-law asked him about his parents. He said that they should return to his parents and then come back again for a visit. So the young man took his wife and his son and the three of them started back up inland. When they got there, they found that the boy's parents still had the girl's dog and had taken care of it. So the young man told his parents what had happened, "Why did you complain when she ate the fat?" he asked his mother. "Never say that again; you see all the trouble you have caused."

And the two couples, the boy's parents and the boy and his wife and son, lived together well after that. And after a while, the young people visited again among the polar bears but they never had trouble with aŋusil^{y}uq again.

THE KUKUWEAQ (TEN-LEGGED POLAR BEAR)

There were some people living between Icy Cape and Wainwright. They had two houses. In one house there were a man and his wife and their many children. In the other lived quite a few related people. Now it happened that one winter the people in the second house got a walrus. They kept all the meat for themselves and gave none to the family with the many children. The father of the family with the many children, a man named kucirak, was very unhappy. Food was scarce and he didn't know how he was going to provide for his children.

The next day he decided to go out sealing. He went out on the ice. In among the pressure ridges, he noticed a huge glacier, bigger at the top than at the bottom. Walking by it, he saw a big hole. In the hole there were seal lungs floating about. And he knew at once what he had stumbled into—the lair of the kukuweaq, the 10-legged polar bear. He was very frightened but he decided that his family needed food too badly. So he sat down by the hole and waited. Soon the huge head of the kukuweaq came out of the water. Taking his seal spears, kucirak blinded the monster, stabbing out first one eye, then the other. The bear came up out of the water roaring. It followed the man by the smell of his footprints. As the man ran, he saw the ten-legged bear gaining on him. He began to circle around but still the bear followed him, coming closer and closer. Soon he doubled back to the inverted glacier. He circled again, noticing that there was a narrow passage in between the ridges. He ran in between and the monster, following him, was caught tight. The man crawled around behind it and stabbed it to death.

Then he cut off one of its ten legs and brought it home as food to his family. As soon as the people in the other house heard of his catch, they came over with plenty of walrus meat. Next day, he and his wife went out and began butchering the carcass. It was just as though they were cutting whale. And they gave freely of their food to those people in the other house.

THE THREE ESKIMO KINGS

Note: The following tale was written in English by Eddie uŋaruk, age 25. It is presented here with no editing beyond an orthographic change or two. By "kings" the writer refers, of course, to the umealiq.

There was a big village up inland. The village was divided into three sections. And they had three kings to rule them. The usual name was given by these people as east, middle, and west. The east-side king had an adopted son and he was supposed to train him as a strong boy. This boy was about 12 or 15 years of age.

This happened during the month of July, at about 7:00 in the evening. The wife of the king went to empty the garbage can and it disappeared. It was believed that it was caught by someone, some evil spirit or some magic. And the kings' wives disappeared.

These three kings didn't know what happened to them. Sadly they went to bed. The east king and his son went to bed, too. But about midnight that boy got up and went 2 or 3 miles where there was a tree. All night long he wrestled with that tree, trying to pull it up by the roots. Next morning, the father of that boy noticed that his clothing was wet from sweating but he didn't ask him about that.

The three kings waited nearly a week. And finally they agreed to look for their wives. They planned to go the next morning.

The boy wanted to go with them but his adopted father refused and told him he could stay with the people. But he begged to go with them. When he begged three times, they let him come along. And they started out without any food. They mentioned that there would be animals along the way.

They traveled for weeks and weeks without any food because the three kings were not good hunters. They spied some rabbits but they couldn't outrun them. Finally, the boy decided to try to catch or grab some rabbits because this was the only animal they could find. The boy grabbed one and tossed it in the air and killed it. They ate for the first time since they had left their home town. So the boy became their hunter after all.

They traveled until they came to the mountains. Then they camped for a couple of days and started off to the coast, following the river. And finally, they saw two villages, about 20 or 25 yards apart. They didn't rush to the villages because they wanted to take them by surprise. Also, they saw that the villages were playing football. This was their usual custom in the evening. Finally, one side won. The three kings stood watching about 75 yards away. And the people finished and went home about 6.:00 p. m.

After the people went inside, the boy's adopted father led his companions under the bank of the houses because they did not want to be seen. They stood outside a house and waited. It was dark. Finally, someone came out of the house. It was a lady. She looked up at them in surprise and without asking any questions, she went inside as quickly as possible. About 30 minutes later that same lady came and invited the strangers in. The lady led them through an inside passage covered with ugruk skin.

When they came into the house, they saw some families with one father and mother. The old man and his wife were in the middle of the room and the others sat by the sides of the house. The old man asked the strangers where they came from. And he asked them what it was they were looking for. The boy's father answered and told what had happened in their village, how all three had lost their wives.

The old man said: "I think that the dwarf brothers have taken your wives. They rob men of their wives. It is the usual custom of that village." This old man was head of one village. The other village had as its leaders the two dwarfs. They were dangerous men because they took wives and they usually took their husbands as well and they took out their left eye and treated them as their slaves. And the old man said: "Today we had a ball game with that village and we won. Tomorrow we will start early with the sunrise and we will play all day." Then they had a supper and went to bed because the ball game should be played on time.

Early the next morning, the dwarf younger brother was playing with the ball while the older watched from the top of a house. The old man invited the strangers to be on his team. They all started to play but the strangers didn't get into the group right away. The dwarf said in pride that this time they would win. Then the boy came to the dwarf and asked him to let him play in the game. But the dwarf refused, saying that in their country boys couldn't play. But the boy said he would join them even if they wouldn't allow him in the game. They didn't quarrel but started to kick the ball. They kicked it sideways and struggled with it until it burst. Then the dwarf ordered another ball from his brother and they did the same to that. Then he begged another ball. The older dwarf brother told his brother to try to get it away because it was the last one.

Then the dwarf kicked the ball. As the boy looked, it went toward the winning stake. The boy had to fight through the crowd to get at it. Then the boy kicked it back. They played 2 to 4 hours, kicking the ball back and forth. At last the boy won. Then after the ball game, the people went home as usual.

The next morning, the older dwarf brother invited the strangers into the big sod house used for gathering together (karigi). When they went inside, they saw quite a few people which the dwarves kept there. Finally, the older dwarf ordered one of the men to get a pot of cooked meat for his supper. And a few minutes later, one of the women came up with the meat. Other women came, and the strangers recognized their wives. The women went out as soon as possible, fearing the older dwarf.

Then the boy got angry and kicked over the pot of meat. The older dwarf looked up in suprise and said that the boy did not obey his commands. He told the boy to come over. Then he grabbed him and tried to pull him to a stone he he had there. But the boy wrestled with him and dragged him around. The boy got hold of his arm and lifted him off his feet. He circled with him and threw him onto his own stone and killed him there.

Then the boy started for the younger dwarf brother. This man begged for his life and said he would not rough the people up like his brother did. But the boy refused to believe him and grabbing him by the arms and legs, threw him through the window.

And afterward, the three kings got their wives back and all of them went home in victory.

Texts

I.

tapkoak	irinʸereeik	aŋuneaatiŋak
Those two	parent and son	hunting

igłu	igalaaiga	aasi	igalaaŋanun	tuttu
house	through skylight	and	into skylight	caribou

kataxłuutin	aasi	irinʸereeik	anilermata	tuttu
falling in	and	parent and son	not remove	caribou

tavraŋa	tiriannellu	aasi	aγnaq	kupiluktuwak
from there	fox	and	woman	walked

kataganetsuq	taaptumuwa	aasi	suliiliŋiktapkoak
fall into	that place	and	those, those two

kalanilluakkalekamik	ariyuuniraaq	tamna	aasi
when almost fall in	they quit	that	and

saqovłuutiq	aalaamun	nirerunmik	aŋuneksek
they two turned	other way	other animals	they catch

arervirmik	tapkoak	aŋatkuvłuutik	aasi
whale	those two	two shamans	and

sull	aγnaq	awłaŋaruuak	kataganetsuq
that	woman	was away	fall into

taaptumuwa	aravaγvennu	aasi	iŋyugunik
that place	of catching whale	and	other people

peaaksimman	saakuminnirak
they fell	they two broke it

Free Translation

A man and his son in their hunting so arranged it that the animals they took would come directly to their house and fall through into the house from the skylight. They took caribou and foxes in this way. But a woman also fell in and they themselves were drawn to their own skylight and almost fell in. Being shamans, they turned their attention to the sea. A whale was drawn to their skylight and fell through. But then the woman fell in again. And when others too began to be drawn to the house and fall through the skylight, the two shamans gave up their hunting and broke their skylight.

[The informant remarked that he considered this a true story. He had seen the house full of caribou bones and a whale backbone had been seen in the house itself.]

II.

irinʸereeik	innexsuq	taareeum	sinʸaanne	nuwukaamme
parent and son	they were	the sea	alongside	at the point

tukuttane	innexsuq	inʸunnexluq	taanna	ireniŋa	aasi
at tukut (n. pr.)	they were	big man	that man	her son	and

kayaaktukłunne	kaluweak	tuxłuwic	kayemmiq	arvaγuniksuk
was in kayak	with spear	he speared	from kayak	he caught a whale

arvaaniŋyik	aasi	tuttuneaktuwat	naγvammi	innexsut
young whale	and	caribou hunters	in lagoon	they were

kapuxłuwic	kayemmin	tuttutuγoonexsut	aasi	tawkserea γooneksut
spearing	from kayak	they hunted caribou	and	they traded

oxerunik	taptumaŋa	arvaktuami	okumaatinik	aasi
blubber	from that	whaler	for caribou skins	and

tulakaamme	isiverexłiyunneaaminik	nakoorawnik	pikarooneksuk
he came ashore	he examined them	good ones	he took for himself

aasi	taapkua	tukuculiinʸiraat	nukurawnik	pisuwumaan	aasi
and	those men	finally wanted to kill	when he wanted	good skins	and

kayman	inʸuminnik	acuktukniraat	ilowanun	kayeŋata	aasi
he came	to people	they stuffed it	inside	to his kayak	and

awłayumineγman	kapuaanirat	aasi	anawlaxluwic	iliaŋic
he cannot move	they begin spearing	and	he hit them	some

tukutkaloaaniraic	aasi	kaymata	miloxługu	umeaŋaat	aliŋman
he killed them	and	they came	he threw stones	their umeak	hole

kivixłiwic	tulakselivłuwic	nuunamun	aasi	kupuxługu
they sank	he prevented them	the shore	and	they speared him

tukunniraat	aasi	tukuvłutik	aasi	tamna	tukuman
they killed him	and	he died	and	(after) that	he died

panerenexsut	oxerunikammi	tukunnamicuŋ	tamna	aasi	aakeŋa
they starved	with no blubber	when they killed	that (man)	and	his mother

tukuvłunne	irenʸinne	tukumman	suluq
died	her son	after him	(n. pr.)

Free Translation

There lived a mother and son out by the point at tukut. He was a strong man who would take whales in his kayak. The inland people who hunted caribou came down and would trade their caribou skins for the blubber which the whaler had. When they traded, the whaler would examine the skins and take the best ones for himself. The inland people finally wanted to kill him. When he came to the inland people in his kayak, they stuffed the cockpit of the kayak with skins so that he couldn't free himself. Then they started throwing harpoons at him. He was able to kill some of them and threw stones at their umeak, making a hole in the bottom so that it sank. Then he kept them from reaching the shore. But some of them managed to spear him and kill him. After he was dead, they, having no blubber, starved. When the whaler was dead, his mother also died. His name was suluq.

III. A HERO TALE

inʸuwic	inʸuneaanuksuat	tareeum	sinʸaanne
They were	peoples' habitations	sea	alongside

inʸuneaanuksuq	tapkunani	inawruani	aananilʸu
they lived	with those	with others	grandparent and child

sekunaksimeoγłu	aanaluwiik	inʸuŋ
when time to sleep	grandmother and grandchild	man

tukularaic	igalaakun	umealugumγo	imma	ireniŋa
he called in	through skylight	of the chief	his	his son

piicaq	tapkoak	aananilʸu	nelumiinʸerak	umealugum
he is gone	they both	grandparent grandchild	didn't know it	the chief

akilʸuutineraa	ivaakuvłuγu	nukatpeeanum	akilʸuutivłu
paid them	searching him	young people	paying them

awłaaniksut	sumuupaya	pakaciŋinʸasut
go out seeking	everywhere	they did not find him

tupsiŋicitunʸit iilʸepuk okallaneksuq
they did not track him orphan boy he said

uvuŋaleatawvuŋa aneŋen anʸiraniraa aasi
I try to find him grandmother she agreed and

taaxsiman paranavłuniq taaxsiman aninexsuq
when dark he got ready when dark he went out

umealugum iγłuuata sivowaŋanu paaŋata
the chief to his house in front of his door

qiqaaneksuq sumaroq suwunamutkeeaq ireniŋa umealugum
he stood he thought to which way he the son of the chief

awłaanetpaq tenna isumaanikamme sutilaani
he went out when he thought so suddenly

tavraŋaceaq nalunira kawriruq kitaxikatikaxłune
he knew not nothing he noticed he stood next to him

nukatpeeamik nukatpeean okalawtigaa apa aytkumatin
young man young man said father told me

ayyikpin iilʸepom aperiga sumiitpisi
I came for you poor boy asked where house

uvanikiraaksemma awławtiga alaytkaraak tareeum
right over here he took him he could see the sea

tawtuknaaneksuq iγłu tikitkaa ikirakaaneksuq
he could observe house he approached it had racks

malaroinik naypektuŋmawn piyakoominʸaktuamik
two of them he looked to see what would happen

pinʸaksuq isermaŋnik inexsuq nuleearik
what happened they came in there were man and wife

aŋayokaxruk inexsuq niveaxseak ataataruruq
were old there was young girl old man

nalaneksuq tavrasi akuvixłuniyu okalawtiga
he lay down and then he got up he said

iilʸepuk nuleearanu tekuŋa qilovarin
orphan boy to your wife over there to that place

kilowaktuq akuvuktuq saŋiranu niveaxseam
when he went he sat down at side of young girl

akuvitaniŋman makixłune aniruq niveaxseak
when he sat she got up went out young girl

puyuttamik tigumiragunne aniruq niveaxseak
with pan she carried went out young girl

pisallexuneisattuq puyutaŋa imaqaaneksuq aseanik
came back inside her pan it was filled berries

kanuciniklikaa nirigaic nageanikami ataataruruq
all kinds they ate after eating old man

okallatuq siniksanarearuxłuni okallatuq ataataruruq
he said I want to sleep early he said old man

uvulaaku uvulamme awłaamawk ireniŋyalu iilʸapugłu
tomorrow in morning they go with his son poor boy

tevretutaaktut aasi niveaxseam tutaaktuq ataataruruq
they went to bed and young girl went to bed old man

sinʸiksak palemagenit iilʸepom apexruax nuleeani
maybe they slept poor boy he asked his wife

nalumivarok nukatpeeak malakataktilaŋanik ilsimaruŋa
does not know young man they ran after him I know

aapa wixiramnik tilisuuniraa irinʸe kaxreritkovłuγu
father for husband he sent him his son say to bring

tennaasi pilirosikaamisun awłaktinneraasik akutukiraak
and then as usual let them go fat caribou

saresimivsiŋa uvuluupuk sinʸiktillu pilirosikaamisun
you better get today sleeping as usual

okalanereluktuq niŋaw kannak sinʸaktuvat
he suddenly said son-in-law too much he sleeps

awłarasuawooŋitpat itektuq ireniŋalo iterimaan
they should go quick he awoke his son when he awoke

winʸi koruveŋaluaraa iilʸepuk kamaasumicok
husband when her tears fell orphan he did not care

koruvemun nuleeane tavrasi awłaktuq irrim
her tears his wife and then he went mountain

tuŋaanu irrik tikinʸamiku okalawtigaa nukatpeeam
toward mountain he arrived at he said young man

avatkuluγu kasutisawγulutik awłaqenikamiq iilʸepuk
go around each get together ahead he started orphan

suaγoomuna kuwaraq suaγuγuna pagenuq
and there was river there was fat caribou

iilʸoaane kuwarum kilirakłuγu pisiktirạa tuttu
in sight of river being he shot bow caribou

aasi awłaksetkikaaluaknanne piliyakaa tuttu
and before he started again he skinned caribou

aasi tunuŋnik mumuraaniγulu nanmexłune
and fat hind quarter after on his back

aysaktuq awłaniŋmeoγlu tunuaaniŋ tikisaniŋnaksuq
started home after he left behind him it came from behind

niptaylaq avuŋa kanirenaylaq niptaypayłune
fog over there can't see too foggy

pisuqutanellamme tutinniraa suaγokmanna pisiksi
while he walked he stepped on that was bow

tigumiriyutigaa tavra isigani tawtuleraik
he picked it up and then his feet he can't see

niptaypayłune putukisaleksuq kisamatemma areγanne
too foggy starts falling and then his hands

tawtuleraleqpe pisukatanʸiraknelaamme putukisalekpu
could hardly see while he was walking he falls down

tavrasi nutkakaame okalaktuq tavrallekka ataataruruq
and then when he stopped he said that's it old man

inaxłuwic tukuttaknire taynaqaxłuni aanarawni
he did that way he killed them After he that his amulet

itkaaniraa aanalukeaq avrumma sukuramnik
he remembered old lady that what for

oyamitkoaalenʸekpaŋa tavraŋasi isakłu puuŋa
she gave amulet to me from there he got it bag

alikłuγu aasi okumiriutivłu tavrasi makixłune
he carried it and he put it in mouth and then he stood up

suvłuaaniraa okumiiraykanni tavrasi kaniŋani inexsuq
he blew it in his mouth and then close by there was

nipteruaq inʸuŋnamaŋa nipteruamu tamatumunnasi
clearing for the man clear on that

aylaktuxłune	nipteruakuŋ	tikinmeoγłu	iγłumun
started home	where clear	he got there	to the house

nanmayganikmeoγłu	aniŋyeksuq	arnaq	koyavaytłune
he took it off (what he carried)	went out	woman	was so glad

aγnaata	okalawtineraa	ayliguroaaneksutin
his woman	told him	finally got home

nanmaŋiitkotige	aarnata	kuyaroq	iserimaan
he took (his load)	his woman	was glad	when he entered

iilʸepuk	naganeksuq	ataataruruq	temma	akavłune
orphan	he ate	old man	and then	he sat down

ataataruruq	okallaktuq	niŋawak	pisawyuminaytkaluwaaneksuq
old man	said	son-in-law	can't get into trouble

aymaŋniq	sinʸiksalawγneksuq	uvulami	awłaγovsik
when comes	wants to sleep quick	in morning	you go

ugruceaktuq	ticarevsiŋa	aasi	ataataruruq	sekumman
hunting ugruk	let me eat	and	old man	slept

okallawtineraa	nuleeni	suknamun	awłakneakinʸuksamna
he told her	his wife	which way	are we going to go

apiyamma	awłutinearaatin	iteqamiq	nirigaluanatik
my brother	will take you	when wake up	without eating

awłatiliika	kayernik	paluŋaneksuq	kayak	onaniγłu
he took him out	in kayak	turned it over	kayak	with spear

kamukawrakeniγłu	nukatpeeam	okalawtigaa	avatayrun
using little sled	young man	told him	different ways

sikum	awłaresiruqsamna	aŋusaaxiran	ugeruniŋ
ice	start that way	what is caught	of ugruk

alawrak	awłaktuq	avannmu	siku	sinʸikraasiga
different	they went	each way	ice	he started on the edge

ayuγaloakanne	tawtuka	uguruumin	alawrak	suaγunna
before he got far	he saw	ugruk	different	right by

kiliŋaγun	kayaŋata	puivilyune	kasigeaq	temmasi
near it	his kayak	came up	spotted seal	and then

aŋunminʸik	anawvłu	nekaktiteraa	suagurunna
his paddle	hit him	it went down	and then

puivilyune	uguruumin	alawrak	tigumigallu
came up	ugruk	different	he took hold

nawlikanne	suagurunna	kasigeaq	puivilyune	kiliŋagun
with his spear	and then	spotted seal	came up	on edge

kasigeaq	kolawtureaksigaa	kayaŋa	naliksaynaypeakłune
spotted seal	went over jumping	his kayak	so he won't spear

omicaxtexłune	nawlikteraa	kasigeaq	temasi	kiŋulereneksuq
he became angry	he speared	spotted seal	and then	he turned over

temasi	nalulereneksuq	kawrinʸeksuq	nalagum	savirviŋme
and then	he didn't know	when he noticed	there where	place where first departed

tinraaketaqsireneksuq	kayeniru	makinname	tusaaneksuq
ebbing and flowing	his kayak	where he stood	he heard

uvulułuŋani	awłaruuamik	makinname	tawtukka	akłunaaq
toward day	something moving	he stood	he saw	rope

iγłumi	tuŋaanun	ulaksinʸiraa	suagoomenna	iilʸaŋa
house	toward	he started to it	it was	some of it

isiŋaneksuq	kikaktuaksaŋikcukunni	iserineksuq	iserimariγua
was inside	he didn't stand still	he went in	when he went in

onna	nukatpeeak	saγuniuneksuak	kinirimaw	akłunaaq	
that	young man	had pain	he looked	rope	
suagomenna	isuqaaneksuq	saŋiraaŋanu	iilʸepom	aperiγaa	
there was	the end was	on his side	orphan	asked him	
suwitsamna	samaγgo	aniutakakaxane	piyirinʸeriga		
what is matter	that it is	he has pain	I take it out		
awłukcaylilektuqsawmeamawt		iilʸepom	savinʸi	tigulekamiu	
try to keep still		orphan boy	his knife	he got hold of	
akłunaaq	tiguvłuγu	piyiraasigaa	nekiligexłiuγu	aasi	
rope	took hold	going to take it out	he got meat on it	and	
tavrawva	anilʸexune	kiŋyenʸitcokunne	kayaminʸuxłune		
right away	he went out	he didn't look back	went to kayak		
kayeminʸu	ikukammi	awławtigillan	ulaaxłuγu	ataataruruq	
his kayak	he went in	started out	he went	old man	
aasi	tikinʸamme	kayenni	kakisinʸaxłuγu	tikikaŋitkamme	
and	he arrived	his kayak	he pulled up	arriving there	
isereaxłune	nalaliinʸaksewak	aarnata	sakisexłuγu	niyuŋa	
he went in	lying down	his wife	nudged him	his leg	
okalawtiga	niŋawa	uvuŋa	akavitaniŋmin	okalawtiga	
she said	our son-in-law	here	having said	she said	
nakixiran	uva	ataatarurum	tiguua	tigukamiu	okalawtiga
take food	here	old man	got hold	when took hold	he said
niŋawvak	samna	okalawtiklikaa	ataatarurum	uvuŋa	
to son-in-law	this	he said again	old man	here	
sivukamnu	akovłutin	kuleaktoarootiŋa	akuvitkalaroma		
in front of me	sit down	tell me something	if I sit down		
okperanʸenʸikiŋma	anilʸutin	ilʸuqaaqtuamik	keruunmik		
you don't believe me	you go out	hollow	wood		
imerilʸuγu	silumigłu	itkurrii	kiilammik	aneruq	ataataruruq
fill it	with ice	bring in	quickly	went out	old man
isektuq	tigumeaxłune	imaqaaqtuamik	sikumigłu	aasi	ilʸiivłuγu
came in	he carried	inside of it	with ice	and	he put it
iilʸepom	saaŋanu	ataataruruq	okalawtiga		
orphan	in front	old man	he said to him		
akimnuli	akovittin	akavetaniŋman	makittuq		
over there	sit down	after sitting	he stood up		
iilʸepallu	putuγuγunni	misuwaxłuwiq	imerremut		
orphan	his toes	dipped them	in water		
ataatarurum	umasiŋitcuq	kinʸiriniktutilaaŋatu			
old man	not far	as long as he could			
kinʸakoova	makitanealaami	mikilisaynʸaktuq			
looked at him	as he stood	started to get smaller			
ataatarurum	tawtukka	kayaktooneksuq	sikum	kiliŋanu	
old man	he saw	was in kayak	ice	edge of	
kayaktuktilu	puwiroq	uguruceaq	satkuxurutimaw		
as in kayak	came up	ugruk	when took spear		
ilʸuwilʸipeaaxłuγu	kasigeaq	puwigaraxsiru	kisayma		
he was in the way	spotted seal	began to come up	and then		
nawliktatpa	aasi	kiŋuruutiγłu	iilʸepom		
he got his spear in	and	turned him over	orphan		
nuleaŋa	kearutirooq	keaneaktiluγu	akaŋata		
his wife	while she wept	beginning weeping	her mother		

okalawtileaγa	iilʸepuq	awłaanixtiraniksuq	kayanni	
told her	orphan	started out at once	in kayak	
ikulexłuγu	kamukawraminʸu	awłaaneksuq	katipeaŋarun	
getting it	his sled	he went out	to middle	
sikum	kanʸektillunne	kamukawraŋe	sekumineksuq	
of ice	while watching	his sled	it was broken	
sekuminmatu	kamukawrane	exliutivłuγu	kayene	
when broken	his sled	he shouldered it	kayak	
awłaaneksuq	igliraluakamme	nukaaneksuq	uvlureet	
he went off	while going	he stopped	stars	
naypektoonare	taatkeγilʸu	okallaktuq		
he watched	moon	he said		
ukiuraaksinʸeraamnʸa	aanaloaq	sivunerenʸiraa		
winter coming now	grandmother	thinking of her		
awławtigillan	pilʸekami	siniksaktuq	kawmaminʸexsoγłu	
started again	when tired	he slept	it was daylight	
itiktuq	awławtigillan	igluqtuapasaŋikcuq	kayenni	
he awoke	started again	not going far	in kayak	
kalliyuutiga	nutkaxame	tawtukaamiu	kayenni	
pulled it up	when stopped	saw	in kayak	
aligaktuaniγineksuq	puktayumineγune	unʸiteluγu		
it was torn up	it won't float	he left it		
pisuaaxłune	awłaktuq	ayuktoakpasaŋikcuq	nitkaxaneksuq	
he walked	he started	he didn't go far	he stopped	
ilikcoreruq	inminʸun	paneraneksuŋa	tavra	
he found out	to himself	he gets thinner	and then	
sumunaγilaŋŋame	pisuakataktoaleγlaŋa	ayutoakpasaŋikcuq		
as I can	I will walk	he didn't go far		
suamanna	imaq	nutkaŋikcuq	sinʸanutikcuq	immam
there was	water	he didn't stop	it was edge of	water
kanuksawsikiraycuq	tavraakiuvuŋa	paneaniktuŋa		
he didn't know what to do	and then	I am already thin		
tavruŋawvaŋa	tokullaγłaŋa	siniksawtigillan	keyalexłunne	
and there	I had better die	he went to sleep	he got cold	
itiktuq	makinname	pisukataloataŋikcuq		
he awoke	when he stood	he could not walk well		
onaksipayaŋicukunne	narilʸaraneksuq	nakixirayixłune		
he didn't even get warm	he couldn't eat	he had no food		
nagaliksaaleksuq	nakixirayixłune	unʸaralilʸinʸakamme		
he began to suffer	he had no food	he got sleepy again		
kumigineksuq	sekosukłune	kumikamme	savitka	
got arm under	for sleeping	when arm put in	he touched	
oyamitkoanne	isumaroq	sunakeaxsamna	aylxunne	
his amulet	he thought	what is this	put arms out	
igiluaniq	tawtukka	suaγoγonna	mitkotaylum	
with one arm	he saw	it was	of sea bird	
isiganilʸu	neakoalom	issaroŋisa	takinixraŋiq	
the feet	the head	wing feather	the longest	
papinʸiγilu	kinʸillaan	aanani	itkaxniγa	
tail feather	watching	grandmother	he remembered	
kamukawraaniŋa	sikuume	kinʸiriniraat	awłanipayaaŋa	
his sled	on the ice	have seen	every movement	

ilʸeepom aanani tuxłuniraa anaŋ tavruŋavilan
orphan grandmother he called her grandmother right now

tavra inʸuγutiγa isukaksaasiro anaŋan
there my life will end his grandmother

tavrawvaa kiyuuva inʸuγutin isokaxanaŋikcuq
at once there answered your life does not end

oyamitkooren aareserłuγu kanisuŋaynʸaanin
your amulet wet it from your mouth

arinmareksilʸuγu isiganilʸu neakoalo aaresanikuku.
make it very wet the feet the head after wetting

siguukun tiγuluγu tawtuksaaresigin tawtuŋmaγu
on the bill get hold of start to look at it when he saw it

suagoγuna mitkotaylum aameya nuksawsiika
it was sea bird's skin he didn't know what to do

nanŋagaluaneksuq aanane tuxluniraa anaŋ
it was whole his grandmother he called her grandmother

aaresanikaloaneksuq kanuksawsikiγa
it is all wet now I don't know what to do with it

anaŋ atkiulitkaa akovłutin ovlaŋnun
grandmother answered you sit down between your legs

ilʸiyuγu atisaŋŋoaktiru iilʸepom atisaŋoaktiraa
put it down try to put it over orphan he tried to put it on

sikuŋarexłune kikaaniγineksuq qinʸaqamme tawtukke
he closed his eyes already he stood up he observed he saw

iric tayka anaŋ kaniŋane irik kinʸiraananeksuq
mountains there grandmother close by mountains can be seen

ixminʸun suagoγuna kinʸixłune inminʸik
himself he was he looking himself

mitkotaylaγonexłune suagoγuna taliginiyunmukłuwiq
resembling sea bird he was he put his arms up

awłacaktixłuwiq kaŋatakirneksuq kaŋataktikamme
he began to move them he got off ground when off ground

awłaaneksuq sikuktuŋaanu sakoovłune
he started toward the ice he turned back

pilʸeoominʸaaneksuq iniminʸukamme tiŋyineksuq
he won't get tired he went back he flew

aanami tuŋaanu sukatilaamisin tiŋmineksuq
his grandmother toward as fast as he can he was flying

nerisulereneksuq nerisuktilaane ilʸicurikamiu
he wanted to eat wanting to eat he found out

qiveaaneksuq anmun suagoγukua ikalluwaret
he looked down there were small fishes

ilʸanaŋnik naqixiraktirneksuq allamiksule
some of them he obtained for eating still more

nirisuwixsuq awłakitkami owinʸiraalereneksuq
stopped eating when started was again sleepy

sukuramik tawtukamme micaaneksuq sirkotigillan
secure place he saw landing on beach went right to sleep

sinʸisiguruγuneksuq tiŋikamme awławtigillan tiŋikamme
after sleeping a time he flew he started out he flew

sukatellaamisin tawtuke iγłut kallikamme
as fast as he could he saw houses when he arrived

suagu	makoa	illaatun	ittuat	nerin^{y}esuguruuneksut
there	just as	he himself	him	they were eating

tikixłunil^{y}u	nakixiraaneksuq	aasi	nuunemu
as he approached	he got food	and	on dry ground

micaalune	neriniraa	sin^{y}iksawtigillan	kawriruq
he landed	started eating	going to sleep	when he saw

suagoγona	ilitkucimisun	inexsuq	makinman
he was	he was as before	he was	he stood up

suagoγmanna	pisiksi	paketaŋa	taktuooman	aasi
there was that	bow	he found it	when foggy	and

aygaxsivłune	anaamin^{y}u	isirman	aanaŋata
started home	to his grandmother	when he came	his grandmother

oputiγa	ayγuluneksutin	maraa	pisiksi	umealiŋmu
exclaimed	you finally came	this	bow	to chief

tawtukticaktuaruŋ	tamaretualuγu	paketaŋa	ataataruavu
let him see it	it is the only one	found	old man

tukutarunire	aŋataktiguvłune	nukatpeat	aasi
habitually killed	was a shaman	young people	and

ataataruruq	tukuruaq	anaruraq	kuleaktuaneksuq
old people	she died	old lady	he told

taapkuniŋa	iil^{y}epom	kuleaktuaŋinik
to them	orphan	this tale

kowiyero	umealiq	il^{y}isarikamiu	pisiksi
was glad	chief	when he noticed	bow

taymaptawk
it is finished

Free Translation

A group of people were living in a village by the sea. Among them lived an orphan boy and his grandmother. Once when it was time to go to sleep, a man called into the skylight of their house, saying that the son of the chief (umealiq) had disappeared. All were looking for him and although the chief was paying them to find him, they had sought everywhere and were unable to find his tracks. The orphan said to his grandmother that he would try to find the lost boy. She agreed and he got ready. At dark, he came and stood before the house of the chief, thinking of the way in which the chief's son might have disappeared. As he thus stood, a young man came to stand next to him. This was a stranger, who informed that his father had sent him to fetch the orphan boy. The young man informed him that their house was nearby but they walked on far. At last, they came to a house with two racks. When they went in, the orphan boy saw an old man and his wife. With them was a young girl. The old man was lying down but rose up when the orphan boy entered and said: "Go to your wife over there." So he sat down at the side of the young girl.

After he had been seated, the girl arose and, taking a pan, went outside. Presently, she returned, her pan filled with berries of all kinds. When they had eaten, the old man said: "I wish to sleep early." Then he told them that in the morning the orphan boy should go out with his son. Then they slept. The orphan boy asked the girl, his wife, what had happened to the young man (the son of the chief) for whom they were searching. She told him that her father had sent this young man out for caribou. The young man had accompanied her brother. She told him that when they went out this day, he should get many caribou. Then (in the morning) the old man said: "My son-in-law sleeps too much." He wakened his son and they got ready to go. Meanwhile, the wife of the orphan boy cried bitterly. Disregarding her tears, he started off with his brother-in-law. He started off toward the mountains. When they arrived there, he told his brother-in-law that each of them should go around in different ways and come together ahead. The orphan started off alone. He came to a river and saw many fat caribou. He shot them with his bow. Before he started again, he skinned one and removed the hind quarter and slung it over his shoulder and started off. As he walked, there came a fog from behind him and he couldn't find his way. As he walked in the fog, he stumbled over something. Reaching down, he found a bow. He picked it up and carried it along. After a time, it began to be more and more foggy. At last, he couldn't see the ground. He lost his balance and began to fall. As he did so, he exclaimed: "This is the way that old man killed those people" [i. e., by sending a fog].

Suddenly he remembered the amulet an old woman had given him. "This is why it was given to me," he thought. He took it from the bag in which it was carried and, putting it in his mouth, he blew hard. A clearing came in the fog, and following it he was able to get back to the house. His wife received him there, glad that he had come, and taking the caribou haunch, welcomed him. Then he ate. The old man was there and said: "My son-in-law can't get into trouble; he quickly goes to sleep and sleeps in the morning." Then he gave instructions for the following day. He said to the orphan that he wanted him to go off to hunt ugruk (bearded seal). Then the old man went to sleep. As they were in bed, the orphan asked his wife which way they were to go in the morning. She replied that her brother would show him.

In the morning, his brother-in-law took him out in his kayak. They had not eaten. They put the kayak and the spears on a sled and started off. The brother-in-law remarked that they would go different ways out on the ice for their ugruk. The orphan boy took the kayak and a little sled. He started off to the edge of the ice. He had not gone far when he saw an ugruk and then another right near his kayak. Next he saw a spotted seal. He struck at it with his paddle and it went down. Then he saw another ugruk. He took hold of his spear, but the ugruk was gone and the spotted seal came up again. This time the seal came up from the edge of the ice and leaped over his kayak, to avoid being speared. Angry, he speared it. His kayak turned over and he was cast away. He came to himself at a place where the tides were ebbing and flowing and from which he had started out. It was dark. As it grew light, he heard something moving. He saw a house nearby and the rope from his spear led to the house. Without hesitating, he went to the house and entered it. There was his brother-in-law with a harpoon in his side and the line from the harpoon leading through the door. The orphan boy bade him be quiet, saying that he would remove the harpoon point. He took his knife and pulled at the cord. His knife came away with the flesh on it. He got up and without looking backward at all, started off alone. He went to his kayak and started off, going back to his wife and father-in-law.

When he arrived there, he went into the house and lay down. After a while, his wife nudged his leg. "Here is our son-in-law," said the old woman. They offered him food and he took hold of it. The old man said: "Come over here; sit down in front of me and tell me something." The orphan replied: "If I do, you won't believe me." But then he told the old man, his father-in-law, to go out and bring in quickly a hollow piece of wood filled with ice. The old man did as he was told and put the wood in front of the orphan boy. Then the latter said: "Now sit down over there." Then the orphan boy dipped his toes in the water. The old man began to get smaller and suddenly he was in his kayak. In the water, the ugruk and the spotted seal came up again. The orphan boy took his spear and turned the kayak over. The orphan's wife and her mother were weeping at this.

Then the orphan started out from the house. He took his kayak and a small sled along with him. He went out on the ice. Suddenly his sled broke. He shouldered his kayak and sled and started walking over the ice. He paused to look at the stars and moon. He thought to himself that winter was approaching. And he thought of his grandmother at home. After a time, he paused to rest and sleep. When he awoke, it was daylight. He came down to his kayak and saw that it was all torn and wouldn't float. He walked about the ice, marooned. He became thinner, starving. At last, he came to the edge of the ice and could go no further. He didn't know what to do—he was starving. At last, he thought to himself: "I had best die right here." Lying down, he went to sleep. It was cold. When he awoke, he could scarcely walk from hunger and weakness. He could not get warm and he had no food. He lay down again, exhausted.

But this time, as he lay down, he drew his arm inside his parka preparing to rest his head, and suddenly he felt his charm. He reached in and drew it out. It was a charm consisting of parts of the sea bird called mitkotayluq, the feet head, wing feathers, and the longest tail feathers. And he thought that his grandmother would have seen every movement of his sled on the ice. So he called: "Grandmother! My life will end right here." And at once his grandmother answered: "No, your life does not end. Take your amulet and make it wet from your mouth. Make it very wet; wet the feet and the head. Then get hold of the bill and look at it." He did so, and suddenly, the whole bird was there before him. Then he called again: "Grandmother! It is all wet now and I don't know what to do next." She answered: "Sit down, try to draw it (the birdskin) over you." He tried to do this. Then he closed his eyes and stood up. He could see the mountains and he knew that he was near his grandmother. He suddenly realized that he had taken the form of the mitkotayluq. He put his wings up and began to fly. Above ground, he flew over the ice and fearing fatigue went down again. Then he flew toward his grandmother as fast as he could. As he flew, he recalled his hunger. Below him, in the water, he observed numerous small fishes and flew down to gather some of them up. He ate until he was full and then flew on. He reached the beach and, tired, slept again on the beach. Then he flew on until he came to the houses of his people. Pausing, he got some more food, and ate and slept again. This time, when he awoke, he had regained his human form.

He started up, taking the bow that he had found when it was so foggy, and went in to his grandmother. She told him, after exclaiming that he had finally come, that he should take the bow and take it to the chief. "Let him see it," she said, "it is the only one found" (i. e., only evidence of his lost son). And that old man was a shaman who regularly killed young people and the orphan boy destroyed him. And the old lady (the shaman's wife) died after that, too. And the orphan boy told the story to all and the chief was glad when he saw the bow which had belonged to his son.

Note: This tale is interesting as a reflection of a shamanistic contest. The orphan, aided by his grandmother, vanquishes the wicked shaman and returns to his people, ostensibly taking vengeance for the death of the chief's son.

Children's Stories

A few examples of stories told to children were collected. The type of story involved here relates in the main to animals. These were principally told to the very young child. Older children, by age 7 to 8, had begun to develop an appreciation for adult folklore. Most frequently, a song is associated with the child's tale. Such songs were regularly sung by children as part of play. At present, the tales are still virtually universal. The element of the lullaby is present; children were often told such stories on retiring. In all such tales, humor is a significant feature.

THE MOUSE

There was a little mouse on the edge of the skylight. He looked in and saw the stone fireplace. He circled around and missed his step and fell. He fell on the edge of the stones. When he fell, he hurt his belly and his intestines came out, so he thought. But he just hit himself on his little ribs. He began to cry:

isuŋa ŋa ŋaa

iniloat	alitkikaa
intestines	I tore them

LITTLE BLACK RAVEN

It was blowing on the side of the river. It blew hard. And the little black raven sang:

tiŋinaa aa aa
tiŋinaa aa aa
tiŋinaa kucugunaa
turukucuk turukucuk
uyaranoo ee ee ee

Poor little black raven—he had a pain in his belly.

THE RAVEN

There was a raven who flew over two people who couldn't find their son. They asked him: "Raven, can you tell us the story? You are flying over us."

And the raven answered:

suumiŋme	suumiŋme
What then?	what then?

uleaktooanakpik
What shall I tell the two of you?

neariγik piginʸaa
Up at the mountain

akuγunʸaaarane
between them

irinʸereik piŋyaa
there is your son

nerekpukpiŋinʸaa
We have eaten him

tatpiginʸakpiviu
Is he the one you ask about?

And the woman answered, singing:

sumiktukpaγana
I wonder what it is

milukxaaługu
I throw at him

nekemigłu	irimigłu
with meat	with an eye

CONCLUSIONS

It is evident that there is justification for considering North Alaska as a single zone of Eskimo culture. This is an area, as has been shown, bounded on the south by the Brooks Range and the Noatak drainage system, and thus includes the Alaskan Arctic slope, the northwest coast of Alaska, and the Arctic coast as far east as the trading centers of the Colville mouth and Oliktok Point. Despite the ecological differences between the two basic groups resident in the area, and the consequent differences in material culture, there is a high degree of cultural uniformity which further justifies the culture area designation. The foregoing study has sought to raise the question of the extent of the relationship between economy and society, asking in how far the social forms developed in the area relate to the demands of the physical setting. It remains to consider briefly the implications of this hypothesis in the light of the data available. At the same time, the relations between this and other Eskimo areas deserve to be considered, if only to demonstrate how North Alaska represents a particularized zone of Eskimo culture. Lastly, because so much attention has been given to the questions of the temporal development of Eskimo cultures, it seems fitting to conclude with some remarks on the ethnographic implications of this problem as revealed by North Alaskan data.

ECOLOGY AND SOCIETY IN NORTH ALASKA

As was noted in the introductory sections of this study, and following the suggestions advanced by Kroeber (1939), environment can be considered only a limiting factor in the shaping of human society. Among the North Alaskan Eskimo, the physical setting might be considered harsh and inhospitable, demanding concerted human activity in order to promote maximum efficiency to effect survival. That the culture was efficient there can be little doubt, but it was no more so than a host of other Arctic cultures which have succeeded in meeting the problem of survival equally well. Given, indeed, a complex of culture traits which are widely distributed in the circumpolar zone from northern Europe across Asia and America to Greenland, the North Alaskan Eskimo simply offer variations on an Arctic theme. Theirs was a development suited to the environment in which they found themselves. It made capital of whaling and of caribou hunting in a distinctive way, factors which in turn lead to some specialized social forms. These in fact are localized phrasings of a basic Arctic hunting culture and permit a social delimitation of the North Alaskan culture area.

The distinctive aspects of the culture appear to rest primarily in the ecological dichotomy which arose in the region. Unlike the Eskimo farther to the east or, indeed, farther to the south in Alaska, such as in the Kobuk-Selawik drainage and south of this in the areas approaching the Bering Straits, there was less attention given to pronounced changes in economic activity. The fact that the contrast arose between inland caribou hunting and maritime sea-mammal hunting is revealing. It places the two ecological adjustments in rather sharp contrast to each other, a contrast which is not evident among other Eskimo groups, some of whom follow a changing land-sea pattern, shifting from one activity to the other. It must be stated, however, that even in North Alaska, the boundary between the one hunting activity and the other is somewhat blurred, since it is evident that there were maritime dwellers in the area who did hunt caribou intensively, and at the same time there were various inland peoples who might engage in sealing at different points on the coast. But there was associated with each activity a skill which neither group could quite capture from the other. The nuunamiut who might engage in sporadic seal hunting did not engage in the challenging activity of whaling, nor did the maritime dwellers who might engage in caribou drives do so on a scale comparable to that of the inland peoples. Further, if the yardstick of societal integration be applied and if these two ecological systems be viewed in the light of their stabilized internal relationships, the whale and the caribou respectively become the pivotal focus of each setting. There is the same cultural base, it is true, but the distinctive ecological alinements evoke differences of response. The cult of the whale is to be contrasted with that of the caribou. And if one can readily see the parallels and the structural elements shared between the two socioreligious forms, it is evident that factors resident in the physical setting of each group operate differently off the base of a common culture. In general organization, the unity of the area goes far; the concepts of the umealiq, of family and society, of cooperative crew and karigi, and the attitudes toward the natural world are in essence the same in both settings. It is only the primary economic emphasis, either that on the whale or the caribou, which spells the difference.

Where various other Eskimo groups have permitted seasonal variation of activity, North Alaska chose a greater degree of stability. The groups became interdependent and by developing the patterns of trade, made the particularized adjustment of the area possible. Trading thus came to represent a specialized activity, the hallmark of the area. This is not to say that trading is not characteristic of other Eskimo or other Arctic peoples, but it does become for the area in question a crowning achievement. Its remarkable intensity reflects economic interdependence on a massive scale. It served to throw one group in sharp perspective against the other. It meant that the tareumiut and the nuunamiut, for all their community of culture, were distinctive peoples. Where, as among the Central Eskimo, the individual group, having amassed sea-mammal fat in quantity, could then turn to the increase of a meat supply by hunting caribou, and become quite mobile in the process, North Alaska balanced specialists against each other and chose to lay particular emphasis on the trading partnership, effecting thereby a fairly uniform distribution of goods.

It was through the trade and, further, through trade focused in the trading partnerships, that the economic balance was achieved. This, as is evident, was primarily a cooperative institution, one of several selected forms of cooperation characteristic of the area. If environment limits (and among the Eskimo it is perhaps clearest as to just what the limitations of environment are), it follows that the human element can make as wide a series of choices in fashioning a society as the environment itself permits. Indeed, the primary solution which was found in North Alaska was the selection of means by which the cooperative tie could be most effectively achieved. Forms of cooperation, obligations incumbent on the individual to cooperate, appear as two primary principles or premises of North Alaskan culture. The first of these lay in kinship, in the bilateral kinship unit from which mutual aid, economic assistance, and moral support were always forthcoming. No insignificant aspect of this first principle is its corollary: that there were patterned ways in which the whole implicit array of mutual obligations between kin could be extended, under specialized and formalized circumstances, to nonkin. The second formal manifestation of cooperation was basically economic, lying as it did in the social and ceremonial relationships which existed between the members of a hunting group, what has been called in this study a crew, a body working together under the banner of an umealiq and pledged to the concerted activity of the hunt, whether on the sea, for whale, walrus, or ugruk, or inland, in the intensive caribou drive and impound. Only in these basic aspects of cooperation does society in the area come to be. Once developed, these aspects operate as a continuing force to promote societal stability.

The individual was a tareumiut or a nuunamiut by birth. Further, he was identified with a particular locality in the ecological setting. But, as has been frequently noted, this did not mean that he was bound to it or even to the ecological system into which he had been born.

He was free to move in and out of a particular setting if he chose and to seek his associations where he wished. But from a practical point of view, a man generally remained where he received (and was required to give) the support of the bilateral kinship grouping of which he was a part. Clearly, the cultural definition of the happy man bears out the aspect of the kinship tie. He is regarded as fortunate who can count on the backing of his kindred and who can enumerate them widely. Conversely, the worst fate which can befall the human being is to be an "orphan," that is, one lacking in the support of a circle of kinsmen. The kinship structure itself was not highly formalized, relatives being those with whom the kinship tie was affirmed. It could be a widely dispersed, extended family group, but more often it was an affirmation of ties to a relatively limited circle. In practice, it is evident that a good deal of variation existed, as it does even today. Given a bad season at nuwuk, a man might leave to settle at tikeraaq, reaffirming kinship ties there, or seeking a place by virtue of some other kind of formalized association. But the point remains that there was a formalized recognition of such social ties. One defined one's relatives by the fact of cooperation and support, and by the sense of collective responsibility applicable to the group membership. By the same token, partnerships, whether within the same ecological setting or across ecological lines, were formalized, reached only after deliberation and then in patterned ways. The partnership, with its sexual exchange, with the resultant status of quasi-kinship applicable to the respective offspring of partners, was such a formal way of extending kinship privileges to nonkin. On this level, the cooperative patterns may be summed up as being resident in kinship to various bilateral degrees, and in the circle of nonkin who came to occupy a position of quasi-kinship.

This meant that informal associations, apart from the hunting group or crew system, were not only rare but competitive as well. Friendships, outside of partnerships, however conceived, had really no meaning. Indeed, the term iil^{y}onaaruq, meaning an intimate in the sense of "friend," has a joking derogatory sense and suggests competitive status difference and a patronizing usage. karigi memberships and crew composition were infinitely less stable than the formal partnerships, owing to the changing success or lack of success of a leader. The umealiq, whether inland or at the sea, bribed his crew to keep them. Except for his own kin and his associated quasi-kin, he commanded little primary loyalty. Indeed, it was his competitive success which insured him a full crew.

What this situation and societal organization did to other social institutions is obvious. While a village or settlement represented community of interest, it lacked reality as a corporate unit. There were instead coexisting kin groups across which, at specified times of activity, crew membership might cut. It would be incorrect to identify either the village or the crew with a political organization. But even though a political structure was lacking, this was hardly an anarchic society. Social sanctions, customary law, community of interest, and the common cultural bonds of a folk society made for relatively smooth functioning. Only when competitive rivalries came to the fore, as in respect to the competition for status, and particularly for status as represented in the control of women, was a dilemma created. At times, when the unconforming or status-seeking individual arose, bullying his way across the community, since this was the usual pattern of antisocial behavior, the society was at a loss to act. It was then that the otherwise fairly smooth net of interpersonal relations was broken and the kinship units lined up one against the other. Clearly, despite the rather limited kinds of formal association which the social structure permitted, the society followed an even course.

If one's kin group was thus primary, the question as to the place of the marital tie may again be raised. Again in line with the economic aspect, it is evident that, as among other Eskimo (and many so-called primitives), marriage related to a sexual division of labor, to the fact that the defined activities of one sex necessarily complemented those of the other. By this same token, marriages, though conceptually ephemeral and being fairly informally conceived, were fairly permanent. The unmarried individual was so rare as to occasion comment and disapproval. Thus marriage may in effect be compared to the partnership for mutual aid. Indeed, this is precisely what it was. Sexual liaisons did not necessarily result in marriage and although, for the male, prowess over women related to status rivalry, this is wholly apart from the defined reciprocities of the marriage tie. One's affined kin were not conceived to fall into the kinship classification, but because of the emphasis on bilateral organization, a bond with one's in-laws was effected through offspring, whether of blood or by adoption, and further by the lack of formalism in residence. This meant that marriage, tenuous though it might at first glance appear, with its suggestions of polyandry, its polygyny, possibility of divorce, etc., was more of a stabilizing force than not. One cannot forget that there were ceremonial duties imposed on the married couple, something borne out best in the case of the duties imposed on the wife of the umealiq, but true of every hunter's wife as well. The wife of the seal hunter was obliged to offer fresh water to the slain animal, while the wives of both inland and maritime hunters were obliged to remain quiet while their husbands were engaged in the chase. But the obligations of a wife went far beyond these simple ceremonial acts. It followed, too, that the social system, with its emphasis on formalized associations of cooperation, could impose regulations governing the selection of a mate. In the effort to do all possible to increase the circle of cooperative activity, it is easy to explain why the marriage of cousins was, if not ceremonially prohibited, at least regarded by the group at large as the poorest kind of social arrangement. By the same reasoning, the levirate, the sororate, sororal polygyny, or fraternal polyandry were considered outrageous and shocking. Although these forms of marriage might occur, it is clear that they never did so without social stigma.

The social organization which is summarized here applies equally to the interior and to the coast. The differences between the nuunamiut and tareumiut were thus solely those of making a living. The social structure readily permitted either kind of economic life.

Religion emerges in the culture as an important social institution, one which is again intimately related to the ecological system. As has been suggested, religion in the North Alaskan area has three aspects: (1) world view, (2) ceremonialism, (3) shamanism. As in any religious system, the latter two are intimately connected with the first. The religious organization at large relates, of course, to the general patterns of supernaturalism current among the boreal hunting peoples, but it does possess some distinctive facets. A primary theme among the nonagricultural hunters of North America and Asia is that the world of the hunted animals is superior to that of men, and that the animal allows himself to be hunted and taken, that compulsive and imitative magic may succeed in subduing him, and finally, that at all costs no offense may be given him. From this basic premise proceeds the magic of song and amulet, and from it, too, comes the power of the shaman. This study has perhaps added something to the body of knowledge concerning shamans and shamanism among the Eskimo by way of detail, but the affinities of Eskimo shamanism are well understood. Suffice it to add only that the Eskimo, like other Arctic peoples, treat shamanistic power as coming from the environment, that is, from the animal sprits whose presence is conceptually so vital to the continuation of life. If every hunter has his particular magic for game, especially in the compelling songs which he may own, this pattern reaches its extreme in the North Alaskan area in the two cults which characterize the two ecological systems. Ritual directed to the major activities in the economic sphere reaches its peak in respect to the whale among the tareumiut and to the caribou among the nuunamiut.

The umealiq, as has been shown, was usually a man of parts, a good leader, a dominant figure, strong, and a respected hunter. But he need be none of these things. The harpooner and a skilled crew could do the work of whaling, while it was an experienced hunter and several hard-working assistants who could best manage the caribou impound and slaughter. Thus the umealiq was primarily a ritualist, a priest, and it was as much on this as on his wealth and bounty, that his success in holding a crew depended. And it was in this ritual arrangement that one finds the cult, the special phrasing of some basic Eskimo ideas which applies to North Alaska.

North Alaskan Eskimo society thus emerges as a balanced and integrated one. Its common cultural understandings created the possibilities, while the society arranged itself around the two dominant economic modes. The interdependent system which was created was wholly effective, self-perpetuating, and would undoubtedly have remained so, had not forces from without—new interests, new diseases, new modes of life—disrupted and decimated it. The coastal peoples remain, with perhaps a larger population than was true a century ago, but the nuunamiut are virtually gone. In its untrammeled setting, the culture provided for the individual and the group, leaving a wide range of individual latitude and freedom of choice, but at the same time allowing a high degree of security. Limited by environment, forced to focus on the resources of a rather narrow kind which the area provided, this culture, more effectively perhaps than any other among nonliterate peoples, represents a cooperative human triumph over nature.

THE PLACE OF NORTH ALASKA IN ESKIMO CULTURE

No attempt is made here to provide a listing of the distinctive elements of culture which characterize the North Alaskan Eskimo, or to show their general distribution. This task ought to be undertaken, and, indeed, is contemplated for publication elsewhere. It depends, however, on a somewhat fuller analysis of the material aspects of the area than has been given in this study and might better await the results of the intensive archeological work carried on for several seasons at Point Barrow by Harvard University. Restricting the problem to ecological adjustment, omitting for purposes of the present discussion the material culture, and to social and ceremonial organization, it is still possible to offer a comment or two on the cultural position of the North Alaskan Eskimo.

North Alaska suggests a basic Eskimo configuration in which the rather elaborated cultural development of the Alaskan Eskimo generally plays a significant part. But it contains traits which are evidently more generalized and which may be regarded as more characteristic of the Central and Greenland regions. The conclusion is a simple one: North Alaska, despite its economic specializations, is a regional phrasing of Arctic culture, reflecting a particularization of the culture which has been associated with the Eskimo as well as the distinctive patterns of the circumpolar zone. Needless to say, this is borne out by the presence in North Alaska of a great many elements associated with the general Eskimo picture, such as tailored skin clothing, the fanwise dog-trace, the tambourine, the stone (or pottery) lamp, the distinctive harpoon types, semisubterranean houses, shamanism with its associated array of artifacts and world view, and a host of other traits. Further, given an Eskimo base of sea-mammal and caribou hunting, with its many associated material and social aspects, it is possible to determine the elements shared between the North Alaskans and all other Eskimo. Breaking it down still further, there are those elements in North Alaskan culture which point to affinities with the Eskimo of the central and eastern regions of the American Arctic, and those which suggest an overlay of influences from the south in Alaska itself, not omitting in this regard traits suggestive of the strong culture of the Northwest Coast area of western North America. Similarly, and despite these clearly defined historical relationships, it is possible to determine the uniqueness of North Alaskan culture, not so much by virtue of its possession of particular or distinctive culture traits, but rather because of the special phrasing of elements which seem to characterize the Eskimo at large.

This is again apparent in the land-sea dichotomy of livelihood. Parallels exist among other Eskimo groups, to be sure, but nowhere is an integrated pattern of sea-mammal hunting so sharply set off from one of caribou dependence. This, as has been shown, is the characteristic of the area, one so distinctive as to permit its definition as an area of subcultural development. It is worth stressing again that against dissimilarity of ecological adjustment, nuunamiut compared with tareumiut, is set the community of culture and its essential similarity. This being so, it seems fitting to inquire as to the place of the total area, considering especially social and ceremonial organization, in the Eskimo picture at large.

It is here that a problem arises. What, indeed, is Eskimo culture? As De Laguna has pointed out (1947, p. 284), one is tempted to stress the notion of a kind of substratum Eskimo culture from which the historical as well as the contemporary Eskimo patterns have been derived. This would be a kind of Eskimo base, which, if it could be defined, would permit a ready resolution of the problem. But as the data are considered, it is clear that the prehistoric Eskimo cultures are infinitely more diverse than is true of those in the ethnographic present. In other words, it seems indicated that modern Eskimo cultures are less to be explained in terms of a cultural substratum on which, here and there, various extraneous elements are imposed and operate, and rather more in terms of original diversity worked upon by essentially uniform environmental conditions which evoke a convergence toward cultural uniformity. This solution admittedly omits the question of the remarkable similarity which characterizes the Eskimo area as a whole, since, if carried to its logical conclusion, it posits diverse ethnic origins. And by the same token, the uniformity of physical type is suggestive, such being characteristic of the coasts, but not necessarily of the interiors. The point has been made, and the evidence is clearly discernible, that there is a difference in physical type as between the nuunamiut and the tareumiut (Collins, 1951, p. 442). The alternative, considering other possible explanations than an ultimate and original uniformity of culture, language, and physical type, is to lay emphasis on the presence of the Thule culture, conceived as originating in the western regions of Arctic America, spreading eastward and then back again. This, as a whaling culture, with its roots in the Birnirk (piγiniq) culture of Point Barrow, points in turn to the antiquity of the whaling complex in North Alaska (Collins, 1951, pp. 428–429). Language and somatology, as well as general culture, can be explained in their striking similarities only by a recognition that if, indeed, there was any Eskimo substratum, it appears to be late and coincident with the Thule culture (cf. De Laguna, 1947, p. 10).

This implies, therefore, that North Alaska, in its cultural position, is to be identified with a Thule-like configuration. Analysis of the material features offers confirmation of this. Without going further into detail on the problems of the antiquity of the North Alaskan whaling culture, however, it is perhaps sufficient to note that one can relate the patterns of the ethnographic present, at least in their material contexts, to prehistoric horizons in the area. It may be further supposed that the patterns of societal organization as they appear in the area, and considering the distribution of their types, likewise have their roots in the considerable past.

It is somewhat less easy to compare social organization among the Eskimo than it is the patterns of ceremonial life. This is simply because of the absence of full data. In a general way, however, Eskimo society appears to depend on the relatively simple organization of the bilateral family. Variations on this structure arise in different Eskimo groups, emphasis on one form or another being hit upon as a matter of expediency. Given the bilateral family, some differences arise in the matter of its extensions, differences which reflect local phrasings. The hunting group or band, the village, and the concept of community are, among most Eskimo, secondary to the elementary kinship tie. As the North Alaskan data are reviewed, therefore, it seems evident that here is a basic social organization paralleling that of other Eskimo groups to the east. It is borne out further by the kinship terminologies. Here is a variation of the "Eskimo" type of system, even though there has been an evident loss of some categories and the development of one or two specialized terms relating to local social circumstances. The classificatory qataŋun, and what it implies, seems to be a localized example characteristic of North Alaska. It is not until one comes into the Bering Sea area of Alaska and points south that there are the beginnings of a more formalized unilineal social organization, even though, as nearly as can be judged, terminological systems have been less subject to modification. Even in this part of Alaska, until the strong influences of the unilineal organizations from the Northwest Coast of America make themselves felt, one does not capture the sense of clan or moiety; it is rather that of a unilineal structure in its incipient forms, those of lineages (cf. Lantis, 1946, et al.). Among the North Alaskans, whether, under the influence of the adjacent peoples to the south, this might ultimately have become the case, is of little import. The social patterns which were followed reflect the institutions of peoples to the east rather than those of Alaska itself. The admissible conclusions seem to be that the existing social structure of North Alaska has its roots in antiquity and that it can be identified with an organizational type widely distributed among the Eskimo.

Breaking this structure down into some of its component elements, one is struck first by the essential simplicity and the lack of formalism in the familial organization, but at the same time by its intensity and strength. Formality lay only in the definition accorded by the person to his kinship affiliations. Personal interdependence arose in the family not only to the extent of community of labor, sharing, and joint enterprise, but also in the demands of collective responsibility. Like other central and eastern Eskimo, the North Alaskans subordinated all other associations to the family tie. And indeed, it is on the level of extrafamilial association that the patterns which emerge are less suggestive of the basic, generalized Eskimo organization of the central and eastern Arctic, but more reflective of Alaskan arrangements. The formalized association of the hunt group under the ceremonial leader, the umealiq, with all the array of the karigi participation, has its parallels to the south rather than to the east. The karigi itself (kashim, kazhigi, etc.) has been described in the greatest detail for the Alaskan Eskimo, but it is not a phenomenon which proceeds farther east than Point Barrow (cf. Lantis, 1947, pp. 104–107). With the karigi is to be found the socioceremonial arrangement of the Messenger Feast. It is in respect to this festival that some fairly obvious connections with the Northwest Coast are seen, proceeding, as these do, throughout the Alaskan Eskimo cultures. Wealth, it will have been noted, is a complex in the North Alaskan area which is fairly well developed. In a sense it ties into the mutual aid worked out between family members. But it comes to be most effective in a festival complex which is not an integral part of the functioning culture. The Messenger Feast is obviously a secondary configuration, one not vital to the culture and one which may even have arisen within the last 150 years with the introduction of luxury goods, particularly those which had their origins in the south, such as tobacco and iron products. There is the distinct impression that wealth, at the time of contact, was becoming more of a force in the society.

The concept of partnership was fairly well established among most Eskimo. To the east, however, partnership in the formal sense is less well elaborated than in the Alaskan setting generally. It is to be remembered that in North Alaska the partnership idea and institution were primarily means of extending the cooperative bonds of kinship to nonkin. It was frequently, although not always, cemented with wife exchange. The North Alaskans made capital of the concept of partnership as a means of stabilizing the relations between two economic systems. Some reflection of a formal partnership organization, operating somewhat in the same way, is seen in the Alaskan cultures farther to the south. North Alaska, however, does something with the basic Eskimo idea of partnership which no other Eskimo culture does. It can be said that these relationships, next to those inherent in the family, were a primary focus of societal stability. This is not true of the joking partnerships, forms which seem better developed and integrated among other Alaskan Eskimos. These are, it is true, important in establishing certain kinds of social relations, those between men of the same crew or karigi, men who were intimate because they represented the same age grade or the same locality. But there were not the full associations of joking partnership which are described, for example, from Nunivak Island, where these relationships apparently assume a far greater importance (cf. Lantis, 1946, pp. 243–244). To put it in other terms, it is the formalized trading partnership which, although patterned in an Alaskan way and yet characteristic to some degree of all Eskimo, assumes more elaborated proportions in the phrasing of the North Alaskan cultures.

In conclusion, the North Alaskans can be said to represent a basic Eskimo type or pattern (in so far as this is a definable concept), a pattern with its roots in some antiquity. Over this is laid a series of Alaskan Eskimo traits. There is then a particular local phrasing of both aspects. It can be said of the North Alaskan Eskimo that theirs was a marginal culture when viewed in the light of Alaskan Eskimo developments at large.

Nowhere is this so well borne out as in the case of the partnerships, and also in the case of ceremonialism and religion. Mythology of course is generally Eskimo, or, indeed, boreal or subpolar with some local phrasing. Similarly, the world view differs nowise from that of other North American and Asiatic hunters. Shamanism, too, with all its array, its associated behavior and artifacts, is not out of keeping with the patterns found among other Eskimo. But the ceremonialism of North Alaska is basically that of Alaska. The Sedna myth, for example, is not present, nor the ceremonials associated in the central regions with the kinds of attentions devoted to Sedna. Instead, there is the presence of the two cults, that of the whale and of the caribou, with the ritualistic behavior of the kind characteristic of Alaska. The idea of greeting, of distribution of the meat, the treatment of boats and hunting weapons suggest a syncretism, a combining of elements which mark several feasts and ceremonials farther to the south. Two major festivals stand out in North Alaska, the one being the hunting celebrations, the other the Messenger Feast. The latter, as has been suggested, appears to be late. In both, however, appear traces of the festivals which are to be found on a much more elaborated scale in the south—the Bladder Feast, the "Asking" Feast, and many more. These do not appear as such, although their elements fuse in the two major festivals of the north. As Lantis (1947, pp. 114–115.) notes "The absence of public life-crisis ceremonies—birth, boys' lip-piercing, girls' puberty, memorial feasts—and the ritual simplicity of the festivals they did have, particularly in the fewer and more simply carved masks, made Point Barrow life look not different but distinctly *less* than the life of the Bering Sea people." This seems a fair statement. Indeed, as one considers the ritual paraphernalia, from Point Hope to Point Barrow, and again in the adjacent interior, it seems clear that a point of greater elaboration in the area, especially in this regard, lay in tikeraaq (Point Hope.). Here, according to informants and corroborated further by Rainey (1947), the kariyit were more elaborate, masks were more complex, and a kind of extreme, for the area, at least, appears to have been reached in the development of hunting fetishes. Point Hope had permanent kariyit, as indeed, did utkeaaγvik and nuwuk, but those at Point Barrow were said to be smaller and less well furnished. When it became necessary, in fact, the Point Barrow kariyit were implemented with buildings of ice blocks, something seemingly never necessary in the larger and more splendid ceremonial structures of Point Hope. In other words, the temporary karigi of the interior peoples was at times duplicated at Point Barrow. The suggestion may be made, therefore, on the basis of this development, that many of the southern ritual elements were moving into the area at the time of contact and that Point Barrow, being farthest away, had not yet made as full capital or succeeded in effecting such complete integration of them as had the people of Point Hope.

This brief summary touches only a few of the points which could be considered at length in defining the cultural position of North Alaska. The area, marginal to Alaska itself, thus suggests a meeting place of two strains, an eastern and a western. It is its own specialized area. Its economic development arises in far greater dependence than was true of any other Eskimo group on the great baleen whales. This made for a group of specialists, hunters who, in obtaining vast amounts of surplus food, made possible in turn the inland economy of caribou hunting. Maritime life and whaling, with the associated hunting of other sea mammals, seems crucial, for without the stability afforded by the trading of the products of the sea to the inland, the quasi-nomadic inland bands with their exclusive caribou hunting could not have flourished. Theirs would have had to be a variable existence, one of pushing to the sea at times and inland at other times. In North Alaska this was clearly not the case, although when the support of the maritime whalers is lost, as at Hotham Inlet and along the rivers which drain into it, the line between nuunamiut and tareumiut becomes less clear. It is in these areas of the Kobuk and Selawik Rivers, just as at the mouth of the McKenzie to the east, that the culture area of North Alaska begins to shade off.

NORTH ALASKA AND ESKIMO CULTURE HISTORY

The problem of Eskimo origins need not intrude into an ethnological study, one concerned, as this has been, with a people as they were essentially at the time of contact with Europeans—in the present case, roughly between 1800 and 1850. But the data submitted here do possess certain significant implications for the general question of Eskimo culture history, even if no attempt is made to present a conclusive resolution of its problems. Nowhere else among the Eskimo is the nuunamiut-tareumiut distinction so clearly pointed as here in North Alaska. Since this is so, it remains to examine the data further to see whether there are any suggestions which can be made as to the temporal sequence leading to the ethnographic present, if it is possible to determine a priority of one ecological mode over the other. A rapid review of some of the major theoretical points which have been advanced is in order.

By Birket-Smith's theory, the nuunamiut, like the Caribou Eskimo of the Barren Grounds, would represent an earlier stage of Eskimo development. They would, in fact, be survivors from antiquity of the inland groups who, in pushing to the sea from the interior of North America, were to become the Eskimo (cf. Birket-Smith, 1929; 1952). This places them, because of fishing in the ice, in the Paleo-Eskimo stage of development. By this reasoning, the whale hunting and general settled maritime developments, suggestive of the so-called Neo-Eskimo stage, are later in time, representing specializations of the archaic base. This point of view, it will be remembered, can be traced back to early theorists—Rink, Steensby, and also to Franz Boas (Collins, 1951, pp. 423–424). Indeed, the notion of inland American origins for the Eskimo was once fairly widely accepted.

The Ipiutak culture, pertinent to this study because of its location at Point Hope, described by Larsen and Rainey (1948), has suggested to these investigators a rephrasing of Birket-Smith's theory at least in terms of later sequences. This prehistoric culture, with Asiatic affinities and distinguished by several striking features but negatively, by its absence of whaling, is identified with Birket-Smith's Paleo-Eskimo stage of development, one in which the seasonal alternation of activity, between caribou hunting and sealing, comes to the fore. The nuunamiut, by this reasoning, would be identified with the Ipiutak complex. Further, Rainey and Larsen's "Arctic Whale Hunting" culture, developed as it is at Birnirk (at Point Barrow) and in the so-called Thule culture generally, bears out Birket-Smith's Neo-Eskimo stage. Hence, the tareumiut of this study, by the reasoning of both Birket-Smith and of the Ipiutak investigators, represent a later Eskimo level of development.

But conversely, as De Laguna and Collins have demonstrated, even though Eskimo culture permits some distinction of definition, and although its affinities to a Siberian Neolithic are fairly clear, the strains which form it are too diverse, too scattered, and too difficult of definition to permit the kind of conclusive pinpointing which either Birket-Smith or Larsen and Rainey give. This does not invalidate Birket-Smith's hypothesis, but it does in some measure contravene portions of it, since, on the basis of a host of assembled archeological evidence, the Eskimo cultures and Eskimo prehistory suggest an Asiatic source. Or, to put the matter more accurately, and following Collins, it appears that in Alaska, with the recent discoveries of the typologically Mesolithic Denbigh Flint Complex (Collins, 1951, p. 459; Giddings, 1952; Solecki, 1950; et al.) may be seen the type forms from which both the Siberian Neolithic and the ultimate Eskimo development arise. There is a negative distinctness to Eskimo culture in that in its particularistic adaptations, it is what adjacent non-Eskimo cultures are not; it is a boreal culture adjusted to special conditions, suggesting in its affinities and its impetus Asia rather than native America.

But omitting the question of Asiatic origins, and being in agreement with the general hypothesis that there is too much diversity in Eskimo cultures to permit any one explanation of its beginnings and being, the present study suggests, on the basis of the data at hand, that the nuunamiut-tareumiut are not to be resolved in terms of the priority of one system over the other. It would have taken time for the earlier cultures of the region, for example, Ipiutak, to have developed the specialization of whaling. And at this stage of Eskimo development whaling was not practiced. That aspect of Eskimo life which led peoples to push away from the coasts to the land in search of game, and again to the sea after sea mammals seems a not unreasonable solution, one practiced still by some living groups of Eskimo. The suggestion must thus be made that the inland-maritime dichotomy represents not one system which evolves into another, but rather two specialized kinds of developments in the domain of a common culture. When compared, it has been established that the two groups did not differ from each other except in the ways of making a living. Barring local invention on the basis of this or that material, for example, willows in the interior, both groups stand side by side in respect to weapon assemblage, clothing, the house types (with some modifications in the interior because of less permanent settlement), social organization, religious and ceremonial life (with the difference of attention to whale as against caribou), shamanism, and world view. The conclusion is that here are two interdependent ecological variations on a primary cultural theme. And the primary cultural theme is in itself a tangential phrasing of the kinds of adaptations which have come to be associated with the concept Eskimo.

BIBLIOGRAPHY

Aberle, David F.

1952. "Arctic hysteria" and Latah in Mongolia. Trans. New York Acad. Sci., ser. 2, vol. 14, pp. 291–297.

Admiralty, Great Britain.

1854. Papers relative to the recent Arctic Expeditions in search of Sir John Franklin and the crews of H. M. S. *Erebus* and *Terror*. London.

Anderson, H. D., and Eells, W. C.

1935. Alaska natives. Stanford.

Beechey, Capt. F. W., R. N.

1832. Narrative of a voyage to the Pacific and Beering's Strait to cooperate with the Polar Expeditions performed in H. M. S. *Blossom* in the years 1825, 1826, 1827 and 1828. Philadelphia.

Birket-Smith, Kaj.

1929. The caribou Eskimos. Material and social life and their cultural position. Rep. 5th Thule Expedition, 1921–24. (The Danish Expedition to Arctic North America in charge of Knud Rasmussen, vol. 5. Copenhagen.)

1936. The Eskimos. New York.

1952. Present status of the Eskimo problem. *In* Indian tribes of aboriginal America (Selected Papers of the 29th International Congress of Americanists, Sol Tax, ed.), pp. 8–21. Chicago.

1953. The Chugach Eskimo. Nationalmuseets Skrifter, Etnografisk Raekke, vol. 6. Copenhagen.

Boas, Franz.

1888. The Central Eskimo. 6th Ann. Rep. Bur. [Amer.] Ethnol.

1899. Property marks of the Alaskan Eskimo. Amer. Anthrop., vol. 1, pp. 601–613.

1907. The Eskimo of Baffin-Land and Hudson Bay. Amer. Mus. Nat. Hist., Bull. 15.

1916. Tsimshian mythology. 31st Ann. Rep. Bur. Amer. Ethnol, 1909–10, pp. 29–1037. Washington.

Bogoras, W. G.

1902. The folklore of northeastern Asia as compared with that of northwestern America. Amer. Anthrop., vol. 4, pp. 577–683.

1904–1909. The Chukchee. Mem. Amer. Mus. Nat. Hist., vol. 11 (Publ. Jesup North Pacific Exped., No. 7).

1913. The Eskimo of Siberia. Mem. Amer. Mus. Nat. Hist., vol. 12, pp. 417–456, New York. (Publ. Jesup North Pacific Exped., vol. 8, pt. 3.)

1929. Elements of culture of the circumpolar zone. Amer. Anthrop., vol. 31, pp. 465–482.

Brower, Charles D.

1942. Fifty years below zero. . . . New York.

Cantwell, John C.

1887. A narrative account of the exploration of the Kowak River, Alaska. *In* Report of the cruise of the revenue marine steamer "Corwin" in the Arctic Ocean in the year 1885, pp. 21–52. Washington.

1889 a. A narrative account of the exploration of the Kowak River, Alaska. *In* Report of the cruise of the revenue marine steamer "Corwin" in the Arctic Ocean in the year 1884, pp. 49–74. Washington.

1889 b. Exploration of the Kowak River, Alaska: ethnological notes. *In* Report of the cruise of the revenue marine steamer "Corwin" in the Arctic Ocean in the year 1884, pp. 75–98. Washington.

Collins, Henry B., Jr.

1943. Eskimo archaeology and its bearing on the problem of man's antiquity in America. Proc. Amer. Philos. Soc., vol. 86, pp. 220–235.

1951. The origin and antiquity of the Eskimo. Ann. Rep. Smithsonian Institution for 1950, pp. 423–467.

Dall, William Healy.

1870. Alaska and its resources. Boston.

1877. Tribes of the extreme Northwest. Contrib. to North Amer. Ethnol., vol. 1, pp. 1–156. Washington.

1885. On masks, labrets, and certain aboriginal customs, with an inquiry into the bearing of their geographical distribution. 3d Ann. Rep. Bur. [Amer.] Ethnol., 1881–82, pp. 67–202. Washington.

De Laguna, Frederica.

1947. The prehistory of northern North America as seen from the Yukon. Mem. Soc. Amer. Archaeol., vol. 12, No. 3.

Ekblaw, Walter E.

1926. The material response of the Polar Eskimo to their far Arctic environment. Annals, Assoc. Amer. Geogr., vol. 17.

Forde, C. Daryll.

1934. Habitat, economy, and society: A geographical introduction to ethnology. New York.

Franklin, Sir John.

1828. Narrative of a second expedition to the shores of the Polar Sea, in the years 1825, 1826, 1827. London.

Giddings, J. L., Jr.

1944. Dated Eskimo ruins of an inland zone. Amer. Antiq., vol. 10, pp. 113–134.

1949. Early flint horizons on the north Bering Sea coast. Journ. Wash. Acad. Sci., vol. 39, pp. 85–89.

1952. The Arctic Woodland culture of the Kobuk River. Univ. Pennsylvania, Univ. Museum, Mus. Monogr. Philadelphia.

Hammerich, L. L.

1951 a. The cases of Eskimo. Int. Journ. Amer. Linguistics (Kleinschmidt Centennial I), vol. 17, pp. 18–22.

1951 b. Can Eskimo be related to Indo-European? Int. Journ. Amer. Linguistics (Kleinschmidt Centennial VI), vol. 17, pp. 217–223.

Hawkes, E. W.

1914. The dance festivals of the Alaskan Eskimo. Univ. Pennsylvania, Anthrop. Publ., vol. 6, pp. 3–41.

Healy, Capt. M. A., et al.

1887. Report of the cruise of the revenue marine steamer "Corwin" in the Arctic Ocean in the year 1885. Washington.

HEALY, CAPT. M. A., et al—Continued
1889. Report of the cruise of the revenue marine steamer "Corwin" in the Arctic Ocean in the year 1884. Washington.

HERSKOVITS, MELVILLE J.
1952. Economic anthropology. New York.

HOEBEL, E. ADAMSON.
1941. Law-ways of the primitive Eskimos. Journ. Criminal Law and Criminology, vol. 31, pp. 663–683.
1954. The law of primitive man: A study in comparative legal dynamics. Cambridge.

HOLMBERG, H. J.
1856. Ethnographische Skizzen über die Völker russischen Amerikas. Acta Soc. Sci. Fennicae, vol. 4, pp. 281–422. Helsinki.

HRDLIČKA, ALEŠ.
1930. Anthropological survey in Alaska. 46th Ann. Rep. Bur. Amer. Ethnol., 1928–29, pp. 19–374. Washington.

INGSTAD, HELGE.
1952. Nunamiut. Unter den Inland-Eskimos von Alaska. Berlin.

IRVING, LAURENCE.
1953. The naming of birds by Nunamiut Eskimo. Arctic, vol. 6, pp. 35–343.

IRVING, WILLIAM.
1951. Archaeology in the Brooks range of Alaska. Amer. Antiq., vol. 17, pp. 52–53.
1953. Evidence of early tundra cultures in Northern Alaska. Univ. Alaska, Anthrop. Pap., vol. 1, pp. 55–85.
MS. An archaeological reconnaissance of the Lower Colville River and delta regions—final report. (Unpublished manuscript, 1953, filed with Chief, Office of Naval Research, Washington.)

JENNESS, DIAMOND.
1922. The life of the Copper Eskimos. Rep. Canadian Arctic Expedition, 1913–18. (The Southern Party, 1913–16.) Vol. 12. Ottawa.
1924. Eskimo folk-lore. Rep. Canadian Arctic Expedition, 1913–18. (The Southern Party, 1913–16.) Vol. 13. Ottawa. [Part A: Myths and traditions from northern Alaska, the MacKenzie Delta and Coronation Gulf. Part B: Eskimo string figures.]
1928. Eskimo language and technology. Rep. Canadian Arctic Expedition, 1913–18. (The Southern Party, 1913–16.) Vol. 15. Ottawa. [Part A: Comparative vocabulary of the Western Eskimo dialects. Part B: Grammatical notes on some Western Eskimo dialects.]
1953. Stray notes on the Eskimo of Arctic Alaska. Anthrop. Pap., Univ. Alaska, vol. 1, No. 2, pp. 5–13.

JOCHELSON, W. I.
1905–1908. The Koryak. Mem. Amer. Mus. Nat. Hist., vol. 10. (Publ. Jesup North Pacific Exped. No. 6). New York.

KROEBER, A. L.
1939. Cultural and natural areas of native North America. Univ. California Publ. Amer. Archeol. and Ethnol., vol. 38. Berkeley.

LANTIS, MARGARET.
1938. The Alaskan whale cult and its affinities. Amer. Anthrop., vol. 40, pp. 438–464.
1946. The social culture of the Nunivak Eskimo. Trans. Amer. Philos. Soc., vol. 35, pt. 3. Philadelphia.

LANTIS, MARGARET—Continued
1947. Alaskan Eskimo ceremonialism. Amer. Ethnol. Soc. Monogr. 11. J. J. Augustin, New York.
1950 a. The reindeer industry in Alaska. Arctic, vol. 3, pp. 27–44.
1950 b. The religion of the Eskimos. *In* Forgotten religions (V. Ferm, ed.), pp. 309–340. New York.
1952. Eskimo herdsmen: Introduction of reindeer herding to the natives of Alaska. *In* Human problems in technological change (E. H. Spicer, ed.), pp. 127–148. Russell Sage Foundation, New York.
1953. Nunivak Eskimo personality as revealed in mythology. Univ. Alaska, Anthrop. Pap., vol. 2, No. 1, pp. 109–174.
1954. Research on human ecology of the American Arctic. Arctic Institute of North America. (Mimeographed.)

LARSEN, HELGE.
1952. The Ipiutak culture: Its origin and relationships. *In* Indian tribes of Aboriginal America (Selected Papers of the 29th International Congress of Americanists, Sol Tax, ed.), pp. 22–34. Chicago.

LARSEN, HELGE, and RAINEY, FROELICH G.
1948. Ipiutak and the Arctic whale hunting culture. Amer. Mus. Nat. Hist., Anthrop. Pap., vol. 42. New York.

MACCARTHY, ELIZABETH.
1953. Point Barrow today. *In* Societies around the world, selec. 22, pp. 160–164. I. T. Sanders, ed. New York.

MCCLENEGAN, D. B.
1887. Exploration of the Noatak River, Alaska. *In* Report of the cruise of the revenue marine steamer "Corwin" in the Arctic Ocean in the year 1885, pp. 53–80. Washington.

MCCLURE, ROBERT LEM.
1875. The discovery of a northwest passage by H. M. S. *Investigator*, Captain R. LeM. McClure, during the years 1850–1854. Capt. Sherard Osborn, R. N., ed. London.

MARSHALL, ROBERT.
1933. Arctic village. New York.

MATHIASSEN, THERKEL.
1930. Archaeological collections from the western Eskimos. Rep. Fifth Thule Expedition, vol. 10, pp. 1–98.

MILLER, G. S., and KELLOGG, R.
1955. List of recent North American mammals. Smithsonian Institution, U. S. Natl. Mus. Bull. 205.

MURDOCH, JOHN, ET AL.
1885 a. Natural history. *In* Report of the International Polar Expedition to Point Barrow, Alaska, pp. 89–200. Washington.
1885 b. The retrieving harpoon. Amer. Nat., vol. 19, pp. 423–425.
1886. A few legendary fragments from Point Barrow Eskimos. Amer. Nat., vol. 20, pp. 593–599.
1890. Notes on the counting and measuring among the Eskimos of Point Barrow. Amer. Anthrop., o. s., vol. 3, pp. 37–43.
1892. Ethnological results of the Point Barrow Expedition. 9th Ann. Rep. Bur. [Amer.] Ethnol., pp. 19–441.
1893. Seal-catching at Point Barrow. Smithsonian Misc. Coll., vol. 34, pp. 102–108.

MURDOCH, JOHN, ET AL—Continued
1898. The animals known to the Eskimos of Northwestern Alaska. Amer. Nat., vol. 32, pp. 719–734.

MURIE, A.
1935. The wolves of Mount McKinley. U. S. Nat. Park Service, Fauna ser., No. 5. Washington.

MURIE, O. J.
1935. Alaska-Yukon caribou. North American Fauna.

NELSON, EDWARD WILLIAM.
1899. The Eskimo about Bering Strait. 18th Ann. Rep. Bur. [Amer.] Ethnol., vol. 18, pt. 1.

OSBORN, SHERERD. *See* ROBERT LEM. MCCLURE.

PAIGE, SIDNEY; FORAN, W. T.; and GILLULY, JAMES.
1925. A reconnaissance of the Point Barrow region, Alaska. U. S. Geol. Surv., Bull. 772. Washington.

RAINEY, FROELICH G.
1941. Culture changes on the Arctic coast. Trans. New York Acad. Sci., ser. 2, vol. 3, No. 6, pp. 172–176. New York.
1947. The whale hunters of Tigara. Amer. Mus. Nat. Hist. Anthrop. Pap., vol. 41, pt. 2, pp. 231–283. New York.

RASMUSSEN, KNUD.
1927. Across Arctic America, narrative of the Fifth Thule Expedition. London.
1930a. Intellectual culture of the Iglulik Eskimos. Rep. Fifth Thule Expedition, 1921–24, vol. 7, No. 1. Copenhagen.
1930b. Intellectual culture of the Caribou Eskimos. Rep. Fifth Thule Expedition, 1921–24, vol. 7, No. 2. Copenhagen.

RAUSCH, ROBERT.
1951. Notes on the Nunamiut Eskimo and mammals of the Anaktuvuk Pass region, Brooks Range, Alaska. Arctic, vol. 4, pp. 147–195.

RAY, P. H., ET AL.
1885 a. Report of the International Polar Expedition to Point Barrow, Alaska. Washington.
1885 b. Ethnographic sketch of the natives. *In* Report of the International Polar Expedition to Point Barrow, Alaska, pp. 37–87. Washington.
1885 c. Habits and customs of the Inu of the Western Shore and Point Barrow. (Section H, British Association for the Advancement of Science, Montreal. Report of the 54th Meeting.) London.

ROBERTS, PALMER W.
1954. Employment of Eskimos by the Navy at Point Barrow, Alaska. Proc. 3d Alaska Sci. Conf., pp. 40–43. College, Alaska.

SCHRADER, FRANK CHARLES.
1904. A reconnaissance in northern Alaska across the Rocky Mountains, along Koyukuk, John, Anaktuvuk, and Colville Rivers, and the Arctic coast to Cape Lisburne in 1901. U. S. Geol. Surv. Prof. Pap., No. 20.

SHADE, CHARLES J., AND CAIN, THOMAS.
1951. An anthropological survey of the Point Barrow, Alaska, region. Proc. 2d Alaska Sci. Conf., pp. 248–251.

SIMMONDS, P. L.
1854. The Arctic regions (being an account of the American expedition in search of Sir John Franklin). Auburn and Buffalo.

Simpson, John, R. N.

1855. Observations on the western Eskimo and the country they inhabit. *From* Notes taken during two years at Point Barrow (*in* Further papers relative to the recent Arctic Expeditions in Search of Sir John Franklin, Parliamentary Reports, 1855) and reprinted, 1875, in Arctic Geogr. and Ethnol., Roy. Geogr. Soc., pp. 233–275. London.

Simpson, Thomas.

1843. Narrative of the discoveries on the north coast of America . . ., 1836–39. London.

Smith, Middleton.

1902. Superstitions of the Eskimo. *In* The White World (R. Kersting, ed.), pp. 109–130. New York.

Smith, Philip S., and Mertie, J. B., Jr.

1930. Geology and mineral resources of northwestern Alaska. U. S. Geol. Surv., Bull. 815. Washington.

Solecki, Ralph S.

1950. New data on the inland Eskimos of northern Alaska. Journ. Washington Acad. Sci., vol. 40, pp. 137–157.

1951. Archeology and ecology of the Arctic slope of Alaska. Ann. Rep. Smithsonian Institution for 1950, pp. 469–495.

Spencer, Marietta.

1954. The child in the contemporary culture of the Barrow Eskimo. Proc. 3d Alaska Sci. Conf., pp. 130–32. College, Alaska.

Spencer, Robert F.

1953. The hunted and the hunters. California Acad. Sci., Pacific Discovery, vol. 6, pp. 22–27.

1954. Forms of cooperation in the culture of the Barrow Eskimo. Proc. 3d Alaska Sci. Conf., pp. 128–130. College, Alaska.

Spencer, Robert F., and Carter, W. K.

1954. The blind man and the loon: Barrow Eskimo variants. Journ. Amer. Folklore, vol. 67, pp. 65–72.

Spetzman, Lloyd A.

MS. Plant geography and ecology of the Arctic slope of Alaska. Univ. Minnesota, Dept. Botany, unpublished MS. dissertation. Minneapolis. 1951.

Spier, Leslie.

1925. The distribution of kinship systems in North America. Univ. Washington Publ. Anthrop., vol. 1, No. 2, pp. 69–88.

Steensby, P. H.

1910. Contributions to the ethnology and anthropogeography of the Polar Eskimo. Medd. om Grønland, vol. 34, No. 7, pp. 253–407.

Stefansson, Vilhjalmur.

1914 a. Prehistoric and present commerce among the Arctic Coast Eskimo. Mus. Bull. No. 6 (Canada, Department of Mines, Geological Survey, Anthrop. Ser. No. 3).

1914 b. The Stefansson-Anderson Arctic Expedition of the American Museum. Preliminary ethnological report. Amer. Mus. Nat. Hist., Anthrop. Pap., vol. 14, pt. 1.

1924. My life with the Eskimo. New York.

Stoney, George M.

1900. Naval explorations in Alaska. U. S. Naval Institute, Annapolis.

Swadesh, Morris.
1951. Unaaliq and Proto-Eskimo. Internat. Journ. Amer. Linguistics (Kleinschmidt Centennial III), vol. 17, pp. 66–70.
1952 a. Unaaliq and Proto-Eskimo II: Phonemes and Morpho-phonemes. Internat. Journ. Amer. Linguistics, vol. 19, pp. 25–34.
1952 b. Unaaliq and Proto-Eskimo III. Internat. Journ. Amer. Linguistics, vol. 19, pp. 69–76.
1952 c. Unaaliq and Proto-Eskimo IV: Diachronic notes. Internat. Journ. Amer. Linguistics, vol. 19, pp. 166–171.
1952 d. Unaaliq and Proto-Eskimo V: Comparative vocabulary. Internat. Journ. Amer. Linguistics, vol. 19, pp. 241–256.

Thalbitzer, William.
1910. Eskimo. *In* Handbook of American Indian languages. (F. Boas, ed.) Bur. [Amer.] Ethnol. Bull. 40, pt. 1, pp. 971–1069.

Townsend, Charles H.
1887. Notes on the natural history and ethnology of northern Alaska. *In* Report of the cruise of the revenue marine steamer "Corwin" in the Arctic Ocean in the year 1885, pp. 81–102. Washington.

Transehe, N. A.
1928. The ice cover of the Arctic Sea, with a genetic classification of sea ice. *In* Problems of polar research, Amer. Geogr. Soc. Spec. Publ. No. 7, pp. 91–123. New York.

Van Valin, William B.
1944. Eskimoland speaks. Caldwell, Idaho.

Weyer, E. M.
1932. The Eskimos—their environment and folkways. New Haven, Conn.

Wiggins, Ira L.
1953. North of Anaktuvuk. California Acad. Sci., Pacific Discovery, vol. 6, pp. 8–15.

Wissler, C.
1916. Harpoons and darts in the Stefansson collection. Amer. Mus. Nat. Hist., Anthrop. Pap., vol. 14, pp. 397–443.

Wrangell, Ferdinand von.
1840. Narrative of an expedition to the Polar Sea in the years 1820, 1821, 1822, and 1823. (E. Sabine, ed.) London.

APPENDIX I: TOBACCO

Tobacco reached the North Alaskan area in the precontact period. While the advent of tobacco cannot be dated, it seems apparent that it had reached Barrow by diffusion and trade before 1826. Murdoch mentions its description by Beechey's account (Beechey, 1832, p. 308). Elson, of the *Blossom*, describes both the marketable value of tobacco and its universality among the Barrow Eskimo (ibid.). The older pipes, some of which are still seen in use today, appear to be of a Siberian or Russian type. Unquestionably, the presence of tobacco at this early date reflects a widespread and lively aboriginal trade. Murdoch mentions preferences for certain kinds of tobacco at Barrow and points out that both pipe smoking and chewing, by no means limited to adults, were the rule (Murdoch, 1892, p. 66). He further indicates that the pipes were cleaned and that before smoking, a bit of caribou hair was placed in the bottom of the bowl to keep the smaller tobacco flakes from entering the pipe (ibid., p. 70).

Living informants still recall the importance of tobacco to the aboriginal precontact culture. As part of the process of economic and trade specialization, certain families took over the task of obtaining tobacco. These left as soon as the sea was passable and might be gone all summer. Tobacco was obtained from the Cape Prince of Wales and Diomede Island area.

The trades brought pelts of various kinds and had evidently established partnerships in the areas where tobacco was obtainable in quantity. Leaves were sacked in caribou skins, carefully, so as to prevent mold. Such sacks were extremely valuable. They were fairly small, containing 40 leaves. For half a sack, one man paid 5 caribou skins as well as 5 tanned skins of caribou fawn and several lengths of cured sinew. In another case, two men were out hunting at sea; one had tobacco and the other, desiring some, paid one of his labrets for a smoke. While not a beaded labret of higher worth, this ornament was nevertheless considered quite valuable. Tobacco was thus extremely costly.

Certain individuals acted as middlemen in the tobacco trade. This was true not only of the families who went directly to the source of supply, but along the coast there were people who specialized in tobacco trading. For the Barrow groups, contacts with such middlemen, such as those at Icy Cape and even Kotzebue, involved long trading journeys. The trading of skins and pelts for tobacco was the usual procedure.

Tobacco was either sacked in the manner described or placed in pouches of walrus gut. Other types of pouches are described by Murdoch but not recalled today. People made their own pipes after the models which they saw elsewhere. Men smoked a short pipe, easily carried, and cleaned it before each use. Women smoked a longer pipe. Both were carried under the parka. Bowls were often made of ivory, but not infrequently of metal, the latter being imported. Clay pipes were also imported at a later postcontact period. The tobacco was obtained in leaf form. The leaves were crushed and rolled for smoking, while the stems were reserved for chewing. The smoking tobacco was often adulterated with willow bark mainly to stretch the quantity. Unadulterated tobacco was preferred and often requested of one partner by another in the Messenger Feast.

Pipe bowls were quite small. When filled, they afforded two or three drags. The method of smoking, however, was significant. The smoker inhaled directly from the pipe, often holding his breath as long as possible before expelling the smoke. Amusing incidents are still recounted of how such and such a man, after bargaining for a drag on a pipe from a pipe owner, would seek to hold the smoke in his lungs as long as he could, often falling insensible before expelling it. This point is borne out by Murdoch who describes the tears, coughing, and sputtering associated with smoking.

Along the coast, nearly everyone owned a pipe and smoked. There was no feeling against smoking by women or children, although the latter were usually not sufficiently economically productive to get their own tobacco. People coming to Barrow from inland would tend to bargain for a drag on a pipe and would pay high prices for the privilege.

Murdoch mentions that chewing was also universal and notes that 2- and 3-year-old nursing children might be pacified with a quid of tobacco. The juice was swallowed, apparently, as Murdoch notes, without ill effects (Murdoch, 1892, p. 70).

The European whalers seem to have introduced snuff which is still used by some older people. With the advent of money into the community, cigarettes are the usual fare today, although some men smoke modern pipes. A few old women may still be seen smoking the pipe of the precontact period. Many of the older men prefer to chew. In the latter case, tobacco is pared from the cake in small shavings. These are apparently swallowed, since no one has been observed spitting tobacco. The writer has sat with old men for several hours as they put flake after flake of tobacco into their mouths. This was never expelled. Most men smoke today. Many women smoke as well but this is much less frequent, apparently as the result of influence from the church. Cigarettes are the usual fare for women.

While it is known that tobacco reached the various Eskimo groups from abroad and that no Eskimo tribe, so far as can be judged, and unlike the natives of British Columbia, raised its own tobacco, a tale relating to the origin of tobacco was recorded. This is of interest since it not only points up the adoption of a complex and its elevation to an important level in the culture, but as an example of myth making. As a folkloristic study, it might be of significance to trace the tale among other peoples.

The tale follows:

There was an old lady that started tobacco. She had a grandson. When the time came for her to die, she expressed the wish to have her body placed several days' journey away, near the mountains where the streams do not run fast. She made her grandson take her on his back and carry her there. He started out walking with her. At last they came to a place where the streams were moving slowly down from the mountains. He laid her down on some flat rocks there and she said, "This is where I want to be." She told him that when she died, he should leave her body there and come back next spring to see what was growing in that place. He should wait and when the plants got bigger, he should taste them. If he liked the taste, he should make a little pipe and smoke some of that plant in it. And then he should sell it to others.

Every summer he came back to the place and each time the plants had got bigger and each time they tasted better. He had meanwhile married a woman and had two small boys. He took his sons up there with him. Once, on the way, they met a woman whom he invited to taste the plant. She expressed a wish to have some more. "Take it to the other people," he told her, "and see if they want some too." The other people were happy to get this tobacco and bought it from the man. He became very rich. The woman who helped him continued to do so and he made her husband his agent, saying that all who wanted tobacco should buy it through that man.

After he had started doing this, he went up there near the mountains and lived. His sons and he cut the leaves and made them into bundles of 40. After that, the woman's husband came back again and got the bundles for sale. In the summertime, the plants grew again where they had put the old lady's body. This was the best tobacco in the world. It tasted better than the tobacco which the ships brought.

The introduction of a magical origin, that is, from the old woman's body, suggests, as noted, the value with which tobacco was regarded. It is evident that the myth is recent. It lacks the drama and continuity of the older Eskimo tales. The story may be regarded very likely as a rationalization on the part of the Eskimo of the Arctic slope to discover an origin of so important a narcotic as tobacco. As nearly as can be ascertained, prior to the 19th century no narcotic or stimulant of any kind was known. As noted elsewhere, the complete absence of plant utilization would preclude any experimentation in respect to the native flora.

APPENDIX 2: DOGS

Dogs, qimmiq (pl., qimmit), were vital to transportation on land, and they still remain the sole means of winter travel and transport. People without dogs were "poor" and were obliged to depend on others for travel and often for meat. Unquestionably, dog hitching and dog transport are very ancient in the area, as indeed, they seem to be in the entire Eskimo zone, but it is surprising that only in recent years have innovations been applied which make use of dogs as burden carriers more practical. In the aboriginal culture there was no concept of training a lead dog. Instead, dogs were strung out on a single trace, the owner grasping the harness of the first dog and running with the team. Tandem hitching was introduced in 1906–7 by the Native Service school and may depend in part on the influence of reindeer which were also hitched in pairs. One informant was interviewed who carried the mail between Barrow and Kotzebue between 1904 and 1910. He used the single trace until 1906 and was much surprised when in Kotzebue, in 1905, he saw tandem hitching for the first time. He began to use this method in 1906, but it was several years before it came into common use and then, as noted, largely through the school. It is evident that some further research should be done on this subject, since tandem hitching may be aboriginal in the Greenland area.

There were two types of traces in the aboriginal culture. One was the single trace and the other the fanwise trace. The latter was preferred for hunting, since the dogs could be easily released when a polar bear or wolves were in sight. The fanwise trace was fastened to the sled with a pin. The lines in either case were of walrus hide. Murdoch (1892, p. 358) states that the dogs he saw were strung in a single line from the sled, and were hitched alternately on each side of the line. He mentions, too, that there were no lead dogs, although that a bitch in heat might be put at the head of the procession so that the other dogs would follow more readily. He says that a woman or child might run ahead with the lead dog, although anyone might do this, including the owner of the team. Murdoch (1892, p. 360) is also of the opinion that the single trace is superior to the tandem hitch, since it places the burden directly on each dog.

Each dog was named, and learned his name quickly. While dogs "have no souls," their names could be important and there is a suggestion that by naming a dog one could allow a soul to enter it. Thus, if a family had no children, the dog might be given the name of one of the deceased relatives. This was not done too freqently but was well known. When a dog received the name of a human, it was taken into the house and better fed than the other dogs. Names were not descriptive, and there were no dog nicknames. There was a whole range of names which were reserved for dogs and never used for humans unless magically. If several children died in succession, the one surviving might be given a dog's name to break the sequence. This, it was said, always worked and saved the life of a surviving child.

Dogs were trained by women. Puppies were kept in the hallway of the house and prevented from tearing things by being struck with a stick. The dog also learned not to eat in the house. When broken to the team, the puppy was first harnessed and allowed to pull against its mistress. After a time, the dog was put on the sled and the woman stood before him and called him, rewarding him when he came dragging the sled. It was not, however, necessary to reward the dog with food. Dogs were also petted as a reward. A newly broken dog was harnessed behind experienced dogs, and the team called. The best dogs for sleds were those who were "more scared," a fact which remains true today.

At present, with tandem hitching, a lead dog is trained. Both men and women train the leader, selecting a puppy which seems best suited to the task. The leader is a pet, often kept in the house in winter and not staked out in the snow as are the other members of the team. A good leader is trained to respond to the directions of the driver. The dog stops on command and has learned to change direction, either at verbal command or when the driver exclaims, "mawna, mawna!" (turn!) and indicates the direction with his arm. The dog in the latter case will stop and look behind to note the direction indicated by the driver. When the lead dog is lost, the older method is still used, the woman often going ahead and directing the team. A team is started by the command "ku, ku!" and there are like commands to halt a team. To summon a team, one calls, "hay!" In verbal commands, a right turn is indicated by "gi," a left by "ha," stopping by "ou." These cries vary somewhat from town to town and as between inland and maritime people. Dogs may also respond to an arm sign to slow or halt. It is the lead dog which is trained specifically to heed the commands given. It is said that until a dog is actually on the team, one is not sure how it will work out, how it will get on with the other members of the team. A dog was called by saying, "sa!"

A "good" dog is valued by the owner. If it dies, however, it is not customary to show any grief. A child is free to do so. An old dog may be killed. It is not eaten, however, although it may be skinned.

Some groups raised puppies for food and clothing. In traveling, a sick dog might be carried on the sled. If, in traveling, the team tires, a day or two halt may be called to rest the dogs. When not working, the team members are tied. Useless in summer, the teams are underfed and watered infrequently. In winter, however, when the team is again necessary to transport, greater care is given. A team is staked down when not in use in summer or winter. The dogs burrow in the snow in winter and are given shelter only in extremes of wind or weather. Dogs were given meat in winter once a day. Water, blood, and blubber (excluding whale meat or any parts of the whale, this being hateful to the whale) were a usual fare for dogs. If meat was lacking, fish might be given twice a day in winter. Walrus was the usual dog feed, this meat being unpopular with humans. Walrus is still the principal dog food. Fish are also given dogs, as well as caribou droppings mixed with oil, and, not infrequently, human feces.

Pet dogs are more frequent at present than was true in the past. A favorite dog is allowed in the house and may not be broken to a team. English names, the dog names of western culture, are given today, and the custom of giving the dog a name of a deceased person, or indeed, of a dead dog, is pretty much gone. Modern names include: kummiq (chocolate), Stranger, Whitey, Right, Snap, Daisy, Blackie, Nigger, Bruno, John. Some of the older dog names, such as agiilak, are still used.

Small children play with puppies. Little girls treat the puppies as babies and carry them in their parka hoods.

In the aboriginal culture, there were several attitudes toward dogs which play a prominent part in what might be called law or law ways. If a person were bitten by a dog, or if the dog barked too much, annoyed children, or the like, one went to the owner and requested that the dog be tied. If the offense were repeated, one was free to kill the dog. This might have serious repercussions, as one of the foregoing legal cases attests. If, however, the dog owner were warned, and failed to heed the warning, the dog could presumably be killed with impunity.

There were also several supernatural ideas relating to dogs. If a person or a child were bitten by a dog, the dog could under no circumstances be killed. If this were done, the person bitten would die. In the modern scene, a dilemma is thus created for the dog owner, since the advice of older people is always against killing the dogs, while white man's culture might demand the killing of a vicious dog. Dogs might talk to their masters, pulling the skin of the head back and speaking. There were no dog-spirit helpers, however.

Dogs were inherited. If they descended by inheritance to an unskilled person or to an orphan, others might take the dogs and divide them. Relatives might keep dogs for a young person until he had acquired sufficient skill in handling them. Children, boys especially, were trained at the age of about 5 or 6 in the care and handling of dogs. It was considered that a long term of experience was necessary before taking dogs out into the Arctic winter and staking one's life on them.

More dogs were owned by the maritime people than by the inland. Shortages and the nomadic round apparently reduced the inland number. No one inland had more than six dogs. Actually, this number was sufficient for winter travel, since the sled with iced runners was extremely mobile and a few dogs could carry a great load. On the coasts, 14 to 16 dogs in a team was not unusual. Here they were used with the heavier box sled, and for coastal travel the runners were not iced. Today, at Barrow, 14 dogs constitute a large team. Anywhere from 8 to 16 dogs might be used. From personal observation, it may be said that the inland dog type is much larger.

A team is regarded as valuable property. The trained lead dog would never be sold. Indeed, there appears a feeling against selling or trading dogs, except puppies. Once one has trained a dog to one's own liking, it is kept.

One cannot emphasize sufficiently the value of the dog as a means of transport to the cultures of the area, both in the past and at present. The reindeer has failed to supplant the dog as a means of transportation, and as a result the dog team remains paramount, despite the efforts of the Alaska Native Service in favor of reindeer. There is little doubt that the reindeer would be more practical and considerably less expensive to keep, but the feeling against the loneliness of the herdsman required by reindeer herding is still too strong. A dog is said to eat as much as a man, which may mean from 6 to 7 pounds of meat a day when working. This means that the energies of the hunter must be extended toward getting meat for his dogs as well as for his family. While the dog is not the subject of identification, except perhaps for the pet dogs and lead dogs of today, and is not felt to be imbued with feelings and motives like those of humans, it is vital that good care be given. Boots, for example, are made for dogs as protection against ice, and the dogs may be rubbed down with oil or mixed oil and marrow as mosquito protection.

It not infrequently occurs that a team is lost. When out on the ice, for example, a rift may occur which necessitates the abandoning of a team. Two teams were lost in this way early in 1952, one consisting of a sled and 14 dogs. This was a hard blow to the owner, who had then to begin working up a new team and buying puppies from others at about $5 an animal. He had before him the whole process of training and estimated that it would be at least 3 years before he could take his new team out. It is generally felt that a dog must be 2 years old before it is strong enough to work with a team.

The dogs of the area are wholly nondescript. There has evidently been much admixture with outside breeds. The classic Eskimo dog which is described by Murdoch is a rarity. Dogs appear in all shades and sizes. Apparently no attempts are made to effect selective breeding. Nor could any data be had on attempts to interbreed dogs and wolves.

The winter of 1951–52 was a serious one for the Barrow community. Distemper was introduced at this time and decimated the dog population. It is said that over 250 of a dog population of about 750 perished. Inoculations were begun through the local hospital and the local National Guard, and the problem was further studied and inoculations given by the United States Public Health Service in the summer of 1952. Many families were hard hit by the epidemic.

As noted, there was some tendency to anthropomorphize in respect to dogs. In general, however, the feeling is that dogs are primarily a means of transportation. Except for the lead dogs, an innovation, the team, when working, is treated well and pretty much impersonally.

APPENDIX 3: POTTERY

While the present investigation did not devote much time to aboriginal material culture, the presence of pottery, so unusual in so markedly nonagricultural a people as those of the Alaskan Arctic slope, deserved some attention. The detailed studies of pottery styles made by such investigators as De Laguna (cf. 1947) and others, need not be elaborated on here. However, it may be of interest to consider pottery from an ethnological, rather than an archeological point of view. The presence of potsherds in fair amounts in archeological sites of the region attests a fairly extensive use of pottery in the aboriginal period. A brief description of potsherds found in the Barrow area is given by Murdoch, although the latter denies ever seeing a pot either in use or in process of construction (Murdoch, 1882, p. 91). Metal vessels were already being used in the area at the time of the Beechey voyage and point again to the lively precontact trade described by Elson (Beechey, 1832, p. 572). It is true, however, that pottery was being made both during and after Murdoch's visit and the art was still known in 1916, when an old woman made such a vessel for Stefansson at his request. By the late 19th century the need for pottery had begun to disappear with the intensive introduction of metal vessels from abroad. Murdoch's failure to find any pottery in use is hardly surprising in view of the fact that such pottery vessels were made for the inland trade, the coastal people preferring to keep the imported metal vessels for their own use. As will be seen, moreover, there was a special need for such pottery among the nuunamiut.

Pottery generally is known as utkusik. A clay pot is called individually kiku. Both words refer to pottery of clay as distinguished from vessels of other types, such as the wooden tubs which were used much more extensively than pots of clay. The term kiku is apparently a localism at Barrow and Wainwright. It refers to a specific place which bore the name kiku from which the clay used in making the pottery was obtained. utkusik was the common generic term. A word also in common use was naaparuq, "without handles," which referred to the large pointed-bottom, lugless pot. Locally, at Barrow and Wainwright, this was also kiku.

Several types of pottery were known. The principal type was the naaparuq, a simple, largely undecorated, black, pointed-bottom vessel, often with perforations at the lip for suspension with cords. In size, these ranged from 15 to as much as 24 inches long, with a diameter at the lips of 19 to 12 inches. A second type was the smaller cup, a round bomblike vessel 6 to 8 inches in height. This was a ceremonial vessel and used only for giving fresh water to the bodies and bones of slain sea mammals. In the whale expeditions, for example, when a whaling crew had been successful, the snout of the animal was brought up on the offshore ice. The wife of the umealiq came forward with fresh water in the cup and made the formal ritual offering of water, pouring it into the snout of the whale. This cup was kept in a special place in the karigi and could be taken from there by any woman whose husband had taken a sea mammal. Similarly, when a house was moved and the bones of seals, whales, walrus, etc. were collected together and burned, water was again offered them in this cup. This vessel might also be made of wood. A third type of pottery recalled by living informants was a flat-bottomed, panlike vessel, one which might also resemble the stone lamp of the household. The lamp, however, as well as another type of vessel resembling the flat-bottomed pan, was most often made of soapstone and was not regarded as utkusik. The naaparuq type appears to have been the most common.

Pottery making was regarded as women's work and the finished pot as women's property. This held true among the maritime groups. Inland people, however, had special uses for the pottery associated with caribou hunting. This was obtained by trade from the maritime people and became the property of men.

Any woman who had the skill was free to make pottery. A necessary element was a special clay obtainable at the site of kiku, a location some miles down the coast from modern Barrow at the location of Skull Cliff. Women might take a day or two in summer to go down to the site and gather enough clay. At times, the pottery was made at the place where the clay was obtained and the pots left until they could be called for by boat. Some women made a practice of bringing back bags of clay from kiku and trading some of it to other women. Only this reddish clay was adequate for pottery. A living informant recalls that one woman tried to make a pot using the local gray clay but that she was unable to get it to congeal.

As nearly as can be recalled by living residents who have seen pottery made, the steps in making a vessel were as follows:

1. The clay was made into a "loaf," kneaded and watered frequently again and again. From time to time, sand was mixed into it.

2. When sufficiently moist, and of the right texture, the maker rubbed the clay between the hands, gradually adding the down from duck wings as well as a quantity of blood. Murdoch specifically lists bear's blood as the ingredient at this point. Modern informants state that any blood was acceptable. Feathers

and blood, together with clay and sand, and, occasionally, crushed shells, provided a fairly cohesive mass with which to work. This was worked by a kneading process.

3. The pot now being ready to construct, a base was used. This was either a flat stone with one convex side or a few pieces of sinew, tied and braided together. If the former base was used, the stone was removed when the pot was put together; if the latter, it was simply sunk into the clay.

4. Using the base of her choice, the maker, now rolling the clay into a strand between her palms, started the coiling process. The initial coils were drawn around the selected base and from this, the pot was coiled into shape.

5. A flat stone was now held inside the pot and the outside was worked around with a wooden or bone paddle.

6. When the pot was completed as to shaping, it was set in the sun and allowed to dry (pottery could only be made in summer).

7. During the drying process, a series of sinew cords might be tied about the neck and shoulders of the pot. These were sometimes knotted, lending additional strength to the vessel. While the vessel was drying, or in the course of being finished with the paddle, such decoration as might be put on were added. Decoration was often no more than a stamped indentation around the neck. No recollection is had today of any spiral designs. The cord marking was often the only design element and this was more often inadvertent. More frequently than not, pots were undecorated. They were never colored in any way.

8. After drying, the pot was fired. This was a simple process, involving the building of a fire, often with oil, in a depression in the sand. Firing was imperfect, since the pot was simply laid on the fire and turned from time to time. One informant recalls the dried pot being suspended by cords through perforations over a fire. The blackness of the pottery probably relates to the use of oil in the fire to increase heat.

While these general steps appear to have been universally followed, a woman was free to utilize the materials at hand for the making of pottery. Mention is made of various kinds of feathers, of ashes, and of blood in various quantities as congealing agents. All informants are agreed that the blood which was used in the manufacture should be free of oil, since the oil prevented congealing.

When a pot broke, it was repaired by means of additional clay, feathers, and blood, and it was refired.

Pottery among the tareumiut was fairly common. Not every household had it, however. Pottery was stored in the hallway of the house in the cooking area. It was used only for cooking, rarely for storage of food. A woman felt free to borrow a pot from her relative or neighbor should she not own one. Pottery was used for boiling meat and was fairly satisfactory for the purpose. The pottery was never set over the flame but was used with the stone boiling method. The thick-walled, imperfectly fired pots were not always waterproof. Hence, in cooking, they were often lined with a caribou paunch, walrus gut, or some other watertight substance. The pointed-bottom vessels were stood up against stones in cooking.

It is in the various aspects relating to trade that the pottery made along the Alaskan Arctic coast assumes interest. Actually, the maritime Eskimo had not too much need for vessels of this type and preferred wooden tubs to the pottery. The latter were much more easily transported and infinitely less fragile. But there was a demand for pottery among the caribou Eskimo of the interior, for it formed an important part of the ceremonies relating to the principal caribou round-up and slaughter. This activity, corresponding to the whale hunting of the coastal peoples, was fraught with ritual and religious circumspection. Held in spring, the caribou roundup involved a series of ceremonies held both before and after the hunting activity. For example, at this time caribou could not be butchered with a metal knife and the first flesh eaten from the animals in this period had to be cooked in a clay pot. This fact accounts for the demand for pottery. The fact that the nuunamiut were not in a position, by virtue of their nomadic existence, to make pottery and to transport it at any length, necessitated their obtaining it from the settled peoples along the sea. It therefore became most important as an item of trade and was valued accordingly.

Thus a maritime woman who made pottery might make it simply for purposes of trade and not for her own use in the home. For a large naaparuq she could get as many as five caribou skins. Hence, among the items brought by the maritime groups to the great trading point at neγliq were pots in fairly large numbers. There was rough equating of values, in which pottery had a definite place. Thus five caribou skins were generally equivalent to a poke of seal oil. A large pot was equated on about the same level. Another such trading point was at nooataq, located inland along the mountains. Here, too, pottery was extensively traded. As part of the trading process of pottery, agreements were made between trading partners to the effect that on the next contact a certain number of pots, so many pokes of oil, etc., were to be brought and traded for such and such an amount of inland products.

The development of pottery among the Eskimo of northern Alaska is clearly of interest as a cultural oddity. While there is the suggestion that the pottery of the region owes its origins to a diffusion from the peoples of the interior of Alaska, there is also the point that Siberian connections are not to be ignored. Apart from the historical connections, however, a feature deserving of further study, there is the interesting problem of the function of pottery in the cultures of the area. As noted, pottery had little place in the maritime cultures. The little cup in which water was offered to hunted sea mammals was of pottery but was crew property, kept in the karigi, and obtained as needed by the hunter's wife. Such pots would therefore be rare. Murdoch does not even mention them. On the other hand, the large cooking pots, while certainly common among the maritime Eskimo, lacked all the ceremonial implications which they had for the caribou Eskimo of the inland. The difference is an interesting one. It appears that it was through such differences in economic specialization and ceremonial interest that trade and contact were kept alive. It is not to be implied, of course, that there were differences in point of view as between the two groups. Certainly, an inland man in engaging in whaling, if at the sea during the season, followed the same ceremonial restrictions and patterns as did his maritime hosts. And the reverse was true of the seaman hunting caribou with people of the inland regions. Because of the ceremonial use of pottery by the caribou Eskimo, the maritime groups found a market.

There was, as stated, little use for pottery on the coast. The preference was for igaavaktuat, the wooden tubs. These, made with a sewed frame in the shape of a hoop, thus circular, and fitted with a bottom of thin boards, made for infinitely superior water containers. At Barrow and Wainwright, wood was hardly obtainable in sufficient quantities to make these vessels, which, although fairly shallow, were about 30 inches in circumference. It is true that the vessel was copied in the Barrow area in baleen, but the wooden tub was preferred. Such vessels were used for storing water, and ice was placed in them in the house to melt. They were also used to collect the urine which formed so important a part of the tanning process and was also used for washing. The nomadic groups, trading for wood farther inland made these and traded them to the sea. There was also a coastwise trade in them with the kuvuŋmiut, people of kuvuk, south of Kotzbue, who manufactured these items. But while wooden vessels were useful and necessary to the maritime existence, they did not fetch so high a price as the pottery and were not nearly so prized.

APPENDIX 4: TIME RECKONING, ENUMERATION

DAYS OF THE WEEK

tawsiŋutuat	Monday
aypiksuat	Tuesday
piŋacuksut	Wednesday
sisaameksut	Thursday
tallimeksut	Friday
icexireksut	Saturday
savaycut	Sunday

There is no question that the above are loan-translations arising in the postcontact period. Other designations were not known. In view of the variations in respect to names for the months, one should expect similar disagreement for days of the week. The fact that there is none points to a recent development.

MONTH NAMES

The reckoning of months was on a lunar basis. Twelve and thirteen months were named although there was no careful count. The emphasis lay on seasons rather than on the months themselves. However, there were month names which varied with each group. Some reflect the major activities, others are descriptive of some event which occurs seasonally at the time. Month names were collected by the present writer for both nuunamiut and the coastal groups, by Stoney (1900, p. 101), by John Simpson (1855, pp. 260–261), and by Rainey (1947). Some such names are translatable, others are not. Names of the months may be listed as follows:

January	awakłtuavik
	sakinʸerelcraaq, "Sun returning"
	sakinʸaceuq (Stoney), "Sun returning"
	iraasiugarun (Simpson), "Great cold"
	sakinʸaatsiya, "New sun"
February	panaksiivik, "Drying skins"
	sekonaasuguruq (Stoney), "Snow is melting"
	sakinʸaceuq (v. above)
	seksilaawik (Simpson)
March	sakinʸaasuguruq, "Sun gets high"
	kusewiktaguwik (Stoney), "Snow is melting"
	kaatitaaγvik (Simpson), "Whales return"
April	kiliriqtatqeaq, "Little birds come"
	katiteraavik
	kelleriktutkeraat (Stoney), "Owls come"
	kawaytpiviuna (Simpson), "Birds come"

May	suvłuuwevik, "Rivers start running"
	umeakaavik, "Umiak is ready"
	toŋmeretutkeraat (Stoney), "Geese come"
	kawayaniviuna (Simpson), "Birds hatched"
June	sikururguwik (Stoney), "Ice breaks"
	kawaylanraviuna (Simpson), "Birds fledged"
July	mitkoyaxsiivik
	irgeneiwik (Stoney), "Birds lay eggs"
	ecerwik (Stoney), "Moulting"
	amiraaksiuna (Simpson)
August	ecerwik, "Moulting" (v. July)
	itkowaaktuwik (Simpson)
	negaralaaligit (Stoney), "Geese cannot fly"
	ecerreat (Stoney), "Geese lack feathers"
September	sikusaavik, "Ice begins"
	sokaaktitaktuat, "New antlers"
	aarmakseusevik (Stoney), "New velvet"
October	sułirevik
	aruptutkeraat (Stoney), "Water freezes"
	sudłewik (Simpson), "Sewing"
November	kiyeevilwik, "(Shamans) get busy"
	nueleaaγuwik (Stoney), "Caribou cohabit"
	sudłewik aytpa (Simpson), "Sewing"
December	aageluuleraavik, "They shine" (Morning and evening star)
	awłaktuavik, "Time of departure" (i. e., seals and caribou)
	nugeruwaaksiivik (Stoney), "Horns drop"

The above offers a rough equation of month names with those applied by the peoples in question. There was overlapping and no exactness was required. Living informants, although they may know no English, make use of English month names. The native designations reflect activities, preoccupations, and descriptions of conditions. More exact and much more specific were the designations for the seasons.

SEASONS

Winter	uqiiyuq
Spring	upinaakeraax
Summer	upinneraak
Fall	uqeaq

These nouns are a reflection of the basic division of the year into cold and warm periods. It is of interest that any situational description, as in recounting events, in a folktale, requires that the associated season be designated.

THE CARDINAL DIRECTIONS

North	nigit
West	kanaŋnak
South	uŋalak
East	kiloowaganak (palusakkanak)

The peoples of the area recognize only the four cardinal directions. The zenith and nadir, expressed as kunmun and anmun respectively, are not regarded as primary. Exactness, as in sea travel, for example, can be rendered by combinations of the cardinal points, often with saniŋmun, sideways.

ENUMERATION

Several systems of enumeration have been in use among the North Alaskan peoples. These aboriginal methods of counting have for the most part been dropped in favor of English numbers. Informants are agreed that the counting systems were complex and unwieldy in the past, in view of the presence of several parallel numbers derived ostensibly from different sources. The individual was free to count by the system he chose. Basically, the system is decimal, with the first five numbers reappearing as compounds in enumeration above five. The system is variable not only as the result of coexistent terms, but also because of the presence of grammatical numerical classifiers in language. Attention is given here only to one set of numerals:

1	atawsi
2	aypak
3	pinayoak
4	sisamak
5	tallimak
6	icexerat (also arviliγirilic, i.e., six skins to cover an umiak)
7	tallimatmalo (five and two; malo, a variant)
8	tallimatpiŋasut (five and three)
9	xuliŋnoγotayle
10	xulit
11	atawmeak
15	akimmeak; tallimeak
20	in^{y}uin^{y}ak
30	in^{y}uin^{y}ak xulit
40	malirokipeak (fingers and toes of two persons)
50	malirokipeak xulit
60	piŋusipeak (fingers and toes of three persons)
70	piŋusipeak xulit
80	sisamakipeak (fingers and toes of four persons)
90	sisamakipeak xulit
100	tallimakipeak (fingers and toes of five persons)

The numeral 20, which seems irregular, refers to the digits of one person (in^{y}uk).

Counting games were popular and were played between children.

Informants at Point Barrow.

Barrow village today.

a, A sod house in use at Point Lay. *b*, The iccellik, tent of the nuunamiut. *c*, Storage racks, meat cache, and umiak frame, Point Lay.

PLATE 4

a, The 1953 summer settlement of nuunamiut at Anaktuvuk Pass. *b*, A house ruin at Tikeraaq (Point Hope). *c*, Summer house of the Barrow village people at piγiniq (Birnirk), the duck shooting station.

a, The spring whaling camp at an ice lead near Barrow village. (Courtesy W. Wartes.) *b*, An umiak in tow, stern foremost. *c*, Barrow village men shooting walrus from an ice floe.

a, Barrow village women engaged in skinning a polar bear. *b*, nalukataq. The "blanket toss" celebration held at the close of a successful spring whaling season. (Courtesy W. Wartes.) *c*, Informant and interpreter Alfred Hopson, shown with his daughter.

a, Chorus of men singing at a social dance at Barrow village. *b*, The traditional Eskimo tambourine. *c*, Women join the men in singing, seated near or behind them.

a, Informants at Anaktuvuk Pass. Nuunamiut man and wife. *b*, Sikvayuŋgaq shown with the box drum used in the Messenger Feast.

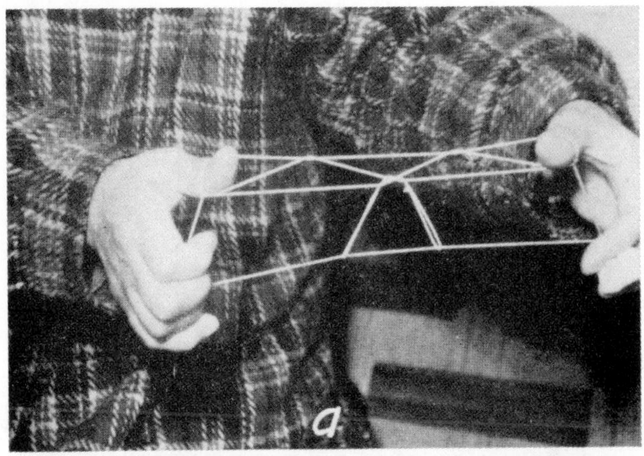

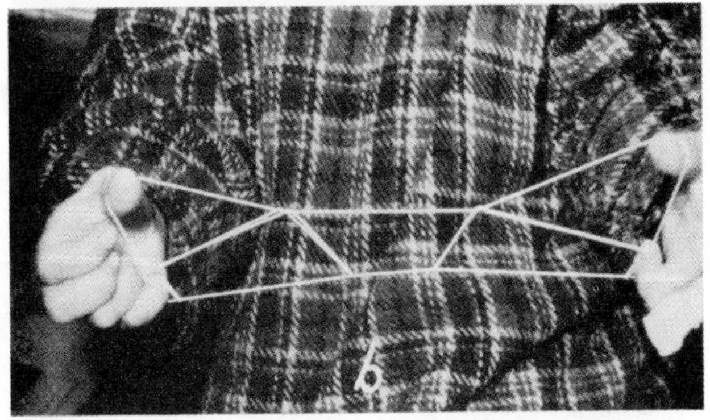

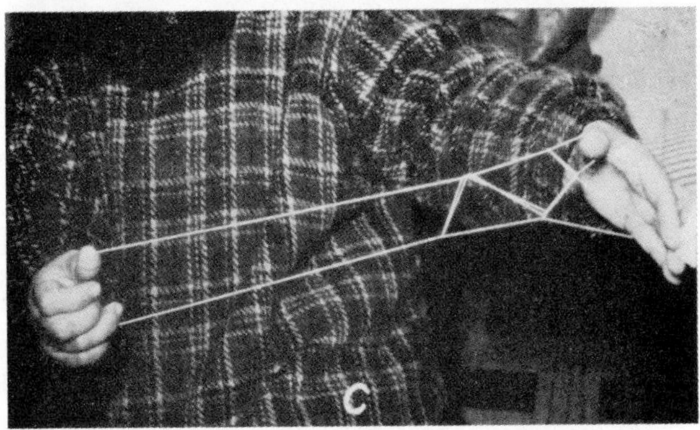

Ayaraq (string figure). *a*, Sawiaxlukak carrying his kayak. *b*, Aakluq, the two brown bears. *c*, Amawk, the wolf.

INDEX

Abandonment, of aged, babies, or infirm, 92–95, 233
Abduction, in marriage, 79, 80–81
Aberle, David F., 301, 455
Abortion, 229
Acculturation, 358–382
Activities, yearly cycle of, 140–143, 331, 366–370
Adopted child, responsibilities of, 90–91
Adoption, 81, 87–92, 95, 144, 166
    attitudes toward, 91
    frequency of, 91–92
    of newborn child, 233
    See also Quasi-kinship.
Adoptive kinship relationships, 69
Adultery, 99
Affection, toward infants, 234
Affinal kinship terms, 68–69
Age classes, absence of, 243
Aged, treatment of, 145
Aggression, patterns of, 161
Alaska, *see* North Alaska.
Alaskan Arctic slope, 9–13, 126
Alaska Native Service (A.N.S.), 5, 358, 359, 360, 361, 362, 363, 382, 465
Alaskan Eskimo cultures, 446–452
Alcohol, 107–108, 114
Amulets, 282–286, 312, 445
    classes of, 282
    curing functions of, 283, 285–286
    food prohibitions with, 283
    given by shamans, 284
    household, 56, 285–286
    inheritance of, 285
    of the dead, 284
    song associations of, 279
    whaling, 332, 337, 338–342, 343
Anaktuvuk Pass, 4, 10, 19, 20, 22, 24, 44, 379
    Christianity, 379
    See also killiγmiut.
Anaktuvuk River, 28
Anglican denomination, 379
Animal and human interrelations, in religion, 261–277
Animal power, in shamanism, 300–301
Animal souls, 264–277
Animal tales, told as moral lessons, 266–267
Animals, supernatural aspects of, 261–277
Anxiety, occasioned by hunting, 262–264
    occasioned by shamans, 299–300
aŋutawken (men who had sexual relations with the same woman), 80, 120
aŋatkoak, *see* Shamanism.
aŋatquq (shaman), *see* Shamanism.
Arctic Contractors, Ltd., 2, 363, 376
Arctic hysteria, 301, 319–320, 455
Arctic Institute of North America, 1
Arctic Research Laboratory, Point Barrow, 1, 26
Artisans, 196
"Asking" feasts, 193, 451
Assemblies of God, denomination, 379
Associations, aboriginal, 166–192, 443–444
    See also Crew (hunting group) association; karigi; Partnerships.
Aurora borealis, 258

Baleen, market for, 361
Baleen basketry, as modern craft, 360–361
Ball games, 190, 207, 351
    See also Football; Messenger Feast.
Band, economic, of nuunamiut, 127–139
Barrow village (modern), 1, 4, 14, 16, 19, 358–382
    Christian church at, 381–382
    reindeer herding at, 364–366
Barter, 193–209
    See also Partnerships; Trade.
Barter Island, 17
Beads (trade), 156–157, 203, 360
Bear (grizzly), hunting of, 32
    relations to supernatural, 266, 270–271
    See also Polar bear.
Beauty, ideals of, 246
Beechey, Capt. F. W., 359, 455, 462, 470
Behavioral ideals, 161
    See also Individual; Personality.
Behavioral prohibitions, religious, *see* Prohibitions.
Beluga, hunting of, 33–34, 276, 374
    relations to supernatural, 276
Bering Strait Eskimo, 24, 172
Berries, 24, 375
Bible, in Eskimo, 379
Bidding, in trade, 195–196
Bilateral descent, 62–63
Birds, *see* Ducks; Fowl.
Birket-Smith, Kaj, 126, 127, 257, 349, 452–453, 455
Birnirk culture (prehistoric), 14, 448, 453
Birth, 231–234
    hut, 231–232
    magic, 231, 232–234
    prohibitions at, 57, 231–234
    See also Childbirth.

Bladder Feast, 451
Blanket-toss, 351–352
See also nalukataq.
Blood, as food, 376
Blood feuds, revenge, *see* Feuds.
Bloodletting, in curing, 329
Boas, Franz, 264, 310, 453, 455
Boat-launching, in whaling, 342, 353
See also umiak.
Bogoras, W., 455
Bola, use of, 35
Bone fractures, 329
Boys' puberty, 241–243
social status, 336
Bride service, 78, 245
Brooks Mountains, 9
Brower, Capt. Charles D., 92, 107, 114, 195, 218, 253, 263, 318, 360, 372, 378, 455
Bullying, as a social mechanism, 238–239

Camps, inland Eskimo, 48
Cannibalism, 95
Cantwell, John C., 456
Cape Denbigh, 13
Cape Prince of Wales, 49
Cape Smythe, 16
whaling company, 51
Cardinal directions, 476
Caribou (*Rangifer arcticus stonei*), 22, 27–32, 132, 135–136, 152, 163, 178, 269–270, 331, 353–357
as food, 374
butchering, 356
ceremonialism associated with, 31, 182, 353–357, 446
See also Cult habits, 27–28
hides as trade items, 203–204
hunting, 22, 27–32, 132, 135–136, 152, 163, 178, 269–270, 331, 353–357
compared with whaling, 354, 357
modern, 366–370
ritual, 182, 353–357
social occasions following, 357
umealiq (leader), functions of, 181–182
in folktale, 413–414
movements of, 27–28
relations to supernatural, 263–264, 269–270, 353–357
Caribou Eskimo, 452
Carter, W. K., 383, 396, 460
Case materials, 97–123
Cat's cradle, 188
Census, *see* Population.
Central Eskimo, 442
Ceremonial house, *see* Karigi.
Ceremonialism, *see* Cult; Whaling.
Chandler Lake, 19, 44
Charms, *see* Amulets
Chastity, absence of demand for, 78–79, 244
Chiefs, absence of, 65
See umealiq.
Childbirth, 231–235
delivery, 232, 233
magic in, 232, 233
relations of shaman to, 232
See also Birth.
Childhood, 237–240
recreation and games, 239–240, 438–439
social controls in, 237–238
temper tantrums, 239
Chipp River, 48
Christianity, 164, 256, 257, 280, 297, 298, 299, 314, 360, 362, 378–382, 384
history of, 379–381
impact on native cultures, 380–381
marriage patterns changed by, 382
social prestige in, 381–382
Church, *see* Christianity.
Climate, 11–12
Clothing, 56–57
modern, 377
Collateral kinship, 67–68, 166
kinship terms, 67–68
Collective responsibility, 65, 71–75, 166
See also Feuds.
Collins, Henry B., Jr., 13, 126, 448, 453, 456
Colville River system, 12, 19, 136
delta trade center, 198–199
Community, solidarity in, 159–165, 227–228
Community council, modern, 378
Compelling, in ritual, 277–281
Competition, 159–165
behavior patterns in, 160–161
social resistances to, 161–162
Conception, native theories about, 230–231
Confession, of ritual violations, 112, 309–310, 323
Consanguineal kinship terminologies, 66–68
Constipation, 329
Construction, of houses, 43–61
Containers, 470–474
Contraception, magical, 229–230
Controls, magical, 277–291
Cooking arrangements, 53–54
Cooperation, 159–165, 362
arising from sexual relations, 84
See also qataŋun.
between nonkin, 86, 166–192
characteristic of native cultures, 442
derived from wife exchange, 84
Copper Eskimo, 265
Coresidence, as a factor in kinship organization, 70–71
Corrals, in caribou hunting, 29–30
Cosmology, 255–259
Counting, 477
Cousin marriage, held improper, 75

Crew (hunting group) association, 64, 163–165, 177–192, 443
membership in, 159
relations to leader, 153, 179–180
See also umealiq.
whaling, ceremonial activities, 332–352
Cross cousin kinship terms, 68
Cult, organization, 331–357
caribou, 269–270, 303, 331, 353–357
whaling, 294, 303, 331, 332–353
Culture, relations of North Alaskan Eskimo, 446–452
Culture change, 358–382
Culture hero (Raven), 257
See also Raven.
Curing, 299, 305, 327–330
power, 266
songs, 280
Customary law, *see* Law.
Cycle, of economic activities, 140–143, 366–370

Dall, William Healy, 228, 456
Dances, social, 191
Death, 252–253
life hereafter, 291–293
Death cult, revivalism, 296–298
Delivery, of child, 232
Demography, *see* North Alaskan Eskimo, population.
Denbigh flint complex, 453
Diapering, of infants, 233, 235–236
Diet, *see* Food.
Diomede Islands, 462
Direction finding, 258
Disease, *see* Illness.
Disposal of the dead, 252–253, 292–293
Disputes, 97–123
Divination, 294, 295, 307–308
Division, of game, 163
See also umeaktuwat.
Division of labor, 65
Divorce, 77, 78, 82–83
custody of children, 83
remarriage, 83
Doctoring, *see* Shamanism
Dogs, 57, 360, 372, 465–469
absence of souls, 289
breeds, 469
eaten, 374–375
hitching in teams, 465–466
names, 289, 465–466, 467
ownership, 467–468
population, 468–469
supernatural ideas about, 335–337, 346–347, 467
taboo to whales, 336–337, 346–347
Dorset culture (prehistoric), 126
Dreams, 293, 305
Drum, in shamanism, 303
See also Messenger Feast; Shamanism.
Duck hunting, 35–36
Ducks, as food, 375
Dwarfs, 259–261

Earth diver, motif in folklore, 385
Eclipses, 258
Ecological areas, *see* nuunamiut, tareumiut.
interrelationships between, *see* Partnerships; Trade; Voluntary associations.
Ecology, inland vs. maritime, 124–146, 440–446
and kinship, 124–125
and religion, 445
Economic organization, 124–146
basis of cults, 331
cooperation, 85, 159–165, 166–192, 362
See also Cooperation.
family involvements in, 84–85, 132–146
specialized skills, 124, 196
Economy and society, problem orientations, 6, 440–446
Eider ducks, 35
Employment, of Eskimos by non-native organizations, 362–364
Endogamy, within settlements, 75
Enumeration, 475, 477
Environment, influences on social organization, 6–8, 124, 440–446
Environmental determinism, fallacy of, 6, 124, 440
Eschato-Eskimo cultures, 127
Eskimo-Aleut linguistic grouping, 39
Eskimo culture, history, 452–454
Eskimo cultures, defined, 447–448
environmental relations, 6–8, 440–446
prehistory, 13–14, 452–454
"Eskimo" kinship system, 70, 449
Etiquette, 58–59
Europeanization, 358–382
Excavations, in house building, 47, 52
Exchange, in partnerships, 168–172
See also Trade.
Exogamy, 75
Extended family, 65–66

Family, 62–96
composition, 145
disorganization, 62
factor in societal integration, 62–96, 358, 440–446
income, modern, 376–377
organization, 62–95, 249
retention of aboriginal, 358, 361–362, 364, 365
system, general Eskimo, 448–449
Famine, 142–143
Fauna, range of use by North Alaskan Eskimo, 25–38
Fear of the dead, 292–293
Federal Council of Churches, 379
Feeding, of infants, 234–235
Feuds, 64, 71, 72–75, 98, 99–107, 108–110, 115, 117–118, 122–123, 161, 281
terminating, 64, 86–87

Fieldwork, in North Alaska, 3-6
Firearms, introduction of, 360
Firemaking, 56
Fish, 36-38, 375
 relations to supernatural, 276
 species utilized in North Alaska, 37
Fishcamps, of Point Barrow area, 38
Fishing, modern, 367-368, 375
Folklore, 188, 315, 383-439
 children's stories, 438-439
 motifs, 384-439
  animal wives, 391-395, 418-425
  dwarfs, 426-427
  earth diver, 385
  kukuweaq, 425-426
  magic flight, 384, 388-390
  "orphans," 386, 387, 388, 391, 402-413
  shamanistic contests, 429-438
  spider, 386
  "trickster" mythology, 395-396
  worms, 414-418
 storytelling, 383-384
Folsom culture, 13
Food quest, aboriginal, 23-38
Food storage, 60-61
 modern, 372-373
Food taboos, 232, 233, 244, 279, 283-285, 306, 307-308, 312, 322
 at childbirth, 232-233
 at first menstruation, 244
 imposed at whaling, 334
 imposed by shaman, 306, 307-308, 312, 322
 seasonal, 265, 272
 violations as a cause of illness, 306
 warding off effects of violations, 284-285
 with amulets, 283-284
 with songs, 279
Football, 190, 207, 351
Footracing, 190, 207, 212, 217-218, 219-220
Foster kinship, 69-70, 81, 87-92
 parenthood, 87-92
Fowl, 35-36, 375
Fox, commercial trapping, 361
 hunting of, 32
 relations to supernatural, 267-268
 varieties, 32
Franklin, Sir John, 456
Friendships, patterning of, 83
 See also Crew (hunting group) association; Joking partnerships; Partnerships.
Fuel, modern problem of, 376-377
Fur trapping, 360, 361

Gambling, 188-189
Game, as property, 147-151
 division of, 163
  See also umeaktuwat.
 supernatural aspects of, 261-277, 331, 332-355
Games, 159-160
 children's, 239-240
 in karigi, 188-191
Generational kinship terminology, 66-67
Generosity, as behavioral ideal, 153, 164, 197
Geology, of North Alaska, 9-13
Ghosts, 287, 291-293
 relations to illness, 291-292
Giants, 261
Giddings, J. L., Jr., 7, 10, 46, 127, 453, 456
Gift giving, *see* Messenger Feast.
Girls' puberty, 243-244
 absence of ritual elaboration, 244
Goods traded, 201-205
Grandparental kinship terms, 66
Grandparents, role in socialization, 236, 252
Grayling, 37
Greenland Eskimo, 39, 465
Greeting, of caribou, 356
 of game, 451
 of whale, 344-347
Guardian spirits, shamanistic associations, 300
Gubik sands (loess), 11

Hammerich, L. L., 39, 456
Harbor seal, 33
Harpooner, 178, 336, 337, 341, 342
 amulets, 339
 social role, 178
 special songs, 343
Harvard University, archeological research at Point Barrow, 446
Hawkes, E. W., 456
Healy, Capt. M. A., 456
Herskovits, M. J., 457
Hoebel, E. A., 457
Homosexuality, absence of, 246
Hospitality, 83
Host-guest relationship, *see* Messenger Feast.
Hostility, in interpersonal relations 310-311
Hotham Inlet, as trade center, 198
House, 43-61
 abandoned, 59
 amulets associated with, 285-286
 building, 43-61
 of nuunamiut, 44-49
 of tareumiut, 49-61
 ownership, 59
 sharing, 58
 trading of, 60
 types, 43-61, 49 (fig. 1)
Howard Pass, 10
Hrdlička, A., 457
Human ecology, 6-7, 440-446
Humor, 190
 See also Joking partnerships.
Hunting group association, 177-182
 cooperative aspects of, 163
  See also Crew (hunting group) association; Cult; umealiq.

Hunting songs, 278
Husband-wife relations, 249–251
Hyperborean languages, 39

iccellik (house type), 44–46
Ice house, distribution, 43
Ice storage, 60
Icy Cape, 16
Ideals of behavior, 161
of personality, 155
See also Individual; Personality.
iil^{y}aruq (joking partner), 172–177
iivłulik (house type), 47, 48
ikpikpaŋmiut, 20, 94
Ikpikpuk River, 20
Illegitimacy, 78–79
Illness, causes of, 305
curing, by shamans, 299, 327–330
prevention, by amulets, 283
psychosomatic aspects of, 327–328
treatment of, 327–330
See also Shamanism.
Incest, 76
native definitions of, 62–63
Individual, areas of economic choice for, 130
competition, 160
cycle of life, 229–254
integrity, 161
personal ideals, 131, 154–155, 161
personality traits, 247–248, 253–254
See also Personality.
Industriousness, as behavioral ideal, 75, 89
Infancy, 233, 234–237
Infant, newborn, treatment of, 233
Infanticide, 87–88, 92–93, 121
Ingstad, Helge, 45, 47, 457
Inheritance, 149, 152, 253
Initiation rites, absence of, 241, 243
Inland and maritime Eskimo, 124–146
See also nuunamiut; tareumiut.
Inland settlements, 18–23, 44–49
Insult songs, 173–176
Integrative factors, in social organization, 62–66, 124–125, 440–446
Interkin feuds, 71–75
Intrusion, as a cause of illness, 306, 316, 321
Ipiutak culture, Point Hope (prehistoric), 13, 14, 126, 453, 454
Irving, L., 457
Irving, William, 7, 127, 457

Jealousy, marital, 250
Jenness, Diamond, 265, 457
Jochelson, W. I., 457
Joking partnerships, 85, 162, 168, 172–177, 178, 226, 248, 443
insult singing between, 173–176

kaγmalliγmiut, 21
kallimmiut, 17, 18
kaŋgianermiut, 21
karigi (ceremonial house), 43, 48, 49–51, 83, 133, 144, 148, 153, 155, 159, 163, 165, 167, 176, 180, 182–192, 249, 265, 310, 311, 332, 333, 334, 335, 336, 347, 348, 349, 350, 353, 355, 356, 441, 449, 451, 473
as formal men's house, 187
at tikeraaq, 183–184
at utkeaaγvik, 183
charms of, 184
description of, 183
distribution of, 182–183
family association of, 185
food in, 187–188
individual association, 186–187
in Messenger Feast, 211–226
interkarigi contests, 190–191
joining, 186–187
names of, 185–186
opening of, ceremonial season, 185
recreational aspects, 188–191
kayaakserevinmiut (Icy Cape), 16, 18
Killer whale (*Orca*), 34
relations to supernatural, 275–276
killiγmiut (anaktuvuŋmiut), 4, 19, 28, 44, 45, 138, 181, 198
Kinship, 62–96, 124–125, 443
ecological relations of, 124–125
extensions, 162
obligations, extended to nonkin, 166–192
organization, 166
relations to umealiq, 179
system, 62–96
terminology, 66–71
terms, combined, 69
See also Quasi-kinship.
kivalinermiut, 18
Kobuk-Noatak river system, 14
koluγuraγmiut, 20
Kotzebue, 20
Kroeber, A. L., 6, 43, 440, 457
kuγmiut, 4, 16
Kuk River, 16

Labrets, 154, 156, 241, 242, 318, 462
Laguna, Frederica de, 447, 448, 453, 456, 470
Lamps, 47, 55–56, 447
in karigi, 184
supernatural aspects of, 286
Language, 39–42, 127
fads in, 39–40
morphology, 40–41
phonology, 40–42
stress patterns, 42
Lantis, Margaret, 65, 70, 150, 183, 211, 303, 330, 349, 353, 449, 450, 451, 457–458
Lapps, 365
Larsen, Helge, 7, 20, 21, 127, 142, 453, 458
Law, 71–75, 97–123, 161, 444
Leadership, 152–155, 163
of hunt group, 177–192
See also umealiq.

Legerdemain, in shamanism, *see* Shamanism.
Lemmings, 34
Lending, of property, 148, 150
 of wives, *see* Wife exchange.
Levirate, banned, 76
Life crises, 229–254
Life hereafter, 291–293
Lineal kinship relationships, terminologies, 66–67
Lip piercing, at boys' puberty, 241–242, 451
Local groups, of North Alaskan Eskimo, 13–23
Lost articles, found by shamans, 311–312

McLenegan, D. B., 20, 458
Magic, compulsive, in songs, 277–281
 for whaling, 332–352
Magical controls, of nature, 277–291, 294–295
Magic flight, motif in folklore, 384, 388–390
Marginal cultural features of North Alaska, 451–452
Maritime and inland Eskimo, 124–146
 See also nuunamiut; tareumiut.
Maritime Eskimo houses, 49–61
 settlements, 16–18, 26–27, 49–61
Marriage, 75–82, 444–445
 abductions in, 79–80
 and kinship, 74, 76
 arrangements, 77–78, 79
 behavior in, 249–251
 between ecological groups, 129–130
 Christian, 382
 following puberty, 242, 243, 244
 kinship responsibilities in, 122–123
Masks, 293–294
 used at close of whaling, 348
Mathiasson, T., 458
Meade River, 20
Meals, contemporary culture, 375–376
Medicines, absence of, 328
Men's house, *see* karigi.
Menstrual prohibitions, 57, 233
Menstruations, first, 243–244
Mermen, 261–262
Merties, J. B., Jr., 9, 460
Mesolithic cultures, 13
Messenger Feast, 22, 49, 136, 147, 153, 157, 159, 160, 170, 171, 172, 174, 183, 185, 190, 191, 207, 210–228, 241, 256, 259, 290, 294, 303, 311, 357, 378, 449, 450, 451, 463
 as element of social integration, 210
 "asking", 226
 ball game, 224–225
 costumes, 214, 221
 dances, 219, 223, 225
 drum, 215, 218, 220, 223, 224, 225
 foot races in, 212, 217–218, 219–220
 gift assemblage, 215–216, 218, 223
 host-guest relationship, 211–227
Messenger Feast—Continued
 insignia of messengers, 212
 intercommunity contacts, 210, 216
 invitations, 212–213
 joking patterns, 217, 226
 karigi, 214–215, 220, 221, 222, 223, 225
 names, 219
 potlatch parallels, 227
 relations to social status, 218
 social functions of, 210, 227–228
 song exchange, 226
 wealth display, 215, 223
Messianism, 296–298
Missing persons, 324–327
Modesty, 248
Money, introduction of, 208
 sources of, contemporary, 360–366
 uses of, 376–377
Monsters, supernatural, 262–264
Month names, 475–476
Moose, as food, 375
Motifs, folklore, *see* Folklore.
Motion pictures, in contemporary Barrow, 377
Mountain sheep, 34
Mourning, 253, 293
 rites absent, 149
Murder, 72, 97
 treatment of corpse in, 117
Murdoch, John, 3, 7, 16, 26, 28, 31, 228, 294, 339, 341, 342, 360, 367, 378, 458–459, 462, 463, 465, 469, 470, 474
Murie, A., 459
Musk ox, 34–35
Myths and cosmology, 257–259, *see* Folklore.

nalukataq (whale festival), 350–352
Names, 286–291
 changing of, 290
 dogs', 467
 for deceased, 287–288
 importance of, 290
 of newborn child, 233
 relations to amulets and songs, 291
 to prevent illness, 289
 transferred from kinship terms, 291
Naming, of children, 233, 287
Narwhal, 34
Native employment, in North Alaska, 19, 360–366, 376–377
Nativism, 257–258, 296–298
Naval Petroleum Base IV, 1, 362, 363
neγliq (trade center at Colville Delta), 199–205
Nelson, Edward William, 183, 349, 459
Neo-Eskimo, stage of cultural development, 453
Neolithic, 453
Noatak River, 21
noataγmiut, 21, 28
Nomadism, 127–139

Nonkinship social relations, *see* Crew (hunting group) association; Joking partnerships; Partnerships; qataŋun; Voluntary associations
North Alaska, as culture area, 440–441, 452
drainage systems, 10–11
geographic limits, 9–13
physiography, 9–13
prehistory, 13–14, 452–454
rainfall, 11
temperatures, 11
North Alaskan Eskimo:
Christianity, *see* Christianity.
communities, 13–23
cooperation, 2, 159–165, 167–172, 177–182
cultural locus, 7, 441, 446–452
culture change, 358–382
dreams, 293
ecology and society, 440–446
See also nuunamiut; tareumiut.
family, 2, 62–96
fauna used by, 25–38
food, 23–38, 371–375
health, 22
houses and settlements, 43–61
hunting cults, 331–357
karigi, 182–192, *see* karigi.
kinship, 22, 62–96
language, 39–42
marginal culture of, 450–451
mobility of population, 21–22
money economy, contemporary, 1–2, 360–366, 376–377
nuunamiut-tareumiut distinctions, 7, 13–23, 43–61, 124–146, 167–172, 193–209, 331, 357
partnerships, 167–177
plant utilization, 23–25
population, *see* Population.
relations to general Eskimo culture, 446–452
relations to geographic environment, 23–38
religion, 255–357
See also Amulets; Cosmology; Names; Shamans; Songs.
settlements and villages, 13–23
shamanism, 299–330
socioeconomic interdependence, *see* nuunamiut, tareumiut.
trade, 193–209
travel, 12, 126–132, 193–209
"tribes," 22
North Pacific Coast (culture area), 147, 153, 211, 227, 449
North Star, *ss*, 5
Nosebleed, 328
Nuclear family, 43, 63–65
Nuclear kinship relationships, terminologies, 66–67
Numerals, 477
Nunivak Island, 450
Nursing, of infants, 234
nuunamiut (inland Eskimo of North Alaska), 3, 14, 15, 18–23, 24, 25, 27–32, 35, 36, 44–49, 51, 56, 60, 61, 75, 76, 94, 124, 127–139, 144, 152, 155, 165, 166, 168, 172, 177, 178, 181, 182, 193, 194, 200–202, 207, 331, 353–357, 359, 441, 442–443, 445, 446, 447, 448, 452, 454
family composition, 134–138
integration of bands, 133
problem of the, 3
reduction in population, 19, 28, 130
See also Population.
relations with tareumiut, 440–446, 452
nuwuk, 15
nuwuŋmiut, 3, 11

Offenses, 97–123
Office of Naval Research, 1
Oil, sea mammal, as trade item, 203–204
Old age, 87, 251–252
Old Bering Sea culture (prehistoric), 14
Old women, role in child rearing, 252
shaman power of, *see* Shamanism.
Oliktuk Point, as trade center, 198, 208
Omens, 293
Orca, *see* Killer whale.
"Orphans," as kinless status, 90, 153
motif in folklore, 386, 387, 388, 391, 402–413
Ownership, 44, 147–151

paamerak (house type), 47
Paleo-Eskimo cultures, 126, 452–453
Parallel cousin kinship terminologies, 67
Parental kinship terminologies, 67
Partnerships, 58, 83, 84, 85, 95, 128, 162, 167–172, 193, 248, 442, 450
"asking" complex, 172
examples of, 170–171
formation of, 168
joking, 172–177
noneconomic, *see* Joking partnerships.
obligations of, 169, 170
relation to social status, 169, 170
wife exchange in, 172
women's, 177
Parturition house, 45, 231–234
Paternal descent, preference for, 74
Paternity, 79, 81
Patrilocal residence, 64, 74
Payment, for labor, services, 196–197
Peard Bay, 16
Permafrost, 10–11
Personal behavior, 97–123, 229–254
See also Individual; Personality.
Personal property, 148–151
disposal of, at death, 253
Personality, 229–254
development of, 237–240
ideals, 71, 73, 81, 89, 98, 178–179, 238, 383

Personality—Continued
status seeking, 98
traits, 247–248
types, 253–254
Phonemes, North Alaskan Eskimo, 41
Physical types, 448
Physiography, of North Alaska, 9–13
Pipes, 462–464
See also Tobacco.
Placenta, treatment of, 232
Plants, used by North Alaskan Eskimo, 23–25
Point Barrow, *see* Barrow village.
Point Barrow Expedition (1881–1882), 3, 18
Point Barrow villages, 15–16
trade relations of, 199–200
Point Belcher, 16
Point Hope (modern village), 17, 19
See also tikeraaq.
Point Lay (modern village), 4, 17, 19, 363
Poisons, absence of, 328
Polar bear, 32
division of meat, 273
relations to supernatural, 272–274
Political organization, absence of, 65
Polyandry, 81, 82, 251
Polygonal ground, 12
Polygyny, 67, 76, 82, 250
Population, 15, 16, 17, 18, 19, 20, 21–22
decline of inland Eskimo, 19, 28, 130, 172, 359
See also nuunamiut.
fluctuations, 140
modern Barrow village, 363
numbers involved in trading, 200
Portents, 293
Potlatch, paralleled in Messenger Feast, 227
Pottery, 470–474
functions of, 473–474
manufacture, 471–472
traded, 473
types, 470–471
Poverty, 153, 155
native definitions of, 162, 166
Predictions, by shamans, 307–309
Pregnancy, 229–231
Preparation for whaling, ceremonial, 332–337
Presbyterian denomination, 379
Prestige and wealth, 151–158
See also Messenger Feast.
Problems of Eskimo ethnology, 6, 446–454
Prohibitions
in pregnancy, 230
land vs. sea animals, 272
menstrual, 243–244
relating to food, 265–266
See also Cults; Religion; Shamanism.
Property, 147–158
communal, 147–148
in sex, 99
marks, 150–151
Property—Continued
of the deceased, 149
personal, 66
rights, as sexual rights, 149–150
vested in residence group, 147–148
Proto-Eskimo cultures, 126
Psychological aspects of shamanism, 301–302
Ptarmigan, 35
Puberty, 241–244
Public opinion, as a social force, 88, 97, 98, 194
Purchase, of goods, 193–198
Purification, in caribou hunt, 356
in whaling, 337

qataŋun (qataŋuutigiit, pl. qataŋuutigiic), 58, 76, 84–87, 95, 166, 237
See also Quasi-kinship.
Quasi-kinship, 63, 74, 84–92, 162, 443
See also qataŋun.

Racing, *see* Footracing.
Racks (storage), 60–61
Rainey, Froelich G., 7, 17, 18, 20, 21, 22, 127, 142, 182, 184, 349, 451, 453, 459, 475–476
Rape, 79–80, 84, 247
Rasmussen, Knud, 21, 39, 51, 459
Rausch, Robert, 7, 27, 31, 32, 44, 204, 459
Raven, culture hero, 257, 296
mythology, 384, 385
Ray, P. H., 3, 7, 15, 16, 18, 228, 378, 459
Reciprocity, in kinship obligations, 65
Recreation, 188–192
children's, 239–240
Reincarnation, vague belief in, 287–291
Reindeer, domesticated, in North Alaska, 360, 364–366
Religion, 255–357, 445
See also Amulets; Christianity; Cosmology; Cults; Names; Shamanism; Songs.
Religious orientations, 255–257
Residence patterns, 43–61, 78
at marriage, 143–144
factor in cooperative activity, 167
relations to kinship, 63–65, 70
Revivalism, 257–258, 296–298
Ribbon seal, 33
Ringed seal, 33
Ritual, of caribou hunting, 353–357
of whaling, 182, 331–353
prohibitions, 264–266
Rivalry, in karigi games, 189
in sex, 121
singing, 173–176
Roberts, Comdr. Palmer W., 363, 459
Roles, sexual, 240
social, 229–254
Romantic attachments, 79, 245–246
Russia, historic influences in North Alaska, 359

Schrader, F. C., 9, 459
Sea mammals, supernatural aspects of, 272–277
Seals, 32, 33, 141–142, 261–262, 274, 366–370, 373–374
  as food, 373–374
  bearded, *see* ugruk.
  hunting, 32, 33, 141–142
    contemporary, 366–370
    nets, location of, 274
  netting, 32, 33
  species taken by North Alaskan Eskimo, 32, 33
  supernatural manifestations of, 261–262, 274
  utilization of, 33
Seasonal activities, aboriginal, 132–133, 140–142
  modern, 366–370
  prohibitions relating to, 265–266
Seasons, designated, 476
Secret society, suggestions of, 348–349
Security systems, individual, 237, 239
  See also Individual; Personality.
Sedna myth, absence of, 265, 310
Selawik River, 20
Selling, of goods, 193–198
Settlement patterns, 43–61
Settlements and villages, North Alaskan Eskimo, 13–23
Sexual behavior, 244–248
  in childhood, 245
Sexual competition, among men, 161
Sexual division of labor, 65, 149
  in childhood, 237
Sexual division of property, 148–149
Sexual freedom, 79
Sexual intercourse, 246, 247
Sexual relations, 80, 120–121, 129, 130, 244–248, 444–445
  avoidance before hunting, 333, 335
  during pregnancy, 230
  in partnerships, 172
  social effects of, 77, 83–87, 162
Sexual rights, 149–150
Shamanism (aŋatkoak) and shamans (aŋatquq), 57–58, 256, 277, 279, 294, 295, 296, 299–330, 445, 451
  amulets given by, 282–283
  behavioral examples, 315–330
  clairvoyance, 319
  compulsive behavior associated with, 302–303
  confessions, 309–310, 323
  credence in, 300, 313
  curing, 123, 305, 322–323
  divination, 307–308
  dramatic aspects, 307
  dress, 305
  drum, 303, 304
  "envy" patterns associated with, 161–162
  female practitioners, 251–252, 303, 324
  finding lost articles, 312, 323
  food taboos imposed by, 322
Shamanism—Continued
  formalized institution, 299–300, 315,
  functions of, 299–300
  helping spirits, 291, 307
  hostile acts associated with, 309–311
  in caribou cult, 355
  instructions in, 302–303
  intrusion as illness cause, 306, 321
  legerdemain, 302–303, 304, 305, 313, 316, 317, 318–319
  lost articles recovered by, 312, 323
  lycanthropy, 324
  malevolence, 306, 309–311
  missing persons located by, 324–327
  native definitions of, 300–301
  numbers of practitioners, 314–315
  opposed by Christianity, 381
  pay for services, 308
  possessional aspects of, 313–314
  power sources, 270, 271, 324
  psychological aspects of, 302–303
  relation to children, 315, 317
  relation to the dead, 312
  removal of intruded object, 302, 303, 321
  seances, 304, 306–307
  skills in, 313
  social controls related to, 161–162, 308–309
  social status in, 303
  songs, 280, 318, 322
  sorcery, 322
  soul loss, as illness cause, 305–306
  sources of power, 270, 271, 300–301, 324
  vengeance patterns associated with, 321
  ventriloquism, 305
  wealth, 308
  weather prophecy, 319
  whaling associations, 334, 338
  wound curing, 322
Shamans, *see* Religion; Shamanism.
Shares of game, 163–164
  See also umeaktuwat.
Sharing, informal, 59
Siberian Neolithic, 453
Sibling rivalry, minimized, 236
Simpson, Dr. John, R.N., 3, 7, 15, 156, 183, 205, 228, 359, 360, 378, 460 475–476
Simpson, Thomas, 156, 359, 378, 460
Singing partnerships, 173–177
Skills and manufactures, 196
  specialized, 155
Sleeping arrangements, 45–68
  of infants, 236
Smith, Middleton, 142, 460
Smith, P. S., 9, 460
Snow goggles, 294
Social classes, absence of, 151–152
Social conformity, 310–311
Social controls, 161–162
  in childhood, 237–239
  songs in, 176
  See also Law.

Social integration, factors in, 362, 364
Social relations, in marriage, 249–250
in trade, 193–198, 206
Social status, 147–158
hunt group relations to, 152
Society, 62–96, 97–123, 124–146, 166–192, 440–446
and economy, problem orientations, 6–7, 124–146, 166–192
relations to ecology, 124–146, 440–446
Solecki, Ralph, 7, 9, 10, 11, 13, 127, 453, 460
Songs, 40, 189, 277–281, 294, 445
amulet associations, 279
caribou ritual, 355
children's, 240, 439
Christian, 380–381
curing, 322
entertainment features of, 174, 191
examples, 175, 316–317
insult, 173–176
magical, 277–281
popular, 174, 191
property, 277–278
purchase, 278, 280
shaman's, 316–317, 318
whaling ritual, 341–343
Sorcery, *see* Shamanism.
Sororate, banned, 76
Soul, 264–277, 287, 291–293, 305, 311
animal, 264–277
human, 291–293
loss, as illness cause, 305, 311
Spencer, M., 6, 460
Spencer, R. F., 383, 396, 460
Spier, Leslie, 67, 460
Spiritual power, 300
See also Shamanism.
Sportmanship, 191
Squirrels, 34
Starvation, 94, 138, 140, 164
Status, based on wealth, 147–158
of umealiq, 151–158, 178–182
relations in Messenger Feast, 218
See also Messenger Feast.
rivalry, 98, 99
sexual aspects of, 161
Steensby, P. H., 453, 460
Stefansson, Vilhjalmur, 7, 20, 21, 31, 51, 193, 198, 320, 460, 470
"Step" relationships, 69
Stoney, Lieut. George M., 7, 23, 24, 46, 47, 48, 50, 184, 203, 355, 460, 475–476
Storage arrangements, 53, 54, 60
Stranger, as social status, 58, 72, 73, 166, 168, 273–274
"Strangers in the Sky," as revivalistic example, 257–258, 296–298, 379
Structured trade, 198–209
Structure of ecological divisions, 124–146
Suicide, 106, 251, 321
Supernatural, 255–357
aspects of amulets, 282–286
aspects of names, 286–291
aspects of songs, 277–281
beings, 259–277
cult organization, 331–357
distinctions between game, 264–265
relation to animals, 255, 261–277
See also Cults; Religion; Shamanism.
Surplus goods, as wealth, 152–153
Survey Pass, 10
Swadesh, Morris, 40, 461
Sweating, absence of institutionalized, 329

Tales, 383–439
See also Folklore.
Tambourine, *see* Drum; Shamanism.
tareumiut (maritime North Alaskan Eskimo), 14, 15, 16–18, 23, 26–27, 31, 34, 35, 36, 49–61, 76, 125, 127–131, 139–145, 155, 165, 166, 168, 172, 177, 193, 194, 198, 200, 201, 207, 252, 331, 332–353, 441, 442–443, 445, 447, 448, 452, 454, 472
nuunamiut interrelations, 198–228, 440–446, 452
seasonal movements, 140
settlements and villages, 139–140
villages, bases of integration, 15–18, 144
Tattooing, of girls, 243
Taxation, of Eskimos, 377
Teams, *see* Dogs.
Tents, 44–49, 60, 137
Territorial divisions, among nuunamiut, 132–133
Texts, in Eskimo, 428–438
Thalbitzer, William, 42, 461
Theft, 121–122
Thule culture (prehistoric), 14, 18, 448
tikeraγmiut, 17, 18
See also Point Hope language, 39.
Time reckoning, 475–477
Tobacco, 24–25, 156, 252, 289, 359, 360, 462–464
Toilet training, of child, 235–236
Tomcod, 36, 37
Toothache, 329
Townsend, C. H., 461
Trade, 76, 127–128, 141, 168–169, 193–209, 473
as area specialization, 441–442
centers, geographic, 198–209
description of trade center, 199–200
goods, 203–204
informalized, 193–198
intercommunity, 198–209
intracommunity, 193–198
items of, 201–205
items of foreign origin, 378
routes, 198–199, 200 (map 3)
social effects of, 208–209

Trading partnerships, 167–172
See also Partnerships.
Transportation, *see* Dogs; Travel; umiak.
Transvestitism, absence of, 246
Travel, 46, 136–137, 165–167
methods of, 136–137
routes, 198–209, 198 (map 2), 200 (map 3), 202 (map 4)
Treatment of illness, 327–330
Trial marriage, 245
Tribes of North Alaskan Eskimo, *see* North Alaskan Eskimo, settlements.
"Trickster" mythology, 257, 395–396
Tuberculosis problem, 362, 371
tulugaγmiut, 19
tunarak (shaman power), *see* Shamanism.
Tundra, 9–13

ugruk (bearded seal), 33, 163, 262
supernatural aspects of, 262, 274
umeaktuwat (communal division of game), 163, 178, 180, 346, 366
See also Caribou hunting; Whaling.
umealiq (hunt group leader, chief, rich man), 65, 144, 152–155, 160, 163, 164, 167, 173, 177–182, 194, 332, 333, 334, 335, 336, 337, 338, 340, 341, 343, 344, 345, 347, 348, 349, 351, 352, 353, 355, 356, 357, 373, 441, 445–446, 471
achievement of status, 179
as host and guest, in Messenger Feast, 210, 211
duties of wife, at whaling, 334, 335, 336, 337, 338, 339, 343, 344–347, 351
in folktale, 402–403, 426–427, 429–438
relations to crew, 177–192
See also Whaling.
relations to kin group, 179
restrictions at whaling, 335–337
rivalry with others, 180
share of whale, 344, 345–346
umiak, 136, 200–201
in trading expeditions, 201, 203
in whaling, 332–352
See also Travel.
Unilineal social organization, 449
Union of Soviet Socialist Republics, 361
United States Navy, petroleum installations in North Alaska, 1–2, 358
United States, Office of Indian Affairs, 358
Public Health Service, 469
Urine, human, uses of, 57, 328–329
utkeaaγvik, 3, 16, 18, 66
language, 39
map showing, 50
See also Barrow.
Utokak River, 17
utokaγmiut (inland Eskimo), 17, 20, 28
uxorilocal residence, 64, 90

Vengence patterns, 71–75
Villages, in North Alaska, 13–23
tareumiut, 139–145
Virilocal residence, 64
Virtues, personal, 247
See also Individual; Personality.
Voluntary associations, 166–192
See also Crew (hunting group) associations; Partnerships; umealiq.

Wainwright (modern village), 16, 19, 363, 365–366
Walrus (Pacific walrus), 33
as food, 374
hunting, modern, 366–370
movement of, 140–141
relations to supernatural, 274–275
Warfare, absence of formalized, 71
Wartes, Rev. W., 379
Water, as ceremonial offering, 272–276, 338
shortage of, 11
supply, modern, 369
Wealth, 147, 151–158, 174, 178, 193, 449–450
as a basis of social status, 152
display, 174
increase in importance, aboriginal, 157–158
See also Messenger Feast.
Weaning, of infants, 235–236
Weasel, 34
Weather control, 308
songs, 278
See also Songs.
Weyer, E. M., 264, 314, 461
Whale (*Balaena mysticetus* Linn.), 17, 26–27, 332–353
as food, 372, 373
ceremonial treatment of, 332–352
disposition of meat, 27
feast, *see* Cult, whaling.
relations to supernatural, 332–352
Whaling, 22, 26–27, 140, 152, 163, 178, 180, 331–353
amulets, 338–342, 343
archeological aspects of, 127
bombs, 360
butchering, 345–347
camp, 336, 337
close of season, 347–350
compared with caribou hunt, 354, 357
cult, 332–352, 446
division of game, 343, 346
dress of umealiq, 340
duties of umealiq, 332–352
festivals, 347–352
greeting the whale, 344–347
in fall, at Point Barrow, 143, 349–350, 368–369
magician for, 334, 341
methods of, 342
modern, 366–370, 372

Whaling—Continued
relations to crew organization, 177–182
ritual, 182, 332–352
Whitefish, 37
Widows, status of, 77
Wife abduction, capture, 77, 79, 80, 81, 115–116, 119–120
Wife exchange, 85, 168, 170, 172
social functions of, 83–84
Wife-husband relations, 249–251
Wife lending, *see* Wife exchange.
Wife of umealiq, ritual functions, 471
Wiggins, Ira L., 1, 10, 461
wiivaksat, as example of revivalism, 257–258, 296–298
See also Culture change, "Strangers in the Sky."
Wilmovsky, Norman, 37
Wissler, Clark, 461
Wolf, hunting of, 32
native utilization of, 32
supernatural associations, 268–269, 318
traps, 268
Wolverine, hunting and utilization, 32
supernatural associations, 269
Women, and old age, 245, 251–252, 309
kinship obligations, 93
shamans, 251–252, 303, 309, 324
Womens' dances, 191
partnerships, 177
status, 158
Wood, use of, by Eskimos, 25
Worm mythology, 295–296
Wounds, 329

Yearly cycle, aboriginal, 140–143, 331, modern, 366–370
Yukon River, 9